A
History of the
A. M. E. Zion Church

Part II

1872-1968

By
DAVID HENRY BRADLEY, SR.

WIPF & STOCK · Eugene, Oregon

Wipf and Stock Publishers
199 W 8th Ave, Suite 3
Eugene, OR 97401

A History of the A.M.E. Zion Church, Part 2
1872-1968
By Bradley, David Henry, Sr.
Copyright©1970 by Bradley, David Henry, Sr.
ISBN 13: 978-1-5326-8827-0
Publication date 4/10/2019
Previously published by Parthenon Press, 1970

To Young Americans
Who must believe in the eventual triumph of freedom and love
Despite that which they may see in areas of government and life
For it is for these ideals black as well as white have worked
and fought and died.
To my son, David Henry Bradley Junior
To George Fauntleroy, the son of a Zion Methodist
minister also,
To Wilma Reneé Lewis, whose father and mother
were joined in wedlock
and who, herself
was baptized by this ministry
To Skyne Uku, a young Biafran girl, who was
sponsored and educated in America
by
Bishop and Mrs. W. A. Hilliard
THIS BOOK IS DEDICATED

CONTENTS

INTRODUCTION 7
I. NEW FACTS FROM OLD HISTORY 11
II. DAYS OF RECONSTRUCTION AND THE
A. M. E. ZION CHURCH 31
III. THE GENERAL CONFERENCES OF 1872 AND 1876 .. 41
IV. NEW CONFERENCES AND MISSIONS, 1864-1956 54
V. EDUCATION IN THE 19TH AND 20TH
CENTURIES—HOME AND CHURCH 65
VI. EDUCATION IN THE 19TH AND 20TH
CENTURIES—HOME AND CHURCH 88
VII. EDUCATION IN THE 19TH AND 20TH
CENTURIES—SCHOOL AND COLLEGE 96
VIII. THE DEVELOPMENT OF THE EPISCOPACY 120
IX. THE DEVELOPMENT OF THE EPISCOPACY 135
X. THE DEPARTMENTS AND THEIR
DEVELOPMENT 149
XI. THE DEPARTMENTS AND THEIR
DEVELOPMENT 169
XII. THE DEPARTMENTS AND THEIR
DEVELOPMENT 187
XIII. A BRIEF GLANCE AT EARLY MISSIONS IN THE
A. M. E. ZION CHURCH 211
XIV. HOME AND FOREIGN MISSIONS IN THE CHURCH .. 222
XV. THE DENOMINATION AND ITS FINANCES 252
XVI. THE DENOMINATION AND ITS FINANCES 276
XVII. ORGANIC UNION AND ZION METHODISM 314
XVIII. ORGANIC UNION AFTER 1868 340
XIX. ORGANIC UNION AFTER 1868 358
XX. THE CHURCH AND THE ECUMENICAL TIES 369
XXI. THE CHURCH THROUGH THE YEARS 384
XXII. THE CHURCH THROUGH THE YEARS 395
XXIII. THE LAYMEN AND THE CHURCH 412
XXIV. THESE CONCLUDING YEARS 420
XXV. THE STORM BREAKS 444
XXVI. THE AUTHORITY OF THE GENERAL
CONFERENCE 459
XXVII. THE CHURCH'S PROGRAM AND BELIEFS 475

INTRODUCTION

FOR MORE than twenty years the thought of the development of the second volume of the History of the A.M.E. Zion Church has been an uppermost idea of our mind. There have been reasons for the delay, however. The A.M.E. Zion Church has a great task within itself to encourage factual knowledge as the basis for its continuing existence. The First Volume, appearing in 1956 not only had rough sledding but the opposition to the presentation of a factual and documented work which undermined much of the legend about our founding and early history brought a sense of discouragement to the writer. At one time, for example, it was our province to state in official circles that the Church must arrive at the place of encouraging writing rather than discouraging it. It is naturally common knowledge of a student of history that the material written is never the final word in the light of the possibility of the uncovering of new material, but any starting point is more agreeable than no point of departure at all.

A close examination of our years of existence as a denomination will reveal the painful fact that not more than ten major works have been written on the total life of the denomination in all of her history. To state that even these have had restrictive circulation is to point up even more vividly an unwise state of affairs.

The collection of material has not only been slow but, in instances, discouraging. The denomination, in the future, should take more care in the keeping of records and the preservation of these records. Time, after time, for example, we have run across references to vital matters only to discover that because of the carelessness of the individual who handled the material or the eventual preservation of it, we have only that—the reference to it.

In many instances the search for material has led down blind alleys and to keen disappointment but because of the need of a sincere *beginning* work there has been always the hope that success could be achieved eventually. In no small measure has been the individual encouragement of three different source groups: the special group who submitted a resolution in the Thirty-seventh Quadrennial session of the general conference: from the Allegheny Conference, Charles H. Foggie, Arthaniel Harris and Henry McCreary III; from the Ohio Conference, J. Dallas Jenkins and Eugene E. Morgan; from the

Michigan Conference, James W. Eichelberger, N. L. Meeks and Richard L. Fisher; from the Philadelphia and Baltimore Conference, John Satterwhite; the Texas Conference, Harrel Gordon Tillman; the West Central Conference (North Carolina) Edgar French and Edgar F. Jones, and Mark Brown whose conference affiliation is not listed;[1] several members of the Board of Bishops including Stephen Gill Spottswood, Herbert Bell Shaw and William Alexander Hilliard, and Mrs. Alice Fauntleroy Royal who has diligently inquired about the progress of the work and aided in its publishing.

The need to faithfully report facts of history, and, if moved to do so, in the light of those facts, present one's own conclusions and opinions, is the imperative duty of any writer. Of course, it goes without saying, facts as they are discoverable are essential before interpretation. In addition, the writer of history, whether it is secular or religious, must lay emphasis upon the conviction that *God is,* that the revelation of faith and man's humility in the universe exists, despite all which may appear or which denies this existence. The belief that if the struggle is meaningful, if the participants are really a part of God's plan, some portions or segments of their actions and their lives are therefore directed to the development of the God Plan.

If the conviction that God has a pattern for His world is valid, someone at some time must stumble upon vestiges of its outline and bring it into human focus. All too frequently the vehicle may be different from current suggestion and desire. Zion Methodism, that is the total Church, priest and people alike, must somehow become aware of the importance of the past and its relationship to the present and future. It is a current belief that only by examination and reexamination of the past can the program of present and future be charted and moved towards their logical and realistic conclusion. Herein, then, one sees the vital need of true and accurate reporting of fact and fact interpretation. To deal carelessly with either from ignorance or studied intent throws everyone who accepts the position off balance, and, off course, and, in instances, into un-Christian thinking and relationships.

As a Christian, such a person may then become unknowingly or unintentionally untruthful. As a teacher of the past and an inter-

---

[1] *Official Journal Thirty-Seventh Quadrennial Session, General Conference,* Indianapolis, Indiana, 1964, 537

INTRODUCTION

preter of the present he or she misguides, and as a priest (and we subscribe to the universal priesthood of all believers) he or she is an uninformed advisor or a false prophet. Two groups are therefore victims of his understanding—the people whom he or she seeks to lead and the people sinned against, for room in every equation must be made for the sincere Christians of today's and yesterday's generations even though we possess the urge to measure beliefs and deeds by the thinking of our time and generation. This appears to be the forgotten dimension of our age,—a great part of our immediate dilemma and fears.

When one uses as a measuring rod of behavior the need that each person must act responsibly, as best he or she can, there comes a new appreciation of the past and its accomplishments. If we do not observe this, do not react to our own responsibility and set out to ignore our God given assignment,—or we seek deliberately to misinterpret it, we betray not only ourselves but our fellowmen, who, by their act, have evinced belief in us. Above all, in this instance, we have ignored as well, the God charge given.

The avid student however, should recognize two things,—the possibility of honest mistake and the inability of the attainment of perfection, both by men and of systems—above the critical analysis of either contemporaries or the future. No doubt this factor is involved in America's present crisis in human relations. Honest ignorance may team up with reluctance of involvement and imperfection to delay the arrival of goals. Races of men, the old and the young, are all caught up in imperfection. When there is no perfection we become critical and even hostile. When there may be no immediate and final solution we may seize upon revolt all to hastily. Howard Grimes, for example, in his Through-The-Week Text: THE CHRISTIAN VIEWS OF HISTORY says: "The question for the Christian is not whether the basic problems of history can be eliminated but rather how they can be alleviated."

The Church, then has merely struggled with immediate problems as they have presented themselves. At times she has been thwarted in her decision making only to be *snowed under* by demanding situations clamoring for attention. When this has occurred, only partial solutions have been devised;—an example of this would be the retirement of Bishops.

Of course, present and future must see and recognize the slow movement of change, and this to a marked degree in the Church which sings and believes in "Give Me That Old Time Religion," no doubt because of the imagined and perhaps, security and familiarity in the lack or the absence of change. Like the great ocean liner that takes hours to reach her berth once she is in the harbor while the small launch comes to port quickly, so the Church assumed time, the time of years and decades to respond to the helm.

The author wishes to thank the following for aid in preparing this manuscript:

> Mrs. Harriette Bradley
> Mrs. James Clair Taylor
> Mrs. Emily Hagar
> Miss Elizabeth Lewis
> Miss Elsie Nelson

The reader should note the difficulty the writer has experienced in the varied spelling of names. In many instances the Secretary of Minutes has not been sure himself so more than one way of spelling a name has been found. For example: *Petty* has many times been *Pettey* etc.

CHAPTER I

New Facts From Old History

THE FIRST volume of the History of the A. M. E. Zion Church, 1796-1872 was written with the underlying thought in mind that there would be new material discovered as time would go on. This has proved correct and as we have run across this matter we have felt that the second book should begin with an acknowledgment of them. We hope that, in years to come that which we have brought together will be of valuable use to any future student interested in the History of this branch of Methodism.

The Minutes of the General Conference of 1848 were printed along with those of the existing four annual conferences of the time, the Baltimore, the Philadelphia, the New York and the New England Conferences. For some reason those of the New England Conference were relatively short, occupying only two printed pages. The little pamphlet was printed by G. W. Okie of 101 Canal Street, New York and was prepared by the Reverend John A. King, Rev. T. Eato, and the Reverend Peter Ross.

MINUTES OF THE GENERAL CONFERENCE

The General Conference of the African Methodist Episcopal Zion Church in America, met according to appointment in Zion's Church, corner of Church and Leonard Streets May 29, 1848.

The session was opened with singing and prayer.

When Reverend C. Rush addressed the conference in a very appropriate manner, touching the general interest of our connection, and also stating that the term for which he had been elected to serve the connection as their Superintendent had expired, &c.

On motion of the house, the Rev. John Dungy was appointed President; Rev. Edward Johnson, Vice President, and J. J. Moore, Secretary, until the proper Superintendent was elected.

By motion the names of the proper members of the General Conference were announced there being 46 in number.

On motion of the house a committee of seven was appointed to nominate a candidate, for the General Superintendent, and also for Assistant Superintendent. Committee On Nomination:—Solomon T. Scott, Pa.: S. T. Gray, New England; Peter Ross, N. Y.; J. J. Moore, Balt.; Ed Johnson, Pa.; William H. Bishop, N. Y.; J. J. Clinton, Pa.

The Committee retired and after a short absence returned, and on motion made the following report: For General Superintendents, Rev. C. Rush and James Simmons. For Assistant Superintendents, Rev. Geo. Gelbreth and J. P. Thompson.

The report was received and the Committee discharged.

By a motion of the Conference, the following persons were appointed Judges of Election: Wm. H. Bishop, George A. Spywood, Edward Johnson.

The Judges took their seats, when, it was on motion,

Resolved, That the General Superintendent be elected first.

The house then proceeded to the election. The votes were cast and counted, which gave the Rev. Christopher Rush a large majority over the opposite candidate. The polls were then reopened. The members cast their votes for Assistant Superintendent. The election resulted in favor of Rev. George Gelbreth, he having a large majority over the opposite candidate. The Judges then proclaimed the Rev. C. Rush, General Superintendent, and the Rev. Geo. Gelbreth, Assistant Superintendent. The Superintendents were then conducted to their seats by three of the oldest elders present.

The ministers of the Conference congratulated the Superintendents on their election on which Superintendent Rush arose and addressed the Conference in a very feeling manner on their general duty, and also alluded to his willingness to labor in the future for their general good to the utmost of his ability, as he had endeavored to do in the past, to which address the house made a general response of favorable feelings.

The Rev. G. Gelbreth then addressed the Conference. He alluded in his remarks to the great responsibility the Conference had imposed upon him and his duty to God and his brethren, and intention to maintain the confidence reposed in him &c. The election of Superintendents being concluded, the Conference adjourned.

Tuesday Morning, 9 O'clock

The Conference assembled on Tuesday morning, agreeable to adjournment—the Rev. Supt. Rush in the chair, associated with the Assistant Superintendent Rev. G. Gelbreth.

Members Present

New York:—Rev. C. Rush, Wm. H. Bishop, John P. Thompson, J. C. Spence, Timothy Eato, George Gennett, J. A. King, Peter Vanhass, Joseph P. Thompson, Henry Johnson, J. W. Louguin, Sampson Talbot, Geo. Tredwell, J. A. Williams, John Tappan, Ed. H. Bishop, Peter Ross.

Pennsylvania:—David Stevens, George Gelbreth, A. Cole, Solomon T. Scott, John J. Moore, S. Golden, Moses Gales, Joseph Sinclair, N. H. Terpin, J. J. Clinton, Basal Mackall, Wm. Jones, Peter Fulman, Jacob Trusty.

New England:—James Simmons, Thomas Hensen, Daniel Vandevere, S. T. Gray, Joseph Hicks.

The house proceeded to business, after being organized, by calling the Roll, reading and adopting the doings of the previous day—when it was on motion,

Resolved, That there be a Committee of nine appointed on Revision of the Discipline, from the different Annual Conferences.

The Circular on Revision was then read. On motion the letters containing the decision of the Quarterly Conferences on the Circular on Revision of 1844, was read in the audience of the Conference prior to their being submitted to the Committee on Revision when on motion the documents from the different Quarterly Conferences on Revision, were submitted to the Committee on Revision for their consideration. The Committee were then appointed as follows:
David Stevens, Pa.; Wm. H. Bishop, N. Y.; J. A. King, N. Y.; Thomas Henson, N. E.; J. J. Moore, Baltimore.

After some remarks on different topics, pertaining to the general interest of the connection, the house adjourned to Wednesday morning, 9 o'clock.

Wednesday Morning, May 31st.
Conference assembled agreeable to adjournment. Supt. Rush in the chair, with his associate Rev. G. Gelbreth. House organized in usual way. Roll was called. Minutes read and adopted. When the Committee on revision retired by resolution. When the remainder of this day and the two following days, Thursday and Friday, June 1st and 2nd, were spent in discussing questions and passing resolutions, pertaining to the general interest of our connection.

Saturday Morning, June 3rd
Conference met according to adjournment. The Rev. Superintendents in the chairs. Organized in the usual way. Roll was called. Minutes of the previous day read and adopted. When the Committee on Revision returned, and on motion made their report, which was on motion received by the house, and the Committee were discharged. On motion, J. J. Moore was appointed to read the Minutes of the Committee on Revision, and that the house take up the subject of the revision by sections or paragraphs, proceeded by calling for the reading of the Title Page, which was as follows: The African Methodist Episcopal Zion Church in America. Brother G. A. Spywood, took the floor to show the great necessity of striking out the word "African," and after he had shown some of the reasons for its removal, S. T. Gray arose to show reasons for its being retained. The discussion continued up to the hour of adjournment.

Monday, Morning, June 5th
The Conference met according to adjournment—Rev. C. Rush in the chair. The Rev. G. Gelbreth also present. House organized in the usual way. Roll was called. Minutes of the previous session read and adopted.

The same discussion arose on the word Zion and the word Connection. That is to say, whether the Title Page should read so as to say Af. M. Ep. Church in America, or read so as to say Af. M. Ep. Zion Connection in America. After much discussion on the subject, several motions were made relative to it. It was finally decided, on motion of the house, that the following be the Title of our connection: The African Methodist Episcopal Zion Church in America.

The General Conference was occupied from the 3d until the 13th of

June mostly with the report of the Committee on Revision of the Discipline, which report, after much debate and many amendments, was finally got through with and adopted by the General Conference, June 13th, 1848.

Wednesday Morning, June 14th

Conference met according to adjournment. The Rev. Superintendents both present. Opened in the usual way, with reading a portion of the Scripture, singing and prayer. Roll of membership was called. Minutes were read and adopted. After which several letters relating to the Conference were read. When it was on motion

Resolved, That the General Conference proceed to set off a Conference embracing such portion of the State of New York, west of the Hudson River, as may be determined upon. And also, on motion, that there be a Conference set off in western Pennsylvania. The house adjourned to 9 o'clock, Thursday morning.

Thursday Morning, June 15th

Conference opened agreeable to adjournment. Rev. Superintendents in their seats. Opened in the usual way. Roll was called. Minutes read and adopted. When, on motion of the house, there was a Committee of five appointed to determine the bounds of the Conference in western New York. Committees names as follows: John Tappan, J. W. Loguin, Joseph P. Thompson, J. A. Williams, John P. Thompson.

The above Committee retired a short time, and returned with the following report, as follows: Making the City of Albany the eastern boundary; from thence a northerly direction, up the Canal to Lake Champlain, and from thence to the Canada line, returning to Albany; then running a line a south-westerly direction to the Eastern boundary line of the Alleghany Conference. The above report was received, adopted, and the Committee discharged. It was, on motion—

Resolved, That the Conference set off as described above, shall be known by the name of Genessee Conference. The Conference set off in western Pennsylvania to be called the Alleghany Conference, is bounded as follows: From Bedford to Hallidaysburg, all that part of the State lying west of the Alleghany Mountain, extending to Lake Erie; then south running to the Ohio line, thence east to the Alleghany Mountain on the Maryland line. Thus forming a district which shall have its location in the city of Pittsburg. It was farther, on motion,

Resolved, That the Genessee Conference meet on the second Saturday in September, 1849, and also that the Alleghany Conference meet on the third Saturday in August, 1849.

The Conference then passed a resolution that there should be Three Book Agents appointed, to be known throughout the connection as the Central Agents, and that the Rev. Superintendent appoint said Central Agents.

The Superintendent proceeded to appoint the following brethren, Book Agents.

REV. JOHN A. KING, *Chairman*
REV. TIMOTHY EATON, *Treasurer*
REV. PETER ROSS, *Secretary*

On motion of the Conference, Rev. Edward Johnson was appointed Book Agent for the Philadelphia District. Rev. John J. Moore, for the Baltimore District, and Rev. James Simmons for the New England District.

House adjourned to Friday, June 16th, 9 o'clock.

Friday Morning, June 16th

Conference met according to adjournment. Rev. Superintendents presiding. Organized in the usual manner. Roll was called, Minutes read and adopted.

The first thing introduced to the Conference this morning for their consideraton, was the Manual Labor School. The Superintendent arose and informed the Conference that he had purchased the land for the connection, in the county of Essex, State of New York, for to establish the institution upon. After which the following preamble and Constitution was read in the audience of the house, and adopted by the General Conference.

Preamble

Whereas, we the ministry of the African Methodist Episcopal Zion Church in America, feeling as we do that many of the difficulties which we have to labor grow out of the fact that there is a great lack of education among us. Man, viewed as being susceptible of happiness and capable of responsible action, sustaining a thousand relations, involving as many duties: whatever, therefore, tends to increase this susceptibility and enlarge this capacity, must exalt his nature and promote the benevolent purpose for which he was created. Such is the tendency of a well-directed education of virtuous example, of sound philosophy and theology, indeed of everything which gives the understanding a controlling influence over the grosser passions, of everything which purifies and regulates the feeling, without diminishing their order or depriving them of their appropriate objects. And among the many causes which conspire to produce this effect, none is so efficient as a well directed education. Therefore, those persons whose names are here connected, do agree to form an institution, having for its object the establishment of prominent schools of education preparatory to the ministry, and with other useful information calculated to elevate our whole people, do agree to be governed by the following Constitution and other By-Laws, which may be found necessary for carrying out the object set forth in this Preamble.

CONSTITUTION

Article I

This institution shall be known by the name of the "Rush Academy," Essex county, State of New York.

Article II

Every subscriber for one dollar and fifty cents, or more, per annum, shall be a member of this institution, and shall be entitled to the privilege of membership.

Article III

The funds raised by annual subscription or otherwise, shall be appropriated under the direction of the Committee of Managers to defraying the necessary expenses, as well as the general expenses of the institution.

Article IV

Every subscriber, at the time of subscribing, shall direct to what particular department the amount of his or their subscription shall be appropriated—all donations shall be deemed the permanent property of the institution. The institution may, however, at its annual meeting or other legal meetings, authorize a sale of any of its permanent property for the purpose of reinvestment for others more desirable or advantageous.

Article V

The officers of this institution shall consist of a President, four Vice Presidents, Corresponding and Recording Secretaries, a Treasurer, a Committee of Twenty-five of which shall be located in and about the city of New York with the Corresponding and Recording Secretaries. Each set of Committee not provided for in this Constitution shall have power to appoint their own Secretaries and Agents.

Article VI

It shall be the duty of the President to preside at the annual meetings of the institution, to watch over its interests generally; to recommend such measures as he may deem calculated to promote the object of the institution, and to call meetings of the same when he may think the good of the institution requires it, or when requested so to do by the Committee of Managers. The Vice Presidents shall set as Chairmen in their different sections of the Committee, possessing all the power of the President in their respective bodies.

Article VII

It shall be the duty of the Corresponding Secretary to institute and carry on the correspondence between the general committee of management, the Secretaries and Agents of the different departments, and to lay before the general committee all letters and communications he shall receive; to pay over to the Recording Secretary monthly, or oftener if required, all monies which shall come into his hands, and to perform such other duties appertaining to his office as may be prescribed by said Committee of Managers.

Article VIII

It shall be the duty of the Recording Secretary to keep the records of the institution and of the General Committee of Management; to receive all the monies of the institution, and to pay over the same monthly, or oftener if required, to the Treasurer, taking his receipt, therefor. He shall have in Charge the seal of the institution, and shall affix the same to such documents and papers and in such manner as shall be ordained by the Committee of Management. And he shall attend to and perform such other duties appertaining to his office as the President may direct.

Article IX

It shall be the duty of the Treasurer to receive all the monies of the institution from the Recording Secretary, and disburse the same as shall be directed by the General Committee or by such subcommittee as they shall appoint or substitute, keeping regular books of entry and accounts of all such receipts and disbursements, and to report to the Committee of Management the state of the Treasury as often as requested to do. He shall, one week previous to the annual meeting of the institution in each year, render to the Committee of Management a full and complete report of all monies received and disbursed by him and of the state of the Treasury.

Article X

The General Committee of Managers shall have the general supervision and management of the interest and affairs of the institution; they shall open and conduct all negotiations for the purchase of any property for the institution, taking care, however, to respect each branch of the committee, and the actual funds of the institution may warrant. They shall provide for the preservation and increase of the property of the institution. They shall have power to appoint Committees or Agents, as the interests of the institution shall seem to them to require; to prescribe their respective duties and fix their compensation, and they may adopt and execute generally such measures as shall to them appear to be proper in emergencies and necessary to carry out the objects of this institution.

Article XI

The Committee of Management shall at every annual meeting of the institution, render a full report of their proceedings during the year, stating the principles governing them in their selection of purchases, entering into such details as they shall think proper, and of interest to their associates.

Article XII

All annual subscriptions to the institution shall be for the current year, expiring on the first day of the following year. No subscriber shall be entitled to the privileges of membership until his subscription has been paid.

Article XIII

It shall be the duty of the Committee of Managers to frame a code of By-Laws for their own as well as the further government of the institution. Providing such By-Laws are not repugnant to this Constitution. Which By-Laws for the latter shall be submitted to the members, at a meeting of the institution for their approval.

Article XIV

This Constitution may be altered or amended by the annual meeting of the institution, or at a meeting called for said purpose by a two-thirds vote of the members present.

The above Constitution was adopted by the General Conference, June 16th, 1848. Adjourned to Saturday morning, 9 o'clock.

Saturday Morning, June 17

Conference assembled according to adjournment. Rev. Superintendents in the chair. Opened with the usual religious ceremony. Roll was called. Minutes read and adopted. After which the following resolutions were passed.

1st, By motion of the house the Rev. Geo. Gelbreth was appointed President of the Rush Academy, and the Rev. Christopher Rush, Treasurer of the said institution. And also the Rev. Peter Ross was appointed by the Conference Vice President of the Rush Academy for the New York Conference.

The General Conference then authorized Superintendent Rush to appoint Secretaries and the other three Vice Presidents of the above institution. It was, on motion—

Resolved, By the General Conference, that the Constitution of the School Fund be so altered or amended as to allow each Vice President appointed by the Conference, from time to time, to organize a Committee in his district sufficient to meet the demands of the Constitution.

It was further, on motion—

Resolved, That the Central Committee draw a plan of said building, and an estimate of the cost of the same, and submit it to their acting committees as soon as possible.

Also, on motion—

Resolved, That the Central Committee of the School Fund are requested to appoint their Agents, and make their appeal to the public as soon as practicable.

On Motion—

Resolved, That the Book Agents are authorized to have printed one thousand copies of the Minutes of the Conferences. And also they are authorized to have three hundred copies of the Discipline bound.

On motion—

Resolved, That in view of the bill presented to the Conference against the Publishing Committee for printing one thousand copies of our Hymn Books, that the General Conference receive the stock bargained for, paying the balance of the printer's bill.

On motion of the House the following Constitution was received and adopted by the General Conference.

CONSTITUTION
Of the Ministers' Mutual Benefit Society

ARTICLE I

This Society shall be called the Preachers' Mutual Benefit Society of the African Methodist Episcopal Zion Church in America, and is established for the benefit of destitute superannuated Preachers, their Widows and Orphans.

ARTICLE II

Any Preacher of this Connection may become a member of this Society by paying one dollar initiation and the further sum of one dollar annually.

ARTICLE III

No minister shall be entitled to share in the benefits of this Society who is not a contributor, and who has not done at least five years effective service in the Itineracy of the Connection.

ARTICLE VI

The funds of this Society shall be paid over to the General Agent of the African Methodist Episcopal Book Concern, and shall be considered a loan to said concern so long as they may be needed.

ARTICLE V

It shall be the duty of the Agent to keep a separate book for such funds, which shall contain the names of each contributor, and the Conference within whose bounds he or she may reside.

ARTICLE VI

Dividends shall be made annually of the interest at six percent, to each yearly Conference, in proportion to the amount which has been paid from within the bounds of each Conference, which dividends shall commence when one thousand dollars have been paid in, and which the Conference may have added to the capital, when there are no such cases as specified in the 1st and 3rd Articles.

ARTICLE VII

The General Agent shall give his receipt for all monies paid him for the above purposes, which receipts shall be entered on a book kept by the several yearly Conferences for that purpose.

ARTICLE VIII

When the permanent funds of this Society are no longer needed in the Book Concern, they shall be loaned at six per cent on security of real estate to at least twice the amount of the loan, and the interest shall be paid annually to the general Agent, who shall pay the same to the several Annual Conferences as specified in Art. 6.

Article IX

The business of this Society shall be conducted by a Committee appointed by the General Conference, to consist of an equal number of ministers from each annual Conference.

Article X

When contributors shall remove from one Conference to another, or when alterations shall be made in the boundaries of Conferences, the Book of the Agent shall be so regulated as to give each Conference its proper claim—he being duly notified.

Article XI

Each yearly Conference shall appropriate its portion of dividends among its proper claimants, according to the judgment of necessities.

Article XII

This Constitution may be altered or amended by a majority of the members at any General Conference of the African Methodist Episcopal Zion Church in America, so as not to effect its general principles.

The following special action of the Council, confirmed by the General Conference, as follows:

At a special meeting called by the Superintendent from emergency, to consider the propriety or impropriety of ordaining Mr. Robert Charles Henderson from Demerara.

Persons were present from the New England and New York Conferences. Rev. C. Rush, General Superintendent; Daniel Vandevere, James Simmons, John P. Thompson, Timothy Eato, Wm. H. Bishop.

The meeting organized by calling the Rev. C. Rush to the chair. D. Vandevere, Secretary. A letter was then presented by the Superintendent from Geo. A. Spywood of Boston, recommending brother R. C. Henderson to favorable notice, with documents from the Church and Society in St. Paul's Parish, East Sea Coast, county of Demerara, W. I., desiring said R. C. Henderson to be set apart or ordained an Elder and sent to them. The documents were then read. It was then, on motion—

Resolved, That the Superintendent open a correspondence with R. C. Henderson on these essential points, relating to his connecting himself with the American Church, and the toleration act of his country.

Which correspondence was had, and his answers were clear and lucid, and very satisfactory extending beyond enquiry. It was then thought best under the circumstances, by the council, that the Superintendent

proceed immediately to Boston and accomplish the wishes of the petitioners.
New York, July 12th, 1847.
Approved by the General Conference, June 12th, 1848.

The General Conference adjourned after eighteen days session, to meet on the fourth Saturday in June in Wesley Church, city of Philadelphia, Pa., 1852.

New York, June 17th, 1848
REV. CHRISTOPHER RUSH, *General Superintendent*
REV. GEORGE GELBRETH, *Assistant Superintendent*
SAMPSON TALBOT, *Secretary*

As the General Conference of 1848 provided for the organization of the two new Annual Conferences it is interesting to note the churches which composed the two areas: The Alleghany, as it was then spelled, was composed of the following circuits and stations: The Pittsburg Circuit consisted of Pittsburg (45 members), Washington, Pa. (22 members), and Bridgewater (13 members). Evidently the first named now is known as Wesley Center and John Wesley in that city. There is still a Washington, Pa. congregation, while the Bridgewater Church no longer exists. The second circuit consisted of Bedford, after which it was named, with 37 members, Hallidaysburg, as it is written, had listed 15 members, Johnstown listed 12 and Blairsville 14. All of these churches are still existent. The Third circuit, now a part of the Philadelphia and Baltimore Conference (Chambersburg, 100 members, Shippensburg with 28 members, Carlisle with 31 and Brownsville, the latter not now known with 30 members) and the fourth group, likewise of that Conference (York, 95 members, Gettysburg, 60 members, Barus, 31 members, Peach Bottom, 22 members, Columbia, 32 members, Chansford, 10 members, Center 15, and Lancaster, 8 members) are noted. It is not clear whether any of the following churches were set off with the Allegheny Conference, although at least one of these points is west of the line drawn: Lewistown (42); Bellefonte (48); Perryville, 14: and Williamsport (45). Listed also is Alleghany Station in the appointments when David Stevens was assigned. Other appointments made to this new Western area were: Pittsburg Circuit, Jacob Trusty, "in his charge" Isaac Coleman, William Burley; Bedford Circuit, Shadrach Golden: Lewistown Circuit, Joseph Sinclair, "in his charge" Peter Fulman, Charles J. Carter.[1] Con-

---
[1] *Minutes of the Philadelphia Conference of* 1848, 17, 18.

ference support was paid by Blairsville and (40¢) and Alleghany Station, $1.00.

While no elaboration is made on one of the resolutions offered at the session, one wonders about a paper which appears to have enjoyed partial Conference support:

> Resolved: That this Conference cannot support the paper published in Pittsburg called the Mystery, as it has become a party paper.[2]

Another resolution evidently had to do with a discussion on the episcopacy for it is stated:

> Resolved, That the African Methodist E. Church repudiates the bishopric set up by any and every church, digressing from the Apostolic principles—and that we, as a connection, will stand on the mode layed down by our father in Methodism.

The Genesee Conference, on its formation, evidently was composed of the following points: Syracuse (23); Little Falls (23); Oswego (no membership listing); Sodus (20); Canandaigua, (14): Ithaca (30); Utica (9). These were members of that which was called the Syracuse Circuit. There were two other circuits in this Conference: Bath Circuit consisting of Bath (13); Elmira (47); Binghampton (35); Montrose (23); and Auburn Station (20): Rochester Circuit, consisting of Rochester (45) and Lockport (18).[3]

In the chapter dealing with the Days of Reconstruction more will be said about the work in Nova Scotia but in the year in which we are dealing Halifax, Nova Scotia, listed as the British America Mission reported 72 members. While in the reporting of appointments made this church was to be supplied, S. Giles was sent as a Missionary to the Province of Nova Scotia.

Frequently the insistence of these early churchmen for equality of opportunity is overlooked so it is of interest to note too, the resolution on this matter:

> Resolved: That the color of a man's skin is no objection to his becoming a member of this Conference.

It was in this Conference as well that John P. Thompson "was suspended from all official standing" for refusing to travel.

---

[2] *Minutes of the Philadelphia Conference of 1848*, 19.
[3] *Minutes of the New York Annual Conference*, 1848, 21.

The New England Conference has one item of extreme interest in that year. The Rev. G. A. Spywood was designated "oversight," an early term for that which we now know as "Presiding Elder." [4]

In the Baltimore Annual Conference minutes of 1851, the controversy over the matter of the title of Superintendent and that of Bishop is exhibited in the following:

> Resolved, That this Conference consider the use of the word, Bishop, and the Third Ordination, as set forth in the new Discipline of 1851, as inconsistent with our form of Church Government.[5]

The Philadelphia Conference concurred in this resolution.[6]

The Genesee Conference evidently ran into difficulty in its first sessions for the New York Conference noted: "Resolved, That the Genesee Conference be held on the second Saturday in September, A.D. 1851." Earlier, Superintendent Rush had stated that an effort should be made to "resuscitate" that Conference. Discussion followed and the resolution resulted. A second resolution was likewise drawn on the subject:

> Resolved, That the Secretary be instructed to write letters to the various societies in the West, informing them of the decision of this Conference, and they that use their influence in procuring means to support the said Conference.[7]

The New York Conference likewise approved of the action re: the Superintendent and Bishop controversy, as noted in the Baltimore area.

At this session of the New York Conference a petition was received from the "People of Liverpool, Nova Scotia" but the matter was laid on the table. Another Church reported from this area as well, Cubbigut Road (with nine members).

The Conference also received a communication from its Missionary in Demerara, Brother Henderson, requesting hymn books.[8] These were not sent simply because they were not available, but the Superintendent hoped this could be remedied.

According to the new plans of the New York Conference, the

---
[4] *Minutes of the Fourth Annual New England Conference*, 23 (1848).
[5] *Minutes of the Baltimore Annual Conference*, 1851, 6.
[6] *Minutes of the Philadelphia Annual Conference of* 1851, 12.
[7] *Ibid.*
[8] *Minutes of the New York Annual Conference of* 1851, 19.

Genesee Conference met in "Zion's Church, in the village of Ithaca, Saturday Afternoon, Sept., 13, 1851." [9] Churches reporting at this session were Binghamton, (40), Elmira (30), Syracuse, Auburn, Montrose (30), Rochester, Ithaca (35), Rockton and Lockport. Sunday Schools were reported from Elmira (40), Binghamton (30), Montrose and Ithaca (25).[10]

Confusion exists where the matter of a J. W. Logain is concerned. It is not clear as to whether this is J. W. Loguen or a different individual. However, J. W. Logain had requested to withdraw from the connexion so this matter was taken up by the Conference. It appeared that some correspondence had gone on between him and the Superintendent and this was brought into the discussion. A motion was finally made that his request be granted but it was lost. The matter was laid aside for the time being but was taken up again the next day when a resolution was passed stating "That the case of J. W. Logain be laid over until the next sitting of the New York Conference, third Saturday in May A. D. 1852." [11] As the Conference concluded John Anderson was appointed to Ithaca Station, Binghamton, Elmira and Montrose were to be pastored by John A. Williams with Leonard Patterson assisting. Edwin H. Bishop was assigned to Rochester and Lockport while the Syracuse Circuit had John Tappan with John Thomas and Geo. Bausley assisting, working with Auburn, Syracuse and Rockton.

By the Conference of 1853 the great division within the Church had taken place and a segment had withdrawn. The Genesee Conference found it necessary to take some type of action. The following is noted: "The house resolved to appoint four brethren to lay before the public some of the facts which caused the rebellious faction to leave the African Methodist Episcopal Zion connection. The President appointed the Rev. J. J. Clinton, J. Trusty, S. Collins, J. A. Williams. Accordingly a note was prepared and read to the public, inviting the people at large to hear these 'brethren make the statements on the afternoon of to-morrow.' " [12]

Meanwhile the Conference took other matters under advisement among them being the statement of the Rev. James Harper of

---

[9] *Minutes of the Genesee Annual Conference,* 1851, 3.
[10] *Ibid.,* 9.
[11] *Ibid.,* 6.
[12] *Minutes of the Genesee Annual Conference,* 1853 (Andrus, Gauntlett and Co's Steam Power Press, Ithaca, N. Y.) 5.

Canada who requested that the Genesee Conference establish an Annual Conference in Canada. The Conference then passed the following resolution: "Resolved, That an annual Conference be held in the city of Hamilton on the 15th of October, 1853." [13]

A period of remembrance was set aside for the late Assistant Superintendent, Rev. George *Galbrath* who had passed away on April 6, 1853.

The situation within the denomination appeared to be one which could not be taken lightly. As the Conference carefully examined and answered each of the disciplinary questions from the very opening of the Conference until its closing day, it finally wound up its work, by again returning to this vexing matter:

synopsis of matter PRESENTED BEFORE THE CHURCH AND CONGREGATION OF ELMIRA, IN REFERENCE TO THE RELIGIOUS FACTION OF SECEDERS FROM THE AFRICAN METHODIST EPISCOPAL ZION CONNEXION.

These were presented in connection with the synopsis printed and published by the New York Annual Conference proper, who met at Williamsburg June 9, 1853, by Rev. Jacob Trusty, of D. C.; Rev. Leonard Collins of Bridgeport; Rev. Joseph J. Clinton of Philadelphia; Rev. John A. Williams of Sackets Harbor, L.I.

1st. By J. Trusty, that Ex-Superintendent Rush, in 1852, at the General Conference held in Philadelphia, came to him, as one of the nominating committee, and told him to keep Rev. Wm. H. Bishop off the ticket and put their's on. It was fully proven that the cause was a wicked aspiration for office. The synopsis of Williamsburg, L. I. here added, will give full satisfaction. (See Synopsis.) [14]

The Conference then adjourned.

SYNOPSIS OF MATTERS

Pertaining to the Interests of the African Methodist Episcopal Zion Church

In accordance with the appointment of the Conference in the selection of a committee of five to lay before the public in circular form the causes which lead to the removal of the New York A.M.E. Zion Annual Conference proper, to Williamsburg, L. I., beg leave to state a few facts out of the many, which are as follows:—

The ejecting of the Rev. W. H. Bishop from the chair, by a portion of the conference members, appointing Rev. John C. Spencer to fill it, the

---
[13] *Ibid.,* 7
[14] *Minutes of the Genesee Annual Conference of* 1853, 12.

reason given by the revolters and usurpers in justification of their rebellious course of procedure, was, a pretended charge against his moral character, the charge was preferred by Joseph P. Thompson, who put it in the hands of Rev. Demsy Kennedy, who was then pastor of Zion Church, New York, he forwarded it to Supt. Bishop, November of 1852, the Supt. was then in Western New York, on official duty; notwithstanding the illegality of the call, Supt. returned from the West, took with him an Elder, repaired forthwith to New York, called on the Rev. D. Kennedy and after informing him of the illegal manner in which he had called him to trial, he stated to Rev. Kennedy that he stood before him an accused person, and after demanding of him the specification of the charge told him he was ready for trial. In answer to which, Elder Kennedy said to Supt. Bishop that he did not know the particulars in the charge and was not prepared to give any specification respecting it, and referred him to Joseph P. Thompson, refusing to take any further action in the premises. The Supt. failing to obtain any satisfaction, and being indifferently treated was from the necessity of the case compelled to give the matter up. Subsequently he called on Rev. Kennedy who solicited him to preach and assist him to administer the Lord's Supper which he complied with, and was more or less in New York for several weeks successively, *occasionally* calling on Rev. Kennedy. The Supt. having learned from reliable sources that he had been grossly and maliciously misrepresented; the Rev. Kennedy having repeated that he (Bishop) had organized societies under another name, instead of the A.M.E.Z. Church in *American,* and furthermore, asserted that he had divided and destroyed the whole connection and that he was no supt., which report was contradicted in the Zion Church by the supt. to a crowded audience; after this contradiction, the Rev. Kennedy became more indignant, and resuming his wonted course, consequently the members of the Quarterly Conference of Zion Church was called together before whom Supt. Bishop laid his grievances, and contradicted there the report the Rev. Kennedy had circulated.—the Rev. Kennedy denied before them of ever circulating the report complained of by the Supt., but many of the members of the body contradicted him (Kennedy) to his face declaring that he had so reported. The members of the board apparently becoming satisfied with the statement made by the Supt. respecting his position and course of his administration, a motion prevailed nearly unanimously that they would sustain the Supt. while he held to the discipline, after which the meeting adjourned. The Supt. having learned that the Rev. Kennedy still continued to go on "Galio like" in the defamation of his character, was finally compelled to proceed against the Rev. Kennedy according to the rule of discipline, (see Article 4, 35th page Discipline, 1848,) and also he the (supt.) at the same time proceeding against Rev. Joseph P. Thompson as above stated who also has defamed the character of the Supt. by repeating falsehoods as well as sowing schisms. They were cited to trial before a committee of three neighboring Elders, evaded it by absenting themselves. The committee in conjunction with the quarterly conference therefore suspended them from all official standing until the sitting of the Annual Conference. When that body assembled the General Supt. was prevented from organizing the Conference as before stated. Several days passed during which time strenuous efforts were made by the Supt. and others for an adjustment of the affair without success. Subsequently a motion prevailed in that body, "that the New York conference do not recognize Wm. H. Bishop to be General Superintendent"; he (Bishop) nevertheless insisted on having the matter cleared up, and challenged any person composing that body to point him to a single instant wherein he had violated the Constitution of the A.M.E.Z. Church at this junction. *Father* C. Rush stated that the Supt. Bishop had been called to trial by the Rev. Kennedy, but evaded it, upon which the Rev. Kennedy arose and *declared* to the audience and a large number of spectators that he (Kennedy) never called Wm. H. Bishop to trial since he was born; the Supt. finally demanded a fair and impartial investigation of the charge preferred against him and failing to obtain satisfaction in any way, he proceeded to organize the New York Annual Conference (proper) of the A.M.E.Z. Church in America, in the basement of Zion's Church, corner of Church and Leonard Sts. but being repulsed by two of the Trustees of said Church, viz, Isaac Burnell and William Burnett; while in session, he was compelled to adjourn to meet in Zion's Church, in the city of Williamsburgh, L. I., demanding all the members of the conference to repair thither. N. B. Supt. Bishop was called to trial by one elder, instead of three, or two elders and one deacon; and at the commencement of the so-called conference, they received the delegates from the different conferences invited by the elder, except J. J. Clinton, who they thought would not agree with their measures after he arrived, and they learned his sentiment, they rejected all the delegates from Philadelphia conference because they were judged to be supported by the general conference action in electing Supt.

The conference having met in Williamsburgh, it was proceeded as announced daily until the business which came before it was finished. During the session the following Elders were expelled from the connection of the A.M.E.Z. Church in America, viz:—Joseph P. Thompson and Demsey Kennedy, for causes before named. The others who were of the *rebellious* and insubordinate party were suspended from all official standing in the above named connection, names as follows: John C. Spence, Christopher Rush, John Dungy, Leven Smith, Timothy Eaton (Ed. note: may have been Eato), Peter Ross, Noah Brooks, Cyrus Bocha, Wm. H. Decker, James R. Levingston, James Davis, Silas Mitchell. Finally, we are decidedly of the opinion that the general Supt. Wm. H. Bishop is not guilty of any act of immorality as charged, but think it was to have been a preconcerted plot and scheme of malicious aspirants, who being defeated in an election to the superintendency, through envy, sought to thrust him from the position he occupies—having declared in word and deed that they would not have Supt. Bishop to rule over them. The foregoing was received and adopted unanimously by the Conference, and commended to a

religious and an intelligent public for their careful perusal.
In Behalf of the Conference
William H. Bishop, General Supt.
John P. Thompson, Secretary.
Williamsburgh, L. I. 1853 [15]

In order to understand the full implications of this situation it is necessary that the reader refer to a History of the A.M.E. Zion Church, Part I, 1796-1872 by David H. Bradley, Sr., Chapter XI, page 131 ff. The above statement is that of the one wing of the Church and needs to be seen in the light of that which has been said previously.

The Baltimore Annual Conference of 1853 took cognizance of the restless condition of the denomination when the following resolution was passed:

Whereas, There are many grievous evils now existing in the various churches composing this wide-spread connection, arising from the non-enforcement of the book of Discipline, by ministers having the charge of circuits and stations.
Therefore,

Resolved, That we the members of the Baltimore Conference will, from this time forth, endeavor to enforce the rules of discipline, and shall also hold any member of this Conference, having the charge of a circuit or station, chargeable that fails to do the same.[16]

The Philadelphia Conference[17] and the New England Conference[18] as well as the New York endorsed this resolution.[19]

The New York Conference likewise adopted another Resolution which said in part:

Resolved, That Bros. Dempsey Kennedy and Joseph P. Thompson, be, and are hereby expelled from the connection for violation of suspension rule.

A second Resolution passed by the Conference contained the following:

Whereas: the Brethren named in the following preamble and resolutions, refused to acknowledge the Superintendent appointed by the

---
[15] *Minutes of the Genesee Annual Conference of* 1853, 13-15.
[16] *Minutes of the Baltimore Annual Conference,* 1853, 8.
[17] *Minutes of the Philadelphia Annual Conference,* 1853, 18.
[18] *Minutes of the New England Annual Conference,* 1853, 32.
[19] *Minutes of the New York Annual Conference,* 1853, 26.

General Conference of A.M.E.Z. Church in America, and whereas an attempt was made on their part to sustain the charges against the Superintendent, William H. Bishop, which were without the slightest foundation, but the result of malice aforethought or envy. Furthermore, when the General Superintendent had proceeded to organize the New York Annual Conference proper, it was discovered that the rebellious faction had influenced two of the trustees of Zion Church to demand said place of worship, which rendered it necessary for the Superintendent to request the Conference to meet him in Williamsburgh Zion Church; the rebellious faction refused so to do, and on being summoned to answer the charge of insubordination, refused;

Therefore, Resolved, That they be suspended from all official standing in the A.M.E.Z. Church, until the next New York Annual Conference, unless they discover their error and retract. In such case they may communicate the same to the General Superintendent, William H. Bishop, in the interval, who may restore them sooner if he deems it expedient.

The names of the persons suspended by the above resolution are: John Dungy, Peter Ross, Wm. H. Decker, Noah Brook, L. Smith, Timothy Eato, Cyrus Bocha, J. C. Spence, Christopher Rush, James Davis, J. R. Livingston and Silas Mitchel.[20]

A final Resolution on this matter was presented by George Washington, and seconded by John Wells. This Resolution also passed.

Resolved, That this Conference prepare charges against James Simmons of the New England Conference, and John Tappan of the Genesee Conference, for insubordination and rebellion against the New York Conference.[21]

Records seem to show that for a time two Annual Conferences were held in New York, the one with the actions noted above and the second, presided over by the Reverend John C. Spence. This Conference tried Superintendent Bishop and stated that he no longer could function in the name of the Church.

Two matters appear to have been the basis for this disagreement within the Church, the subject of the ranking of the Superintendents and the discussion on the dropping of the title *African* and substituing *Wesleyan*. Writers of the period agree that the majority of the members and churches were with the Bishop faction but the group

---

[20] *Minutes of the New York Annual Conference,* 1853, 26, 27.
[21] *Ibid.,* 27.

suffered an irreparable blow in the loss of the Lycoming County Court Case.

This writer would again point out, however, that a new impetus was given the Church in these years of controversy for many new organizations came out of these seemingly dark and tragic days.

CHAPTER II

Days of Reconstruction and the African Methodist Episcopal Zion Church

IT IS almost a brash suggestion for one to endeavor to sum up the work of a denomination which covers a period of the greater part of a half century. And yet, that any work might be broad enough in its view that the reader can at least gain an idea of the magnificent sweep of events, one must at least mention, though not in detail, the hurrying events which made of this people a national church. Few of its present three quarters of a million members could have any concept of the deep consecration and broad interests of its early leaders and followers.

One knows, it would seem, of the work of the Reverend J. W. Hood in North Carolina and Virginia and the story of the delay of the New England Conference's first appointee to this mission work, the Reverend John Williams. The story of the part played by Miss Malvina Fletcher, a maid in the home of the Postmaster General, Honorable Montgomery Blair, may or may not be known.[1] It will be recalled that she became deeply interested in the work of Superintendent Joseph Jackson Clinton, one of her own Church leaders, and made a contribution in gold to the work and than urged Mr. Blair to secure a pass from the then Secretary of War, Stanton, that these missionaries might follow hard after the Union Armies as they struck deeper into the heart of the Southland. The Church remembers her burial place, Harmony Cemetery in the Nation's Capital.

Known too, is the work of the Reverend Wilbur G. Strong, the missionary to Florida, Louisiana and Alabama. Meanwhile the Reverend Butler was at work in Kentucky and the Reverend John Jamison Moore had sailed to the West Coast. But there are some hidden items of history which we would likewise like to mention.

While it is said that the Key West Church is a living testimonial to the work of the Reverend Wilbur Strong it has been noted, for example, that the New England Conference also sent out the Reverend

---

[1] Bishop E. D. W. Jones, *Comprehensive Catechism of the A. M. E. Zion Church*, (Washington, D. C., 1934) 26.

Samuel G. Birchmore to this point.[2] It is said that he organized churches as well in Tampa, Simmons and Hammock, located in Dade and Marion Counties. As was the pattern for pastorates in churches, he remained but two years, however. The Reverend J. W. Lacey, although born in Fauquier County, Virginia, eventually found himself in Hayti as early as 1861. Two years later he was elected a General Superintendent there (1863) and in that same year it is recorded that the Zion Methodist Church and the A.M.E. Church held a joint convention at Gro Mound. The other two Superintendents resigned (Superintendents Pierce and Clingman) and Reverend Lacey led the destinies of the united group with his headquarters at St. Marc. In 1869 Reverend Lacey returned to the United States and joined the Genesee Conference.[3]

The Bahama Islands Conference was organized by Bishop Joseph P. Thompson in 1877 (Dec., 16), with some six elders and four deacons present. Evidently, Wilbur G. Strong, who was connected with the work in Florida, accompanied the Bishop as he set about to organize this work.[4]

Quite frequently one overlooks the original work of J. W. Hood as we point time after time to his significant work in North Carolina and Virginia. After his admittance to the New England Conference he was sent as a missionry to Nova Scotia. He states: "As there were no funds on hand to send him out he returned to New York and went to work in a hotel for thirteen months, at the end of which time he had saved enough money to provide for his family and to take him to his field of labor."[5] He goes on to state that he was ordained a deacon in Boston, the first Sunday in September, 1860, and sailed for Halifax the following Wednesday At the end of the year's work he sent for his family. He, himself states, that his accomplishments were limited but that he succeeded in organizing one church of eleven members.

The Reverend Robert Russell Morris was actually born in Nova Scotia, May 27, 1833. It cannot be ascertained when the first Zion Church was established but his parents were among the first mem-

---

[2] Bishop J. W. Hood, *One Hundred Years of the African Methodist Episcopal Zion Church*, (New York, 1895) 254.
[3] Hood, *loc. cit.*, 277-279.
[4] *Ibid.*, 399.
[5] *Ibid.*, 187.

bers of that group.⁶ No doubt he would have been our first missionary to Africa had he not been dissuaded and instead landed in Hayti. Earlier, he, too, had been appointed to the Nova Scotia area where he spent two years, erecting a combination church and school building at Mauroon Hill. He pastored a second time in Nova Scotia but because of the lack of men and money the main points were lost to the British Methodist Episcopal Church. Later, Morris established a church on the Island of Bermuda, giving strength to the Bermuda Conference.⁷

The Nova Scotia area endeavors were not without their rewards for not only did it produce Robert Russell Morris but also William Harvey Goler, the second President of Livingstone College. Goler was converted in an A.M.E. Zion Church in Halifax then pastored by Rev. Stephen Goosley.⁸

William Harvey Goler was born in Halifax, Nova Scotia, January 1, 1846. He and Morris were personal friends in early life. In 1870, Goler went to Boston, later matriculated at Lincoln University in Pennsylvania (1873). Two years later he met Edward Moore, who later became a Medical Doctor and was asked to serve at Livingstone with Dr. Price. Again these two friends found themselves serving in the same project together. For a time William Harvey Goler pastored but is better known to the Zion Constituency for his work at the college and as a General Officer of the denomination.

Few writers have given great note of the spiritual war which, in many respects, overlapped the American Civil War in the 1860's. The prize over which this new conflict was waged was the religious lives of the black men and women and children of the South. The eventual loser was the Methodist Episcopal Church, South. In another work we have pointed out the existence of this church's deep interest and recognized obligation to the slaves and freedmen of the section of the country where the churches were found. Dwight W. Culver wrote of the period following 1844: "With the restraint in the matter of their attitude toward slavery removed, the Methodist Episcopal Church South looked upon Negro missions as a great opportunity and a special task. No longer a part of a denomination with a strong abolitionist wing, it was able to reach Negroes on plan-

---

⁶ Hood, *loc. cit.*, 414-419.
⁷ *Ibid.*, 419.
⁸ *Ibid.*, 447 ff.

tations where Methodist gospel had been unwelcome earlier. By 1860 Southern Methodism numbered in its membership 207,766 Negroes and over 180,000 Negro children under instruction."

Culver goes on to state: "In the six years after 1860, the Negro membership of the Methodist Episcopal Church South dropped to 78,742 with resultant gains for the independent Negro denominations." However, it appears that not all of these members were lost to Negro Churches but the Methodist Episcopal Church, North benefited from this state of affairs as well.

As the Zion Methodist Church widened its mission outlook to include the Islands of the Sea it was logical that she should early look South as well. The great numbers of free men, freedmen and escaped slaves she had among her membership already established ties with many sections of the South. For example Christopher Rush, the second Superintendent came from the region of New Bern(e), North Carolina, while Jermain Louguen had a mother and brothers and sisters along with himself in slavery in Kentucky and Tennessee. At one time he refused the Superintendency because there was danger that he might have to labor in the South. John Jamison Moore escaped from slavery along with his mother and father and at least one brother, the owner being located somewhere in Virginia or that which is now known as West Virginia. There were many, many other ties to be found as well.

The action of the New England Conference (to foster activity in North Carolina) and the New Conference (to foster work in Louisiana and the Deep South) were logical ones. The Superintendent, and later, Bishop Joseph Jackson Clinton, saw the possibilities and so, leading these conferences, the project of missionary effort got underway.

John Williams, a minister, was accordingly appointed to begin the work. It is intimated that he knew or was aware of the danger involved so delayed most of one year.[9] The Conference being impatient, the Bishop then appointed J. W. Hood in December of the same year. By January Reverend Hood had moved his family to Washington, D.C. and by the twentieth of that month found himself in New Bern(e), North Carolina trying to persuade Andrew Chapel to join Zion Methodism. In the effort to lead the church out of the Methodist Episcopal Church South fold were several other

---

[9] Hood, *loc. cit.*, I, 289.

groups, including the Congregationalists, and two representatives of the A.M.E. Church, working out of Norfolk, Virginia.[10]

Because of a Small Pox epidemic the Union Army head had decreed that no worship services or larger gatherings of people should be held, so the initial jockeying for the Church had to be carried on through its official board, made up of some 40 persons. Because of the presentation of facts made by Hood the Board finally accepted the idea of joining Zion Methodism. However, the matter had to be taken up with the congregation. With the opening victory carried in the Board the struggle then became one between the Methodist Episcopal Church South and the Zion denomination. The question of ministerial credentials came before the General and a communication was forwarded to the Secretary of War, Edward M. Stanton. The communication follows:

> "So far as I am informed both Hood and Round are regularly ordained ministers, and are both men of good character. The point at issue is, shall a congregation of colored people, who have owned their church and worshipped in it for twenty-five years, have the right to elect their own pastor, or are they compelled to have a pastor forced upon them by Bishop Baker's delegate? There is an old church maxim that a Bishop cannot delegate his power."

The Secretary of War replied, using the same communication:

> The congregation worshipping in Andrew Chapel are permitted to select their own pastor.
>
> E. M. Stanton, Secretary of War[11]

Reverend Hood, later Bishop mentions the organizing or the taking in of several churches in this area, among them being Roanoke Island, which rivals New Bern for being the oldest Zion Methodist Church in the South and Beaufort. Clinton Chapel Church was either organized or taken in by the Reverend E. H. Hill who, according to Bishop Hood, "organized" some twenty churches within 50 miles of Charlotte. The Bishop declared that he actually *preached himself to death.*[12] He had been ordained a deacon by Bishop Clinton in the morning and an elder in the afternoon at the Conference and was so impressed with the call that his work has seldom been equaled.

---
[10] *Ibid.*, 291.
[11] Hood, *loc. cit.*, 293.
[12] *Ibid.*, 297.

In May, 1864 Superintendent Clinton arrived in New Bern (e),[13] evidently prior to the meeting of the General Conference in Philadelphia (May 25, 1864).[14] It would not appear likely that he would have left the sessions to make this visit. It is interesting to note that which Hood has to say about the missionary work of the Conference sponsoring the work in the South. He states that from the New York Conference's efforts the following had developed: New England, Genesee (now the Western New York), the New Jersey and Louisiana. Seven or eight conferences were organized from the Louisiana.[15]

The New England Conference, after its organization in 1845 gave birth to the short lived Nova Scotia Conference, the North Carolina (1864) and those conferences which were formed from this Conference; South Carolina, 1866[16] and Central North Carolina in 1879. Meanwhile, the Old Philadelphia Conference which later combined with the Southern Conference to form the Philadelphia and Baltimore Conference (1828—this date is that of the Philadelphia Conference) had a great deal to do with the organizing of the Allegheny (1852) and the Ohio (1891). The Canada and Michigan Conference dates from 1877. It met in Pontiac in 1895, for example.[17]

By 1895 another North Carolina Conference had been organized, the Western (1890). Meanwhile, Wilbur Strong had pushed the work in the deep South organizing and taking in churches in Alabama, Georgia and Florida and David Hill had been sent into North Carolina to aid the work there.[18] The Reverend William F. Butler is credited with much of the work in Kentucky and the mid-west. Bishop Hood states that he had "decided ability, but was not well balanced." As a result of Butler's work and others, the Kentucky Conference was organized in 1866—June 6 by Bishop Sampson D. Talbot. In truth, the work here grew to the point that at one time there were two conferences, the Kentucky and the West Kentucky Conferences. Most of the work, however, was lost because of a disagreement with the Reverend W. H. Miles who, it appeared,

---
[13] *Ibid.*, 296.
[14] J. Harvey Anderson, *Official Directory of* 1895-1896, 30.
[15] Hood, *loc. cit.*, I, 214.
[16] Anderson, *loc. cit.*, 66. Hood states that the South Carolina Conference was organized in 1867, (March 24) 573.
[17] Hood, *loc. cit.*, 87.
[18] *Ibid.*, 86.

wished to become a Bishop of Zion Methodism. Bishop Hood gives the following account as it was written by the Reverend E. H. Curry:

"The membership of the Conference was made up of men of no experience in the itinerant work, and without a knowledge of the polity of the Church. They were sent to their appointments in many places without a church edifice, nay, without any members, nevertheless they went trusting in God for success. The superintendent left and was seen no more until the next Annual Conference, and the only guides left to instruct the conference were Rev. W. F. Butler and Rev. W. H. Miles. The latter was appointed general missionary and supported from Center Street Church by the Daughters of Conference, or at least in part.

"At the reassembling of the Second Annual Conference, William Haywood Bishop, general superintendent, presided. Reverend W. F. Butler was removed from Center Street Church and succeeded by Rev. W. H. Miles. Hence some feeling of unpleasantness sprang up between these two divines. The Superintendent, however, left again, to be seen no more until the sitting of the Third Annual Conference at which the Rev. J. W. Loguen, general superintendent presided. Then began the scene of trouble in the Conference, and the Reverend W. H. Miles tendered his resignation, which was finally received. This created quite a feeling, and many of the leading men of the higher rank left, until the conference was left with only seven elders all told, and many of the churches followed in rapid succession; yet there were a few who dared to hold on to Zion, and continued to struggle against all opposition. Rev. Richard Bridwell, Samuel Elliot, Rev. A. Bunch, Samuel Shurman, Leroy Brannon, J. B. Stansbury, William T. Biddle, with one other man, were all the elders left in the Kentucky Conference. One year later showed a gradual decline in both churches and communicants. This rigor in the conference discouraged both members and ministers, and all the more because the ministers being returned to their former charges it was easy for them to confuse the minds of the people by trying to carry them into the Colored Methodist Episcopal Church, and that by the same men who led them into the Zion Connection at a date still fresh in their memory.

One year later reports show the following churches lost: Falmouth, Ky.; Millersburg, Ky.; Carrollton, Ky.; Flemingsburg, Ky.; Burksville, Ky.; Greenburg, Ky.; with Center St. Church, Louisville, Ky. But there were a faithful few who still stood up for Zion.

The next event worthy of special mention was the appointment of Right Rev. S. T. Jones, D. D. to the Third Episcopal District, which gave new life and impulse to the Kentucky Conference. The work settled to a firmer base during the twelve consecutive years of his administration, notwithstanding there was some dissatisfaction in the Board of Bishops and among leading men about Organic Union with the Methodist Episcopal Church, and the Conference being told by those in authority that the union would be consumated in the near future it was hard for them to tell what they were. This had much to do in shaking their faith in the firmness and stability of Zion Connection. But the fight ended and the faithful few were seen doing what they could to build up Zion. The Kentucky Conference carried the standard of Zion into Indiana, Illinois and Missouri, and organized the Arkansas and the Missouri Annual Conferences.[19]

Bishop Hood gives three men credit for the work in The Rev. A. Y. Carr and the Reverends A. J. Warner, later a Bishop of the denomination and J. M. Washington. The West Coast work owes its origin to the Reverend John J. Moore, who sailed to California in 1852. The Old Starr King Church in San Francisco appears to have been the oldest church on the West Coast, evidently established in that year. At one time every outstanding Negro in the City was a member of Zion Church. However, a setback came several years later. It will be noted that the Church was organized just two years after California was admitted into the union as a state. Negroes, however, had been in California as early as 1840. Reverend Starr King, after which the organization was named, was an outstanding abolitionist. Incidently, Reverend Moore was the first Negro School Teacher in the state. In 1906 the earthquake and fire destroyed the Church building and for three years the people were without a pastor. It was during this time that the ascendancy of Zion appeared to have been lost.[20]

Other organizations on the West Coast were San Jose, which still exists and Napa, which has gone out of existence. The Church at San Jose, for several years had a pew which had been brought around the Horn but in recent years its identity has been lost.

Of deep significance was the Kentucky defection as it related to the newly formed Colored Methodist Episcopal Church and Zion Methodism. The Reverend W. H. Miles, we have stated earlier, resigned from the A.M.E. Zion Church in the controversy involving Reverend Butler. He was born in Springfield, Washington County, Kentucky on December 26, 1828. A slave, he was owned by a Mrs. Mary Miles, who, in her will, as was the custom in that day for many to do, gave him his freedom. It is our understanding that the will was contested to the point that even though the will was probated possibly in 1854, he was not freed until 1864. A year following his being set free he joined the Methodist Episcopal Church, South. A short time after his conversion, he felt the call to preach and

---

[19] Hood, *loc. cit.*, 329, 330.
[20] *Souvenir Program,* First A. M. E. Zion Church, San Francisco, Calif., 1960.

applied for a license in 1856. The request was denied but a year later the Presiding Elder, a Reverend A. H. Redford granted him the license. At the instance of the Quarterly Conference he was recommended for deacon's orders and received them when the Conference met in Bardstown in 1859. Bishop Andrew was presiding over the sessions at the time.

In 1865 Reverend Miles moved to Ohio at a time when the great concern was being felt for the Negro members and churches organized and aided by the Methodist Episcopal Church, South as a result of the activity of Zion and Bethel and the Methodist Episcopal Church, North. This evidently caused Reverend Miles to consider joining one of the Negro denominations, which he did, selecting Zion Methodism. On returning to Kentucky, he naturally joined the Center Street A.M.E. Zion Church and the Zion Conference, the Church in 1865 and the Annual Conference in 1866, as one of the charter members. Two years later he became the pastor of Center Street Church and in that year represented his annual conference as a delegate in the General Conference held in Washington, D.C.

Because of the fact that Jermain Louguen was, at one time a slave in Kentucky and Tennessee, it is said that Reverend Miles supported him for the Bishopric in that year. Just what happened when Louguen was appointed to preside over the Kentucky Conference may never be known but in his first session of that Conference he moved Reverend Miles from Center Street Church and made him a missionary to travel and organize churches but no provision was made for his support. Naturally, he wrote out his resignation and withdrew from the Zion Methodist Church.[21] Later, he joined again the Methodist Episcopal Church, South and naturally became a part of the formation of the C.M.E. Church in December 1870 (December 15). He was listed as a reserve delegate in this General Conference of formation.

In that session, the First General Conference of the C.M.E. Church, the Reverend W. H. Miles was scheduled to preach and was so well received that it is suggested that this sermon aided in his election to the Bishopric. We would state that his organizing ability in the formation of the Kentucky Conference also played a leading part in this election. It is written of Bishop Miles that he always

---

[21] Bishop C. H. Phillips, *The History of the Colored Methodist Episcopal Church in America* (Jackson, Tenn., 1925) 196-204.

made his appointments "without prejudice or revenge," and for upwards of twenty-two years he led the new denomination in its development.

In 1892 Bishop Miles appeared so ill that it was impossible for him to perform the duties of his office. In fact, at that time he was confined to his home. The C.M.E. Kentucky Annual Conference, however, met in Louisville in that year and he attended some of the sessions and before it he made his last speech. Three weeks later he was dead. He was buried from Center Street Church, Thursday, November 17th. And thus ended one of the great and lasting ties with Zion Methodism.

CHAPTER III

The General Conferences of 1872 and 1876

WHEN THE General Conference of 1868 had completed its work Samson D. Talbot, John Jamison Moore, Joseph Jackson Clinton, Singleton T. Jones and John W. Loguen had been elected or re-elected heads of the Church and could now assume the title of Bishop as over against the title *Superintendent,* in vogue in the church since its founding in 1820 as a denomination. A biographical account of these men can be found in the first volume of the History.[1] Joseph Jackson Clinton, of course, not only from the standpoint of election and age but because of his great leadership of the denomination was the acknowledged head of the Board. However, the great acclaim accorded Singleton T. Jones at the Methodist General Conference (1868) in Chicago gave him a type of prominence not usually known to a man serving his first term on the Bench. He was evidently a progressive, one of those who *followed* the Wesleyan movement in 1852 and was actually the one who drew up the discipline of that group.[2]

The law of the denomination followed was that each General Conference would, before adjournment, select the meeting place of the next session. It appears that the 1868 General Conference had selected New York for the 1872 session. Just what caused a change of plans is not known definitely, but the Board of Bishops changed the meeting to Charlotte, North Carolina, in violation of custom and law. Singleton T. Jones insisted that the sessions be held in New York and at the time specified. The Board of Bishops in selecting Charlotte had stated that broad interpretation should be made of membership. Jones suggests that this was to insure a majority of delegates. He states: "Elder J. W. Hood (on the first day of the conference) presented the following which was adopted; viz: whereas the Board of Bishops have invited all the elders and lay delegates whether appointed by the lay convention or churches, shall be admit-

---

[1] David H. Bradley, Sr., *A History of the A. M. E. Zion Church,* 1796-1872, (Parthenon, 1956) 140, 141; 163-167.
[2] Bishop E. D. W. Jones, *Comprehensive Catechism, A. M. E. Zion Church,* (Washington, D. C. 1934) 24.

ted as members of this General Conference if in good standing in their several churches.³

The New York General Conference met in Dr. Henry Highland Garnett's Church (Presbyterian). The Charlotte General Conference met June 19th in Clinton Chapel Church. It appears that fifteen (Hood says 16) of the Annual Conferences had agreed to the time and place of the Charlotte meeting along with the Board of Bishops. Finally, Bishop Jones adjourned the New York Conference and proceeded to Charlotte.

Again, it is asserted that many angles of this circumstance remains hidden but there can be conjectures with a reasonable amount of certainty. It will be recalled that an effort was made to re-unite Zion with the Mother Church, when Singleton T. Jones served as Fraternal Delegate to the General Conference of that Church.⁴ It is supposed that an unofficial statement was made re: the matter of Organic Union and the willingness of the Mother Church to accept certain but not all of the Board of Bishops in any plan of union. Singleton Jones felt it wise that the Zion Methodist group meet as he felt it was scheduled, in New York City, where they would have the opportunity of instant and free conversations with the Methodist Episcopal Church. Certainly there was sufficient strength for the movement that the 1868 General Conference, is supposed to have selected that city for its meeting place.

Bishop Hood states that it was Bishop Haven of the Methodist Episcopal Church who attempted to spearhead this effort at union, but he was not able to persuade his denomination to accept the *pro rata* idea where the Board of Bishops was concerned. He goes on to state that "in all other respects we (Zion) should have such recognition as our numbers entitled us to," but again, it appears that this was not possible. It appears that Singleton Jones returned from Chicago and took up the matter to select the meeting place of the next General Conference but was informed that this had already been set. However, according to Hood, the matter was *reconsidered,* but in the rush of closing nothing was done at the time and the next day the General Conference adjourned without action on the matter. According to Hood, Charlotte, North Carolina had been selected prior to the move to reconsider.

---
³ *Ibid.,* 27.
⁴ See Chapter XVIII for the background of this matter.

THE GENERAL CONFERENCES OF 1872 AND 1876

A year before the sitting of the General Conference, the board of Bishops met and endeavored to decide the issue. Bishop Jones was presiding and even though the Board voted to go to Charlotte, objected and endeavored to overrule them. The other members of the Board appealed to the Annual Conferences and (one number is 15) (However, according to our count there were only seventeen conferences organized), sixteen accepted the majority decision. Bishop Jones, however (again the number of Conferences appears to be in dispute) with two or three of the Annual Conference delegates met in New York on the date legally set by the Quadrennial Body. Not having a quorum they adjourned to meet in Charlotte on the 19th of June, the date specified by the Majority of the Board.

Bishop Hood agrees that the change of date was in violation of law but the matter of change of place was an open matter. The meeting and adjournment in New York, Jones stated, legalized the Charlotte sessions. Incidentally, the Methdist Episcopal Church was meeting in Brooklyn.

Hood states had a vote been taken after the four hour speech of Jones, he would have carried the Conference, but the next day, Clinton responded in another four hour speech and the action noted was then taken.

Behind the scenes many discussions evidently were carried on. The majority of the Board naturally saw a danger in going to the city of the denomination's birth in the light of the supposed stand on Zion's Episcopacy. Naturally the Church had fewer churches and members for each Bishop selected because of the wide dispersion of Negroes over the Nation. In many cases too, churches were smaller in numbers than companionate white organizations. The extensive distance Zion Bishops had to travel made it well-nigh impossible to have as high a ratio as that of the Mother Church.

As in the early stages of the formation of the first organization, the matter of educational qualifications entered the controversy—this time on the level of the Bishopric. Bishop Moore gives only the barest details of the situation, once the two groups met in Charlotte. He states, for example, that the "Bishop (Jones) rose and read to the conference several eulogies he had received from various Annual Conferences in regard to his course (of action); he also read his diploma from Avery College, which had been conferred on him as

Doctor of Divinity; the Bishop continued his remarks in defense of the course he had taken until the adjournment of the session." [5]

One can imagine that the question of educational qualifications had come up in the controversy, a point lending credence to the belief that this acceptance of Zion Methodist Bishops was a key factor in the situation.

The next day, June 25, 1872, Bishop Joseph Jackson Clinton was selected to answer the statement of Bishop Jones. The entire morning was taken up with his reply in which he defended the action of the Board of Bishops and supporting action of *fifteen* of the Annual Conferences. At the conclusion of his statement he was accorded a vote of thanks by the Conference. Bishop Jones was then asked if he considered himself a Bishop on the basis of his election by the New York General Conference. His answer evidently satisfied the General Conference along with his statements made earlier regarding Elders J. P. Hamer and J. B. Trusty. Following the rule, his character was then passed and he received the right hand of fellowship.[6]

It must be asserted that Bishop Jones was not entirely in the wrong in his going ahead with General Conference supposedly assigned to New York. Evidently the controversy was so intense that it was not feasible to utilize the Mother Zion Church. This can be clearly seen. The Conferences had followed its right no doubt to select its next meeting place and 1872 did not abrogate this right. This mode existed at least until the end of the century—the leadership being so careful at one time as to actually open the General Sessions in Mobile before adjourning to the nearer site—Montgomery, to save travel costs and perhaps, a health hazard.

The change of meeting place of the 1872 General Conference was made possible for many reasons, chief among them being the fact that the balance of voting strength had shifted to the Southern Conferences. The desire to meet in the South was thereby aided by this movement. From this point on it will be noted that the projects of the denomination and the growth were to be seen in the South—the establishment of a periodical, the establishment of the University or College; in truth, all educational efforts turned to the section of the country where the major part of the people lived.

Earlier, we have made the statement that the change of meeting

---

[5] Moore, John J. Bishop, *loc. cit.*, 276, 277.
[6] *Ibid.*, 277.

THE GENERAL CONFERENCES OF 1872 AND 1876

place was in part due to that which many of the Bishops of Zion Methodism believed regarding unification. As late as the Sixteenth Session of the North Carolina Conference (November 26-December 3, 1879) Bishop Hood was stating: "The Methodist Episcopal Church had led many of us to believe that the desire on its part for us to become a part of its body was so great that it would offer us a honorable basis of union. Dazzled with the idea of becoming a part of that great body, a few have left us and tried to break up the conference. One of them told me he had 40 pledged to go with him. It looked at that time as though the first colored conference organized in the South was about to go to pieces. On the day that the conference assembled there was only a small number present. At that time I hardly knew whom to talk to as friends of Zion." [7]

This statement likewise gives another reason for the change of the meeting place for the General Conference as seen from so many years away—the necessity of welding together the gains the denomination had made in the post-Civil War years. Since most of the older Churches were Methodist Churches evidently established by the Southern branch of Methodism there would be less hesitation to join the Methodist Episcopal Church, North. In truth, it was stated that the rumors of unification with that body persuaded many persons to defect.

The depth of the controversy and feeling is to be noted in the Message of the Board of Bishops to the General Conference: "Dear Brethren, you can more fully appreciate our need of money to extend and support our connection, when we remind you of the two great monied religious bodies we have to grapple with—the M.E. Church north, and the M.E. Church south, who make their money a means of proselyting our preachers, in many cases especially the former body, and the steps taken by our body at our last General Conference toward consolidation with the M.E. Church has been used by unscrupulous agents of that church to proselyte our ministers and members, creating distraction among us and sometimes ruptures in our churches, which course no Christian body could sanction, in the light of the Golden Rule: Do unto others as you would have them do unto you. In relation to the question of affiliation and consolidation with the M.E. Church, we would wish as expressed in our General

---

[7] *Minutes of the Sixteenth Session of the North Carolina Conference,* November 26-Dec. 3, 1879, Lincolnton, N. C.

Conference in 1868, that all branches of Methodism on this continent were united; but from unfortunate developments connected with this movement, we are compelled to recommend the suspension of future action on the subject until the great obstacle to this happy result is farther removed: that is the prejudice of caste that still exists in the mother (the M.E.) church, yet we shall cultivate a friendly and Christian feeling toward our mother until she has reached the proper position on this question of caste.[8]

Despite this statement, however, there were areas of cooperation between the Methodist Episcopal Church and Zion Methodism. This statement appears, for example, in an extant copy of a hymnal used in Zion Methodist Churches:

Bishop' Address

Members and Friends of the African Methodist Episcopal Zion Church in America

Beloved Brethren: In consequence of the great difficulties our societies have labored under for the want of a suitable Collection of Hymns, the General Conference at its session of 1872, adopted the following book as used by the Methodist Episcopal Church. That the Triune God may make it a blessing to all into whose hands it may come is the sincere and earnest prayer of your humble pastors and companions in tribulation, and in the Kingdom and patience of Jesus Christ.

> BISHOPS
> JOSEPH JACKSON CLINTON
> SAMPSON D. TALBOT
> J. W. LOGUEN
> S. T. JONES
> JOHN J. MOORE
> J. W. HOOD

While the General Conference of 1872 was known in some circles as the "Battle of the Giants" or the "Struggle of the Giants," as Joseph Jackson Clinton and Singleton T. Jones struggled over points of ecclesiastical law,[9] the adoption of the Hymn Book will certainly be one of the milestones of attainment for that session. It was voted too, at this Conference, that a majority of the Board of Bishops could change the place of meeting of the Quadrennial sessions.[10] Other matters were recorded as well. Bishop Hood states that, un-

---

[8] Moore, *loc. cit.*, 286.
[9] F. Claude Spurgeion, ed., *A. M. E. Zion Handbook*, 1952-1956, 28.
[10] Jones, *loc. cit.*, 27.

THE GENERAL CONFERENCES OF 1872 AND 1876

noticed, another matter of importance came before the Conference: He writes: "In 1872 there was a desire to retire two of the Bishops and for that reason some insisted upon re-election, which for harmony sake, was agreed to; but it was realized that it was a questionable course, and therefore a committee was appointed to draw up a law governing the Board of Bishops, in which it was made plain that the Bishops had a life term to the Episcopal office, and that the re-election only decided whether or not they should be active or retired Bishops. If they failed re-election that retired them. But they were still Bishops and liable to be called into active service in case of a vacancy or on the formation of a new district in the interval of the General Conference, and to place the matter beyond all question each Bishop was given a certificate on parchment declaring them to hold the office so long as their spirit and practice were such as becomes the gospel. The certificates were signed by the Senior Bishop and General Secretary." [11]

Moore states that it was at this session that a provision was made that the Board of Bishops should meet semi-annually. The Conference voted as well that the General Conference Secretary should be elected at the time of the election of Bishops and should serve for a term of four years.[12] A ritual for the ordination of elders, deacons and the laying of cornerstones of churches was also adopted. Other significant legislation involved the right of lay people in the annual conferences to vote on all matters except the examination of ministers' characters and the election of ministerial delegates to the General Conference.

Too frequently overlooked are other matters at this session, such as the calling of attention to the need of an adequate financial structure, the matter of the Book Concern, the need of an educational institution in which candidates for the ministry might be trained and the establishment of a "connectional journal." The next eight years should see the General Conference facing these problems.

At least two additional statements should be made about the 1872 Conference. Keen admiration certainly must be held for a Church leadership who, in the final analysis, recognize a mistake, regardless of the reasons for it. The 1872 General Conference sensed the great

---

[11] J. W. Hood, *Sketch of The Early History of the African Methodist Episcopal Zion Church will Jubilee Souvenir and Appendix*, 26.
[12] Moore, *loc. cit.*, 280, 281.

responsibility of leadership to obey the law, and where it concerns them, to carefully follow it. There may have been reasons for the delay in holding the session but it was convenient that this Quadrennial meeting came *after* the General Conference of the Methodist Episcopal Church, North. Wounds were healed as Singleton T. Jones was elected again by the Charlotte Conference and went on, in his day, to feel the full weight of responsibility for the destiny of the Church. The session adjourned and by vote to meet in Louisville, Ky. in 1876.

THE FOURTEENTH QUADRENNIAL SESSION

The Fifteenth Street Church, Louisville, Ky., was the host to the Fourteenth Quadrennial Session as it opened June 1, 1876. Bishop Loguen and Bishop Brooks had passed away. Others from the days of the Superintendency also had died, among them being Father Christopher Rush, James Simmons and William H. Bishop. Since the Reverend James A. Jones, the elected Secretary of the General Conference, too had died, Prof. William Howard Day of Harrisburg, Pennsylvania was appointed in his place.

It should be stated that there appears to be no printed minutes for the Quadrennial years of 1872 (evidently because of the lack of funds) and 1876 when William Howard Day, who was charged with the readying the manuscript for the printers and seeing to it they were published, did not carry out his assignment. More then is to be found in the echoing accounts of the Fourteenth Session than that which appears to have been written.

The North Carolina Conference in its Thirteenth Annual Session reveals much of that which transpired.

In Bishop Hood's address and reporting to the North Carolina Conference he stated that because of the "hardness of the times" (one of the periodic economic depressions of the 19th Century) only two-thirds of the elected delegates were in attendance. He stated that the Third District alone was seventeen short of a full delegation and yet he "never had met a General Conference more pleasant." He went on to state that a great deal of business was accomplished in a short time. They were able to make several vital revisions of the Discipline which (because of the necessity of saving money) would be so printed that each minister and layman who had an earlier

THE GENERAL CONFERENCES OF 1872 AND 1876

discipline could paste the revisions in the front or back of the book. The cost would be five cents for the sheet, or copy.[13]

Provisions were made for larger classes in the churches—"about 20 to 30," and penitents, for the first time, were to be admitted to the Love Feasts as well as the probationers. However, no person was to be taken into full connection unless he had been converted. In other words each new member must have a positive faith in the saving grace of Jesus Christ.

Another striking provision was the law governing Deacons. They were to be permitted to perform the semi-Sacrament of matrimony and perform the rite of baptism without the presence of an elder.

A new regulation regarding delegates to the General Conference was adopted as well. No person should be elected as a delegate from the Annual Conferences unless he had "traveled" at least four years from the time he was admitted to that conference. Provision was also made outlining the business of the Annual Conference; Devotionals, Roll Call, Election of Officers, Delivery of the Episcopal Address and Examination of Characters. Each District within the Conference could have two or more elected representatives in the Annual Conference.[14]

It will be recalled that the Board of Bishops suggested in 1872 that something be done about a denominational paper. The listed resolution was offered in the North Carolina Conference following the 1876 General Conference:

Whereas: The General Conference in June last set out to publish a paper for the Connection, provided that any minister or person might take stock in said paper and Whereas: many of the ministers wishing to do something in that way but are not able to take stock to the amount required in a stock:

Resolved: That this Conference take stock in said paper to the amount of its ability, and said stock be raised by each member of the Conference contributing 50¢ and upward, further, this stock shall be called the stock of the North Carolina Conference; also the following brothers, R. H. Simmons, E. H. Hill, and William H. Pitts be appointed as the Annual Conference Committee and said Committee shall be appointed annually.[15]

---

[13] *Minutes of the North Carolina Annual Conference, loc. cit.,*
[14] *Ibid.*
[15] *Minutes of the North Carolina Annual Conference,* Washington, N. C., Nov., 22-29, 1876.

The Louisville meeting covered a period of thirteen days during which re-elections to the Bishopric were announced for Joseph Jackson Clinton, John Jamison Moore, J. W. Hood and Singleton T. Jones. To this group were added William H. Hillery, Joseph P. Thompson and Thomas H. Lomax. Approximately 150 delegates were in attendance.

Time was likewise taken to adjust and set the salary of the episcopacy and provide for the establishment of a periodical for the denomination in this quadrennial session.

When one looks back on this period fraught with its financial problems he is amazed at the results of slow and painful planning. Educational efforts had reached a frustrating end as the Charlotte Conference received from the hands of the Trustees the property and assets of Rush Academy, for example. The body authorized the Reverend Thomas H. Lomax to sell the land belonging to the school and purchase property in Fayetteville, North Carolina. Moore states that he did not sell the land but "an agent was sent out to collect money with which to purchase property and establish an institution." [16] The property in Essex County, New York, could well have been a fine investment for the denomination, had it been retained and cared for. Within five years the beginnings of Livingstone College were to be seen in the work of Cicero Harris, Elder Thurber and others, and on May 8, 1878, Bishop J. W. Hood became the first Chairman of the Board of Trustees.

Jermain W. Loguen

Of all of the Bishops of the Church Bishop Jermain W. Loguen appears to be the only one to have had written a full length history of his life and the happenings therein. However, because he was the son of a slave (his father being his master) the date and actual place of birth appears to be lacking. As near as can be ascertained, he was born in Davidson County, Tennessee. He escaped into free territory and settled in Canada and Western New York State. He was licensed to preach in Syracuse in 1841 and joined the conference June 20, 1843. He was ordained deacon in May 1844 and elder in May 1845. Bishop Hood states that he was an intimate friend of Frederick Douglas, whose son married Loguen's daughter. Bishop Hood goes on to state that he was not a great preacher but was more suited to

---
[16] Moore, *loc. cit.*, 313.

THE GENERAL CONFERENCES OF 1872 AND 1876

the platform as a public lecturer, especially on the subject of slavery. He was elected a Superintendent in 1864 but declined when it was discovered he may have had to do work in the South where he was still a fugitive from law. His name was proposed in 1868 and he was again elected, this time as a Bishop (the title having been changed that year) of the Church. He was consecrated a Bishop on May 29, 1868 and was assigned to the Allegheny and Kentucky Conferences. At the end of two years he exchanged with Bishop Jones and served over the Genesee (The Western New York) and the Philadelphia and Baltimore Conferences. In 1872 he was assigned to the West Coast. Bishop Hood states that he did not think that he ever reached that field as he died in 1873.[17]

THOMAS H. LOMAX

Bishop Thomas H. Lomax was born in Cumberland County, North Carolina, June 15, 1832. Bishop Hood, however, gives the date as 1836. He was the son of Enoch Lomax and the grandson of William Lomax who came to America with General La Fayette from the French colony in Africa. We quote from Bishop Hood's History: "William Lomax joined the Revolutionary War under General George Washington and General La Fayette, fighting faithfully to the close of the war to secure liberty of America. He was a pensioner to the day of his death. He died in full triumph of the gospel faith as a Methodist at the ripe age of one hundred and five years. He was honored with a military burial by the remnant of his regiment."

"Enoch Lomax, the father of our subject, was united in marriage to Rechel Hammonds, the daughter of Isaac and Dicy Hammonds, and was of Indian descent. Thomas Henry Lomax joined the Methodist Episcopal Church, South in 1848. He was converted in 1858 and licensed to preach in 1867. He joined the North Carolina Conference the same year, and was ordained deacon in November, 1867 and elder in 1868, receiving his orders from Bishop Joseph Jackson Clinton and Bishop J. J. Moore. He pastored churches at Whiteville, Flemington, Swamp and Christian Plains and reorganized churches at Shady Grove, Brown's Chapel and Goose Creek. He also pastored Laurinburg and Little Rock Church, Charlotte, N. C. He was elected and consecrated a Bishop in 1876

---

[17] J. Harvey Anderson, *Official Directory* of 1895, 35. Hood, Vol. I, *loc. cit.,* 180, 181.

and was appointed to the Missionary field which included Canada, where he organized the Michigan and Canada Annual Conference. He ordained twenty-nine elders and deacons at this conference and brought in twenty-nine churches. He died April 8, 1908.[18]

Joseph P. Thompson

Bishop Joseph P. Thompson was born in slavery in Winchester, Virginia. Two dates are given for his birth, December 20, 1818 and April 18, the same year. The birth place in the second instance is listed as being Frederick County, Virginia. He escaped into free territory (Pennsylvania) and was aided in every way by some kind-hearted people, attending night school and being permitted to attend the District School as well. He studied medicine with a physician who resided at Middletown Point, now Matawan, New Jersey, "a study which he continued through his life." He eventually decided in favor of the ministry and studied under a Reverend Dr. Mills of Auburn. He was licensed to preach in 1839 and in 1853 was sent to Halifax, Nova Scotia. He graduated from the "University of Medicine in the City of Philadelphia with a degree of Doctor of Medicine April 1, 1858." He was three times pastor of the church in Newburg, New York. In 1881 he attended the Ecumenical Methodist Conference in London, England and read a paper before that group. He was ordained a deacon in 1846 and an elder in 1847. He was elected to the Bishopric at Louisville, in 1876.[19] He died in December 21, 1894.

William H. Hillery

William H. Hillery was born in Virginia, January 19, 1842. He was converted in 1856 and licensed to preach in 1860. He joined the Conference in November 1863 and was ordained deacon, November 10, 1864 and elder, November 16, 1866. He was elected and consecrated a Bishop in 1876 at Louisville, Ky. and deposed after trial in the General Conference of 1884, in New York City. He died July 22, 1893.[20]

---

[18] J. Harvey Anderson, *Official Directory, loc. cit.*, 35; Hood, Vol. I, *loc. cit.*, 191-195; Attorney Samuel Madison Dudley, The African Methodist Episcopal Church *Year Book*, 1942-1943, 103.
[19] Hood, *loc. cit.*, II ,188-191; Anderson, *loc. cit.*, 35.
[20] Anderson, *loc. cit.*, 35.

THE GENERAL CONFERENCES OF 1872 AND 1876

JAMES WALKER HOOD

Bishop James Walker Hood was born in Kennett Township, Chester County, Pennsylvania, May 30, 1831. He was called to preach, according to his own records, at the age of 21 but did not actively take up the ministry until much later. In 1856, while he was a resident of New York City he applied for his license prior to moving to New Haven, Conn. He became the pastor of that church two years later when the pulpit became vacant. At the end of the conference year he was sent as a missionary to Nova Scotia. He states that he found it necessary to work in a hotel for more than 13 months in order that his family would have sufficient support while he was on this assignment.

The greatest work of Bishop Hood was accomplished in North Carolina as the New England Conference appointed him to follow the Union armies south and serve as a missionary in that section. He is credited with organization of the vast Zion holdings in that State as he organized the mother Conference, the North Carolina, and went on to aid in the organization of others in the State as well as those in Virginia.

Bishop Hood was elected to the Episcopacy of the Church in the famed 1872 General Conference at Charlotte, North Carolina and served until his retirement in 1916—a service of 44 years. He died in October 1918.

Bishop Hood wrote the third History of the A.M.E. Zion Church, the work appearing in time for the Centennial Celebration of the denomination in 1896. He is likewise credited with two other works, an addenda to his History and a book of sermons. He is credited also as Assistant Superintendent of Public Instruction for the drawing up of the North Carolina Public School laws, the successful launching of the Church Weekly, The Star of Zion, and its major institution of learning, Livingstone College at Salisbury, North Carolina.

From James Walker Hood. *One Hundred Years of the A.M.E. Zion Church,* 185-188 and other sources.

CHAPTER IV

New Conferences and Missions 1864—1956

WHEN THE General Conference of 1864 adjourned the following assignments were made: Superintendent Bishop who resided in Newark, New Jersey was to preside over the New York Conference (organized 1821) and the New England Conference (organized 1845). Superintendent J. D. Brooks was assigned the Philadelphia (1828) and the Genesee (now the Western New York organized 1850) Conferences. Superintendent Sampson Talbot was to preside over the Baltimore and the Alleghany (set apart by the General Conference of 1848 to meet the third Saturday in August 1849, Anderson has the date 1852, however) Conferences. The Fourth District, presided over by Superintendent Joseph Jackson Clinton was composed of North Carolina (1864), Louisiana (1865) and California (1868) Conferences. It will be noted that some of these Conferences were projected by the General Conference and yet, assigned to them was Joseph Jackson Clinton who should have had seniority and according to the custom of our day, would not have been located on the Mission field.

In connection with this matter of Conferences, the following is interesting as found in the Episcopal Address of the Superintendents: "The Church at Bedford, Pa. was remodeled under the pastorate of Rev. S. T. Scott. It is out of debt."[1] On the matter of Missionary Fields this likewise was added: "Some of the Missions are not in a very prosperous condition; others are doing well.

"Nova Scotia Mission: The Church at Halifax which seceded from us, but is about to return again. The Church at Liverpool is not in a very prosperous condition. Cornwallace was doing well when last heard from.

"West India Mission: Missionary Urling writes that he is engaged in building a Church at Friendship Village, and has secured the Church at Essequebo, formerly under the charge of Rev. Henderson, deceased. The Church is much embarrassed. We would recommend the Mission Boards to make an appropriation for the new Church at Friendship Village and also for the Church as Essequebo.

---

[1] *The General Conference of the African Methodist Episcopal Zion Church of* 1864, *with an Appendix* (Published by S. M. Giles, Hartford 1864) 63, 4, 5.

NEW CONFERENCES AND MISSIONS 1864-1956

"North Carolina Mission:—This mission has exceeded our most sanguine expectations. Missionaries Hood and Williams have been quite successful. Nearly two thousand members have been brought into the mission with three fine churches.

"Arlington Heights and Brightwood Missions:—are doing well. A new mission field has been opened in Louisiana. A society of one hundred members has been received with the pastor, Rev. Joseph Duck, who was ordained at the New York Conference.

"New England Conference District.

"We would most respectfully recommend the General Conference to set off a Conference in Nova Scotia, California, North Carolina and Louisiana." [2]

Where the Baltimore Conference is concerned, Bishop Hood acknowledges its existence by 1860. He states: (speaking of the Southern Conference) "This Conference was comparatively short-lived. We find it represented in the General Conference of 1860. At a later period its title was changed and it was called the Baltimore Conference. In 1872 it was combined with the Philadelphia Conference and called the Philadelphia and Baltimore Conference." [3] In this Bishop Hood appears to be in error for as early as 1848 it was known as the Baltimore Conference. At the time, its composition appears to have been the churches in and around Baltimore only. The minutes of that year record Baltimore Station (this may have been Park Street Tabernacle where the sessions were held), and Spring Street Chapel. The Columbia Circuit is also mentioned. Only one elder (Solomon T. Scott), one deacon (Wesley C. Marshall) and two preachers are listed (Jacob P. Hamer, Jr. and William Johnson).[4]

It should be stated that the Rev. Christopher Rush, Superintendent, presided at this session. Three years later, April 12, 1851. the sessions met in Howard Street Chapel, Baltimore. On hand were both Christopher Rush and George Galbraith, Superintendents. John J. Moore was the Secretary with the following present from the Conference: Nelson H. Turpin, Robert Squirrel, Charles Johnson and Charles Wright. Two representatives attended from each of the following areas: Pennsylvania, New York and Washington, the two from Washington being Rev. Abram Cole and John Cox.[5]

[2] *The General Conference of the A.M.E. Zion Church*, 1864, *loc. cit.*, 4, 5. Where the Baltimore conference is concerned, Bishop Hood recognizes its existence.
[3] Hood, *loc. cit.*, 282.
[4] *Minutes of the Baltimore Annual Conference*, 1848, 2.
[5] *Minutes of the Baltimore Annual Conference*, 1851, 3.

The presence of the two representatives from Washington leads this writer to believe that mistakingly Hood has thought that the Southern Conference and the Baltimore Conference were one and the same, but this is not so, apparently. The resolutions of this 1851 session of the Baltimore Conference are interesting:

GENERAL RESOLUTIONS

1. *Resolved,* That this Conference consider the practice of adminstering the Sacrament to local preachers and exhorters at the same time impossible.

2. *Resolved,* That this Conference recommend the Elders having charges to license none to exhort to preach but such as come up to the Rules of Discipline on that subject.

3. *Resolved,* That this Conference consider the use of the word Bishop, and the Third Ordination, as set forth in the new Discipline of 1851, as inconsistent with our form of Church Government.

4. *Resolved,* That James A. Jones receive Deacon's orders.

5. *Resolved,* That Robert Squirrel receive Deacon's orders.

6. *Resolved,* That the Spring Street Chapel acted wrong in objecting to the appointment of Conference in 1850, when they had nothing in the least against Brother Brooks.

7. *Resolved,* That a vote of thanks be tendered to the United Daughters of Scott for their liberal contribution.

8. *Resolved,* That a vote of thanks be tendered to the Missionary Daughters of N. H. Turpin for their liberal contribution.

9. *Resolved,* That a vote of thanks be tendered to the Daughters of J. J. Moore for their liberal contribution.

10. *Resolved,* That the Conference make a present of the twenty-one dollars collected for this conference, to the Trustees of Howard Street Chapel, for said Church, as it is much embarrassed at this time.

11. *Resolved,* That this Conference receive the apology of the Officiary of Spring Street Chapel, and that it was an oversight on their part in not receiving Brother Brooks.[6] The Baltimore Annual Conference met again in 1853 with the Reverend William H. Bishop, General Superintendent, April 13. This time the sessions were held in South Howard Street Church or Chapel. Ministers from the Conference present were: Bazill Mackall, Joseph J. Clinton, Robert Squirrel, Charles Wright and Jacob P. Hamer. Five representatives came from Pennsylvania. The Reverend Joseph J. Clinton was elected Secretary.

In this session of the Conference Sunday Schools were reported, recognition was taken of the death of Rev. George Galbreath ("therefore, be it resolved, that we the members of the Baltimore Conference wear a mourning band on our hats for one year, as an exhibition of respect to his memory,") the Superintendent. Note was also taken of the unrest within the denomination by the following resolutions:

Whereas: There are many grievous evils now existing in the various

---

[6] *Minutes of the Baltimore Conference of* 1851, 6.

NEW CONFERENCES AND MISSIONS 1864-1956

churches composing this wide-spread connection, arising from the non-enforcement of the book of discipline, by ministers, having the charge of circuits and stations. Therefore

Resolved, That we the members of the Baltimore Conference will, from this time forth, endeavor to enforce the rules of discipline, and shall also hold any member of this conference, having the charge of a circuit or station, chargeable, that fails to do the same.[7]

Bishop Moore makes no mention of the Southern Conference and yet, from time to time this identification comes up. The only reference, therefore, is that of Bishop Hood as stated above.

In 1868 Bishop S. D. Talbot was assigned the New York and New England Conferences, while the Second District, composed of Genesee, Philadelphia and Baltimore Conferences was assigned to Singleton T. Jones. The Third District, composed of the Virginia Conference, (1865), the North Carolina, the South Carolina (1866), and Georgia (1867) Conferences was assigned to Bishop J. J. Moore. The Louisiana, Florida (1869), Alabama (1867) and Tennessee (1867) Conferences were assigned to Bishop Joseph Jackson Clinton. Bishop J. W. Loguen received the Kentucky (1866), Allegheny, Missouri (?), Iowa, Kansas, Illinois and Indiana Conferences "including Western Mission."[8]

The Sixth District composed of California (1868), Pacific Coast (Oregon 1893) was assigned to Bishop J. D. Brooks.

The Episcopal Address of the Board of Bishops in 1872 had the following to say on the growth of the Church:

> First, Of our episcopal arrangements: As the General Conference convened at Washington, D. C. 1868, there were six episcopal officers appointed over an equal number of districts; in these six districts were established seventeen Annual Conferences, operating in twenty-seven States of the Union and two territories; in these Annual Conferences were 1,000 itinerant ministers, 200,000 laymen, or communicants, 18,000 Sunday-School teachers, 85,000 Sunday School pupils; church property in value, $14,000,000; expenditures for support of mission work, $70,000 in twelve years.[9]

As the Minutes for this General Conference have not been located we can merely say that by its convening one additional Conference

---

[7] *Minutes of the Baltimore Annual Conference,* 1853, 8.

[8] Moore, *loc. cit.,* 265. Evidently most of these Conferences were projected rather than already in existence as Missouri did not become a Conference until 1889. The same is true of Texas, which was not organized until 1881. Texas was assigned to Bishop Clinton.

[9] Moore, *loc. cit.,* 285.

had been organized, other than those listed in 1868, and this was the West Tennessee and Mississippi, established in 1871. Hood intimates that it may have been organized earlier, however.[10]

The sessions of the 1876 General Conference met in Louisville, Ky., June First. In the intervening years since the Quadrennial meeting in Charlotte, North Carolina, the New Jersey Conference had been set up, comprising, originally of the New York Conference Churches located in New Jersey along with the Staten Island (Richmond Borough) organizations of the City. The organizing session was held in Red Bank July 2, 1874 with the Rev. Joseph Jackson Clinton, Bishop, presiding. Within the next few years the new Conference petitioned the Philadelphia Conference for a transfer of all the organizations of that Conference located in the Western part of New Jersey. Eventually this was accomplished and in April (16) 1879 the sessions met in Camden with the Rev. J. J. Moore, Bishop, presiding.

Note should be taken of the Bahama Island Conference which held its first session in Nassau, December 26, 1877 with Bishop Joseph P. Thompson, presiding. Fourteen ministers of the Conference were present along with a ministerial delegation (evidently from the mainland) of four. In attendance also were two lay delegates, reporting 190 members, four Sunday Schools with 129 students, and 17 teachers and officers. The report showed 78 books in the libraries, one of the must items reported in these mid-century Annual Conferences.

One of the major reasons for the growth of the Church was the missionary zeal of the Bishops themselves. One can hardly understand how they were able to travel so much on so little. One of the Bishops reported in the General Conference of 1880 that during the last four years he had traveled "a little over 85,000 miles in the interest of my beloved Zion during my quadrennial term, and to deliver 1,510 sermons and lectures...." [11]

The Bishop of the Seventh Episcopal District (T. H. Lomax) reported to this same session of the General Conference: "This was laid off at the last General Conference as a Missionary District. There was no Mission Fund in hand to aid the Bishop appointed to

---

[10] Hood, *loc. cit.*, 381.
[11] *Daily Journal of the Sixteenth Quadrennial Session of the General Conference* 1880, 19.

NEW CONFERENCES AND MISSIONS 1864-1956

this field, in commencing operations. The Bishop of the Third District, not thinking it best to make any other appointment for the Church at Charlotte, the Church at that place being quite willing to receive such service as Bishop Lomax could give them, he was thereby enabled to visit his field in October 1877, and to organize the Michigan and Canada Conference on the second Wednesday in that month, with four elders and five preachers. This Conference was held in the city of Windsor, and adjourned to meet in the City of Grand Rapids on the third Wednesday of September 1878." [12]

The report of Bishop Lomax goes on to say: "At this second session all the ministers reported progress. We had an addition of elders and five preachers. Adjourned to meet in the city of Detroit, Michigan on the third Wednesday of September 1879, at which time the Conference roll increased to twenty-eight members and five delegates. It adjourned to meet in the city of Chicago on the third Wednesday in September 1880 at 10:00 A.M."

The growth of the Michigan-Canada Conference appears unbelievable. Bishop Lomax stated that at the time of his report there were six districts with a presiding elder over each. Fourteen Churches were evidently established, while the Bishop himself, had traveled some 15,000 miles.

The Central North Carolina Conference was set apart in 1879. In Alabama the West Alabama Conference was organized the same year. Moore seems to believe that the West Alabama Conference was established in 1880. Hood states that it was organized in 1881 (December 14) by Bishop Joseph P. Thompson. J. Harvey Anderson gives the 1879 date which we have quoted. However, by 1881 it appears the Conference had 114 preachers and 17,144 members.[13] Moore agrees on the number of preachers but lists only, 4,689 members in 1881.

In the report of the Fifth Episcopal District to the General Conference of 1880 we note the following: "In compliance with repeated solicitation from our brethren of the State of Arkansas, who formerly belonged to the West Tennessee and Mississippi Conferences, that Conference set off the State of Arkansas as a separate Conference District, in January 1870, fixing its organization at Little Rock, for November of that year. In conformity with order, I had the honor to

---

[12] *Ibid.*, 20.
[13] Hood, *loc. cit.*, 423.

organize said Conference on the 13th of November last, under the name of the Arkansas Conference of the A. M. E. Zion Church in American, subject to the ratification of the General Conference.[14]

Bishop E. D. W. Jones in his Historical Catechism says that the Arkansas Conference was organized March 1882 by Bishop Singleton Jones. Reverend J. Harvey Anderson gives the date as 1881, which would be the first session following approval by the General Conference. Bishop Hood states that the date was 1882 and again lists Bishop Singleton Jones. It would appear that the actual first session was held in 1879.

In the assignment of Bishops for the quadrennium 1884-1888, the following was announced:

REPORT ON DISTRICTS

We, your Committee on Districts, beg leave to submit the following:

First District: New York, New England, Virginia and Central North Carolina. Bishop Singleton T. Jones.

Second District: Allegheny, Canada and Michigan, South Carolina and Florida. Bishop J. J. Moore

Third District: North Carolina, Georgia, West Alabama and Louisiana. Bishop T. H. Lomax

Fifth District: Philadelphia and Baltimore, Kentucky, East Tennessee, East Alabama and California. Bishop J. W. Hood

African Mission: Rev. Andrew Cartwright

We further recommend that after two years the Bishops shall rotate. The Bishop on the First District shall go to the second, and the second to the third, the third to the fourth, the fourth to the fifth, and the fifth to the first. They shall remain two years on a district.

Yours Respectfully,
S. C. BIRCHMORE, *Chairman*
A. WALTER, *Secretary*[15]

No mention is made in this report of the Fourth District which must have been composed of New Jersey, Genesee, Arkansas, Texas (1883 by Bishop T. H. Lomax). It is presumed that East Tennessee was really the Tennessee Conference, organized by Joseph Jackson Clinton in 1868. Anderson gives the date of the Texas Conference as 1881.

According to J. Harvey Anderson, the Statistical Secretary of the

---

[14] *Daily Journal of the Sixteenth Quadrennial Session of the General Conference* (1880), 18.

[15] *Daily Proceedings of the Seventeenth Quadrennial Session of the General Conference,* 1884, 132, 133.

NEW CONFERENCES AND MISSIONS 1864-1956

time by the close of the century Missouri (1889—Jones states this Conference was organized by Bishop Lomax, September 17, 1890), Palmetto (1890—again Jones differs giving the date as Dec., 1891 with Bishop I. C. Clinton organizing), South Florida (1890—again there is a difference with Jones who lists the organizing date as January 14, 1891 with Bishop Lomax organizing; North Louisiana, now the South Mississippi (1890—again Jones places the date January 14, 1891 with Bishop C. C. Petty organizing); South Mississippi (1891, with both Anderson and Jones agreeing—December of that year with Bishop C. R. Harris organizing) and Oregon (1893 - Jones gives the date as 1892 with Bishop Petty organizing) as having been established. Confusion exists in the Alabama Conferences for East Alabama, with Anderson listed as having been formed or organized in 1867. Evidently the Alabama Conference is this Conference. Central Alabama, according to Jones, was organized in 1881. Anderson does not list this Conference at all. He does list North Georgia, giving the date of 1885.[16]

A difference of opinion does not exist in the date for the organization of the Ohio Conference. Bishop Jones gives it as being September 1891 with Bishop Hood organizing the Conference while J. Harvey Anderson states the same, but they cannot agree as to the founding date of the Western North Carolina Conference, Jones stating November 1889 with Bishop Moore presiding while Anderson lists the date as 1890. Bishop Hood agrees with Bishop Jones or vice versa.

Bishop Jones, thereafter, is actually our major source of information where the younger Conferences are concerned. He states that Bishop Holliday organized the North Arkansas Conference in 1896. Two years prior to this date Bishop Petty had set up the North Alabama (1894). Incidentally Jones states that the Blue Ridge Conference was set apart in October 1892 by Bishop Lomax. In 1897 Bishop Holliday organized the Oklahoma Conference, thus completing the work of the Century.

As one looks over the progress of the denomination it is clear that there were actually three major missionary thrusts of the Church after its formative years. A distinct emphasis must be placed on the

---

[16] J. Harvey Anderson, *Statistical Year Book of* 1895, 66; E. D. W. Jones, *Comprehensive Catechism*, 61, 62; Hood, James Walker, *One Hundred Years of the A.M.E. Zion Church.*

years immediately after and during the Civil War. As this thrust tapered off a new one commenced which brought the denomination into the closing two decades of the Nineteenth Century. Fruitful too, were these years of the second half of the period as the departments of the Church were organized and the educational program established. This rounding out of effort is to be noted where the Episcopacy is concerned, Church mission and interpretation as well as the matter of communication. The pace slowed in the opening years of the Twentieth Century as the denomination entered a period of ecumenics, Christian Education and the formation of a high interest in Foreign Missions. At home, the revival was to be noted as well, as new Conferences emerged.

The West Central North Carolina Conference became an imperative in 1910 (November 18) as Bishop Hood was beginning to wind up his great work in the South and in North Carolina. Bishop Blackwell turned to the task of organizing the Indiana Conference a year earlier, in 1909. The Southwest Virginia Conference—later the East Tennessee and Virginia Conference, was organized October 15, 1910 by Bishop C. R. Harris, while on the West Coast Bishop J. S. Caldwell re-organized the Oregon-Washington Conference (Oct. 23, 1910). Meanwhile, Bishop Hood and Bishop G. W. Clinton brought about the organization of the Albemarle Conference (November 30, 1910). In Alabama, the grand old leader, J. W. Alstork brought into being the South Alabama Conference (Dec. 2, 1911) and the Cahaba Conference (November 20, 1912).

But of equal note was the re-organization of Mission work abroad. Bishop Alexander Walters set about organizing the Cape Coast Conference (March 1910), West Gold Coast and Liberia, all in the same year—1910.

It does not seem logical but it appears that it is a more difficult task to pin-point the organization dates of later Annual Conferences than those formed earlier. For example, Jones lists a "Cape" Conference organized by Bishop Alexander Walters on November 27, 1911. He also lists the Cape Coast Conference organized by the same Bishop in March of the same year. As there is no listing of delegates or conferences as such in the 1916 General Conference Minutes, one is at a loss to interpret his meaning. It appears that the Cape Fear Conference was listed in 1912 but does not appear in the Discipline of 1905. It therefore, came into existence either in the General Con-

NEW CONFERENCES AND MISSIONS 1864-1956

ference of 1908 or in the intervening years.[17] One is led to believe that approval or tacit approval for its formation had to be given in the General Conference of this earlier year.

Confusion is likewise found in the formation of the present South and Georgia Conferences. It will be recalled that the Georgia Conference goes all the way back to 1867. The North Georgia Conference appears to carry the date 1885. Later, mention is made of the South Georgia Conference. It appears, therefore, that one of these two Conferences later took the South Georgia title.

Some confusion may exist where the Michigan Conference is concerned. Bishop George Lincoln Blackwell reported to the General Conference of 1912 that distances made it imperative to organize the Chicago area as the Michigan Conference in 1910. Just what happened to the old Michigan and Canada Conference is not clear. The original number of points in the 1910 Michigan Conference was ten.

Alabama likewise posed a question as conference after conference was formed from the original one established. As late as 1924 there was a Southeast Alabama Conference. Since Jones makes no mention of this Conference in 1932 it is presumed that here again was a mere change of names. No delegates from the Pee Dee Conference are listed in 1920, but reports from this area are found in the Minutes of 1924 which shows that it had to be in existence as early as 1920. One must conclude that the Twenty-sixth Quadrennial session, therefore, set apart this Conference and that it met in the Fall of that year (1920).

It is just as illusive to trace the origin of the West Kentucky Conference, for it, too, appears in the Minutes of 1920 and in truth in the Minutes of 1916 as well, but it had no listed delegates in 1912. At that time the Statistical Secretary made no mention of it so it is presumed that it was formed after the rise of the General Conference in that year. The South-west Rocky Mountain Conference was evidently formed in 1920 after the rise of that quadrennial session. Reports for that Conference appear first in 1921 in the episcopal report of Bishop Lynwood Westinghouse Kyles.

One of the youngest conferences of the denomination, the Colorado, was organized by Bishop Stephen Gill Spottswood (organized

---

[17] *Minutes of The General Conference of* 1912, 498.

December 7, 1952) and reported to the General Conference of 1956.[18]

The Jamaica Conference, according to our understanding, was organized by Bishop Herbert Bell Shaw in 1968 and therefore becomes the youngest conference of the denomination.

[18] *Official Journal of the Thirty-fifth General Conference,* 1956, 223.

CHAPTER V

Education in the 19th and 20th Centuries— Home and Church

JUST WHEN the African Methodist Episcopal Zion Church established its first Sunday School is not clear, but the mere fact that by 1860 the Negro was educationally conscious leads one to believe that early experimentation of this form of training was to be had. Certainly, again the Church was influenced not only by the times but by the early stand of all Methodism where the training of children was concerned. Brief mention of some type of training of children was to be noted as early as 1834—fourteen years after the separation from the Mother Church. By 1851, nine organizations were listed in the New York Conference alone, engaged exclusively or in part with the religious training of children.[1] Bishop Walls in a thesis in preparation, states that the Sunday School movement was authorized in the General Conference of 1860, and schools were in evidence in New England in 1858.

In the Baltimore Annual Conference Minutes of 1850 a short *Sabbath School Report* is noted: "James A. Jones Sup't. This Sabbath School consists of five male teachers, two female teachers, also thirty-nine male scholars and twenty female scholars."[2] It is interesting to note in the Philadelphia Annual Conference Minutes of the same year that the preachers who joined the conference were expected to study. The Second Resolution stated: Resolved: That each preacher after joining the Annual Conference shall, the first year, study Porter's Homiletic and Homes Introduction, and on the Second year he shall study Wesley's Sermons, Mosheim's Church History.[3]

The same Minutes carry the following report:

REPORTS OF SABBATH SCHOOLS

Philadelphia, May 12, 1850

A report of the Wesley Church Sabbath School, for the year ending 1849: the number at present, scholars, 100; superintendent of the school, William B. Banton; teachers 13

---

[1] John Jamison Moore, *History of the A.M.E. Zion Church*, (New York, Pa., 1884), 114.
[2] *Minutes of the Baltimore Annual Conference* (New York, 1850), 5.
[3] *Minutes of the Philadelphia Annual Conference* (New York, 1850), 10.

Report of Sabbath School in York, Pa., Stephen D. Davage, superintendent; scholars, 36; teachers, 5.
Report of Sabbath School, Columbia, Lancaster County, Pa., Allen W. C. Bonsin, superintendent; teachers 5, scholars, 55.
Report of Chambersburg Sabbath School: superintendent, Daniel Lundon; teachers 11, scholars, 63.
Report of Sabbath School Brownsville: superintendent, Elias Hall; teachers, 5, scholars, 25.[4]

Incidentally, the Superintendents of this conference were: Christopher Rush and George Galbraith. The Resolution of thanks is interesting since it makes no use of the word Bishop but utilizes the word Superintendent.

Resolved, That a vote of thanks be tendered to the Superintendents for the able manner in which they have conducted the affairs of this conference.[5]

The New York Conference of the same year was more rigid in the qualifications for preachers for the Resolution concerning ministerial studies stated: "That it shall be the duty of each minister in charge, to inform each preacher who proposes to join the Conference, that he shall procure and study the Bible and our discipline, English Grammar, Watts on the Mind, and Mason on Self-Knowledge, anterior to his joining the Conference." [6] There appears to have been record of Sabbath Schools.

The New England Conference of the same year did report the following, however:

Sabbath School in Boston, 18 scholars; Middletown, 55; in Demarara Friendship Village, East Sea Coast, Guiana, last year's report, scholars, 138 and 28 church members; Bentervenwagting, 11 Church members, and 120 Sabbath School scholars, day school, 30 scholars.[7]

The above report lists Sabbath Schools in New England as early as 1850 so one can conclude that they were organized in that area prior to that time. By 1874 Church Sunday Schools were well established in the New Jersey Conference, eight being listed in this first yearly conference, with 427 students, 47 teachers and 1,690 books in the libraries, required item.[8] The next year, 1875, six more schools were

---
[4] *Minutes of the Philadelphia Annual Conference,* 1850, 10.
[5] *Ibid.,* 10.
[6] *Minutes of the New York Annual Conference,* 1850, 24.
[7] *New England Conference Minutes,* 1850, 30.
[8] *New Jersey Conference Minutes of* 1874 (unprinted).

EDUCATION IN THE 19TH AND 20TH CENTURIES—HOME AND CHURCH

listed with an addition of 184 pupils.[9] Shortly thereafter another increase was noted, particularly because of the inclusion of the Philadelphia and Baltimore Conference churches located in the Western section of the state.[10] Thus the fact that by 1878 Sunday Schools had increased to 27 with 786 students and 3,317 books in the libraries, attest to the fact that the church was well aware of the need and moved to meet it.

The Sunday School movement among Methodists had really found a beginning when the Methodist Episcopal Conference meeting in Charleston, South Carolina, resolved to establish schools for Whites and Blacks in 1790. Earlier, Bishop Asbury had established such a school in the house of a Mr. Thomas Crenshaw in Hanover County, Virginia sometime during the year of 1786. Record is found of one established in New York by a colored woman named Katy Fergerson in 1793.[11] By 1827 some organization was found in the Methodist Church and by 1840 the General Conference began to recognize and organize the department.

Perhaps we should not overlook the famous question asked in the Conference of 1784, when this was written: "What shall be done for the rising generation?" Answer: "Where there are ten whose parents are in the society, meet them at least once a week."

Additional facts have been discovered which point to the holding of an annual Sunday School Convention in the Philadelphia and Baltimore Conference as early as 1881. A printed minute is in the author's possession which lists the convention of 1888 as the Seventh Annual Session.[12] This conference was held in Harrisburg, October 17, 18, 19 of that year. William Howard Day, who had received the ire of some members of the denomination where Sunday School work was concerned, was the compiler of these minutes and the publisher as well.

The Philadelphia and Baltimore Conference Sunday School Convention had in attendance ten delegates, sixteen officers and ministers and eleven visitors. The work consisted of the examination and passage of resolutions and the listening to prepared papers and

---

[9] *Ibid.*, 1875.
[10] *Ibid.*, 1878.
[11] *Minutes of the Sunday School Convention, Philadelphia and Baltimore Conference*, Carlisle, Pa., 1887, 36.
[12] *Minutes of the Sunday School Convention of the Philadelphia and Baltimore Conference*, (Carlisle, Pa., 1888).

essays. The latter numbered among the group: History of the Sunday School Movement, Education, Parental Responsibility, etc. Some of the resolutions presented immediately claim our attention: Resolved, That it be recommended to the Sunday Schools to organize a Temperance Society in each school, and especially among the children. "Resolved, That it be made obligatory upon each Sunday School to organize A SEPARATE primary department wherever it can possibly be done, and that wherever a separate room is possible, a primary superintendent be elected to take charge." A Sinking Fund was created to aid the *weak* schools, music was stressed and superintendents were urged to form Sunday School Choirs.[13] G. W. Offley was listed as President of this organization while Prof. William Howard Day was General Superientendent of the Conference. Highly significant is the following resolution:

> Whereas, the question during the session of the convention was asked: "How can the children be retained in Zion after arriving at the age of Maturity?" and that thus far we have not been able to use the paraphanalia of our own composition, and
> Whereas: That now we are to have such of our own; be it therefore Resolved: that we use what influence we have as a convention, to compel all schools within our convention District to use the Zion lesson leaf and Catechism.
> Resolved, that we further impress upon all the schools to teach as far as possible the doctrine of the A. M. E. Zion Church.
>
> F. M. Jacobs
J. Harvey Anderson[14]

Perhaps the early pioneer for interdenominational contacts where religious education as we now know it, was concerned, was Bishop Alexander Walters. Prior to his elevation to the Episcopacy he attended the First World's Sunday School Convention held in London, England, in 1887. Bishop Walters, then the Reverend Walters, represented the New York Conference and Sunday School Association. The Bishop later stated to the late Secretary of Christian Education, James W. Eichelberger, that he made a request to two leaders of the World Union as to a Negro being placed on the Lesson Committee. The astounded leaders exclaimed, "Dr., a Negro on the Lesson Committee!" the Bishop declared; "When they told me that, I was through."

---

[13] *Ibid.*, 20, 21, 22.
[14] *Ibid.*, 21.

EDUCATION IN THE 19TH AND 20TH CENTURIES—HOME AND CHURCH

The need of a uniform system of teaching in the Sunday Schools had been seen as early as 1866 when Dr. Vincent, later a Bishop in the Methodist Episcopal Church, advanced the idea of common lessons. In 1870 the Berean Series came into existence, while in 1873, the International lessons and the Chatauqua courses were drawn up. It was the thought of the Bishop that some representation should have been had in their development.

The visit of Bishop Walters to the World Sunday School Association Convention had a real effect on the church. The following year, 1888, the General Conference meeting at New Bern, N.C. agreed to the establishment of a Sunday School Department.[15] In 1889, the Board of Bishops appointed Dr. R. R. Morris as the Superintendent of the A.M.E. Zion Sunday Schools and Editor of the Sunday School Literature. Dr. T. A. Weathington became Financial Secretary of the Sunday School Department at the same time. This was not the first action taken however, in a General Conference, for the Conference of 1880, meeting in Montgomery, Alabama, accepted the report of the Committee on temperance which recommended that "the Juvenile Templar's Lesson leaves be introduced into our Sabbath Schools." [16]

The same General Conference undertook three other significant actions, two, dealing with the Sunday School and the other having to do with Baptized Children.

REPORT OF THE COMMITTEE ON SUNDAY SCHOOLS

To the Bishops and members of the General Conference of the A. M. E. Zion Church in America.

We, your Committee on Sunday Schools hail with delight the task assigned to us, that important subject, the Sunday-school of our beloved Zion. In view of the fact that the Sunday School is the nursery of the Church of God, and youth, the only hope of the future, and

Whereas, Our Sunday-schools should have more attention, and be better governed, and whereas there is much need of a uniform model by which all of our Sunday School work may be carried on with more success; after carefully considering this important subject, we find that a constitution for the better government of our Sunday-schools is much needed. We therefore recommend the following as a Constitution for the regulation and general government of the Sunday-schools of the A. M. E. Zion Church.[17]

---

[15] *Minutes of the General Conference* 1888, 74.
[16] *Minutes of The General Conference of* 1880, 74.
[17] *Minutes of The General Conference of* 1880, loc. cit., 74.

According to the Report on Sunday Schools of 1892 no major action was taken in this field at the New Bern General Conference of 1888. "The Report states: "For want of time for its consideration by the General Conference it was referred to the Board of Bishops for their consideration, and at the Board meeting succeeding the General Conference of 1888 the Bishops did create the Sunday School Union of the African Methodist Episcopal Zion Church and located the same in the city of Montgomery, Alabama (which is the capital of the state), with Dr. R. R. Morris General Superintendent and Rev. T. A. Weathington Financial Secretary." The complaint of the committee is evident in that which it states. "The department was started without a dollar to help it. The superintendent was placed in charge of one of our churches in the city, as was also the secretary, in order to give them a support while they were establishing the department—one with a church of 1,300 and the other with 380 members to look after as pastors and do their other church work. Nothwithstanding their being on double duty, they have made this department a credit to our Zion." [18]

The 1892 General Conference proposed the following:

Resolved: There shall be held in each year a District Sabbath School Convention, which may meet at the time and place of the District Conference, which shall be composed of all pastors, superintendents, two lay delegates from each Sunday School. The Convention shall have power to elect its own officers, *provided,* this does not prohibit an Annual Conference from holding a conference district convention when it deems necessary.[19]

The report of the Committee on Sunday Schools and the subsequent actions of the General Conference were no doubt carryovers from proposals from 1888 and the interval actions of the Board of Bishops. In the Episcopal message of the Nineteenth Session of the General Conference the Board of Bishops stated in part that the Union was not only important but necessary. It insisted that the union continue under "devout Christian men" who had more than ordinary religious experience. It proposed too, that somehow Zion Methodist literature be prepared for use in the schools of the denomination. The third suggestion was that "We should make it an

---

[18] *Minutes of the Nineteenth Quadrennial Session of the General Conference, A.M.E. Zion Church,* Pittsburgh, Pa., 1892, 142.
[19] *Ibid., Nineteenth Session, General Conference,* 127.

organic part and parcel of the Book Concern" and that proper financial provisions be made for the department.[20]

Two other significant proposals were made by the Board in this message: the establishment of a Preachers Institute "1. To cultivate Christian fellowship and helpfulness between its members. 2. To aid its members to gain knowledge as shall be of use in the discharge of their duties as required by the Discipline, and 3, To pursue a course of instruction or reading for the purpose of cultivating their moral, spiritual and intellectual powers." The institute should meet once a week and should require the presence of every exhorter and local preacher of the charge. Reports should be made at each Quarterly Conference.[21]

Another move proposed by the Board of Bishops was the establishment of that which was known as THE CORRESPONDENCE SCHOOL. Some of its provisions were:

> At the first quarterly conference held each year an educational session shall be held, at which all the travelling and local preachers residing in the circuit or station, together with the exhorters, shall be examined by the presiding elder, or his proxy, in the studies designated for them by the Book of Discipline, including those of the Correspondence School.
>
> All failing to pass said examinations shall pursue the studies prescribed for them in the Correspondence School.

Other suggestions involved periodic examination in the succeeding Quarterly Conferences, the receiving of an offering in each church for ministerial education, the maintenance of a library, providing books and literature for all those who wished to study with all surplus funds being spent for the Sunday School library.[22]

In 1896 George Lincoln Blackwell, later Bishop, became the manager of the Publishing House and was given the additional duty of preparing and producing the Sunday School Literature. In 1898, realizing that the dual responsibilities were too taxing R. B. Bruce was selected to take over the editorial duties. Reverend Bruce served in this capacity until he was elected to the episcopacy in 1916.

Dr. J. Francis Lee was elected the Editor of Sunday School Literature when the General Conference met in Louisville, Ky. and

---
[20] *Ibid.*, 40.
[21] *Ibid.*, 40, 41.
[22] *Ibid.*, 41.

served continuously until his death in 1931 when the Rev. Dr. Buford F. Gordon was assigned by the Board of Bishops. He served as Editor until 1944, when he was elected to the episcopacy. He, in turn was succeeded by Dr. J. S. Nathaniel Tross. Dr. Tross served for the succeeding eight years when the Rev. Dr. J. Van Catledge was elected to the office. His death in 1962 brought Rev. Dr. L. J. Baptiste to the office as Editor of the Church School literature.

By 1905 a few leaders throughout the Zion Methodist Church had become quite aware of the possibilities of Religious Education. Again the Church benefited from a laymen's movement, this time headed by James W. Eichelberger, who was then serving as an instructor at Clinton Junior College, Rock Hill, South Carolina. Through the District Conferences of North and South Carolina as well as Alabama, five individuals were selected to represent the Church at the International Convention (Sunday School) in Toronto, Canada in that year. The group included James W. Eichelberger, Jr., Miss Emma Andrews of Williamston, North Carolina, Miss Nettie C. Crockette and J. S. Stanback of Chester, South Carolina and J. S. Jackson of Birmingham, Alabama.

The impressive item of this convention as far as the Zion delegates were concerned was a publishers' exhibit, Professor Eichelberger being so moved that when he returned to his father's home in Gladen Grove, South Carolina, he brought the matter to that minister's attention asking why Zion did not do something in that line.

Professor Eichelberger was so interested in the possibilities of greater interest and emphasis on Sunday School work that he wrote a series of articles which appeared in the Star of Zion on the Sunday School problem. These articles were published over a space of several months.

As the result of the impetus given the movement by these articles and the attendance of the five Zion representatives at Toronto, three of the group, headed by Professor Eichelberger (the others being Miss Nettie C. Crockette and J. S. Stanback) proposed a State Convention for South Carolina. The three agreed that efforts at a permanent movement should be pushed as much as possible in the interim of the General Conference, and then, when that body met, endorsement for the project would be solicited. If the General Conference should refuse to lend its endorsement plans would be dropped.

EDUCATION IN THE 19TH AND 20TH CENTURIES—HOME AND CHURCH

In the Fall of 1905 the first state convention was held at Rock Hill, South Carolina, the sessions being held in the Mount Olivet Church. James E. Shepherd, field superintendent for Negro work of the International Sunday School Association attended and spoke. The following year the second state convention was held at Union, South Carolina. Every Presiding Elder's district in the state was represented, bringing the enrollment to well over 100 persons.

It should be stated that the movement involving Sunday Schools in this early period was one sponsored mainly by outstanding laymen who took this phase of church work as a prime responsibility. More will be said about this angle later.

When the World's Sunday School Convention opened May 18, 1907 in Rome, Italy, Professor Eichelberger, now thoroughly aroused to the need for such contacts, attended, representing the Zion Church.[23] Returning from the Convention in time for the Third State Convention which was scheduled to meet at Chester, South Carolina, he lent encouragement to the leadership so much so that they were determined to persevere. Attending this Convention, too, was the Reverend W. J. Walls, now a Bishop, retired.

Soon after this third statewide meeting a Sunday School newspaper was decided upon. It first appeared as *The Sunday School Headlight* and was presented to the General Conference meeting in Philadelphia, Pennsylvania, in 1908. After a few issues under General supervision, the publication was permanently suspended.

The work of this South Carolina group so impressed Dr. R. B. Bruce, the Editor of the Sunday School Literature, that he introduced Professor Eichelberger to the General Conference and gave him a part of his allotted time to present the South Carolina plan. It was at this time that the *Headlight* was presented to the General Conference.

The 1908 Conference was memorialized mainly at the instance of the South Carolina group to create the office of Administrator and promotional worker for Sunday School work. While it was reported favorably by the committee to which it was assigned, the General Conference refused to pass the measure. The purpose of the request was to restrict the work of the Editor to editing where heretofore it was his job to promote Sunday School work as well. In 1912 the mat-

---

[23] See Listing of Delegates and Observors.

ter was again presented favorably by the committee but when the report was called for it was in the possession of an absent member.

Again we note that these efforts in South Carolina came several years after the ventures in some other Conferences. For example, the Philadelphia and Baltimore Conference to whom we have alluded was noting "an increase of interests in the important work of the Sunday School," but progress, according to the Committee was slow.[24]

The Conference was interested in the future of the denomination and said as much. It deplored, as well, the unwillingness of churches to use the materials prepared by the denomination. Such men as J. P. Thompson, J. C. Dancy, F. M. Jacobs, who acted as Secretary, composed the Committee.

A program of the Allegheny District Conference and Sunday School Convention shows that this Conference was holding Conventions prior to 1907. The Convention met that year in Meyersdale, Pa., July 17, 18, 19th. Some of the papers presented at that meeting are interesting: *What Methods Should Be Used to Interest Children? Character, and How to Develop It in the Sunday School, The Sunday School as a Factor in the Salvation of the World.* Daniel Francis Bradley was then one of the Presiding Elders of the Allegheny Conference.

By 1908, too, the denomination had been gradually formulating its policy towards the Sunday School movement. In that year, as the General Conference met in Philadelphia, Robert Blair Bruce reported that 96,000 Picture Lesson Cards, 480,000 Junior Lesson Quarterlies, 48,000 Teachers' Journals, 64,000 *Cluster* Rolls (Cradle?) and 250,000 Catechisms had been sent out during the quadrennium. He went on to say:

> We have been connected with the Editorship of the Sunday-School Department for 14 years. At the death of Dr. R. R. Morris, we were placed in charge of the Department for 2 years. We assisted Dr. G. L. Blackwell in preparing lessons 4 years and we have had absolute charge for 8 years.[25]

Meanwhile the International Sunday School Association had been vitally interested in plans for promoting the work among Negroes.

---

[24] *Minutes of the Philadelphia and Baltimore Conference,* 1888, 37.
[25] *Quadrennial Report of the Sunday School Department* of the A.M.E. Zion Church, May 6, 1908. R. B. Bruce, Editor.

EDUCATION IN THE 19TH AND 20TH CENTURIES—HOME AND CHURCH

The International movement as well as the World's Convention claimed the attention of some of the most outstanding business leaders of the day, among them being John Wanamaker of Philadelphia, H. J. Heinz of Pittsburgh, Pa., Edward K. Warren of Michigan; B. F. Jacobs of Chicago; W. N. Hartshorn of Clifton, Mass., whom we will have occasion to mention later. In addition, in many small communities or cities business men of lesser rank were likewise engaged in furthering Sunday School work, individuals such as Henry Heckerman of Bedford, Pa., who later gave a great amount of his wealth to advance the Kingdom.

In 1895, the Reverend L. B. Maxwell was employed by the Sunday School group. When he died in March 1902, and the second worker, Silas X. Floyd, employed in 1896, resigned, in the same year (1902), Prof. G. H. Marcus and James E. Shephard were employed. Prof. Marcus died in 1904 and James Shephard left the Association in 1908.

The Central Committee of the International Executive group met at Dyk Rock Cottage, Clifton, Mass., home of Mr. Hartshorn, to consider its Negro work. A Plan was formed whereby if five Southern States would organize and agree to pay a State Secretary $450 per year, the Association would match the amount. Five states promptly selected secretaries. These individuals were charged with contacting pastors and Superintendents of Sunday Schools in the local churches and thereby attempting the setting up of interdenominational Conventions.

The first problem encountered by the movement had to do with finance. Evidently the state conventions faced too great a task in raising the $450 without authoritative backing since each denomination was endeavoring to carry on some type of work itself. It appears that the Committee on Work Among Negroes made the blunder of expecting that which was not and is not being practiced 40 or 50 years later by white denominations, submerging denominational rivalry to secure results. At any rate, difficulties existed.

The secretaries were considered inefficient because of their inability to provide reliable information. It was conceded, however, that the financial ability of the Negro made it hard or well nigh impossible to support denominational and interdenominational conventions at one and the same time. Furthermore, the fact that "comparatively few Negroes were able to control their own time, presented a serious obstacle to our work." These circumstances as to the failure to accomplish very much were brought out at a conference held at Greensboro, N.C. early in 1907.

In December of the same year another conference, this time interracial, was called to meet at Raleigh, North Carolina. Ten states were represented, all attending being guests of the Committee on Work Among Negroes. As a result of this conference it was decided to abandon efforts to further Negro Sunday School work as practiced by the Association. Instead, the plan suggested was to utilize Negro educational institutions as a means of training workers. Since it was planned that these courses should be a part of the regular curriculum of the participating schools it was felt that something would be accomplished with the smallest cost.[26]

The idea presumed (unwisely) that these students would be the Sunday School teachers in their home communities. Again, someone failed to see that in all too many cases he, or she, who was a teacher in these Sunday Schools would be a teacher still, preparation or no.

To put over the Raleigh Plan, Negroes were invited to another Conference,—this time at Clifton, Mass., and again the Committee on Work Among Negroes bore all the travelling and other expense.[27]

On August 19, 1908, to Clifton came practically every outstanding Negro leader of the Nation, there to think through the problem of Religious Education among their group. As Zion's representative came Bishop George Clinton, who, by his presence, began the active participation of our church into interdenominational religious education work.[28] And for the first time Zion was on the *inside* of the International Sunday School Association.

The Clifton Conference closed a period of disappointment and opened an era of hope, insofar as the Association was concerned. Disappointment was voiced in the statement, "The methods employed have been those familiar to the work among white people. More than $24,000 have been expended in salaries. The results have been disappointing. The needs of the Negroes have not been met." However, closing the section entitled: "The What and The Why of This Book" the Editor has said that twelve things could be held as

---

[26] *The Development of the Sunday School*, 1780-1905 (Fort Hill Press), 701-702.
[27] *The Encyclopaedia of Sunday Schools and Religious Education in three vols.* II, III, Thos. Nelsons and Sons, 1915.
[28] *Ibid.*

promising. Chief among them were the interest of the white churches, the improved mutual understanding between Christians of the Nation, Negro institutions of learning, opportunities opened to Negroes, the increase in the number of trained leaders, the growing efficiency of Negro churches, and finally, the growing ability of Negroes to help themselves.[29]

As a result of the Clifton Conference Dr. H. C. Lyman, a professor in one of the Negro schools, was asked to assume the task of organizing Sunday School training classes in the institutions which subscribed to the Clifton Plan. According to the Consulting General Secretary of the Council, approximately 35,000 students were enrolled in these leadership training classes from 1908 to 1922.[30]

Towards the close of Dr. Lyman's period of service in 1922, nearly 200 answers to a questionnaire sent out, commended the work. Dr. James W. Eichelberger, at the time of the report serving the Church as General Sunday School Secretary was mentioned in the report of the Consulting General Secretary as one who could verify the statements on the work since he, himself had taught such a course at Walters Normal School in Warren, Arkansas.

To an individual attending a District Convention at the close of the 19th Century,—the apparent disregard of that which is commonly accepted educational practice today,—keen disappointment would be felt. It was not extraordinary procedure for sessions having to do with Sunday School and Christian Endeavor practices and procedures to be postponed from day to day until the close of the Conference when ministers as well as other interested people had departed. The agitation continued, however, for adequate recognition of religious education needs. In the South, the Carolina area was the experimental grounds, while in the North, the Philadelphia and Baltimore, the Allegheny and Ohio Conferences came into the limelight as individuals, such as the Reverend C. E. West and Mrs. Dillard, or William Howard Day pioneered in the struggle. When James W. Eichelberger Jr. returned from the Zurich, Switzerland meeting of the World's Sunday School Association in 1913, he requested the Board of Bishops meeting in Pittsburgh, to appoint a Sunday School Commission, to study the work and its

---

[29] *The Encyclopaedia of Sunday Schools and Religious Education* III.
[30] *Ibid.*

needs. Twelve members were appointed to this commission among them being Sarah Janifer and Mary Frances Terrell.

Dr. George C. Clement, Editor of the *Star* and later Bishop of the Church, aided in alerting the denomination to its needs. Yeoman service was done likewise by the Reverend William Jacob Walls, later Bishop, who wrote, no doubt, the most critical and sharpest articles on the subject in the *Star of Zion*. In one such article he declared that the Bishops should refrain from placing themselves on so many inter-denominational boards and appoint the younger men who were close to the work, thereby giving these men the benefit of contacts.

Reverend Walls' article stirred up that which might be termed a hornet's nest, for when the Bishops met in New Bern in 1914 many of them were determined to show resentment at this criticism. The struggle for a revamped program was at white heat and the leaders of the move staked all to put over their ideas. To climax the whole controversy the Committee of Twelve reported. They made two significant recommendations. First, it was suggested that a General Sunday School and Christian Endeavor Convention be held the next year, in 1915, as an experiment. Their second suggestion recommended that in the editing of the Junior Quarterly, comments should be added or we should cease to publish this leaflet.

It may be stated here that at this time the Church was issuing, through its Editor of Sunday School literature, in addition to the picture lesson cards, three quarterlies, The Teachers', The Senior and the Junior editions. This last leaflet gave only the barest items such as the text, the time and place of the lesson and the golden text. There were no comments.

After much debate and discussion, bringing with these elements frayed nerves, their recommendations were approved and the time and place selected for the Convention. It was decided that this General Convention should be held the following year, 1915, in connection with the General Convention of the Women's Home and Foreign Missionary Society.

This experimental convention opened Thursday, August 5, 1915, in Washington Metropolitan Church, St. Louis, Mo. Mrs. Mary Jane Small, President of the Women's Home and Foreign Missionary Society, presided at the opening session. At the afternoon session, Professor Aaron Brown, Secretary of the Varick Christian Endeavor Society, was in charge. The session time was used in discussing the obstacles to a good Christian Endeavor from the standpoint of the Conference, the district and the local society. The Reverend O. H. Banks of the Indiana Conference, Mrs. Louisa B. Pringle of the Ohio Conference and Miss Lydia E. Lee of the Missouri Conference, served as leaders. Mrs. Belle Riley Conrad of Washington, D.C. delivered the address: *The Religious Motive Fundamental in Young People's Work.*

The evening session was taken up with a welcome program while the next day, morning and afternoon, was allotted to the Missionary group. Friday evening Professor Brown gave his annual address. Bishop Walters, another interested churchman, also spoke.[31]

Sunday, the Reverend R. B. Bruce presided. Such matters as grading the school, the pastor's place in the Sunday School and the Teacher's Meeting were taken up. Dr. Eichelberger conducted an open parliament on the subject to close the morning session. The afternoon hour brought simultaneous conferences on the various departments of the Sunday School such as the Cradle Roll, Primary, Home and that which was known as the ABC Departments. This first effort at a General Convention was climaxed with the Sunday School Parade on Monday afternoon.

The success of the St. Louis Convention lent impetus to the religious education movement, so much so, that when the General Conference met in Broadway Temple Church, Louisville in 1916 the work of the General Sunday School Superintendent was separated from that of the Editor of the Church School Literature. Dr. J. Francis Lee was elected Editor and James W. Eichelberger Jr. was selected Superintendent on half salary.[32] At this time Dr. Eichelberger was likewise principal of that which is now known as Walter-Southland School. The salary of the General Superintendent was to be paid by an assessment of one and two dollars on each church, if he were paid at all.[33]

Meanwhile a struggle was going on between the clergy and laity from an interdenominational standpoint over the control of Sunday School Literature. As is probably known, up to 1910, the literature of all Sunday Schools was based on the planning of the International and World Sunday School Association. As noted before, these

---

[31] From the Program of 1915.
[32] Minutes of the Twenty-fifth Quadrennial Session of the General Conference, Louisville, Ky., 1916, unpublished items.
[33] Interview, Dr. James W. Eichelberger.

organizations were dominated by lay people. To break this stranglehold, a new organization was formed in that year called the Sunday School Council of Evangelical Denominations.[34] Negro groups were slow to request membership in the new organization probably because of the friendly relationships with the Association. By 1917 only one Negro group had actually taken membership and that was the National Baptist Publishing Board of Nashville. In the 1917 Annual Meeting Zion Church, through Dr. Eichelberger, applied for membership and was accepted. James W. Powell and B. W. Swain aided in this move.

Important actions were taken by the General Conference meeting in Knoxville, Tenn. This time the General Superintendent of Sunday School work was placed on a full time basis.[35] The following year offices were opened in Chicago in the Michigan Avenue Church, 3947 Michigan Avenue, now the site of the South Side Boys' Club. Later the office was moved to 438 East 46th Street where the property was purchased. The final move was made to 128 East 58th Street in 1936, the property being secured one year earlier.

The Second General Sunday School Convention convened in Hopkins Chapel Church, Asheville, North Carolina, August 2nd through the 6th, 1922. The Third Convention was held in Saint Paul Church, Cleveland, Ohio, August 1-5, 1923. Emphasis at this conference was placed on curriculum, rural schools, leadership training and on group organization, i.e. children, youth and adult work. This plan of procedure had been utilized in the Asheville meeting as well. It may be interesting to some to note the themes of these conventions: the first general convention had no general theme while that of the second was "The Child in The Midst," and the third, "Religious Education in the New Social Order."

After the first General Convention the Christian Endeavor group decided against a general session, so it will be noted that the Asheville and Cleveland Conference Meetings were styled "General Sunday School Conventions."

In 1924, the General Conference meeting in Indianapolis, coordinated the Sunday School and Christian Endeavor Departments and changed the name to the Department of Religious Education. Aaron

---

[34] Interview, Dr. James W. Eichelberger.
[35] Minutes of the Twenty-sixth Quadrennial Session of the General Conference, unpublished items.

EDUCATION IN THE 19TH AND 20TH CENTURIES—HOME AND CHURCH

Brown, formerly the Secretary of the Varick Christian Endeavor was made Director of Promotion for the Department and James W. Eichelberger was to become Director of Religious Education. Dr. Eichelberger was to oversee the work of the Department supervised by a Board of Religious Education.[36]

The Indianapolis Conference likewise made significant change in the editorial staff. Heretofore, the Christian Endeavor literature was edited by the Secretary of the Varick Christian Endeavor Union. This duty was now transferred to the Editor of Sunday School Literature and this title was changed to the *Editor of Church School Literature*.[37] Dr. J. Francis Lee, the Editor, never assumed this task, however, declaring the additional work too much of a responsibility and so it was not until Dr. Buford F. Gordon (later Bishop) assumed the office on the death of Dr. Lee, that the will of the General Conference was carried out. In the meantime Professor Brown continued to edit the material.

Few members or non-members of the Church will dispute the conviction that the Christian Education Department in this century has found its rightful place in the inner-denominational circles of study and participation. In addition to participation in the original agencies of Sunday School work and Christian Endeavor, the Department has seen to representation in every major movement, both at home and abroad. The World Sunday School Conventions, since the first attended by Alexander Walters, have found Zion Methodist people in every session. The International Conventions, here on this Continent, likewise have had their Zion Methodist adherents present.

The First Youth Assembly meeting in Amsterdam, Holland, had in attendance, Dr. Buford F. Gordon (later Bishop), Margaret L. Lewis, Youth Council President, Charles L. Black and Martin L. Harvey (1939).[38]

The second Assembly of Christain Youth convened in Oslo, Norway when, in 1947, the then Miss Rena J. Weller and James W. Eichelberger Jr. were the official delegates of the denomination. Majorie Stiggers (Lyda) was sent to Travencore, India by her denomination while Marian Marsh was the youth representative at

---

[36] *Minutes of the 27th Quadrennial Session* of the General Conference (Indianapolis, Ind., 1924) 88.
[37] *Ibid.*, 232.
[38] The source material for this information has been the Quadrennial Printed reports of the Christian Education Department.

Tokyo, Japan, along with adults Bishop H. B. Shaw, James W. Eichelberger Sr., and Mr. and Mrs. David Wisdom. Enoch B. Rochester made the second conference held in India, this time at New Delhi.

Representation too, has been high at world meets of the Council of Churches and World Council of Christian Education, while for many years it has been the habit of Zion Methodism to be represented in the World Methodist Conferences. These assemblies and Zion's participation will be dealt with later.

The participation of the Church in the International gatherings has been even more spectacular, the numbers attending having grown immensely since the days of Alexander Walters and G. W. Clinton.

Since the early days of the first General Convention in 1915 no less than ten General Church School Conventions have been held with the largest attendance being that recorded at Livingstone College, Salisbury, North Carolina in 1962. A listing of these Conventions shows that these sources of Christian Education emphasis have been held in such places as Hopkins Chapel, Asheville in 1922, St. Paul, Cleveland, Ohio, 1923, Washington, D.C., 1926 Detroit, 1930, Knoxville, 1934, St. John Church, Cincinnati, 1938, Livingstone College, Salisbury, N.C. in 1942, Mother Zion Church, New York City, 1946, Hood Temple, Richmond, Va. 1950, Broadway Temple, Louisville, Ky. 1954; Caldwell Temple, Columbus, Ohio, 1958; Livingstone College, Salisbury, N.C. in 1962 and again, Salisbury, N.C. in 1966.

Many ministers and members have been involved in these projects as they have served as host pastors, J. L. Black, President W. J. Trent, Benjamin Robeson, C. W. Turns, Felix S. Anderson (later Bishop), J. Dallas Jenkins, and President Samuel Duncan, being a few of the later ones.

The Department, too, has worked in Educational Evangelism, the Protestant Film Commission, a pioneering organization formed to project the denominations into the realms of audio-visual (Zion Methodism was one of the early members of this group, and perhaps, the only member among black denominations), the Boy Scout movement among Protestants and organizations dealing with higher education. At times, too, it has aided in the work of the Protestant Chaplaincy; participated in All-Negro promotion of vital agencies, advanced Family Life Study; encouraged Social Education and action and aided research in many fields.

A subject, no doubt, of special study should be the work of the Department and the Church in the field of human relations. Christian Education has gone hand in hand with the insistence of equality of opportunity and freedom for all peoples. Its impact in the field of race relations has been a lasting one—from the incidents of Birmingham and Atlanta to these days when Christian Conventions meet without comment in such places in the South as Dallas, Texas. United Protestantism has fought this battle all the way from Grand Rapids to Houston.

The formation of the International Council of Religious Education which combined the agencies interested in the promotion of Sunday School work was reported by James W. Eichelberger to the 1924 General Conference. As noted in this work previously, the major agency for Sunday Schools had been the International Sunday School Association, one made up mainly and controlled by lay people. The rival organization, The Sunday School Council of Evangelical Denominations was formed in 1910 to break this lay strangle hold. The new combined group now became responsible for the production of basic material for all Sunday School work which eventually included Group Graded, Closely Graded and Uniform series. Committees of each series met each year for projected study and planning. They were made up of the outstanding religious scholars in their various fields and allowed all denominations to have common benefit of their thinking and planning.

The most recent innovation in Sunday School studies has been made by joint undertakings of the denominations, that which has been known as THE COOPERATIVE CURRICULUM PROJECT and the COOPERATIVE CURRICULUM DEVELOPMENT, the latter participated in actively by the A.M.E. Zion Christian Education Department with David H. Bradley Sr. as the designated representative. The work of the groups has been completed and is now available for denominational study and use.

In the development of these new trends of study many churches have formed *cluster* groups to share the high expense of producing study materials. However, the denomination at present has not committed itself to moving into the field singly or cooperatively. A decision it appears must eventually come on this matter.

James W. Eichelberger passed away, January 30, 1967 and was replaced by action of the Board of Bishops by Reverend George L. Blackwell, in February of that year.

JAMES W. EICHELBERGER

James W. Eichelberger, (August 30, 1886—January 30, 1967), son of James Washington and Josephine (Myers) Eichelberger, was born in Columbia, South Carolina. His father who died in December 1936 was a successful minister of the A.M.E. Zion Church.

Baptized when he was six weeks old, he was admitted to full membership in Jones Chapel A.M.E. Zion Church on Main Street in Columbia, South Carolina several years later.

He attended Howard Graded School, Columbia, S.C., and was later taught by his step-mother in the seventh grade class.

He was employed as a printer in the A.M.E. Zion Publishing House at Charlotte, North Carolina upon graduation from Livingstone. He served on the faculty of Clinton Institute (now College) at Rock Hill, S.C., spending three years in this post (1904-1907). For two years he then conducted his own printing establishment at Columbia. It was during this period (1905) that James W. Eichelberger attended the International Sunday School Convention of Toronto, Canada.

On his return he attended several conventions held in North and South Carolina. In the latter states several district and state conventions of the Sunday School movement and Christian Endeavor were promoted. Three are recalled at this time: one held at Mount Olivet, Rock Hill in 1905, the following year at Union, S.C., and in 1907 in the Metropolitan Church, Chester, S.C.

The Fifth World's Sunday School Convention was held in Rome, Italy in 1907. Through the generosity of South Carolina friends and his own means, James W. Eichelberger was privileged to attend.

In 1909 James W. Eichelberger was elected principal of Walters' Institute and served until 1921.

The Sixth World's Sunday School Convention met in Washington, D.C. and James W. Eichelberger attended.

At Zurich, Switzerland, when the Seventh World's Sunday School Convention was held in 1913 only two individuals from Zion Methodism were in attendance, James W. Eichelberger and the Reverend R. M. Boulden, minister of Mother Zion Church.

EDUCATION IN THE 19TH AND 20TH CENTURIES—HOME AND CHURCH

The 1916 General Conference, meeting in Louisville, Kentucy and having as its host this Reverend W. J. Walls, reacted to this interest in the Sunday School movement by providing for the first Sunday School Board. At the same time James W. Eichelberger was elected General Superintendent of Sunday Schools on half time.

A year after his election (1917) as General Superintendent of Sunday Schools, the Sunday School Bulletin made its appearance and was published by the Superintendent until 1924.

In 1924 when the General Conference met in Indianapolis, Indiana, the Sunday School and Varick Christian Endeavor Union were merged. Dr. J. Francis Lee was elected Editor of Church School Literature while James W. Eichelberger was elected Director of Religious Education. Prof. Aaron Brown was elected Director of Religious Education Promotion. James W. Younge was elected Secretary of Education.

In 1938 James W. Eichelberger married Helen Herndon. Meanwhile, he was active on many boards of an international and World flavor. Among them being The North American Committee of the World Council and the World Council itself, and membership in Council of Church Boards of Education, the American Association of School Administrators, The American Teachers' Association, The N.A.A.C.P., the Chicago Urban League. The Association for the Study of Negro Life and History and American Adult Education Association; the American Council of Education, National Education Association and American Education Fellowship. A trustee of Livingstone College, and the International Society of Christian Endeavor, he held an official relationship to the National and World Council of Churches as well. In 1924, the Sunday School Bulletin was succeeded by the Church School Herald and was edited by Dr. Eichelberger until 1932.

James W. Eichelberger was a member of the General Conference of the A.M.E. Zion Church in every session since 1908 until 1964.

From the minutes of the General Conference of 1864:

IV

SUNDAY SCHOOL UNION

This institution was organized by electing a Board of Officers; but the General Conference having established no method for operation, the officers elect framed and adopted the following Constitution:

CONSTITUTION
Of The Sunday School Union of the African Methodist Episcopal Church

PREAMBLE

Whereas: the mind in childhood is more susceptible than in riper years, no better method can be adopted for the cultivation of religious principles among the rising generation than the Sabbath Schools. In view of this fact, this institution is established to concentrate our efforts to carry out that purpose.

CONSTITUTION

Article I

This institution shall be known as the Sunday School Union of the African Methodist Episcopal Zion Church. Its object shall be to aid, encourage, and establish Sunday Schools in our churches, in accordance to the provision herein made or as may be determined by the Board of Officers.

Article II

The affairs of the institution shall be under the control of the officers elected by the General Conference, who shall constitute a Board to serve for the term of four years, except removed by unavoidable circumstances, in event of which the vacancy may be filled by the annual meeting, or if necessity require it, by the President in the interval of the annual meeting.

Article III

The officers shall consist of a President, four Vice Presidents, (or more when deemed necessary) Secretary, Treasurer, Corresponding Secretary, and a Standing Committee of three, whose duty shall be as follows:

The President shall conduct the affairs of the institution, preside at the annual meetings and all meetings of the Board.

The Vice Presidents shall be the presiding officers of the auxiliaries in each Annual Conference of their district, and act in cooperation with the President. The Secretary shall keep a record of all proceedings of the institution.

The Treasurer shall hold all funds put in his hands, and disburse it in no other way than authorized by the Board, or determined by the annual meeting, and report annually.

The Corresponding Secretary shall conduct the entire correspondence of the institution.

The standing Committee shall attend to such matters as they may be authorized to do by the Board of officers, or annual meeting. Matters of importance requiring attention in the interval, shall be under their control to regulate so long as it does not conflict with any previous arrangement of the Board, or detrimental to the institution. Any matter requiring consultation, they may call any of the officers (two or more) in counsel, and act accordingly.

Article IV

Whenever and wherever it is practicable and necessity require it, there may be an agent in each conference who shall visit the Sabbath Schools, organize them where they are needed, and keep a journal of the same, the result of which he shall report to the Board of Officers and Annual meeting. He shall solicit aid for the same purpose, and all funds thus collected shall be remitted to the Treasurer, and his account submitted to the Secretary once in four months for inspection.

Article V

The members of the Union shall consist of all persons who will contribute fifty cents per annum. Any person contributing ten dollars and upwards at one time, is constituted a life member, or if contributing twenty dollars at one time, is constituted a life manager, with privileges to speak, but not to vote, in the Board of Managers.

Articles VI

There shall be an annual meeting of the Society held at such a time and place as said meeting may determine, and shall consist of the Board of Officers, members of the institution, and such representatives as may be delegated by the Annual Conference and Sabbath Schools.

Article VII

The appropriation of the funds shall be exclusively for Sabbath School purposes, to be determined by the Board of Officers, except as much as may be necessary to defray the expenses of the Board.

Article VIII

All expediencies not herein provided for or implied, shall be regulated by the Board at their Annual Meeting, or a special meeting when urgent necessity demands it, which regulation shall be final, provided it does not conflict with the interest of the institution, or determined otherwise by the General Conference.

Article IX

There shall be auxiliaries organized or collections taken up in each Church or Sabbath School, to aid the institution.

Article X

This Constitution shall be revised by the General Conference, whenever expedient; but by-laws for the regulation of the Board or Annual Meeting may be adopted by them at any of their meetings, provided they are not contrary to the Constitution or detrimental to the institution.

CHAPTER VI

Education in the 19th and 20th Centuries —Home and Church

THE REVEREND JESSE E. COLBERT has written a little work called the History of the Varick Christian Endeavor Society of the A. M. E. Zion Church. While it brings to mind many points as to the phenomenal beginnings of this youth work among Zion Churches, many important details appear to have been omitted.

The Christian Endeavor movement began in a minister's home in Williston Congregational Church of that city at the time. The movement spread rapidly from that date of beginning (February 2, 1881). The first convention was held in that city in 1882 when 200 young people attended. Colbert states that a later one held in London, England, less than 20 years later, had in attendance 40,000 persons (1900).[1]

Early beginnings of the Christian Endeavor work in the A.M.E. Zion Church are credited to such individuals as the Rev. R. H. Stitt. Rev. Stitt was a product of Livingstone College and one of the first ministers of Grace Church, Charlotte, North Carolina. He was transferred to the New York Conference and stationed at Newburgh, Williamsburg and then Fleet Street (now First Church, Brooklyn.)[2] Here, he organized what was known as the Progressive Literary Society for the youth of the Church.[3] Following a revival he placed all young people joining during the meetings in a group called the Sons and Daughters of Zion.

In 1893, Stitt organized the young people's Society of Christian Endeavor with eighty-five members and in the same year attended the International Convention of Christian Endeavor Societies at Montreal. From this early interest he felt that some sort of instructional and communication media was needed so he began editing that which was known as "The Christian Endeavor Advocate." He continued this publication until his death.

---

[1] Rev. Jesse E. Colbert, *History of the Varick Christian Endeavor Society* (no date or place given) 13.
[2] Bishop J. W. Hood, *One Hundred Years of the African Methodist Episcopal Zion Church* (New York, 1895) 422.
[3] *Ibid.*

There is also a strong indication that soon after the organization of the first Christian Endeavor Societies within the denomination that the Reverend Alexander Walters became interested as well as the Reverend J. S. Caldwell. Bishop Walls states that the former attended several early conventions of the society. It is known too, that he both wrote and worked for the advancement of the Christian Endeavor cause.[4]

In the light of the Reverend's Stitt's contribution, one has to carefully analyze the statement of Colbert when he says that the first Varick Christian Endeavor Society was organized in Clinton Chapel Church in Lancaster, South Carolina.[5] This is no doubt true when the designation is Varick. Reverend W. A. Blackwell was the pastor at the time. However, Colbert later states the church was Mount Zion in the same city. This can be one and the same Church with a change of name. The date given for organization is August, 1896.

By 1889, the Church as a whole was accepting the new idea of Christian Endeavors. The movement had spread to the mission field to such an extent that the Second report from these fields noted a Society at Brewerville.[6]

In the General Conference of 1896, meeting in Mobile, Alabama, the following is noted: "We recommend that Christian Endeavor Society to your consideration and also recommend a distinct organization of our own to be known as the Varick Alliance.[7] In the discussion which followed the recommendation was referred to the Committee on Christian Endeavor. The Committee reported, recommending two organizations. "The previous question was called and prevailed. . . . Mr. Dancey and Rev. J. B. Colbert supported the word *Zion* instead of *Varick*. . . . The substitute of Mr. Dancy to substitute *Zion* for *Varick* was put and lost. . . . The main proposition was put which is, that the organization be known as the Varick Christian Endeavor Society of the A.M.E. Zion Church and prevailed.[8]

"By motion of Dr. W. D. Clinton, of Pittsburgh, Pa., the Report of the Committee on Episcopal Address was adopted as amended.

---

[4] Colbert, *loc. cit.*, 42.
[5] *Ibid.*, 42.
[6] *Minutes* of the General Conference, Nineteenth Quadrennial Session, 1892, 176. *Minutes* of Twentieth Session, 1896, 40.
[7] *Minutes of the Twentieth Quadrennial Session*, 1896, *loc. cit.* 115.
[8] *Ibid.*, 74.

Hence the recommendation of the Committee on Christian Endeavor was amended to read as above." [9]

It appears that the impetus to the Christian Endeavor movement came as a result of a memorial drawn up by a group of workers at a meeting in Jersey City, N. J. Rev. Stitt was the moving spirit of this meeting but did not live long enough to see his work bear fruit.[10]

The Rev. Colbert took up the leadership and no doubt carried the idea to the General Conference.

Others who were concerned with the movement, besides Bishop Alexander Walters, who became a trustee of the Internatonal Society were the Reverend J. H. White, who acted as Secretary of the Board of Control for four years, Bishop George W. Clinton and Bishop J. S. Caldwell, the last named one of those most vitally concerned with the furtherance of Christian Endeavor.

Once associations were established the link of the denomination was continued by other men such as Bishop Lynwood Westinghouse Kyles, and later, Bishop William Jacob Walls.

Bishop Caldwell and Reverend Colbert (Josiah Caldwell, however, had not yet been elevated to the episcopacy) launched, just three months after the adjournment of the 1896 General Conference, THE VARICK CHRISTIAN ENDEAVOR. Four years later, when the General Conference met in Washington, D.C., they declined to continue editing the paper so this organ was separated from the Varick Christian Endeavor Union. And the Rev. B. J. Bolding was elected editor. At the St. Louis General Conference in 1904, the Rev. J. T. McMillan was elected editor as well as President of the Union. In time Aaron Brown and Buford F. Gordon, produced the material.[11]

Reverend Colbert served as President of the Union from its beginning in 1896 to 1904, leaving the pastorate in 1898 to devote his entire time to this and other duties of the connection. It is said that when he came to the society there were 600 members. At the close of 1900 there were more than 35,000.[12] Dr. Colbert was followed in offfice by the Rev. J. T. McMillan who served until 1912 when Prof. Aaron Brown was elected to the position.[13]

---
[9] *Ibid.*, 75.
[10] Colbert, *loc. cit.*, 21.
[11] Jones, *Comprehensive Catechism, loc. cit.*, 60.
[12] Jesse Colbert, History of the Varick Christian Endeavor of the A.M.E. Zion Church, 13.
[13] Official Journal of the Twenty-fourth Quadrennial Session of the General Conference, 129.

EDUCATION IN THE 19TH AND 20TH CENTURIES—HOME AND CHURCH

The General Conference at Indianapolis, Indiana in 1924 merged the Sunday School union and the Christian Endeavor Union into that which thereafter was to be known as the Religious Education Department under one Board of Religious Education.[14] Three coordinate executive officers, Director of Religious Education, Director of Promotion, and Editor of Sunday Church School Literature and Christian Endeavor Literature, were elected and their work designated on a functional basis.[15] Heretofore, the salaries of the executives of both the Sunday School and Varick Christian Endeavor Union were paid by special assessments from local Sunday Schools and Varick Christian Endeavor Societies respectively, although the amount of their salaries was fixed by the General Conference. The Indianapolis General Conference provided for the payment of their salaries from the denominational fund.[16]

In the General Conference of 1932 which met in Pittsburgh, Pa., the Department of Education and the Department of Religious Education were merged into that which is now known as the Christian Education Department with one executive and the Editor of Church School Literature. Thus, the separate identity of the Varick Christian Endeavor was lost.[17]

A humorous note serves to close this brief account of the development of the Christian Endeavor as a separate organization. It is said time after time ministers would write in asking about the Christian Endeavor movement, for it was thought that it was a secret organization. Everyone seemed to want a sign and a grip. In order to meet this challenge a picture of the Holy Bible was drawn above which towered the Cross as the sign, the whole was held by a hand which was labeled the grip.

Within the Christian Education Department full and close relationships have been maintained with the Christian Endeavor movement despite its membership in the youth organization maintained by the majority of Protestant denominations, The United Christian Youth Movement. In many respects the programs are similar to the point that adherence to either by a local group is possible. Literature

---

[14] Minutes of the Twenty-seventh Quadrennial Session of the General Conference, 88.
[15] *Minutes of the Twenty-seventh Quadrennial Session, loc. cit.,* (Indianapolis, 1924) 231, 232, 88, 89.
[16] Minutes of the Twenty-seventh Quadrennial Session, 55.
[17] Journal of the Twenty-ninth General Conference, 238.

for the Varick Society is still published and used by many churches.

In an Episcopal Address before the Sixty-second Session of the New England Conference Bishop Alexander Walters had this to say:

> I know of no plan so well adapted to the development of young Christians as the one inaugurated by the United Society of Christian Endeavor, with its executive, prayer meeting, look-out, flower and other committees. It exactly meets the needs of our young people and can be made effective if the pastors and officers will take the proper interest in the work. The society must have the guiding hand of the pastor. Wherever a society has ceased to exist, it is for want of proper attention. The Christian Endeavor, like other societies of our Church, can only be kept alive by earnest effort. A society for young people is an absolute necessity in this highly social age. We need not hope to hold the intelligent young people of our Church, if we fail to organize and find something for them to do.
> The able President of the Union deserves a great deal of praise and credit for his efforts in keeping the work going.[18]

THE RELATION OF BAPTIZED CHILDREN TO THE CHURCH

Section 18—We hold that all children, by virtue of the unconditional benefits of the atonement, are members of the Kingdom of God, and therefore graciously entitled to Baptism; but as Infant Baptism contemplates a course of religious instruction and discipline, it is expected of all parents or guardians who present their children for Baptism, that they use all diligence in bringing them up in conformity to the word of God, and that they should be solemnly admonished of this obligation, and earnestly exhorted to faithfulness therein.

Section 2—We regard all children who have been baptized as placed in visible covenant relations to God, and under the special care and supervision of the church.

Section 3—The preacher in charge shall preserve a full and accurate register of the names of all the baptized children within his pastoral care, the dates of their births, baptism, their parentage, and place of residence.

Section 4—The preacher in charge shall organize the baptized

---

[18] *The A.M.E. Zion Quarterly Review*, Vol. V, No. 3, 1906, 1.

children of the church, at the age of ten years or younger, into classes, and appoint suitable teachers (male or female), whose duty it shall be to meet them in class once a week, and instruct them in the nature, design, and obligations of baptism, and the truths of religion necessary to make them wise unto salvation; urge them to give regular attendance upon the means of grace; to advise, exhort, and encourage them to an immediate consecration of their hearts and lives to God, and inquire into the state of their religious experience.

Section 5—Whenever baptized children shall have attained an age sufficient to understand the obligations of religion, and shall give evidence of piety, they may be admitted into full membership in our church, on the recommendations of a leader with whom they have met at least six months in class, by publicly assenting before the church to the baptismal covenant, and also to the usual questions on doctrines and discipline.

Section 6—Whenever a baptized child, orphan or otherwise, becomes deprived of Christian guardianship, the preacher in charge shall ascertain and report to the leaders and stewards' meeting the facts in the case; and such provision shall be made for the Christian training of the child and the circumstances of the case admit and require. Offered by M. M. Bell.

ALFRED DAY, *Chairman*
J. C. DACEY, *Secretary*[19]

J. S. COWLES	J. McH FARLEY	E. D. TAYLOR
J. F. PAGE	R. H. SIMMONS	C. SMITH
W. H. FERGUSON	R. H. G. DYSON	W. C. VESTA
T. A. HOPKINS	A. JACKSON	J. W. MOSSEY
E. H. CURRY	J. THOMAS	H. L. SIMMONS
C. C. PETTY	M. M. BELL	A. BOLIN
A. W. ALLISON	S. W. JONES	LAWSON IRWIN
A. F. MOORE	THOMAS DARLEY	W. T. BIDDLE

CONSTITUTION OF THE A. M. E. ZION SUNDAY SCHOOLS

ARTICLE I

Our Schools shall be known as the A. M. E. Zion Sunday Schools.

---

[19] From the *Daily Journal of the Sixteenth Session* of the General Conference A.M.E. Zion Church, 1880, p. 66, 67.

Article II

Our Sunday Schools shall be governed by a Committee of not less than three nor more than nine, appointed by the Quarterly Conference and the teachers and officers of the school, the minister in charge being the chairman.

Article III

The officers of the school shall be the minister in charge, one male or female superintendent, and Assistant Secretary, Treasurer, and a Librarian. The Superintendent and other officers to be elected annually by the teachers and the adult scholars, but the right of nomination shall always be with the preacher in charge, in the organization of a Sunday School. The superintendent and teachers at the first teachers' meeting after the appointment of the Superintendent and teachers (?).

Article IV

It shall be the duty of the minister in charge to take the general oversight of the school, to attend the teachers' meetings as often as practicable.

Article V

The Superintendent shall preside at the teachers' meetings, and give all necessary encouragement to teachers, to a faithful performance of their relative duties, and frequently to lecture them. He shall see that his school or schools are furnished with copies of this Constitution, and that it be carried out, so that the design of our Church relative to Sunday Schools, as expressed in the Discipline, be fully realized.

Articles VI through X dealt with the duties of officers and teachers, while XI established the Committee or Board controlling the work of the Sunday School. Article XII provided for the selection of new Teachers while XIII stated:

Teachers are strictly admonished against conversations with each other during the session, unless upon purely school matters. Any negligence upon the part of teachers, or any misdemeanor, shall be settled at the teachers' meeting; in failing to do so, let the whole matter go before the Board.

Articles XIV listed the order of Business of the Sunday School and the rules for the school. It also included the following:

1. *Resolved,* That one portion of the Sabbath be devoted to the instruction of the children in the Scripture, the doctrines and Catechism of our Church.
2. *Resolved,* That the Juvenile Missionary Societies be formed in our Sabbath Schools.

3. *Resolved,* That we do endorse the "International Series" of lessons.
All of which is most respectfully submitted.
S. S. Wales, M. Page, Thomas Darley, W. G. Strong, A. Tasker, W. A. Foreman, Lawson Irwin, T. A. Hopkins, S. Sherman, J. H. Jackson, A. W. Goslin, E. S. Reeves, J. McH. Farley, A. Anderson, G. E. Smith, J. W. Brown, A. F. Moore, D. J. Walker. Committee[20]

[20] *Daily Journal of the Sixteenth Quadrennial Session* of the General Conference, Montgomery, Ala., 1880, 74-77.

CHAPTER VII

Education in the A.M.E. Zion Church School and College

AS A denomination increases in age there is the likelihood of its members losing sight of the reasons for its existence. As one looks back on the formation of Zion Methodism in the 18th Century it is not hard to discern at least six basic reasons for its birth: the necessity of a wider Christian fellowship among African believers and the descendants of Africans; the urgency of evangelism among this same group; the necessity of economic development among free black men and freed men; the advancement of social and educational concerns, including the working for the abolition of slavery; the development of an indigenous ministry; and the concern for expansion and development of Christian experience among black people. In this and a succeeding chapter we will deal with the development of educational work and opportunities.

In the construction of the second church building in New York City in 1820, the decision of the Board of Trustees to provide for education by including schoolroom facilities was not a matter for light consideration.[1] This need was paramount in the eyes of Negro lay leadership. While there is little doubt that some facilities for Negro education were available[2] these could not have been wholly adequate or the move of the Board of Trustees would not have been necessary.

According to the Minutes of the Common Council of New York City, the plan of these trustees had evidently been carried out at a much earlier date than the time of the building of the second structure, for these accounts appear as early as 1804, and perhaps earlier.[3] An earlier estimation of the success of this venture, therefore, needs to be revised, for evidently the school fulfilled a satisfactory mission.

One would be forced to confess that several factors produced this interest in education. Certainly a strong incentive was the essential training of Negro preachers. This was a factor in the forming of the

---

[1] Christopher Rush, *A Short Account of the Rise and Progress of the African Methodist Episcopal Church in America*, (New York, 1843) p. 30.
[2] Benjamin F. Wheeler, *The Varick Family*, (Mobile, Ala., 1906) 12.
[3] *Minutes of the Common Council of the City of New York, 1784-1831.*

organization and it played its part as well in the advancement of leadership. Ill-prepared ministers were not welcome[4] even among the Africans of Zion Church, themselves, for they were quite well aware of the standards for preaching. It is significant that years later the common notion that a call to preach alone was the needed qualification to occupy a pulpit displaced the earlier and beginning concept of preparation first.

The Wesley tradition of a "saddle bag of books" affected Methodist America profoundly. Bishop Allen of the Bethel Church is said to have attempted the education of "Black Harry, Bishop Asbury's aide, who could neither read nor write." When Black Harry took up this task of being educated he lost his effectiveness as a preacher so he decided to remain ignorant.

Of the nine trustees of the Chapel (the original number), four could write.[5] While this appears to have been commendable the fact remains that the Chapel had among its number the most respected and forward-looking Negroes of the City. The outstanding men of this group were selected as officers of the new organization. Thus it can be seen that educational needs were ever-present with the group.

Bishop Hood states that the early annual conferences were in essence Theological Schools as they were the only means available for the training of the ministry.[6] Dr. Gray, evidently of Mother Zion Church, was one of the early ministers who served as an instructor at these long annual conferences. Usually perhaps, for that reason and others, the conferences were closed affairs. Later the public was admitted.

The first official note we have of denominational interest in education appears in the statement of Bishop E. D. W. Jones who states that Rush Academy was first proposed in 1844.[7] In this, as in the case of the founding of the denomination the welfare of the laymen was expressly considered. The name chosen for the first venture was "Connectional Manual Labor School." A committee was appointed

---

[4] Rush, *loc. cit.*, 32.
[5] See The Charter of the African Chapel, Copy included in Rush, *loc. cit.*, 15-22. Also, *Bradley, 1796-1872*, 50-54.
[6] Bishop J. W. Hood, *One Hundred Years of the African Methodist Episcopal Zion Church*, (New York, 1895) 85. Also note Original (unpublished) *Minutes of the New Jersey Annual Conference* (deposited at Livingstone College).
[7] Jones, *loc. cit.*, 28.

to draw up a constitution for the new enterprise, it consisting of Reverends J. C. Beaman, John P. Thompson and Peter Ross.

In 1847, Jones states that a Literary Connectional Convention was called to meet at York, Pennsylvania to aid the committee in "drafting plans to present to the General Conference in 1848." [8]

A famous abolitionist, Gerritt Smith had offered land in Essex County, New York, for the purpose of educating ex-slaves and so the committee proposed to utilize the ground for the new institution.

In the General Conference of 1848 a Committee on the Revision of the Discipline and the proposed Rush Academy was appointed.[9] Later at this same conference Superintendent Galbreath was elected President of the Academy.

Little could have been done in the General Conference of 1852 as the time was consumed with the differences involving the Superintendency. In the Conference of 1856, however, the subject was again brought up. A Reverend J. F. Wright of the Methodist Episcopal Church, spoke on the Ohio African University while another individual, Rev. Dr. C. Adamson, represented another institution.[10] As a result of this renewed interest in education, the Committee on Education recommended the following:

> Consideration of the Ohio African University.
> That a Committee of Three be appointed by the General Conference to visit "the agent of the institution and inquire on what terms a right may be secured."
> That the Conference inquire into the state of funds of Rush Academy. Also to require Rev. Rush to give this Conference perfect understanding of the deed of the institution.[11]

From this latter statement it is clear that one of the handicaps of the Rush Academy movement was the uncertainty as to ownership. Before the Conference adjourned, however, a definite endorsement was made of the Ohio African University and a new setup made for the Rush Academy.[12] Reverend S. T. Scott was elected President, Joseph P. Thompson and George A. Spywood were made Vice-Presidents while Christopher Rush was elected Treasurer. Not being fully satisfied with this arrangement the Conference appointed a

---

[8] *Ibid.*, 29.
[9] John J. Moore, *History of the A.M.E. Zion Church in America*, (York, Pa. 1884) 211.
[10] *Ibid.*, 217.
[11] *Minutes of the General Conference of* 1856, see Moore, *loc. cit.*, 218.
[12] Moore, *loc. cit.*, 221.

Committee "to investigate the Constitution to clear the deed angle," and a Board of Trustees was appointed to "hold the property of the institution in trust for the African Methodist Episcopal General Conference." [13]

In the Committee assignments of the General Conference of 1864, William Sanford, G. H. Washington and J. Anderson were members of the Committee on Sabbath Schools. On Education, the following appeared: William F. Butler, S. T. Jones, and J. D. Brooks. Another interesting item appearing in the minutes of the same year was the resolution to provide for the establishment of an agricultural organization.[14]

Bishop Joseph Jackson Clinton has been well remembered for his work of expanding the borders of the denomination and very often this great achievement has dwarfed his companionate interest in education. Jones, in his work: *The Comprehensive Catechism* perhaps sums up this great interest when he states of Bishop Clinton (Of the failure of Zion Collegiate Institute in or near Pittsburgh, Pa.) "in the language of another, 'it broke his heart' from which stroke he never recovered." [15]

One could see just why Bishop Clinton was so affected by the failure of his educational hopes as one senses the difficulties and reasons for the failures. Bishop Clinton was fully aware of the great necessity of a trained leadership and the association educational efforts had to the eventual economic improvement of his people. The zeal with which he undertook the spiritual freedom of the Negro had its beginning counter-part in the educational enterprises. Rush University, or Academy as it was first known, was but one of at least three ventures—the other two being the Ohio African School and the Zion Hill Collegiate Institute.

To William Howard Day is attributed a great part of Bishop Clinton's failures. Of this astute leader a Harrisburg Newspaper had this to say:

> Reverend Dr. William Howard Day, perhaps the most prominent Negro citizen of Pennsylvania and one of the most prominent of his race, died this morning at 7 o'clock at his home, 625 Briggs Street. He devoted his life and the best energies of a trained and astute mind to the uplifting of his race and he was very generally respected by both

---
[13] *Ibid.*, 221.
[14] *Minutes of the General Conference of* 1864, p.
[15] Jones, *loc. cit.*, 30.

races. He was a friend of Booker T. Washington, President of Tuskegee Industrial College.

Dr. Day had been ill for a year with paralysis and a complication of diseases. He had been confined to the house since last May, but spent most of the time in an easy chair. He was always hopeful of his condition and up to the time he lost consciousness, fully expected to recover. He was about 78 years of age which materially interfered with his regaining his health.

He is survived by a wife, but no children and few, if any near relatives. The funeral services will be held on Friday morning at Wesley Union A. M. E. (Zion) Church, South Street, and several Bishops and General Officers of the A. M. E. Zion Church will be in attendance. Dr. Day was a member of the Masons and the Odd Fellows and these bodies will attend the services.

William Howard Day, General Secretary of the A. M. E. Zion Church, and chief Secretary of the Philadelphia (and Baltimore) Conference, was born October 16, 1825 in New York City and was baptized by Bishop (Superintendent) Varick, the founder of the Zion Church. He was the son of John Day, 1783-1828, and Eliza Dixon, 1793-1869. He was educated in the public schools of his native city and in the private school of Rev. Frederick Jones, and prepared for college in the high school of Northampton, Mass., then in charge of Rev. Randolph B. Hubbard and Tutor Dwight, subsequently of Yale University.

In 1843 he entered Oberlin College, graduating in 1847. He learned the art of printing in the Hampshire "Gazette" office at Northampton and afterwards turned his attention to teaching and lecturing. In 1850 he was elected by the colored citizens of Ohio at a state conference, to plead their cause before the Ohio Constitutional Convention. He received the degree of A. M. from Oberlin in 1859, and later the degree of D. D. was conferred upon him by Livingstone College. He was elected professor of language by two colleges in 1857, and was offered the Latin tutorship at Lincoln, England in 1862.

From 1852 to 1855 he edited the ALLENDED AMERICAN of Cleveland, having previously been local editor of the Cleveland TRUE DEMOCRAT, now THE LEADER. In 1866 he was invited to take the lecture platform in Great Britain, and remained there at the request of the American residents from the north to explain to the people of England the issues at stake in the great civil conflict then at its height in this country. He was received by the Earl of Spencer at Spencer House, England. Subsequently he was received by the Lord Provost of Edinburgh, Scotland. He was the Principal speaker at a meeting of 3,000 persons in the Music Hall, Dublin, which was presided over by the Lord Mayor.

In 1866 he was ordained deacon and elder at Petersburg, Virginia, by Bishop J. J. Clinton, and was elected General Secretary of the General Conference in 1876, 1888, 1892, 1896, and 1900. In 1867 and 1868 he was superintendent of schools in the district of Maryland and Delaware under the United States Government. He held a clerkship in the auditor general's office in 1872-1875, during the incumbency of General Harrison Allen.

EDUCATION IN THE A.M.E. ZION CHURCH SCHOOL AND COLLEGE

He was elected to the school board of this city in 1878 from the eighth ward and served until ill health compelled him to relinquish his seat in 1898. He is the only colored man who has even had a seat on the school board. He was elected president of the board in 1891-92, the only instance on record in the United States where a colored man has been successfully elected president of twenty-five men. He was also elected president of the Dauphin County Directors' association for five successive years, from 1891-96, he being the only colored member of the body.

William Howard Day died December 3, 1900.[16]

The controversy between the Board of Bishops and William Howard Day is not clearly understood for there are several angles about which little has been written. For example, Bishop Hood writes in his history, "Brother Day (William Howard) was ordained an elder at this session. (1866 session of the Virginia Conference). If he had taken work in that conference at that time, and had bent his best effort to the work of building up the work in that Conference, Zion might easily have been as strong in Virginia as she is in North Carolina. He was very much better equipped than any other man we had in the South at that time." [17] While the statement of Bishop Hood no doubt was wholly true, the life and existence Day had built in Ohio and Pennsylvania for himself would have had to have been sacrificed had he moved to Virginia.

The Daily Journal of the Sixteenth Quadrennial Session of the denomination brings to light two other matters which, to this writer, are of paramount importance, both to the denomination and to the educational projects of Bishop Clinton. The account is merely headed: THE SECRETARY OF THE GENERAL CONFERENCE and is here given in its entirety:

> Prof. William Howard Day, Secretary of the General Conference, and Compiler of the Minutes, having failed to publish the Minutes up to Jan. 1878, the Board of Bishops resolved to publish them. We were informed by good authority that Prof. Day had them compiled, and as two years had passed and he was paid $25 for compiling them, we had no thought to the contrary. We should have taken it for granted that the compilation was ready for publication, if no one had seen it. Therefore, having resolved to publish the Minutes, we sent to Prof. Day for the *Manuscript Minutes.* In anticipation of this action he had been notified to send the Minutes to the Board. After considerable delay, he sent the Journal of the General Conference through a party whose pledge he took that it should be returned to him. Up to that

---
[16] From a Harrisburg, Pa. newspaper of that date.
[17] Hood, *loc. cit.*, 353.

time we had no thought of anything criminal on his part; we supposed the delay was the result of neglect; we had no thought of sending for the journal of the General Conference.

It was not what we wanted; we had no use for it; we dispatched repeatedly for the manuscript. In our last dispatch we told him he would be held as in contempt; he pretended not to know what we wanted. He did not say that he had not the manuscript written. As we could not get the manuscript and had not time, if we had the authority, to prepare a compilation, nor were we willing to pay someone else to do the work that Prof. Day had been so well paid for. Therefore we had to give up publishing the Minutes.

As we understood that Prof. Day was working against the Zion Hill Collegiate Institute, and that he otherwise appeared disaffected toward the connection, Bishop Clinton was instructed to hold the journal until further developments. He was also instructed to prepare charges against Prof. Day, and place them in the hands of a Committee.

At our last meeting in Petersburg, we were informed that the Virginia Conference had suspended Prof. Day, thus making a vacancy in the office of General Conference Secretary.

PROF. DAY, SECRETARY OF THE GENERAL CONFERENCE..

Charges having been made against Prof. Day by Bishop Clinton at the request of the Board, and placed in the hands of an elder, who reported that Prof. Day had been tried and suspended, the Professor was summoned to appear at the Virginia Conference, where his case would be finally determined.

Learning from him that he would not be present, his case was taken up with Bishop Lomax in the chair. Bishop Lomax was not present at the meeting of the Board of Bishops, at which the offense charged against Prof. Day was committed.

In Prof. Day's defense sent to the Conference, expressed a doubt of the Committee's right to call him, took issue with the composition of the Committee, and stated that one member of the Committee was not fit to sit upon his case.

Although it was thought that had Prof. Day condescended to meet the Committee, he could have had all our clergy in Washington City added to the Committee, yet the Conference decided to drop the papers coming to the Committee on Complaints, who brought in the following report.[18]

REPORT OF COMMITTEE ON COMPLAINTS..

For the Bishop and Members of the Virginia Annual Conference of the African Methodist Episcopal Zion Church in America.

We your committee, to whom was referred the matter of complaint against Prof. W. H. Day, have had the matter under careful consideration.

We find that Prof. Day was charged with contempt in refusing to send to the Board of Bishops the manuscript minutes of the last General Conference.

---

[18] *Daily Journal of the Sixteenth Quadrennial Session of the General Conference A.M.E. Zion Church in America.* (New York, 1880) 45, 46.

This charge was placed in the hands of an elder who called a committee and summoned Prof. Day to meet and answer to the charge. This, Prof. Day refused to do. A majority of the committee voted to suspend him.

Prof. Day, in a letter of defense, claims that the committee was improperly formed, that a portion of them had pre-judged the case and were not competent to try him.

In order to give him the benefit of all he claims, we decided not to take the committee's actions or findings into account in making up our judgment. It however appears to us from the information before us, especially from the letters of Prof. Day to the committee and to this Conference, that he is guilty of contempt.

We therefore most respectfully submit the following:

Whereas: Prof. W. H. Day has been charged with contempt in refusing to send to the Board of Bishops the manuscript minutes of the last General Conference. And whereas, the said Prof. Day has sent to this Conference a document which indicates his contempt, both of this Conference and of the Bishops; boasting of his attempt to sow discord in the Sabbath Schools and of his success in reducing it to about one-half of its former strength. And whereas: Prof. Day has been repeatedly summoned to this Conference to answer to the complaint against him, and has failed to do so, therefore

Resolved, that he be suspended from all official standing and church privileges, until he meets this Conference and answers to the charges preferred against him.

Respectfully submitted,
A. PAXTON
W. H. PITTS
W. JONES
S. STORY
H. H. WHIDBEE
Committee

The report was adopted.[19]

Of significance is the statement concerning Zion Hill Collegiate Institute at this point. It appears that the State Legislature of Pennsylvania had voted to appropriate to the institution $5,000, which, at that time, was a significant sum. It is said that William Howard Day was opposed to segregated schools and that he persuaded the Governor at the time to veto the bill, thus the amount was lost to the institution. It is known that he had considerable influence with the Governor at that period of the State's history.

While we shall deal elsewhere with the matter of the holding of the two General Conferences in 1872 it should be stated here that the *evident balance of power* from two angles was exhibited in that

---

[19] *Daily Journal of the Sixteenth Session*, 1880, loc. cit., 47.

year. So frequently each generation feels that it plays a unique place in the challenge of the old and assumption of responsibility, but this is not the case, for this challenge of responsibility and assumption of responsibility is an ever-recurring event. Bishop Joseph Jackson Clinton had ably led the denomination through its most fruitful period which should come to a close in the final two decades of the Nineteenth Century. In truth, the New York and Charlotte General Conferences were but an indication of restlessness. From this time on there would be new challenges of leadership and new challenges of participation as the voting strength of the denomination moved ever Southward, away from New York, Pennsylvania, Maryland and the Middle East to new area of Virginia, North and South Carolina and Alabama.

Challenges not only came in leadership but in the re-building of the denomination and educational efforts, naturally, felt the full impact of this change. The seemingly futile efforts to establish a College in the North failed for several reasons, chief among them being economic strength, the liberal policy of many white schools which allowed eligible Negroes to enroll and evident opposition to the *separate* school idea.

By the time the General Conference met in Charlotte in 1872 (the New York General Conference adjourned to meet with this Southern Wing) the handwriting was on the wall. The struggle was more than that as recorded between *the Giants,* as Jones puts it.[20] Moore writes of the proposal of actually *two General districts* "Providing for two General Book Agencies for the Book Concern." [21]

In the absence of the Minutes of 1872 the Tenth Session of the North Carolina Conference in session at Wilmington, North Carolina (November 26-December 3, 1873) carries the following resolution based on the action of the General Conference:

> *Whereas;* The General Conference at its last session in Charlotte, N. C. authorized the Trustees of the Rush Academy, located in New York, to transfer that institution to Fayetteville, N. C., and Whereas: it was contemplated that the General Agents would be able to raise sufficient funds to open that institution within a few months after the close of the General Conference; and, Whereas: nothing has been done in this important matter, and to wait longer for the action of the Trustees would be detrimental to every interest of the institution, therefore

---

[20] Jones, E. D. W., *Comprehensive Catechism, loc. cit.,* 27.
[21] Moore, *loc. cit.,* 275.

Resolved; That this Conference proceed to organize a Board and establish a fund to be known as the Rush University Fund of the North Carolina Annual Conference of the A. M. E. Zion Church, to aid in establishing an educational institution at Fayetteville, as was contemplated by the General Conference.

Resolved: that the Bishop appoint an agent to travel through the district, and collect means on behalf of said fund, and the names of all who contribute 25 cents and upwards be published in The Advocate; those contributing one dollar and upwards to be published in a Roll of Honor.[22]

The Committee assigned to handle this fund were: Bishop J. W. Hood, Reverends, J. A. Tyler, Vice President, C. R. Harris, Secretary, E. H. Hill, Treas., Amos York, Thomas Henderson, and Francis House, J. McH. Farley was appointed the Traveling Agent.[23]

When the Conference met in New Berne (as it was then written) North Carolina, the records showed that a total of $667.72 had been collected for the project.[24] Of course, from this sum there had to be deducted the travel and salary of the agent which left little amount in the Treasury. The Conference assembled the next year at New Berne as well (1875) and the ardor seemed to have cooled, somewhat for the only mention of the project appears to have been one of *progress.*

Our records not being complete the action of the Annual Conference is not known for the next four years. In the Minutes of the 16th Session (Lincolnton, 1879) the Reverend C. R. Harris made his second annual report. This of course means that he was evidently appointed or elected to the position in 1878. His report reads:

> Brethren: I have no rose-colored report to offer, but such as I have give I unto you. In accordance with a resolution of the last annual conference, Diplomas of Honor were prepared by Prof. A. S. Richardson. From January 13 to February 21st, fifty ministers were supplied with them, express charges being paid from the Treasury. A few others were supplied afterwards, the total number distributed being five hundred. Nine hundred and thirty-five were printed, eleven sold by the Secretary, and three were returned by Deacon Vandenburg, leaving a balance on hand of four hundred and twenty-seven. Of scholarships 476 were printed, two of them being sold last year by Elder Bonner of Tarboro and two this year by Elder Harris at Salisbury.
>
> One or two ministers wrote saying thay intended to comply, but up

---

[22] *Minutes of the North Carolina Conference of 1873.*
[23] *Minutes of the Tenth Session* of the North Carolina Conference, 1873.
[24] *Minutes of the Eleventh Session of the North Carolina Conference,* 1874.

to the assembling of Conference none had responded to that appeal but Jerry M. McNeil, who sent two dollars from Swann's Station. All honor to him. Let this epitaph be written over his grave: "He hath done what he could."

As further aid in raising funds for the Institute, the Trustees, at an informal meeting held at Concord in August, agreed that the diplomas might be sold on time, by paying one dollar yearly. The Secretary was to inform the financial agents of the arrangements and furnish them with blank due bills to be signed by the parties purchasing the diplomas. At the same time several brethren present agreed to advance certain sums, to supply the demand while the building was in process of erection. Of these Bishop J. W. Hood forwarded to the Treasurer fifty dollars, forty dollars being the balance of the educational fund of this Conference then in his hands, and ten dollars donated by himself.

No receipts yet from the scholarship diplomas.

On the 19th inst. the idea occurred to me that the apathy of the ministers in regard to the collection of funds, might be due to the fact that the deed to the land had not yet been placed in the hands of the Trustees. Although it had been agreed that no improvement should be made 'til this was done, and the Chairman of the Building Committee had been instructed to get the deed as soon as possible.

I then thought I would secure a piece of land in Salisbury, and have it presented to the institution. However, on the 21st I dropped a card to Warren Coleman, Esq. of Concord, one of the most prominent of the Trustees, who dedicated the land to Zion Wesley, asking if there was any possibility of having a deed for that land to be presented to this Annual Conference and be placed in possession of the Trustees of Zion Wesley Institute. I will not press the application from Salisbury.

I have said I have no rose-colored report to offer, but as some cloudy days end with a golden sunset, so may this report close with a cheering statement. Since coming to Conference the following brethren have paid $55.25 into the Treasurey, which amounts they have raised during the year, viz: W. J. Moore, A. York, W. H. Thurber, J. C. Dancy, R. S. Rieves, A. G. Kesler, John Hooper, A. P. Smyer, Z. T. Pearsall and J. H. Mattocks, with a donation of ten dollars from Bishop Lomax. Besides this, owing to happy fore-thought of our silver-tongued orator, and the generosity of the Conference and the congregation of this Church $36.11 have been received as the proceeds of the Thanksgiving collection.

I now offer my report as Treasurer of the Institution:

Balance on hand at last Conference	$ 23.13
Receipts on scholarships	37.87
Receipts on Diplomas	32.25
Collections from churches	4.00
Thanksgiving collection	36.11
North Carolina Conference Education Fund	40.00
Donation from Bishop J. W. Hood	10.00

EDUCATION IN THE A.M.E. ZION CHURCH SCHOOL AND COLLEGE

Donation from Bishop T. H. Lomax 10.00

Total $193.36
Expended for printing and distributing Diplomas ....$ 27.92
Expended for 11 copies of Star sent to Trustees 3.70
Expended for Circulars and Due bills...................... 3.60
Expended for Lecturer's board at Wilson 2.75
Expended for Envelopes and postage...................... .35

Total ....$ 38.32
Balance on hand in the Treasury $155.04

Zion Wesley Institute as an institution of learning concerned in, and thus far fostered and sustained alone by the North Carolina Conference, appeals to your warmest sympathies and most energetic labors. I trust that though divided in name, we are not, in heart, and that every member, both ministerial and lay delegates, will push forward the roll of diplomas and scholarships, and by no means neglect the public collections provided for at this session of Conference.

Respectfully submitted,
C. R. HARRIS
Secretary and Treasurer of A. W. I.[25]

In the same session of the Annual Conference (North Carolina) the following appears in the Minutes:

> It was ordered that the Secretary be required to secure an engrossed copy of the Act of Incorporation from the Secretary of State for the benefit of the Institute.
> It was further ordered that the words "Zion Wesley Institute Fund" be inserted in the statistical table instead of Rush University Fund. The Trustees of Zion Wesley Institute were instructed to open school on the First Monday in January, 1880.[26]

It will be noted that Cicero Harris mentioned in his report the matter of division. For the benefit of the casual reader it should be said that as early as 1876, when the Thirteenth Session of the North Carolina Conference met in Washington, N. C. the creation of the Central North Carolina Conference was discussed. A minority report stated the following: 1. It would make the burden of sustaining the Conference lighter; 2. More time could be given for the work of the Conference; 3. The conference could be taken to a greater number of places; 4. Traveling expenses would be less; 5. There could be a more rapid spreading of the Church; 6. And the Transfer System

---
[25] *Minutes of the Sixteenth Session of the North Carolina Conference,* 1879.
[26] *Minutes of the North Carolina Conference,* 1879.

could give the same advantages. The report called for an Eastern and a Western Conference. The minority report was made by C. R. Harris. Those who voted with the majority stated that the privilege of greeting men from the East and those from the West, or North or South, was a distinct advantage. Their second point declared that the people in the churches would be dissatisfied and there was really no burden at present. W. J. Moore and A. M. Barrett advanced the major contentions.

As the discussion continued it was suggested that the matter be referred to the Quarterly Conferences, requesting a two-thirds ruling. This was later withdrawn and the proposition to divide was defeated by a vote of 52 to 47.[27]

The matter of the creation of the Central North Carolina Conference came up again in the Sixteenth Session of the North Carolina Conference (1879) when a Resolution was offered by J. C. Tyler. It stated: "resolved that this Conference do now divide, hereafter to be known as the North Carolina and the Central North Carolina Conference." While J. C. Dancy opposed the resolution, it carried by a vote of 76 to 16.[28]

J. C. Dancy moved, after the vote, that the North Carolina Conference would meet at Tarboro, North Carolina the fourth Wednesday in November, 1880; and that the Central North Carolina Conference would meet at Fayetteville, North Carolina on the Second Wednesday in November, 1880.

The Third Report of the Reverend C. R. Harris for the Zion Wesley Institute was given before the First Session of the Central North Carolina Conference which met on November 10-18, 1880 in Fayetteville, North Carolina. It follows:

REPORT OF THE SECRETARY-TREASURER OF ZION WESLEY INSTITUTE TO THE PRESIDENT AND MEMBERS OF ZION WESLEY INSTITUTE

In accordance with ordinary usage, I present you this, my Third annual report as Secretary-Treasurer of the Board.

From the indications of the previous year and results of our last Annual Conference (North Carolina) I am impressed with the opinion that it would be best for the interests of the Institute to open at the earliest moment practicable, and carry it on in a rented house until our Institute building should be erected. Immediately after the ad-

---

[27] *Minutes of the Thirteenth Session, North Carolina Conference,* Washington, N. C., 1876.

[28] *Minutes of the North Carolina Conference, Sixteenth Session,* Nov., 26-Dec. 3, 1879.

journment of the North Carolina Annual Conference I suggested that a meeting of the Board be called to take the matter into consideration. This was done and on the 16th of December, 1879, the Board met at Charlotte, North Carolina; the following members being present, viz: Bishops J. W. Hood and T. H. Lomax, R. H. Simmons, T. F. H. Blackman and C. R. Harris. After consultation, the Secretary, in view of the scarcity of funds in the treasury and the acknowledged need of the school, agreed to take the position of principal of the school for the first session at a salary of seventy-five cents per month per scholar. A room was rented for twenty dollars per year, and incidental expenses to be paid from the treasury. A schedule of studies was presented; it was adopted, and 500 copies ordered to be printed. A faculty was elected and it was ordered that the school open on the first Monday in January, 1880, in Concord, North Carolina.

Accordingly the school was opened and continued with one week intermission 'til July 23rd—a period of seven months, with an enrollment of eleven scholars.

Just before the beginning of the second session in October 4th, 1880, finding that the additional duties of the General Steward and Business Manager of the Star of Zion imposed upon me by the General Conference, it would be impossible for me to properly fill the position of Principal, I secured the services of Prof. A. S. Richardson as Assistant Teacher at 25 dollars per month, and presented my resignation to the Board. This was afterwards accepted. I recommend that Prof. Richardson be elected Principal with the same powers heretofore granted to that officer, and with the present salary. I herewith present my account as principal of the School.

ZION WESLEY INSTITUTE

In Acct with C. R. Harris, Principal

Dr.

To furniture for school room	$ 11.37
To Books	8.24
To incidentals, fuel, etc.	6.50
To Books for W. D. Dickenson, a member of Conference	2.75
To salary of Principal, First session	28.50
To salary of A. R. Richardson, Assistant, 1 mo.	25.00
To rent from Jan. 1, 1880 to Jan. 1, 1881	20.00
Total	$103.06

Cr.

By tuition from scholars	$ 22.75
By Balance	80.31
Total	$103.06

I insert the item of W. D. Dickenson for books and have no tuition from him from due precedent set heretofore, in paying the tuition and cost of books of members of the Conference who attend Howard School in Fayettewille. If it be disallowed I will willingly refund the money.

At the General Conference, owing to the exertions of the Trustees of the A. M. E. Zion Church, Concord, North Carolina, and of Mr. Warren C. Coleman, a deed for seven acres of land was presented to the conference for the erection of a building for Zion Wesley Institute. It was then ordered also that the property in Fayetteville, N. C. known as Rush University property be turned over to the use of Zion Wesley Institute. A portion of the surplus arising from the General Fund was appropriated to the maintenance of the school, and a collection for the same purpose ordered to be raised annually in all the churches, and forwarded to the Treasurer of the Institute.

It will be seen that we have sufficient legislation, if carried into effect, to place the Zion Wesley Institute on a firm and enduring basis. In the name of our beloved Zion, I call upon every one of her ministers and members to do their duty as pointed out by our highest ecclesiastical body, the General Conference of the A. M. E. Zion Church.

We need at once a building for a schoolroom and boarding hall. Many are applying for admission and we can hardly find suitable accommodations for them. Donations of books and newspapers would be very acceptable to our library.

In conclusion, I would say that the interest manifested in the Institute by persons in South Carolina, who have become or desire to become students, justifies the location of the school in easy reach of the residents of that state. I now offer you my report as Treasurer.[29]

Earlier, Cicero Harris had stated his preference for the removal of the Institute to Salisbury, setting forth the advantages of the railroad to the South and another to the West as well as the North-Southwestern main line route. In part, he stated: "Salisbury is undoubtedly the better location for the Institute, both because it is easier of access from the Western part of the state, and because there being no high school in the place it offers a fairer prospect of academical students."

To Elder William H. Thurber and Prof. A. S. Richardson must go the major share of the credit for the firm establishment of the school. The story, often told about the decision is carried in Jones' Catechism. Reverend Thurber, who had been assigned to the church at Tarboro had pastored the Cherry family whose two daughters later attended Barber-Scotia Seminary in Concord. Bishop Jones says that while he was seated on the parsonage porch of the Zion Church in Concord to which Thurber had been recently assigned he noted the girls on the Campus of Scotia. He rushed over to greet them at the

---

[29] *Report to the First Session of the Central North Carolina Conference.*

fence, something which was against the rules. From this incident, the interest in the removal of Zion Wesley Institute began.[30]

In the General Conference of 1880 the following is found in the Report of the Committee on Education, or as it was styled: *Reports on Educational Interests:*

> "The need of a Theological and Collegiate Institution, sustained by our Church has been increasingly felt for several years, in the whole connection; especially in the South and West, where the most of our own people reside.
>
> "This urgent necessity found a voice in the N. C. Conference which met in Salisbury, N. C., in November 1877.
>
> "Here a plan was drawn up for the establishment of a Theological Seminary, to be located in Concord, N. C. . . .
>
> "We recommend that Zion W Conference (Institute) be made the chief Theological Institute for the entire connection." [31]

Mentioned in the same report were the following institutions: Petty's High School (located in Lancaster, S. C. The first session was held beginning November 17, 1879) where two acres of land had been secured and a building; the following resolution called attention to another significant project: "Whereas, we have been informed that ten acres of land at TosKeegu (Tuskegee) have been donated to the Alabama Conference of the A.M.E. Zion Church for educational purposes, and Whereas: Said Annual Conference is making strenuous efforts to establish an educational institution in this Episcopal District, we therefore heartily endorse such an enterprise, and recommend that the institution be one of the high schools of the connection, as provided for in this report." [32]

The following was said of Zion Hill Collegiate Institute:

> "This institution, though not belonging to the connection, has for some time been conducted in its interest. It is offered for sale to this connection, but owing to its indebtedness, we cannot commend it to the support of our connection. We recommend that no steps be taken to purchase the property at present, but refer the matter to the Allegheny Conference, within whose bounds it is located, and if, at any time said Conference choose to make it a Conference or District Institute, it shall do so." [33]

---

[30] Jones, *loc. cit.*, 30.
[31] *Daily Journal of the Sixteenth Quadrennial Session, loc. cit.,* 82, (1880).
[32] *Ibid.,* 83.
[33] *Daily Journal, Sixteenth Quadrennial Session, General Conference,* 83.

The General Conference of 1884 heard a report from the Committee on Education which dealt with but the one institution—Zion Wesley Institute. It spoke of the incorporation of the school, its Board of Trustees, its session and the improvements which had been made. By this time it is noted that the school had been moved to Salisbury and was carrying on there in its first permanent buildings. The report urged that each church send students to the school and that since the President had been made a General Officer his salary should be set by the General Conference.[34]

By 1895, J. Harvey Anderson lists, in addition Zion Wesley Institute, now Livingstone College, Petty High School, previously referred to, (founded by Rev. C. C. Petty in Sept. 1879), Jones University in Tuscaloosa, Alabama which, in that year reported over 200 students, Greenville High School, located in Greenville, Tenn., (1889) Atkinson College, Madisonville, Ky., (opened in 1894), 1889; Greenville, High School in Alabama (Greenville, Ala., now Lomax-Hannon (1893); Zion High School in Norfolk, Va.; Sherwood Orphan School (1894) Petersburg, Va.[35]

Others which were organized later included Walters Institute (1907); Dinwiddie, Va. 1908.[35] The Bishops' Quadrennial address of 1908 adds to this list the following: Zionite Institute, Mobile, Ala., Eastern North Carolina Industrial Academy, and Edenton High School. Two other institutions must be mentioned here, Clinton High School at Rock Hill, or Clinton Institute, and Johnson Rural High School, later moved to Batesville and renamed Johnson Memorial Institute. Most of these schools listed have either ceased to exist or are inactive. The active schools are Livingstone College, which has just completed a Six Million Dollar Expansion plan, Clinton Junior College, which is now in the process of building the second unit in its expansion services, a girls' dormitory, and Lomax-Hannon at Greenville, Alabama, also in the midst of an expansion undertaking.

Inactive schools at present are: Walters Southland at Warren Ark., Atkinson in Madisonville, Kentucky, Dinwiddie in Virginia, and Johnson Memorial in Batesville, Miss. These schools have been

---

[34] *Daily Proceedings of the Seventeenth Quadrennial Session of the General Conference* (1884), 126.
[35] J. Harvey Anderson, *Official Directory for 1896.* 60, 61. Jones, loc. cit., 58.

utilized for in-service training of ministers and lay people. Their future at the present has not been definitely determined.

The later history of Zion Wesley Institute is well known and perhaps should be taken up in full detail in another work. The General Conference of 1880 selected the institution as the successor of all of its educational attempts and turned over to it the Rush University property located in Fayetteville, and, according to J. Harvey Anderson in his *Official Directory* of 1896 (58) "delegated the Rev. J. C. Price, a recent graduate from Lincoln University, to the Ecumenical Conference in London, England, in 1881, and authorized him to solicit funds for the Institution while in that country." Reverend Price succeeded in raising $10,000 and on his return from Europe, was appointed President of the Institution. During his administration the old mansion house on the Campus was remodeled, Dodge Hall was built from funds donated by William E. Dodge of New York and several other buildings constructed, a full story of which is given in a book on Price written by Bishop W. J. Walls.[36]

In 1886, the name of the College was changed to Livingstone, the name being submitted to the several annual conferences for their approval.[37]

Following the death of Dr. Price in 1893, the General Conference elected William Harvey Goler to succeed him. Upon his retirement in 1917 he was followed by the third President, D. C. Suggs. William Johnson Trent was elected to the Presidency in 1925 and served until his retirement in 1957 when Samuel E. Duncan assumed the presidency June, 1958, serving until his death in July 10, 1968. He was succeeded in February, 1969 by Dr. F. George Shipman. There have been at least two interim acting Presidents, John Henry Brockett (1957-1958) and Victor J. Tulane, (1968-1969).

When J. Harvey Anderson drew up his Official Directory in 1896 the College boasted a total of four large buildings, one frame and the others brick. Huntington Hall was the main building and contained the kitchen and dining room, the parlor, library two class rooms and chapel, plus a dormitory for teachers and 40 students. Stanford Seminary, as it was called, was a brick edifice and was the dormitory of women. It also contained two small and one large room, the latter,

---
[36] William Jacob Walls, *Joseph Charles Price*, (Christopher, 1943).
[37] See Report of College for that year.

an assembly room. Dodge Hall, one of the two remaining on the campus was at that time four stories and housed the young men. Ballard Industrial Hall, was likewise four stories, but one of these floors, evidently, at the time, was the basement. The half-story, evidently later removed, was used as a dormitory.

Four buildings were added soon after this early period, The Chapel (1903) which was a very large structure; The Library, (1908); The Hood Seminary Building, (1910); Goler Hall, a dormitory for women, (1917). During the late President W. J. Trent's presidency, the Price Memorial Building, (1943), (which, because of the recession, stood unfinished a number of years); the enlarged Library; The Central Heating Plant, (1944); The W. J. Trent Gymnasium, (1947); The Moore Apartments, (1948) for teachers; Harris Hall, a men's dormitory, (1954); and the President's Home (this last was purchased), were added.

The great period of physical expansion came during the ten years of President Duncan. The loss by fire of the Chapel made it necessary to build a new Auditorium in 1962. This, coupled with the original Ballard Hall, has made a Music-Auditorium complex. Through the R. J. Reynolds Foundation, a second Women's Dormitory (1962) has been built and is called Babcock Hall. The new Student Union Building (1962) was constructed on a line with the original Gymnasium. This latter building has received an extensive addition—in truth a new building. The W. J. Walls Center of Hood Seminary (1964), occupies a plot of land to the rear of the main Campus. The Science Building (1967) and the Communications Building (1968) were the last additions while the contract has been let for the first of two additional dormitories. A girls' dormitory (1969) is under construction. The Walls Heritage House was completed in 1968.

When William Johnson Trent was called to the Presidency in 1925, the institution had reached a low ebb. The task of securing accreditation was a major undertaking, demanding the rebuilding of the faculty, revamping courses, building adequate library material, and securing imperative facilities. Before his retirement most of these items had been accomplished and it was out of the ranks of the products of these years that his successor came. However, the struggle to maintain its rightful place among colleges of standing still goes on.

While the major College of the denomination is governed, as it has been from its beginning as Zion Wesley Institute, by its own Board of Trustees, a self-perpetuating group, the other schools of the Zion system are regulated by a system of dual control, a Board of Christian Education, School and College, with the direction in the hands of the Secretary of Christian Education, and a Trustee Board for each of the institutions, both active and inactive.

The Board of Christian Education evidently had its origin in an action taken by the General Conference of 1892 when the Nineteenth Session convened in John Wesley Church, Pittsburgh, Pa. Prof. S. G. Atkins read the report which recommended the following:

> In order that our entire field of educational work may be encouraged, especially that our various institutions in our episcopal and conference districts may be fostered in their noble efforts to honor the connection, and far and wide raise the standard of intelligence in Zion, we recommend that a Department of Education be and is hereby created by this General Conference; that the scope of its operation shall include the working up and development of the Children's Day, the raising of funds for educational purposes everywhere, and in every way possible, as well as representing the Church in everything that pertains to the work of education, not in conflict with the legitimate and peculiar functions of the Board of Trustees and faculty of Livingstone College.

On motion, the above recommendations were adopted.[37]

A few days later, the Third, Fourth and Fifth sections of the report were read. They included:

> Third, that this Department may be operated and developed according to system, and with uniformity and success, be it
> Resolved, That this General Conference elect for its head, one who shall be known as the Secretary of Education for the African Methodist Episcopal Zion Church, whose duties and powers shall be prescribed as hereinafter provided for. That he shall receive a salary of not less than $800 per annum, to be taken from the Children's Day Fund, subject to modifications as hereafter provided for, provided that the Children's Day be reimbursed to the amount of the salary from funds collected by him, and traveling expenses, provided that said traveling expenses shall be raised by himself. Provided, further, that when not in conflict with some special arrangement of pastors and congregations (of) all the churches in our connection shall be open to his appeals in aid of his cause.

This resolution was adopted without discussion.

---

[37] *Minutes of the General Conference of* 1892, Pittsburgh, Pa., 72.

> For the better equipment and management of this Department, be it Resolved, further, That a Board of Education be appointed by this General Conference, to consist of one member from each episcopal district, which Board shall have general control of the Department of Education, with the power to prescribe rules for its operation and management. Said Board shall have power to locate the headquarters of the Department, by and with the consent of the Secretary, and shall instruct the Secretary as to the best method of developing the Department and prosecuting its work; and shall have power also to specify the Secretary's powers and duties, and to modify his salary in a way not inconsistent with anything heretofore authorized. That it shall be the duty of said Board to organize with the election of a President and a Secretary during the sitting of this Conference, and to hold annual sessions at such time and place as they shall choose, until their successors are elected, provided that special meetings may be called by the President upon the advice of a majority of the members.

After Professor Evans called for a second reading of the above the resolution was adopted.[38]

The fifth Section stated:

> *Resolved*, further, That the Secretary of Education be an *ex officio* member of the Board, provided that he shall have only advisory functions, without privilege to vote; that the General Steward of the Church be the Treasurer of the Board; and that the funds of the Department be paid out only upon warrant, signed by the President and Secretary of the Board of Education of the African Methodist Episcopal Zion Church.

After debate on an opening statement by Reverend Smith Claiborne, who objected to the General Steward being Treasurer, this part of the resolution was amended to designate a member of the Board as Treasurer. The resolution was adopted.[39]

The Reverend R. S. Rives offered the following amendment to the Report:

> Resolved, That the Treasurer of The Educational Department shall give a justified bond in suitable sum for the safety of all moneys that shall come into his hands from time to time from any source for the benefit of said Educational Department.

This amendment was adopted.[40] And on motion, after debate, the full report as amended was approved, and adopted.

As the result of the legislation of 1892, Dr. S. G. Atkins was elected

---
[38] *Minutes of the General Conference*, 1892, 74.
[39] *Ibid., Nineteenth Session, General Conference,* 74.
[40] *Ibid., loc. cit.,* 75.

as Secretary of Education. He served until 1896 when Dr. B. F. Wheeler was selected for the post. Dr. Wheeler, like his predecessor, served only one term, to 1900, when Dr. Atkins again became Secretary. This time Dr. Atkins served in the position until 1916. As the Secretary completed his report in that year the Secretary of the General Conference wrote: "The enthusiastic and scholarly way in which the report was rendered was truly characteristic of the speaker. In spite of the financial embarrassment which greatly hampered the Department, it had been kept intact. A vote of thanks was tendered Professor Atkins and the report was referred to the proper committee." [41]

Dr. S. G. Atkins was succeeded by Reverend J. W. Martin.[42] When Dr. Martin was elected to the bishopric in 1924 he was succeeded by Prof. J. W. Younge, who served until the work of Education and Christian Education was consolidated in 1932. Professor Younge was given the office of Treasurer of Livingstone College while James W. Eichelberger assumed the responsibility for the new joint Department. At his passing in 1967, Reverend George Blackwell assumed charge of the office.

By 1912 the following institutions were listed in the Zion Methodist School system: Edenton High School, Atkinson College, Lomax-Hannon College or High School, Clinton Institute, Greenville College (Tenn.), Dinwiddie Agricultural and Industrial School, Eastern North Carolina High School, Lancaster Normal and Industrial School, Zion Institute, Macon High School, the African Mission Schools and Livingstone College.[43]

MEMORIAL

Trustees of the Rush Academy to the Annual Conference of the Methodist Episcopal Zion Church, in Session.

The Board of Managers of the Rush Academy, feeling a desire that the laity of our churches ought to be fairly represented on all matters pertaining to the school, we therefore hope that this Conference will consider and recommend to the other Annual Conferences, meeting in the interval of the General Conference, the following resolutions, viz: Resolved that we recommend the General

---

[41] *Minutes of the Twenty-fifth Quadrennial Session of the General Conference* (1916), 15.
[42] *Ibid.*, 27.
[43] *Official Journal of the Twenty-fourth Quadrennial Session*, 428.

Conference of the Methodist Episcopal Zion Church so to amend these laws, pertaining to the Academy, as to allow the laity of the churches of our connection a fair representation; say, *per ratio*, one for every hundred or two hundred members, or such number as the Conference may decide on, and such delegates shall have full power to act on all subjects pertaining to the school, and that such representation shall be chosen by election of the male members of the church. The above resolution we hope will meet the views of your Conference, and have the decisive influence of working the redemption of miners from the thralldom of darkness, and your petitioners will ever pray. Signed,

P. Ross	John Darnells	Ambrose Hutchinson
Thos. Harris	Wm. Burnett	Wm Burnett
James Jeffries	Patrick Brown	Avea Bush
H. Francis	Thomas Johnson	Lewis Valentine
		Edward V. Clark

New York, May 29, 1850 [44]

According to the Reports of 1904 the following schools and colleges were on the official lists of the denomination: Livingstone College, Salisbury, N. C., William Harvey Goler, President; Eastern North Carolina Industrial School, Newbern, N. C., William Sutton, Principal; Lancaster Normal and Industrial Institute, Lancaster, S. C., M. D. Lee, President; Clinton Institute, Rock Hill, South Carolina, Robert J. Crockett, President; Edenton High School, C. M. Gaines, Principal (Edenton, N. C.); Lomax-Hannon High School, Greenville, Ala., S. B. Boyd, Principal; Zion Institute, Mobile, Ala., B. F. Wheeler, Principal; Greenville College, J. C. Chandler, President (Greenville, Tenn.); Atkinson College, Madisonville, Ky., Bishop G. W. Clinton, President; Walters Institute, Wilmot, Arkansas.

By 1912 H. V. Taylor had replaced J. C. Chandler at Greenville College in Tennessee; Prof. R. J. Crockett was at Lancaster and R. J. Boulware was at Clinton. John W. Martin had taken charge of Atkinson in Kentucky and J. R. Wingfield was at Lomax-Hannon. At Walter Institute James W. Eichelberger had become Principal and Mrs. J. B. Allen was at Zion Institute. J. B. Bridges reported for

---

[44] *New York Annual Conference Minutes,* 1850 (New York, 1850) 26.

a new institution, Macon High School in Georgia while, for the first time Dinwiddie College is noted in Virginia with T. C. Irwin as Principal. Meanwhile, W. E. Woodyared had taken charge of Edenton High School. At the time C. D. Hazel was in charge of that which was known the Theological Circle.

CHAPTER VIII

The Development of the Episcopacy

GERALD F. MOEDE, in his recent work *The Office of Bishop in Methodism* writes that the first period in Episcopal development actually was underway by 1740 and lasted until 1784.[1] This early phase, however, appears to have involved mainly the expedient idea of John Wesley who appeared reluctant to consider any church government so elaborately conceived, Moede quotes from the second annual conference:

> Is Episcopal, Presbyterian or independent Church government most agreeable to reason? The answer given was: each is the development of the other. A preacher preaches and forms an independent congregation; he then forms another and another in the immediate vicinity of the first; this obliges him to appoint deacons, who look on their first pastor as their common Father; and as these congregations increase, and as their deacons grow in years and grace, they need other subordinate deacons, or helpers; in respect of whom they are called presbyters, or elders, as their father in the Lord may be called a bishop, or overseer of all.[2]

It is interesting to note Moede's reference to the following as he quotes Wesley, who, in 1746, based his conclusion on Lord King's *An Inquiry Into The Constitution, Discipline Unity and Worship of the Primitive Church:*

> In spite of the vehement prejudice of my education, I was ready to believe that this was a fair and impartial thought, but if so, it would follow that bishops and presbyters are (essentially) of one order, and that originally, every Christian congregation was a Church independent of all others.[3]

While discussions on the subject in these early days appear to have been influenced by the existing Church of England system, a new and more complex angle was being evolved in America. One notes, for example, that ready acceptance of lay involvement in the American Church, even as early as its founding, almost demanded a

---
[1] Gerald F. Moede, *The Office of Bishop in Methodism* (Publishing House of the Methodist Church, Zurich, Switzerland, 1964), 15.
[2] Moede, op. cit. from *The Life and Times of the Rev. John Wesley, M.A.* (1872, I 310) 18.
[3] John Wesley, *Works*, Zondervan Ed., II, 6 reprint, 1872.

different type of interpretation from the original thesis of Wesley. Moede, for example, openly states "Methodist Societies had been planted in the New World, not by missionaries sent for that purpose, but by lay people." A Student of Zion Methodism's history immediately sees the implication for, unlike the two other Negro Methodist groups, Zion effectively fits the pattern of early development. This, writer, for example, has insisted, that efforts to erase lay importance in the church is a misinterpretation of historical fact, for even when these whose responsibility in our development is accepted without reservation, we must concede that many of them were lay people as they labored.

Perhaps the wisdom of these early church founders must be clearly noted as Methodism rapidly spread. The problems of closely evaluating the original stand on the non-administration of the sacraments is clearly seen, and unlike many later situations, the church met the crisis head-on. No longer thereafter, was the church mainly interested in preaching. The authority of the historic church became vital. Men who could transmit such authority were therefore, a must. The problem, of course, was deep. Who could lay on hands? What area of authority could Wesley discern to grant him, a simple elder of the Church of England, this right?

Writing of Thomas Coke Drew mentions the following:

> That keeping his eye upon the conduct of the primitive churches, in the ages of unadulterated Christianity, he had much admired the mode of ordaining bishops which the Church of Alexandria had practiced. That to preserve its purity that church would never suffer the interference of a foreign bishop in any of their ordinations; but that the presbyters of the venerable apostolic Church, on the death of a bishop, exercised the right of ordaining another from their own body, by the laying on of their own hands; and this practice continued among them for two hundred years, till the day of Dionysius. And finally, that being himself a presbyter he wished Dr. Coke to accept ordination from his hands, and to proceed in that character to the Continent of America, to Superintend the Societies in the United States.[4]

One must conclude from these early conversations and writings that the Wesleyan interpretation of the Episcopacy was not then the creation of a new ecclesiastical order. His interpretation of himself as a presbyter merely denoted that he was an elder of the church with authority to rule,[5] as was noted in the early Christian Church.

---
[4] Moede, loc. cit. 34.
[5] Webster's *New School and Office Dictionary*, 1961.

The African Methodist Episcopal Zion Church, from its beginning as a denomination, had a sharply different approach to the leadership of the movement from that conceived either by the Mother Methodist movement or any of her daughters. While we clearly note the dangers of conjecture, it appears to have been the thinking of these early Church leaders (Zion) that leadership should be definitely limited in nature. Despite the pattern of the American Methodist Episcopal Church the first discipline of Zion utilized the term *Superintendent* rather than bishop. To indicate that no thought had been given to this interpretation would be to ignore all that we know of the matter.

When the first yearly conference was held in June 21, 1821, the Zion-Asbury group proceeded to elect one of the bishops of the Methodist Episcopal Church as "Their Superintendent."[6] None being present they chose Dr. William Phoebus as President of the Conference pro ax viso (as noted). As late as May 1822 the matter of leadership of the conference was not settled for at that time the Methodist Episcopal Bishops feeling that they could not attend the conference and the conference noting that Zekiel Cooper was not available elected Abraham Thompson as President.[7] It should be noted that Bishops Roberts and George "called on them during the time of the conference in order to advise them to wait until the meeting of their General Conference."

The discipline drawn up by the new group appears to have provided for the election of a chief officer styled a "Superintendent," who was to act in case no bishops were present.[8] This provision eventually carried over for the next several years, with the alternative evidently having been dropped after the eventual separation from the Mother Church.

With the selection of the second Superintendent, Christopher Rush, the matter of the Episcopacy became more of a basic concern. While it is not clear as to this revival of interest it can be gleaned from Rush's writings that some were endeavoring to look down on the new denomination simply because they did not have bishops. Evidently the relations with Bethel, headed by Bishop Allen intensified this discussion. This, however, must remain simply conjec-

---

[6] Christopher Rush, *Rise and Progress of the African M. E. Church*, (New York 1866) 69.
[7] Rush, *loc. cit.*, 73.
[8] *Ibid.*, 76.

ture on our part. Rush opens the door to this belief as he appends the following to his history:

> We now proceed, according to promise in the preface to give a view of our thoughts and knowledge of Church Government, as an Episcopal Church; showing for the information and satisfaction of the ministers and members of our connexion, especially, and the public in general, that our present mode of church government, as an Episcopal Church, is as established upon as good a basis as any other church, according to the custom of ancient Christians and the expressions in Scripture of some of the Apostles of our Lord. And in order to be understood by the reader we will endeavor to do it in as plain a manner as we can, and proceed after the following order, viz:
>
> 1. The Bishop or Superintendent, and his power or authority in the church.
> 2. The Elder and his duty, and
> 3. The Deacon and his duty.
>
> In order to take up the first proposition, we shall begin with the word Episcopacy, or Episcopal, appertaining to the Bishopric. As we from our commencement took this title, we have been judged by some unfriendly persons, to claim a name that did not belong to us, according to our present mode of government, by a superintendent elected and not particularly or especially ordained for a Bishop; and invalidate our connexion as having no Bishop, and therefore, have no right to the name of Episcopal, and, in consequence of this unfriendly practice, many of our brethren were much annoyed, being not able to confute them by contrary information. In order to meet this objection and stop the mouths of these gainsayers, it will be necessary to inquire into the origin of a Bishop and thereby find out from whence the term Episcopal arose.
>
> We proceed them to say that Buck's Theological Dictionary informs us that the word Bishop comes from the Saxons, and that they derived it from the Greeks, and that these people used it as a title for the chief clerk of the market who inspects all that is bought and sold therein. James Wood brings it from the Hebrew, Greek and Latin, and agrees with the above information, and when the title was brought into the church Lord King shows that the man who bore it was only a priest, a presbyter, or elder, and examining the New Testament we find nothing therein which makes him anything more, as to ordination, than an elder. How then, does he become a Bishop, or Superintendent, as he is called among us? He is virtually elected by the Church. How does the Church elect him? They have granted this power to the yearly Conference according to our discipline, which consists of a body of itinerant ministers, and by them he is actually elected for term of years by ballot, and, at the expiration of that term, he is re-elected, or another person elected in his stead, if the Yearly Conference think proper, at one of those meetings which the discipline designates for making new rules and regulations.

In confirmation of the foregoing, relative to the origin of the word Bishop, and to their being originally but two orders in the church, see Buck's and Wood's Theological Dictionaries; also Lord King's account of the same and Scripture references: see St. Paul's Epistle to the Philippians, 1st Chapter and 1st Verse—I Peter, 5th Chapter and 1st verse—The Acts of the Apostles, 20th Chapter and 17th verse—and 28th verses—Titus, 1st Chapter, and 5th and 7th verses—I Timothy, 3rd Chapter, 1st and 8th verses—making but two orders of ministers in the Primitive Church; and as the Reverend John Wesley, the founder of the Methodist Church, was a regularly ordained priest of the Protestant Church of England, we see no difficulty nor impropriety in claiming the name of Episcopal, although the venerable Wesley refused to do so for himself, because he would not interfere with the established order of the Church of which he was a member, but he submitted to the term Superintendent which we are satisfied to claim; and with these views we follow John Wesley's mode of government, with some slight alterations, in consequence of being under a Republican government.

We shall now proceed to give some extracts from the writings of Lord King who has given us a view of Church Government from the days of the apostles down, for three hundred succeeding years, so that we may be informed how Bishops were made by the ancient Churches. We have said, relative to our own method, that a Bishop was virtually elected by the Church, and actually by the yearly Conference, and now see Lord King:

"When a Bishop of a Church was dead all the people of that Church met together in one place to elect a new Bishop—so Sabimus was elected Bishop of Emerita, by the suffrage of all the brotherhood, which was also the custom throughout all Africa, for the Bishop to be chosen in the presence of the people, and so Fabianus was chosen Bishop of Rome by all the brethren, who were met together in one place to that very end." 37th Page and 7th verse.

And now a reference to our discipline, as having given to the Yearly Conference, by the whole Church, the power of election will satisfy us on this head; and what is now to the point, this Bishop, so elected by the Church, being but an Elder or Priest, is evidently called an Episcopalian. But that all concerned may be satisfied, we give an extract in the author's own words as follows:

"Now the manner of electing a Bishop I find to be thus: When a Parish or Bishopric was vacant, through the death of the incumbent, all the members of that Parish, both the Clergy and Laity, met together in the Church, commonly to choose a fit person for his successor to whom they might commit the care and government of their Church. Thus when Alexander was chosen Bishop of Jerusalem, it was by the compulsion of choice of the members of that church. And as to the Bishopric of Rome, we have a memorable instance of this kind of the Advancement of Fabianus to that See.

"Upon the death of Bishop Anterus, all the people met together in the Church to choose a successor, proposing several illustrious and eminent personages as fit for that office, whilst no one so much as thought upon Fabianus, then present, till a dove miraculously sat upon his head, in the same manner as did the Holy Ghost formerly descend on our Saviour, and then all the people, guided, as it were, with one Divine spirit, cried out, with one mind and soul, that Fabianus was worthy of the Bishopric and straightway taking him, they placed him on the Episcopal throne. And as Fabianus, so likewise his successor, Cornelius was elected by the suffrage of the clergy and the laity." See Lord King, pages 55 and 56, 3rd verse.

The titles given to this supreme personage by Cyprian are Bishop, President, Pastor, Governor or Superintendent. And having given the origin of the Bishop, we shall now say something of his duty, in a very brief manner, and for this purpose we shall make another extract from the writings of Lord King, in his own words:

"The Bishop's flock, having been so largely discussed, it will now be necessary to speak of the Bishop's duty towards them, and the several particulars of his honorable office. I shall not be tedious—since about this there is no great difference—only briefly enumerate the several actions belonging to his charge. In brief, therefore, the particular acts of his function were such as these, viz., preaching the word, praying with his people, administering the Sacrament of Baptism and the Lord's Supper, taking care of the poor, ordaining of ministers, governing his flock, excommunicating of offenders, absolving penitents, and, in a word, whatever acts can be comprised under these three general heads of preaching, worship and government, were part of the Bishop's functions and office." See Lord King, page 51, 1st verse.

Having thus given our views of primitive Bishops from the first three hundred years succeeding the Apostles, we will here briefly show the difference between their manner of government and ours.

The primitive Church formed no connection of several Societies, as we do, for every pastor of a congregation was a Bishop and had the control of his own Society, but with us it is essentially necessary to form a connexion of our several societies, and, they being located in different parts of the United States, it becomes needful to have one central point, where our ministers have interviews, from time to time, hence, our Yearly Conference is formed for that purpose, and therefore our Bishop or Superintendent must travel and oversee the whole, that every branch of our Church may harmonize.[9]

Several observations are needed here as we examine all that Rush has to say about the Superintendency and Episcopacy. John Wesley, for example, according to Moede, had a *strong repugnance* against any of his preachers being addressed as *Bishop*.[10] This writer is not certain that Rush's viewpoint had not changed in the intervening years since the writing of the first discipline for its wording was clear in its interpretation of the office of the Superintendency and its relationship to that of the Bishop. It will be noted that it had been stated that when a Bishop was present (of the Methodist Episcopal

---

[9] Rush, *loc. cit.*, 93-99.
[10] Moede, *loc. cit.*, 45.

Church) he took precedence over the Superintendent. Rush had aided in the drawing up of this first discipline and certainly knew the wording and intent. Unless this relationship had changed either by vote or inference of the Yearly Conference, which was entirely possible, he had to be aware of the first interpretation.

Since there is only one early writer of our Church History where Zion Methodism is concerned on the subject, we are forced to conclude two or three understandings. Our earlier and first premise would be the Wesleyan influence, that of the free and freed men, coupled with the basic desire of a church organization which would be strictly in keeping with the democratic thinking of the time. It will be recalled that Rush styles this a *Republican influence.* A second conclusion has the undertone of Mother Church and the African Churches in New York and Philadelphia, The third conclusion which also has merit since almost 45 years went by without significant change, that the founders of Zion Methodism actually set out to create a different type of Church government. In this we refer again to Joshua Soul's letter to Bishop McKendree dated Sept., 1820.[11]

Rush and Wesley, along with the early writers which Rush quotes, agree on the point that Superintendency or Bishopric creates no new ecclesiastical order. Each Superintendent or Bishop is merely an elder elected to supervise the work.

At one point Rush appears to labor a bit as he refers time after time to the election of the Superintendent or Bishop by the full congregation. This leads us to feel that the peculiar nature of Zion Methodism which permitted lay people to enter into deliberations and elections had been under criticism as well. While this may have created controversy with or in other denominations it is now an established fact and at that early time was certainly in keeping with the agitations of the period.

Later writers on the Episcopacy have settled on certain characteristics common to the office of Bishop. They state that the individual selected must bear that title. This, Zion evidently did not permit until the General Conference of 1864,[12] when as a compromise

---

[11] See David H. Bradley, Sr., *A History of the A.M.E. Zion Church*, 1796-1872 (Parthenon, 1956) 19.

[12] It is the opinion of this writer that the grounds for the General Conference acceptance of this change was based upon the lay representation carried in the General Conference—one of the provisions which Zion Methodism refused to relinquish in the conversations. The change of title was definitely a constitutional change and was not

with the A.M.E. Church in the conversations on Organic Union the title of Superintendent was changed to Bishop. It is this writer's conviction that legally this term cannot be used to designate any of our Superintendents until that date.[13]

The second provision, calling for lifetime election did not take place until the General Conference of 1880. On Wednesday, May 19, 1880, Samuel Sherman of the Kentucky Conference offered the following resolution:

> 1st. *Resolved* that the Committee on the Revision of the Discipline are hereby instructed to report an amendment to article, 12th, Section 1, so that Bishops of the A.M.E. Zion Church shall be elected for life.
>
> 2nd. To report a form for ordination of Bishops to take the place of our present form of installation.
>
> 3rd. To report a provision that a Bishop may be placed upon the retired list for neglect of duty, unprofitableness or disability.

The Resolutions were lost: yeas, 39—nays 70.[14]

The matter of lifetime election was not taken up again until several days later, May 24th—the 18th day of the Conference. The Reverend W. A. Foreman, evidently a substitute or alternate delegate as his name does not appear in the official listing of the General Conference delegates, offered the following resolutions:

> *Resolved:* That the present Bishops remain in office during good behaviour.
> *Resolved:* That we do away with quadrennial elections.[15]

In the discussion which followed J. B. Trusty of the Philadelphia and Baltimore Conference moved to lay the resolutions on the table. This motion was lost. Smith Claiborn of the Kentucky Conference, J. B. Trusty of the Philadelphia Conference, Mark M. Bell of the same conference, John Bryan Small of New England and William T. Biddle of the Genesee Conference all spoke against the resolutions.[16]

---

submitted either to the Quarterly or Annual Conferences. This contention must be accepted at this early date to legalize later acts of the General Conference.
Also. Bradley, *loc. cit.*, 151 ff.
Bishop Moore states that this law did not pass until 1868, John J. Moore, *History of the A.M.E. Zion Church*, York, Pa., 1884, 81.
[13] Bradley, *loc. cit.*, 151 ff.
[14] *Daily Journal* of the 16th Quadrennial Session of the General Conference of the A.M.E. Zion Church, in America, Montgomery, Ala., May, AD 1880 (N. Y. 1880) 34.
[15] *Ibid.*, 44.
[16] *Ibid.*, 44.

The following were listed as speaking for the change: Joseph Charles Price, North Carolina Conference, Jacob Thomas of New York, J. L. H. Severes of Tennessee; Alfred Day of the Philadelphia and Baltimore Conference, along with others whose names were not listed, were noted as speaking for the measure.

The argument of these against the measure encouched the thought that to change the organic law of the church, without the same being submitted to our people, and at so late a stage of the Conference too, might prove disasterous to the Church instead of a blessing.[17]

The previous question was finally called for and the resolutions were adopted by the following recorded vote: yeas, 73, nays 17.[18]

The General Conference is likewise significant where the episcopacy is concerned as a Committee functioned on the examination of the characters of the Bishops.[19] A report was made by the Committee but the Conference recommitted the report because of an error.[20] At this session, too, a nominating committee functioned.[21]

The report of the Committee on the Examination of the Bishops follows:

"Dear Fathers and Brethren: Your Committee on the examination of the Bishops beg leave to report the following:
Whereas: Bishop J. J. Clinton is prevented from meeting the General Conference by reason of his affliction and
Whereas: we know nothing against his religious or moral character,
Therefore be it Resolved: That his character pass. Also the characters of Bishop S. T. Jones, J. J. Moore, J. W. Hood, J. P. Thompson, W. H. Hilliary and Thomas H. Lomax (Present). All of which we, your Committee most respectfully submit.
J. M. WASHINGTON, *Chairman*
Wallace Jones, Abram Anderson, A. Holmes, J. H. Washington, D. I. Walker, E. D. Taylor, P. J. Wesley, E. W. Simpson, J. Saxton, Alfred English, J. W. Davis, G. Paxton, P. Jackson, W. T. Biddle, J. B. Trusty, H. J. Thomas, A. Jackson, Amos York, Secretary.[22]

As an added note to the discussion of the Episcopacy in the A.M.E. Zion Church we would turn to the writings of Bishop John Jamison

---

[17] *Ibid.*, 44.
[18] *Daily Journal, Sixteenth Quadrennial Session, op. cit.*, 44.
[19] *Ibid.*, 31.
[20] *Ibid.*, 32.
[21] *Ibid.*, 80.
[22] *Ibid.*

Moore, one of the most astute and prolific writers of the early Church. While it is not clear just how much of his material was drawn from the thinking and writing of Christopher Rush, the fact that so much of his life overlapped the later years of Rush to the point that these earlier conversations had to be fresh in the minds of the church gives them a place here. Moore records the following as the result of a special committee's work requested by the Methodist Episcopal Bishop during the conversations over relationships with the Mother Church. Since only the third and fourth items pertain to the subject now under discussion, we include these only:

> "Thirdly: We think the foregoing desire can be accomplished if one of the Bishops be allowed to preside at the Yearly African Methodist Conference from time to time, and in case of his absence, the Superintendent contemplated by the aforesaid discipline of the African M.E. Conference shall have full power to preside and perform the duties of a Bishop, so far as it shall become essentially necessary for the prosperity of the aforesaid connexion and without any opposition to the interests of the Mother Church.
>
> "Fourthly: That in order to accomplish the object of the third item, reciprocal regulations can be adopted, to secure the bishops of the Mother Church the perogative of superintending at the African Conference from time to time; also, to secure to him compensation for his extra services and expense; also that the said African Conferences be so convened as to suit the convenience of the bishops, and not too laborious or expensive for the African preachers to attend." [23]

The matter of the growth of the Episcopacy in Zion Methodism is not hazy. Perhaps there has been the overlooking of facts but they all have been evident over the years. Bishop E. D. W. Jones in his *Comprehensive Catechism*, for example states:

Q. When were the Superintendents styled Bishops?
A. In 1864 and onwards.[24]

Turning again to Bishop Moore in his History we find the following:

> "Our Ecclesiastical Economy. The Hierarchical arrangements, clerical and common licentiates are as follows:
>
> 1. Exhorters: They are religious public speakers, licensed by the Quarterly Conference, a local Court of the Society. For particulars on their appointment, see our Book of Discipline.

---

[23] John Jamison Moore, *History of the A.M.E. Zion Church in America*, York, Pa. 1884, 94, 95.
[24] Bishop E. D. W. Jones, *Comprehensive Catechism of the A.M.E. Zion Church* (Washington, D. C., 1934) 76.

2. Local Preachers. A higher order of Licentiates. They are licensed by the same local Court of the Society, to preach as local clergymen.
3. Itinerant Preachers. Are those sent out by an Annual Conference, appointed by a bishop to their field of labor to collect and organize societies, and to serve those already organized as pastors. In relation to them see our Book of Discipline.
4. Ordained Ministers. Consisting of two orders as Deacons and Elders, sacredly set apart by the Church, and elected by the Annual Conference, and ordained by elders and a Bishop, by the imposition of hands.
5. Our Bishops. A third modern Episcopal order in the Christian Church. They are elected by the General Conference, consecrated and installed into that office, and appointed to their diocese by that body. The Bishop remains in office during good standing and efficiency for duty. Until 1880, he was quadrennially elected but at that time the quadrennial election was abolished. The title of our Episcopal officers was changed in the General Conference of 1868, from Superintendent to Bishop, in the modern sense as used by Episcopal Methodists. "Although bigots have questioned the Christian authenticity of validity of our Bishopric, the ablest writers on Primitive Church government sustain the ground upon which we base our Episcopal Economy; writers whom we have already mentioned in this work.

That Elders can ordain Elders legitimately or can constitute or set apart a modern Bishop, no one can successfully controvert. That Elders and Presbyters were the only two sacred orders in the Primitive Christian Church, is a settled point with the best Biblical expositors. That Elders and Presbyters were in the Primitive Church also styled Bishops, and exercised similar functions to those of a Methodist Bishop, as far as was necessary in that period of the Church, is also fully established by Scripture. Elders or Presbyters regulated in the Primitive Christian Church or Churches their ecclesiastical interests, as do the executives we now set apart and entitle *Bishop* who are our general overseers. Let us examine the word *Bishop* derived from the Saxon word *Biscop*. The Saxon word is a corruption of the Latinized Greek word, *Episcopus*. Its analogy to the second and third syllables of the latter is obvious. Then the English word *Bishop* is derived from the Saxon word *Biscop*, which is from the Latin word *Episcopus*, which is from the Greek word, *Episkopos*, which Greek word signifies overseer or Superintendent. Thus the word from which we get our English word Bishop, was used by the Apostle to express or represent the office or function of an elder in the Church of God, and of no higher office. The word Bishop is used five times in the New Testament and in each case, it is evidently synonymous with presbyter or Elder (Acts XX; 17-

28), "Take heed to yourselves and to all the flock over which the Holy Ghost hath made you Bishops' which means overseers or Superintendents or Bishops in our English text: in the Greek text Episkopos: which means overseers or Superintendents. In the seventeenth verse the Apostle sent for the Elders or ordained ministers and in the twenty-eightth verse he reminds them of their high relation to the church as ordained ministers, they were overseers or superintendents or Bishops, all being synonymous terms. Again Phil. I: 1. Here he addresses the Church at Philippi.
1. The members whom he calls saints.
2. Then the Bishops and Deacons.

Surely if the Bishops had been a separate and distinct order of the ministry of the Church from Elder and presbyters he would not have passed them in his address and descended to the deacons, the order below elders in the church. See A. Stevens (of M.E.C.) work. In Titus I: 7 it is said: "For a Bishop must be blameless as the Steward of God," The Apostle had left Titus in Crete to organize the Christian converts into churches, and ordain pastors among them. He describes the qualification of these pastors. What were those pastors? Were they Elders? He tells us in the fifth verse, "For this cause I left thee in Crete that thous shouldst set in order the things that are wanting, and ordain elders in every city." After describing the necessary qualification of these elders, he assigns the reasons that a Bishop or *Episkopus* or an overseer, must be blameless. That a Bishop and an elder were identical what could be more evident? The word occurs again (I Tim. III: 2. "A Bishop must be blameless, the husband of one wife." The Apostle in this chapter instructs Timothy respecting the qualifications of a Bishop and then immediately describes those of a deacon without a single reference to presbyters though these were an unquestionable order of Pastors in the Ancient Church and though he was expressly directing Timothy in the appointment of its necessary officers. This fact in connection with the passages already examined renders it evident that he calls presbyters Bishops and that he did not neglect them by oversight. (See Coleman on Primitive Church, also Rev. Abel Stevens of the M. E. Church and also Dr. Campbell, the able writer on Philosophy of Rhetoric).

Now, if it be admitted, which it must be, that the elders were the highest order of pastors and Gospel ministers in the Christian Church then it must be admitted that there is no higher ordaining power than they are in the Church since the Apostles' time and that they were an ordaining power in the time of the Apostles, then the elders have the power to ordain elders, and to appoint them as local Bishops, with Elders or presbyters were in the primitive church, and with the consent of the churches, they had power to appoint an elder or presbyter or Bishop (which were synonymous terms in the

Scripture), over several local churches, and the elder so appointed would be a Bishop in a general sense and in accordance with our more modern episcopacy.

THE SOURCE OF ORDINATION IN THE ZION'S CONNECTION

The African Methodist Episcopal Zion Church in America obtained its ordination from the M.E. Church (The Mother Church); our first ordination of elders was by elders, ordained in the M.E.C. who were in good standing, and those elders ordained in our church by them, established our episcopacy; establishing it upon the same principles our Mother Church (the M.E. Church) established her episcopacy.

We have the great satisfaction and pleasure to know one of the most eminent Bishops of the M.E. Church, Bishop Scott, in a letter to Bishop S. T. Jones of the A. M. E. Zion Church, acknowledges our episcopacy as being as valid as theirs. Hence, let the mouths of all Zion's gain-sayers on her episcopacy be stopped, if it is possible for bigotry and ignorance to stop.[25]

The discipline of 1884 carries the form for the consecration of a Bishop. The strange thing, however, is it appears that little is said concerning his qualifications. In fact, one gathers by close examination of its pages that the interpretation of Rush and Moore evidently were so generally accepted that the regulations applying to the Elder were the regulations affecting those who were proposed for the office of Bishop.[26] No section on this subject appeared in the changes listed as being accepted in the General Conference on 1888 which met in New Bern.[27] However, the new printing of the discipline which evidently occured in 1889 carried the following:

Question: How shall a Bishop be constituted:

Answer: By the election of a majority of the General Conference and consecration by the Bishops, or Elders appointed by the General Conference for that purpose.

Question: How long shall a Bishop serve?

Answer: So long as his spirit and practice are such as become the Gospel. Provided that no person shall be elected to the office who has not been four years a traveling Elder, nor one who has at any time been expelled from the connection.

---

[25] Moore, *loc. cit.*, 80-85.
[26] *The Doctrine and Discipline of the African Methodist Episcopal Zion Church in America*, (New York, 1886) (General Conference of 1884).
[27] *Ibid.*, see section following page 264 *Revisions made by the General Conference* at New Berne, N. C., May, 1888. (A.M.E. Zion Book Concern, Sept. 1888.

THE DEVELOPMENT OF THE EPISCOPACY

Question: What are the duties of a Bishop?

Answer: To preside in our annual Conferences; fix the districts according to his judgment; to make out the appointments of the preachers: provided he shall not allow any preacher to remain in the same station more than four years, by the request of the people, except he be engaged in building a church; otherwise he shall not continue in the same station for more than three years successively; except the General Agents, the Editors of our periodicals and teachers of our seminaries and academies. He shall have authority, when requested by an annual conference, to appoint an agent, whose duty it shall be to travel throughout the bounds of such conference, for the purpose of collecting money for the benefit of the institutions belonging to such Conference; in the interim to change, receive and transfer preachers when necessary, but he shall not transfer a preacher from one conference district to another without his consent; he shall travel through his entire district once a year, if possible, to oversee the spiritual and temporal affairs of the churches, to ordain Deacons and Elders who have been elected by the Annual Conference, and to furnish them credentials; and to decide all questions of law in the Annual Conference, subject to an appeal to the General Conference.

The Bishop and Annual Conference shall appoint presiding elders when, in their judgment, it is necessary for the efficiency of the work.

The Bishop shall nominate and the Annual Conference shall elect. Presiding Elders shall be elected for two years, subject to re-election.[28]

Bishop Hood in his Volume II, in a sense, disagrees with the findings which we have noted as stated above. However, it is hard to accept that which he says in the light of developments unless one concedes that there was controversy regarding the status of the Episcopacy. For example, he alludes to the convention held on Organic Union in 1864 (held in Philadelphia). It appears that he deals with a bit of cloudiness with the subject since he admits that involved were two questions, one, the change of title from Superintendent to Bishop and the other, the election of the individual for life. On the former subject he states:

> We hope that we have made plain, that which our fathers failed to ordain Bishops for life at the beginning, it was not for the lack of authority to do so, but at the beginning the General Superintendent was elected for four years at a time because that was preferred. This may be accounted for to some extent by the fact that congregationalism largely predominated in the East, especially in New England. The ministers in Zion were all Abolitionists and they would not extend far South where the Episcopal sentiment was stronger. The idea of larger

[28] *The Doctrines and Discipline of the African Methodist Episcopal Zion Church in America.* (New York, 1889) containing the revisions of 1888. 51-53.

freedom was associated with an elective superintendency. And it was not until the emancipation and the extension of the Church to the Southland, where the Methodist people had no idea of a church without a bishop, that many of the early preachers realized the importance that an episcopacy which is free from any display of arrogance or unseemly assumption of power, is capable of the best possible results.[29]

---
[29] Hood, *loc. cit.*, Vol. II, 27, 28.

CHAPTER IX

The Development of the Episcopacy

IN THE previous chapter we would call attention to the statement of Bishop Hood as he lays stress on the fact that the sectionalism of Zion Methodism had an important part to play in the use of the term SUPERINTENDENT and the limitation of power. However, we would suggest as well the relationships of the New York Conference of the Methodist Episcopal Church and the controversy then in progress leading to the Stillwell Secession as another important cause as well as the clear understanding at that time of the thinking of the Founder of Methodism, John Wesley. Still another possibility is the relationship of some of the members to the English or British brand of Methodism as over against American Methodism, as no doubt, some of the early members of the Church were from the Islands.

Between 1864 and 1868, Hood states that the matter of change of title and the election for life proposition were submitted to the Quarterly Conferences. Jones makes no mention of this. However, the entire matter was tabled following the General Conference of 1868. At the same time we note no mentioning of this vote in the General Conference minutes of 1868.[1] Hood does state that the General Conference ratified the election of Bishops for life in that session with two dissenting voices—Peter Ross and Dempsey Canady.[2]

The confusion, however, comes as we note that which Hood has to say later on the matter.

> In 1872 there was a desire to retire two of the Bishops and for that reason some insisted upon re-election, which for harmony sake was agreed to, but it was realized that it was a questionable course, and therefore a committee was appointed to draw up a law governing the Board of Bishops, in which it was made plain that the Bishops had a life term to the episcopal office, and that the re-election only decided whether or not they should be active or retired Bishops. If they failed a re-election, that retired them. But they were still Bishops and liable to be called into active service in case of a vacancy, or on the formation of a new district in the interval of a General Conference, and to place the matter beyond all question, each Bishop was given a certificate on

---
[1] *Minutes of the General Conference of* 1868.
[2] Hood, *loc. cit.*, II, 26.

parchment declaring them to hold the office as long as their spirit and practice were such as becomes the gospel. The certificates were signed by the Senior Bishop and the General Secretary.[3]

The General Conference of 1872, according to Hood stated:

ARTICLE II OF BOARD OF BISHOPS

Section I—The Board of Bishops shall meet semi-annually to counsel for general interest of the Connection, and to attend to such duties as are required by law, and shall hold other meetings as may be necessary.

Section II—A majority of all the active Bishops shall be necessary to form a quorum for the transaction of business, provided that retired Bishops shall have a seat in the Board as honorary members. Retired Bishops are those who have been elected and installed, but are without an Episcopal charge. Active Bishops are those in charge of an Episcopal District.

Section III—At each semi-annual meeting the Board shall elect a President and Secretary. Provided, that said President and Secretary shall have no extraordinary powers in the interval, except to call special meetings when in their judgment it may be necessary or at the request of two or more members. They shall also appoint the time and place of holding the semi-annual meeting when not fixed by the Board.

Section IV—The Board shall have a general supervision over the entire Connection in the interval of the General Conference, but as individual Bishops they shall not interfere with each other's work or charge. They shall make Provision for new Episcopal Districts when necessary, and shall also provide for any vacancy that may occur in any existing district by death, resignation or otherwise, by appointment from among the retired Bishops, provided there be a retired Bishop able to travel; provided, further that they shall consult the wishes of the Conferences embraced in the vacant district.[4]

Hood, of course, states that at this time ther were two classes of Bishops, the active and the retired. *If they failed of re-election, they were retired.*[5] Other writers, including Jones, declare that election for life did not begin until the action of the General Conference of 1880.[6] The reader will be forced to conclude the matter on the facts as related.

The Reverend J. W. Brown, writing in the A. M. E. Zion Quarterly Review[7] has a great deal to say about the Episcopacy, much of

---

[3] Hood, *loc. cit.*, II, 26.
[4] Hood, *loc. cit.*, II, 26, 27.
[5] *Ibid.*, 27.
[6] Bishop E. D. W. Jones, *Comprehensive Catechism*, 37.
  Minutes of the General Conference of 1880, 44.
[7] *The A.M.E. Zion Quarterly Review*, Vol. XII, No. 1, 3.

which has been noted in earlier writings. The basic significance of Brown's article, however, appears to be the new interest in the nature and duties of the office. The writer reiterates the belief that the office was not a new order. Evidently, too, the matter of qualifications had been in the minds of many for he likewise mentions this angle.

This interest in the Episcopacy is likewise reflected in the continuing of the Committee on the Examination of the Bishops[8] which reported to the General Conference of 1880.[9] Since no mention of this being an extraordinary committee one can assume that this had been the custom in prior session. The added significance is noted here since the 1880 sessions finally decided to elect the Bishops for life. The report of the group was adopted in sections. The first section, using the words of the compiler, was adopted. The second section ran into considerable debate and at the conclusion of the day had not as yet been accepted.[10]

The next day, May 17th, the report of the committee, with the provision that there be six active Bishops was accepted by a vote of 88 to 32.[11] Two other matters regarding the Episcopacy were taken care of at the same time—the selection of one ministerial member from each Annual Conference to draw up the districts and a Committee on Nomination for the office of Bishop.[12] Both of these matters are of vital importance in the light of later developments. It should be noted, however, that an election of Bishops was held at this General Conference. Evidently, because of his illness the

---

[8] *Daily Journal, Sixteenth Quadrennial Session,* General Conference, A.M.E. Zion Church, 1880, 31.

[9] *Ibid.,* 80.
Dear Fathers and Brethren: Your committee on the examination of the Bishops beg leave to report the following:
Whereas: Bishop J. J. Clinton is prevented from meeting the General Conference by reason of his affliction, and whereas we know nothing against his religious or moral character, therefore be it
Resolved, That his character pass. Also the characters of Bishops S. T. Jones, J. J. Moore, J. E. Hood, J. P. Thompson, W. H. Hilliary, and Thomas H. Lomax (present).
All of which we your committee most respectfully submit.
                                              J. M. Washington, Chairman
Wallace Jones, Abram Anderson, A. Holmes, J. H. Washington, D. I. Walker, E. D. Taylor, P. J. Wesley, E. W. Simpson, J. Saxton, Alfred English, J. W. Davis, G. Paxton, P. Jackson, W. T. Biddle, J. B. Trusty, H. J. Thomas, A. Jackson.
                                              Amos York, Secretary

[10] *Daily Journal, Sixteenth Quadrennial Session, loc. cit.,* 31.

[11] *Daily Journal* or *Minutes* of the Sixteenth Session, *loc. cit.,* 31.

[12] *Ibid.,* 31.

Committee proposed no opponent for Bishop J. J. Clinton. Samuel Sherman opposed Bishop Singleton T. Jones, while Bishop J. J. Moore had as his opponent, A. Anderson; Bishop J. W. Hood ran against W. H. Thurber while Bishop J. P. Thompson ran opposite A. Hannon. The Reverend R. H. G. Dyson was the opponent of Bishop W. H. Hilliary and Bishop T. H. Lomax had A. York as his opposition.[13]

When the General Conference met in Mother Zion Church, New York City (West Tenth and Bleeker Streets) May 7, 1884, the matter of the examination of the characters of the Bishops was opened by Reverend N. H. Williams who desired that a Committee for this examination be appointed. Bishop Jones stated that while it had always been the custom "there was not the shadow of a shade of law for the procedure." [14] A significant statement was thereafter made by the Reverend C. C. Pettey who, in referring to the question of Reverend Williams intimated that there had been a great amount of dissatisfaction, "because certain matters had not been submitted to the Quarterly Conference action." [15] While it is impossible to state the basis for this dissatisfaction, it appears that it had to do with the election of Bishops for life. If this premise is true then the position of Bishop Hood on the matter is not correct. At the time Reverend Pettey (later a Bishop of the Church himself) made his assertion the Chairman, Bishop Singleton T. Jones "Said that previous to 1852 everything done in General Conference before becoming law, had to be submitted to the Quarterly Conferences, thus requiring four years to elapse before anything could be settled upon. But in that year, in order to obviate this difficulty, lay delegates were given a seat in the General Conference, with full power to speak and vote, thus giving the lay element in the Church their rights in legislating for the whole connection." [16]

"Bishop Moore said, the difficulty was, that a great many of the brethren were hanging on to the old Discipline published prior to 1852, and refused to get the new Discipline containing the present law of the Church, and then, as the Chair had said, they endeavored

---

[13] *Ibid.*, 85.
[14] *Daily Proceedings of the Seventeenth Session of the General Conference,* 1884, 11.
[15] *Ibid.,* 11.
[16] *Daily Proceedings of the Seventeenth Quadrennial Session, loc. cit.,* 12.

to get behind the people to accomplish certain ends. They ought to get new Disciplines." [17]

The method of placing in the hands of a committee the naming of the candidates for the Bishopric who would be elected was again proposed by Reverend J. H. Anderson.[18] On a motion proposed by the Reverend G. W. Clinton the resolution of Reverend Anderson was to be taken up the following day. When this was done, the matter was tabled.[19]

The General Conference of 1884 will be remembered as that session which had before it the matter of Bishop W. H. Hillery. The famous trial has within it too many ramifications to occupy our attentions in this chapter, so this controversy will be taken up in another place. It should be mentioned here that two charges were brought against Bishop Hillery: (1) drinking whiskey at a public grocery bar, and, (2) owing a grocery bill.[20]

An examination of the Journal of the General Conference of 1884 appears to suggest an interest in the clarification of the laws and regulations having to do with the trial of ministers of each of the several ranks. This, evidently, was occasioned by the confusion brought about in the matter of the trial of Bishop Hillery. The Journal, for example, lists insertions dealing with The Trial of Local Preachers and Exhorters and provision for the Courts of Appeal where ministers are convicted by the Annual Conference.[21] As one examines the proceedings of this affair one is alerted to the fact that many of the members of the General Conference had his particular doubts as to the jurisdiction of the General Conference, since, evidently, the appeal came at the hands of the prosecution rather than at that of the defendant.

The discipline of 1884 (published in 1886) lists the following where the Episcopacy was concerned:

Question: How shall a Bishop be constituted?
Answer: By the election of a majority of the General Conference and consecration by the Bishops, or Elders appointed by the General Conference for that purpose.
Question: How long shall a Bishop serve?

---
[17] *Ibid.*, 12.
[18] *Ibid.*, 99.
[19] *Ibid.*, 101.
[20] *Proceedings of the Seventeenth Quadrennial Session of the General Conference*, 37.
[21] *Ibid.*, 140, 141.

Answer: So long as his spirit and practice are such as become the Gospel. Provided that no person shall be elected to this office who has not been four years a traveling Elder, nor one who has at any time been expelled from the connection.[22]

There was no change in these qualifications as listed in the 1889 Discipline (1888 General Conference).[23]

The General Conference of 1892, which met in the John Wesley Church, 40 Arthur Street, Pittsburgh, Pennsylvania, appeared to have been satisfied with the rules thus far developed where the Episcopacy was concerned. The Committee for the Examination of Bishops' characters appears to have disappeared by this time as no record of such a group is to be noted. Bishop Thompson requested that the Bishops themselves be allowed to make out the districts without the benefit of a Committee. The Chairman, Calvin, C. Pettey ruled the suggestion out of order "for the time."[24] As one notes that the Committee on Districts (composed of 30 members) did make a report [25] the Chairman could as well have said the suggestion was out of order.

The 1892 General Conference also had a Committee on The Episcopacy, which evidently received several items of business, but either this Committee did not report or its report was not included, or it has been misplaced. However, this last seems impossible for no action on the report appears to have been made by the General Conference. The Committee, itself, was made up of 29 or 30 ministers.[26]

It is not clear as to whether the Committee did come to the floor with a partial report, but the following resolution was reported by the committee on Revision:

> PP 51. Question. How long shall a Bishop serve?
> It was voted that the following words be added to the answer to the above question: "Nor any minister who has been expelled from this or any other connection for gross immorality." [27]

Another resolution up for ratification passed earlier:

---

[22] *The Doctrines and Discipline of the African Methodist Episcopal Zion Church* 1886, 51.
[23] *Ibid.*, 1889, 51.
[24] *Journal of the General Conference of the A.M.E. Zion Church, the Nineteenth Quadrennial Session,* 1892, 90.
[25] *Ibid.*, 185.
[26] *Ibid.*, 10.
[27] *Ibid.*, 101.

THE DEVELOPMENT OF THE EPISCOPACY

Whereas: We see the evil that is being done by the use of tobacco; therefore be it,
Resolved, That it be the sense of this General Conference that hereafter no man shall be elected to the office of Bishop in our Church who uses tobacco in any shape or form.[28]

It should be noted as well that in the General Conference of 1892 the matter of votes necessary for election was set by that body itself and not by any action of an earlier quadrennial session. At that time on motion of the Hon. J. C. Dancy "the two candidates receiving the highest number of votes and having a majority be declared elected, and the motion was carried." [29]

The Reverend W. H. Snowden offered the following resolution which was referred to the Committee on Episcopacy:

Whereas: The election of Bishops is over; therefore, be it
Resolved, That we hereafter elect no elder to the office of Bishop who is under forty or over sixty years of age.[30]

While a historical work is not the place for conjecture it would not be amiss to call to the attention of the reader evident developments which may escape note. With the final passage of the provision to elect Bishops for life one can note a distinct change in the attitude of the Bishops. The elimination of the Committee on the Examination of the Characters of the Bishops appears to have been the first step. At no time prior to this step had the authority of the General Conference where the Episcopacy was concerned, come into question. With the elimination of this Committee, trial alone, stemming from charges filed in the Annual or General Conference, could bring the person under review.

Just what was actually discussed by the membership and clergy of the Church may never be known, for again, the absence of written discussion, leaves too much for conjecture. However it can be noted that both Episcopacy[31] and ministry[32] were represented in the writings on ecclesiastical law of the period. One could reasonably ask, was the inquiring mind awakened because of the trial of Bishop Hillery

---

[28] *The Journal of the Nineteenth Session of the General Conference, op. cit,* 79.
[29] *Ibid.,* 77.
[30] *Ibid.,* 118.
[31] Right Rev. S. T. Jones, *Hand-Book of The Discipline of the African Methodist Episcopal Zion Church* (Hunt and Eaton, New York, 1890).
[32] Bishop John Bryan Small, *Code On The Discipline of the African Methodist Episcopal Zion Church* (York Dispatch Print, 1898).

and the new Zion interpretations of the Episcopacy? It is significant that Bishop Singleton T. Jones wrote, in his work, on the *Trials of the General Conference*.[33] The writer states: "Law, rules, regulations, and not character, are subjects for the consideration of the General Conference, therefore no cognizance may be taken of any crime or improper conduct by the General Conference dating behind its sitting, save in the form of an appeal from a lower court, or matter of a strictly legal character.[34]" This, of course, is in line with the earlier ruling that the Committee on the Examination of the Character of Bishops had no legal status.

While the work of Bishop John Byran Small was issued after his election to the Episcopacy certainly several of his interpretations come out of his experiences as a minister of the period. Both works were approved by the Board of Bishops and the General Conference, and both authors hold the original thesis of Zion where the election of Superintendents was concerned—that the episcopacy was not originally a favorite child of Methodism. Bishop Small goes on to state: "The African Methodist Episcopal Zion Church in her incipiency, loyal, not only to her mother, but to her grandmother—Wesleyan Methodism—termed her chief ministers, though bishops to all intent and purposes—'Superintendents.'" [35]

One notes a parallel discussion within the Church at this time as well—that on divorce. Readings of the period support the theory that the Church appeared to be gaining a sense of concern where divorce was involved. The two Bishops who wrote on ecclesiastical law appeared more interested in the marriage of a Christian *to* an *unconverted* person, the necessity of clarification on this point evidently being paramount.[36] In 1884, Elder A. Walters had proposed a series of resolutions on divorce.[37] It appears that no action was taken on the resolution as they are not reported by the Committee on Revision.

The Disciplines of 1884 and 1888 carry identical qualifications for the Bishopric of the Church. They each state (Page 51, Ch. II, Article 1) of the election and consecration of Bishops and their duty:

---

[33] Jones, *Hand-Book of the Discipline*, loc. cit., 21.
[34] *Ibid.*, 21.
[35] Bishop John Bryan Small, loc. cit., 143.
[36] Singleton T. Jones, *Handbook*, loc. cit., 7.
[37] *Daily Proceedings of the Seventeenth Quadrennial Session*, loc. cit., 87.

Question. How shall a Bishop be constituted?
Answer. By the election of a majority of the General Conference and the consecration by the Bishops or Elders appointed by the General Conference for that purpose.
Question. How long shall a Bishop serve?
Answer. So long as his spirit and practice are such as becomes the Gospel. Provided that no person shall be elected to this office who has not been for four years a traveling Elder, nor has at any time been expelled from the connection.[38]

Changes in the qualifications for the Episcopacy, therefore, had to come in the Twentieth Century since no reference to additional qualifications appear in the Minutes of the General Conference which met in Mobile, Alabama in 1896. By vote of the Mobile Session, the General Conference of 1900 was scheduled to meet in Washington, D. C. with the church which is now known as Metropolitan Wesley. No doubt it was the basic intent of the denomination to bring into focus all of her accepted pronouncements where the Episcopacy was and is concerned. Yet, because there has been a tendency to either overlook, forget or ignore items of the law it appears to this writer that somewhat of confusion does exist. The acceptance of the writings of Singleton T. Jones, commissioned by the General Conference and eventually receiving a stamp of approval on the part of that body leaves one in a peculiar position as he declares: "Laws, rules, regulation and not character" are matters for the General Conference. Is he stating that investigation of character must be a matter of the Annual or Quarterly Conference? The denomination has an obligation to clear this point, for much depends upon that which is determined.

The controversy on the Episcopacy was evidently vivid as the Nineteenth Century drew to a close. Some of the evidences of this discussion is to be seen in references appearing in church periodicals and annual conference minutes. Caught up in these writings were such individuals as John C. Dancy and Bishop C. C. Petty. The latter had drawn up several qualifications for the Bishopric, which several Conferences had approved.[39] After the election of 1892 the following resolution was offered and referred to the Committee on the Episcopacy: "Whereas: The election of Bishops is over: therefore

---

[38] *The Doctrines and Discipline of the African Methodist Episcopal Zion Church in America.* (New York, 1886) (New York, 1889).

[39] *A.M.E. Zion Quarterly Review.*

Be it Resolved: That we hereafter elect no elder to the office of Bishop who is under 40 or over 60 years of age." [40]

It is difficult for one not to come to a decision to criticize the Church in many of its crucial conversations, for time after time it must be conceded that the impatience of delegates to return home has worked against the fulfillment of a task. Measures which evidently would not pass in the early stages of the Quadrennial Sessions have been brought up near the close of these sessions to receive the affirmative vote of the General Conference. This was true in the vote on election for life for the Episcopacy. It appears true where added restrictions on that Episcopacy as far as eligibility is concerned.

Controversy, one must again note, was rife throughout the closing twenty years of the Nineteenth Century but the General Conference of 1896 adjourned with no major change except the service and age qualifications.

The Twenty-first Quadrennial Session met as scheduled in Wesley Metropolitan Church, Washington, D.C., the Reverend W. H. Snowden, pastor. Few know of the deep significance of the session for several important items faced the delegation. Among these was the matter of the Episcopacy. Bishop Petty, as stated above, had been urging some regulations but so far we have been unable to uncover a copy of them. The battle on the matters at hand commenced when the Reverend B. F. Wheeler offered a resolution for immediate consideration asking the Bishops on the Episcopal Committee to resign (Official Journal of the Daily Proceedings of the Twenty-first Quadrennial Session (1900). 169). The matter was so volatile that it was decided that an executive session was necessary. It was made the order of the day for Monday at 10:00 A. M. The Reverend J. H. McMullen read the resolution of Reverend Wheeler at that time and after discussion a vote was taken defeating the resolution.

The Committee on Episcopal Matters and Assignment, at the time, had as General Conference members the following: Reverend G. W. Lewis, M. S. Kell, W. J. Holland, and I. W. Selectman. It made a partial report on these affairs but evidently did not bring in a complete report until sometime later. Bishop Hood's resolution, which appears to have had something to do with the election of the

---

[40] *Minutes* of the General Conference of 1892, *loc. cit.*, 118.

number of Bishops was discussed Tuesday, May 8th at 11:00 A. M. (See Page 41). Again this matter was deeply moving to the point that it was decided that four speakers for each side were to be given ten minutes each while all others were to be limited to five minutes. Evidently as a result of the vote only one Bishop was agreed upon (186-80). J. W. Alstork was subsequently elected.

The crucial matter regarding the Episcopacy was not brought up until sometime later. The question arose again as to quorum, something which we repeat, has plagued the General Conference in practically every session. On a motion of the Reverend T. B. McClain the resolution which stated that the "majority of the members present at any regular session of the General Conference would constitute a quorum." (See P. 75). Thus the way was paved for the consideration of the matter at hand.

On the twentieth day of the session the following resolution was offered:

1. No man having two living wives will be eligible for election to the bishopric.
2. No Bishop of Annual Conference is to be allowed to use a minister who has been expelled or who has deserted his family unless he has been restored by the Conference which suspended him.
3. That no man be elected to the office of Bishop who is under 40 years of age.[41]

In a subsequent session, evidently, the following elaborations have been added:

1. Who has not been twenty years a Traveling Minister
2. Who has been expelled from our Church or from any other Denomination for gross immorality.

As we conclude this Chapter it is well to recall the statement of the Church on divorce as it appeared in the Minutes of the General Conference of 1864, page 61:

Resolution of the late General Conference, which from oversight was not compiled in the Minutes.
Resolved: That no man who has two living wives, or a woman who has two living husbands, shall be a member of our church.

---
[41] *Official Journal of the Daily Proceedings of the Twenty-first Quadrennial Session of the General Conference* (1900) 84, 85.

The matter of the Episcopacy flared again into prominence as the decade of the 1940s opened. Bishops, General Officers and ministers were in turn brought into the discussion as the open forum prevailed on the nature and the meaning of the Bishopric was debated. The late Dr. James Clair Taylor, Editor of the Review, and later Bishop, traced in detail not only the historical background of the office but wrote on the interpretation of John Wesley as well.[42] Here again, there is a need for the denomination to clear its stand as a Methodist body, keeping in mind its own traditional stand in the first period of our Church history and the companionate second period as well, for the Church cannot exist as a Methodist body only when it suits its purpose and lean heavily to the interpretation of Episcopalianism when it is deemed expedient.

Coupled with the hazy notion of function has come the recurring need to settle the retirement situation. Each struggle, along this line, has left the denomination with much to be desired, for retirement has always meant a shifting of denominational emphasis along one line or another when to the best interests of its membership, gradual change should be the process rather than the building of a particular power structure. Too much energy is wasted merely to depose a dynasty and install a new one, which, in turn occupies a major part of its time seeking it own perpetual rule.

In the Quadrennial address of 1940 the Board of Bishops said of the Episcopacy:

"One hundred and fifty-six years ago the Episcopacy of the Methodist Church was established by the laying on of hands by John Wesley, assisted by a Presbyter of the establishment and two elders of the Methodist Church. On Friday the 24th of December 1784, was begun the first 'General Conference' in which both Dr. Coke and Reverend Francis Asbury were elected and the latter consecrated 'Bishop' or Superintendent as they were then designated.

"The exigencies growing out of the Revolutionary War made Wesley's action inevitable. 'Methodism,' says Abel Stevenson, 'was the only form of religion that had thrived during the Revolution. The colonial English Church had been generally disabled, if not extinguished; its clergy fleeing the country, or entering political or military life. By this measure, American Methodism was to take

---

[42] *The A.M.E. Zion Quarterly Review*, Vol., LII, No. 3, p. 3, 46, No. 4, 44: LIII, No. 1, 64: No. 2, 82, for the years, 1942, 1943.

precedence of the Colonial Episcopal Church in the dates of their reorganization after the Revolution. The Methodist Bishops were the first Protestant Bishops, and Methodism the first Protestant Episcopal Church of the New World.'

"The historic references are not submitted to argue the validity of our Episcopacy: that has been long ago established. We do not waste words in theoretically declaring the 'Apostolic Succession.' We rather emphasize the 'Spiritual procession' of those commissioned to feed Christ's sheep and to be true shepherds of the flock. In our disciplinary exhortion we are admonished to 'Be to the flock of Christ a Shepherd, not a wolf.'

"It is assumed that Episcopates are called by the Holy Ghost and those who present them for consecration describe them as 'Holy Men.' The background of the office is such that they cannot but be examples of the flock. Peter in the first epistle urges: 'Feed the flock of God which is among you, taking the oversight thereof, not by constraint, but willingly; not for filty lucre, but of a ready mind. Neither as being lords over God's heritage.'

"We are of opinion that our Episcopacy should not be thought of has functioned throughout the quadrennium; giving no offence in anything that this higher office be not blamed.

"Those who have been ordained to the ministry have a special relationship to our Episcopates, having promised 'Reverently to obey your chief ministers, unto whom is committed the charge and government over you, following with a glad mind and will their godly admonitions, and submitting yourselves to their godly judgment.'

"We are of opinion that our Episcopacy should not be thought of merely as the appointing power or collecting agency of the General Church. Our Episcopacy has a definite place in the life of our several churches and oversight by the disciplinary demand that a bishop travel at large among the people, to oversee the spiritual and temporal affairs of the work.

"The Bishops, although set apart for special work, must still be thought of as fellow-workers, cooperating with the humblest minister or member in the building of the kingdom of Jesus Christ. Let it be remembered that we are one body. Paul wrote: 'For I say, through the grace given unto me, to every man that is among you, not to think of himself more highly than he ought to think; but to think soberly, according as God has dealt to every man the measure of faith. For as we have many members in one body, and all members have not the same office; So we, being many are one body in Christ, and every one, members one of another.' If this is realized and remembered by the Bishops, general officers, pastors and members, it will greatly enhance the stability and growth of our Zion Methodism." [43]

---

[43] *Official Journal of the Thirty-first Quadrennial Session of the General Conference* (Washington, D. C., 1940) 78, 79.

CHAPTER X

The Departments and Their Development

THE FIRST General Secretary of the African Methodist Episcopal Zion Church evidently was George Collins, who, it appears, also worked on the first copy of the Discipline.[1] Others involved were James Varick, Charles Anderson, Christopher Rush and William Miller. George Collins evidently was well educated for the times as he aided Christopher Rush in the writing of the first account of our Church's history.

It was not until the General Conference of 1840 that record is found of another appointment, this time, the Reverend Joseph P. Thompson with the Reverend John A. King as his assistant.[2] It appears that secretaries were appointed to serve Conferences only in this early period. Much later, as we will note, the secretary was empowered to serve in the interval of the General Conferences as well.

The Reverend Sampson Talbot became Secretary in 1844, when this General Conference met. Reverend John J. Moore served in the 1848 session.[3] He was replaced by the Reverend J. D. Brooks in 1852. The Reverend Samuel M. Giles succeeded him in 1856. In the Tenth General Session (Philadelphia, Pa.) the Reverend William F. Butler was elected. He served in 1864 as well, but resigned and was replaced by William Sanford.

Statistics of this Conference showed the following:

Conference	Traveling and Local Preachers	Members	Probationers
New York	146	3,826	500
New England	29	1,126	64
Philadelphia	77	2,262	346
Allegheny	55	779	96
Genesee	37	750	5
Baltimore	19	857	79
North Carolina	10	2,300	300

When the Session of 1868 was called to order in Wesley Zion Church, Washington, D.C. (the Twelfth Quadrennial Session)

---

[1] Christopher Rush, *A Short Account of the Rise and Progress of the African M. E. Church in America* (New York, 1866) 44.
[2] John Jamison Moore, *History of the A.M.E. Zion Church* (York, Pa., 1884), 205.
[3] Moore, *loc. cit.*, 208.

Bishop William H. Bishop was in the chair as Singleton T. Jones moved the election of William F. Butler as Secretary. Following his permanent election Butler selected four others to act as his assistants, this privilege being granted him by the Conference.

The Thirteenth Session of the General Conference meeting in Charlotte, North Carolina (Clinton Chapel Church) elected Reverend William H. Hilliary as General Secretary and the Reverend Robert Harris "recorder of the Minutes."[4] James A. Jones was to compile them. One does not know what events or action prompted this move, but it is known that the Minutes of 1872 were not published as planned. In this General Conference, too, the rule of electing a Secretary for the duration of the session was dispensed with and thereafter, the General Secretary was elected to serve four years and was charged with the task of furnishing the Bishops with certificates of Ordination and for the self-same Bishops Certificates of election. The Certificates of Ordination evidently were to be used by the Bishops as men were admitted to the two orders. Under this law Reverend J. A. Jones was selected General Conference Secretary.

Later a further duty was added, the compiling of the official lists of General Conference delegates, both ministerial and lay—these to be forwarded to him by the Secretaries of each annual conference.[5] Reverend Jones passed away during the interval of the General Conferences so that when the next session met as selected in Louisville, Kentucky in 1876, the Bishops announced the appointment of William Howard Day as General Secretary. On motion, he was permitted to name his assistants at the Conference. C. R. Harris from North Carolina, W. H. Fergeson (Tennessee) and L. J. Shurlock of Mississippi were subsequently named. Two others, M. M. Bell (of the Philadelphia and Baltimore Conference) and J. McH. Farley of Virginia were named Statistical Secretaries.[6]

Elsewhere, in this work we have gone into detail regarding the matters which led to the fact that no minutes of the 1876 session were printed. As a result of actions taken by Dr. Day he was summoned to trial in the Philadelphia and Baltimore Conference and subsequently replaced when the important session of 1880 met in Montgomery, Alabama. The Reverend Cicero R. Harris acted as

---
[4] Moore, *loc. cit.*, 273.
[5] Moore, *loc. cit.*, 282.
[6] Moore, *loc. cit.*, 290.

THE DEPARTMENTS AND THEIR DEVELOPMENT

Secretary at that time. Working with him were the Reverend Alfred Day, Assistant with the Reverend Calvin C. Pettey of South Carolina listed as Journal Secretary. The Reverend John Bryan Small of the New England Conference served as Statistical Secretary along with Rev. B. Max Manning of the Georgia Conference.[7] It will be noted that Cicero Harris was likewise elected General Financial Steward.

In 1884, Cicero Harris gave up the work of the General Secretary and devoted his time to that of the General Steward. He was succeeded in the General Secretary's office by the Reverend Calvin C Pettey of Montgomery, Alabama.[8]

The duties of the General Secretary were revised again when the General Conference met in New Bern, North Carolina in 1888. He was charged to make quarterly, annual and quadrennial reports of "all monies collected for general purposes of our church, and the distribution of the same, the Bishops' salary and traveling expenses, Livingstone College, the Book Concern, the Star of Zion, the Superannuated Ministers, the Missionary in Africa, the salaries of the General Secretary and General Steward, and widows and orphans."[9] Incidentally, his salary was to be $300 per year. The Superintendent of African Missions was to get $400.

Calvin C. Pettey was elected to the Bishopric in the New Bern General Conference so it was necessary to replace him as General Secretary. Again, William Howard Day was elected and was so listed when the General Conference met in Pittsburgh, Pennsylvania in 1892. He was re-elected at that session as well, and in Mobile in 1896.[10]

William Howard Day was again elected to the office of General Secretary in 1900 but passed away in December of the same year. George Lincoln Blackwell was evidently selected by the Board of Bishops to succeed him and was elected to the office in 1904.[11] Ac-

---
[7] *Daily Journal of the Sixteenth Quadrennial Session of the General Conference*, 2.
[8] *Daily Proceedings of the Seventeenth Quadrennial Session of the General Conference*, 2.
[9] *Supplement to the Discipline of* 1884 (printed, 1886) 9.
[10] *Minutes of the Twentieth Quadrennial Session of the General Conference*, Mobile, Ala., 1896, 80.
[11] *The Doctrines and Discipline of the African Methodist Episcopal Zion Church*, 1905, 358

William Howard Day is listed in the Souvenir Program of 1900 when the General Conference met in Washington, D. C. In 1904, the General Conference met in St. Louis.

cording to the Year Book of 1956-1960, issued by Mrs. Willie G. Alstork, then General Secretary, the Reverend Dr. Blackwell served until 1908 when he was elected Bishop. The Reverend Dr. M. D. Lee succeeded him. Reverend Lee had opposition in 1912 but was finally re-elected when other candidates withdrew.[12] The Minutes of the Twenty-fifth session are strangely silent on the election of a General Secretary but it is assumed that Reverend M. D. Lee was re-elected. He served two years of this 1916-1920 term and when the Board of Bishops met in Chicago in 1918 the Reverend Dr. F. M. Jacobs was assigned the office. He served until he was elected to the Bishopric in 1928. Dr. H. C. Weeden then became General Secretary. Before the Quadrennial Session of 1940, Dr. Weeden passed away and was succeeded by Mr. Samuel Madison Dudley, the Board of Bishops having appointed him to the position. He was elected in 1940 and again in 1944 as the General Sessions met in St. Paul Church (Now Metropolitan), Detroit, Michigan. His death occurred January 6, 1947. In the January meeting of the Board of Bishops the Reverend Dr. R. Farley Fisher was assigned the work of the General Secretary. That year the Board met in Oakland, California. Dr. Fisher won election in 1948 (Louisville) and 1952 (Brooklyn). He passed away in March 1953, and was succeeded by Dr. F. Claude Spurgeon on appointment of the Board of Bishops. He was elected to the office in 1956 and served until his passing, June 2, 1959 when again the Board of Bishops was called upon to fill the office, this time appointing Mrs. Willie G. Alstork to the position, (August, 1959).

While Mrs. Alstork ran for election in her own right in 1960 she was defeated by Mr. E. M. Graham in the Thirty-sixth Quadrennial session (Brooklyn, New York.)[13] Mr. Graham was re-elected in 1964. In the months prior to his death, in June, 1967, Mrs. Willie G. Alstork was assigned major tasks in the office and then, the Secretary's work was placed in the hands of a Committee. The Reverend Dr. R. H. Collins Lee was selected by the Board of Bishops in Brooklyn, 1967 and was elected by the General Conference in 1968.

THE BOOK CONCERN AND PUBLISHING HOUSE
According to the Year Book issued in 1942, by Attorney Samuel

---
[12] *Official Journal of the Twenty-fourth Quadrennial Session*, (Charlotte, 1912) 118.
[13] *Official Journal, Thirty-sixth Quadrennial Session*, General Conference, 80.

Madison Dudley, the A.M.E. Zion Book Concern was established first in 1841.[14] Bishop John Jamison Moore, in his History records no mention of the office in the General Conference of 1840 where it should have been created. He does mention the Book Steward in the Sixth General Session.[15]

This omission apparently is linked to the statement of Bishop E. D. W. Jones as he states that the Book Concern was first established by the New York Annual Conference and therefore, was not a denominational enterprise in the beginning.[16] The Reverend John D. Richardson was evidently the first Book Steward and with him was associated Reverend Nathan Blount. Jones states that it became a denominational enterprise in 1844, which does meet approval of the known records.

In the General Conference of 1848 a resolution was passed which provided for three Book Agents, one for each annual conference. Those appointed were: Reverend Edward Johnson, Philadelphia Conference, Rev. John J. Moore, Baltimore Conference and Reverend James Simmons, New England Conference. New York was not represented since the headquarters of the Book Concern were in that Conference. Officers appointed were: Reverend John A. King, Chairman, Reverend Timothy Eato, Treasurer and Reverend Peter Ross, Secretary.[17]

Two other actions regarding the Book Concern were also taken in this session. The Concern was authorized to publish "One thousand copies of the Minutes of the General Conference and three hundred copies of the Discipline." [18] The second interesting note regarding the Department was that of authorizing one thousand copies of "our hymn book," the General Conference to "receive the stock bargained for, paying the balance of the printer's bill." [19]

Moore states that the Minutes of the General Conference of 1852 were never published. The records available deal mainly with the controversy over the Superintendency and nothing is said concerning the Book Concern or the reports of the Book Agents.

By 1856, the denomination was in the midst of its first major crisis.

---

[14] *The A.M.E. Zion Year Book*, 1942-1943 (Washington, D. C.) 75.
[15] Moore, *loc. cit.*, 209.
[16] Bishop E. D. W. Jones, *Comprehensive Catechism*, 28.
[17] *Minutes of the General Conference of* 1848 (See Vol. LXXXI, No. 2 Summer, 1969) A.M.E. Zion Quarterly Review.
[18] *Ibid.*
[19] *Ibid.*

While, no doubt the Book Concern came in for its share of attention, major interest centered around education (the Ohio African University and Rush Academy), the Antislavery Question and the efforts at reconciliation within the Church.

By 1860, the breach, apparently, had been healed and a united Church, at least on the surface, met in Wesley Church, Philadelphia (Wednesday, May 30). It is interesting to note that in this session a Board of Home and Foreign Missions (President, George A. Spywood; Secretary, Samuel M. Giles; Corresponding Secretary, Clinton Leonard; Treasurer, R. R. Morris and C. G. Washington and Jos. G. Smith) is listed.

To insure the perfect healing of the breach the sessions adjourned from the Philadelphia site on the Fifth of June to meet in Mother Zion on the Sixth, thus showing deference to each faction.

The General Book Steward, appointed at the 1864 Quadrennial Session was Isaac Coleman. Trustees selected were Singleton T. Jones, William H. Decker, William H. Pitts, Jeptha Bancroft and Jacob Thomas.[20]

The apparent growth of the work in the South and the shifting of the balance of power is noted first in the General Conference of 1872—a session concerning which minutes were not printed. However, in the scanty record Moore gives, this shifting is evident in his brief account concerning the Book Concern. It appears that while no decision was arrived at, a resolution was offered providing for two "General Book Agencies." [21] A second indication of this new state of affairs is dimly seen in the resolution to establish a school or college in the District of Columbia. The resolution urged the purchase of "suitable lots for the purpose be procured in a suitable locality." [22]

It is not stated as to that which happened to this resolution.

This General session also provided for an imprint edition of the Methodist Episcopal, North, Hymnal as that Church, through its own Book Concern, had "offered our connection the use of their hymnbook, with the privilege of placing the title page of the African M. E. Zion Church Hymnbook and our Bishops' names in place of

---
[20] *Minutes of the General Conference of* 1864, p.
[21] Moore, *loc. cit.*, 275.
[22] *Ibid.*, 276.

THE DEPARTMENTS AND THEIR DEVELOPMENT

theirs in the preface, and they to publish it for our exclusive use at a reduced cost per copy." [23] This resolution was passed.

In writing the account of the Hymnal, Moore, inadvertently, includes the note that the purchase of property for a school house or college at Fayetteville, North Carolina, was also authorized.

It appears that the Reverend Jacob Thomas, who was first elected in 1868,[24] was again elected in 1876, and, according to Jones, he held this position until 1900 when it was apparently eliminated.[25]

In 1880 an executive Board as well as an Auditing Committee was selected by the General Conference as it met in Montgomery, Alabama. At that time the following were elected: Executive Board: A. M. Wilson, George H. Washington, C. W. Robinson, M. M. Bell and J. B. Small. The Auditing Committee consisted of A. Day, A. Jackson and A. Anderson.[26] The Minutes of the General Conference also carry a Constitution for the Executive Board.

The report of Reverend Thomas for 1884 is interesting. He reported that "we have printed 50,000 love-feast tickets, 4,000 disciplines, 5,000 catechisms, 1,000 catalogues, 300 hymnbooks of different descriptions, and purchased a lot of 500 hymns, already to put on the market, besides printing all other requisites necessary to publish our business, such as cards, advertisements and circulars. . . . No debt has been created save that on salary of General Agent." [27]

The Auditing Committee reported that $8,529.68 was received for the four year period, while the Concern had $1,584.92 over liabilities.[28]

At this session an effort was made to move the site of the Book Concern to St. Louis, Missouri, but on motion of Joseph Charles Price it was decided that the Concern should remain in New York City. Again Elder Jacob Thomas was elected General Book Agent, despite another effort to place the work in the hands of annual conferences. This may have been merely to collect funds due the Concern rather than doing away with the General Book Agent. The Executive Committee this time consisted of H. M. Wilson, President,

---

[23] Moore, *loc. cit.*, 278.
[24] *Minutes of the General Conference of* 1868.
[25] Jones, *loc. cit.*, 63.
[26] *Daily Journal of the Sixteenth Quadrennial Session of the General Conference,* 1880, 36.
[27] Daily Proceedings of the Seventeenth Quadrennial Session of the General Conference 1884, 127.
[28] *Ibid.*, 129, 130.

G. H. Washington, Vice-President, J. H. Anderson, Secretary, G. E. Smith, A. Anderson, W. H. Decker, George Jackson, Anthony Jackson. This group appears to have contained the names of the auditing committee as well.

While the record does not appear clear on the matter of the election of the General Book Concern Agents, the revised constitution of the agency in 1884 has some items one may suggest is of vital interest to the reader. For example: the Book concern Constitution called for two General Agents, "one of the General Agents shall be a member of an Annual Conference, the other a layman of the A.M.E. Zion Church distinguished for commercial ability. Three of the clerical members of the Executive Board must be connected with the New York Annual Conference. The remaining three (clerical members) must be members of conferences adjacent thereto, the seventh member being a layman." [29]

These regulations evidently had a great deal to do with the effort to change the headquarters of the Concern as noted above. Provision was made in the Constitution for Local Agents "appointed in each Annual Conference, with whom books may be deposited by the General Agents as provided for in Section 7th." [30] The ministry was expected to support the Concern through purchases but there was a penalty for preachers who failed to pay their accounts—the stoppage of the "passage of their characters until their accounts are settled, or otherwise provided by their Conference." [31]

The changes noted above in the Constitution of the Book Concern evidently were in vogue when the General Conference met in New Bern, North Carolina, in 1884. They appear to have remained unchanged in 1888. In that year Jacob Thomas was re-elected General Agent of the Book Concern.[32]

At this point the writer is somewhat confused since Jones states that Jacob Thomas served until 1900. That which may have happened we may have difficulty in knowing. The name of Jacob Thomas is not noted in the listing of the outstanding men who died during 1888-1892. Yet his name is not listed in 1892. By this time the

---

[29] *The Doctrines and Discipline of the African Methodist Episcopal Zion Church in America,* 1884, p. 240.
[30] *Ibid.,* 243.
[31] *Ibid.,* 243.
[32] See Revisions of the General Conference of May 1888, appearing in Discipline of 1884, 265.

THE DEPARTMENTS AND THEIR DEVELOPMENT

Concern had evidently suffered some reverses, contrary to the report of 1888. On October 15, 1889, the Reverend Alexander Walters became the General Agent and moved the headquarters from the basement of 182 Bleeker Street to 353 Bleeker street, "next door to Mother Zion Church." The following year the plates of the Discipline were burned, the hymnal was not giving satisfaction and there was the nonpayment of bills.[33] The Executive Board proposed several changes at this time as well.

1. The Book Room to be maintained in New York City.
2. All orders, as much as possible should be cash.
3. A sub-book department to be conducted in each Episcopal District.
4. The Star of Zion to be located in New York City.

The General Conference of 1892 proceeded to elect the Reverend John Holliday Book Agent for the succeeding four years.[34] He was evidently the last of the General Agents of the Book Concern for in 1896 the Reverend Dr. G. L. Blackwell was designated the General Manager of the Publishing Department, located at Charlotte, North Carolina. The motion to do so was made by Reverend J. B. Colbert.[35]

One cannot say that Bishop Jones is in error as he lists the General Officers of this period, but evidently, George Lincoln Blackwell served as Manager of the Publishing Department until the General Conference of 1900. Following the death of William Howard Day in December of 1900 he was appointed General Secretary. This writer cannot be sure of these facts however. Bishop Jones lists him as Manager 1896-1900. If this is correct, then Blackwell served the office for this period and again as General Secretary and Corresponding Secretary of Foreign Missions, or Missions for another period. Bishop Jones states that Dr. Blackwell was elected General Secretary in 1904—serving until 1908.[36] He lists him as Missionary Secretary for the same period. This is borne our in the Discipline of the period as well.[37]

---

[33] *The Minutes of the General Conference of* 1892, 135.
[34] *Minutes of the General Conference of* 1892, 86.
[35] *Minutes of the Twentieth Quadrennial Session of the General Conference,* (Mobile, Ala.) 80, 81.
[36] Jones, *loc. cit.,* 63, 65.
[37] *The Doctrines and Discipline of the African Methodist Episcopal Zion Church,* 1905, 358, 359.

Bishop Jones states that the Reverend J. M. Hill became Manager of the Publishing House in 1900, and served until April, 1904 when Bishop G. W. Clinton took over for the two month period ending June first.

According to the records, the Reverend John F. Moreland was elected Manager of the Publishing House in 1904 and served until 1908. He was succeeded by Reverend F. K. Bird who served until 1914 when he passed away. He was followed in office by Reverend George C. Clement. We are not sure as to whether he stood for election in 1916, but he, in turn, was succeeded by Mr. J. W. Crockett in that year.[38] Mr. Crockett was defeated for re-election in 1920 and was succeeded by the Reverend S. D. Watkins who served until 1928. Mr. R. W. Sherrill began his tenure of office in that year and served until 1948 when he refused to stand for re-election.[39] The Reverend W. A. Blackwell was selected to succeed him, he, evidently, did not stand for re-election in 1952. The Reverend L. L. Boyd was subsequently elected.[40] He was re-elected in 1956 without opposition.[41]

When the General Conference met in Buffalo, New York in 1960, affairs at the Publishing House had reached a state that the Board of Bishops saw fit to appoint a special committee to look into the matter. The Committee on the Publishing House referred to this Commission as it made its report. The General Conference adopted the report. Major points of the report are herein listed:

> Whereas, the A.M.E. Zion Church Publishing House has for years operated without the desired efficiency and minus the anticipated profit, and Whereas the effective managerial system has fallen short of the purposes for such a Publishing House, and Whereas, the Board of Bishops appointed a Commission to study the Publishing House, and Whereas, the Board of Bishops and the Manager's report recommended relocation and the construction of a new building for use as the A.M.E. Zion Publishing House,
> Be it therefore Resolved that the A.M.E. Zion Church Publishing House be relocated and that a new building be constructed on such a site as the Board of Bishops and the Board for the Publication House shall agree, and Be It Further Resolved, that paragraphs 413, page 152 of the Book of Discipline be revised so as to read "The Board of

---

[38] *Minutes of the Twenty-fifth Session of the General Conference,* 1916, 27.
[39] *Official Journal of the Thirty-third Quadrennial Session of the General Conference,* 1948, 66.
[40] *Official Journal, Thirty-fourth Session, General Conference,* 1952, 73.
[41] *Official Journal, Thirty-fifth Quadrennial Session, General Conference,* 1956, 120.

Publication shall be empowered to hire a manager of the Publication House." That Section 2 will read, "The Board of Publication shall have the power to replace the manager for sufficient cause, subject to the approval of the Board of Bishops." Also, "That the Board of Publication shall have the power to determine the salary of the manager of the Publishing House, subject to the approval of the Board of Bishops." [42]

The Board of Publication, following the subsequent resignation of Reverend L. L. Boyd appointed to the position D. L. Blakey, who is the incumbent at the present time. Under the Board of Bishops' and Board of Publication's direction the new building for the Publication House has since been constructed and now houses the work of that department.

THE CHURCH EXTENSION DEPARTMENT

It appears that this total work could well have been utilized to relate and interpret the work of the Sixteenth Quadrennial Session of the General Conference of the A.M.E. Zion Church. It appears trite to state again that the organization of the Woman's Home and Foreign Missionary Society was merely one of the high-lights of this historic session. The Reverend James M. Hill was a diligent Secretary as he reported the full work of this Committee, dividing its contributions into three major sections: the first dealing with Foreign work called to the denominational attention the need to give to the *West India Mission* special consideration. The report stated that the Church needed to furnish "them with men and means, and any other foreign mission, that may come under their observation."

The second section dealt with Home Missions and stated:

> The Territory or State of Kansas, opens to us a good field for missionary labor, for thousands of our people are emigrating there, and among them a large number of our members, and Whereas, We your committee, believe it would be conducive to the good of our beloved Zion, we further recommend that our Bishops appoint competent missionaries for that work, also any other mission referred to in the Episcopal Addresses of the Bishops.[43]

The third section is more directly concerned with the subject of Church Extension as the Committee wrote:

---

[42] *Official Journal, Thirty-sixth Quadrennial Session, General Conference,* 1960, 438.
[43] *Daily Journal of the Sixteenth Quadrennial Session of the A.M.E. Zion Church,* Montgomery, Ala., 1880, 79.

After carefully considering the subject of Church Extension, we rejoice to find from the reports of the different Episcopal Districts, that the Connection is increasing in Church property. We therefore recommend there be an agreement between trustees and members for purchasing land for churches and parsonages etc.

By a conjoint meeting or meetings, for the purpose of purchasing such property, having the counsel and cooperation of the pastor, we do further recommend that they shall see that a clear title be given for such property, and that the deed be in accordance with our discipline.

We further recommend the adoption of the following preamble and constitutions of the Home and Foreign Missions Board, and Ladies Home and Foreign Missionary Society. (Offered by Elder M. M. Bell.) (See Constitution of the General Missionary Board.) All of which we your Committee most respectfully submit.

J. P. Hamer, Chairman

J. A. Anderson, W. A. Forman, A. Coleman, A. Tasker, H. J. Thomas, H. Clinton, W. H. Thurber, J. B. Trusty, N. H. Turpin, J. W. Brown, W. H. Ferguson, T. A. Hopkins, James A. Thomas, R. S. Evans, George Sexton, A. Newby, J. W. Davis.[44]

It appears that the General Conference of 1884 was silent on the matter of Church Extension as such and no concrete action appears to have been taken on the subject when the General Conference met in New Bern in 1888.

The Committee on Church Extension in 1892 called the attention of the Nineteenth Quadrennial session to more definite tasks. It spoke of the building of Metropolitan Church in Washington, the new building under construction in St. Louis and other undertakings in various parts of the country. Especially did it call attention to the work in Oklahoma and the needs there. Strange to say, they also tried to arouse interest in the Far West. Then, as it began its report proper it stated:

> Now, to do this, to further this grand work, it is clear to your committee, that some new steps must be taken in this direction. We therefore recommend the establishment of General and Sub Church Extension Boards, with the following constitutions:

CONSTITUTION OF THE GENERAL BOARD

Article I

Section 1. The Board shall be composed of all the Bishops of the connection, the General Secretary and the General Steward of the connection, nominated and elected by the General Conference. They shall

---

[44] *Daily Journal of the Sixteenth Quadrennial Session*, 80.

hold in trust moneys and properties for the ministers and members of the African Methodist Episcopal Zion Church in America.

Section 2. The object of said moneys shall be to aid in the erection and improving of churches and parsonages in the African Methodist Episcopal Zion Church; said moneys to be loaned to societies or the trustees of said societies, upon proper security, at two per cent interest per year,

Section 3. The cost of searching the title, drawing papers, and the like to be paid by the society or trustee board obtaining the loan.

Section 4. The officers of the Board shall consist of President, Vice-President, Secretary and Treasurer. The Board shall meet semi-annually, and their traveling expenses shall be paid from money coming into the hands of the Treasurer.

Article II dealt with the duties of the respective officers and the following unique features:

Power of the Board

Section 4. The Board shall have power to assess per year each Conference district for the benefit of its funds, which amount so assessed shall be proportioned among the churches by the sub-board in each respective Annual Conference. In no case shall the assessment exceed six cents per member; provided, however, this shall not prevent the Board from receiving any amount per year that may be voluntarily donated by any society or individual.

The Minister in Charge

Section 5. It shall be the duty of the minister in charge of a circuit or station to raise the amount assessed by collections or otherwise, and forward the same to the Treasurer of the sub-Board of his Conference.

Section 6. The sub-Treasurer shall furnish a receipt to each minister for all moneys sent to him.

According to Article III the organization of the sub-Boards is outlined—the Board consisting of five elders nominated by the Bishop and elected by the Conference for a two-year period. All loans were to be made to the sub-Board and forwarded through them to the General Board who would have the right to accept or reject the application for funds. A regular corps of officers was provided for, their expenses to be paid by the Treasurer of the sub-Board.[45]

The Constitution of the Church Extension Society, as it was then called, underwent major changes in the next two General Conferences, 1900 and 1904. It was incorporated under the laws of the

---

[45] *The Minutes of the Nineteenth Quadrennial Session of the General Conference* (Pittsburgh, Pa. 1892), 147-150.

State of Pennsylvania, July 10, 1905;[46] and by this date the General Conference was electing a "Corresponding Secretary who served for four years, traveling, lecturing, soliciting and otherwise." [47] The salary of the Corresponding Secretary was to be $1,200 per year. The Society provided for four different funds: The Emergency Fund, The Loan Fund, The Annuity Fund and The Memorial Fund.

The following report was made to the Twenty-second Quadrennial session of the General Conference, meeting in St. Louis, May, 1904:

> It is with profound reverence and heartfelt gratitude to our Heavenly Father who doeth all things well, that I now make my first report, as Church Extension Secretary, to this honorable body.
> In August, 1901, at Atlantic City, N. J., (I think), by a motion made by Dr. E. D. W. Jones, Dr. Curry and I changed places, he becoming President of the Church Extension Board and I Secretary of the Church Extension Society.
> On the sixth of May, 1902, at Hartford, Conn., with fears and trembling and a very dark future, and no promise of support, except the cheerful words and sunlight smiles from that great churchman, Bishop J. W. Hood and the kind and loving words of Drs. Biddle and Bloice, I took the field, knowing not what should befall me. I soon found that the great and good Bishops Walters and Geo. W. Clinton were heart and hand with Bishop Hood to organize this Society and to give it their unrestricted support. And as I passed around from Conference to Conference, I found the other good Bishops with the same determined spirit to make the work go, which greatly encouraged me and relieved me of many doubts.
> In June, 1902, in Dr. Caldwell's office, 1825 Lombard Street, Philadelphia, Pa., the Church Extension Society was organized, and Bishop Hood became responsible for $300 to tide us over the Summer months. In August of the same year we were about to go adrift, and Bishop Hood threw out the life-boat of $100 and rescued us from drowning. That $100 some day will be worth millions to Zion. It was "Bread cast upon the water," "A mustard seed sown." A very few people know the worth of Bishop Hood to our beloved Zion, and possibly will never know it fully until it is revealed in the "Sweet Bye and Bye."
> So we cut loose from a first class appointment and started out to do the best we could to fully organize and develop this important Society—The General Conference in Mobile, Ala. in 1896, inaugurated and elected Dr. A. J. Warner Secretary of the Church Extension Society. Dr. Warner started out, like a new born star from among the constellation of mighty lights, and swept over the connection until he so attracted the members of Zion that the cry was heard everywhere,

---

[46] *The Year Book*, 1942-1943, 76.
[47] *Church Extension Society of the A.M.E. Zion Church* (a pamphlet).

"Come see the Star from the South." He suggested many good and wholesome ideas, which, had they been fully carried out, the Church Extension Society of Zion would be equal today to the Church Extension Society of any Negro denomination in the world.

The General Conference of 1900 elected Dr. E. H. Curry as Secretary of this Society to succeed Dr. Warner. Dr. Curry very wisely remained in the pastorate, so that he would have something to fall back on, and hence, did not experience some of the sufferings that Dr. Warner and myself had to pass through.[48]

It will be noted that the Corresponding Secretary calls attention to the fact that the Society actually had roots as far back as 1896. Reverend W. H. Coffey was the one who made the report as noted above. His report allows us to go beyond the seemingly known facts to at least the 1900 date for the full existence of the Society and allows us to understand even earlier facts for the formation of the Society. It appears that the Committee on Episcopal Address had provided for the election of one Secretary for the Missionary and Church Extension offices. This action was approved by the General Conference.[49]

On motion of the Reverend J. F. Moreland, the Reverend A. J. Warner became the Secretary of the joint Departments.[50]

It would appear, therefore that action in 1900 again separated the Departments when Dr. E. H. Curry assumed charge, followed by William H. Coffey. Reverend Coffey made his concluding report to the Twenty-fourth Quadrennial session as it met in Clinton Chapel Church, Charlotte, North Carolina in 1912. While there appeared to have been no adverse criticism in the Bishops' Message of that year regarding Church Extension the Reverend Mr. Coffey did not stand for re-election. He did report many problems and trying experiences as he made his report, however.[51] He was succeeded by Dr. J. C. Dancy when the report of the Committee considering the re-uniting of this Department with Missions voted non-concurrence with the Bishops' recommendation and was sustained by the General Conference. Evidently, according to the vote cast, Dr. Coffey did not run for re-election. Since he passed away in the new quadrennium it is

---

[48] In the *INFORMER* of the Church Extension Society, see Corresponding Secretary's report, 9-11.
[49] *Minutes of the Twentieth Quadrennial Session of the General Conference,* Mobile, Ala., 1896, 72.
[50] *Ibid.*, 81.
[51] *Official Journal, Twenty-fourth Quadrennial Session, General Conference,* 1912, 437-439.

presumed that his health was impaired. Dr. J. C. Dancy was reelected in 1916 as well, and went on to another term in 1920. He died soon after this final election in 1920. Professor S. G. Atkins replaced him as Corresponding Secretary of Church Extension and Home Missions.

It is interesting to note that the matter of combining these two offices, Church Extension and Home Missions apparently did not work out to a satisfactory end. As one reads the Address of the Board of Bishops he runs across these words: "The Church Extension Department was perhaps the first well ordered Department established by our Church and for the organization of this Department the credit is due the late Reverend W. H. Coffey. It is true that the Church has all along established and developed many influential churches. But we have seen our most phenomenal growth in the large congested cities in every section of the country since the establishment of the Church Extension Department."

"Prior to the Louisville, General Conference in 1916 the Church Extension Department was operated separate and distinct from any other department. But as the result of the slogan 'Elimination by combination' which had been advocated for years by a number of our leading men the Home Mission Department was combined with the Church Extension Department. . . . We have had eight years of experiment with the Combination theory and ample opportunity to determine its merits. . . . There are many who feel that the success of the Church Extension Department has been secured at the expense of the Home Mission Department and the sacrifice of the interest of the mission preachers." [52]

The statement of the Board of Bishops urging that something be done about the combined status of the Church Extension and Home Missions Department appears to have been accepted by the Committee,[53] as they reported: "It is recommended that there be established a Home Mission Department with full-time, full-salaried Corresponding Secretary." However, it appears that this was not the feeling of the entire committee. After debate the motion to again have the one Secretary for the two Departments was carried by 222 to 96. Subsequently Prof. S. M. Dudley was elected to this office.[54]

---

[52] *Minutes of the Twenty-seventh Quadrennial Session of the General Conference,* (Indianapolis, Ind., 1924) 110, 111.
[53] *Ibid.,* 68.
[54] *Ibid.,* 74.

THE DEPARTMENTS AND THEIR DEVELOPMENT

As the Twenty-ninth Quadrennial Session of the General Conference was meeting in Pittsburgh, Pennsylvania, the impact of the 1929 Market Crash and subsequent depression was so fully felt that most minds were on retrenchment and consolidation. In the matter of Education this was done, combining the work of three Departments, Christian Education or Superintendent of Sunday Schools and its Director, Education and Varick Christian Endeavor work, under one head. Dr. James W. Eichelberger was elected to this post. In the matter of Church Extension and Home Missions the Bishops had noted heavy indebtedness and diminished financial means so it was recommended that there exist a Board of Church Extension without a paid Secretary. This was accepted by the General Conference.[55] No Secretary was elected.

At the conclusion of four years endeavor to operate the Church Extension Department without a Secretary, Resolution No. 56 was offered by H. R. Jackson and accepted by the General Conference. It stated: "Whereas we have tried the committee idea for four years on the Church Extension Department and the results were nothing like satisfactory. Therefore, Be it resolved, that the Church Extension be put back as it was before the Pittsburgh General Conference. Signed, H. R. Jackson." [56] It should be noted that the decision to elect a full-time Secretary was not without opposition, although it prevailed.

Oscar W. Adams was therefore elected to the office.[57] In his report, four years later, he stated that he found debts and claims against the office totaling $122,960.22. The amount turned over to him by the Committee was $90.17. His report as found in the Minutes is both detailed and interesting. He was re-elected in 1940 and 1944, passing away in this final term. He was replaced by the Reverend Dr. C. W. Lawrence by vote of the Board of Bishops. Mr. D. W. Andrews succeeded him as a result of the vote of the General Conference in 1948.

No essential changes have been made in the structure of the Church Extension Department during the past thirty-two years. Mr. Andrews failed of re-election in 1968 and was replaced by Mr. Lem Long.

---

[55] *Journal of the Twenty-ninth Session of the General Conference,* 70, 71.
[56] *Journal of the Thirtieth Quadrennial Session of the General Conference,* (Greensboro, N. C., 1936) 279.
[57] *Journal of the Thirtieth Quadrennial Session,* 56.

In the Discipline of 1884 and 1888 the following appears re: Church Extension:

> Every pastor in charge shall make an annual collection in every congregation for church extension purposes; and the money so collected shall be lodged in the hands of trustees or stewards, to be sent to the Annual Conference.

THE STATISTICAL SECRETARY

In 1884, the mystery of the election of the Secretaries evidently is cleared up, as the custom had developed to allow the General Secretary to name his assistants. The statistical Secretary appears to have been in this number so named. In that year J. Harvey Anderson was selected as the Statistician of the General Conference and of the Church while General F. M. Chester was listed as the *Stenographic Secretary*. Aiding these three were four assistants.

In 1892 it is noted that a Bureau of Statistics was named consisting of J. W. White, Secretary, N. J. Green and J. S. Caldwell. Four years later the group consisted of L. H. Taylor, who served as chairman, J. H. Anderson, Secretary and P. H. Williams, Treasurer. The Committee made its report in this General Conference as well.[58]

The Minutes of the General Conference show the election of a Statistical Secretary in 1896 [59] and again, in 1904, and 1908. In these instances the Reverend J. Harvey Anderson was elected. In the Official Journal of the 1912 General Conference he is listed as Editor, *Statistical Year Book*. No record appears to state whether a Statistical Secretary was elected in 1912. Thereafter, it appears that no election for this office was held. (See note)

THE AUDITOR

The office of Auditor appears at no place in the Minutes of the 19th Century. It is therefore, an office of this Century. It should be stated, however, that there was such an office as Assistant Secretary to the General Secretary, Reverend Frederick M. Jacobs acting in this capacity in 1904 (evidently having been elected in that year). An auditing committee was listed in this period of the Church's

---

[58] *Minutes of the General Conference of* 1896, 97.
[59] *Ibid.*, 81.
Note: The Statistical Secretaries of 1880 were: Rev. J. B. Small and Rev. C. Max Manning. The Bureau existed in 1892 and 1896.

history, this being the twenty-sixth item in the report made to the General Conference.[60]

The first recorded note of the election of an Auditor appears in the Minutes of the General Conference of 1908 when evidently the Rev. Dr. F. H. Hill was elected to the office, or at least served in the office.[61] He could not have been elected to the office in 1912 as the Board of Bishops referred to him as an ex-General Officer, in their Message to the General Conference.[62] In the 1920 General Conference, Attorney Samuel Madison Dudley reported on the Religious Census but there appears to have been no report of an auditor.

No report for the auditor is noted again in 1924. However, in that General Conference on motion of the Reverend C. C. Stewart the offices of Auditor and General Secretary were combined. Dr. F. M. Jacobs therefore became General Secretary-Auditor upon his election to the post.[63] The Reverend W. L. Hamblin appears to have been the Auditor at the time, along with others who composed the Board of Audit.

THE CONNECTIONAL EVANGELIST

It was in 1884 that the Reverend L. D. Blockson moved that the General Conference provide for two or more Connectional Evangelists.[64] On motion of Cicero R. Harris it was decided that the matter of the creation of this office and the appointment(s) be left to the Board of Bishops. The office carried no salary in these formative days and there is every possibility that reports in the beginning were not made to the General Conference.

In 1912, it appears that the Reverend A. McLeese was being listed as Connectional Evangelist. Four years later one can suppose that there was an election to the post or posts with the office again carrying no salary.[65] The Reverend William Lyons evidently held the post from 1912 to 1916. In that year the Reverend F. D. Douglas became the Connectional Evangelist, along with Reverend Lyons.[66] In 1920 the Reverend Benjamin Garland Shaw was elected, serving until 1924 when he was elected to the Episcopacy.

---

[60] *The Doctrines and Discipline of the A.M.E. Zion Church,* 1904, 65.
[61] *Official Journal, Twenty-fourth Quadrennial Session,* 329.
[62] *Minutes of the Twenty-fifth Quadrennial Session,* 37.
[63] *Minutes of the Twenty-seventh Quadrennial Session,* 66.
[64] *Minutes of the General Conference of* 1884, 112.
[65] *Minutes of the General Conference of* 1916, 121.
[66] *Ibid.,* 121.

The Reverend W. W. Slade was elected Connectional Evangelist or Director of the Bureau of Evangelism in 1928. He was re-elected in 1932 and 1936. In 1940, the Rev. Dr. W. S. Dacons was selected for the post and served continuously until 1960 when the Reverend Dr. E. S. Hardge succeeded him. In 1968 the Reverend J. Dallas Jenkins assumed charge of the Bureau.

According to the discipline of 1944, the amount allocated for the support and maintenance of the Department of Evangelism was only $400. Four years later, 1948, the Director was made a full-time General Officer, the Committee recommending the following:

> A.—Since the chief business of the church is to save souls, to win men and women to the Christ way of life, and to do this effectively there must be a well-organized department operated by an efficient and capable head whose sole duty shall be to direct activities for the purpose of winning souls: We recommend that there shall be a Bureau of Evangelism with a full-time General Officer to be known as the Director of the Bureau of Evangelism.[67]

This recommendation was accepted by the General Conference.

The Christian Education Department of the denomination has not neglected the education work of evangelism as it has developed within the framework of cooperative enterprises. The National Christian Teaching Mission was not only fostered but engaged in by several churches as a result of educational participation. Later, as the National Council of Churches entered the field through its Commission on Educational Evangelism and its Central Department, the Christian Education Department of the denomination participated.

---

[67] *Official Journal of the Thirty-third Quadrennial Session* of the General Conference, 288.

CHAPTER XI

The Departments and Their Development
The Department of Home Missions, Pensions and Relief

THE THIN thread of history where charitable intent is concerned and the denomination is at times so faint that it is acknowledged that a full account is impossible. The examination of the brief records available, however may lead one to conclude that care of the ministry was early in the minds of Zion Methodism. Elsewhere we have alluded to the fact that the development of indigenous leadership was one of the basic reasons for the establishment of the denomination. Accounts are available which establish the theory that concern went beyond payment for services to the necessity of caring for underprivileged, retired or mission preachers as well as the widows and orphans of the clergy.

Nineteen years after the formation of the denomination, in 1839, the New York Conference drew up the following:

THE ANNUAL CONFERENCE FUND

Whereas, on account of the people's delinquency in many of our stations, and circuits, our preachers fail to get means to support their families and are compelled to neglect their duties as ministers or suffer. We have therefore agreed in our associated capacity as ministers, to establish a fund to be used in relief of our brother ministers connected with this conference, when they are in want of relief or help. We therefore adopt the following constitution: In consequence of the delinquency of the people in many of our stations and circuits, the preachers have not received a sufficiency to support themselves and families; they have therefore been compelled to neglect their duties as ministers, or suffer; we have agreed, therefore, in our associated capacity, for the purpose of raising a fund to be appropriated to our members, to adopt the following:

CONSTITUTION
Article I

Section 1. The fund shall be known by the name of the New York Annual Conference Fund.

Sec. 2. The members of this fund shall consist of all of the preachers belonging to the conference who shall pay into the treasury one dollar annually, or such sum as the conference may determine.

ARTICLE II

Sec. 1. The officers of this fund shall consist of nine persons who shall be members of this conference, to be elected annually, (President and Vice President excepted); the Superintendent, shall be President, and Senior Elder, Vice-president; a Secretary, Treasurer and a Board of Managers, consisting of three elders and two deacons or preachers.

Editor's Note (Section 2 continues to outline the duties of officers, while Section 3, lists the duties of the Board of Managers which included the formation of auxiliaries, "wherever and whenever it is within their power." They should also determine who should be recipients of aid.)

Article III called for the Board to meet monthly, have an audited report and provided for the change in Constitution.[1]

Moore appears to have listed no further reference to relief or pensions even as he writes the account of the Committees of the General Conference until he lists those of 1876, the Fourteenth Quadrennial session. Number 14 was listed as the Superannuated Preachers' Fund.[2]

Recently, the Minutes of the 1848 General Conference have come to light, agreeing with the statement of Bishop Hood in his book, ONE HUNDRED YEARS OF THE AFRICAN METHODIST EPISCOPAL ZION CHURCH when he states that a Mutual Benefit Society was established in that General Session. The Constitution of the same may be found in the Chapter, New Facts of Old History.

In the Seventeenth Quadrennial Session of the General Conference (New York, 1884) the Committee on Miscellaneous Matter reported.

> We, your Committee on Miscellaneous Matter beg leave to report: First We have examined the papers referred to as Paper No. 1, entitled Recommendation on Superannuated Preachers' presented by the New Jersey Annual Conference, we recommend that an organization be instituted by this General Conference, to be known as Preachers' Aid and Endowment Society of the African M. E. Zion Church, and that it be organized under the Constitution proposed by said Conference.[3]

The paper alluded to does not seem to be a part of the printed record and that which happened to the above report is not known. It

---
[1] Bishop John J. Moore, *A History of the A.M.E. Zion Church,* 108, 109.
[2] *Ibid.,* 292.
[3] *Daily Proceedings of the Seventeenth Quadrennial Session* of the General Conference (New York, 1884) 123.

is supposed that the report was accepted.

As one examines the Discipline of 1884, however the following is noted:

> *Section I.* There shall be regular public collections made in all our congregations every quarter, and also quarterly collections by the leaders in each class, at the time of giving out the love feast tickets, which money so collected shall be separately kept from that for the church and poor, and shall be lodged in the hands of the preacher's steward for the support of the ministry in our church.
>
> *II.* In such places where the State Legislature does not interfere the money collected as aforesaid, shall be distributed according to the judgment of the Annual Conference, to the best interest of the ministers, their wives, widows and children.
>
> *III.* In those places where the acts of the State Legislature have appointed the mode, and make it the business of the male members of the society to determine upon the allowance of ministers, it must be done accordingly; nevertheless the Annual Conference shall be consulted; and its advice shall be communicated through the medium of the Quarterly Conference previous to the determination of the members on the subject.[4]

The Discipline drawn up as a result of the work of the General Conference of 1904 contains a chapter dealing with widows and orphans. It provided for a Board known as the Widows' and Orphans' Board, consisting of the Bishops and a member from each Episcopal District. It was their task to distribute the funds which should come from two major sources,—one-third of the Benevolent assessment, (If the law had been followed this sum would have been $15,833 per year from this source) and another amount from the Widows' and Orphans' Fund brought to the Annual Conference from the various churches. Only one-half of the money reported to the Annual Conference should be distributed by that Annual Conference, the other 50% was to be sent to the Financial Secretary. All children under 14 were to share in the Annual Conference fund remaining and the collective fund from the denomination. The ratio, however, was to be for the children one-third of the widows' fund. Distribution of these moneys on the denominational level was to take place at the time of the Connectional Council.[5]

Dissatisfaction with this arrangement evidently existed, for the

---

[4] *The Doctrines and Discipline of the African Methodist Episcopal Zion Church in America,* New York, 1886 (General Conference of 1884), 93, 94.
[5] *The Doctrines and Discipline of the A.M.E. Zion Church* (St. Louis, Mo., 1904) 202, 203.

Board of Bishops in their Quadrennial Address to the 1908 session at Philadelphia stated:

> After dealing this most important department a most stunning and almost fatal blow, the last General Conference proceeded to elect the Reverend Dr. H. L. Simmons, secretary, to operate it, and put life in it, if he possessed such power.
> Dr. Simmons has made it possible for this General Conference to have an organization duly chartered and intact as a basis for devising ways and means by which the Brotherhood may be made what it was intended to be, viz. a helpful agency to our superannuated and worn-out preachers, their widows and orphans, also a protection to the families of active ministers, who may die and leave their families without adequate support. The present Secretary has had the Brotherhood chartered, prepared such literature as needed to conform to the erquirements of the charter, and has kept the organization constantly before the Church. His report will show the number of active supporters composing the Brotherhood, also its financial status.
> We have examined the charter and literature and desire to express our approval of the course which has been pursued by the Secretary.
> We wish also to again impress upon the General Conference the urgent need of such an organization, both as the means of strengthening the meagre stipend already provided for the class of persons the Brotherhood is designed to benefit; and as an evidence of gratitude to those whose labors have helped give to us and preserve the goodly heritage which we now enjoy.
> We believe that the weak should be helped by the strong, therefore, we regard the Brotherhood as an agency that gives every loyal son of Zion an opportunity to contribute to that end. We ask the General Conference to make such provisions for the future operation of the Brotherhood as will enlist the sympathy and hearty cooperation of our ministry through out the entire connection.[6]

The Reverend John F. Moreland was elected Secretary of the Brotherhood in 1908. The fund, according to the Discipline of 1904, had been granted an allocation of $1,500 from the General Fund. Along with this had gone one-third of the Benevolent Assessment. Whether this was at all possible in the light of that which has been stated above, is not clear. No doubt this is one of the items which troubled the Board of Bishops.[7]

Dr. Moreland issued a printed report for the first 18 months of the quadrennium showing that 774 persons had joined within "seven-

---

[6] *The Quadrennial Address* of the Bishops of the A.M.E. Zion Church to the delegates of the Twenty-third Session of the General Conference (Philadelphia, 1908) 18.

[7] *Doctrines and Discipline of the A.M.E. Zion Church of* 1904 (printed 1905), 200, 201.

teen months." Later, he stated that 237 *lapsed* in 1909 which, according to his records showed only 434 in benefit. The goal, according to the report was 500 persons. At the time both members of the denomination and ministers were admitted to the Brotherhood. When the report was issued two lay people had died and the survivors had been paid $20.00 each. One was listed from Birmingham, Ala. and the other from Monroe, Ga. In the same period eight ministers had passed—the survivors of whom each received $80.00, except in one case when only $7.40 was paid.[8]

The Board of Bishops reviewed the scene where the Brotherhood was concerned as the General Conference met in Charlotte, North Carolina in 1912. In part, they stated: "The general church has seen the need of this department for years, and for the last twelve years has been trying to perfect an indissoluble association for the protection of the ministerial and lay members of our Zion. The first attempt ran for four years—from 1900 to 1904. That plan was destroyed by the action of the General Conference at St. Louis. At the same General Conference a new plan was adopted. This was an optional plan. For four years it made little headway. From 1904 to 1908 at the General Conference at Philadelphia 1908, here the department was rearranged and the constitution simplified. It was sent forth on its great mission of relief with the endorsement of the general church. There is no reason why this department should not become so strong that it will answer, or serve the purpose of life insurance and protection among our membership.

"This department is in better shape than it has ever been. This has been brought about by the hard and constant strokes of Rev. John F. Moreland, D.D., that wonderful financier, great preacher and business man."[9]

The underlying cause of the dissatisfaction with the Brotherhood actually began prior to the 1904 General Conference as is noted in the A.M.E. Zion Quarterly Review. The Editor, John C. Dancy wrote: "The small sums that have been paid to families of deceased ministers during the quadrennium out of the Brotherhood Fund proves conclusively that the fund is totally inadequate to the demands supposed to be made upon it. The law governing it needs

---
[8] *Report of the A.M.E. Zion Brotherhood*, June 1, 1908-Dec. 31, 1909, 28.
[9] *Official Journal of the Twenty-fourth Quadrennial Session* of the General Conference (Charlotte, N. C., 1912), 150, 151.

drastic remedial legislation. It is not fair to have a fund where meagre results are realized. At least $100 should be paid the family of any deceased minister who belongs to the Brotherhood. Anything less than that looks ridiculous to a man who has given the least study to insurance matters, and who is up on insurance schemes." [10]

The distress the Editor felt is clearly stated as he continues: "The purpose of this organization is to help the ministers, and to relieve their families of immediate distress when they pass away. To say that a man shall not have at least all he has paid into the Brotherhood, if he lives only a few years, is ridiculous on its face. He should have at least all that and more, as the existence of the Brotherhood is contingent on the regular paying of every minister into that fund a sufficient amount to meet the ordinary death claims.

"It is highly important therefore, that such action be taken at the approaching General Conference as will make it not merely optional, but obligatory, upon the officer holding the Brotherhood fund to pay to the family of every deceased minister who contributes to the maintenance of the Brotherhood fund, at least one hundred dollars and increase that sum in proportion to the increased amount paid annually by the beneficiary."

In his report to the General Conference the Reverend Dr. Moreland stated that as he took office all which was available were the seal, some Literature, the incorporation papers and a debt ot $43.79. During the quadrennium, 1908-1912, however, he had been able to pay every death claim and restore confidence in the Department. His recommendations included the enrollment of "all those whose names were on the Annual Conference rolls" with a payment of $2.50 per year, and the sending of all money to the Brotherhood office, rather than leaving a part in each Annual Conference. He likewise recommended a full-time Secretary who would take care of the Superannuated and worn-out preachers and the widows and orphans as well.[11]

The Committee on Ministerial Brotherhood agreed with the Secretary on this combination of interests as they made their report. They likewise agreed with him regarding the payment of sums, removing them from the Annual Conference and giving them de-

---

[10] *The A.M.E. Zion Quarterly Review*, Vol. XIII, No. 1, 93, 94.
[11] Official Journal of the Twenty-fourth Quadrennial Session of the General Conference, 455, 456.

nominational status. They likewise suggested that there be three classes of superannuates, those in the 20-30 years of service bracket, those in 10-20 year service group and those who had served from 1-10 years. This appeared to mean that there would be like gradations of payment. The report was accepted and adopted by the General Conference.[12] Dr. Moreland was re-elected at this Session of the General Conference. He died prior to the meeting of the next quadrennial session. To replace him the Board of Bishops assigned Reverend L. W. Kyles, Editor of the A.M.E. Zion Quarterly Review.

At this, the Twenty-fifth Quadrennial Session of the General Conference, the Reverend C. S. Whitted was elected to the office.[13]

In the Twenty-sixth Quadrennial Session there appears to have been no written report for the Ministerial Brotherhood Department. A financial statement, however, does appear. The Bishops, in their message add this: "The establishment of the Relief Department in a regular way at our last session has proved to have been wise legislation. At no time in our past history have we been able to give our superannuated ministers, widows and orphans, the support that has been given them this quadrennium. This is very gratifying from every point of view. The law was so fixed that there accrues a larger revenue than ever before for this purpose, and we hope that nothing we do at this session will lessen the stipend now available." [14] Dr. Whitted was again elected to the Secretaryship, in 1920 and 1924.

Dr. Whitted was elected again to the office of Ministerial Relief and Brotherhood when the Twenty-eighth Quadrennial Session met in St. Louis, Mo. (1928). In August of the same year he passed away. At the Connectional Council the Board of Bishops announced the appointment of the Reverend Dr. Thomas W. Wallace as his successor.

Dr. Wallace received from the two accounts then open for this Department a total of $10.01 as he moved the headquarters to Washington, D. C. As the Secretary of the denomination went over the accounts a total shortage of $2,174.43 was discovered. There were "no assets from which we could recover." [15] Dr. Wallace in his

---

[12] *Ibid.*, 541.
[13] *Minutes of the Twenty-fifth Quadrennial Session* of the General Conference, 120.
[14] *Ibid, The Twenty-sixth Session* of the General Conference, 75.
[15] *Journal of the Twenty-ninth Quadrennial Session* of the General Conference (Pittsburgh, Pa. 1932), 159.

report stated that the bank "in which these amounts were ($10.01) deposited failed so nothing was brought over from the previous administrations." [16]

In his report Dr. Wallace stated that he, along with Bishop William Jacob Walls and Secretary Weeden had paid a visit to Barber Camp, a farm of 310 acres willed to the A.M.E. Zion Church for superannuated ministers, widows and orphans. While the property was well situated out from West Granville, Mass. nothing had been done to that time to fully utilize it. He recommended that a house be erected on acreage which would be open to any superannuated or retired minister who might care to take up residence there and that suitable facilities be provided for camping for the young people of the denomination. He suggested as well the establishment of a chatauqua for ministers and lay leaders and proposed that Summer meetings of Connectional Council be held there.[17] It should be stated that throughout his life, Dr. Wallace maintained a great interest in the Barber Camp property.

The Committee on Ministerial Brotherhood made some strong recommendations to this session of the General Conference, criticizing the lending of funds of the Department and insisting that amounts so allocated should be disbursed as intended. It suggested that the General Conference prohibit the Executive Secretary from doing so in the future. It likewise suggested that the Eighteen year Paid Up endowment policy be eliminated but this item was not approved by the Conference. It urged too, that "these Departments be kept separate and distinct from other departments." [18]

A companionate report from the Committee on Schools and Colleges recommended that "the property of Atkinson College at Madisonville, Ky., be used for an aged Ministers' Home." [19] This last matter evinced a comment from the General Secretary in the 1936 session when he labeled this "a wise act" but stated that the property was involved in heavy debt which had to be assumed and eventually liquidated by the Brotherhood and Relief Department.[20]

The Board of Bishops in their message of 1940 brought again the

---

[16] *Ibid.,* 203.
[17] *Journal of the Twenty-ninth Quadrennial Session* of the General Conference, 201.
[18] *Ibid.,* 226, 227.
[19] *Ibid.,* 227.
[20] *Journal of the Thirtieth Quadrennial Session of the General Conference* (Greensboro, N. C., 1936), 149.

matter of the Ministerial Brotherhood and Relief to the attention of the General Conference as it met in Washington, D. C. The message acknowledged that the Ministerial Brotherhood was merely a beginning and, at best, was inadequate. It went on to say "This Department under the direction of Dr. Thomas W. Wallace, has been able only to give a gesture in trying to meet the needs of the many calls of our wornout preachers and widows. It is a known fact that the small amount given to our disabled ministers is far inadequate for their needs." [21]

The message also called attention to the establishment, at the order of the General Conference, of the Home for the Superannuated Preachers at Madisonville, Ky. The Reverend C. C. Ellis was in charge. They could well have said few ministers appeared to request such services, however.

The re-vamping of the Brotherhood Department actually began in the sessions of 1940. Bishop W. C. Brown, who was vitally interested in an adequate insurance arrangement worked with the Committee which was chaired by the Reverend J. L. Black. The Reverend M. P. Sawyer was the chairman of the Committee on Ministerial Brotherhood. The Committee on Superannuated Ministers, Widows and Orphans reported favorably on Bishop Brown's Plan which had to do with an adequate Pension Service. They suggested that the Rev. David Bradley's proposed Pension Plan be turned over to the Board of Relief for investigation and study.[22] It does not appear that the report was adopted by the General Conference, except in its barest outlines, however.

The Thirty-first Quadrennial session again elected Dr. Thomas W. Wallace to the office of Home Missions and Relief. In September, 1942, he passed away and the Board of Bishops appointed Dr. Herbert Bell Shaw of the Cape Fear Conference to succeed him.

In Dr. Shaw's report to the Thirty-second Quadrennial Session of the General Conference meeting in Detroit, Michigan, the broad outlines of the proposed Pension Plan was revealed with the earnest suggestion that the Conference adopt it. Dr. Shaw said:

> The law set up in our "Book of Discipline," Paragraph 390, Page 201, states that there are two policies offered to our ministry;

---

[21] Proceedings of the Thirty-first Quadrennial Session of the General Conference (Washington, D. C. 1940), 88, 89.
[22] Ibid., 222.

Class A provides $100.00 at death. The annual fee for Class A is $5.00. Class B provides $50.00 at death. The fee is $2.50. In the Brotherhood Department we have paid all death claims as soon as they were filed according to our law.

The Commission on Pension Plan of which Bishop W. C. Brown is the Chairman, will offer a resolution for the merging of the Ministerial Brotherhood into an organization to be hereafter known as the Brotherhood Pension Service. The Plan is the very thing needed to assure our ministers not only of a death benefit but guarantees an income for our faithful preachers after their years of usefulness are over. The plan is simple and adequate. The minister pays $12.50 per year, and the church, churches, districts or departments he serves, pays the same amount. The Annual Conference shall pay one half of the annual dues for the Bishop. Under the provision of the Brotherhood Pension Service when the minister is retired he receives $25.00 per month or $300 per year for life. When death occurs the family of the deceased minister receives a death benefit of $100.00. Should the minister die before retirement his family receives a death benefit of $100.00. A double premium doubles all benefits. If we will enact this measure in this General Conference and cause it to be written in our Discipline, a new day will be heralded in Zion for our ministry.[23]

This proposal was accepted by the General Conference.[24]

The Thirty-third Quadrennial Session, meeting in Louisville, Ky (1948) made only slight changes in the law. For example, the Committee deemed it wise that the three Departments (Home Missions, Brotherhood, Pension Service) remain under "one Corresponding Secretary." They likewise voted that "retired ministers be relieved of responsibility of paying annual dues in the Brotherhood Pension Service." These changes, along with the recommendation of the Secretary that Mother's Day be retained as Pension Service Day when the local church would raise its share of the pension, were all accepted by the General Conference.[25]

In all, Dr. Shaw made fifteen recommendations regarding Home Missions, as well as proposing the second item in the Committee's report.

A most exhaustive report of the work of the Department was made to the Thirty-fourth Quadrennial Session which met in Brooklyn, New York by the Secretary, Herbert Bell Shaw. The report covers some seventy pages and concludes with fourteen recommendations in

---

[23] *Official Journal of the Thirty-second Quadrennial Session of the General Conference* (Detroit, 1944), 174.
[24] *The Doctrines and Discipline of the A.M.E. Zion Church*, 1944, 205-209.
[25] *Official Journal, Thirty-third Quadrennial Session of the General Conference* (Louisville, Ky., 1948), 289, 284.

the Home Missions Department, three in the Brotherhood Pension Service and a request for additional funds for the superannuated ministers in the Relief Department. A most significant note is made of the assertion that more than $143,000 was expended in the quadrennium for Home Missions alone. The Secretary also informed the Conference of the work at the Harriet Tubman Home, Auburn, New York and Barber Camp, West Granville, Mass.[26]

Two added notes should be made in connection with the Department. Agreeing with a resolution offered by the Board of Bishops, and Committee the Harriet Tubman Home was taken over by the Home Missions Department in 1948.[27] The Bishops stated of the Brotherhood Pension Service the following: "Bishop W. C. Brown is to be given credit for keeping before the Church the need of a pension plan during the quadrennium ending at the meeting at Detroit. So when the plan for merging the Ministerial Brotherhood, which only provided a death benefit, with the pension service was presented by Rev. H. B. Shaw it was accepted heartily. This plan promised to pay a death benefit to the families of our deceased ministers, and also a liberal pension to our retiring ministers. By order of the General Conference this organization was incorporated in the State of North Carolina in the year 1945. At the Connectional Council in Wilmington, N. C., 1947 the Secretary-Treasurer of this organization announced that they had on hand the amount of $100,000 for the Reserve Fund required by the State to guarantee the fulfillment of all promises made by the organization. All of this had been accomplished within the brief span of three years. This department announced that it would be ready to begin payment of pensions in the month of January, 1948. It was also announced that the policies of certificates of membership would be issued during the first part of the year. We are pleased to say to this General Conference that the Department of Brotherhood Pension Service has kept every one of its promises and today has in its treasury more than one hundred thousand dollars." [28]

Dr. Shaw was elected to the Episcopacy in May 1952 and was suc-

---

[26] *Official Journal of the Thirty-fourth Quadrennial Session of the General Conference* (Brooklyn, N. Y. 1952), 281-351.
[27] *Official Journal, Thirty-third Quadrennial Session,* 289.
[28] *Official Journal of the Thirty-third Quadrennial Session of the General Conference,* (Louisville, Ky., 1948), 312, 313.

ceeded in the office of Brotherhood Pension Service and Relief by the Reverend Dr. S. Seay.[29]

The Committee on Pension Service and Relief presented some recommendations with the understanding that before they could be placed into effect the State of North Carolina, under which the Department was incorporated, would have to agree. However, the General Conference suggested further study by the Committee with the results of their additional study to be reported at the Connectional Council.[30]

When the Thirty-fifth Quadrennial session of the General Conference met in Pittsburgh, Pennsylvania in May 1956, the Board of Bishops stated in their message the following:

> Your chief pastors have been put to the painful responsibility of removing from office, two general officers and the treasurer of an auxiliary within the reach of two years.
> It is a palpable fact that we had to become awakened to the trend towards breakdown in the honest administration and the faithfulness to duty in some of our departments. We share the regrets of the church that this climate has come upon us, but being the responsible group to execute the laws and regulate the affairs of our Zion, your chief pastors found it seriously imperative to take corrective action. Using the due process of our law, we exhausted all the methods of dealing in these departmental matters, through investigation and exhaustive trial, in order to reach our conclusions. And we found that we could no longer face you with an excuse for continuing conditions that would bring the church to greater calamity. We therefore moved from office two officials whose departments showed gross irregularities in handling the funds, that had left serious losses of our people's hard-earned and sacrificial money, that could not be accounted for by the officers.
> In one case, the person was dealt with by civil law which went beyond our authorization, but this was found necessary by the banks and bonding company before the accounts could be protected. No member of the Board of Bishops and no one else issued any indictment for the church. However, this whole matter was brought on by the unfaithfulness of the officer whom we were forced to dismiss.[31]

Elsewhere in their statement the Board of Bishops said: "The Board of Bishops brings to the attention of the delegates of this General Conference that we are solely responsible for the type of persons we elect to fill these very important offices. Your Bishops feel that persons elected to these General Offices should have some previous training to fit them

---

[29] *Official Journal, Thirty-fourth Quadrennial Session of the General Conference* (Brooklyn, N.Y., 1952), 76.

[30] *Ibid.*, 79, 80.

[31] Official Journal Thirty-fifth Quadrennial Session of the General Conference (Pittsburgh, Pa., 1956), 49.

THE DEPARTMENTS AND THEIR DEVELOPMENT

for the heavy and exacting responsibilities that shall be theirs, if and when elected." [32]

The Certified Public Accountant Audit of the Brotherhood Pension, Home Missions and Relief was presented and portions read by the Acting Secretary, Bishop Herbert Bell Shaw "who supervised the departments for the past six months." A statement re: the matter was made by Bishop Brown after which the report was, on motion of Rev. James A. Clement, referred to the Special Committee handling the matter.[33]

After several ballots the Reverend Dr. A. P. Morris was elected to the office of Brotherhood Pension, Home Missions, and Relief.[34] On motion of Mrs. Willie Alstork the office was to be located in Charlotte, North Carolina.

When Dr. Morris made his first quadrennial report in 1960 he suggested that an auxiliary of Ministers' wives and widows be organized in each local church and district that the sums distributed to the widows and children of ministers would be substantially increased. The four years prior to 1964 would be utilized in building these additional moneys with quarterly disbursements to begin June 1, 1964. At the same time he recommended an increase in Home Missions Funds with concentration to begin in "certain areas." Present premiums of $25.00 and $50.00 would be considered minimum payments with the ministers requested to pay five per cent of their salaries into the Pension Service. This would allow for increased pension benefits. After June 1, 1964, if this system were to be accepted the minister would receive on retirement, the usual sum of $25.00 or $50.00, depending on the class, plus 1% for each year's service above the basic amount. Retirement would be allowed after the age of 70 or after 35 year's service.[35] It is not clear as to that which happened to these recommendations but it appears that they are not a part of the Discipline issued for that General Conference so it is assumed that they were not accepted.

In the 1964 Quadrennial session the Secretary requested increased sums for Home Missions and Pensions and Relief. The amount appropriated fell $15,000 short of his asking, and while the requested 10% was given (and more, 10.8%) for Pension and Relief, it was scattered through five areas: Ministerial Relief, Superannuated ministers (who now would receive $150.00 per year), Bishops' widows, Ministers' widows (at $120.00 per year), Pension supplement, and Ministers' minimum salary.[36] Dr. Morris was re-elected in 1968.

Where the Home Missions Department is concerned, the Board of Bishops recommended that it be attached to the Brotherhood, Pension Service and Relief (as it is now designated) in their Message

---
[32] Official Journal of the Thirty-fifth Quadrennial Session, 59.
[33] *Ibid.*, 119.
[34] *Ibid.*, 124.
[35] *Official Journal of the Thirty-sixth Quadrennial Session of the General Conference,* 319, 320.
[36] *Official Journal of the Thirty-seventh Quadrennial Session of the General Conference,* 546.

to the General Conference of 1932 at Pittsburgh, Pa.[87] The Committee on Elimination and Consolidation agreed and the report was adopted.[38]

Forty per cent of the Budget of the Woman's Home and Foreign Missionary Society goes to this Department for Home Missions, amounting, under the present budget, to $40,000.

Bishop E. D. W. Jones, in his listing of Home Missions Secretaries omits the name of Samuel Madison Dudley, which should have been carried.

THE A.M.E. ZION HISTORICAL SOCIETY

The formation of a Historical Society or some type of organization to safe-guard the founding and development of the denomination may have come to the attention of the General Conference in prior years to its first official mentioning by Bishop William Jacob Walls, but no reference to this effect can be found at this time. As a result the Church appears to have suffered along many lines because of the delay. To the credit of those of the past it should be indicated that one marvels at their meticulous manner in which minutes were kept or published, even though, and this is self-evident, financial concerns were a constant companion of the conferences and the General Conference. To them, we owe far more than can be stated as with limited means they preserved that which they could.

The General Conference was meeting in historic St. Paul Church, Detroit (now the Metropolitan Church edifice) when the following took place:

> Bishop Walls moved that a non-salaried historian be appointed for the time being until plans can be worked out. The motion was seconded by Senator Brokenburr. The Reverend H. R. Jackson stated that because of the importance of the position, a salary should be paid. Bishop Walls expressed himself as agreeable to this if a plan could be worked out for compensation. The motion was adopted. Bishop Martin moved that Dr. R. E. Clement be elected head of the Society. Seconded by Rev. J. W. I. Tunstall. The motion prevailed.[39]

The motion which was passed as noted was occasioned by the reading of a resolution on the History of the A.M.E. Zion Church. In or-

---

[87] *Minutes of the Twenty-ninth Quadrennial Session of the General Conference*, (Pittsburgh, Pa., 1932), 245.
[38] *Ibid.*, 238.
[39] *Official Journal of the Thirty-second Quadrennial Session, General Conference*, 58.

der to understand the matter the resolution was again read following discussion in which Bishop Walls spoke. It had been offered by the Reverend Dr. James Clair Taylor who "made it clear what prompted him to write it." Others speaking on the resolution were: Dr. W. J. Trent, and Rev. S. S. Seay.

In this session of the General Conference a resolution to provide $5,000 to Bishop Walls for the writing of the History of the Church was voted down.[40] No further action was taken on the subject it appears, until 1956 when the Rev. David H. Bradley submitted the following resolution:

1. In order that valuable historical records and history of the denomination may be maintained, the General Conference shall establish a Historical Department in which shall be gathered the original minutes of the several Annual Conferences, the said Minute Books to be turned over periodically by the Conference Secretaries.
2. The General Conference shall further direct the maintenance at a place designated, of Annual and General Conference Minutes or copies, published books and pamphlets of interest to the denomination, and of any other work which may have a bearing on Denominational, Church or Annual Conference history.
3. A Secretary of this Historical Department shall be elected and shall hold office for four years or until his successor is elected. He shall devote at least half-time to this service. He shall report semi-annually to the Board of Bishops, annually to the Connectional Council and every four years to the General Conference.
4. The General Conference shall provide a budget whereby the Secretary of the Historical Department shall be able to maintain an office, travel, purchase aforementioned books or pamphlets, provide the Annual Conferences with a standard Minute book suited for filing, and he shall maintain reasonable relationships with the International and World Methodist Historical Society.
5. Any pamphlets or books written or edited by the Secretary of the Historical Department shall be the copyrighted property of the denomination provided the denomination assumes responsibility either through the General Conference, the Board of Bishops or the Connectional Council. If neither group takes action within one year after completion of any manuscript, permission may be granted for private publication.[41]

With the acceptance of the resolution it should be noted that the Ministers' and Laymen's Association, meeting in Durham, North Carolina had endorsed this establishment of the Historical Depart-

---

[40] *Official Journal of the Thirty-second Quadrennial Session,* 58.
[41] *Official Journal, Thirty-fifth Quadrennial Session, General Conference,* 460, 120.

ment and so assured its passage. The General Conference likewise approved a budget of $1,250 per year for the work, plus one-half salary of a General Officer. The Rev. David H. Bradley was elected as Secretary of the reconstituted Society and re-elected in each session to date (1968), the office carrying one-half a General Officer's salary.

The matter of a low budget has prevented this Department from fulfilling its over-all intent but at least a beginning has been made to collect and preserve historical facts and records of the Church.

THE PUBLIC RELATIONS AND SOCIAL SERVICE DEPARTMENT

No mention of Public Relations and Social Service appears to exist in official documents of the Church prior to 1944, especially as the duties were outlined for the General Secretary of that year. Just how much discussion developed in the next four years may not be known but the discussions had developed to the point that the General Conference took some action at that time. The sessions convened in Louisville, Kentucky at the time and the Board of Bishops suggested: "We recommend that a Public Relations Department and Social Action Committee be established, and that a means of operation be determined by the General Conference." [42] The General Conference assigned this suggestion to the proper committee and the following resulted:

BUREAU OF STATISTICS AND PUBLIC RELATIONS

In view of the need of accurate records and statistics; and in view of the need of a medium by which the voice and influence of the Church might be heard and felt in public affairs; and because these times demand that the Church speak out more accurately and forcefully than ever before: we recommend the establishment of a Bureau of Statistics and Public Relations and the duties of this department be performed by the General Secretary, who shall be made a full-time General Officer.

The General Conference sustained the concurrence of the Committee.[43]

---

[42] *Official Journal of the Thirty-third Quadrennial Session of the General Conference,* 320.
[43] *Ibid.,* 290.

THE DEPARTMENTS AND THEIR DEVELOPMENT

To undergird this recommendation and change in the duties of the General Secretary the General Conference appropriated 1% of the denominational budget.

The sense of the importance of these new tasks, however, was such that four years later, in 1952, the Committee stated as follows:

> RESOLUTION, ESTABLISHING SEPARATE PUBLIC RELATIONS DEPT.
> We feel that the results received from the present Public Relations Department setup is inadequate compared with the amount of money spent for that purpose during the last quadrennium ($3,000.00 per year or $12,000.00 per quadrennium.)
> We feel that the General Secretary and Auditor has so much other connectional responsibilities that he is unable to do a Public Relations job commensurate with the progressive needs of the great African Methodist Episcopal Zion Church.
>
> RESOLUTION:
> Be it resolved that a Public Relations Commissioner be elected by this General Conference—a part-time officer—who shall not be the Secretary-Auditor of the Church and that he be given the amount of $3,000.00 per year, for the operation of the department, whose report shall be made to the Board of Bishops, Connectional Council and General Conference as all other General Officers.

The General Conference referred the matter to the Board of Bishops for action.[44]

At the Connectional Council meeting in Boston, Mass., the Board of Bishops appointed the Reverend J. W. Findley (August, 1952) to the office of Director of Public Relations. He established an office in Mother Zion Church and began setting up the department. He reported to the General Conference of 1956, as the resolution stated.[45]

The Committee on Revision reported the following on May 14th, during the sessions of General Conference (the Rev. Dr. Felix S. Anderson, Chairman):

> Mr. Chairman, Bishops, General Officers, and delegates to the thirty-fifth session of the General Conference:
> *Whereas:* we have received the report of the Public Relations Officer separated for several years of this quadrennium, and having given satisfactory service in publishing the activities, functions, and projects of the A.M.E. Zion Church.

---

[44] *Official Journal, Thirty-fourth Quadrennial Session of the General Conference,* 399.
[45] *Official Journal, Thirty-fifth Quadrennial Session,* 1956, 395-399 incl.

Be It Resolved: That the Public Relations Department shall become the Public Relations and Social Service with regular office.

Rev. Felix S. Anderson
John F. Sawyer
Daniel F. Martinez
Andrades L. Brown

The General Conference agreed with the Committee. As a result Mr. Alexander Barnes was elected to the office at that session and has continued in office since (1968).

CHAPTER XII

The Departments and Their Development
PERIODICALS

THE LATE Mrs. Dancy Reid had in her possession some of the most valuable records of the A. M. E. Zion Church, among them being several copies of Minutes of the North Carolina Annual Conference. In these Minutes the development of two great institutions of the denomination is noted: Zion Wesley Institute, later Livingstone College and the early beginnings of the Star of Zion, the weekly paper of the Church.

Were it not for another great source of our early History, John Jamison Moore, little would be known of the middle period of the Church, including the beginning of the Star. Moore states that, as with many other movements, the New York Conference saw the early need of a periodical. Their beginning efforts evidently are first noted in the Annual session of 1841 when the following action was taken:

> *Whereas,* a connectional Journal is indespensible as a proper exponent and advocate of our connectional interests; therefore be it Resolved, That a committee of three be appointed from this body, to draft a prospectus for a connectional newspaper; which paper shall be named the *Zion Wesley;*
> *Resolved,* That said committee be authorized to issue monthly the said paper, as soon as sufficient number of subscribers can be obtained to justify the publishing of it; with the concurrence of the Philadelphia Conference, the first sheet to contain the prospectus.

According to Moore the committee named was composed of the following men: Jehial C. Beaman, Jacob D. Richardson and Nathan Blunt.[1]

In addition to this enabling group of resolutions the following also was passed by the Conference:

> *Resolved,* That each preacher be required to act as an agent for the paper, and that he remit monthly to the Senior Superintendent or Bishop the subscription money, the concluding resolution only to apply to the N. Y. Conference.

---
[1] John Jamison Moore, *History of the A.M.E. Zion Church* (York, Penna., 1884), 333, 334.

Accordingly, the Philadelphia Annual Conference passed the following Resolution:

> *Resolved,* That the Philadelphia conference concur with the New York Conference on the subject of the publication of a paper for our connection.
> *Resolved,* That a committee of three be appointed from the conference to confer with the New York Committee on the subject of publishing a paper.
> The following persons were appointed: David Stevens, G. Galbreath and L. Collins.

Evidently the venture as seen by the New York Conference was not successful, for it appears that Moore believes the next venture was to be made through the General Conference in 1860. While the writer has little to substantiate the assertion, this appears to have been an oversight on Moore's part, for the Minutes of the Philadelphia Conference do mention another venture in which this body appeared at first to be interested. The following resolution was passed in the session of 1848: Resolved, That the Conference cannot support the paper published in Pittsburg called the *Mystery,* as it has become a party paper.[2]

Wording here enters the picture in that the Conference recognized that at one time it could lend its support to the paper.

The Mystery was first published in Pittsburgh, Pennsylvania in the early part of 1843, five years prior to the action of the Philadelphia Conference. Edited by Major Martin R. Delaney, this weekly, like many other race enterprises, was born out of necessity since actually there was no voice for the Negro insofar as the press was concerned. Since few if any papers printed either news, comments or complaints of Negroes, they had a difficult time being *heard* in the communities and nation. This kept many of them from finding a favorable climate for progress.

It should be said that survival of these enterprises was always a question for three basic reasons. Funds to underwrite their establishment was often lacking. Many of these early efforts had to be financially fostered by one person, the owner and very often, the Editor. Then, too, the fact that reading was not a common art made purchase of copies, once they were off the press, a trying problem. Literary talent was limited in many instances. All these handicaps

---

[2] *Minutes of the Philadelphia Annual Conference,* 1848, 19.

had to be faced and overcome. Block support of churches, therefore, was desirable, for, as in the case of the Philadelphia Conference, thirty-four congregatons would be reached through its endorsement.[3] The New York Conference had approximately 54 congregations at the time.[4]

Major Delaney had ability, and placed his own money into the launching of *The Mystery*, yet he could keep it going only nine months with these resources. After that time he had to resort to a joint stock Company of six others, while he retained the Editorship.[5]

It is said that due to Delaney's *editorial influence* the Avery Fund was given. In Garland Penn's book the following appear:

> He (Delaney) was the only editor from 1827 to '70, to our knowledge, who was ever arrested for what his enemies would term libel; certainly he was the first. A verdict of guilt was rendered in the suit for libel, and he was fined. Mr. Delaney stood well with his newspaper friends. They were loud in praises of his and his editorial work; and upon the occasion of the suit for libel, this was fully exemplified, for as soon as they found out that the court had fined him, they proceeded immediately to start a subscription paper to pay the fine. Happily, it had been remitted and the money was not needed.
>
> Mr. Delaney was a physician of great skill. He was among the first Afro-Americans to graduate from Harvard College. . . . He died January 24, 1885.[6]

Penn goes on to state that *The Mystery* suspended publication in 1847, one year prior to the action of the Philadelphia Conference which evidently was an effort on the part of its owners to revive it.

The next reference Moore makes to the undertaking of a periodical within the denomination is confusing. He states: "the subject was again brought before the General Conference in 1860"[7] It is not clear as to that which he intends to say or convey here. Does he mean that the bringing of the matter before the two Annual Conferences was considered the first such conversation, and when this failed it was brought before the General Conference? In the light of the fact that the General Conference Minutes are not before us we have no way of clearing this situation.

---

[3] *Minutes of the Philadelphia Conference, A.M.E. Zion Church,* 1850, 7.
[4] *Minutes of the New York Conference, A.M.E. Zion Church,* 1850, 22, 23.
[5] I. Garland Penn, *The Afro-American Press and Its Editors* (Springfield, Mass., 1891), 56.
[6] Penn, *loc. cit.*, 56, 57.
[7] Moore, *loc. cit.*, 325.

At the General Conference of 1860 action on a periodical took the form of the following resolutions:

Resolved, That some plan be adopted to start a monthly periodical for the benefit of the connection.

Having taken this action the General Conference went on to state:

Whereas, A paper has been started in this city, entitled the *Weekly Anglo-African,* and said paper being devoted to the interest and general good of our people; therefore

Resolved, That we as a body in General Conference, will give it our hearty cooperation and support, recommending it to our respective charges as the proper organ of our people, it being worthy of the highest regard and merits the influence of every minister of the connection.[8]

According to Penn, Thomas Hamilton (who earlier had been connected with the People's Press, founded in 1843) launched the *Anglo-African* sometime around 1859, its first number appearing July 23 of that year. This coincides with the action of the 1860 General Conference. Hamilton was sole owner but evidently his brother Robert aided him with the work of the paper. Frederick Douglass said of it, "It had more promise, and more journalistic ability about it than any of the other papers." At the time the most respected Negro Journalist was Douglass, Negro papers vying for his assistance in editorial work.

Penn goes on to say: "The Anglo-African was a large sheet of four pages, with seven columns to a page. These were larger than ordinary newspaper columns." It was published every Saturday at 43 Beekman Street, New York City, and sold for $2.00 per year, four cents per copy. According to Penn it was a very respectable paper: "We will not venture the opinion that it was the best paper published, but we will say it was the largest." He continues: "The great feature of the Anglo-African was that it did not seek to make itself a paper whose matter should originate in the Hamilton family alone; and some of its contributors were known to embrace the best Afro-American talent of those days; the result being a genuine Afro-American newspaper."[9]

---

[8] Moore, *loc. cit.,* 325, quoting from the General Conference Journal of 1860, 66, 122, 126.
[9] Penn, *loc. cit.,* 84.

The motto of the Anglo-African, a common practice of the papers of the time, was: "Men must be free; if not through the law, then above the law."

It is understood that Thomas Hamilton continued to edit the Anglo-African until it was purchased by James Redpath, an Abolitionist. It was then styled the *Weekly Anglo-African* for a short time and finally its name was changed to the *Pine and Palm*. In 1861 the paper reverted again into the hands of the Hamilton family, this time, Robert Hamilton, since Thomas had died. It increased in size and aggressiveness as it added to its staff Henry Highland Garnett who was in charge of the *Southern Department* of the paper.

Later, headquarters were moved to 50 Beekman Street and then to 184 Church Street. William G. Hamilton, son of the former owner, became associated with the work and this, too strengthened the paper as he worked as Business Manager. Penn states that the *Anglo-African* lived to see the Afro-American a "free man" and "on the march to an intellectual position." [10] It should be stated that the paper was later changed back to its original name, The Anglo-African from *Pine and Palm*.

In the General Conference of 1864 the following was ordered:

> *Whereas,* The paper known as the *Anglo-African* has been used by members of this connection as a medium of communication for several years in the interest of our church; therefore Resolved, That it is the duty of each minister to labor for the increase of its circulation, as well for the interest of our connection as for the paper;
> *Resolved,* That a committee be appointed by the chairman to consult with the editor to the end of gaining information in regard to purchasing a press.

The following committee was appointed: W. F. Butler, R. H. G. Dyson, J. W. Hood, J. H. Smith, B. Pulpress, J. J. Smith.[11]

According to Moore, between this General Conference (1864) and the next session (1868), the trustees of Zion's Church in New York "and some laymen" began work on a weekly paper. At the time the Reverend Singleton T. Jones was the pastor and became the religious editor. William Howard Day was the secular editor. The paper was called the *Zion Standard and Weekly Review*. Two other

---
[10] Penn, *loc. cit.,* 87, 88.
[11] Minutes of the General Conference of 1864.

members of Zion's Church were charged with the business arrangements for the paper: Samuel Howard and M. B. Coss. Moore states that at the General Conference of 1868 the type, printing press and debts were all turned over to the General Conference. The report of the Committee of the Conference is herewith given:

I. Report of the Committee on *Zion Standard.*
The Committee on *Zion Standard* respectfully submits the following for adoption by the General Conference: We find the whole amount due to the Trustees of Zion Church of New York, as $8,749, and we recommend the General Conference to assume the debt, and take possession of the paper on the 1st day of June, 1868.

M. B. Coss, Sec'y.   J. P. Thompson, Pres.

II. Report of the Committee on *Zion Standard*
The committee respectfully states that of the amount due to Zion Church of New York, she will donate to the General Conference $4,500, upon the fulfillment of the following conditions namely:
That the conference pay $1,200 cash, $1,000 in six months, and $2,000 in two years from the first installment, making the total amount to be paid $4,200. Your committee recommends that we take the paper upon the above condition.

M. B. Coss, Sec'y.   Jos. P. Thompson, Pres.

On the recommendation of the committee the following action was taken by the General Conference:

III. Report of the Committee on *Zion Standard*
The purchase of the paper: We the members of the General Conference of the A. M. E. Zion Church, now in session in the City of Washington, District of Columbia, May 20, 1868, do hereby promise and agree, and have now entered upon that agreement with the Trustees of the A. M. E. Zion Church, New York City, for the purchase of *Zion Standard and Weekly Review,* of the said city, now the property of the said Trustees; to purchase the said paper with all its appurtenances (all its outstanding debts, obligations or encumbrance excepted) from the 1st of June, 1868 for the sum of $8,750. The said corporation of said church, the second party of the above contract, agree upon the fulfillment of the said terms, that is to unite upon signing this agreement; the first party of the contract, the General Conference of the A. M. E. Zion Church, do promise to pay the said corporation, of the second part, the sum of $600, and the further sum of $600 on the 1st of August, 1868, and the further sum of $1,000 on February 1869 and the further sum of $2,000 on June 1st, 1870 with interest at seven per cent, except the last payment of $2,000 which is to be without interest. We the parties of the second part, Trustees of the A. M. E. Zion Church corporation, do bind ourselves, and suces-

sors in office, to fully comply with the terms of this agreement, and to donate to the conference the sum of $4,550 out of the $8,750 mentioned in the contract of purchase. Signed, sealed, and delivered in behalf of the General Conference.

M. B. Coss, Sec'y.   J. P. Thompson, Pres.

IV. Report of Committee on Editor of *Zion Standard*
Your committee recommend: 1st That the Editor receive $1,200 for one year; 2nd, That he pay his clerk and office hire out of his salary; 3rd, That he have the business management of the paper, subject to the advice and control of the following named Board of Managers: J. P. Thompson, Elder of Zion Church, New York; W. H. Decker, G. H. Washington and Jacob Thomas.

M. B. Coss, Secretary[12]

It will be recalled that Singleton T. Jones had been elected to the Bishopric so was no longer pastor of Zion Church. Moore utilizes a peculiar statement as he notes the above. He writes: "From this action of the General Conference in the purchase of the paper its fate was soon sealed and soon the *Zion Standard and Weekly Review* was defunct, leaving the connection without an organ." [13]

The Reverend William Howard Day did not come to the project at Mother Zion Church without experience in journalism. While in Cleveland, Ohio he had edited (1852) *The Alienated American* "after he had graduated from Oberlin in 1847" [14] Again this was one of the Freedom Journals, serving the cause of the Anti-Slavery movement. The publication was suspended while Prof. Day was in England, (1856-1857).

Between the years, 1868 and 1872 Moore states that the Reverends Jacob P. Hamer and J. E. Price put out another paper called the *Zion Church Advocate*. While both Hood and Moore mention this venture, Bishop Hood states that Jacob B. Trusty was also involved along with others.[15]

Both these writers (Hood and Moore) agree that the venture was turned over to the General Conference in 1872 or 1876. Hood again states that since the Minutes of 1876 were never published "we have only memory to rely upon." The General Conference accepted the paper and William Howard Day was made editor. Bishop Hood makes two statements which have a tinge of humor. Regarding this

---

[12] *Minutes of the General Conference of* 1868.
[13] Moore, *loc. cit.*, 328, 329.
[14] Penn, *loc. cit.*, 74, 75.
[15] Moore, *loc. cit.*, 329, J. W. Hood, One Hundred Years of the African Methodist Episcopal Zion Church (New York, 1895), 108.

venture he intimates that each minister was to pledge $4.50, "the price of three copies per year; but for some cause not a copy was issued after the General Conference." [16]

The earlier statement which has a bit of humor has to do with the *Zion Standard and Weekly Review*. Of this publication Hood writes: "The collapse was so complete that the record of the succeeding General Conference contains no mention of it." [17] Three numbers of the Zion Standard were finally issued.

While Hood alludes to the Minutes of 1876 as not having been published he must have meant as well, 1872, for it appears that the writers are not in agreement on the date of this venture. Moore says that the *Zion Church Advocate* was offered in 1872. Hood gives the date as 1876. In this he may have been right for the below was given in 1877.

Bishop Hood was a very careful person when it came to the obligation of reporting the happenings to his annual conferences. So before his North Carolina Conference he makes the following statement:

CHURCH ORGAN

I have frequently urged the inportance of an organ through which the church could speak to all the world and tell whatever is important for the world to know. The General Conference at its last session attempted to establish a journal, but the effort proved a failure. Your money deposited with the Secretary at the last Conference was sent to the Editor, since which we have received no paper from that source. Tired of being harassed by persons who had sent their money and could get no paper, I went to New Berne and arranged with Brother Tyler for the publication of a paper. The Star of Zion is the result of that effort. While this paper was started to supply a need resulting from the failure of the *Zion Church Advocate*, its grand success has stamped it as a permanent organ of the connection, whatever may be the success of other emterprises. Let us make it a power in this land—a star so bright that no cloud can hide the beauty of its days.

The selection of the name *The Star of Zion*, should recall to all members of the denomination the work of one of her local preachers from the New Bedford, Massachusetts Church, who began his career as a public speaker from that church's pulpit. Perhaps the greatest Negro Abolitionist of them all, Frederick Douglass later moved to the City of Rochester, New York and there, it is said, in the Church now styled the Memorial A.M.E. Zion Church, edited his famed paper, *The North Star*. Its first edition was issued November 1, 1847.

---

[16] Hood, *loc. cit.*, 108.
[17] *Ibid*.

Penn states, for example, that *The North Star* was a new era in the black man's literature. It found its way into American homes regardless of color. So well did it carry the standard of its Editor that it was styled Fredrick Douglass' paper.

Bishop Hood put down the first $5.00 for the Star of Zion and from this beginning the people of the Church were asked to subscribe $1 per month until it was self-sustaining. Hood states that "about twenty-five persons responded." At least $30.00 was needed per month to keep the paper in business.

The response of the North Carolina Conference to the Bishop's move is recorded as follows:

REPORT OF THE COMMITTEE ON CHURCH ORGAN
Whereas: The General Conference in its effort to establish a connectional organ did hereby show the great necessity for the same: and Whereas, The plan fixed upon the General Conference has thus far been a failure,
Resolved, That we, the members of the North Carolina Conference do agree to perpetuate the plan and intention of the said General Conference by a hearty support of the paper gotten up through the wisdom of Right Rev. J. W. Hood and edited by. Rev. J. A. Tyler with artistic skill through the unshrinking love and zeal he has for the advancement of the Kingdom of our Lord Jesus Christ and the cause of our beloved Zion; and Whereas, This is the first time the Southern portion of the connection has ever attempted to establish a paper, and a paper is much needed in our midst, therefore,
Resolved, That every minister of this Conference be urged to take the paper himself and become an agent to solicit subscribers for the same,
And
Whereas, Elder J. A. Tyler has been so faithful in editing and upholding and continuing the paper until the sitting of the Conference,
Resolved, That the members of this Conference do pay the sum of $25 by way of respect.
Resolved, That we do pledge ourselves to maintain and support, in all honorable ways, the paper above mentioned, known as the Star of Zion.

                              Respectfully submitted,
                              H. C. Phillips
                              J. McNeil Farley
                              J. W. Davis
                              E. S. Rieves
                              Committee[18]

These North Carolina Conference Minutes were cherished possessions of Mrs. Dancy Reid of Salisbury, N. C.

[18] *Minutes of the North Carolina Conference* of 1877.

The action of the General Conference to which the North Carolina Conference referred was based on the report of the Committee on the Journal. Their report follows:

> To the Bishops and members of the General Conference of the A. M. E. Zion Connection. Fathers and Brethren: Your committee on Journal, or Church Organ, respectfully report that they have carefully considered the matter relative to the subject placed in their hands, and recommend the following:
> 1. The establishment as soon as possible of a Journal or Organ of the connection, with as little outlay of money as possible, consistent with making it efficient upon the plan marked "A" and submitted to the conference.
> 2. That the Journal be kept separate from the Book Concern, as far as its sustenance is concerned. 3. That this General Conference, or the Bishops elect a Religious Editor, to assist in carrying out the editorial portion of this plan, and edit said journal as soon as practicable. 4. That each delegation present elect now for the Annual Conference which they represent, and elect annually an assistant editor to represent that conference in the editorial conduct of the journal. 5. That we recommend the establishment and publication of a Sunday-School paper, to be named the A. M. E. Zion Sunday-School Banner, under the auspices of the A. M. E. Zion Connection, at as early a date and as cheap as possible, the International Lessons forming a feature of the Sunday School Journal. 6. That to make this work a success each elder or preacher in charge of a circuit or station, throughout the extent of our connection, shall personally carry out the 13th article of the plan, viz: to subscribe and pay for two copies, at least, of the journal, at $2.25 per copy each year in advance. If this be not done, a good reason should be shown at the Annual Conference, of which the Conference shall be the judge. 7. That the editor or publisher, elected by the General Conference, or the Bishops, shall also be held amenable to his Quarterly, Annual or General Conference for dereliction of duty in connection with this work. 8. That the members of this conference, and other ministers and friends present, be offered an opportunity to subscribe either for the paper or the stock, or for both, before we finally adjourn.
>
> Respectfully submitted on behalf of Committee,
William T. Biddle, Secretary
William Howard Day, Chairman

The Plan "A" mentioned in the report is listed as follows; as it was presented by William Howard Day, the Chairman:

> To the Rt. Rev. J. J. Moore, and Board of Bishops of the A. M. E. Zion Church in America:
> Plan for establishing a newspaper which shall also be the general organ of the A. M. E. Zion Connection:
> 1. Name: *Our National Standard*

2. The place of publication: At Harrisburg, Pa., with other places suggested. See Conference Journal, 284.

3. The character of the paper: A weekly home journal of the North, South, East and West.

4. Motto: Mind constitutes the majesty of man, or taking the motto from the Burning Bush, *nec tamen:* Not yet consumed

5. Size of paper: During the first year five or six columns on each page; second year seven columns.

6. Departments of paper: Educational, religious, including church news; political, defending the rights of the people; industrial, local, etc.

7. Editors: Educational editor-in-chief, religious editor-in-chief, with assistants in every Annual Conference; local editors for general news in every part of every state in the Union, etc: conferences, conventions, and general important meetings to be specially reported; the religious editor-in-chief always to be named by the General Conference or the Board of Bishops, to whom he shall be subject.

8. Stock of paper: Ten thousand shares (10,000).

9. How owned: One half or five thousand shares to be offered to and to be owned in the interest of the connection, and one-half to be offered and owned outside of the church interest, the connection to have the privilege of purchasing the whole ten thousand shares if so desired.

10. Value of shares: Each share valued at par at five ($5.00) dollars making the value of the stock fifty thousand dollars.

11. After expenses are paid, at the close of each paper year, a dividend interest of six per cent shall be paid, or as large an amount as the business will justify.

12. Control of the paper: Each share shall count as one vote in the choice of trustees or business board and in all questions of general business, but the connection shall be entitled to two members of the Board of Control or directors at all times, and more, including these two in proportion to the shares of church stock held.

13. Each elder or preacher in charge throughout the connection to subscribe and pay for two copies at least in his circuit or station in the interest of the connection each year.

14. The Board of Control or Directors shall consist of thirteen members, five of whom shall be a quorum to transact business.

15. For the present, two pages of the paper to be devoted to church matters and religious news, subsequently one half of the paper.

16. No one to be responsible for any debts beyond the par value of his or her share or stock.

Respectfully submitted,
Wm. Howard Day

The General Conference accepted in full the plan as outlined. Moore states, however, that "the plan failed in it application on account of many of its operators' apathy and their not conforming with its requirements."[19] William Howard Day was made Editor-in-Chief with an assistant from every annual conference.

The three issues of the paper which finally appeared did not make a sufficient impression on the times to be long remembered so there appears to be no record of them except the brief statement of Bishop Hood who acknowledges that "Since the above (a statement of complaint made) was written we have learned that three numbers were issued, and the amount sent from North Carolina being all that was sent, was thus used up."[20]

Moore acknowledges that the members of the General Conference returned home "with high hopes." He believes that an effort was made to increase circulation and enthusiasm was high. Bishop Hood concurred in this feeling.

When Bishop Hood reported on the periodical at the 1880 General Conference he told again how the delegates had gone home from the last General Conference with high hopes that the Connectional Journal was at last underway. Some funds for example, had been given prior to adjournment. Much more had been promised but no paper made its appearance. Evidently Elder Tyler was the North Carolina representative for he had taken the lead in getting subscribers so when the paper was not forthcoming the Bishop stated that he "was pretty roughly handled." In order to quiet many of the protesting people Elder (later Bishop) C. R. Harris placed subscriptions with The *Weekly Witness,* paying the amounts out of his own pocket. The Bishop with Reverend Tyler took action on the matter and the Star of Zion was the result. He reported:

> A number of circulars were sent out, asking persons to pay a dollar a month for the support of a monthly paper until it should become self-sustaining.
> It is regretted that the circulars were not sent to more persons at first, but it was an oversight at the time. Much effort has been made since to increase the number of stockholders, but not much has been accomplished in that direction.

The Bishop stated that The Star *has been continued,* a press has been purchased, all conducted by the members of the Annual Conference. He gave credit to Elders Tyler, Moore, Harris and Pettey.[21]

---

[19] Moore, *loc. cit.,* 333.
[20] Hood, *loc. cit.,* 108, footnote.
[21] Daily Journal of the Sixteenth Quadrennial Session of the General Conference (Montgomery, Ala., 1880), 13, 14.

THE DEPARTMENTS AND THEIR DEVELOPMENT

The report of the Committee on Press recommended the purchase of the North Carolina Conference project.[22] Evidently, too, the Reverend J. A. Tyler was continued in office for the next four years since it is noted that he is listed as the Editor of the Star of Zion in the Minutes of the session. Trusteees for the Star of Zion were appointed and the General Conference proceeded to elect Reverend J. A. Tyler as Editor. He, however, refused "except he could be assured that he would receive a salary." Mr. A. S. Richardson was therefore elected.[23] The nine trustees provided for to govern the paper, and who were supposed to have been listed in the appendix, cannot be noted.

According to Moore, Cicero R. Harris was considered the publisher or manager of The Star. At first it was evidently published in Charlotte and later moved to Concord, N.C. and more recently, Salisbury, N.C.

Richardson either gave up the Editorship or, in reviewing the work, the Board of Bishops meeting in Chester, South Carolina in 1882, saw a need for a change. They, therefore appointed the Reverend J. McH. Farley, who became both Editor and publisher. The paper was then removed to Petersburg, Va. Two years later, Reverend Farley purchased a new press and type at "a cost of seven hundred dollars." [24]

The Report of the Committee on The Star of Zion in 1884 was very encouraging to the General Conference. In part the report said:

> We recommend that The Star of Zion receive the cordial and unwavering support of every minister and member of the Zion connection.
> We recommend that an editor, or an associate editor be elected to contribute editorials upon the leading questions of the day, for the benefit of the paper's many readers.
> We recommend that the bill of the Rev. J. McH. Farley, for $40.94, for amount furnished out of his own means, for the benefit of The Star be allowed.
> We recommend that some arrangements be made, whereby The Star and Zion's Banner can be consolidated, so that the influence of the entire connection con be exerted in behalf of one organ.
> We further recommend that the sum of $50.00 for material and indi-

---
[22] *Ibid.*, 88.
[23] *Ibid.*, 44.
[24] Moore, *loc. cit.*, 335.

vidual interest in Zion's Banner be paid, to the end that the consolidation may be speedily effected.

J. C. Dancy, Chairman[25]

The Committee praised the work of Reverend McH. Farley as it said: "We rejoice in the success which has attended the labors of Rev. J. McFarley, the present Editor of *The Star of Zion* at Petersburg, Va., and earnestly hope that our whole church, ministers and laymen will heartly cooperate with him in placing this paper in all the families throughout our wide-extended connection."

The Committee on Miscellaneous Matter suggested to the General Conference that the Book Concern and The Star of Zion he placed under one management.[26] The General Conference laid this suggestion on the table.[27] In the balloting for the Manager and editing of the paper the Rev. J. McH. Farley was elected manager and the Rev. A. L. Scott, Editor.[28]

One should not lose sight of the fact that others were involved in the successful launching of The Star of Zion. For example, W. C. Smith was connected with the venture as early as 1879, when The Star was being printed in Charlotte, North Carolina. Smith was in charge of the "mechanical work of the paper" while J. A. Tyler was the Editor. It is said that "his heaviest fight (as an Editor, no doubt), and the most signal victory this Editor boasts of, was the controversy between Bishop Singleton T. Jones and himself. He dared to criticize certain remarks in a sermon delivered by the Bishop, which he regarded as calculated to injure his race and church. The Bishop called him to account at some length, in his usual sarcastic way; but after this he will inform himself as to the size of the game before he makes another attack on a Smith." [29] Another battle in which Smith was involved was that regarding the establishment of a female seminary for his church. Penn states that "he completely demolished the brilliant Dancy and all others who dared oppose it." Incidentally, the press on which *The Star* was being printed at the time was the second one in the State run by Negroes.

In the General Conference of 1888, John C. Dancy reported for

---

[25] *Daily Proceedings of the Eighteenth Quadrennial Session of the General Conference*, (New York, 1884).
[26] *Daily Proceedings of the Seventeenth Quadrennial Session*, 123.
[27] *Ibid.*, 105.
[28] *Ibid.*, 107.
[29] Penn, *loc. cit.*, 272.

The Star of Zion since he had been elected by the Board of Bishops to fill the office after the rise of the preceding quadrennial session as Rev. Scott declined to serve. In 1888, Dancy was elected by the General Conference and served until 1892 when George W. Clinton was assigned to the Editorship.

In Dancy's report to the General Conference, he noted that he had been severely criticized about the paper. He pointed out that it was through his other work that The Star actually existed for funds were needed badly for the running of the paper. This was aggravated because the General Conference of 1888 actually reduced the amount of support to the paper. Prior to 1888 Dancy had seen fit to enlarge the publication by eight columns and then was faced with the reduced appropriation. He agreed to hold the office until the General Conference but for more than a year he had served without salary.

In a portion of the quadrennium D. C. Suggs had served as Business Manager. He later left the state and was replaced by Rev. R. S. Rives. Dancy noted that the cost of publishing had increased since the office was moved from Salisbury.[30]

Space will not allow us to completely detail the history of The Star from 1892. Dr. Clinton served as Editor until 1896, when the Rev. J. W. Smith became Editor.

Again, no doubt the paper received a reverse when the Board of Bishops suggested that its appropriation be cut from $1,500 to $1,000 and this sum given to the Sunday School Department. The Reverend J. W. Smith succeeded Reverend Clinton as Editor of The Star of Zion while the Reverend Dr. Blackwell became Manager of the Publication House. In this session, too, the law was enacted that all ministers subscribe to The Star of Zion.

The Reverend J. W. Smith served until 1904. In that General Conference he was replaced by Dr. George C. Clement who served until he was elected to the Bishopric in 1916. He, in turn, was succeeded by the Reverend J. Harvey Anderson, one time Statistical Secretary of the Church. Dr. W. J. Walls succeeded to the office in 1920 and served for the next four years, until 1924, when he too, was elected to the Board of Bishops. Dr. W. H. Davenport was elected in

---

[30] *Minutes of the Nineteenth Quadrennial Session of the Genearl Conference*, 1892, 152, 153. It should be stated that Dr. Dancy had been appointed to the office of Collector of Customs at Wilmington, N. C. in April by President Harrison.

that year and re-elected in 1928 as well as 1932. He was again elected in 1936.[31] Before the adjournment of the sessions, Dr. Davenport passed away (May 20, 1936). The Minutes are not clear regarding the selection of Rev. W. A. Blackwell, but in the report of his successor, Reverend Walter Raleigh Lovell in 1940 it is stated that he was selected "in a special election." [32] Dr. Lovell served as Editor until early in 1952 when the Board of Bishops, after investigation, removed him from office and placed the periodical in the hands of a Special Committee. The Board stated in their Address:

> One of our general officers had to be removed for neglect of duty, and for permitting our main organ to become a means of denominational self-destruction. After many times being cautioned and cajoled to be more constant and alert on his job, and more positive and constructive and less disintegrating in methods and utterances, he failed in this counsel. Because he continued in this misconception of the scope of his duties, as a spokesman for the denomination which allowed himself and the paper to become a means for creating an atmosphere for destructionists to monopolize its columns uncensored, discontinued waywardness compelled your chief pastors to take unanimous action. A climate had arisen around The Star of Zion where such loose freedom obtained that the church and its officials could be easily attacked and libeled to the dismay of us all, high and low, and to our disparagement before the world. All of this forces us to rise to the occasion of saving the honor, standards, and good name of our Zion before a critical and game-making world, because of this misunderstanding of the use and meaning of our official weekly church bulletin. Page 34 of the Discipline, Paragraph 90, sections 3 and 4, empower us to dismiss a general officer upon such discoveries as here described. We went one step further by invoking the law of investigation by the Publication Board, which we were not compelled to do because we received the facts directly from our own investigation with several members of the Board of Publication,
>
> P. 157 Paragraph 427, Section 5
> The Editor of The Star of Zion shall be amenable to the Board of Publication for his official Conduct, who shall have the right for cause to them sufficient, to report him to the Board of Bishops, who shall have power to remove him and fill the vacancy.
>
> P. 155 Paragraph 425
> The Board of Publication shall have the right, for cause to them sufficient to report any Editor, for neglect of his official duty, or for erroneous doctrines, mischievous statements of their own or those they permit to be printed under their supervision, and utterances in-

---

[31] *Official Journal of the Thirtieth Quadrennial Session of the General Conference* (Greensboro, N. C., 1936), 49.

[32] *Proceedings of the Thirty-first Quadrennial Session of the General Conference* (Washington, D. C., 1940), 176.

consistent to the Scriptures, as we understand them, or contrary to our Book of Discipline, to the Board of Bishops who shall have the power to remove him from office and fill the vacancy.

But the nature of the matter, and the clear and informed justification of any final action, caused us to use gradualness and refer the matter to the board for a fuller and longer time investigation of the particular incidents that touched off the calamity to which our attention was rudely called, and based upon the findings of the Publication Board, which did not change the facts first discovered, but reaffirmed and riveted them, we converted the temporary suspension into a permanent dismissal.

These events bring us to observe that it is unfortunate for any person selected by the franchise of the Church as custodian of its funds and operator of a department, to either by motive or imagined necessity, or otherwise, misappropriate funds or distribute them contrary to the law and to permit or act as the principal in forgeries and malfeasance. The church deserves to have uttermost honesty in administration, because it teaches it and it is supposed to live through its members and agents. We advise and urge all persons in the future accepting and assuming office to be forewarned, that the office belongs to the church and must not be usurped as his or her own by an officer or agent officially selected under law. They must give full recognition to all authorities.

Your chief pastors admit that we have no other reasons to offer you for these actions than that we seek, with our best collective judgment and prayerful decision, to save the church intact for operation in the contemporary world in respectability, Christian honor, and to pass it on to the coming generations in a status that commands continual respect of the world in growth of a proud and loyal membership among youth and adults.[33]

It should be stated that the message of the Board of Bishops, listed above dealt with three areas: The Brotherhood Pension Service and Relief, the Woman's Home and Foreign Missionary Treasury and The Star of Zion. The Editor of The Star of Zion, having small funds to handle, would not fall under the full impact of the above statement.

The Committee selected by the Board of Bishops to take over the work of the Editor was composed of the following: Bishop W. W. Slade, Mr. Brockett, Reverends P. L. Deberry, and F. R. Blakey. They made their report to the General Conference. The Committee on Periodicals of that body reported of the Star: "We heartily concur with the Board of Bishops in their Quadrennial Address read by Bishop W. W. Slade, page 25, last clause in which it is stated, 'we

---

[33] *Official Journal, Thirty-fifth General Conference,* (Pittsburgh, Pa., 1956), 49, 50.

regret that there have been some well-founded complaints about the character of some editorials and new column matter appearing in the Star of Zion. Regulatory steps have been taken, and we do not anticipate further trouble in that regard.' " [34]

The reaction of the General Conference to the report of the Board of Bishops and its Committee is not so clearly seen as one reflects on the matter. Those who lived through the period might differ with the writer on this but in the light of attendant tones and happenings it chose to turn away from the decision of the Board of Bishops and the statement of its own committee and return Dr. Walter Raleigh Lovell to office. The reader can therefore bring to the situation his own judgment. The vote for the Editor of The Star of Zion on Tuesday, May 15th was as follows: Lee, 7; Fisher, 24; Lomax, 10; Moncur, 23; Medford, 26; Siler, 26; Lovell, 272. Bishop Brown declared Walter Raleigh Lovell elected Editor of The Star of Zion.[35]

Dr. Walter Raleigh Lovell served through the 1956-1960 term, was re-elected in 1960 and again in 1964 and 1968. He died November 16, 1968. In January, 1969 the Board of Bishops selected the Reverend M. B. Robinson as his successor.

THE A.M.E. ZION QUARTERLY REVIEW

The Reverend George Wylie Clinton was no novice at editorial work when he assumed the pastorate of John Wesley A.M.E. Zion Church in Pittsburgh, Pennsylvania. He had gained renown for several articles and poems in the Afro-American Press of the time, and was listed on the editorial staff of The Star of Zion. He renewed his personal interest in publishing by editing in Pittsburgh a paper called *The Afro-American Spokesman,* then the only paper among Negroes in that area. This venture was supported by a stock company composed "principally of the ministers of the city." According to I. Garland Penn it began operations May 30, possibly 1889 "without a subscriber or helper, except those of the stock company with their capital shares." [36]

Just how long this venture lasted it is not known. It is known, however, that a very short time elapsed between the establishment of

---
[34] *Official Journal of the Thirty-fifth General Conference,* 451.
[35] *Ibid.,* 120.
[36] Penn, *loc. cit.,* 310.

the *Afro-American Spokesman* and that of the A.M.E. Zion Quarterly Review. The Year Book of 1942-43 sets the date of the first issue 1890.[37] By 1891 it was styled *The Church Quarterly* and was distinctly an A.M.E. Zion Church publication for it contained biographies of Bishop Singleton Jones, another of the Reverend Isom Caleb Clinton, General Steward of the denomination and a third of the Reverend Thomas Page R. Moore.

Articles in this 1891 copy of the Review were written by the Reverend M. W. Story of Oxford, Pa., the Rev. Robert E. Wilson, then pastor of the Johnstown, Pa. Church, and a sermon by Bishop John Jamison Moore.

For the following months the Reverend George Wylie Clinton edited *The Church Quarterly,* through 1891 and into 1892 when he played host pastor to the Quadrennial Session of the A.M.E. Zion Church. At that time the magazine was offered then to the denomination and was accepted.

In the Quadrennial Address of the Board of Bishops of 1892 the following was stated: "In this connection we would also call attention to another periodical, the African Methodist Episcopal Zion Quarterly, now published by Rev. G. W. Clinton, in Pittsburgh, which is a very interesting and worthy periodical, published for the benefit of the African Methodist Episcopal Zion Church. This periodical was established by Rev. Clinton through his own efforts, and our connection ought to feel a deep interest, and second so important an effort, and sustain this Church's instrumentality in ad- from undue criticism, such a periodical is the most convenient and best medium at the disposal of a Church. A quarterly gives more ample space for elaborateness and a more immediate consecutive connection of views than any other system of periodicals. To keep pace with religious progress, Zion Church must have a quarterly under her own supervision, and as one has already been established by one of her own enterprising, energetic, and devoted sons, it is but for her to sanction his praiseworthy efforts, and adopt his enterprise, and make it by adoption a connectional institution. There are many questions which the Church wishes to bring before our whole people and the public which the Church cannot secure in a common journal, and at most with very brief insertions, and often to the

---

[37] *The African Methodist Episcopal Zion Church Year Book,* 1942-1943, edited by Attorney Samuel Madison Dudley (Washington, D. C.), 82.

dissatisfaction of ministers of the writers. Indeed, a Church Quarterly is the best means to transmit to coming generations Church departures in tenets or doctrines or *modus operandi* that ours or any church can adopt on a simple and general scale. Hence, we will see herein the advantage and feasibility of at once adopting Rev. G. W. Clinton's *Quarterly,* now published at Pittsburg, Pa." [38]

On Friday, May 14th the Reverend J. H. McMullen offered the following resolution:

> *Whereas,* The long-felt need of the African Methodist Episcopal Zion Church has been met in the establishment of the *Quarterly* by the Rev. George W. Clinton; and
> *Whereas,* It is now the equal of any magazine of the kind published by the race; and
> *Whereas,* It should be taken as a connectional periodical, through which subjects of vital interest may be discussed; therefore, be it Resolved, That the General Conference receive the African Methodist Episcopal Zion *Quarterly* now published by Rev. George W. Clinton as a connectional periodical, and that the editor of said *Quarterly* be elected along with the other general officers of the connection.[39]

It was voted to suspend the rules for the consideration of the resolution and on vote, the resolution regarding the *Quarterly* was adopted.

Since it was known that John C. Dancy was not considering the Editorship of the Star of Zion, which he had held to the sitting of the General Conference, the Reverend G. W. Clinton was given this office. Then, on motion of the Rev. M. A. Bradley, with discussion by many of the "brethren" the Honorable John C. Dancy was elected Editor of the Quarterly.[40]

The Honorable John C. Dancy served as Editor of the Quarterly, or as it is now known, *The A.M.E. Zion Quarterly Review* from 1892 until 1912, a total of twenty years. In 1908 the Reverend L. W. Kyles was elected the Editor of the Homiletic Department of the Quarterly and succeeded John C. Dancy as Editor in 1912.[41] In 1916 Reverend Kyles was elected to the Episcopacy and was succeeded by the Reverend Cameron Chesterfield Alleyne, who served until 1924

---

[38] *Minutes of the General Conference of* 1892 (Pittsburgh, Pa.) , 39, 40.
[39] *Ibid.,* 83.
[40] *Minutes of the General Conference of* 1892, 92.
[41] *Official Journal of the Twenty-fourth Quadrennial Session of the General Conference* (Charlotte, N. C., 1912) , 126.

when he was likewise elected to the Bishopric. His successor was the Reverend Dr. W. O. Carrington.[42]

The Reverend Dr. W. O. Carrington served from 1924 to 1932 when the Reverend P. K. Fonville was elected. The Reverend Dr. James Clair Taylor succeeded Reverend Fonville in 1936 and served until 1948 when he was elected to the Bishopric. The Reverend David H. Bradley was elected to succeed Bishop Taylor and is the present incumbent (1969) having been elected by acclamation in 1952 through 1968.

One period of the *Review* brought the magazine near extinction. In 1932, the Committee on Elimination and Consolidation suggested: "that the publishing of the Quarterly Review for the present quadrennium be discontinued."[43] The General Conference refused to concur. In 1936, the General Secretary, the Reverend H. C. Weeden said: "I recommend that the Quarterly Review be placed in charge of the Editor of the Sunday School Literature and all subscriptions for the same be sent to the manager of the Publication House."[44] No action appeared to have been taken on this suggestion, however.

As a contrast to retrenchment, in 1912, it was suggested that the Quarterly Review be made a monthly. On motion it was decided that it should remain a quarterly.[45]

THE MISSIONARY SEER

Bishop John Bryan Small is listed as the founder of the Missionary Seer, the monthly periodical of the denomination. It appeared soon after the beginning of the century (1901) and was accepted by the General Conference of 1904, when the General Conference met in St. Louis, Missouri. Its major purpose, as Bishop Small, himself stated, was to "bring before the connection the work and working of the Foreign field."[46]

The A.M.E. Zion Quarterly Review speaks of its Editor in the

---

[42] *Minutes of the Twenty-seventh Quadrennial Session of the General Conference,* 69.
[43] *Journal of the Twenty-ninth General Conference,* 238.
[44] *Journal of the Thirtieth General Conference* (1936), 151.
[45] *Official Journal, Twenty-fourth Quadrennial Session, General Conference,* 1912, 26.
[46] Jones, *Comprehensive Catechism of the A.M.E. Zion Church,* 60.

First Quarter of its 1905 issue. At the time the Reverend G. L. Blackwell was listed as the Editor.[47]

The history of the *Missionary Seer* is difficult to chronicle since the work of the Editor is mainly that of Secretary of Home and Foreign Missions. Other Editors of the *Seer* have been, J. W. Wood, later Bishop; W. W. Matthews, later Bishop; H. T. Medford, later Bishop; Daniel Carleton Pope, later Bishop and at present the Editor is the Reverend Dr. J. Clinton Hoggard.

OTHER PERIODICALS

The A.M.E. Zion Church has had other periodicals which we have not named. Among them one would list Zion Trumpet, edited by the Reverend Eli George Biddle.[48] This magazine was listed in the Discipline of 1904 (1905). J. Harvey Anderson, for several years Statistical Secretary edited several Year Books, one appearing as early as 1895. Copies of this Year Book can still be seen. In this light every General Secretary since Attorney Samuel Madison Dudley (his year book appeared first in 1942-43) has issued a year book. Bishop E. D. W. Jones in his Comprehensive Catechism mentions several other publications which will be taken up shortly.

Reverend Jesse Colbert has stated the following about the *Christian Endeavor Advocate,* published by Reverend R. Haywood Stitt and the *Varick Christian Endeavorer,* established by Reverend J. S. Caldwell and Reverend Colbert, the first editors. He states that the Advocate Endeavorer, ceased Publication at the death of Reverend Stitt, who passed away prior to the General Conference of 1896. Three months after the rising of the General Conference the *Endeavorer* began publication. When the General Conference met in Washington in 1900 Reverend Caldwell and Colbert declined to be continued as editors of the periodical. At that time it was separated from the Varick Christian Endeavor Union and the Reverend B. J. Bolding was elected editor. Four years later, the Union and the Endeavorer were placed together and the Reverend J. T. McMillan was elected Editor and President of the Union.[49] Reverend McMillan served until 1912 and was followed by Prof. Aaron Brown, who

---

[47] It was accepted by the General Conference of 1896.
[47] *A.M.E. Zion Quarterly Review,* First Quarter 1905, 88.
[48] It was accepted by the General Conference of 1896.
[49] Rev. Jesse Colbert, *History of the Varick Christian Endeavor Society, A.M.E. Zion Church,* 19.

served until 1932 when the re-organization of departments took place.

THE SUNDAY SCHOOL BULLETIN AND CHURCH SCHOOL HERALD

The Sunday School Bulletin evidently made its first appearance in July or August, 1917. It was a monthly magazine with James W. Eichelberger as Editor and the Reverend J. Francis Lee as Associate. While the *Bulletin* was mentioned in 1924, nothing was said about the *Teachers' Journal*, which evidently was a regular part of the assignment of the Editor of Church School Literature.

At the 1924 General Conference, meeting in Indianapolis, Indiana, it was recommended that there be a re-structuring of the Christian Education Department. It was suggested that there would be three major divisions: The Editorial Section which would involve the issuance of Church Sunday School Literature and the preparation and publishing of Christian Endeavor material. The second area would prepare and issue standards of Sunday School work, Christian Endeavor departments, deal with building and equipment materials, prepare programs of leadership education etc., and jointly, with the General Secretary of the Varick Christian Endeavor Union, edit the official newspaper of the Department. The third officer would be responsible for both Varick Christian Endeavor and Sunday Schools on the field, and for joint responsibility for the official newspaper. The Editor of Sunday Church School material would be in charge of the Editorial section (it should be said that until the election or assumption of responsibilities of Dr. Buford Gordon, the Editor of this section prepared no material for Christian Endeavor.), the former Superintendent of Sunday Schools would be in charge of the educational section while the former head of the Varick Christian Endeavor Union would be in charge of the Promotion section. He, however, continued to edit Varick Christian Endeavor material since this was not being done by the Editor. These changes were agreed to by the General Conference and appear in the Discipline of 1924.

The General Conference of 1928 ordered the merging of the *Bulletin*, now called the *Church School Herald* and the *Sunday School Teachers' Journal*. The content according to the report of 1932 "was greatly improved" along with its size. Later, it was turned over to the Editorial Department and remains the Church School-Herald-Journal. In the beginning, it was a monthly. At present it is a quarterly.

THE STRENGTH OF MY LIFE

The Strength of My Life was founded by Bishop Raymond L. Jones and is a daily devotional magazine issued through the Hood Theological Seminary. It has been adopted by the General Conference (1968) and is now an official publication of the denomination.

CHAPTER XIII

A Brief Glance of Early Missions in the A.M.E. Zion Church

IT IS difficult to actually trace the beginnings of Missions in the denomination for many reasons, among them being the fact that organizations were formed which evidently gave no indication of this work. Nevertheless many of them carried on such functions, aiding in the development of the denomination wherever they could. However, the first indication of a true Missionary Society appears to have been noted in the Minutes of the New England Annual Conference in 1851 when the following is noted:

> *Resolved:* That a committee of three be appointed to draw a plan for establishing a Home and Foreign Missionary Society in the New England Conference District.[1]

Fifteen years later the Superintendents wrote in their message:

MISSIONARY FIELDS

Some of the missions are not in a very prosperous condition; others are doing well.
Nova Scotia Mission—The Church at Halifax which seceded from us, but is about to return again. The church at Liverpool is not in a very prosperous condition. Cornwallace was doing well when last heard from.

Then followed an account of all the mission fields which we have recorded in a prior chapter.

The account, however, is amplified in the Minutes of the Baltimore Annual Conference of 1866, where the report of its Mission Board is recorded as well as the constitution. These follow.

THE THIRD ANNUAL REPORT
BALTIMORE ANNUAL CONFERENCE MISSION BOARD

The success attending our Missionary operations, especially the past year, will no doubt afford much satisfaction to all who feel interested in its welfare. In presenting this Report to the public, no pains have been spared to ascertain the progress of the mission in each of our sister Conferences in the Connection: though we did not succeed in procuring all the information desired, yet sufficient facts have been produced to show how gloriously the work is going on.

---

[1] *The New England Annual Conference Minutes of* 1851, p. 31.

The favorable results from the zealous labors of our Missionaries, the increasing interest manifested by our Churches, evinced by their contributions; and the glowing prospects with which we are surrounded are not only encouraging but urges us to greater exertions in the upbuilding of Zion. If there is anything to be regretted it is a want of Missionaries, especially those who are willing to teach school, and funds to sustain those who are thus employed. However, these deficiencies do not stop the work but render the labors of the Missionaries more arduous and prevents them from devoting as much time in each locality as necessity requires: nevertheless the people are satisfied; and it is gratifying to see the willingness of local preachers to aid in laboring where necessity requires their assistance, some of whom left their homes and became Missionaries.

Finance

The increasing interest for the Mission cause is strongly evinced by the finance, the receipts of which having never been so large as at present; notwithstanding this great increase it is insufficient to meet the constantly increasing demands. It is true some of our Churches are not so prompt or free in aiding us in this laudable work, yet we have no right to complain, there being reasonable cause for the seeming indifference: First, our people are generally poor. Second, they were never instructed on the importance of contributing for such purposes. *Third, its necessity was never considered until within the last four years when circumstances urged it; hence when the occasion occurred they were unprepared, and their limited contribution not being sufficient to meet the demand, we were obliged to solicit aid from other sources, but it is believed before long there will not be a church among us that will not respond to the Mission call with a large contribution. The receipts of the (Baltimore Conference) past year ending April 18, 1866, were $1,466.27, all of which has been exhausted leaving claims still pending of more than $400, an increase in the receipts of over last year of $987.01. The latest returns from Philadelphia, New England, Genessee, Alleghany, and North Carolina Conference Districts, commencing June 1864 and ending September 1865, the receipts amounted to $4,037.82, of this amount $554.50 were donations from the New England District sent to relieve the necessities of the freedmen in Washington, D. C.

The General Conference at its last sitting, in order to meet the wants of missions, prescribed a collection to be taken up in each congregation annually. Had the provision been complied with the result of the first year would have been at least $2,684.27. It is gratifying to know that the Conference has urged its compliance, and it is hoped that each sister conference will do the same. For the information of all who feel interested to know what the provision is, it is here appended to the report as follows:

---

* The New England Annual Conference is an exception, they organized a Mission Board in 1857 and continued in operation, sending out Missionaries. When the emergency or demand was made for a Mission South, it sent two, viz: Revs. Hood and Williams to Newbern, N. C. and subsequently sent Supt. J. J. Clinton in 1864.

THE GENERAL CONFERENCE

Report on Missions

The Committee on Missions respectfully represent that so far as their limited time would permit, they have considered the subject of Missionary operations in the A.M.E. Zion Church, and are of opinion that too little interest is manifested in the very efficient means of enlarging the borders of Zion. The Missionary work of our church during the last four years is not by any means of an encouraging character, with the exception of very recent operations in North Carolina and the District of Columbia. The Conference having set off Conferences in the South, contemplating immediate operations in that quarter, the necessity for suggesting any particular action in reference to that great missionary field is superseded, as the Superintendent presiding in that region will be much better prepared to govern the matter than the Committee.

The great difficulty in the way of missionary operations, however, is the want of means to send the persons willing to go and labor in distant fields, and to sustain them while there. Societies have been formed for this purpose, some of which are doing well, but as the funds secured by this means are still inadequate, it is suggested that each member of the church and each member of the Sunday School be taxed one cent per month for missionary purposes, and that the preachers in charge of circuits and stations shall cause to be taken up for the same, a monthly collection in each society, and all money so collected shall be held by a member of the Quarterly Conference, chosen for that purpose, called the Missionary Steward, who shall deliver all money so collected during the year to the Annual Conference, or to the agent appointed to receive it in the interval. Such funds shall be for missionary purposes only, and appropriated by the Annual Conferences respectively.

S. TALBOT, *Secretary*   S. T. JONES, *Chairman*

MISSION

An allusion having been made respecting the progress of the mission under the indefatigable labors of our missionaries, further remarks are not necessary; the facts will speak for themselves.

MARYLAND AND THE DISTRICT OF COLUMBIA

We have several missions in this vicinity, some of which have been recently established. The inhabitants of this section a year ago were quite unsettled, owing to the state of the country, but the termination of the war having removed the embarrassments, the prospects are quite encouraging, while the Church and congregation is on the increase and schools are being established in which the children are advancing rapidly.

VIRGINIA

Last year Superintendent Brooks opened missions in Richmond and Petersburg. The latter place is in a flourishing condition and has become self-sustaining; it being in the bounds of the North Carolina Conference, it has been given up to that District.

In Richmond we were not so successful. Superintendent Brooks established our Church there, but from opposition which arose after he left, it became disorganized, and thus our first efforts were blasted. A reorganization, however, was subsequently effected by Rev. R. Tompkins, aided by Rev. J. Trusty, which remained under the oversight of the latter until Rev. Mr. Hicks, from the New England Conference, took the pastoral charge, who afterwards purchased the church which the people had agreed to buy for $3,250. While every effort was being used to meet the second payment, we were all shocked as with electricity at the sad intelligence of the sudden death of Rev. Joseph Hicks. Though called upon to mourn the loss of an esteemed and worthy brother whose death cast a deep gloom upon the church as well as his numerous friends, there was no time to stand still, hence, Rev. J. Trusty once more assumed the oversight thereof, and sent Rev. Walker, a deacon, to take the pastoral care. Since then, Rev. Dyson has been sent by the Conference as being an efficient (leader) for that important station, and we believe no better selection could have been made under the present emergency. May God bless his labors and let success crown his effort.

In this enterprise we have had many difficulties, of which only one has been mentioned, but prudence dictates to us to pass the others in silence, as they have been referred to by the Rev. J. B. Trusty, and his letter to the Anglo-African. Notwithstanding all we have passed through we are not discouraged, neither has the Lord forsaken us, hence we will trust Him, and in His name we will set up our banner in Richmond, believing He will fulfill all our petitions. There are several other smaller missions in this State, all of which are progressing rapidly.

Kentucky

Last Conference, from an organization being made in this State, a mission was opened. Rev. Mr. Butler was sent to Louisville with authority to exert every effort to advance the cause of Christ. With the aid of Rev. Mr. Bridwell, the result has been the organization of fifteen congregations and the establishment of several Day Schools. The Church membership has increased near two thousand since last year with a number of intelligent laborers, some of whom are ordained. There has been a request made to set off an Annual Conference in this State; from the returns made and the encouraging prospects the request has been acceded to, and the Conference will be organized June 6.

The foregoing is the progress of the Mission cause in the Baltimore Conference of which we have not named every place as the tabular contains all the information desired. The following statements refer to those Missions of the Connection not in this Conference.

North Carolina Conference

The Mission of this State is increasing rapidly, a brief extract of which we make from the Minutes of that Conference hoping it will give equal satisfaction. There have been organized during the past year, ending December 1865, 35 congregations being an increase in membership of 5,158. The increase in the Sunday Schools is 1,448, but this is far short of the real increase there being a very large number of schools yet to report. There are many Day Schools organized in this District but we have not ascertained their aggregate.

THE LOUISIANA (OR SOUTHERN) CONFERENCE

This Conference District extends nearly over the entire southern States. Our cause here is advancing also, although not as fast as it would were we able to make up for those deficiencies previously mentioned; however, with all embarrassments, the increase in membership since last year is over 4,000. Of Sunday Schools we cannot say what the increase is but no doubt it is in proportion to the Church. Of Day Schools we have not heard, yet we believe that as efforts are used to establish them with our Churches, it is not likely it will be overlooked in this vicinity.

TENNESSEE

The Genesee Conference, at its last sitting, through the energetic labors of our worthy esteemed, and tried Brother, Rev. J. W. Loguen, a Mission was opened in this State. Since that time we have learned from the Rev. Superintendent J. J. Clinton, that the Mission cause is doing a great work in that section and from the apparent rapid progress a Conference will have to be organized there within twelve months. A few months ago there were fifteen organizations but we only give the probable statistics as we cannot ascertain the real aggregate; no doubt we shall be in possession of it in a few months. School teachers are in great demand in that State, but we shall refer to that hereaf-

INCREASE

The following is the aggregate increase of membership and Sunday Schools since General Conference 1864, through the Missionary operations, so far as can be obtained at present. If the reports were full, or if we could get the returns that will be issued in a few weeks, the numbers, no doubt, would be far greater. We wish it to be understood that this statement only includes our Missionary operations.

AGGREGATE MEMBERSHIP *

Baltimore Conference	1,645
North Carolina Conference	7,267
Louisiana Conference	6,000
Tennessee Conference	1,500
Total	16,412

* Those in italic are the Conferences from which we have not full reports.

SUNDAY SCHOOLS

Baltimore Conference	1,440
North Carolina Conference	1,671
Louisiana Conference	1,428

DAY SCHOOLS

This subject has become one of the most important items to our en-

---

* There is no proscription respecting teachers; white or colored are acceptable provided they have the requisite abilities.

terprise. Our Missionaries are instructed to exert their efforts in this direction, and teach school themselves where necessity demands it. It is our intention to establish schools as well as preach Christ. The demand for school teachers is as great, and in some respects, greater than for Missionaries; therefore, while we call for Missionaries to travel, the services of any who will volunteer to travel to teach schools as well as preach Christ, will be equally acceptable; and anyone desiring a situation as school teacher even if he does not belong to the class alluded to above, will not be rejected, provided he has the ability to perform the duty.

The Baltimore Conference and its Mission Board have agreed to cooperate with the "American and British Commission" which is organized for the benefit of the Freedmen, especially for their education. The aim of this institution is for the elevation of the freedmen, and is aided in this work by kindred associations in England, therefore, it pledges itself to establish schools wherever practicable in the South, or furnish teachers* for any organized under its auspices. Rev. Superintendent J. J. Clinton is its President, Prof. Wm. H. Day, the corresponding Secretary, and Rev. William F. Butler, Superintendent of Schools, for the State of Kentucky. This institution has an organ through which the condition and progress of schools is made known monthly.

It is regretted that we are unable to give the statistics of the day schools in our mission but probably it was deemed not essential in view of the returns or reports being published by the above institution; the following are the returns from the Baltimore Conference:—Schools, 1,325 members, and 22 teachers, all in good condition, and children advancing rapidly.

Books are of great demand in some of the schools, hence donations in books, old or new, or funds for that purpose will be thankfully received by those appointed to receive them. (See list of officers).

Moral and Religious Conditions

It is gratifying to learn that the religious feeling in our mission is progressing gloriously, in many of the churches there have been revivals and large accessions. The Lord is doing great work among the freedmen, and our prayer is that it may continue until every place in the South where the gospel banner is unfurled, shall echo with the praise of God.

In morals they do not advance as fast as desirable, but as fast probably as circumstances will permit, considering how long they have been kept in darkness. But there is no doubt that the efforts now in progress from education and religious instruction will shortly effect such a change as will utterly efface all the evils produced by slavery.

Missionaries

We have forty-five missionaries in the field besides those who are in charge of the Churches in the mission district, all of whom deserve great credit for their zeal in this good cause. Among many the following are named:

A BRIEF GLANCE OF EARLY MISSIONS IN THE A.M.E. ZION CHURCH

We cannot overlook Rev. Superintendent J. J. Clinton, though not a missionary, strictly speaking, but can be with propriety regarded as a missionary Superintendent, who by persevering and unwearied exertions, contending with the worst of opposition, and that right and left he has been instrumental in raising the standard of the Lord Jesus among the freedmen of the South under the auspices of our Connection. The result of this achievement is 15,000 members. More could be said but it is not needful. It is sincerely hoped that this appeal to his associate Superintendents and their Conferences will secure their sympathy and speedily be responded to.

We record with satisfaction the name of our own worthy and esteemed Brother, Rev. J. W. Loguen, who has had the honor of raising the standard in his own native State, which no doubt will add some thousands more to our army; his effort is highly appreciated, and we hope he may succeed in his labors as an agent to sustain the missionary cause.

The effectual service of Rev. Thomas James in Kentucky, will not soon be forgotten: after he had established our church in Louisville, he witnessed with pain the sufferings of our own people who were incarcerated in prison. Appealing to General Palmer* he was authorized to release them. From that period he never ceased until he emptied the prison and every place where the oppressed has been secured to be sold into slavery.

Whether he really (has) done a missionary work is not difficult for any to decide. The successful efforts of Rev. W. F. Butler and Rev. Richard Bridwell, whose services have rendered it essential that a Conference be established in Kentucky, require no encomiums from us, for the records of that Conference will show the names of its founders to future generations. Nor can we pass in silence those local brethren under Rev. Mr. Butler's charge, who, like Isaiah, seemed to be touched with hallowed fire from Jehovah's altar; for when laborers were needed and the word was spoken who will go, each was ready to say, "Here am I, send me." God bless their labors, and ever make them useful.

Long will the memory of Rev. Joseph Hicks be cherished for his successful labors and usefulness in establishing our church permanently in Richmond. It is doubtful whether the property would have been secured as satisfactorily had it not been for him. Owing to the opposition against us, and the inexperience of the people, through his ability all difficulty is obviated if we meet our demands. He had only just succeeded in his effort when he was called from labor to reward, and his lifeless form was conveyed from before its altar to its last resting place in Providence, R. I.

Rev. Mr. Tompkins has distinguished himself by the improvements and additions to his Mission in the District of Columbia and State of Virginia. There are others that could be added to the list; but this is sufficient to show we have those who have a mind to work, and will

---

* The name of General Palmer will ever be held or regarded with the highest esteem not by us alone, but all who may become acquainted with the interest he manifested in behalf of the colored people in the vicinity of his command not merely in words but in noble deeds that can never be forgotten. May the blessing of God attend him through life.

spare no pains to advance the cause of Zion. All that we ask is pecuniary aid to carry on the good work.

Conclusion

Having completed the report, in which we have referred to every feature of this great work that might be considered of interest to those concerned, it is hoped that it will be read with satisfaction. It may be thought by some too long. However, as we have been generally brief and short, it has been thought that the report was not full enough. We admit that this report is more extensive than it ever has been previously, but it was done in compliance to the request of the Executive and we believe will be productive of good.

As we have been aided most bountifully in our undertaking the past year, the report should not be closed without some expression to those friends who manifested their appreciation of our labors by their liberality. We hope that it may be in our power to give some expression of gratitude by something better than the few sentiments that follow:

With pleasure we record the name of our worthy Superintendent, Rev. Sampson Talbot, whose magnanimity contributed to our success in Richmond. The New England Mission Board have our grateful acknowledgment for their liberality in responding to our order. The same feeling will be reciprocated when necessity demands it. If the unanimity now existing between us continue—provided it be not interrupted by a concentration to establish a Connectional fund, which is certainly desirable,—our united effort will contribute largely toward the progress of the Gospel among our people.

The ladies of the Soldiers Relief Association in Bridgeport, Conn. will please to accept our sincere thanks for their benevolent donation to our Agent, Rev. Joseph Hicks, for the Richmond Church.

The interest manifested by Mr. Samuel J. Howard will be held in grateful remembrance for his kind assistance toward obtaining an edifice for Divine worship for the Richmond Church.

Nor should we overlook our Church in Louisville, Ky., which during the last year manifested their interest toward the Mission by responding so liberally and cheerfully notwithstanding the frequent appeals. May the Lord reward its liberal contributors, bless the Church with prosperity, and scatter its enemies. Zion Church, New York; Wesley Church, Philadelphia; Zion Church, Petersburg, Va., and any other which may have borne a part, will accept our grateful thanks for the interest manifested to our people in Richmond, who were struggling against heavy opposition to secure a place for the worship of God. May their united efforts with ours be not spent in vain!

We close by soliciting the earnest prayers of the followers of Jesus, that the beauty of the Lord Our God may be upon us, and that He may establish forever the work of our hands.

Signed by the Missionary Committee,
SAM'L M. GILES
JOHN A. WILLIAMS
ROBT. H. DYSON

A BRIEF GLANCE OF EARLY MISSIONS IN THE A.M.E. ZION CHURCH

CONTRIBUTIONS 1865-66

Wesley Zion Church, Washington, D. C.	$ 43.45
Wesley Zion Sunday School, Washington, D. C.	7.00
Union Wesley, do	24.88
John Wesley, do	8.26
Galbraith Chapel, do	24.18
Jones' Chapel, Virginia	16.14
A Joint Committee of Ladies	73.00
Soldiers' Relief Association, Bridgeport, Conn.	25.00
Sunday Resources	463.00
New England Conference Mission Board	40.00
South Howard Street, Baltimore, Maryland	14.48
Rock Creek, D. C.	78.72
Brightwood, do	53.72
Freedmen's Village, D. C.	4.73
Arlington, Va.	48.84
Zion Church, Louisville, Kentucky	383.50
Agency	11.87
Zion Church, Petersburg, Va.	20.00
Wesley Church, Philadelphia, Pa.	55.00
Zion Church, New York	70.50
Total	$1,466.27

CONSTITUTION
OF THE
BALTIMORE ANNUAL CONFERENCE MISSION FUND

PREAMBLE

Whereas the cause of religion depends much upon missionary efforts, this institution is established under the following regulations for that purpose.

I

This institution shall be known as the Baltimore Annual Conference Mission Fund of the African Methodist Episcopal Zion Church. Its object shall be to sustain those missionaries who are duly appointed by the Conference or Superintendent, according to the provision hereafter mentioned. It shall be supported by voluntary contributions, public collection or otherwise.

II

The affairs of the institution shall be under the entire control of a board of officers subject to the Annual Conference, to whom they shall report the state of the funds, the progress of the mission, and all matters touching the same. Its officers shall consist of a President, Vice President, Secretary, Corresponding Secretary, and Finance Committee of three, all of whom shall be elected annually by the Conference. When a full board cannot be elected because of a deficiency of Conference members, the Finance Committee and Secretary may be omitted, and the remainder of the officers elected, who shall constitute a missionary committee, and be invested with all the powers of the Board, under the same responsibility to act until a full Board can be elected.

The President shall preside at all meetings of the institution, call special meetings of the Board when necessity requires it, and direct the affairs of the institution. When absent, the Vice-president shall perform the same duties.

The Secretary shall keep a record of the entire proceedings of the institution, and present an annual report of the same to the Conference in behalf of the Board, as prescribed in this article, not however, not having been first approved of by the Board.

The Treasurer shall hold all moneys belonging to the Society, nor disburse them otherwise than authorized by the Constitution or Board.

The Corresponding Secretary shall correspond for and in behalf of the institution, and, if necessity requires, visit the Mission.

The Finance Committee shall disburse the funds of the institution, as directed by the annual meeting, and the appropriation then made may be left in their hands but if additional funds are needed in the interval, they shall draw upon the Treasurer, as herein provided.

III

The Board shall meet annually, and determine the time of its own sitting, which may be anterior to the sitting of the Conference, and at the same place. Special meetings may be held in the interval, when necessary, but it shall require two-thirds of the members of the Board at such meetings to do the business. A correct minute of the proceedings shall be kept, subject to the approval of the annual meeting.

There shall be a Missionary Meeting held while the Annual Conference is in session, at which the annual report shall be read, accompanied with any other exercises deemed essential for the good of the fund. Missionary meetings shall be held in the interval of the Conference at any of our churches, if practicable, and collections solicited for the fund. Such meetings may choose their own chairman.

IV

Each church shall be regarded as an auxiliary to the fund, and where practicable other organizations shall be formed for said purposes. When any auxiliary shall request that their contribution be devoted to any particular mission in the Connection, their request shall be granted.

V

No money shall be drawn from the fund except by an order made out by the Chairman of the Finance Committee, (or Vice-President of the Missionary Committee) who shall affix his name thereto, and be signed by the President and Secretary.

VI

All missionaries are obliged to correspond with the Corresponding Secretary, and annually present their report of the moral and religious condition of the mission, statistics of the church community, schools, finance, and whatever they may deem of importance to the Board. No Missionary shall act as President, Secretary, or Treasurer of the Board.

VII

The Board shall appoint an agent when they deem it expedient. When such selection is made from the Conference, it shall be one who can be exonerated from taking an appointment in the Conference. Such agent shall hold no office in the Board.

VIII

Any expediency not herein provided for or implied, shall be regulated by the Board so as not to conflict with the constitution, or determined otherwise by the Conference. These rules may by revised or amended by the Board when necessary, with the consent of the Annual Conference.

—The Minutes of the Baltimore Annual Conference, 1866

CHAPTER XIV

Home and Foreign Missions and the Church

A SEGMENT of the Home and Foreign Missions account has been related in the Chapter: *Days of Reconstruction and the A. M. E. Zion Church*. This, in truth, gives an account of the many projects in which the Church spent time and energy having to do primarily with the work of varied sections of the home front and areas to the North as well as islands of the sea.

The Reverend William B. Bowens gives us a clear picture of the intent of the denomination as he wrote: "The A.M.E. Zion Church is distinctly a Missionary Church. All of her great leaders, laymen, ministers and Bishops have done yeoman work on the mission fields . . . the founders of Zion believed that the field is the world; they saw an open door for a grand, glorious and extensive missionary effort among their brothers and sisters who lived in the large towns and cities of New England, Middle and Western States and the British Province, who were starving for the Bread of Life. . . . They wanted an Afro-American Missionary, the Afro-American Sabbath School teacher, the Afro-American educator, and more, the Afro-American divine, ordained and clothed with all the authority of an ecclesiastic, equal to that conferred by any other church. . . . The states of New York and Pennsylvania (were) our first field of mission operation. They soon sped across the rocky and snowy hills of New England where they planted among its cultured inhabitants in nearly every populous town and city, Zion Missions, most of which have become influential churches. Across the St. Lawrence, the Zion Missionary traversed the British Provinces of the Canadas and Nova Scotia in the midst of wintry blasts and mountains of snow: they preached the everlasting gospel, opened missions and erected churches. . . ."[1]

Earlier, Bowens declared: "The genial clime and flowery island of Bermuda and the West Indies have also been fields of Missionary labor.[2] One of the most populous and flourishing churches in Hamilton, the capital city of Bermuda, was organized and pastored by the

---
[1] *The A.M.E. Zion Quarterly Review—The Centennial Jubilee Number, Vol. X, No. 2,* 15.
[2] *Ibid.,* 16, 17.

late Dr. R. R. Morris." Speaking of the work here at home he stated: "The late War and abolition of Slavery opened up a wide and opportune door for Christian humane and philanthropic work and endeavor among the millions of Afro-Americans of the South. Bishop J. J. Clinton, D.D. was commander-in-chief of the forces of our beloved Zion. He enlisted as chaplain of the 54th Mass. Volunteers and went to the front with them, and while the Union Army was fighting to put down the rebellion, Bishop Clinton was preaching and fighting for God to establish in the Southland Zion Church. He organized thirteen conferences, ordained hundreds of preachers, thousands were converted, and hundreds of churches and missions were organized. Bishop S. T. Jones in the Southwest, Bishop Moore in California, Bishop J. W. Hood, T. H. Lomax and J. P. Thompson in the Middle and Southern Atlantic States and other heroes and valiant soldiers of the cross too numerous to mention, immortalized themselves by their devotion to God and the uplifting of humanity." [3] Bishop Hood, writing in another number of the Centennial edition stated: "The A.M.E. Zion Church is truly a missionary effort. The Mother Zion Church was incorporated in 1801 as the African Methodist Episcopal Church called Zion. At a little later period the Church at Flushing on Long Island, was formed. No later than 1812 the Asbury Church was organized. . . . We may also add to the foregoing, the fact that in the States where our greatest efforts were made there were but few colored people to support a minister, and yet, the New England Conference supported six missions within those states and three in Nova Scotia. This Conference was also among the first to send missionaries to the freedmen in the South." [4]

Bishop Hood continues: "The New York Conference, numbering less than twenty-five Churches maintained several missions in the West Indies Islands, and also sent missionaries to the South as soon as the way was open."

Where the women of the Church are concerned, it is well known that they had a vital interest in the spreading of the Gospel. While much conjecture has been available as to their work our major link to the past is that created through a writing of Aurora Evans who clears up a number of misconceptions: She wrote in the A.M.E. Zion

---

[3] *A.M.E. Zion Quarterly Review, loc. cit.,* 17.
[4] *Ibid.,* 1896, 5.

HISTORY OF THE A.M.E. ZION CHURCH

Quarterly Review: "The origin and work of the Daughters of Conference are as replete with interest as it is full of self-sacrifice and devotion to the cause of missions and promulgation of the Gospel."

Aurora Evans further states:

> The story of their heroic and golden deeds should be as incentives and should instill in our young women much of their love and heroic spirit. They were organized in the year 1821. Zion Church and its missionary operation were in their infancy and the cry came from New England and all over New York and New Jersey, "Send us the Gospel, send a minister; we need a church:" and the great need was money to aid the ministers in going to their mission fields and to assist in erecting churches. Today, we would place our loveliest and most fragrant garland on the brow of that magnamimous and sainted woman, Mary Roberts, who was the founder and for forty years president of the daughters of Conference. She was the woman who exerted a mighty influence over the women of her day in rallying them to the support and aid of Missions, education and other needs of the Church.
>
> There were other great workers and illustrious members of this original society of the Daughters of Conference whose names have long since been recorded on the Lamb's Book of Life.
>
> Sarah Ennals, Eliza Gardner Sr., Elizabeth A. Purnell, Sarah J. Eato, Marie Vogalsang, Matilda Busle, Ellen Stevens and others who gave largely of their means.
>
> The beautiful example and fervent zeal of the older sisters spread, and the young women of the Church expressed the wish to be organized to be known as the young daughters of the Conference, that they too, might take part in the glorious work of sending the blessed Gospel to the lost. The Young Daughters of Conference were gladly organized by the president of the older society, Sister Mary Roberts, with that energetic woman, Ellen Stevens, as president of the junior daughters. One of these laborers, Sister Jane Finch, is with us today.—
>
> Such women as Sojourner Truth and Harriet Davis were as familiarly known as Mother Tubman is today—were as remarkable for their love for their race and their emancipation as Frederick Douglas and John Brown were. Mother Tubman went South several times during the days of slavery, leading out twenty and thirty at a time. Just like the old hero, John Brown, she imperiled her life, but was more successful than he, in that she escaped with those she loved. Her latest great act was to give to the Genesee Conference her homestead as a home for the aged.
>
> We know that several million dollars have been given by them for missions, education and other Church interests. When the Rev. J. W. Hood, D. D. LLD. and other missionaries went South the Daughters of Conference furnished the money and bade them God-speed.
>
> Our Ex-Superintendent Rev. Andrew Cartwright of Africa has been

aided by the Daughters of Conference, but not until the day of rewards when God shall recompense His children, shall be known what God has done for them. The mission of the Daughters of Conference will not be ended until the world is saved, and the shout goes up, Hallelujah! Christ reigneth! [5]

Anna L. Anderson originally of the Allegheny Conference, in her compilation of the Manual of the Woman's Home and Foreign Missionary Society states that the first organization styled The Daughters of Varick was organized in 1845. As is noted in the *Historical Synopsis* of the Woman's Home and Foreign Missionary Society Mrs. Anderson may have had access to material compiled by the late Singleton T. Jones or his son, E. D. W. Jones. Again we state, however, that her work (Mrs. Anderson's) was written in 1933 while Aurora Evans wrote in 1896, (note correction with the *Historical Synopsis*) thirty-seven years prior to Mrs. Anderson's work. As stated, Aurora Evans mentions Sarah J. Eato, a name common to Zion Methodism which supports the possibility of correct information. As stated elsewhere, Timothy Eatto (note spelling) was a preacher according to the rolls of the Conference of 1821. Miss Evans gives no date for the formation of the Young Daughters of Conference, evidently styled the Young Daughters of Rush. Utilizing the title, Daughters of Varick would be in keeping with the sentiment at the time—taking the first Superintendent's name for the older group and the Second Superintendent's name for the younger.

As stated in the *Historical Synopsis* when the General Conference met in Philadelphia in 1864 financial reports were noted as coming from the Daughters of Conference from Newburgh, New York, New York City, Hartford, Bridgeport, New Haven, Norwich, Conn., Boston, Mass., Philadelphia, Pa., Baltimore, Md., and Washington, D. C. Moore states that $2,883.13 was expended for Missionary purposes at this conference.

We take the liberty to quote the following from the *Historical Synopsis*: "In the Discipline of 1852 and the revised section of 1856, the question arose: 'What shall be done to defray the expenses of our Home and Foreign Missionaries?' The answer was: 'Each Annual Conference shall organize a Missionary Society, the members of which shall pay such sums as shall be determined from year to year by the Conference.'"

---

[5] *The A.M.E. Zion Quarterly Review*, Centennial Number 1896, 66-69 (evidently final quarter of that year).

There is a possibility that Dr. Yates in his work on Foreign Missions will be able to clear up the basic reasons that prompted the Rev. Andrew Cartwright to decide on work in Africa. He and his wife were natives of Elizabeth City, North Carolina, when they decided to give their lives in the service of Missions. Accordingly, they sailed from New York in January 1876 and arrived in Monrovia, Liberia the next month. When Reverend Cartwright rendered his reports to the General Conference he reported missions established in Brewerville (1879) and Cape Palamas the same year. It is to be noted that the Cartwrights were handicapped in their labors because of the lack of finance and the second lack was that of authorization. When the Board of Bishops heard Reverend Cartwright's report at their meeting in Petersburg, Virginia in 1883 they endeavored to deal with the matter of authorization. At that time he evidently asked for the status of the early interpretation of Superintendent. Ecclesiastical obstacles evidently were involved but the Board of Bishops agreed that he should be authorized to make appointments and ordain deacons and elders, these powers subject to ratification of the General Conference when next in session. The statement which was given in the General Conference Conference follows:

1. There is our Foreign Mission. Four years ago but little was known of that work or those engaged in it, except one of the Bishops. There was no general interest manifested in it; but today the interest in that work is not only felt by one, but by all the Bishops, and is being diffused among the ministry and membership. Our missionaries received such hearty and substantial encouragement while on this side of the water, that they have returned to the Dark Continent filled with new vigor and inspired with new zeal, so that the outlook for Zion is bright and cheering.

    The Reverend Andrew Cartwright our chief missionary to Africa, met the Bishop's Meeting in Petersburg, Va., March 26, 1883, and made his report of the work. It was very satisfactory to the Board, and the following resolutions were offered by Bishop S. T. Jones: *Whereas,* The work in Africa, as just presented by Brother Cartwright, commends itself to our highest consideration and regard, therefore,

    Resolved, That for the purpose of conserving the interests of the Church and giving proper encouragement to our brethren in that far off field, Rev. Andrew Cartwright be, and is hereby authorized and empowered to hold Annual Conferences in Africa, and to authorize and appoint suitable persons to preach and to teach our people, subject to the ratification or modification of the General Conference.[6]

Nine years later the Reverend Andrew Cartwright made his first report to the General Conference meeting in Pittsburgh, Pa. in 1892. He likewise reported for his wife, Mrs. Cartwright.

REPORT OF THE REV. A. CARTWRIGHT, AFRICAN MISSIONARY

To the Bishops and Members of the General Conference of the African Methodist Episcopal Zion Church, here assembled in Pittsburgh, Pa.:

Dear Brethren and collaborators in the cause of the common Lord and Savior Jesus Christ, through the divine hand of him who holdeth the destinies of nations in his hand, and wisely conducts the affairs of all well and unimpeachable. I thank God through the vicissitudes of life and the meandering scenes of nature, I sailed from New York, January 1876 and landed at Monrovia, February 1876, and engaged in the work of my mission. In 1878 I organized a church in Brewerville with 49 members; and in 1879 organized a church in Clay Ashland with 15 members. Eight miles off I organized a church in Cape Palamas in 1879, with 20 members. The preacher's name at this point was Joshua Neal. He died, and thus the flock scattered.

In 1886 I organized a church with 40 members and 50 Sunday School scholars by a letter. This was because my financial embarrassment was such as to prevent my traveling. The next preacher put in charge at Cape Palamas was R. R. Massa, and I, not being able to reach there for want of means to travel with, have never seen him. This brother wrote to me for money, and as I had not received any salary at that time, I could not send him what he needed. The Episcopalians took advantage of the situation and offered him a salary, and he left us and went to them.

When the people at Grand Bassa County heard of our organization—that is, Zion—in Brewersville, they petitioned to come to Zion, but I had not the money to travel to them. Thus I lost ground. I wrote to the *Star,* so that my letters were seen by the connection as they appeared in it from time to time, for aid in that far-off land. Could I have received a salary I might have had a good work in Sarelone before the ministers of the African Methodist Episcopal Church left, as also in Grand Bassa and Palamas. I came home to America and met the Bishops, and informed them of the situation of things. I saw the need also of lady teachers to teach the children, or girls at least, and I wrote to the editor, Hon. J. C. Dancy, and he published it. But that was the end of it. I then came over again to America all the way from Africa, and informed the connection how a teacher could be supported. The Bethels went to those places that I couldn't reach for want of means to travel with.

The work has been hindered greatly in Africa on account of not hav-

---

[6] *Daily Proceedings of the Seventeenth Quadrennial Session of the General Conference,* (1884) 25, 26.

ing means sufficient to advance it. This is why the work goes slowly, and I want it understood that I am blameless as to its present state, for according to my means I have worked.

FINANCIAL FOOTINGS

I have for my services from 1884 to 1888 received as follows:

First payment in 1884-1885 by C. R. Harris	$ 200.00
In 1885 by C. R. Harris	200.00
December 26, 1885 by C. R. Harris	200.00
May 23, 1887 by C. R. Harris	200.00
From the L. H. and F. M. Society, January, 1888	200.00
From the L. H. and F. M. Society, May 25, 1888	200.00
Whole Amount received from 1884 to 1888 as apportioned by General Conference	1,200.00
From L. C. Clinton, October 4, 1888	60.00
From William H. Day, August 28, 1889	75.00
April 12, 1890	25.00
February 7, 1891	200.00
Total	410.00
November 7, 1890 from Bishop J. P. Thompson through Yates and Porterfield to R. A. Sherman, Monrovia	43.50
From 1884 to 1888	1,200.00
From 1888 to 1891	553.50
Total	1,753.00
Amount received before last payment	1,753.50
At last payment	300.00
Total	2,053.50
Expended for traveling to and from Africa in the year 1887	250.00
Teacher's traveling expense to Africa	125.00
Expenses to meet the Board of Bishops 1891-1892	250.00
Whole amount of traveling expense	625.00
Salary for teacher	43.50
Traveling expense all told and teacher's Salary	668.50

This deducted from what I have received leaves a balance due of $285.00. The first four years my salary was $800.00 per year, and the last four years the salary was cut down to $400.00 making this $1,600.00. I have received for the whole eight years $2,053.50. I have expended, as seen, for traveling expenses $668.50, leaving actual pay to me $1,385, and the balance due of $3,415.

Now as to the membership of Africa. This I claim to have a right to know better than any of you on this side of the water, if my statement is accepted as truth, Mrs. Cartwright, the teacher, has two scholars, prepared for Livingstone College, and two more were expected to be ready, and would have been had no one disturbed us.

As she has given four years service as a teacher, I ask this General Conference what they will allow her per year for services thus rendered, she having received at one time $43.50, and since I have been here Rt.

Rev. J. W. Hood, D. D. paid me for her $19.34, making a total paid her $62.84.

Respectfully submitted,
A. CARTWRIGHT,
Supt. of African Mission Work[7]

REPORT OF A. M. E. ZION MISSION SCHOOL

Brewersville, Liberia, West Central Africa
March 1892

To the A.M.E. Zion General Conference, May 1892
1888—No. scholars, 80 Males—Congo 6; Native 1; Female 60—Congo 3
1889—No. scholars, 80 Males 48—Congo 8; Native 2, Females 32
1890—No. scholars 58, Males 29—Congo 1; Native 1; Females 29
1891—No. scholars, 19, Males 11, Females 8

The shortness for 1891 comes by the stir which rose against us, and is the number of scholars up to the time the Board called Elder Cartwright in June 1891, after which I had to resort to another route for peace sake, but taught on 'til the close of the year, which was November 1891.

And one more school was added, which makes twenty. In connection with the school there was a temperance Band of Hope, forty in number, and of other denominations, too. The children were being quite interested in this little society, and the fireside manners, of which so many were neglected, together with little politeness that ought to exist among them, are being taught. We patiently wait, hoping the Lord will provide, heal up the wounds, and cast up a highway for Zion yet in this neglected land.

CARRIE E. S. CARTWRIGHT[8]

The controversy over the status and support of the Cartwrights occupied the attention of the Church and the General Conferences from 1880 to 1896. For example, in the Seventeenth Quadrennial session the following appears:

> On motion of Rev. A. Walters, the salary of Rev. A. Cartwright, Supt. of African Mission, was set at $800 per annum. The salary to be paid by the Missionary Societies, supplemented, if need be, by the General Fund.[9]

It appears that back salary was due Reverend Cartwright simply because adequate funds were not to be had. In 1884 Elder C. R. Har-

---

[7] *Daily Proceedings of the Nineteenth Quadrennial Session of the General Conference, Pittsburgh, Pa.* 1892, 175,176.
[8] *Daily Proceedings of the Nineteenth Quadrennial Session of the General Conference,* 1892, 176, 177.
[9] *Minutes of the Seventeenth Quadrennial Session of the General Conference* (1884) 113.

ris had offered the following resolution as matters pertained to the salary item:

> An addition to Section 3 Article 6 of the Financial Plan:
> *Provided further,* That no account be taken of the salary of the Superintendent of African Missions until the semi-annual meeting of the Board of Bishops; at which time all moneys received for foreign missionary purposes not exceeding $800, be applied to the payment of said salary, and whatever deficiency there may be shall be met from the receipts on General Fund for the current year.[10]

The resolution was adopted.

The effort to increase the efficiency of Missions in the denomination got underway in the General Conference of 1880. The session was opened by Bishop Joseph P. Thompson in State Street Church, Mobile, Alabama, May fifth. The Board of Bishops had recommended a change to Clinton Chapel Church, Montgomery "in order to reduce the traveling expenses of the delegates from the Northern Conferences" and to get around the health hazard which going to Mobile entailed. After Scripture, prayer, singing and the election of Rev. A. English as Secretary *pro tem,* Bishop Thompson spoke and the session was adjourned with benediction to meet the next day in Montgomery.[11]

The Bishops' address to the Sixteenth session stated: "For a view of the vast mission fields open before us, we refer you to the reports from the Third, Fourth, Fifth and Seventh Districts; not only have we the missionary district of Canada and the great northwest, but Kansas at this time presents one of the finest openings for missionary effort that can be desired. Also from Liberia and West India Islands the Macedonian cry is heard." [12]

The Message of the Board appears to have been placed in the Minutes in two different sections, for in another section it is stated: "Beside our home mission work we have established a mission in Liberia. Rev. Andrew Cartwright is our pioneer missionary in that field: He has organized three churches, and is now building a fine church at Brownsville. We have recently received the following from that field.

Brownville, Liberia
March 10th, 1880

To the Bishops and members of the General Conference of the A.M.E. Zion Church, to assemble in Montgomery, Alabama, on the first Wednesday in May 1880:

We the members of the A.M.E. Zion Church in Liberia, on the West Coast of Africa, do request Rt. Rev. J. W. Hood to represent us in your honorable body, as we are so far off that we cannot send a delegation at this time.

---

[10] *Minutes of the Seventeenth Quadrennial Session (1884) General Conference,* 114.
[11] *Daily Proceedings of the Sixteenth Quadrennial Session of the General Conference,* 1880, 7.
[12] *Ibid.,* 48.

We, the members of the Quarterly Conference, including Brownsville, Claysland and Antherton, wish to say that the work is going on finely as could be expected in this land. We have had a hard fight, and the battle is going on yet, but we feel that we shall go on to the victory. Zion has had her conflicts all the way, but she has not taken in her sails as yet. In 1796 the company was small but she is an army today. We are few in Liberia, but we remember how the Lord blessed our fathers, and we know that our Captain is a man of war. We ask the General Conference, if in her power to do so, to give Brother A. Cartwright power to call a conference here. We know it would enable him to get some more men with us, who would do us a great good.

One of our preachers died in June 1879, and an elder from Bethel joined with us, and thought to get the helm in his hands, and steer for Bethel Coast, but Elder Cartwright was too sharp for him. We have no church at Claysland, but use a large building. We are building a church in Brownsville. Rev. A. Cartwright is conducting the work. We expect to dedicate it on the third Sunday in May, the Lord willing. This is the mother church. We had a common house but are now building a nice church, and we beg you to aid us. A common bell, two large lamps and reflectors, a large Bible and hymnbook. Pray God to give us success. We have a good lot and house. Our church is incorporated, and we hope the General Conference will grant our request for the good of the church in Liberia. You will please receive our report through Bishop Hood. We have a church, also a building at Antherton, and next desire and mean to build a church at Claysland. We hope the Conference will help us a little. We want to open a day school as soon as we can.

Yours truly,
JOSEPHUS SAMUEL BAKER, and others

The Board of Bishops added:

We have other letters to lay before the Committee on Missions, which will throw light on this important work. In regard to the request made for aid, we may remark that Rev. Jacob Thomas desired information as to what was needed to aid that work, and this is the response.[13]

The Committee on Home and Foreign Missions and Church Extension reacted favorably as is noted in their report:

REPORT OF THE COMMITTEE ON HOME AND FOREIGN MISSIONS, AND CHURCH EXTENSION

We, your committee beg leave to submit the following report. We have carefully examined into the Mission Field in Liberia, on the West Coast of Africa, where we find there are three churches, organized by our beloved brother Rev. Andrew Cartwright.

Whereas, as the brethren do most respectfully petition this General Conference for a Bible, one hymn book, and one common bell and

---

[13] *Daily Journal of the Sixteenth Quadrennial Session of the General Conference,* 1880, 15, 16.

two lamps, we do recommend that their request be granted as early as possible.

We recommend that this General Conference authorize the General Agent of our Book Concern, to send them the Bible and hymn books, at the earliest convenience. We further recommend that the Board of Missions be so authorized by this General Conference to furnish them two lamps and a bell at the earliest convenience. We further recommend that the request of the Quarterly Conference at Brewerville, Liberia, in regard to granting Elder A. Cartwright the privilege to hold an Annual Conference, be referred to the Board of Bishops, to take action in the case.

We further recommend that the Bishops give special attention to the West India Mission in furnishing them with men and means, and any other foreign mission, that may come under their observation.[14]

The Reverend Mark M. Bell, who at that time was the Secretary of the General Home and Foreign Missionary Board, with Bishop Singleton T. Jones as Chairman, offered the following resolutions in the sessions of the Conference:

Whereas: The progress of our church in Home and Foreign Missions has been much impeded through the want of sufficient means to send missionaries thereto, and to support those who have been already sent, and that the call for more missionaries in Africa, Liberia, and in other distant lands, (as well as in our own), has been heard and,

Whereas: We have found the ladies of our church always willing to do all in their power to forward the Gospel, in a benighted land and whose willingness has been and is now being demonstrated by them in their liberal contributions, annually received for the support of our Conference and Home Missions, therefore, be it

Resolved: That this General Conference do constitute a fund to be known as the *Ladies Home and Foreign Missionary Society, of the African Methodist Episcopal Zion Church.*

Resolved: That the officers of this Society shall be chosen from among the wives and daughters of our bishops and elders, and other influential ladies of our churches, in the several Episcopal Districts; further

Resolved: That the following Constitutions be adopted for the government of the General Missionary Board and Ladies Home and Foreign Missionary herein before mentioned.[15]

From the Minutes of this Sixteenth Quadrennial session it appears that there was little opposition to the resolutions but E. H. Curry spoke against printing them stating that the Church was entering in-

---

[14] *Daily Journal of the Sixteenth Quadrennial Session, General Conference,* 1880, 79.

[15] *Daily Journal of the Sixteenth Quadrennial Session of the General Conference,* 1880, 63, 64.

to something which would call for greater expense. Reverend Bell stated that this was the only way to properly introduce and interpret the new organization to the constituency of the Church. Others spoke for the printing of both the resolutions and the constitutions and the motion eventually was carried.

As the Constitutions as introduced are carried in the booklet: *Historical Synopsis*, published in 1967, we are not listing these constitutions here. Accompanying the Constitutions and resolutions was the following:

> "Each elder, deacon or preacher in charge of a church is requested (in addition to his regular missionary collections, which his conference directs to be taken), to form a missionary society in his church as soon as practicable, to meet monthly, and more, to forward the Gospel of the Kingdom of our blessed Redeemer. Each preacher will see that said society, appointed in his conference District, once in every three months, prior to the quarterly meetings, of the L. H. and F. Missionary Society shall have proper credit for the amount of money paid over. If the above course be adopted by the preachers in charge, each Vice-President will be greatly encouraged and aided in performing her duties and the work of missions largely increased, and the borders of God's Zion will spread more rapidly and His name be glorified. (For further information, see Constitution).
>
> BISHOP SINGLETON T. JONES, *President*
> M. M. BELL
> *Secretary of the General Mission Board* [16]

It appears that the first officers of the Ladies Home and Foreign Missionary Society were not elected by the General Conference. At least, the Minutes of the General sessions do not indicate that this was done. A ruling of Bishop Hood in 1884 stated that the officers of the Ladies Auxiliary *were not* members of the General Conference. He was sustained by the General Conference in this ruling.[17]

By 1884, the President and other members of the official family of the Ladies Society were being elected by the General Conference. This state of affairs appears to have existed until 1916, at least.[18] This same year likewise saw the breaking away of the election of Bishops' wives as President of the organization when, after two ballots, the incumbent, Mrs. Mary Jane Small, withdrew from the

---

[16] *Daily Journal, Sixteenth Quadrennial Session of the General Conference* 57, 58.

[17] *Daily Proceedings, Seventeenth Quadrennial Session of the General Conference,* 1884.

[18] *Minutes of the Twenty-fifth Quadrennial Session of the General Conference,* 1916, 120.

race and Reverend Dr. Florence Randolph of the New Jersey Conference was elected. While no law or ruling existed which prevented the Bishops' wives from being elected, it appears that from this year on none have been elected or have shown an inclination to seek the office, confining themselves to direction of the Episcopal Districts as designated by the Bishops. While the Accounts of the General Convention of 1919 are not before us it appears that this change may have taken place in that Convention. Seven years earlier the following was noted:

> That the Bishop's wives and widows be Vice Presidents of the W. H. and F. M. Society, to be active members of the Executive Board and that they be empowered to organize and assist in the furtherance of the work of the Connection.[19]

The Reverend Dr. W. J. Wood, in his report to the General Conference in 1920 stated:

> Nor must the Bishop's wives be forgotten. They contributed largely to the success of the Department. They were the pivots around which Missionary workers swung in their respective Episcopal Districts. They worked in season and out of season, braving summer's heat and winter's cold—as Trojans—that the good work might carry on according as it needs be. They served the Foreign Missionary cause well, working alongside their husbands in rural places far from their homes of comfort, in order that jungle-bred individuals, perhaps, might get into the drift of the new order of things. The honor of success is shared with them. They have done well, and they enter immediately unto the joy that cometh in the morning.[20]

The matter of appointing Episcopal Supervisors evidently developed between the period of 1912 and 1920, or following. The active Mrs. Blackwell laid the ground-work for such an appointment when she submitted the recommendation in 1912. It is possible that the change from Vice-President to Supervisor was voted in the Seventh General Convention of the Society held in Birmingham, Alabama in August 1931.[21] It appears that the term *Vice-President* was being utilized as late as 1924-1928.[22] By 1932 the term *Super-*

---

[19] *Minutes of the Twenty-fourth Quadrennial Session, General Conference,* 1912, 540.
[20] *Minutes of the Twenty-sixth Quadrennial Session of the General Conference,* 1920, 214.
[21] *Minutes of the Twenty-ninth Quadrennial Session, General Conference,* 1932, 194.
[22] *Sixth Quadrennial Report of the W. H. and F. M. Society,* 1924-1928.

HOME AND FOREIGN MISSIONS AND THE CHURCH

visor was being used and at that time the Supervisor became a member of the Executive Board, evidently in place of the Vice President as noted in 1912. Reviewing these developments and utilizing the scant record on hand it appears that between the time of the election of Mrs. Hood in 1896 as President of the Society and the time of the election of Mrs. Annie L. Blackwell as Corresponding Secretary, a restructuring program had been underway within the group. This is borne out by the procedures which appeared to exist up to and prior to 1896 and that which appeared to pertain from 1904. These changes may have been discussed and drawn up immediately before 1900, or, as we would suggest, either before, at or after the Atlantic City Conference in 1902. If this is true, then the changes may have been proposed by the Executive Committee or Board in the two years intervening. One will note that when the General Conference met in 1896 Mrs. Hood assumed the responsibility of making the report of the Society. By 1904, however, the job description of the Corresponding Secretary was listed as follows:

> PP555.3 The Corresponding Secretary shall conduct the correspondence of the Society. She shall keep in touch with Missionary Societies of other Churches, and with all the District Presidents and Organizers, and as far as possible, with the Local Societies; prepare the literature and programs for the societies and Conventions and report her transactions to the Executive Board, and for the Society to the Board of Bishops, and to the Connectional Council and the General Conference.[23]

It appears that it was under these rules, Mrs. Blackwell served. It is not clear as to the election of the one who immediately preceded her, Miss Eliza Ann Gardner, who served from 1888 to 1904. Mrs. Blackwell brought the office to a high state of efficiency and respect. She died December 7, 1922 and was succeeded by Mrs. Annie L. Anderson of the Allegheny Conference. Mrs. Anderson served until her voluntary retirement in 1935, when again the Society was restructured—this time when the General sessions of the group were held in Indianapolis, Indiana in August of that year. The major change at the time was the selection of an Executive Secretary.

According to the new interpretation the following was written:

> (d) The Executive Secretary of the Woman's Home and Foreign Missionary Society shall keep in touch with the Supervisors and

---
[23] *The Discipline of the A.M.E. Zion Church*, 1904, 258.

president; send notifications of elections and apportionments, and of special meetings to district officers, and cooperate with the president, secretary of Young Women, superintendent of Buds of Promise in the general supervision of the work of all groups, and in the preparation of all programs for the Societies and Conventions. She shall cooperate with the Committee on Missionary Education and recommend such studies as are suitable for the age groups. She shall, in agreement with the president, prepare the agenda for the regular meetings of the Executive Board. She shall receive all funds and reports from the district and local societies, giving receipts for the same.

She shall, in agreement with the Executive Board, specify to the Foreign Missionary Secretary purposes for which appropriations to the foreign work are made. She shall prepare and recommend money raising devises for the Society. She shall report for her transactions to the Executive Board and shall make regular reports for the Woman Home and Foreign Missionary Society to the Foreign Board and to the Board of Bishops. She may travel, lecture and assist in conventions, etc., in the interest of the promotion of the Society's program. She shall keep a statistical and financial record of her department in a book provided for the purpose and a file of correspondence and copies of reports, etc., all of which shall be preserved for her successor. She shall, by virtue of her office, be a member of the Literature Committee and of the Finance Committee. She shall report quarterly through the Missionary Seer all of her receipts and transfers of cash. She shall be bonded in the sum of Five Thousand Dollars ($5,000) in an acceptable Bonding Company.

The salary of the Executive Secretary shall be twelve hundred dollars ($1,200) per annum. She shall have a secretary whose salary shall be determined by the Execuitve Board.

It should be noted that by this time there were two Executive groups which should not be confused, one, the Board of Foreign Missions—the over-all body emanating from the General Conference of the denomination and the Executive Board, made up of the official family of the women, themselves. The first Executive Secretary of the Society was Mrs. Creola B. Cowan who took office at the adjournment of the Indianapolis meeting. She served the allotted two terms and turned the office over to Mrs. Abbie Clement Jackson (1943-1951). Mrs. Emma B. Watson succeeded her, serving until 1959. Mrs. Margaret May was then elected, serving until her tragic death in a car accident in November 1964. Mrs. Grace L. Holmes was then elected by the Executive Board and was re-elected by the Convention in 1967.

Presidents of the Society have been: Mrs. Mary J. Jones, Mrs. K. P. Hood, Mrs. Mary J. Small, Reverend Dr. Florence Randolph, Mrs. Daisy V. Johnson, Mrs. Henrietta Davis, Mrs. M. Anna Hauser, Mrs.

Rosa L. Weller, Mrs. Elsie G. Keyes, Mrs. Abbie Clement Jackson and Mrs. Emma B. Watson.

The Departments of the Society along with the dates of formation are: Buds of Promise (young children) founded by Mrs. Marie L. Clinton in 1904; Young Women, founded by Miss Victoria Richardson (1909) and accepted 1912; Bureau of Supplies, recommended by Dr. Randolph, August 1911, and accepted 1912; Life Members Council, recommended by Mrs. Anna L. Anderson 1916.

The listing of the General meetings of the Society are not easily traced. It is known that Bishop Alexander Walters called such a session in August 1901 (noted above). Others were evidently held as is noted in the statement of the Board of Bishops which says:

> When our last General Conference closed, the Woman's Home and Foreign Missionary Society was a subordinate branch of our General Missionary Department. By compliance with the request of the officers and working missionary women of the Church, the Council which convened in Allegheny, Pa. (North-side, Pittsburgh), at Avery Memorial Church about three years ago, arranged that this helpful adjunct of our great Church should be operated and controlled solely by the women of the Church. They held their first General meeting at Boston, Massachusetts and Louisville, Kentucky in August and September of last year. They have adopted devices and put into service plans and achieved such a measure of success as have fully justified their action in asking, and the Council in deciding, the present plan be put in force. Nothing has done more to give the Church a more vigorous and healthy growth and awaken the men to take a deeper interest in its forward movements for mission work and the general amelioration of the human family than the great awakening which has been given its most powerful momentum by consecrated and self-sacrificing women . . . . We are convinced from the success of this first general effort made by our own women from the increased activity and results following the efforts of our missionary women workers and from the benefits which the Church is receiving, and the larger benefits which it is destined to receive because of the organization and zeal of our women, and because of the organization and training of the Children of the Church, for systematic, intelligent and charitable service, that the future outcome of this Department furnish showers of spiritual blessings and at the same time greatly increase the missionary funds of the Church. We advise the General Conference to hear the women attentively and give them such legislation and encouragement as will enable them to do what their devoted hearts seem desirous of doing to further our missionary work.[24]

It appears, then that if one calls the Atlantic City Conference the

---

[24] *The Quadrennial Address of the Board of Bishops to the Twenty-third General Conference,* 1908.

First General Convention, the second would be the Boston-Louisville meeting. The Bishops, however, style this the first session. One should not lose sight of the Atlantic City meeting, however. The listed First Convention met in August and September 1907, the second then would be August 11-15, 16-21, 1911.[25] The Third session was held in Washington Metropolitan Church, St. Louis, Missouri, August 5-10, 1915. The last in this early series of General sessions was held in Asbury Park, New Jersey in 1919. The next session should have been held in 1923 but instead met with the General Conference in Indianapolis in 1924. At this time, as was noted, a critical point had arisen in Foreign Missions.

The death of the assigned Bishops John Wesley Alstork and George W. Clinton made it necessary to make changes in the supervision of a major part of the Church, including the Foreign Mission field. Bishop Wood, who had charge of the Seventh District, could not agree with the Reverend Frank A. Pinanko on certain points of law and AUTHORITY. The matter of the old Superintendent idea as interpreted in the case of Andrew Cartwright brought the Bishop and Reverend Pinanko into conflict. The Bishop, for example, stated: "He questioned my authority and gave as a reason that the General Conference gave him power to superintend, to supervise and to ordain in absence of the Bishop of the Foreign Work. With this authority he felt that he had the right under his commission to do what he felt that was right, since I was not on the field, regardless of my instructions as to the things that should be done for the interest of the work.[26]

The explanation of Bishop Wood continued: "On his return from America to take up his duties in Africa, I instructed him not to interfere with Rev. and Mrs. Peters, who had charge of the work at Quittah and the first thing he did was to disobey my instructions. He proceded at once with a corps of teachers to Quittah Station with a determination to oust Rev. and Mrs. Peters from the Quittah Station. They were ordered to leave the Mission House and to leave the employ of the Missions at Quittah."

"I was aware of the fact that I could not suspend him, but to protect our American Missionaries, Rev. and Mrs. Peters who had been

---

[25] *From a Quadrennial Missionary Program of that date.*
[26] *Minutes of the Twenty-seventh Quadrennial Session of the General Conference,* 1924, 298.

so faithful and who had made so many sacrifices for our Zion Church there, I made a feeble attempt to protect them by sending a cablegram to Reverend Frank Arthur Pinanko, that his authority to supervise the African work is hereby suspended. This retarded his progress for a few days and Rev. and Mrs. Peters were able to remain in the mission home and supervise the work. A point of law was raised as to whether I had the right to order the suspension of his authority, since he was authorized to supervise by the General Conference."

"Bishop Clement felt that his authority could not be suspended, therefore informed Rev. F. A. Pinanko that he was not suspended, and of course this gave Rev. Pinanko liberties to take such steps as he desired in the matter of the quarrel between Rev. and Mrs. Peters and himself. Finally, the question of Rev. Pinanko's authority to supervise was brought before the Board of Bishops. We talked the matter over carefully but no decision rendered. At this meeting I resigned and gave up the African work. Bishop Clement assumed the responsibility of carrying on the work. You have his report and I am sure that you are satisfied with what he has had to say in reference to the missionaries and the work accomplished by them in Africa." [27]

It is no doubt possible that Bishop Clement had something to say concerning the African work but it does not appear in his report as appearing in the Minutes of the General Conference. The Reverend Dr. W. W. Matthews, Secretary of Foreign Missions lauded Rev. Pinanko's Annual Address stating that "it was a comprehensive survey in itself of the Gold Coast work." [28] Earlier, he stated: "The annual address of Rev. F. A. Osam-Pinanko, the General Superintendent of the work in the West Conference, will convince the most skeptical that Zion Methodism is not only on the way, but has arrived, set up her camps and way stations and unfurled her banners to the morning breezes of golden Africa."

Here, alone appears to have been a cleavage in the Missionary ranks, Bishop Wood stating his side of the question and the Secretary, along with Bishop Clement evidently taking the other side of the issue. This may have had a great deal to do with the visit of the

---
[27] *Ibid.*, 299.
[28] *Ibid.*, 254.

Reverend Dr. Florence Randolph, the ex-President of the Woman's Home and Foreign Missionary Society. The Secretary stated: "No report could be complete without mentioning the visit of the gifted Rev. Mrs. Florence Randolph, ex-President of the Woman's Home and Foreign Missionary Society. She spent several months in the field in Quittah district assisting Rev. Mrs. Henrietta Peters and preaching uplifting sermons. Then she spent three days at Winnebah with Reverend Ntedu-Kyirbuwa and his congregation and ten days with Rev. Pinanko at Cape Coast preaching on Sunday and on Christmas Day. That she made a very favorable impression and infused a new life in the work may be seen from the passage of Reverend Pinanko's address when it said: 'We wished it were possible for her to have stayed longer on the Eastern, Central and Western Provinces of Gold Coast.' Mrs. Randolph visited the work in Brewerville, Liberia, also." [29]

The Committee on Foreign Missions recognized the existence of dissatisfaction with affairs in Africa when they stated: "That whereas there is considerable dissatisfaction on the field, growing out of certain complaints made by the missionaries and rumors detrimental to the future progress of our missionary activities both at home and abroad, we recommend that a special commission composed of three members of the Foreign Mission Board, three officers of the W. H. and F. M. Society, and three others to be duly appointed, be authorized to examine and investigate the handling of the W. H. and F. M. S. and the Secretary of Missions and determine to what extent our missionaries and their work have been supported financially." [30] The Committee also concurred with the Episcopal address in its recommending a Bishop for Africa. The matter of the African Bishop or rather, a Bishop for Africa was likewise endorsed by the Secretary of Foreign Missions. He suggested: "one who is willing to enter heartily into their lives and problems, willing to live among them, to sympathize with them, to supervise and direct affairs and Zion's destinies in the fatherland." He went on to state that the Conference had in attendance several delegates from Africa who would endorse such a move. As a result of these suggestions the Episcopal Committee recommended the establishment of a Twelfth

---
[29] *Minutes of the Twenty-seventh Quadrennial Session, General Conference* 256, 257.
[30] *Ibid.*, 193, 194.

District made up of this Foreign work. Subsequently, Bishop Cameron Chesterfield Alleyne was assigned to this District. A return to Quadrennial sessions for the Missionary organization was experienced in 1931, the delegates called in that year to meet in Birmingham, Alabama. The 1935 session met in Indianapolis, Ind., as previously reported, while the General Convention selected Detroit, Michigan for its 1939 sessions. Brooklyn was selected in 1943 and Wilmington, N. C. in 1947. Goler Metropolitan Church, Winston-Salem, N. C. was host in 1951, and in 1955, for the first time a General Meeting of the Church met on the West Coast, at Los Angeles. Hartford, Connecticut hosted the group in 1959; St. Louis in 1963 and Brooklyn, First Church, again in 1967.

The following Bishops succeeded Bishop Alleyne as resident Bishops in Africa: W. W. Matthews, J. W. Brown, and upon his tragic passing, Bishop Alleyne again assumed charge: E. W. Watson, H. T. Medford, S. Dorme Lartey, the first native African, serving with W. A. Hilliard and then, with A. G. Dunston, and until his (Lartey's) recent death, during this quadrennium, as the only Bishop assigned to the African field.

Work has continued as well in bases closer to America. Bishops Alleyne, Gordon, Spottswood, Shaw and Smith have worked and some are working in this area today. These fields are the South America, Virgin Islands and Bahamas Conferences.

Since the days of the Rev. Mark M. Bell, who served as Secretary to the Board of Foreign Missions 1880-1892, the following have served as Secretaries: J. H. Manley, 1892-1896; A. J. Warner, 1896-1898; Jesse B. Colbert, 1898-1904; G. L. Blackwell, 1904-1908; R. A. Morrisey, 1908-1912; John W. Wood, 1912-1920; W. W. Matthews, 1920-1928; H. T. Medford, 1928-1948; D. C. Pope, 1948-1952; J. C. Hoggard, 1952.

Few would deny that the impetus of work in Africa came at the hands of Bishop John Bryan Small. An only child of John Bryan and Kittie Ann Small, he could trace his ancestry as far back as 1720. He was born March 14, 1845 at Frazer, St. Joseph's Parish, Barbadoes, West Indies. He was educated at home and at St. John's Lodge. In 1862 he went to Jamaica and other islands of the West Indies and then on to West Africa where he learned to speak the Fantee language. In all, he spent three years and three months in Africa, observing the customs, languages, etc. He had an opportunity to see, at first hand such regions as Sierra Leone, Cape Coast, Elmena, Dix Cove, Accra Lagos, Badagry, Ganbia and Fort Bullin. On his return from Africa he spent time in British Honduras.

Bishop Small was one of the best educated of our Bishops, having studied earlier for the ministry in the Episcopalian Church. On his way to England he came to the United States (1871) and through the Rev. R. H. G. Dyson and Bishop J. J. Clinton was persuaded to join the A.M.E. Zion Church. He was elected to the Bishopric in May 1896 and died January 15, 1915. When John Bryan Small was elected to the episcopacy he signified his willingness to go to Africa, thus establishing the first phase of episcopal supervision in this part of the world for Zion Methodism. He left for his assignment June 22, 1897 and arrived in Sierra Leone July 16th. At this point he tarried until August, going on to Liberia, Saturday, August 7, 1897. It is said that he visited every Zion Church as far as Belize, British Honduras.[31]

Perhaps the most outstanding contribution of Bishop Small to Foreign Mission work is his vast endeavor to train an indigenous leadership. Bishop Alleyne in his book, Gold Coast At A Glance, wrote the following:

> During the disturbances incident to the Ashanti uprisings against the English, there came to Cape Coast with one of the West Indian regiments, as a clerk, a young man who had been trained for the ministry of the Church of England, in his island home of Barbadoes, John Bryan Small, large of stature, soldierly in bearing, cultured in mind and soul, saw many things which seared his cultured soul and offended his refined feelings. He purposed that he would seek membership in an American Church operated and governed by those who were kin to the folks among whom he then lived. That accomplished, he determined to return and introduce that African Church to the African people of the Gold Coast.
>
> He conceived the idea that the ideal way of making entree to the hidden excellencies of the African was by educating and utilizing Africans in the field of social and religious activity. He therefore made arrangements with the Rev. Fynn Egyir-Assam of Cape Coast to select a few young men of piety and promise for training in Livingstone College at Salisbury, North Carolina.[32]

---

[31] *E. D. W. Jones, Comprehensive Catechism of the A.M.E. Zion Church*, 69.
[32] *Bishop Cameron Chesterfield Alleyne, Godl Coast At a Glance* (Norfolk, Va.), 85.

HOME AND FOREIGN MISSIONS AND THE CHURCH

In the selection of young men to study in America James Emman Kwegyir Aggrey (1898) and Frank Osam-Pinanko are well known. Frank Osam-Pinanko returned to Africa in 1903 and labored incessantly among his people. It was he who precipitated the situation which led to the assigning of Bishop Alleyne to the Foreign Missions field. Others brought to America included Walter K. Dolly, Charles Acolatze and Beresford Cole. Mrs. Peters brought over Princess Ayina Adamah in 1916 and Reverend Peters sponsored the Rev. A. A. Adjahoe.[33] Reverend Adjahoe later returned and was assigned to work in Keta. Others evidently followed among them being Isaac D. Osabutey and F. K. Fiawoo, sponsored by Bishop Alleyne and Charity Zomolo of Keta who was sponsored by Reverend Randolph. Bishop and Mrs. W. A. Hilliard have sponsored Skyne Uku from Ogwas Owerri Province, Nigeria, the first young woman from her nation to enroll at Livingstone College. She is at present doing graduate studies since it is impossible for her to return to her home area because of the Civil War. Bishop Alfred G. Dunston has sponsored the following young men during his assignment:

> The educating of these young people has no doubt allowed the A.M.E. Zion Church to exist and progress in the areas where the denomination has endeavored to serve. Today, the listing of Americans working on the Foreign field is indeed scanty. The Reverend Dr. Joseph Drybauld Taylor, arriving in Nigeria in 1931, laid the groundwork of Zion Methodism here. As Bishop Dunston states: "He was able to travel to America to represent Nigeria A.M.E. Zion Church in the Quadrennial General Conference of 1932." He further states: "When Dr. Taylor returned from America in 1932 he broke the good tidings of the recognition of the Nigeria A.M.E. Zion Church as a part of an Episcopal District. He said that Bishop W. W. Matthews was assigned to supervise Nigeria. The effect of this good news spread far and wide with the result that some of the Churches in the Zion Temple of Rev. Young broke away and joined the A.M.E. Zion Church. Rev. P. D. Ofosuhene arrived in Nigeria from Ghana to assist Dr. Taylor in 1932." [34] Earlier, Bishop Dunston explained the Zion Temple Church movement as he states: "Originally, there was an enterprise in the name of Zion Temple under the leadership of one Rev. Archibong Young of Calabar, popularly known as Patnach Young. Rev. Young was a Government Schoolmaster at Ikot Ekan. When he retired he

---

[33] *Ibid.,* 86.
[34] Indonia Rogerson, ed., *Historical Synopsis of the Woman's Home and Foreign Missionary Society* (1967) 79.

made himself a minister and organized churches. He names his enterprise ZION TEMPLE. The mission of Zion Temple spread to few places in Eastern Nigeria, particularly Old Calabar Province . . . There were no churches for the Zion Temple in Ibo land." [35]

It should be stated that the work in Africa has demanded not only close study but improved communication and supervision since 1924, especially. It will be recalled that the Committee in that General Conference proposed such a course of action. When Bishop Alleyne arrived on the field in that year he states that he "found a rather tense situation." It appears that because of the financial difficulties "a majority of the churches and preachers had voted to withdraw from the A.M.E. Zion Connection. With the aid of Dr. J. E. Kwegyir Aggrey, negotiations were carried on with the people and ministry and a reconciliation was effected.

The situation remained tense in some respects in 1932 as well. Appended is a petition from the West African Conference leaders which shows a portion of this unrest and the decision of the Executive and Judiciary Committee. The Committee's report follows:

> To the Bishops, General Officers and Members of the General Conference
>
> The Committee on Executive and Judicial Business reports as follows:
>
> We had before the Episcopal Committee, Drs. Pinanko and Taylor. We were attempting to solve the question relating to the supervision of the African work.
>
> It was decided in the following manner, after much discussion on both sides, to the satisfaction of all.
>
> Dr. Pinanko is to be the Supervisor of the Gold Coast Conference (East and West).
>
> Dr. Taylor is to supervise the Nigerian work. The entire African work is to remain in the Eleventh Episcopal District under Bishop W. W. Matthews.
>
> Supervisor as defined to mean that the person thus appointed is to have power to hold Annual Conferences in the absence of the Bishop; and is answerable to the Bishop annually, and the supervisor is to perform such other functions as required by the Bishop in charge. It was further decided that the Bishop and Foreign Missions Board handle all money for that field.
>
> The Committee is very thankful to all parties concerned for agreeing so readily to these our findings.
>
> THE COMMITTEE

---

[35] *Ibid.*, 78.

PETITION FROM WEST AFRICAN MISSIONS
(To the Twenty-ninth Quadrennial Session of the General Conference, Pittsburgh, Pa., 1932)

Pittsburgh, Pa., May 4, 1932

The petition of your humble servants who are the accredited representatives of the West African Conferences and accredited delegates of the Twenty-ninth Quadrennial Session of the African Methodist Episcopal Zion General Conference assembled in the Wesley Centre Church, Pittsburgh, Pa., sheweth:

1. That as members of the Episcopal Committee of the General Conference in session, we have not been accorded the rights and privileges due us in the disposition made of the African work, in that the valuable representations made to that committee and unanimously carried in its meeting, to the effect that all matters having reference to the future supervision of the work in Africa should be transferred to the Board of Bishops, were unlawfully miscarried.

2. That we verily realize that as Native Africans with no small measure of qualifications to represent Africa in all of her phases and needs, and having been working unceasingly on the field as Pioneer Missionaries for the last 29 or 30 years, that no man can truly represent the present and future needs of Africa as your humble, dutiful servants can do.

3. That your humble Petitioners desire to remind the General Conefrence in Session that it was in the year 1924 when the General Conference first in the history of the Connection appointed Bishop C. C. Alleyne as the resident Bishop of the West African work for the express purpose of giving the African work the needed close Episcopal supervision; and if that is true, your Petitioners would want to know why after the lapse of two terms in which the Missions on the Gold Coast during the last quadrennium has greatly suffered from lack of Mission support—the $15,000 received by the African work alleged to have spent on Liberia—the African work should go back to the unsympathetic hand of the Episcopate who has been assigned to four Conferences in America—an action which defeats the purpose of this General Conference measures to meet the economic depression.

4. That since your humble Petitioners are aware of the supreme sacrifices of the Connection is making generally, and Woman's Home and Foreign Missionary Society is making in particular for Africa in

raising funds for the redemption of Africa, and yet not even half of the money goes to the field for which the money is raised, your Petitioners humbly but emphatically and unequivocally enter their solemn protest against placing Africa on the Eleventh Episcopal District during this quadrennium.

5. That your Petitioners are in position to know as well as the Connection that the necessary close Episcopal Supervision due the African work for which so many thousands of dollars were paid during the past quadrennium, was not given: and therefore it could be readily seen that the monetary sacrifices made by the Woman's (Home and Foreign Missionary) Society and the general Church have not been profitable.

6. That your humble Petitioners during the last quadrennium were the only responsible persons who saved the Gold Coast Zion Missions from disgrace when the property of three of our strategic mission points was to be lost to us.

7. That your humble Petitioners feel that the only reasonable measure to save the African Mission today is to give it an indigenous leadership and supervision with a view to saving thousands of dollars in transportation, missionary equipment and all other non-essentials to the Field which defeat the purpose of carrying on missionary activities in Africa of today.

8. Your humble Petitioners feel as never before that this Connection owes to the Petitioners at least a favorable urgent hearing to the end that their request may be complied with.

9. And that in the name of common justice, and economy, equality of rights and privileges, in the name of this great Church of God and in the name of Christ who has no respect of persons, this burning Petition of your humble Petitioners may be favorably answered and for that your humble Petitioners shall forever pray.

Your humble and dutiful Petitioners
F. A. OSAM PINANKO
J. DRYMAULD TAYLOR
For West African Missions

While it is impossible to record all the results of study in one work on the History of the denomination in most respects and particularly where Missions are concerned, it is felt that additional facts on Foreign work should be listed to give a general idea of the Church's work. For example, according to the records it appears that the East

Gold Coast Conference, as it was then known, was organized and first met March 31, 1910.[36] At the same session Bishop J. W. Alstork reported: "the Rev. E. C. Dean is now building in Nassau. The Church has been partly wrecked. He has stone enough on the grounds to put up the walls—"[37] The Minutes of the Twenty-fifth and Twenty-sixth sessions record the following "Bishop J. W. Alstork was able to visit the West India Islands and part of South America where he gave new impetus to our brethren down there. There seems to be a good and effectual door opening to the A.M.E. Zion Church in South America."

The Demerara South American Conference was organized in 1911 by Bishop Alexander Walters. Bishop J. W. Alstork replaced him at the end of his term. It is presumed that one of the founders of this Conference, if not the entire work, was the late Reverend W. A. Deane, who in subsequent General Conferences gave reports. By 1942, the work had grown to the point that six organizations were reported at that time. In that year, too, one high school and a grade school were listed.[38] Reverend W. A. Deane was succeeded by the Reverend Glascoe Deane, who matriculated at Livingstone College.

In the Minutes of the Twenty-seventh session of the General Conference the following is stated: "Bishop L. W. Kyles introduced the Rev. Jas. A. Agaard, of St. Croix, Virgin Islands. Rev. Agaard pointed out that it was just four years ago that he had visited the General Conference at Knoxville, Tenn. He told of some of the sacrifices made on his field with fifty people, that under the blessings of God had increased to 120." As stated in the Historical Synopsis of the Woman's Home and Foreign Missionary Society, it is disappointing to note that so little is said about this work in the General Conference Minutes of the period. Were it not for the brief statement made by Attorney Samuel Madison Dudley in his Year Book we would lose valuable knowledge of this work. Attorney Dudley notes as recorded by the then Dr. Hampton Thomas Medford: "In the Virgin Islands at St. Croix in 1919, upon completion of negotiations of Bishop R. A. Carter of the Colored Methodist Episcopal Church

---
[36] *Minutes of the Twenty-fourth Quadrennial Session of the General Conference,* 198.
[37] *Ibid.,* 249.
[38] *Minutes of the Twenty-seventh Quadrennial Session of the General Conference,* 39.

and Bishop J. W. Alstork of the African Methodist Episcopal Zion Church which resulted in the bringing of the C. M. E. Church there with its pastor, The Reverend James A. Agaard into the A.M.E. Zion Church." [39]

No mention is made of this move, however, in the report of the Bishop Alstork or by the then Foreign Missions Secretary in his report. Elsewhere we have stated perhaps there is a possibility that the date given is incorrect but a search of the 1924 Minutes has so far failed to reveal anything further on this work except that a Committee recommended that the Reverend Mr. Agaard be reimbursed $2,000 from funds available.[40]

The C.M.E. Church appears to have little to say on the situation as well. In its fourteenth Quadrennial Session of the General Conference, however, we run across the following:

> Our women furnish an example of consecration, zeal and efficiency without parallel in any period of the Church. Their Missionary efforts have been realized and localized for enterprises in charges, districts and Annual Conferences.[41]

Earlier, it is noted that the C.M.E. Church endeavored to build up a cooperative Missionary relationship with another related group. No doubt the conversations on Organic Union and the other work of the A.M.E. Zion Church in the area prompted this unusual move on the part of these two Negro Methodist groups.

Missions in the A.M.E. Zion Church have always called for a great sacrifice, first on the part of the Missionaries sent out from the Home Base, themselves. This has been true both for the Home Missionaries as well as those sent overseas. One finds a feeling of sorrow as the casual sufferings of these pioneers are noted. To a great extent, especially in the latter years of the Church's history, the sufferings recorded abroad have not been matched by a like zeal for suffering at home. Some have offered all, others, little and still others, perhaps, nothing.

The late Bishop John Bryan Small gave much to the work. In his Episcopal Address to the 55th Session of the Allegheny-Ohio Conference, he mentions, for example, having been instrumental in

---

[39] *The A.M.E. Zion Year Book,* 1942-1943 (Washington, D.C.), 79.

[40] *Minutes of the Twenty-seventh Quadrennial Session of the General Conference,* 192.

[41] Bishop C. H. Phillips, *The History of the Colored Methodist Episcopal Church in America* (Jackson, Tenn.) 504.

bringing Mr. William Hockman from Africa to America where he attended Livingstone College. He also tells that, "We received a letter from Rev. Carl H. Williams, Santo Domingo, West Indies. Reverend Williams is pastoring a flourishing mission work on that island and has again and again urged us to give him some financial assistance." . . . Bishop Small further states to clear up the matter of Rev. Ottley: "We received some of the most heart-rending letters from Rev. O. E. Ottley, Belize, British Honduras." Later, too, Bishop Small mentions another young man, Rev. Frank Arthur, who after graduation was sent by the Bishop to Cape Coast, West Africa, to erect a church. Along with the young man the Bishop also sent an organ.[42]

The Twenty-seventh Quadrennial Session of the General Conference records the further extension of Zion's Missionary effort.

> Our venture in Rio de Janerio, and Bahia, Brazil, did not bring forth the expected results hoped for. Under the exhuberance of our zeal for world-wide expansion, I am persuaded to think that we attempted to enter the field before the time was ripe. Our Commission in the person of Bishop George C. Clement, Drs. J. W. Martin and A. A. Crooke, was sent to the place under escort of one Dr. Borchello, passing as a sort of envoy for those whom he claimed were waiting in large numbers to come into our communion. His representations smacked of absurdities, and it looked like we were merely on a chase of the will-O'-the-wisp.
>
> But the Commission decided to leave Dr. Crooke on the field for further try out. He stayed at Bahia for two years and five months, after which time he voluntarily gave up and asked to be brought back to the United States. We gladly complied with his request.[43]

The writer suggests that a broader account of Missions work will be found in the Historical Synopsis and the projected work of Dr. Yates. So, therefore we would close this brief account on Missions with this statement of Bishop Small. "To us it seems a little strange that the Connection should allow the bulk of the foreign work to rest upon our shoulders, and that so little provision should be made to sustain it. The present condition of the work demands that special attention shall be given thereto, and we hope that the delegates sent to the next General Conference will see that special provision is made for the sustentation of foreign missions. The Connection must do one of two things, give up the foreign mission work, or make special provision to sustain it. To give up the work would remove from our Zion the crown of its rejoic-

---

[42] *Journal of the Fifty-fifth Session, Allegheny-Ohio Conference*, 24.
[43] *Minutes of the Twenty-seventh Quadrennial Session of the General Conference*, 260.

ing. We dislike to be placed in a position or situation where we cannot sustain ourselves." [44]

A listing of Missionaries as reported by the late Bishop H. T. Medford when he was Secretary of Foreign Missions.

LIBERIA

Rev. Andrew Cartwright	1876-1903
Mrs. Andrew Cartwright	
Rev. Henry Ghesson	1903-1904
Rev. H. T. Wright	1904-1908
Rev. J. D. Taylor (a native of Gold Coast)	1908-1911
Rev. J. J. Pierce	1911-1915
Rev. and Mrs. Thomas E. Davis	1919-1922
Rev. and Mrs. D. G. Garland	1922-1923
Rev. and Mrs. D. C. Pope	1923-1930
Mr. Oliver L. Sims	1929-1936
Rev. Miss Almena J. Smith	1931-1936
Miss Arwilda G. Robinson	1934-1938
Rev. and Mrs. A. W. Ricks	1936*
Rev. and Mrs. S. W. Peacock	1939*

GOLD COAST

Rev. W. E. Shaw	†
Rev. J. J. Pierce	1910†
Rev. and Mrs. R. E. Peters	1915-1925
Rev. and Mrs. W. D. Francis	1925-1926
Rev. and Mrs. R. F. Pile	1926-1930

While we are not certain where the following served we list their names as well:

Dr. and Mrs. J. A. Babington-Johnson
Reverend and Mrs. A. A. Adjahoe
Dr. and Mrs. D. G. Garland

It should be added also that the change to Quadrennial Convention was voted in the General Conference of 1928.

This listing of Foreign Missionaries is corrected only to 1942, African Missionaries and their term of service:

A. LIBERIA

Reverend and Mrs. Andrew Cartwright	1876-1903
Rev. Henry Chessin	1903-1904

---

[44] *Journal of the 55th session of the Allegheny-Ohio Conference,* 25.
Samuel Madison Dudley, *Year Book,* 1942-1943, 80.
* It is presumed that these missionaries had not completed their term at the time so were still serving.
† The author is not clear as to length of time served.
The return to quadrennial conventions was voted in the General Conference of 1928. The law provided that the meetings should take place the year prior to the meeting of the General Conference.

HOME AND FOREIGN MISSIONS AND THE CHURCH

Rev. H. T. Wright 1904-1908
Rev. J. D. Taylor (native of Gold Coast) 1908-1911
Rev. J. J. Pierce 1911-1915
No American Superintendent 1915-1919
Rev. and Mrs. Thomas E. Davis 1919-1922
Rev. and Mrs. D. G. Garland 1922-1923
Rev. and Mrs. Daniel C. Pope 1923-1930
Mr. Oliver L. Simms 1929-1936
Rev. Almena J. Smith 1931-1936
Miss Arwelda G. Robinson 1934-1938
Rev. and Mrs. A. W. Ricks 1936-
Rev. and Mrs. S. W. Peacock 1939

B. GOLD COAST

Rev. W. E. Shaw 1909
Rev. J. J. Pierce 1910
Rev. and Mrs. R. E. Peters 1915-1925
Rev. and Mrs. R. F. Pile 1926-1930

BISHOPS TO AFRICA

Bishop John Bryan Small 1896-1904
Bishop Alexander Walters 1904-1908
Bishop George L. Blackwell 1912-1916
Bishop G. C. Clement 1916-1920
Bishop Cameron Chesterfield Alleyne, (resident) 1924-1928
Bishop William W. Matthews 1928-1936
Bishop James W. Brown, (resident) 1936-1941
Bishop Alleyne may have supervised interval
Bishop E. B. Watson, (resident) 1944-1948
Bishop H. T. Medford, (resident) 1948-1952
Bishop D. C. Pope, (resident) 1952-1960
Bishop S. Dorme Lartey, (Native resident) 1960-1969
Bishop William A. Hilliard, (resident) 1960-1964
Bishop Alfred G. Dunston, (resident) 1964-1968

CHAPTER XV

The Denomination and Its Finances

ANY organization which undertakes an independent existence, early finds itself concerned rather deeply with financial matters. The Zion Methodist Church was no exception to this state of affairs. Only a short time had passed when the new Church found itself face to face with a monetary situation as it sought to fulfill its mission. There was the matter of adequate housing for the congregation; the desire to foster and maintain a school; and the matter of sustaining an efficient ministry. All these needs appeared to have been noted but that which must have been overlooked, or not considered, was that of missions and evangelism. The early church was therefore handicapped simply because the preachers did not have the funds to travel.

The attainment of the first goal, the matter of housing for the organization, found a sympathetic ear in the city inhabitants, and, after some disappointments and mistakes, lots were leased for twenty-one years and a frame building was constructed. The money for the venture was secured through gifts of the congregation and other Negroes as well as subscriptions paid by the residents of the city.[1] This was the Church's second home. Later, when additional land was offered for sale in the rear of the Church and Leonard Street property the Trustees also bought this parcel.

Rush states that a few years before the expiration of the twenty-one year lease on the original lots a drive got underway to secure $750 for outright purchase. This was accomplished by April 8, 1801. A sizable amount of money was given in this drive by the Negroes of the City. Seventeen years later, it was necessary to undertake a drive for funds to build a new church.[2] This time, the task was greater and the problems more varied. The new structure was to be larger and was to contain a school room.

Money was more difficult to find as the young organization soon understood. The Legislature of the State of New York was petitioned for aid in the building of the school room, the sums to come from the

---

[1] Christopher Rush, *Rise and Progress of the African M.E. Church in America* (New York, 1866) 12.
[2] *Ibid.*, 30.

public school funds. According to Rush in this the Church was disappointed.[3] However, it is noted that funds were later given through the Common Council of the City of New York, for the maintenance of this school.[4] The foundation of the structure had to be covered for the winter months and until added funds could be had. Finally, when Spring came, $3,000 was borrowed on special permission from the Mastery in Chancery, to complete the building.

The third imperative for funds had been a concern of the first early preachers as well as the others who were later called to preach. Practically all available money not allocated to building purposes was given for ministerial services of the preachers appointed by the Methodist Episcopal New York Conference. This left little or nothing for the Negro ministry, thus defeating one of the early purposes of the formation of the organization—the development of an indigenous leadership. Later the question of mission work brought the response that "some of them complained of the want of money as a hindrance to their traveling."[5] The Church was actually poverty-stricken for a note is made of the fact that Reverend Stillwell returned to the Trustees of the organization the full amount given him by the congregation for the year—$10.37½.[6]

On the matter of the development of indigenous leadership the Discipline of 1852 gives this clue as it states the thinking of the early Church:

> Beloved Brethren:
> We think it proper to state briefly, that after due consideration, the official members of the African Methodist Episcopal Zion and Asbury Churches in the City of New York, have been led to conclude that such was the relation in which we stood to the white Bishops and Conference, relative to the ecclesiastical government of the African Methodist Episcopal Church or Society in America. So long as we remain in that situation, our preachers would never to able to enjoy these privileges, which the Discipline of the white Church holds out to all its members, that are called of God to preach, in consequence of the limited access our brethren had to those privileges, and particularly in consequence of the difference of color. They have been led also to conclude, that the usefulness of our preachers has been very much hindered, and our African brethren in general, have been deprived of those blessings which Almighty God may have designed to grant them,

---

[3] *Ibid.*, 30.
[4] David H. Bradley, Sr., *A History of the A.M.E. Zion Church*, 1796-1872, (Nashville, 1956) 65-68.
[5] Rush, *loc. cit.*, 48, 49.
[6] *Ibid.*, 57.

through the means of these preachers, which He has, from time to time raised up from among them, because there having been no means adopted, by the said Bishops and Conference, for our preachers to travel through the Connexion, and promulgate the Gospel of our Lord, Jesus Christ;—and they have had no access to the only source from which they might have obtained a support, at least while they traveled. Under these considerations they believe that the formation of an itinerant plan, an establishment of a conference for the African Methodist preachers in the United States, who are not yet attached to any conference of that nature, would be essential to the prosperity of the spiritual concerns of our Colored brethren in general, and would be the means of advancing our preachers (who are now in regular standing in the Connexion with the white preachers of the Methodist Episcopal Church) whenever it should be found necessary for the advancement of the Redeemer's Kingdom among our African brethren, to bring forward for ordination those who are called of God to preach the Gospel of our Lord, which may be done from time to time, according to the best of our judgment of the necessity thereof, and not according to the method which it is natural, to suppose our white brethren would pursue to determine upon the necessity of such ordination. We are under strong impression of mind, that such measures would induce many of our African brethren to attend on Divine worship, who are yet careless about their eternal welfare, and thereby prove effectual in the hands of God, in the awakening and conversion of their souls to the knowledge of truth.

And, whereas, Almighty God, in His all-wise and gracious Providence, and recently offered a favorable opportunity, whereby these societies may be regularly organized as an Evangelical African Methodist Church they have therefore

Resolved to embrace the said opportunity, and have agreed that the title of the connexion shall be the African Methodist Episcopal Church in America, and they have selected a form of Discipline, from that of our Mother Church, which selection, with a little alteration, we recommend to you, for the Doctrines and Discipline of our Church, hoping that the great Shepherd and Bishop of souls, the all wise and gracious God, will be pleased to approve the above measures, and grant that we may obtain and preserve these privileges, which we have been heretofore deprived of, that thereby we may unite our mutual efforts for the prosperity of the Redeemer's Kingdom among us, and for the encouragement of our Colored brethren in the ministry.

Earnestly soliciting your prayers and united endeavors for the same, we remain your affectionate brethren and servants in the Kingdom of our ever adorable Lord.

Abraham Thompson
James Varick
William Miller[7]

---

[7] *The Discipline of 1852* (Copies of the above will also be found in each of our present Disciplines.).

THE DENOMINATION AND ITS FINANCES

Prior to the formation of the denomination, financial statements were made by the Mother Church where the building project was concerned. For example: George Collins reported that in three years $4,654 had been raised. With the money borrowed the total was listed as $7,232.78 (amount paid out on new building. The sum of $415.91½ remained on hand).[8]

While the new denomination showed a total of 1,426 members in its first yearly conference only $35.08 was reported for the support of the session.[9] Rush does not state how this was allocated.

It appears that to this time there were two major items of the Financial system, one, money given every fourth year (eventually) for the support of the General Conference (these funds were given voluntarily by individual churches and organizations of those churches), and the money evidently given by the Churches or annual Conferences for the support of the General Superintendent. Evidently in the beginning there was no set amount allocated for this officer. Later, two other interests were advanced—the school or college project and sums for the church publication or periodical.

While the writer cannot be sure, owing to the lack of detailed records, the printed minutes of 1848 make no mention of Superintendent support, nor any asking on the part of the General Conference for denominational projects or enterprises.

By 1852, however, the financial structure of the denomination appears to have begun taking shape. They were concerned with the advancement of some of their projects and where home and foreign voluntarily by individual churches and organizations of those missions were concerned the following appears:

> What shall be done in order to defray the expenses of our Home and Foreign Missionaries?
> Answer: Each Annual Conference shall organize a missionary society, the members of which shall pay such sums as shall be determined from year to year by the Conference.
> 2. It shall be the duty of each minister in charge to organize missionary societies wherever it is convenient in his charge—the same to be auxiliaries for the Annual Conference Society for that district.

One might add that, for the first time, we believe, there appears a section in the Discipline on TEMPORAL Economy, Sec. II).

---

[8] Bradley, *loc. cit.*, 64.
[9] Moore, *loc. cit.*

So little is said about the finances of the denomination in the writings that it is difficult to trace true development. A General Conference Fund Agent appears to have been appointed from New York in the General Conference of 1860.[10] One can conclude that this was common practice even though no listing is noted for any other Conference. Support of the Superintendency therefore, had to be a matter of each Annual Conference. The Reverend J. B. Trusty was thus named in the New York area. In the same General Conference (1860) mention is made of a Treasurer of the General Conference Fund—a fund for the support of the General Conference, no doubt. One cannot state whether this individual was William H. Bishop or some other person however.

Four years later a Finance Committee was named consisting of J. B. Trusty, Jos. G. Smith, Robert Dyson, while another Committee on Salary was named consisting of W. F. Butler, S. T. Jones and William Wilson.[11] Again, it can be concluded that this committee was charged with the task of dealing with the Superintendents' salary rather than that of ministers in the local churches since this was a purely local church matter.

In this same General Conference a total of $698.50 was given for the support of the Quadrennial session as noted in the Minutes.[12]

In 1868 one notes again a Committee on Finance as well as another on Ways and Means, and that which is more definite, a Committee on Bishops' Salary (the term Bishop at this time was official). At the time $1,500 was recommended to be the salary of the Bishop.[13]

Incidentally, one can note the trend in these early years as one refers to the case of Superintendent Ross, who was tried by the Church for ceasing to travel. His excuse was that in the rotation system the "field had been gleaned" (by the other Superintendents) so he could not make a living. After expenses, he had received only $200, so he secured a set of cobbler's tools and returned to his trade.[14]

In the report of the Committee on Ministers' Salary noted in the General Conference of 1868, it is stated that the annual allowance

---

[10] Moore, *loc. cit.*, 222.
[11] Moore, *Ibid.*, 233.
[12] *Minutes of the General Conference of 1864.*
[13] *Ibid.*
[14] Bradley, *loc. cit.*, 152.

THE DENOMINATION AND ITS FINANCES

for a minister in charge should be not less than $700.00 per year with parsonage and $800.00 without parsonage. However, if the people were not able to pay these amounts, the minister and people should make such contracts as they were able to agree upon. The minister should receive traveling expense to all meetings called by the Bishop as well.[15]

In the General Conference of 1872 (Thirteenth Quadrennial Session meeting in Charlotte, North Carolina) the Committee on Bishops' Salaries reported the following: that the amount should be "not less than $1200.00 per year and not more than $1500.00." The salaries should be raised by taxing each member twenty-five cents per year, the same to be collected by the minister in charge and paid to the Bishops of the district.[16] No doubt this is the beginning of the calling of General Claims "Bishops' Money."

The statistics of this General Conference, on which this assessment had to be based is vital. The six Bishops reported annual conferences operating in twenty-seven states and two territories, with 1,000 itinerant ministers pastoring 200,000 laymen or communicants. Connected with these churches were 18,000 Sunday School teachers and 85,000 students. Church property was valued at $14,000,000 and $70,000 had been given over a twelve year period for mission work.[17]

The Bishops' address had this to say about the Financial problem:

> Thirdly, Financial matters: Financial embarrassment has been one of the difficulties we have had to grapple with; through it our connectional Journal has been suspended for nearly two years; also our missionary work has been much hindered; also from pecuniary embarrassment we have been prevented from making the desired progress in the work of the establishment of educational institutions for the education of ministers. Dear Brethren, you can more fully appreciate our need of money to extend and support our connection, when we remind you that the two great monied religious bodies we have to grapple with—the M. E. Church north, and the M. E. Church south, who make their money a means of proselyting our preachers, in many cases, especially the former body. . . .[18]

---

[15] *Minutes of the General Conference of 1868.*
Note: Resolved: That each elder of this Conference attend to the collection for the Superintendent's salary. The New England Conference Minutes of 1848.
[16] Moore, *loc. cit.*, 280.
[17] *Ibid.*, 285.
[18] Moore, *loc. cit.*, 287.

The matter of Finance not only brought the above response but in the list of recommendations one notes the following:

II. Proper legislation to permanently secure or establish the Book Concern.
III. We must adopt a general practical financial system; such a system as will secure a general support to our connectional institutions.
IV. We must adopt some plan for the establishment of a suitable educational institution for our young ministers entering our itinerancy.
V. We should take necessary steps to establish a connectional Journal.[19]

The General Conference which met in Louisville, Ky., listed no less than 16 committees, several dealing with finances. Among these were: On Book Concern, Journal, Business for the General Conference, Education, Mission Work, Financial System, Superannuated Preachers' Fund, Finances and Bishops' Salaries.[20] Moore, who is our major source of information for the period, says that all of these committees reported.

The Philadelphia Conference, meanwhile, in 1853 was collecting money for the Superintendent in its annual sessions.[21] In that year $74.57 was reported, thus lending a belief that each Annual Conference collected that which it could for the Superintendent, and, later, the Bishop. The Baltimore Conference reported a total of $10.47 Superintendent's money in the same year.[22] The New York Conference, evidently, because of the division, reported only $14.00.[23] The New England Conference listed no Superintendent's money. At this date, it appears that there was no Annual Conference Steward, so one can conclude that this office developed after 1856. Financial reports are noted as far back as 1848 in the New England Annual Conference but there appears to be no separation of the funds so one cannot say that which was paid to the Superintendent.

In the New York Annual Conference Minutes of 1848, however, $31.95 was given for the Superintendent.[24] This was much less than that which was allocated for the Conference, for Zion's Church, as it was then called, sent $85.64. The Daughters of Conference

---

[19] *Ibid.*, 287.
[20] Moore, *loc. cit.*, 292.
[21] *Minutes* of the Philadelphia Conference of 1853, 16.
[22] *Minutes* of the Baltimore Annual Conference of 1853, 6.
[23] *Minutes* of the New York Annual Conference of 1853, 27.
[24] *Minutes* of the New York Annual Conference of 1848, 22.

reported $60.00 and a donation from the Sabath School of $40.00 was received.

One can see, then that the system of paying the Superintendent was not too well advanced at the time. If a stated amount was to be raised one can run across no reference to it.

Bishop Hood, in his history of the denomination brings to light a very interesting item concerning the Sixteenth Quadrennial session of the General Conference. While we have long known of that session's creation of the Woman's Home and Foreign Missionary Society, few, if any people, have given it high credit for the beginnings of our Financial system. The report of the Committee on Financial Plan is herewith given:

> To the Bishops and Members of the General Conference of the A. M. E. Zion Church:
> Your Committee, to whom has been referred the suggestions relative to a financial system, recommended by the North and South Carolina Conferences, to the General Conference, and by a vote of this Conference referred to us for certifications, respectfully beg leave to submit the following report of our labors: 1. In accordance with the wise and well-digested thoughts of Bishops J. W. Hood, in his address to those Annual Conferences, and also the forcible words to the same effect in the Address of the College of Bishops, proposing and urging a General Financial System, that would be general in its bearing and application to all parts of our widely spread Zion, we, your Committee, have endeavored from the basis of the plan submitted, and the approved matter in our hands, concluded to offer the following system for your approval or rejection:
>
> ### Article I
> Section 1—*Whereas* the sum of fifty cents per annum has been and is assessed upon each and every member of our Church, we your Committee, recommend that there be no change in said assessment.
>
> ### Article II
> Section 1—It shall be the duty of each minister and preacher in charge of a Circuit or Station in the A. M. E. Zion Connection, to collect and forward to the Annual Conference's Steward, monthly, such proportion of the General tax as he may have collected.
>
> Section 2—He shall put forth every effort to collect the whole amount of General tax assessed to his charge before the assembling of the Annual Conference of which he is a member.
>
> ### Article III
> Section 1—The Bishops shall see that each minister or preacher appointed to a charge, faithfully performs his duty, in accordance with Article II.

Article IV

Section 1—It shall be the duty of each Annual Conference to cause a rigid examination of each minister and preacher having a charge, and upon discovering that any minister or preacher has wilfully neglected, or has not put forth proper efforts to collect the whole amount assessed, or having collected the same and failed to remit promptly to the Annual Conference Steward, shall, upon conviction, be suspended or located, as the Conference shall determine.

Article V

Section 1—There shall be a Steward elected by each Annual Conference, upon nomination of the presiding Bishop.

Section 2—It shall be the duty of said Annual Conference Steward to receive all the General Tax collected by the ministers and preachers in said Conference Districts and give receipts for the same.

Section 3—It shall be the duty of the Annual Conference Steward to forward the moneys to the Episcopal District Steward as soon as received from each minister and preacher, and it is made his duty to furnish the District Steward with the amount assessed to that Conference District from the statistical records of the same.

Section 4—It is also made the duty of the Annual Conference Steward, to write to each minister or preacher as may not be making prompt reports, requiring him to make remittances, and shall inform the Bishop or such minister as may be neglecting or failing to make remittances.

Section 5—No Annual Conference Steward shall pay or cause to be paid any moneys arising from the general tax for Annual Conference purposes or for any other purpose whatever.

Article VI
Concerning District Stewards

Section 1—There shall be elected by the General Conference, upon the nomination of the Bishop of the Episcopal Districts, for which he is to act, an elder, to be known and designated as the Episcopal District Steward.

Section 2—It shall be his duty to receive all moneys from the Annual Conference Stewards and give receipt for the same.

Section 3—It shall be his duty to pay to the Bishop of his District at any and all times from such moneys as may come into his hands the salary due him without hesitation. But in no case shall he pay more money then the amount of salary due the Bishop of his District.

Section 4—He shall, after paying the bishop his salary, semi-annually forward the surplus money to the General Steward hereafter provided for.

Section 5—He shall report at the end of every three months to the General Steward the amount of money received and expended and the amount in hand.

Article VII
Concerning General Steward

Section 1—The General Conference Secretary shall be, and he is hereby made the General Steward, and, in addition to his other duties, as Secretary to the General Conference, he is to receive all moneys which may not be used, arising from the general tax, exclusive of that which may have been paid by the District Stewards to the Bishops and holders, and retain such moneys subject to the order of the College of Bishops.

Section 2—It is made the duty of said Secretary or Steward to meet the College of Bishops, and render a full report of any and all moneys in his hand, with a full report of all the District Stewards so far as is made known to him; and he shall keep a correct record of all the proceedings of the College of Bishops, and answer all correspondence, reserving all letters and papers as the property of this General Conference.

Section 3—It shall be his duty to send reports to each Annual Conference of the condition of the General Treasury and the action of the College of Bishops, and prepare to make a full report of his transactions to the General Conference at its sitting.

Article VIII
Executive Board

Section 1—The College of Bishops shall constitute an Executive Committee, a majority constituting a quorum.

Section 2—It shall be their duty to cause an examination of the Books of the General Secretary and see that his reports are correct, and they shall cause to be apportioned and paid upon application of the proper agents, out of whatever moneys there are in the hands of the General Steward, as follows: First, the deficiency, if any due the bishops on their salaries; second, what salary, if any, due any other general officers; third, to the Educational Board or Agent, thirty per cent; Book Concern Ten percent; Foreign Missions, Ten percent; Church Organ, ten percent; to worn-out preachers, twenty per cent; Home Missions, ten per cent, of all the surplus moneys remaining after the general officers have been paid.

We further recommend that the above report be printed in pamphlet form, and sent to each church and minister or preacher in charge.

All of which we most respectfully submit,

G. H. Washington, *Chairman*
C. Max Manning, *Secretary*.[25]

S. W. Jones, J. Sexton, A. Losker, R. H. Simmons, A. Paxton, G. E. Smith, Z. T. Pearsall, E. W. Gibson, C. C. Petty, A. Day, L. A. Hopkins, J. P. Humer, M. L. Gale, J. F. Page.

The report was adopted May 20, 1880 and thus became the first intensive financial plan of the denomination. It should be noted that in the plan the General Secretary of the denomination likewise became the General Steward, handling the surplus moneys turned over to him from the District Stewards.

---

[25] *Daily Journal of the Sixteenth Quadrennial Session of the General Conference* (Montgomery, Ala., 1880) 67-70.

While the matter of finance as far as the General Conference was concerned is not in the main stream of our thinking at this time, it is interesting to note the following report of the Finance Committee of the Sixteenth Quadrennial session:

REPORT OF THE COMMITTEE ON FINANCE
Receipts from all sources $311.40

Expended
As per agreement to Trustees of Clinton Chapel $111.77
To incidentals of Conference— (Appropriations
   made by the General Conference) 49.21
To C. R. Harris, for Secretary's service 20.00
" M. M. Bell, Compiler 30.00
" Assistant Secretary, A. Day 10.00
" Journal Secretary, C. C. Petty 10.00
" Statistical Secretary, J. B. Small 5.00
" Statistical Secretary, C. M. Manning 5.00
" J. C. Dancy, Reporter 10.00
" J. A. Tyler, Reporter 5.00
" J. McH. Farley 5.00
" Sexton of the Church 10.00
" Mail Carrier, W. G. Strong 10.00
" Bread and wine for sacrament 2.00

$238.28

Leaving a balance of $28.12, which will be divided among certain brethren to assist in paying their traveling expenses.

Respectfully submitted,
E. H. HILL, *Chairman*
G. STRONG, *Treasurer*[26]

After four years of the new Financial Plan the Board of Bishops reported some major weak points. For example, under the system it was noted that the Bishops could not carry out fully the mandate of the General Conference where rotation was concerned. To adjust this and other lesser problems they stated that "At our meeting at Chester, S. C., September, 1882, to accommodate the notion of some of the District Stewards, we permitted them to continue to pay the Bishops as before, but agreed among ourselves to turn all moneys over to the General Steward, to be divided equally among us." [27] They stated that because of this new arrangement they were able to

---

[26] *Daily Journal of the Sixteenth Quadrennial Session of the General Conference,* 70.
[27] *Daily Proceedings of the Seventeenth Quadrennial Session of the General Conference* (New York City, May, 1884) 25.

THE DENOMINATION AND ITS FINANCES

visit all sections of the connection and gain an acquaintance with conditions, aid the various institutions, lend impetus to the work and bring a sense of unity to the denomination. They had stated that the District system "brought a localizing tendency, fostering local interests and preventing unity of effort."

The Board pointed to the following accomplishments:

1. The Foreign Mission Work with the Reverend Andrew Cartwright.
2. The Star of Zion
3. The Book Concern
4. The Zion Wesley Institute
5. Church Extension Efforts.[28]

Among the recommendations of the Board was the need for a much larger financial income to support the existing needs and undergird all of the "general connectional institutions." They felt that more revenue could be had by increasing the assessment on each individual member and by absolutely following the law as enacted in 1880. In line with this they stated the following as well:

> Our necessity for a disciplinary provision by which each preacher that makes application to connect with the Annual Conference, shall be required to put himself under the tuition of an Elder for one year, to learn the rules of a preacher; the duties of a deacon; of an elder, and of trustees and class leaders; and that he be required to recite before the Conference those rules relative to the deportment of a preacher, and the duty of a deacon. That no preacher shall be ordained a deacon or an elder who cannot recite before the Annual Conference the duty of a deacon, of an elder and of the trustees, and who has not a knowledge of our financial plan.
> 6. We need a provision in our general law or Discipline that will require any preacher or minister coming from another denomination to join us, to be able to recite before the Annual Conference a sufficient portion of the duties of an elder, deacon and preacher, and have a considerable knowledge of our financial plans as laid down in the Discipline.[29]

Revisions were naturally made in the Financial Plan of 1880. One provision stated that all would be taxed, Bishops, ministers and people. Children under fifteen years of age were not required to pay the full amount, however, but they were to be encouraged to pay that which they could. Those who were enrolled under that which was termed the "Poor List" and "aided from the fund for the poor" were

---

[28] *Ibid.*, 25-28.
[29] *Daily Proceedings of the Seventeenth Quadrennial Session of the General Conference,* 30.

not to be taxed. Preachers or ministers who failed to carry out the provisions of the Financial Plan were to be tried, and "upon conviction, be suspended or located, as the Conference shall determine." Another change was the responsibility placed on the presiding Elder to see that these collections were made and reported.[30]

The general Steward, in this tightening up process, was to receive the money promptly—the Annual Conference Steward, to render an audit of his books *before* adjournment of the Annual Conference. The General Steward was to be bonded. He was charged to apportion all funds on the *fourth Wednesday of every month* on a *pro rata* basis. The listing was as follows:

1. The Bishop's salary and traveling expense incurred in their regular Episcopal tours. The expense of special visits shall be met by the churches requiring their services.
2. The Zion Wesley Institute
3. The Book Concern
4. The Star of Zion
5. The Superannuated Ministers
6. The salaries of the General Steward and Secretary

The appropriations of the General Conference showed the following: Bishops should receive $1,500 each; Evidently in each year $3,000 should be allocated for the collective travelling expenses of the Bishops. Zion Wesley Institute should receive $6,000; the Star of Zion $1,200; the Book Concern, $1,500; Superannuated Ministers, $1,000. For salary of the General Steward $650; the General Secretary, $150 and Superintendent of the African Work, $800.[31]

Surplus money should be allocated by the Board of Apportionment (consisting of the Board of Bishops, the General Steward and three of the Annual Conference Stewards residing nearest to the meeting places of the semi-annual sessions of the Board). Here, too, there was a formula. Money was to go 1, to back salaries of the Bishops, 2, to provide a fund for transportation of students at the Zion Wesley Institute; 3, and to increase the efficiency of the Book Concern and the Star of Zion.

If an area, such as a Presiding Elder's District (or where there were no Presiding Elders), ten circuits or stations, had raised a sum

---
[30] *Ibid.* 31ff.
Note: The offices of General Secretary and General Steward were separated in the Seventeenth Quadrennial session, 1884, 107.
[31] *Daily Proceedings, the Seventeenth Session,* 33.

equal to $700, the obligation to the denomination would be considered discharged. All sums over this amount should be "applied to as many of the following purposes as the Annual Conference may determine: The Superannuated and Worn-out Ministers, the Widows and Orphans of Deceased Ministers, Church Extension, Conference, Educational Institutions, Local Missions, and incidental expenses of the conference." [32]

Another interesting provision of the Financial Plan as amended in 1884 stated that the "collections taken to meet the Bishops' travelling expenses when on their regular tours, shall be accredited to the church as General fund; provided that each Bishop, at their semi-annual meetings shall render an itemized account of the receipts from said collections, and of his travelling expenses." If, for example, The Bishop collected more than this incurred expense he shall pay the same to the General Steward. Of course, there were interpretations of this rule where expense was concerned but these appear to be the main matters. According to the Discipline of 1888 (published in 1889) the essential provisions, along with the appropriations, remained the same.

When William Howard Day made his report to the General Conference of 1892 he stated that a deficit of $20,000 appeared in the four years ending in 1888. He further states that the deficit for the 1888-1892 quadrennium would be shown at the conclusion of the report, but this, we are unable to ascertain.[33] However, in the same Minutes he makes this comment in a supplementary report: "It is proper to say that the General Steward's figures as to the aggregate collected as General Fund differ somewhat from the figures of the General Secretary (that which has happened to the movement to combine these two officers is not clear, despite the thinking they were separate in 1884), because, as the General Steward says, he receives amounts of which the General Secretary has no cognizance; but taking his $69,000 as the amount reported as collected as General Fund during four years past, it must be gratifying as it is creditable to the connection that $13,318.19 can be added thereto, making $82,318.19 as the grand record of our four years. This is very gratifying." [34]

---

[32] *Daily Proceedings of the Seventeenth Quadrennial Session,* 33-34.
[33] *Minutes of the Nineteenth Quadrennial Session of the General Conference,* 1892, 180.
[34] *Minutes of the Nineteenth Quadrennial Session of the General Conference,* 1892, 168.

A partial report on *deficit* in the General Fund was reported by Secretary William Howard Day to the Centennial Session of the General Conference when it met in Mobile, Alabama in 1896. At that time he stated that $43,517.75 was in arrears.[35] This matter concerned the Conference to the extent that the Financial Plan Committee was asked to work out a solution. When the group made the report, however, it was not accepted but an alternate one was substituted (Proposed by Bishop J. W. Hood) for it. The main provisions were to levy an additional 10 cents for each of the following causes: educational purposes, worn-out preachers, their widows and orphans and Church extension and Missionary projects. Only 50% of this additional money should be utilized by the denomination as a whole, the other 50% was to be administered by the Annual Conferences. This change should not become a law until ratified by three-fourths of the Annual and Quarterly Conferences.[36]

The proposed salary of a Bishop at this time appears to have been $2,000, but in the report of the Committee of General Financial Plan it was recommended that this be returned to the prior figure of $1,500. A heated debate was held on this angle but it appears that the adjustment was finally agreed to. Bishop I. C. Clinton readily agreed to the change. The minutes state that Bishop Lomax remained silent on the proposition. Bishop Harris agreed with the Committee and the report was finally accepted.[37]

In the recommendations of the Board of Bishops and others, the Committee on Episcopal Addresss refused to concur with the thinking that the Business Manager of the Publication House and General Steward should be combined. They did recommend that the Book Concern should be under the direction of the Publishing Department, which clears up a point where the General Agent was involved. They set aside $5,000 from the proposed Varick Memorial Fund for the Varick Memorial Building (Publishing House), and refused to agree that the General Secretary and Missionary Secretary should be combined. They suggested instead, that the Church Extension Department and Missionary Secretary be merged. They likewise suggested that the increase in Denominational asking by 25¢. The Conference accepted the combining of the Church Ex-

---

[35] *Minutes of the Twentieth Quadrennial Session of the General Conference*, 1896, 153.
[36] *Ibid.*, 87.
[37] *Ibid.*, 83.

THE DENOMINATION AND ITS FINANCES

tension and Missionary Secretary,[38] but refused to endorse, as has been noted, the 25¢ additional to the General Fund, accepting the proposition of Bishop Hood instead.[39]

Major changes were made in the Financial System again in 1900. Much of the interpretation of change can be found in the following statement which appeared in the A. M. E. Zion Quarterly Review.[40]

> This quadrennium has been the most successful, all things considered in the history of the Church. There were those who prophesied all sorts of happenings during the last General Conference, because of certain apparent drastic legislation looking to certain improvements and reforms. Time has fully justified them all, but none more so than the change from the Conference Steward to that of the present plan, throwing the whole responsibility on the General Steward with the several Conferences and churches as his immediate representatives. It is just simply wonderful to observe the changes.
>
> The church assessment plan too, has worked like a charm. The old system kept the preacher always engaged collecting the fifty cents, whereas now he can resort to any method consistent with church government to raise the amount, whether it be by a church rally, per capita assessment or entertainment. And when the amount is raised the pastor is at once free from further discussion or reminder of the subject.
>
> Added to all this at Connectional headquarters the General Steward is in constant touch with every church in the connection, and therefore, has a better knowledge of every individual pastor and church, than any Bishop of the Board. His office is therefore a training school, which instructs him into the minutae of every church membership throughout the Connection.
>
> That legislation at the last General Conference has brought about more cooperation in work and suggestion, so that all the Departments of the Church will go to the next General Conference less involved than at any time in our history and in better condition to enter upon the work of the next quadrennium.

By 1904 (as a result of the General Conference of that year) the Bishops were to receive $2,000 per year, the General Secretary $600 (nothing is said of payment of the Assistant General Secretary provided for in the Discipline and who was, at the time, Reverend F. M. Jacobs), Financial Secretary (name changed from General Steward), $1,200; Livingstone College, $6,000; Manager of the Publication House, $1,000; Editor of the Star of Zion, $1,000; Editor of Sunday

---
[38] *Minutes of the Twentieth Quadrennial Session of the General Conference,* 81.
[39] *Ibid.,* 252.
[40] *The A.M.E. Zion Quarterly Review,* Vol. XIII, No. One, 1904, 94.

School Literature, $1,000; Educational Secretary, $600; Editor of the Quarterly Review $500. Four estate claimants were to receive $1,500 while the Miscellaneous Claimants were to receive:

1. Superannuated Ministers $1,500
2. Foreign Missions 2,000
3. Contingencies 2,500
4. Chicago Church 1,000
5. Texas Conference 500
6. Hood Theological Seminary[41] 2,000

Total Appropriated $42,900

The total General Fund apportioned was $47,500.00. However the churches were asked to pay the following as well:

1. One-fourth of the General Fund Assessment for Education
2. One-fourth of the General Fund Assessment for Church Extension
3. One-fourth of the General Fund Assessment for Missions
4. One-fourth of the General Fund Assessment for Superannuated ministers, Widows and Orphans and Contingencies.

It appears that the Secretary of Education and Corresponding Secretary of Church Extension were to return to the Annual Conference in which the money was raised, ten per cent of the amount, evidently for local within-Conference work. It is a little more difficult to interpret the purpose of the following:

> The Corresponding Secretary of Missions and the Financial Secretary are required to return to each Annual Conference at the time of its sitting, one-half of the amount they have received from each Conference.[42]

The Discipline refers to Paragraph 534 in which it is stated that the portion of the Mission money returned shall be used for mission work, within the conference, the payment of the salary of the Corresponding Secretary "and the other official Expenses." The Discipline is silent, however, as to the duties of this Corresponding Secretary, so it is supposed that this officer was more of a Home Missions Secretary than that connected with the Woman's Home and Foreign Missionary Society.

---

[41] *The Discipline of the A.M.E. Zion Church* as revised at St. Louis, Mo., 1904, 175.
[42] *Ibid.*, 177.

THE DENOMINATION AND ITS FINANCES

In place of the old Conference Steward there should be appointed in each Annual Conference a General Fund Secretary. His duty was to receive and report all General Funds from his Conference, and, with the Financial Secretary, if he happened to be present, give receipts for the same. All such collections must be sent to the Financial Secretary, if he were not present, prior to the adjournment of the Annual Conference. Ministers who failed to raise their apportionment would have their characters stopped, the General Fund Secretary being charged to do so in the absence of the Financial Secretary.[43] The sum expected from each member at the time was fifty cents.

By the General Conference of 1912, which met in Clinton Chapel Church, Charlotte, North Carolina (The 1908 session had met in Philadelphia, Pennsylvania) the quadrennial General Fund money had risen to $189,493.11. The total amount of General Fund and Benevolences had reached $222,130.61.[44] The Committee's report is herein listed but one cannot be sure as to that which finally prevailed for the concluding statement of the Journal says: "On motion of Bishop Blackwell the whole matter was postponed."[45]

The matter at hand appeared to have been the amount of Bishops' salary and the item of traveling expense. The report, as rendered by the Committee gave each Bishop $2,000 salary and $200 traveling expense. The report follows:

Episcopal Fund and Bishops' salaries	$17,600
General Secretary	600
Financial Secretary	1,200
Livingstone College	8,000
Hood Theological Seminary	4,000
For School	2,000
For Building	2,000
Lomax-Hannon for Theological Purposes	500
Editor of Star of Zion	1,200
Editor Sunday School Literature	1,200
Editor of the Quarterly Review	600
Editor, Western Star of Zion	600
Varick Monument	4,000
To save Rush Church, New York	5,000
Educational Schools other than Livingstone	11,000
Church Extension	10,000

---
[43] *The Discipline of the A.M.E. Zion Church,* 1904, 184, 185.
[44] *Official Journal of the Twenty-fourth Quadrennial Session of the General Conference,* 397.
[45] *Ibid.,* 134.

Mission Board (Home)	7,200
Superannuated Ministers	4,500
Widows and Orphans	4,500
Contingencies	4,500
Total [46]	$90,200

The over-all assessment was raised from $91,600 to $95,300.

The struggle to adjust the finances of the Church had received a set back in 1908, when the General Conference met in Philadelphia. The statement of Bishop Hood before the New York Conference not only pointed this up but brought into focus other matters:

> The General Conference, necessarily, causes an extra expense to the Connection. I do not think that the last General Conference cost the Connection less than $15,000.00. This makes the General Conference year a hard year, financially. Then, it seems impossible to keep the General Conference from appropriating more money than they are willing to assess. If the General Conference had adopted the report of the Committee on Apportionment without change, we would have been within the amount of the assessment. But the General Conference added a considerable amount to what the committee recommended.
>
> If I could have my way, I would conduct the business of the church exactly as I conduct my own. I never make obligations beyond my ability to meet.—This heedless going ahead without being sure of the coming-out place, is what causes embarrassment. For this reason we have not yet been able to publish the minutes of the last General Conference. The minutes are ready, but the money is not in hand to print them.
>
> Very little change was made which will not be thus indicated. The blank for personal contributions indicates that the Quarterly Review, the Trumpet, The Seer, and the Endeavor-Headlight have all been put on the same plane as the Star of Zion and each minister who has an appointment is required to subscribe for them. The General Conference also made it obligatory on each minister to organize a Varick Christian Endeavor Society and to hold an anniversary service in the month of May, or at some time in the year and take a collection for the V. C. Endeavor Union.[47]

The denomination came to the General Conference of 1916 with a bit of anxiety. This is somewhat reflected in the necessity of combining the Minutes of 1916 and 1920, the Twenty-fifth and Twenty-sixth quadrennial sessions. Naturally, little of the undertones of that which had happened appears in the brief writings in these Journals. On the sixth day of the Twenty-fifth session (meeting in Louisville,

---

[46] *Official Journal*, Twenty-fifth session, 539.
[47] *The A.M.E. Zion Quarterly Review*, Vol. XX, No. 3, 5.

Ky., 1916) a brief note of the happenings appear as the Report of the Auditing Committee, "with reference to J. S. Jackson, former Financial Secretary's account was referred to the General Conference. Bishop Walters stated that it should be referred to a special appointed committee. Dr. J. H. McMullen offered the following as substitute for the whole: That the report of the Auditing Committee be accepted as far as it has gone, and the report of the Financial Secretary as submitted to the Board of Bishops for the basis of further action by the Auditing Committee, who shall report their findings to the General Conference. This motion passed." [48]

The Board of Bishops in their address to the Conference stated as follows:

> "We started out from Charlotte, N. C., the seat of our last General Conference, with a revised financial plan. We had not gone very far when we discovered that the plan and some of its parts had not been studied closely. As a result the income has not been adequate to the needs of the Church. This made it necessary for the chief pastors to inaugurate plans to supplement the income. The Church Extension and Missionary Departments have been taxed heavily in an effort to brace the Financial Department; hence, little or no Missionary or Church Extension monies, as such, have been available during the Quadrennium.
> "The centralization of our funds was a step forward. With some changes or modifications, which you will no doubt order during this Conference, you will give us a Financial Plan which will yield more revenue and be easier to operate. The falling off of about $20,000 the 2nd year of the Quadrennium which was due to short crops and a general financial depression, gave the church a financial setback.
> "The shortage in the Financial Secretary's account which was discovered in December of last year, tied up little over $9,000 on his account, and the suspension of the Alabama Penny Prudential Savings Bank tied up about $6,000 more, making in all about $15,000.00." [49]

According to the printed Minutes of the General Conference of the time the Honorable Dr. John C. Dancy was placed in charge of the Finance Department when the matter of irregularities was discovered in the accounts of Dr. Jackson. It was he who made the report for the Department at the Quadrennial meeting. The account states: "This report was given the closest attention and was marked by conciseness and revealed carefully every detail of the office as con-

---

[48] *Minutes of the Twenty-fifth Quadrennial Session of the General Conference* (Louisville, Ky., 1916) 11.
[49] *Minutes of the Twenty-fifth Quadrennial Session, loc. cit.*, 33.

ducted by the Acting Secretary, and how very successful the Connection had tided through an unprecedented financial stringency. Dr. J. S. Jackson, the suspended Financial Secretary, rose to a question of personal privilege, but it was ruled by Bishop Walters that nothing concerning the report could be heard and that the former Secretary should turn all books over to the Auditing Committee, and that the Bishops and Finance Committee also submit whatever they had in their possession to said Committee. All reports were referred to Auditing Committee." [50]

Dr. William Harvey Goler, who stated that he wished to be relieved of the responsibility as President of Livingstone College[51] was elected Financial Secretary,[52] and re-elected to the same office in 1920.[53]

Again changes were made in the Financial Plan, this time, for example, each member was expected to pay $1.00 per year. The Committee stated that this should be the basis of assessment but that an Apportionment Committee or Board should place the amounts on the local churches. No church should be required to raise less than the amount collected and reported at the preceding Annual Conference prior to the meeting of the General Conference. Bishops were charged to assist the ministers in raising the desired amounts—"the collections at the time of his visit should be forwarded at once by the pastor to the Financial Secretary, as part of the assessment of the charge to be credited to the Annual Conference in which it was collected. The Pastor shall send all General Claims to the Financial Secretary monthly." [54]

The Conference recognized that there had been an increase in the cost of living and expense for travel so the committee proposed that "The annual allowance of the Bishop shall be the sum of $2,700 and $300 traveling." [55] The General Officers' salaries evidently followed but these appear not to have been printed. The Board of Apportionment in the Annual Conference was to consist of the Presiding Bishop, the Presiding Elders, the Secretary of the Conference and

---
[50] *Ibid.*, 9.
[51] *Ibid.*, 13.
[52] *Ibid.*, 27.
[53] *Minutes of the Twenty-six Quadrennial Session of the General Conference* (Knoxville, Tenn., 1920) 256.
[54] *Minutes of the Twenty-sixth Quadrennial Session of the General Conference*, 250, 251.
[55] *Ibid.*, 250, 251.

one pastor and one layman from each of the Presiding Elder districts.

The struggle to attain a workable Financial Plan appears to have been one of those continuing matters which occupied the attention of many General Conferences. Certainly the Indianapolis Session of 1924 could be placed in this category. The major kinks in the system were evidently observed by the Financial Secretary, William Harvey Goler who took note of them in his report. First of all, he felt that legislation should be enacted which would allow the Department to make payments to all who were dependent upon it for funds on either a "monthly or a quarterly" basis. To accomplish better bookkeeping he urged that it would be unlawful for any person to "receive salary otherwise than through the regular channel and provision made by this General Conference." The reader can surmise the condition which prompted this complaint. He further stated that the General Conference should make it unlawful for Presiding Elders to either "solicit or receive General Claims either from the preachers or members of his district."

Evidently, funds reported as General Claims had been diverted from time to time as Dr. Goler stated: "That it should be unlawful to use General Claims taken at the Annual Conference for any other purpose than that specified for the use of General Claims." He was concerned too, because practically all funds were allocated and so there was no contingency fund. He insisted that if the Plan was to work the ministers should be strongly urged to report all funds "on the fourth Wednesday in each Month." He suggested that this be rigidly enforced. Salaries of the Manager of the Publication House, and Editors of the Star of Zion, Sunday Church School Literature and Quarterly Review should be paid by their respective Departments.

Another significant recommendation had to do with the elimination of the 7½% of the claims going to the Annual Conferences. Dr. Goler stated that they already had large amounts at their disposal. He felt, too, that salary payments should be distributed on a percentage basis regardless of the officer. Meanwhile, Bishops should cease collecting General Claims personally.[56]

On their part, the Board of Bishops recommended that the fiscal

---

[56] *Minutes of the Twenty-seventh Quadrennial Session of the General Conference*, (Indianapolis, Ind., 1924) 402, 403.

year run from July 1st to June 30 instead of from January 1st to December 31st. They recommended a budget of $220,000 "with provisions for gradual increase," and that of this amount that "the appropriation of Livingstone College increase to thirty thousand dollars, an amount equal to six percent of $500,000." Incidentally, they suggested that the Manager of the Publication House be selected by the Board of Managers. This suggestion was finally taken in 1960.[57]

In the Address of the Board of Bishops it was stated that legislation should be passed preventing the diversion of funds from the Financial Department.

Regulations of the Financial Department as noted in the Discipline of 1924 set up a Board of Finance whose task should be to oversee the work of the Department. The appropriations were as follows:

Total General Fund and Benevolences	$220,000.00
Bishops—12 @ $3,500	$ 42,000.00
General Official Claimants including Traveling Expenses	
General Secretary	$ 1,200.00
Financial Secretary	2,000.00
Manager of the Publication House	2,000.00
Editor of the Star of Zion	2,000.00
Editor of the Quarterly Review	1,000.00
Editor of the Sunday School Literature	2,000.00
Secretary of Education	2,000.00
Secretary of Church Extension	2,000.00
Secretary of Foreign Missions	2,000.00
Secretary of Ministerial Brotherhood	2,000.00
Secretary of V. C. E. Society	2,000.00
Superintendent of Sunday Schools	2,000.00
Total	$ 22,200.00
Benevolent Claimants	
Six Estates ($500 each)	$ 3,000.00
9 Bishops' Widows ($300 each)	2,700.00
Mrs. J. C. Price (Widow)	300.00
Total	$ 6,000.00
Departmental Claimants	
Education	$ 50,000.00
Church Extension	25,000.00
Home Missions	15,000.00
Foreign Missions	10,000.00
Relief Department	15,000.00

[57] *Ibid.*, 119.

Sunday School Department	3,000.00
V. C. E. Department	3,000.00
Mother Zion Church	10,000.00
Debts and Contingents	10,000.00
Publishing Department	5,000.00
Total	$146,000.00

The regulations established a Budget Committee in each Annual Conference of not less than three and not more than five individuals who should collect all General Claims and transmit the same to the Financial Secretary. The Department should disburse money monthly to the claimants and Departments.[58]

---

[58] *The Doctrines and Discipline of the African Methodist Episcopal Zion Church,* 1925, 166, 167.

CHAPTER XVI

The Denomination and Its Finances

THERE IS little doubt that the denomination has been derelict in attempting a thorough-going study of its financial structure and has, therefore, from time to time, found itself in difficulty where the needs for its program are concerned. As one turns again to the situation as it appeared to have developed in 1912 he sees a concise picture of the problem. In that session, for example, as the Board of Bishops recommended the change from *General Fund* to *General Claims* they suggested a budget of $105,000 but evidently intended that the General Conference should base the spending budget on $90,000. The weak point was, however, that "all above the amount of $90,000 was to be applied on the building of a Girl's Dormitory at Livingstone College. There was also another weakness. They suggested that while all money should be sent to the Financial Secretary each Bishop should be allowed to collect and retain $500 as Traveling expenses.[1]

As one looks back at that budget, it appears to this writer it would have been well to have postponed the idea of a Varick Monument until it could be noted how well the new system would actually work. Added strains were placed on the vital areas of the Church's program as it was expected that the Educational Secretary would secure his salary from his appropriation and the same was true in that of the Church Extension Secretary. They decided that the Church no longer needed a Statistician or an auditor. Again, this may have been a costly mistake, for it was supposed that a grossly underpaid General Secretary could assume these tasks.

The difficulty on the situation began almost immediately when the Committee assigned the task, seemed to have been unwilling to report more than the existing assessment. At least an increase of under $4,000 is to be noted. Evidently some person, in the heat of the moment, hastened to the aid of Rush Church (New York City) and tacked on an additional $5,000 while the *Western Star of Zion* was granted another $600. All these changes were accepted, many of them on the motion of Bishops Caldwell and Walters.

---

[1] *Official Journal of the Twenty-fourth Quadrennial Session*, 1912, 23.

A greater mistake was made in the areas from which *added* money was to be expected. Western New York was dropped from $1,500 to $1,000. This may be a misprint. South Georgia was dropped from $800 to $600 but South Carolina was increased from $5,200 to $6,000. Indiana saw an increase of $400 to $1,000 and West Tennessee and Mississippi went from $1,600 to $1,800. Oklahoma received an increase of $400 to $600 and North Arkansas was assessed $900, a $300 increase.

The shock of the shortages discovered at the end of 1915 left small room for any major changes in 1916. As this occurred a scant five or six months prior to the sitting of the General Conference, the situation was fresh in the minds of the delegates. The Board of Bishops was aware that even before this happening there was experienced difficulty in the provisions of the measure.

While a direct relationship between these critical years and the future is not to be noted, it appears to this writer that the difficulty experienced, affected the denomination in the eight years ahead and may have produced the background for other complications. For example, where Church Extension is concerned, expansion concentrated in eight areas would have brought the denomination into better position financially. Yet this Department was weakened at a time when the first great migration of the Black man from the South was getting underway. Overseas, the total Missionary effort was affected as funds were diverted from these enterprises as well. In this Department a crisis was finally to come in 1924, forcing the denomination into a new plan of action.

The Board of Bishops acknowledged that some aspects of the plan of 1912 were good, but the measures were too inadequate so new avenues of revenue were sought and evidently found. However, there was a *bad taste* left in the minds of the leadership even as they responded. Meanwhile the small planning was having its effect as well.

The Committee of the General Conference had made little provision for the building of the Girls' Dormitory at Livingstone College and a special effort was begun which netted $37,500. From the regular educational appropriations another $12,500 was gleaned which amounted to the $50,000 needed.

Four years later (Washington, N.C. January 1919) it became necessary to launch another special drive—the Tercentenary. The original plan involved raising $400,000 and increasing church membership by 100,000. There appears to have been no records kept on this second goal. Subsequently the amount to be raise was increased to $1,000,000 as the Council met in Paterson, New Jersey, Of this amount it appears that $22,386.81 was collected at the 1920 General Conference.[2]

By 1924 the following had been reported from this Tercentenary Drive:

Second Episcopal District	$ 84,653.55
Third Episcopal District	89,562.00
Fourth Episcopal District	59,599.73
Fifth Episcopal District	44,457.40
Sixth Episcopal District	38,320.24
Seventh Episcopal District	9,224.88
Eighth Episcopal District	26,242.75
Total amount reported	$353,060.65[3]

One of the reasons that the effort fell so short of the anticipated goal no doubt, was the fact that it appears that an over-lapping campaign was being waged styled a Debt Paying Rally. This was occasioned by $60,000 worth of obligations due and payable. An effort was made to borrow this amount but this failed. At the time the Council was meeting in Atlantic City (August, 1919). The Tercentenary remained the final hope. In a partial effort to secure the needed sum a total of $19,000 was set as an immediate goal when the group had met in Chicago two years prior to the Atlantic City meeting. By the following January, 1918, over $18,000 had been raised.

To intimate that the Board of Bishops was deeply concerned about the finances of the denomination would be to put it mildly. It will be recalled that in 1924 they had said: "We recommend that this General Conference adopt the Budget System on a minimum basis of Two Hundred and Twenty Thousand Dollars with a provision for a gradual increase."[4] Earlier they had said: "Because of the central and determining position of this Department (the Financial), we feel that it should be placed upon the most practical and business-

---

[2] *Minutes of the Twenty-sixth Quadrennial Session of the General Conference,* 252.
[3] *Minutes of the Twenty-seventh Quadrennial Session of the General Conference,* 81.
[4] *Minutes of the Twenty-seventh Quadrennial Session of the General Conference,* 1924, 119.

like basis, and that it should represent in its managment the highest type of business efficiency." [5]

On the third day of the session Bishop George C. Clement offered a resolution concerning the "Proposed Financial Plan." [6] The next day, the Rev. E. M. Argyle and Bishop L. W. Kyles offered resolutions along the same line. The report of the Budget Committee came on the ninth day and is herein given:

REPORT OF THE BUDGET COMMITTEE

To the Bishops, and members of the General Conference of the African Methodist Episcopal Zion Church in General Conference assembled.

We, your Committee on Budget apportionment, for the next four years beg leave to submit the following:

1. We recommend that the basis of General Fund assessment be $110,000. That an equal amount for benevolences shall be raised of $110,000, making a total minimum budget for the Church of $220,000.

2. That the assessment shall be raised as follows:
(Editors Note: General Fund amount is given with the understanding that the Benevolent amount is the same)

FIRST EPISCOPAL DISTRICT

New England	$2,600.00	Western North Carolina	$8,000.00
New Jersey	3,000.00	Alabama	2,000.00

SECOND EPISCOPAL DISTRICT

New York	$3,200.00	Phila. and Balto.	$6,000.00
Palmetto	3,300.00	North Carolina	5,200.00
North Alabama	3,000.00		

THIRD EPISCOPAL DISTRICT

Michigan	$1,800.00	Allegheny	$2,000.00
Albemarle	3,200.00	Virginia	4,000.00
West Central N. C.	5,400.00		

FOURTH EPISCOPAL DISTRICT

Central, N. C.	$5,400.00	Blue Ridge	$2,200.00
California	500.00	East Tenn. and Va.	2,200.00
So. Georgia	600.00	So. Fla.	700.00
Oregon-Washington	100.00	So. West R. M.	300.00

FIFTH EPISCOPAL DISTRICT

Western N. Y.	$1,400.00	Cape Fear	$5,400.00
South Carolina	3,600.00	Pee Dee	3,600.00
Georgia	800.00		

[5] *Ibid.*, 115.
[6] *Ibid.*, 23.

Sixth Episcopal District

Ohio	$2,500.00	Kentucky	$1,500.00
West Kentucky	1,200.00	Tennessee	2,500.00
West Tenn. and Miss.	2,000.00		

Seventh Episcopal District

Central Ala.	$2,200.00	Southeast Ala.	$1,200.00
South Ala.	2,200.00	West Alabama	3,000.00
Cahaba	1,800.00	So. Mississippi	1,400.00

Eighth Episcopal District

Missouri	$1,600.00	Indiana	$1,200.00
Arkansas	1,200.00	North Arkansas	700.00
Oklahoma	200.00	Texas	200.00
Louisiana	1,000.00	Florida	800.00

The total assessments, including duplicate amounts for Benevolences were $233,800.00. Bishops were to receive $3,500.00 including traveling expenses while ten General Officers were to receive $2,000 each, the Editor of the Quarterly Review, $1,000 and the General Secretary-Auditor was to receive $1,200.00. These ten included both the Secretary of Christian Endeavor and the Superintendent of the Sunday Schools. Appropriations to the Departments were as follows: Education, $50,000; Church Extension $25,000.00; Home Missions, $15,000.00; Foreign Missions (from the General Claims) $10,000.00; Debts and "contingents" $10,000.00; Relief Dept. $15,000.00; Sunday School Dept., $3,000.00; Varick Christian Endeavor, $3,000.00; Publication House, $5,000.00; Mother Zion Church, $10,000.00; The Bishops' widows, (10) $3,000.00; Six Estate claimants, $3,000.00 ($500 each).[7]

The Committee made the following provisions as well. Settlement with the Departments should be made monthly, Bishop's Receipts should be discontinued, Budget Committees should be established in each Annual Conference with three but not more than five members whose duty it should be to collect all moneys. Five per cent of the General Claims evidently could be assessed for the local annual conference expense.

A supplementary report of the Budget Committee of the General Conference also was made. In this document it was stated:

To the General Conference:

---

[7] *Minutes of the Twenty-seventh Quadrennial Session, loc. cit.,* 55, 56.

The Budget Committee recommends the following: First to make effective the Budget system adopted, the plan must be strictly carried out and that the Financial Secretary must be held to strict account for its execution.

Therefore we recommend that it shall be unlawful for the Bishops or any General Officer to collect any funds and give receipt for the same, as provided in budget plan adopted.

We further recommend that there shall be no preferred claimants in the payment and distribution of said funds, provided that Bishops and all salaried officers shall be paid before allotment to the departments otherwise are made.

We further recommend that to enable the Financial Secretary to promptly handle the business of his office that he be allowed sufficient clerical help.

We further recommend that the surplus be held as a Reserve Fund subject to the action of the Board of Finance.[8]

The supplementary report was adopted on a motion made by Bishop Kyles with a second by Bishop P. A. Wallace.

On the full report on motion by P. R. Flack it was decided to accept the report *by sections*. The two sections in the controversy concerned the collection of funds by other than the Financial Secretary or the Budget Committee of the Annual Conference, and both were adopted.[9]

Four years later the Board of Bishops stated: "The last General Conference adopted what is known as the Budget System which has been fairly tried during the four years now passed. This is time enough to know its merits and reveal its faults. The principal involved is beyond question, having been accepted as sound and sane by both Church and State. As we have anticipated it has taken the full quadrennium to approximate the apportionment made at Indianapolis. We levied an assessment of Two Hundred and Twenty Thousand Dollars, and appropriated Two Hundred and Sixteen Thousand. We have raised a maximum of One Hundred and Eighty-One Thousand in the year just ended, and the total deficit for the four years is about Two Hundred Thousand Dollars, which means that an amount equal to the largest sum collected in any one year is the aggregate shortage. Our chief mistake was the appropriation on the basis of the maximum expected instead of a graded and increasing appropriation based on actual per annum receipts. In declaring claimants proferred and setting aside a definite sum for their satisfac-

---

[8] *Minutes of the Twenty-seventh Quadrennial Session*, 1924, 56, 57.
[9] *Minutes of the General Conference, Twenty-seventh Session*, 85.

tion, and at the same time naming the definite sums for other non-preferred claimants, we made a grave blunder. Only two alternatives existed, one was to have no preferred claimants and hence make monthly prorata disbursements to all claimants of all the money received, and the other was to pay the preferred claimants in full monthly and then distribute the balance on a prorata plan to all other claimants without preference or prejudice. The failure to have so provided and so proceeded from the outset is the main ground of complaint and grievance. It is well also to notice both the advantages and disadvantages in the administration of the Budget System as it now operates. The simplicity of the system as it comes before the pastor and the church is without dispute. It is easy to present a plan to cover all interests under one head. It is simple enough to remit to one Treasurer all Connectional monies. On the other hand the consolidation of all claims with special reference to the great benevolent cause of Missions, Education, Ministerial Relief, precludes the emphasizing and illuminating of them, and a consequent loss of the educational and inspirational value of such emphasis and illumination. Our consolidation reacted unwisely also in the handicap it gave to the former activity and assistance on the field of the Executives of our Benevolent Departments, in that, it automatically separated them from direct contact with pastors and churches. While we need to be grateful for the successes of the system we must not be blind to its defects, and our experience should enable us to so modify and revise the Budget System as to more nearly perfect it that it may more fully meet our demands." [10]

When the report of the Committee on Budget Apportionments was brought before the session the Reverend J. F. Moreland moved that "the report be referred to the Committee on Executive Business." [11] Just what this entailed is not known as no further statement is made. In other actions the Bishops' salaries were raised to $4,000 and General Officers were to receive $2,200. Again, an effort was made to add ten percent to the budget for schools and colleges but on a motion of Bishop Kyles, supported by Rev. D. G. Garland this suggestion was tabled. An effort to change Paragraph #316 so

---

[10] *Official Journal of the Twenty-eighth Quadrennial Session of the General Conference*, 1928, 43, 44.
[11] *Ibid.*, 96.

that it would read that 5% of the General Claims would be left in the Annual Conference was likewise tabled.

In the afternoon session of the same day, it was again voted that the "Minimum apportionment for General Claims shall be $220,000.00." It was likewise voted that the $10,000 appropriation for Mother Zion Church be restricted to three years.[12] Departmental claimants were to be paid on a pro rata basis.

In the final apportionment measure the amount allocated was $400.00 above the figure first voted.[13]

As one looks back over the developments of the efforts to solve the vexing financial problems of the denomination it is clear to see that the General Conference has constantly resisted the increase of the denominational budget, so time after time it is to be noted that grudgingly small, almost token, increases have been all the Committees and the General Conference have been willing to grant. There is the hint therefore, that the entire matter is deeper than that which is seen. Taxation, one would agree, has always been an odious item and the delegates, recognizing the possibility of increases on the Annual Conferences and eventually, the churches, have stood as a stone wall against heavy apportionment. We would state, nevertheless, that perhaps one of the major difficulties has been the lack of an over-all program of education where finance is concerned. The membership of the Church has at no time been affluent but it must be recognized that those least able to bear the cost of the programs have been the ones most willing to assume financial responsibility.

The Bishops seemed to grasp the over-all need as they spoke concerning the basic relationship of Executives to pastors and churches. Perhaps, too little attention over the years has been paid to the function of the General Officers where this relationship was concerned.

There is the hint, too, that the matter of finance itself, was not the only reason for this reluctance. One would gather that the General Conference has yet to speak plainly along this line. Since official records say nothing of these underlying causes, a writer can merely suggest that they may exist. It appears that the Church, for example, has never been able to separate finance from the power struggle going on within the organization. One might, see, for example, the

---
[12] *Ibid.*, 97.
[13] *Ibid.*, 105.

roots of this struggle as far back as 1880 with a growth in intensity down to the present.

The ministry caught up in this situation, must confess that in their hands has been a force studiously overlooked, which would have educated the membership to larger giving. Instead, more and more the feeling has grown that the major control of the denomination rests, in the final analysis, with the holding of the purse strings. So long as the General Conference can bring a sense of restraint here, ministers and lay people have a check on the episcopacy.

In this struggle to maintain control the denomination has entered a dangerous period of its existence. Common statements have been heard, for example, that Methodism and Zion Methodism in particular, is pricing itself out of the market. Untrue as this ought to be, it is aided and abetted by the lack of a full stewardship program at a time when the desire for a higher standard of living, good housing and education claim much of the earnings of the membership. It appears, then, that the General Conference must look to its Stewardship programs as well as endeavoring to bring to every official of the Church concern and consideration for the situations faced.

In recent years, the effort has been made to curtail expenses by looking at the organizational structure of the denomination. It appears that all too many fail to see the lack of wisdom in this approach for a greater intensity of program and results is needed, not a lessening of the same. Salvation may rest in the endeavor to attract to the leadership of departments higher and higher calibers rather than the desire to lean heavily upon other means.

Many of the Church's members have overlooked the fact, for example, that since 1912 its connectional budget has allocated from one-fourth to one-third of all receipts to educational enterprises. At the same time, she has not appeared to have held the people whom she has endeavored to educate. Too frequently, those people have drifted to the more sophisticated denominations. Meanwhile, little has been done to encourage tithing, explain the work of the Church, and state just where the limited finance has truthfully gone. Membership training, the matter of indoctrination, the purpose of the Church,—all have been approached solely on the basis of the ministerial interests in the local congregation. An evaluation of the Black Church would definitely point out many of the distinct advantages which have come down to the succeeding generations of people who have lived both in America and around the world. Chief among these advantages has been the demonstration of ability along many lines. In the struggle to maturity the worth of this demonstration cannot be assessed as to overall value.

In the struggle to maintain a program worthy of the name, there is the urgency of imperative change where power and its maintenance is concerned. Somewhere there has to be a middle ground on which leadership and lesser clergy and laity can agree. It must, however, be at a point where all can again discover the goals both of the past and present and wholeheartedly seek these as the fulfillment of the Christian life.

In the light of the above the on-going phase of the denominational Financial program must be seen; if indeed it can be impartially observed with the insecurity of the ministry of the present. By this insecurity we mean the lack of adequate provisions for retirement and the care of the widows and orphans of that clergy.

As we have stated before, one has to clearly see the undercurrents of the Church and the basic spirit of restlessness before he can really understand the Financial revolution of the past ten years—the final phase of the monetary development of this work. This writer suggests that these developments have not been isolated situations but rather the effect of many things. So let us again turn to the matter of ultimate control of the Church and of the individual. We suggest the latter with the hope that individual control will forestall disaster or ultra-revolutionary restrictions.

One can detect the beginnings of change as far back as 1940, when the General Conference met in the National Church of Zion Methodism, Washington, D. C. It will be recalled that efforts were successfully made to prevent the election of any bishop at that session of the General Conference. The methods utilized were simple. The person receiving the highest votes merely experienced the loss of votes on the next ballot. On motion of the Reverend J. E. Garrett and seconded by Reverend M. S. Rudd it was suggested that two more ballots be taken in an effort to elect a bishop and then the Conference should turn to other business. Bishop Cameron Chesterfield Alleyne amended the motion to allow for four ballots instead of two. The amended motion was carried.[14] No election resulted.

---

[14] *Official Journal of the Thirty-first Quadrennial Session of the General Conference*, 1940, 67.

There is little doubt that had an election resulted the course of events for the succeeding years would have been altered drastically. Leading candidates on the first and second ballots were Frank W. Alstork, H. T. Medford and William Orlando Carrington, and it is supposed that any one of these men would have voted with the then constituted majority on the Board of Bishops. Before another General Conference would meet Bishop Lynwood Westinghouse Kyles would pass into the great Beyond. (note) The Conferences assigned to him at the 1940 General Sessions were therefore reassigned (New York going to Bishop Walls, Western North Carolina, Bishop B. G. Shaw and Central North Carolina, Bishop W. W. Matthews).

When Bishop Wallace made his report in 1944 at Detroit he closed his statement with the following: "I was born April 17, 1870. At the General Conference in Louisville, Kentucky, 1916, the law fixing the age for retiring a bishop was enacted. I have reached that age." [15] "Dr. C. Eubank Tucker of the Indiana Conference, offered a constitutional point of order, stating that the pending resolution (suspension of law on retirement) seeking to recall Bishop Wallace for four years was a direct violation to Section 72, sub section 2, page 59 of the 1940 Discipline." He stated it was an attempt to alter a part of our government dealing with the Episcopacy and to create a bishopric for a four year term. The point of order was not sustained by the chair." [16] The vote for suspending the rule on retirement was taken and resulted in its loss, 223 for retention of the law, 218 for the suspension.[17]

On the Eighth day of the 1944 General Sessions the Reverend Dr. A. P. Morris offered a resolution to recall Bishop Paris Arthur Wallace. "The Bishops conferred, bringing Bishop J. W. Martin who was presiding at the time the resolution was offered, and who said that he did not refer the resolution."

Mr. S. M. Dudley was called to read Dr. A. P. Morris' resolution, Dr. Robeson urged the chair to refer this resolution."

"Attorney Eubanks Tucker moved that the resolution be laid on the table. The motion was seconded by Dr. J. W. Frazier. The vote

---

Note: Bishop J. W. Brown had also died.

[15] *Official Journal of the Thirty-second Quadrennial Session of the General Conference,* 1944, 47.

[16] *Official Journal of the Thirty-second Quardennial Session,* 48.

[17] *Ibid.,* 48.

was 149, to lay it on the table, to 114, against. The vote was contested." [18]

"Dr. B. C. Robeson moved that the vote be taken by ballot. It was seconded by H. P. Lankford. It was carried that the vote be taken by ballot."

"Dr. R. E. Clement stated that we should secure unanimous consent and face the issue. 'We ought to decide here and now if we are going to keep the law of retirement,' said he. 'The only thing to do is to vote our conviction.' He asked for unanimous consent for sustaining the law."

"Bishop W. J. Walls came to the floor. He said 'That the rule stated that a man cannot be elected under a certain age, and that we retire at a certain age. Let us face the future as well as the present. If our voting on this that we are suspending the law, then we must suspend it again. Are we doing this for a friend or for the Church?' "

"There was much applause. Bishop Wallace stated, "I am retired; I stated the time of my birth. I am not a candidate to be retained for another four years. I am here to do what the General Conference says. I am obedient to the laws. I dislike very much all this talk and confusion. Drop the whole matter as it relates to me and go on with the business of the conference.' "

Bishop W. J. Walls arose and moved that in keeping with the trends of all Methodism that this General Conference authorize the Board of Bishops to recall a retired bishop, in an emergency caused by death or necessity, during the interim of the General Conference. Mr. Roland Corus of Hartford, Conn., seconded the motion. It was passed." [19]

At no time in prior years have the Minutes of the General Conference noted the situation which arose in the 1944 General Conference. When the Episcopal Committee stated, through its chairman that the report was ready the Conference immediately turned to the hearing of the document. It appeared that the report had to do mainly with "the ages of the Bishops." Bishop Alleyne ruled that because it was incomplete, and inaccurate that it should be recommitted. Dr. G. F. Hall demanded that the Committee resign. The motion to call for the resignation of the Committee was lost.[20]

---

[18] *Ibid.*, 53.
[19] *Official Journal of the Thirty-second Quadrennial Session*, 53.
[20] *Ibid.*, 51.

HISTORY OF THE A.M.E. ZION CHURCH

On May 15, 1944 the Episcopal Committee made its report assigning the Bishops to their various districts. "There was a minority (report) lead by Dr. E. S. Hardge, whose report provoked much discussion. It was moved that we receive the minority report. A voice vote was taken and the division of the house was called. It was decided to vote by ballot. The ballot was counted on the house. Yes —258—No—113. The motion to receive the report of the minority was carried. Rev. E. C. Tucker offered motions to adopt the majority report. Motion out of order. A substitute motion to adopt the report of the minority and make it the report of the committee was adopted. Yes—258. No—113.[21]

As the Committee on Budget and Apportionment came before the General Conference one is puzzled about the words as listed in the report and Minutes "Nonconcurrence." We list the report as it is given in the Minutes:

REPORT OF COMMITTEE ON BUDGET AND APPORTIONMENT
(Non-concurrence)

1. We recommend that the present budget of $146,575.00 be increased to $161,232.50.
2. That the salaries of Bishops and General Officers remain the same but that the Bishops be given $400.00 each for expenses. That ten General Officers be given $3,200.00 for expenses.
   That salaries be paid as follows:

Bishops (11 at $3,600)	$39,600.00
Bishops (expense) @ $400.00	4,400.00
Retired Bishop @ $1,800	1,800.00
General Officers @ $2,000.00	16,000.00
General Officers (Expense) $400.00	3,200.00
General Secretary	1,080.00
General Secretary (Expense) $250.00	250.00
Editor of the Quarterly Review	600.00
Editor of the Quarterly Revew (Expense)	150.00
Editor of the Quarterly Review (Expense)	150.00
Total salaries and expense	$67,080.00

3. We recommend that the 10% Debt Paying be now known as 10% Bishop's and the General Officers' Expenses.
4. It is recommended by the Chairman, Dr. H. R. Jackson that the salaries of Bishops and General Officers remain the same; that each church be asked to contribute $.25 per capita for Bishops and General Officers expenses. That the Financial Secretary pro rate this fund on a basis of 3 to 2.

---

[21] *Official Journal of the Thirty-second Quadrennial Session,* 66.

THE DENOMINATION AND ITS FINANCES

5. That the First Sunday known as Church School Rally Day be observed and that the voluntary offering from the Church School and Varick Christian Endeavor be sent to the Financial Secretary to be paid to the Home and Church School Section.
6. It is recommended that in lieu of $2.00, each minister be asked to pay $5.00 for Hood Theological Seminary to help raise the $20,000.00.

APPORTIONMENT

5%	Annual Conferences	$ 8,061.62
40%	Financial Department	64,493.00
24%	Christian Education	38,695.80
9%	Church Extension	14,510.93
7%	Ministerial Relief	11,286.28
7%	Home Missions	11,286.27
2%	Publication House	3,224.65
1%	Church School Editorial Sec.	1,612.32
1%	Contingent	1,612.32
4%	Foreign Missions	6,449.30
	Total	**$161,232.50**

Note: The Bishops were asked to balance the Budget. A motion prevailed to that effect. For correct budget see the report of Bishops.[22]

The Minutes of the Thirty-second Quadrennial session, naturally do not reflect the full picture of the discussion concerning the finances of the denomination. Bishop E. L. Madison, for example, made extensive remarks as to the full income of the Bishops, declaring that he did not have one of the more lucrative areas but that his income was in excess of $7,000. The Bishops had stated in their message: "It must not be that money will ever become the paramount concern of our Zion, but in the quadrennium this has become imminent among us. The Church and its agents have been prospered beyond anything we have had in two decades. Some unprecedented things have occurred. The largest single church rallies have been had in our history." [23]

Among the six recommendations of the Board of Bishops in 1948 that dealing with the finances of the Church stated: "We recommend a General Claims Budget of Two Hundred and Twenty Thousand Dollars. Observing our dire need of education and Home Missions, we further recommend that Fifty Thousand Dollars other than the General Claims Budget, be raised for education, and Thirty

---
[22] *Official Journal of the Thirty-second Quadrennial Session of the General Conference,* Detroit, Mich., 1944, 192, 193.
[23] *Official Journal of the Thirty-second Quadrennial Session,* 225.

Thousand Dollars for Home Missions. We further recommend that Founder's Day for Livingstone College and the ten (10%) per cent Children's Day money for Secondary Schools be continued." [24]

When the Budget Committee reported on May 19, 1948, it recommended a budget of $250,000 General Claims and $125,000 education. A motion by Rev. C. Coleman, supported by Rev. J. C. Corrothers to approve was made but after comments by Bishop C. C. Alleyne and Dr. James W. Eichelberger a substitute motion was offered to defer action until the Budget Committee had had an opportunity to mimeograph its report for distribution. The following day this was done and the Committee reported as follows:

COMMITTEE ON BUDGET AND APPORTIONMENT

To the Board of Bishops, Delegates and Friends, Greetings:

We, your Committee on Budget and Apportionment, request the high honor and privilege to make the following report:

After prayerful and careful study we recommend that our budget shall include two items only; these to be:
1. General Claims Budget $300,000.00
2. Education Budget 125,000.00

PART II
SPECIAL RECOMMENDATIONS AND PROVISIONS

1. We recommend that the General Conference apportion the amount of General Budget and Education Budget to be raised annually by each Episcopal District.

2. We request that each annual conference elect a Board of Apportionment consisting of the Presiding Bishop, the Presiding Elders, equal number of pastors and equal number of laymen of said conference.

3. We urge that the finance Department be the clearing house for General Claims Budget for all departments of the church, and that said Finance Department be obliged to make settlement with each department quarterly.

4. We recommend that the Education Budget be sent directly to the Secretary of Education. However, we request, that exceptions be allowed so as to make possible the assurance of a full and balanced report for Founder's Day of $70,000, which sum is included in the total Education Budget.

5. We recommend that the Secretary of Education be required to make disbursements to the schools quarterly, and that he be obliged to refund all surplus monies to the Annual Conference Treasurer from which said surplus was sent.

---

[24] *Official Journal of the Thirty-third Quadrennial Session*, Louisville, Ky., 1948, 320.

THE DENOMINATION AND ITS FINANCES

Part III
PRO RATA OF BUDGET

Finance Department	46%	$138,000
Christian Education	20%	60,000
Church Extension	7%	21,000
Home Mission	8%	24,000
Foreign Mission	4%	12,000
Relief	7%	21,000
Gen. Conf. Delegate Fund	4%	12,000
Editorial Section	1%	3,000
Public Relations	1%	3,000
Contingent Fund	1%	3,000
Publication House	1%	3,000

Part IV

To the General Departments	$162,000
Episcopal Claimants (12 full time and one half-time)	62,500
W. W. Matthews as a stipend	2,100
General Officers (10)	36,000
One part-time General Officer	1,800
Bishops' widows ($500 each—7)	3,500
For Holding Annual Conferences	9,800
Operating Expense Finance Department	5,000
Office Expense, General Secretary, Director Public Relations	1,200
Office Expense of Director, Bureau of Evangelism	1,200
Publication and Distribution of Budget Bulletin	750
American Bible Society	2,000
Representation in International Organizations	2,500
Reserve for Emergencies	10,250
Surplus for allocation	1,400

Apportionment of Education Budget

Livingstone College (Founder's Day included)	$70,000
Hood Seminary	5,000
Lomax-Hannon	10,000
Clinton	10,000
Walters-Southland	10,000
Johnson Memorial	10,000
Atkinson	2,000
Dinwiddie	2,000
Administration and Promotion	2,000
Leadership Training and Ministers' Institute	4,000

Respectfully submitted
The Committee

Motion made by Bishop Walls, seconded by C. H. Foggie, prevailed that the Publication House be listed as an item for the Budget and the money be taken out of the reserve fund.

(A motion was made that Item 1 and 2 of Part I be adopted and prevailed)

Rev. A. Marshall Jr. made an amendment to the motion as stated that Items III, IV, and V be considered prior to adoption of Item I. This was seconded by Rev. J. W. Watson. Motion prevailed.

Rev. R. E. Clement offered a substitute motion that the General (Conference) Claims apportionment be $300,000; the Education Budget be $125,000; with the provision that no additional items be assessed the local church, (with clarification that the Annual Conference be free to work out its local setup). The Rev. J. R. Respass seconded the motion. Motion prevailed.

In the afternoon session of May 19, 1948, the following changes were made in the report of the Budget Committee. Both Section 2 of Part II and Section III were amended and adopted.[25] It is presumed that the changes were to be carried either in the Budget Bulletin or the Discipline. It appears that the Budget Bulletin was not issued. The item Section Two appears to have been changed to read: "Each Annual Conference shall elect a Board of Apportionment, consisting of Presiding Bishop, Presiding Elders, three ministers and as many laymen as there are presiding elders and ministers." [26] It appears that Section 3 of Part II does not appear in the Discipline in recognized form so rather than being amended may have been drastically changed. The Journal states that Sections 4, 5, and 6 were automatically deleted but we note no reference to a Section 6 in the original. According to the action of the General Conference the Educational money was to be sent to the "Secretary." It is assumed that the Secretary indicated was the Secretary of Christian Education. Founder's Day Money was not to go to this office, however.

One major change came in the discussion of the Budget report. The General Secretary, with his work as Public Relations officer was to be a Full-time General Officer. The idea was fully noted in the report of the Committee, itself. On motion of Rev. E. Franklin Jackson Section 4 was adopted. Earler, it appears that these three sections were deleted. It may have been that originally there were other sections which were deleted, thereby moving the one accepted to No. 4. The reader must conclude that when Section III is mentioned the writer meant to state Part III as this was accepted by the General Conference on motion of the Rev. E. Franklin Jackson. Just what happened to other items of the Budget are not clear. For example, the 5% allocated to Annual Conferences evidently was eliminated.

---

[25] *Official Journal, Thirty-third Quadrennial Session, General Conference,* 77-80.
[26] *Doctrines and Disciplines of the A.M.E. Zion Church,* 1948, 164, 165.

The $200 allocated to each Annual Conference would then be the amount allowed.

It is not known just what happened to the suggestion of Bishop John W. Martin that the $200 be deducted from the total amount of the General Claims raised in each Annual Conference as his was merely a suggestion.

On motion of Dr. James W. Eichelberger the sum to be raised on each Founder's Day for Livingstone College should be $75,000 instead of the original amount, $70,000. The added $5,000 was to be allocated to the Hood Theological Seminary.[27] On a motion of Rev. C. C. Coleman the budget was approved with the changes indicated.

The final day of the Thirty-third session clarified several matters, one including the matter of the retention of the Two Hundred Dollars from General Claims within the Annual Conference. All collections of General Claims should be sent to the Financial Secretary who should remit to each Annual Conference the $200. One reason for this procedure was that the smaller conferences could not withhold the amount and still make reports, or, in cases, might not report as much. This was explained by the Chairman of the Budget Committee. On motion of the Rev. A. P. Morris it was ordered that the Financial Secretary send the said $200 before or during the session of that annual conference. The Chairman, Dr. Jackson, suggested that the rule apply to the overseas conferences as well.[28]

Again a difficult confrontation faced the General Conference at its meeting in Brooklyn, New York at First Church four years later, in 1952. The Chairman of the Budget Committee, the Reverend J. Clinton Hoggard stated that his committee was "in need of a decision by the General Conference in order to continue its work."[29] The Secretary of the Committee, Mrs. Elsie G. Keys read the following proposal: "The Budget Committee respectfully requests that this General Conference approve a General Claims Budget of $400,000.00 for the 1952-56 Quadrennium." It was moved by the Chairman, Reverend Hoggard and supported by the Rev. J. E. McCall that the request be granted. "After much discussion a mo-

---

[27] *Official Journal of the Thirty-third Quadrennial Session*, 80.
[28] *Ibid.*, 81.
[29] *Official Journal of the Thirty-fourth Quadrennial Session of the General Conference* 1952, 57.

tion by the Rev. C. H. Foggie supported by Rev. J. W. Shaw prevailed that the matter be laid on the table." [30]

The Budget, identically the same for the previous quadrennium was evidently presented on the Fourteenth Day of the session. Dr. S. C. Coleman made the motion for approval with a second by the Rev. J. C. Corrothers. Mrs. Abbie Clement Jackson offered an amendment "that the budget be accepted as presented with the provision that the $1,600.00 for Livingstone College be an item of the budget not included in the $15,000 allocated for Home Missions. The motion carried." [31]

It is not clear that which the Committee presented later on the same day. The Minutes merely state: "The Budget Committee headed by Rev. J. Clinton Hoggard reported through its secretary, Mrs. Elsie G. Keys.

"It was moved by Rev. A. G. Dunston Jr. and seconded by Rev. W. A. Hilliard that the Budget Committee return, consult the Bishops and Delegation leaders and bring recommendations. The motion prevailed." [32]

This writer can see but one change in the apportionment and budget of 1952, from that of 1948. It appears that a portion of the contingent or Surplus Fund was allocated to the Harriet Tubman Home, giving this project $6,000 per year. Otherwise both salaries and appropriations remained the same. Again, the reluctance of the denomination to recognize that changes had occurred in the quadrennium between sessions is hard to understand.

To suggest that every member of the 1956 General Conference recognized that something had to be done concerning the finances of the Church is indisputable, but again there are acts which lead one to believe that other underlying causes were present as the group looked at the monetary affairs of the denomination. This is more clearly pointed out as one examines the actions of the Thirty-fifth quadrennial session. It is well to read the entire report or statement of the Board of Bishops for few areas of life were not touched upon in that message. Budget found its way into the statement rather far down the listing. The Board recognized the "inadequacy" of funds made available. They minced few words in declaring "The Depart-

---

[30] *Official Journal of the Thirty-fourth Quadrennial Session,* 57.
[31] *Ibid.,* 75.
[32] *Ibid.,* 77.

ments of the Church cannot expand and grow on the present budget. The General Conference of 1948 observing that the budget was too small for progressive legislation, arose to the occasion and increased the budget of the denomination—the general claims budget from $162,000 to the present $302,388 and the education budget to $125,529, making our total budget $428,917." [33]

The Board went on to say: "Two quadrenniums have passed since the adoption of this budget; commodities of all descriptions have mounted in cost; living conditions have soared; the worth of the dollar has inflated greatly—and yet the income of the respective departments and salary scales, as per discipline, are the same as in 1948. We are raising more money today than we have raised at any time. This matter has given your chief pastors no little concern—as per discipline the finance department receives $138,000.00 of the General Claims budget, the Christian Education department—$60,000 etc." The Board went on to acknowledge that which has always prevailed when the General Conference refused to act according to assignment: "We have been called upon during the quadrennium to raise, for example, a sum equal to 10 percent of the General Claims budget for the Publishing House. We have been called upon to raise an amount equal to 8 percent for delegates' expense. Each annual conference is a patronizing conference to some school, each year there has been a healthy plus on Founder's Day; besides in many conferences tremendous amounts have been raised for local conference home missions, conference workers, district projects, interchurch movements, et cetera."

They (the Bishops) concluded the statement on budget by stating that the recommendation suggested a budget of $350,000 "with special days set aside for Missions and Church Extension at which time we are to give emphasis to educating our constituency and the raising of $100,000 to be divided between the Home Missions, Foreign Missions and Church Extension Departments." [34]

The casual reader of these statements naturally would begin to wonder why the reluctance of the General Conference to act, even after eight years of a set budget. The Bishops had pointed out, for example, that unprecedented financial growth had been observed.

---
[33] *Official Journal of the Thirty-fifth Quadrennial Session*, 1956, 69.
[34] *Official Journal of the Thirty-fifth Quadrennial Session*, 1956, 69.

However, they said little about over-all membership growth. Perhaps this was because the Church did not have these facts at hand. Time after time it must be acknowledged that the Church kept two sets of membership books, one for General Claims purposes and the other for actual growth of membership. This second set of figures seems not to have been available when a budget was to be made.

It is hard to conceive that normal financial growth would not be in the minds of ministry and lay people alike. Favorable reports as to finance and membership are, themselves encouragements to growth in finance and membership. So again, one must either consider the General Conference far from visionary or look elsewhere for the real reason. And yet, one notes all along the line that educational needs have struck a sympathetic chord.

It should be stated that several studies on budget had been submitted and studied particularly by the Ministers' and Laymen's Association of the Church. An exhaustive discussion was had, for example, at the Hartford (Conn.) sessions where it was suggested that a budget of a million dollars or more was not unreasonable. When the General Conference met in Pittsburgh, therefore, the groundwork had been laid and a perfect understanding of the basic problems which would be faced were in the hands of the Committee.

On Tuesday, May 8, the first communication from the Budget Committee was presented for action by the Reverend Dr. E. Franklin Jackson who was the vice-chairman. The Resolution, No. 8, provided for the voluntary raising of $100,000 for Missionary purposes. He suggested that the rules be suspended that immediate action be taken on the measure. His motion to do so was supported by the Reverend Dr. J. R. Funderburk. After the expression of several unreadinesses and efforts to lay the proposition on the table or otherwise amend it, Mrs. Abbie Clement Jackson insisted that the total increase of all sections of the budget be placed before the House before action on Resolution No. 8. Since the action to suspend the rules was the matter at hand the vote was taken and the motion lost.[35]

On Tuesday, May 16, the Budget Committee brought before the Conference its mimeographed proposed budget for the denomination. Reverend M. C. Williams made a motion that the Conference approve the work of the Committee with thanks to them for their labors. The Rev. C. L. Wilcox supported the motion. Dr. Ernest

---

[35] *Official Journal, Thirty-fifth Quadrennial Session,* 1956, 84.

Robinson complimented the Committee also. Several unreadinesses were noted, one suggesting that the report be adopted item for item. Dr. Rufus Clement declared that the "denomination had gone eight years without changing our budget, that if our church was going to keep pace with other great churches, it was obvious that we needed an increase." [36] Discussion along many lines followed with dissatisfaction being expressed as to amounts for some departments and the general over all increase. No quorum being present the Conference adjourned on motion of the Rev. Felix S. Anderson. The next day, the Budget was called again, reported, and the budget along with the accompanying resolutions were adopted.[37] The report follows:

COMMITTEE ON BUDGET AND APPORTIONMENT

Your Committee on Budget and Apportionment has prayerfully and thoughtfully considered every phase of the work assigned to it and has sought help and guidance from every source available. Your Committee has been, in some instances, stimulated and in others greatly depressed. (The news of a 3.2 million dollar all inclusive Budget adopted by another denomination and the determination of many within our own church to resist any increase at all, are respective examples.)

Constantly before us has been and is the welfare of our Zion and consideration of its growth and expansion the motivating influence in this preparation. We have had before us many resolutions and requests and in each and every case the call has been for an increase in funds allocated to them, some with provisions and others with none. After careful study of the plight of General Officers and Bishops from the standpoint of stated salary and pay scale, and at the same time being aware of the nearness to the saturation point we have attempted to secure pledges and promises from fathers of the Church, (our Bishops) to take any increase we may now propose out of funds already required of churches and pastors in order that there will be no increases in individual churches per se. Some of the Bishops are so agreed. Aware of the need for an unanimous voice in this matter we make the following recommendations:

1. That the resolution restricting the asking assessment, or requirements on a church, charge, pastor or persons within a church, for use within an annual conference to an amount which does not exceed the equal of 40% of the General Claims, be approved and become the law of the Church.

2. That the resolution calling for a voluntary effort for Missions and Expansion be approved with these provisions: (a) that one common date (preferably the fourth Sunday in September be set for the denomination and, (b) that no amount be stipulated but that each

---
[36] *Ibid.*, 124.
[37] *Official Journal of the Thirty-fifth Quadrennial Session*, 126.

area conference, and church be urged to lend every effort for the three departments, Foreign Missions, Home Missions, Church Extension.

3. That the resolution calling for a common Founder's Day for the operating secondary schools and Junior Colleges with a goal of One Hundred thousand dollars, be approved in principle but supplemented by combining this effort with Children's Day and without additional assessment we seek to double our Children's Day report bringing that amount to One hundred thousand dollars, or an anticipated voluntary free-will increase of Fifty thousand.

4. That in the light of the challenge of our times, and the disgracefully low salaries and the lack of anything near adequate apportionment for our departments, we recommend, that our Education budget remain the same except that conference assessments be adjusted so as to relieve strain on our weaker conferences, and that our General Claims budget be increased to Three hundred seventy-five thousand dollars but that the amount of increase be apportioned so as to relieve the burden on conferences now ever-assessed and to transfer the responsibility to those conferences better able to bear the load because of economic potential, industrial setting and numerical strength. Note the following budget we have decreased assessment on 8 conferences, raised assessment less than $1,000 on 17 conferences. Placed the bulk of assessment on the 8 larger conferences. Therefore, we present the following budget:

PROPOSED BUDGET FOR 1956-60

Item	Percentage	Amount
Finance Department	48%	$180,000.00
Christian Education Dept.	17	63,750.00
Church Extension Department	7	26,250.00
Home Missions Department	7	26,250.00
Foreign Missions Department	4	15,000.00
Relief Department	7	26,250.00
General Conference Delegate Expense	5	18,750.00
Pension Service	1	3,750.00
Publishing House	1	3,750.00
Editorial Section	1	3,750.00
Public Relations Dept.	1	3,750.00
Contingent Fund	1	3,750.00
	100	$375,000.00

DISBURSEMENTS OF FINANCE DEPARTMENT

To all Departments	$195,000.00
Episcopal Claimants 12 @ $7,000	84,000.00
Matthews stipend	2,100.00
African Bishop's Foreign Service stipened	1,000.00
General Officers, 11 @ $4,600.00	50,600.00
General Officers, 1 part time @ $2,300.00	2,300.00
Bishops' widows, 13 @ $600.00	7,800.00
Annual Conference support, 21 @ $225.00	4,725.00

THE DENOMINATION AND ITS FINANCES

Operating Expense, Finance Department	6,000.00
General Secretary-Auditor Expense	1,200.00
Bureau of Evangelism	1,200.00
Star of Zion (Editor's office)	500.00
American Bible Society	2,000.00
Publishing House (Additional)	3,000.00
Representation International Organizations	6,000.00
Harriet Tubman Foundation	6,000.00
Historical Society Operational Expense	1,250.00
Quarterly Review supplement	500.00
Surplus	325.00
	$375,500.00

Listed also in the report was the individual assessment on each Annual Conference. The General Claims assessment appears to have been $500.00 short of the appropriation, while $127,610.00 was allocated to Education, excluding the above allocation. The total budget was $502,610.00. The Reverend W. M. Smith was the Chairman of the Committee, Reverend E. Franklin Jackson was Vice Chairman and Mrs. Maggie Hines, Secretary.[38]

The Thirty-seventh Quadrennial session of the General Conference met in the Farmers' Building of the Indiana State Fairgrounds, Indianapolis, Indiana following the first Day opening session at Jones Tabernacle Church. It would not be far from the truth were one to state that the 1964 session was perhaps the most crucial in the history of the denomination, except, perhaps that which occasioned the division of 1852. In a sense, the 1964 session was more critical as one notes the threatened possibility of fragmentation. One could hear, for example, suggestions that home churches be informed of proceedings that they might take action. To those who had given their lives in behalf of the denomination such statements were fearful for the tone of the delegation was not one to brook argument. The major question was one of the supremacy of the General Conference,—whether the leadership it creates is supreme to the creator. One would be forced to admit that reasoning along this line, leadership limits the General Conference, places a low estimate on the makeup of that body. In truth, in every phase, the General Conference must be supreme—even to the changes within the denomination where its power is limited, for in those instances the body can order Quarterly Conference examination of

---

[38] *Official Journal, Thirty-fifth Quadrennial Session*, 440-443.

any and all proposed changes, or a valid vote in the several annual conferences.

Indianapolis needs to be examined in the light of a spirit of growing restlessness on the part of membership. Resistance to financial improvement, as stated before, cannot be said to have been the basic reason for all of its actions in the General meetings. The delegation was aware of the fact that in the Sixties alone, the cost of living index went up approximately 17%.[39] This would normally mean that to produce the same services in 1968 which one had in 1960 would have meant an increase in budget of close to $100,000.00. The budget of 1964, for example, was $1,250,000, but the reader must note that $400,000.00 of this amount was allocated to education,—an increase of $300,000.00. At no time in the Church's history has active opposition existed to the amounts spent for education. Of the existing budget, following the General Conference of 1968, $100,000 more was moved from other allocations to schools and colleges, which means that $500,000.00 of the present budget is allocated to schools and colleges. Of the balance, $300,000.00 is allocated to Departmental support and $135,000.00 to Ministerial Relief while $258,560.00 is distributed to that which is called "Connectional Claimants (Bishops, General Officers and Episcopal Assistance).

However, it should be remembered that under the pre-1964 budget there was a Founder's Day effort and a Children's Day project, so that the net increase is still not that which it appears on the surface.

Careful scrutiny of the acts undergirding the budget of 1964 will show that one major effort was in the mind of the Committee, the tapping of sources already drifting into the hands of the Annual Conferences so that the Church must realize that very little *new* money is being raised even under the adjustments of 1968.

The budget of 1964, which we are listing in full, was not balanced in the first quadrennium for obvious reasons. Here, again, the dependence of the Church's future rests upon the willingness of full cooperation of every person concerned. It was said by one individual in 1952, "where will these assessments end?" The necessity of dedication, and consecration with a return to the original purposes of the Church appears to be our only salvation. The Black Church has been

---

[39] *Ladies Home Journal,* September 1968, 58.

given, through present-day circumstances, a brief lease on life. No matter how we look at that which is called the *Black Revolution* with its *Black is Beautiful* slogan, it serves this day if the Church can only rise to her full height and meet the challenge to be fully Christian.

BUDGET COMMITTEE REPORT

Whereas the 37th Session of the General Conference in session adopted on Friday, May 15 an enabling resolution on a Connectional Budget which says in its closing paragraph:

"*Be it further resolved* that the resolutions specifically delineating the function and office of the Connectional Budget Board and the direction for control, collection and distribution of the Connectional Budget shall be presented and adopted by the General Conference before such apportionments be made." The Budget Committee herewith offers the following Legislative Resolutions for immediate enactment to pave the way for the adoption of the Connectional Budget with a Central Treasury.

Be it further resolved that this 37th session of the General Conference direct that a Connectional Budget Board of 25 members shall be elected by and at this session of the General Conference in the following manner:

1. That one member (ministerial or lay) shall be nominated by each Episcopal District and elected by the General Conference.

2. That the remaining number of members shall be members-at-large (providing for a diversity of talents and experience) who shall be nominated by the Board of Bishops and elected by the General Conference. Three of this number shall be Bishops with special insight on financial matters.

Be it further resolved that the Chairman and Vice Chairman shall be bishops of the A.M.E. Zion Church, and that the Secretary and Assistant Secretary shall be a minister and/or layman. And that such officers be elected by the Connectional Budget Board at its first meeting which shall be held at the Connectional Council next ensuing.

That the Connectional Budget Board shall elect an Executive Committee consisting of the elected officers (Chairman, Vice Chairman, Secretary, Assistant Secretary) and five members of the Connectional Budget Board.

That this Executive Committee shall meet every six months or on call by the Chairman to review the work of the Financial Secretary who shall be Executive Officer of the Connectional Budget Board. The Executive Committee shall make annual reports to the Connectional Budget Board at the time and place of the Connectional Council.

Be it further resolved that the Connectional Budget Board shall decide and pass upon all actions of the Financial Secretary and the Executive Committee, subject to review by the Connectional Council and the Board of Bishops.

Be it further resolved that any and all laws, rule, or other legislation contrary to the afore-mentioned resolution be hereby declared null and void and that the committee on revision of the Discipline of the A.M.E.

Zion Church be authorized and instructed to bring our rules and regulations into line with the afore-mentioned resolutions.

SUPPORT OF THE CONNECTIONAL BUDGET

That the Connectional Budget be adequately supported and financed for the good of all our Zion and that no church, annual conference or Episcopal Area be required to report to the Connectional Budget any increase in assessment; be it therefore enacted that each Church or Charge, annual conference or Episcopal District be required to report to the Connectional Budget the sum total of all of its assessments, General Claims, Education, Conference assessments, including Conference Workers, Home Missions Workers, special workers, District Workers, etc. (no more, no less) than the amount raised for the conference year 1963-64, excluding Quadrennial Testimonial and Freedom Fund.

That each and every existing obligation of the Annual Conference for projects already in operation will be met in the following manner:

The Conference Treasurer shall make requisition for sufficient funds to meet the needs of the Annual Conference Projects on the basis of need and the record of the year 1963-64 expenditures. The Connectional Budget Board authorizes its Financial Secretary to pay from the fund marked Annual Conference Projects under Church Extension.

Annual Conference expenses for personnel and visiting speakers who are not conference members shall be met in the same manner; however, the resource shall be from items noted as Annual Conference Expenses. The basis shall be the 1963-64 expenditure sheet. However, no amounts shall be allowed for visitors honoraria.

CONNECTIONAL BUDGET WITH CENTRAL TREASURY

Be It Resolved that the following shall be the order setting forth a Connectional Budget with a Central Treasury in order that the stewardship of the African Methodist Episcopal Zion Church may be fully developed and that the Church receive the full support on a connectional level of every one through participation in connection interest to the maximum of his ability, let there be adopted the following financial program in the African Methodist Episcopal Zion Church.

1. That there be established a Connectional Budget with a Central Treasury which shall be known as the Connectional Budget.
2. The manifold interests, causes and services existing and to be created shall be included in the Connectional Budget and grouped under the following:
1. Connectional Claimants
2. Administration
3. Departments
4. Educational Institutions
5. Pension-Relief & Ministerial Support
6. Publications and Periodicals
7. Inter-group Representation
8. **Reserve Fund**

That the General Conference in its quadrennial session approve a budget which shall cover the expenses of all department(s) and institutions of the A.M.E. Zion Church, its benevolent causes, projects and claimants. Included in this budget shall be all funds allocated for the existing causes and such as shall hereinafter be created. This amount when adopted by the General Conference shall be the Connectional Budget. The General Conference shall make apportionment of the Connectional Budget to the various Episcopal Districts and Annual Conferences in amounts commensurate with the strength of such Episcopal District and Annual Conference. This amount may not exceed the total amount raised 1963-1964 excluding Freedom and Quadrennial Testimonial.

3. When this amount has been determined, allocations made and approved by the General Conference, shall constitute the entire assessment of an Episcopal District or Annual Conference. The power of assessment is to remain solely with the General Conference, except as hereinafter provided for the distribution of the Annual Conference assessment to local churches; these churches shall be assessed in accordance with Chapter XII, paragraph 322-324. At each quadrennial session of the General Conference, there shall be elected a Connectional Budget Board. This Board shall through its fiduciary officer (Financial Secretary) receive, allocate and disburse all funds raised through the denomination for the Episcopal Districts, Annual Conferences and connectional operations. Included shall be funds raised by Annual Conferences, Episcopal Districts, Special projects, Home Missions, Home Missions Workers, Conference Workers, or specially designated workers by any other name.

1. Episcopal Claimants

The salary and expense of the active bishops and the support of retired bishops shall be paid from the allocation for Connectional Claimants. The fund shall be administered by the Financial Secretary under the direction of the Connectional Budget Board as authorized by the General Conference.

The salary of a Bishop shall be determined by the General Conference upon the recommendation of the Connectional Budget Board, which Board shall submit to the General Conference after careful study of the needs of a bishop and of the ability of the Church to raise the necessary funds that which it deems to be proper salary for a bishop.

The 37th session of the General Conference designated that a bishop actively engaged in administering the affairs of the A.M.E. Zion Church in accordance with the discipline shall receive an annual salary of $12,500, and $2,000.00 for assistance. The entire amount shall be paid by the Financial Secretary from the allocation for Connectional claimants. The total of $14,500.00 shall be paid in twelve equally divided monthly installments. No further amounts for honorarium, expense, travel or any other purpose shall be requested or received by a bishop from the Financial Secretary, local A.M.E. Zion Church, member or officer thereof, a General Officer, District Conference, Annual Conference, special or regularly established conference or conventions or meetings, educational institutions, boards or other institutions of the A.M.E. Zion Church, such expense being included in the salary and expenses delineated above.

The 37th session of (the) General Conference designates that the salary of a retired Bishop shall be $5,000.00 annually and shall be paid by the Financial Secretary in twelve equal monthly installments; however, no travel or support shall be included except that travel and sustentation to the meetings of the Board of Bishops, the Connectional Council and the General Conference shall be made at the rate established by the Connectional Budget Board. It shall be the same as that of an active Bishop. The Bishop of the African and South American work however, shall receive extra travel allowance to permit him and/or his family to visit the work. This amount shall be the prevailing fare charged by plane or boat (Whichever is convenient) at the time of the trip. In the case of a bishop residing in America who serves in Africa, this amount shall be paid only twice during the quadrennium. The travel and sustentation of bishops in attendance to the Bishops' meeting, the Connectional Council, inter-group organizations and inter-denominational meetings shall be paid from the administration allocation at the rate agreed by the Connectional Budget Board.

Any bishop who requests or accepts any travel expense or honorarium from a pastor, presiding elder, local elder, local church, member or officer, annual or district conference, meetings and conventions regular or otherwise or other institutions of the A.M.E. Zion Church shall be guilty of malfeasance of office and shall be brought to trial as provided in Chapter 6, paragraphs 267-273, 1960 Discipline, inclusive. A bishop found guilty of accepting money from any source of the A.M.E. Zion Church other than that provided for by the Connectional Budget Board for official services or gratuities shall be suspended until the ensuing General Conference, forfeiting all unpaid salaries.

I (a) GENERAL OFFICERS SUPPORT

The salary of an active General Officer of the A.M.E. Zion Church shall be paid from the allocation for connectional claimants. This fund shall be administered by the Financial Secretary under the direction of the Connectional Budget Board as authorized by the General Conference.

The salary of a General Officer shall be determined by the General Conference upon recommendations of the Connectional Budget Board, which Board shall submit its recommendations as a part of the Connectional Budget for each quadrennium. A General Officer shall receive an annual salary of $5,000, $1,100.00 for office and $1,100.00 for travel. The total of $7,200.00 shall be paid in twelve monthly installments. The travel and sustentation of General Officer(s) shall be paid to the Board of Bishops Meeting, Connectional Council and General Conference at the rate approved by the Connectional Budget Board and shall be paid from the Administration Fund.

THE DENOMINATION AND ITS FINANCES

II Administration

To effectively provide for the administration of the business of the A.M.E. Zion Church there shall be an allocation from the Connectional Budget for administration. From this allocation shall be paid the expenses of the General Conference, Connectional Council, Board of Bishops Meeting, Connectional Budget Board, the travel and sustentation of Bishops and General Officers to these meetings, the executive Committee, the office of financial secretary, commissions and committees created by the General Conference and inter-group organizations authorized by the General Conference. The expense of the General Secretary and Public Relations Officers.

The Financial Secretary shall disburse such allocations for Administration as authorized by the General Conference under the direction of the Connectional Budget Board where the General Conference has not allocated a definite amount to commissions and committees, inter-group organizations, etc., not hereinafter provided for, the Connectional Budget Board by a two-thirds vote shall determine the amount to be paid.

III Departmental Support

That the various departments of our church may be effectively operated, the Financial Secretary shall allocate and appropriate on a quarterly basis the following amounts to be administered by the Secretary-Treasurer of the respective departments under the direction of the boards governing his office. Each board shall through its chairman make semi-annual reports to the Connectional Budget Board, that is, at the Board of Bishops' Meeting and the Connectional Council. The allocations to departments shall be as follows: Church Extension $130,000; Home Missions $40,000; Foreign Missions $75,000; Christian Education Administration $20,000; Home Church and Evangelism $30,000.

IV Educational Institutions

The Connectional Board shall allocate from the Connectional Budget the amount of $400,000.00 for the support of our operating schools which are: Livingstone College, Hood Seminary, Clinton College, Lomax-Hannon. The maintenance of other schools including Johnson Memorial Institute, Walters Institute, Dinwiddie Institute and Atkinson College, be under the direction of the Christian Education Department and that they be used for Institutes and such other profitable use as the Christian (Education) Department may designate, and that such revenues as may be derived from rent of land or buildings be used by Christian Education Department for the upkeep of these projects. That specific and direct attention be given to raising the Educational portion of the Connectional Budget let there be two major report days.
(1) Founders Day, Livingstone College and
(2) Fourth Sunday in September at which time each pastor, district or annual conference and Episcopal area be required to report at least 25% of the assessment at each of these checkup meetings to be

disbursed by the Financial Secretary on a quarterly basis. Such disbursements shall be made directly to Treasurer of operating schools.

V Pension Relief and Ministerial Support

That the various areas of Ministerial Relief-Pensions and minimum salary may be effectively operated—let there be appropriated from the Connectional Budget Board the amount of $135,000.00 to be used in the following manner: $67,500.00 for support of widows of bishops and ministers; $7,500.00 for Superannuated ministers and ministers' orphans, and $60,000.00 for minimum salary for ministers and presiding elders.

(a) Pensions: Paragraph 387-395 shall remain intact.

(b) Relief: The widow of a bishop who has not remarried shall receive $700.00 per year; the widows of ministers and general officers who have not remarried shall receive $120.00 per year and such appropriation to superannuated ministers and orphans of ministers as the residue will allow.

(c) Minimum salary for Ministers and Presiding Elders (see Resolution attached.)

VI Publications and Periodicals

The Connectional Budget Board will allocate from its total budget for operation of Publishing House and to subsidize the Quarterly Review, Church School Herald literature and Star of Zion editorial staffs. The manager of the Publishing House shall use the appropriation for operation and promotion of the Publishing House upon authorization from Board of Publication and Periodicals. However, no part of this amount is to be used for the manager's salary. The Editors shall report to the Board of Publication and Periodicals the use made of their subsidy.

VII Inter-group Representations

The fund allocated for Inter-group Representations shall be disbursed by the Financial Secretary in accordance with the recommendation of the Board of Bishops approved by the Connectional Budget Board.

VIII The Reserve Fund

That there be always on hand a fund for emergency and undesignated needs that may be approved by the Connectional Budget Board. The amount of $31,440.00 shall be allocated to this fund and at the expiration of each fiscal year all unused funds from any section of the Budget shall be deposited in the Reserve Fund.

Any rule or law to the contrary of the aforementioned legislation shall become null and void upon enactment of this legislation.

To facilitate the collection of this Connectional Budget, this General Conference authorizes that each Annual Conference shall strive to

report at least ¼ of the total reported in 1963-64 on the following dates:
Founder's Day (Checkup)
Easter (Checkup)
Woman's Day (Checkup)
Annual Conference (Total)

In order that the Connectional Budget shall have time to build up its resources, this 37th session of the General Conferences orders and directs all salaries to remain as is until January 1, 1965. Salaries in accordance with this budget shall become effective on this date. Retroactive increase for months June-December 1964 will be paid December 1965 or at an earlier time if deemed proper by the Connectional Budget Board.

Be it further resolved that this General Conference direct that an Annual Conference may not elect to ignore this new budget proposal and that any Bishop, Elder, Pastor or layman acting as agent for or officer of the Annual Conference who hinders, prevents or opposes the collection and remittance of the Connectional Budget shall be guilty of malfeasance and misfeasance of office and shall be handled in accordance with our discipline and that

This General Conference direct that all sections of the discipline dealing with the Financial Department, Educational Department or and other fiduciary matter be revised and amended to comply with the resolutions aforementioned.

CONNECTIONAL BUDGET WITH CENTRAL TREASURY

I. Connectional Claimants

Bishops' salary 12 at $12,500	$ 150,000.00
Episcopal Assistance 12 at $2,000	24,000.00
Retired Bishop 1 at $5,000	5,000.00
General Officers' salary 11½ at $7,200	79,560.00
	$ 258,560.00

II. Administration

Connectional Budget Office	$ 10,000.00
General Conference Delegate Expense	25,000.00
Travel and sustentation	15,000.00
Annual Conference Expenses	25,000.00
General Secretary's office	5,000.00
Public Relations Office	5,000.00
	$ 85,000.00

III. Departmental support
   Church Extension .... $ 130,000.00
      (camps, projects of annual conferences)
   Home Missions 45,000.00
   Foreign Missions 75,000.00
   Christian Education
      Home and Church—Evangelism 30,000.00
      Administration 20,000.00

                                                  $ 300,000.00

IV. Educational Institutions
   Livingstone College .... $ 270,000.00
   Hood Seminary 20,000.00
   Clinton Jr. College 50,000.00
   Lomax-Hannon Jr. College 50,000.00
   Others (inoperative schools) 10,000.00

                                                  $ 400,000.00

V. Ministerial Relief
   Superannuated ministers at $150.00 .... $ 7,500.00
   *Bishops' Widows 67,500.00
   Ministers' Widows at $120.00

               MINISTERS MINIMUM SALARY
                                                  $ 60,000.00

                                                  $ 135,000.00

         * Figure appears to be high (ed.)

VI. Publication House and Periodicals
   Historical Society .... $ 1,000.00
   Editors' Expense 1,500.00
   Publication House 20,000.00
   Editorial Section (Literature) 2,500.00

                                                  $ 25,000.00

VII. Organization Representation
   National and International Membership .... $ 10,000.00
   Zion's office, Nat. Council of Churches Bldg. ..   5,000.00

                                                  $ 15,000.00

VIII. Reserve .... $ 31,440.00
   I. Connectional Claimants .... $ 258,560.00
   II. Administration 85,000.00
   III. Departmental Support 300,000.00
   IV. Educational Institutions 400,000.00
   V. Ministerial Relief 135,000.00
   VI. Publications and Periodicals 25,000.00

THE DENOMINATION AND ITS FINANCES

VII. Representation 15,000.00
VIII. Reserve 31,440.00

Total $1,250,000.00

BUDGET COMMITTEE

M. C. Williams, Chairman, E. Franklin Jackson, 1st Vice-Chairman, G. A. Brooks, 2nd Vice-Chairman, O. D. Carson, Secretary, Joseph Jackson, Assistant Secretary, George J. Leake, J. E. Spruill, S. P. Spottswood, R. A. Council, L. R. Rogers, J. W. Wactor, C. R. Thompson, A. J. Blake, A. F. Johnson, Margaret J. May, Eugene Williams, M. Ardelle Shaw, Elizabeth Davis, Carrie Spaulding, Marvin Mobley, Abbie Clement Jackson, E. B. Patton, Mattie D. Egan, Chief Brown Nyenfuah, Richard Gray.

RESOLUTION

MINIMUM SALARY

Be it resolved that this Thirty Seventh Quadrennial Session of the General Conference of the A.M.E. Zion Church adopt and enact a plan for minimum salary for full time pastors and Presiding Elders in the A.M.E. Zion Church and that such full time pastors and Presiding Elders who are not engaged in gainful employment requiring the time and energy and talent which in due course would be directed toward improving their charges. However, pastors or presiding elders of full time status in this plan shall not be prohibited from pursuing graduate studies in any recognized schools, colleges and universities.

Be it further Resolved that the Thirty seventh Quadrennial Session of the General Conference enact the following:

A. That a portion of the Connectional Budget be allocated to the minimum Pastors Salary Fund.

B. That after a period of four years or as soon thereafter as the Connectional Budget Board finds that sufficient funds are in hand.

 1. Full time pastors who are ordained elders having traveled at least eight years or any ordained elder in full time service holding a degree from a college and seminary and who has traveled at least one year shall receive a minimum salary of $3,600.00.

 2. That pastors of the same category who are not married shall receive a minimum of $3,000.00.

 3. That the minimum annual salary for pastors who are not ordained elders or who have not traveled for at least two years shall be $2,400.00

 4. That the minimum salary of a presiding elder shall be $3,600.00 which salary shall include amount received from District Conference and Sunday School Convention.

Be it further resolved that the allocation from the Connectional Budget for minimum salaries be held in trust until the beginning of the fiscal year 1968 or at such time thereafter as the Connectional Budget Board shall deem such funds are available, at that time payments shall begin in accordance with the aforementioned schedule and the hereinafter mentioned provisions.

Be it further resolved that requests for supplement to make the minimum salary for any given church shall be presented first to the Quarterly Conference which shall decide upon the legitimacy of such claim determined by the ability or the inability of the Church to meet the minimum standard. Upon approval, the presiding elder shall sign the request which shall be forwarded to the secretary of Pension-Relief and Ministerial Support who is authorized to make the payment. In no case shall a requisition be made or honored from a pastor of a Church which is able to meet the minimum requirement but unwilling to do so. In the case of a presiding elder's district the request shall come from the District Conference and must be approved by the Annual Conference at the time of the presiding elder's report. The Annual Conference shall have the power to accept or reject the claim—if claim is accepted, the Bishop of the Annual Conference will then sign the request and forward it in the proper manner for payment.

Upon the establishment of a claim, the pastor shall receive his supplement quarterly, and in the case of a presiding elder, payment shall be made annually. The removal of a pastor or presiding elder whose claim has been submitted and approved shall in no wise stop, curtail or hinder such approved payment provided he is not removed under charges.

The resolution was approved.[40]

The 1968 General Conference (Thirty-eighth Quadrennial Session) met in St. Paul Church, Detroit Michigan. In many respects the Budget had been a vast improvement over that of prior years. Disappointment was noted, however, in the fact that the expected results had not been fully achieved. Speculation, naturally, was in evidence as to the basic reasons. It was supposed by some that there had been an overestimation of the amounts of unallocated funds coming into the Annual Conferences. This is a matter of individual conjecture. Others assessed the failure on lack of united effort to reach the expected goal, stating that initiative had been dwarfed when these funds were diverted from Annual Conference control to Connectional Budget. The reader, himself, will be forced to reach his personal conclusions.

Immediate complaint came in the matter of *restrictions*. The cry was expressed that anyone could do anything he willed with his own money. This writer would state that somewhere in the equation the paramount interests of the Church should take a type of precedence over personal desires and wishes. If actual hardships were evidenced then the Church had no right to demand this withholding of

---

[40] *Official Journal of the Thirty-seventh Quadrennial Session of the General Conference*, 1964, 72-80 incl.

personal funds. The General Conference was seeking to correct that which it termed a matter derogatory to the denomination. As a legislative body, it had the right to seek to control its membership, lay and clergy alike. It sought, as all well knew, to look beyond the immediate to the future. No person then, had a personal privilege over the desires of the whole.

The Connectional Council heard these complaints both unofficially and officially.

As it did so the assault on the system began, forcing at least one major retreat in the first quadrennium and leading to a more serious setback in the second. In order to make up for the shortages incurred as less than the expected amounts came in from the Annual Conferences, the Board endeavored to curtail expenses of the local Annual Conferences. Conferences were rated according to recognized ability and instead of the sending in of requisition sheets for expense the amount sent from the Financial Secretary was based on a preconceived formula. Still shortages developed.

As the Budget Committee endeavored to find a way out of the situation in the Detroit General Conference, they suggested that each Annual Conference set a figure above the old assessment which they would be willing to meet. It should be stated, as one examines the original concept, no Church was expected to contribute more than it had for all causes in the year prior to the General Conference of 1964. With the tone of the Conference ever in mind there was but one suggestion which the Committee could make—the balancing of the 1964-1968 budget and this they did. All other suggestions were ignored.

The General Conference (1968) after losing several days dealing with sustentation and other minor items, found itself with a *raising budget* to cover the needs of 1964 but with the guidelines of the spending budget of the earlier year. So the matter rested in the hands of the Budget Committee, the Connectional Budget Board, the Board of Bishops and the Connectional Council.

The immediate need was to find $100,000.00 additional for Education. The appropriations of the two or three major departments were tapped, along with *all* the allocations to Annual Conferences, save perhaps, the very small Conferences. This meant that regulations on sending in all money raised and reported at the Annual Conferences had to be loosened, so again, the Church returned to the days prior to 1964. At this point it now stands.

Changes in the appropriation at Durham were made as follows; of course some of these items had been voted at the General Conference: Retired Bishop, $6,250.00, Connectional Budget Office, increased by $2,000; General Conference Delegate Expense reduced by $5,000.00; Annual Conference Expense reduced from $25,000.00 to $16,935.00; Public Relations Office and General Secretary's Office expense increased by $200.00 each; Church Extension allocation reduced by $20,000.00; Christian Education reduced from $50,000.00 (which included Evangelism) to $35,000.00; Evangelism (new) $2,400.00; Laymen's Council (new) $1,200.00; Livingstone College increased from $270,000.00 to $325,000.00; Clinton Junior College and Lomax-Hannon increased from $50,000.00 to $70,000.00 each; Inoperative Schools (same) $10,000.00; Superannuated Ministers reduced from $7,500.00 to $1,000.00 (some of this may have been absorbed in the Pension Service); ministers' Widows, $60,000.00 (Bishop's Widows, likewise remained the same at $6,300.00); Ministers' Minimum salary Fund $20,000.00; Pension Supplement $10,000.00; Historical Society, increased by $200.00, Quarterly Review Supplement (the same) $1,500.00; Publication House, increased by $30,000.00 to $50,000.00; Sunday School Literature Editorial Section, increased from $2,500.00 to $5,200.00; Star of Zion (new) $2,400.00; Representation increased by $2,500.00 to $12,500.00, Zion Office at 475 Riverside Drive (same) $5,000.00; Historian (new) $5,000.00. Therefore changes were noted in the following areas: Connectional Claimants increased from $258,560.00 (because of retired Bishop) to $263,050.00; Administration down from $85,000.00 to $74,335.00; Departmental support down from $300,000.00 to 243,600.00; Educational Institutions up from $400,000.00 to $500,000.00; Ministerial Relief down from $135,000.00 to $97,300.00; Publication House and Periodicals up from $25,000.00 to $60,300.00 and Representation up from $15,000.00 to $22,500.00.

An examination of these changes will say a great deal to the Church at large. And while this writer acknowledges that the adjustments no doubt were the best which could be worked out, it appears to us that the points at which the structure has been weakened will eventually affect those which have been strengthened. The Church, as all others, and especially Black organizations, is facing an unprecedented time in which common questions of usefulness are abounding. It appears to us that the agencies which would serve to offset these criticisms are in a much poorer position now to do so. This may well prove the crucial area of the denomination in the years ahead.

CHAPTER XVII

Organic Union and Zion Methodism

AS ONE looks backward on the opening chapters of the History of Zion Methodism he is struck by the decision of non-conformity to the ways and organization of American Methodism, the sensitivity to the matter of the exercising of unChristian advantage and yet, beyond this, a desire to meet more than half-way kindred forces at every level. No critical reader of the times, for example, would state that the new denomination was not receptive to overtures of friendship with the Mother Church, and for a time, it appeared that there would be a return to the fold. Assuredly, ample time was given for the development of just this type of action. So it was only when the glimmer of the hope for reconciliation vanished that the Church forgot this possibility—if it ever did erase the possibility from its memory.

The movement into the City of New York by the forces of Richard Allen left a bad taste in the mouths of the Negro Methodists of that city, and laid the groundwork for a spirit of antagonism which was visible for some time, for the struggling congregations of the City felt that there should be no impediment to their progress, and in this few could condemn them. It remained for several years to pass and a full generation to leave the stage of action before the first thoughts of the Negro Methodists of New York City and those of Philadelphia were harmonious to the unification of that which came to be known as Zion Methodism and Bethel. Once, opened, these conversations were to span more than a century and eventually would involve a third branch of Negro Methodism, The Colored Methodist Episcopal Church later styled the Christian Methodist Episcopal Church.

While it appears that the conversations on Organic Union were in evidence prior to 1860, official note is not seen before this date. The major task of the re-unification of Zion, herself, may have been a cause for so little to be said on the wider subject. The nature with which the subject of union with the A.M.E. Church was presented in the Minutes of 1864 lends validity to the belief that the matter had been much in the membership's mind prior to that time.[1]

---

[1] *The General Conference of the A.M.E. Zion Church of 1864,* 6.

On the second day of the General session, as Moore states it and as it appears in the Minutes of that time[2] "The first business brought up was the report of the committee on union of the two bodies: the A.M.E. Zion Church and the A.M.E. Church. The report was as follows: At a meeting of a joint committee consisting of nine members with the bench of Bishops or Superintendents from the A.M.E. Zion General Conference (the following resulted):

"The Conference met according to appointment in Bethel Church, Sixth Street, Philadelphia, Friday evening, May 27th, 1864. The meeting was organized by Superintendent Clinton with singing and prayer; Bishop J. D. Brooks was called to the chair; Reverends J. M. Brown and J. P. Hamer were chosen Secretaries. After deliveration it was decided that this should be a formal meeting. The object of the meeting was stated, whereupon the proceedings of the committee who originated the matter in the A.M.E. General Conference were read, but the resolutions in those proceedings not being sufficiently full, they were laid upon the table and the matter referred to the following committee: Revs. Birch, S. T. Jones, J. H. Williams, J. W. Loguen, S. M. Giles; these persons were instructed to draw up resolutions expressing the sentiments of the Joint Committee on the subject. The committee withdrew, and after an absence of half an hour, returned and reported as follows":

REPORT OF SUB-COMMITTEE

Whereas: the committee of the A.M.E. Zion and the A.M.E. General Conferences met in joint committee, and having interchanged sentiments on the great question of union between the bodies represented by them; therefore,

Resolved, that is the opinion of this meeting that the great question of consolidation may be safely committed to a convention to consumate a union upon a basis which will be satisfactory to all concerned.

Resolved, that it is the sense of this joint committee that such a convention be held in the city of Philadelphia, commencing on the second Tuesday in June, 1864 in Wesley Church on Lombard Street, at 10 o'clock A.M. and that twenty-five delegates from each convention shall be submitted to the Annual Conferences of both Churches,

---

[2] *Ibid.,* 11.

and if agreed to by a majority of each, shall be final; all of which is respectfully submitted." [3]

The Reverend J. W. Hood felt that something further should be done prior to the submission of the matter to the Annual Conferences, or even before the matter was submitted to the General Conferences. He therefore, suggested the following:

"*Whereas*, it is indispensibly necessary that the minds of the people of both organizations be prepared for the important event contemplated; therefore,

Resolved, that a committee of three be appointed to issue an address to the churches through the columns of the Christian Recorder and the Anglo-African, setting forth clearly the object for which the convention is called."

According to Moore the above resolution was accepted by the Joint Commission and three men were thereafter appointed,—J. W. Hood, Singleton T. Jones and E. Weaver. The matter thereafter rested in the hands of the General Conference.[4]

The General Conference debated the suggestions from the Committee and finally decided that the following would represent the Zion Methodist Church: New York Conference; William H. Pitts, Jeptha Bancroft, Isaac Coleman, Jacob Thomas. The Philadelphia Conference was represented by Sampson Talbot, Singleton T. Jones, Charles Carter and J. B. Trusty. New England; S. M. Giles, G. H. Washington, W. F. Butler and J. W. Hood. From the Southern Conference; J. D. Brooks, J. P. Hamer, R. H. Dyson and J. A. Williams was appointed. The Allegheny Conference was represented by A. Cole, James A. Jones and J. B. Cox. The Genessee Conference; J. W. Loguen, Williams Sanford and J. H. Smith. Several alternates or *reserves* were likewise appointed among them being J. P. Thompson, (New York Conference; Jacob Anderson (Philadelphia Conference); G. E. Spywood (New England); H. A. Gibson (Southern Conference); P. G. Laws (Allegheny Conference) and John Thomas (Genessee Conference).[5]

The work of this first Joint-Committee of Zion and Bethel is set forth in detail in the History written by the late Bishop J. W. Hood. It appears that the legal technicalities which stood in the way of the

---

[3] John Jamison Moore, *History of the A.M.E. Zion Church* (York, 1884) 234-236.
[4] Moore, *loc. cit.*, 236.
[5] Moore, *loc. cit.*, 237.

union were brought into focus by two men, Bishop Payne of the A.M.E. Church and Singleton T. Jones of the A.M.E. Zion Church.[6] In the work of the Joint Committee Jermain Loguen, noting the depth of the differences, suggested that the simple problems and those easily resolved should be dealt with first.[7] Hood states that all these minor differences were cleared up and they came again to the problems of the episcopacy.

Two problems presented themselves to the Commission: 1. The type of Superintendency in vogue in the A.M.E. Zion Church with its title and election for four years with no special mode of induction into office and, 2. The life-time Bishopric of the A.M.E. Church. Hood states that Zion was perfectly willing to, first change the title of Superintendent to Bishop and second, elect for life. However, when the vote was taken the mode utilized in the Zion Church was defeated by a narrow margin. The second proposition, the title of Bishop and election for life was accepted by another close vote. The results of these votes proved that at least some of the Zion men had voted against the Superintendency and evidently some had voted for the Bishopric and election for life.

It will be remembered that the delegations were equal in size. The difficulty appeared to have developed when it was proposed that the A.M.E. Zion Church call a special session of its General Conference and there proceed to elect its Bishops for life and consecrate them. Hood states that the vote on this proposition was a tie. Since Superintendent Joseph Jackson Clinton was in the chair he proceeded to break the tie in favor of the proposal.[8]

In the discussion which followed this vote a request came for another session of the Joint Commission and while the Zion Methodist men saw no real purpose for another session they consented. Hood states that it was the turn of the Zion Church to be represented in the Chair but Bishop Campbell of the A.M.E. Church, presided. At this session a new resolution was submitted either by *Chaplain Hunter or A. L. Stanford* suggesting that the *matter of the final consumation* of the union be put off for four years, *each party doing all which it could for its own side during that*

---

[6] Bishop J. W. Hood, *One Hundred Years of the A.M.E. Zion Church* (New York, 1895) 148.
[7] *Ibid.*, 149.
[8] Hood, *loc. cit.*, 151.

time.[9] The Zion delegation voted against the resolution when the A.M.E. group voted for it—the deciding vote being cast by Bishop Campbell.

According to Hood, who was part of this early venture, the A.M.E. Zion Church preceeded to have printed "thousands of copies of the platform" which were distributed to the ministry and laity of the denomination. This evidently is a true statement since evidence of votes are to be noted among local congregations.[10]

The General Conference of 1864 had, naturally, its own questions to answer where the movement of Organic Union was concerned. On the fourth day of the session Moore states that "A discussion upon Organic Union was inaugurated from a remark made by some of the lay delegates, who deemed it essential that some instruction should be given the delegates in order that they might know what course to adopt." It should be stated that the place of lay delegates was one of the major questions before the Joint Commission. The Zion Methodist Church felt that the rights of the lay people had to be protected[11] and this, as well as any other reason may have been the cause of failure. Singleton T. Jones stated that the General Conference had no right to instruct the delegates of the Joint Commission (A.M.E. Zion delegates) but that the denomination and the General Conference should rely on their judgment, he further insisted that the General Conference should not discuss the matter but rely as well on the Convention. From the Convention the matter would be submitted to the Annual Conferences and the decisions of these bodies would be final. Since, it appears, there were no lay people in the Convention others suggested that the General Conference was the only place where the matter could be fully discussed.[12]

A full picture of all that transpired within the denomination where Organic Union was concerned between the adjournment of the 1864 General Conference and the opening of the next session which met at *Wesley Zion* Church, Washington, D.C. is not to be had. However, it is noted that a Committee on Union and Affiliation was named at the beginning of the session which was composed of 24

---
[9] *Ibid.*, 152.
[10] *Minutes of The General Conference of* 1868.
[11] Moore, *loc. cit.*, 238.
[12] *Ibid.*, 238, 239. The General Conference of the A.M.E. Zion Church of 1864, 23.

men, with, evidently, Singleton T. Jones as Chairman.[13] On May 11th the Committee received from the General Conference "several reports from the Annual Conferences concerning consolidation." The first concrete action, however, did not come until the Sixth Day when the matter of the change of the title of "Superintendent" to Bishop was acted upon and subsequently passed.[14]

Evidence of activity in the intervening years is to be found in several instances. The Baltimore Conference, meeting in Union Wesley Church, Washington, D.C., April 7-18, 1866, with James A. Jones acting as Secretary and assisted by William Sanford, passed the following resolutions:

> 1st. Resolved, That it is the sense of this executive session that it will be to the interest of the A.M.E. Zion Church to adopt the third ordination in our episcopal form and that an extra session of the General Conference be called by the Superintendents for the purpose as soon as the consent of the majority of the Annual Conferences shall have been secured.
> 2nd. Resolved, That in the event General Conference being convened it is the wish of this session that one of the Bishops of the M.E. Church be secured to ordain us, but failing in that, it is our purpose to ordain them in the same manner in which the M. E. Church originally ordained Bishop Asbury.[15]

With the disappointment involved in the failure of unification with the A.M.E. Church, the Zion General Conference took up the proposal of unification with the Mother Church. A Committee was selected to draft proposals and reported the following to the session:

> To the Bishops and Members of the M. E. General Conference:
> We are ready to enter into arrangements by which to affiliate on the basis of equality, and to become one and inseparable now and forever. On the condition of full equality with the most favored of the church, we desire the further stipulation that a sufficient number of those whom we may select to exercise the episcopal oversight of the colored element, of the body may be set apart to that office, on the basis of perfect equality with all other Bishops of the M. E. Church; as we have practically demonstrated that a lay representation, especially in the law-making department of the church, is at once sound, safe and productive of harmony among the people,

---
[13] *Minutes of the Twelfth Session of the General Conference of the A.M.E. Zion Church.*
[14] *Ibid.*
[15] *Baltimore Conference Minutes* 1866, 12.

We hope if at all compatible with view of religious progress that you will adopt the same as the rule of the church.

J. J. MOORE, *Chairman*
J. N. GLOUCESTER, *Secretary*

The Reverend Singleton T. Jones had earlier been selected as the delegate of the A.M.E. Zion Church to the Chicago General Conference of the Methodist Episcopal Church. Few people, according to the record, have been so well received by anybody as he was by the Methodist General Conference. While absent on this mission he was elected a Bishop of the Zion Methodist Church and returned to receive the grateful thanks of that body. The following action was taken:

Resolved: That while we gratefully acknowledge our thanks to Almighty God for the safe return to us of our beloved bishop, Singleton T. Jones, from his mission to the M.E. General Conference, in session at Chicago, Ill., we return our thanks for the manner in which he expressed the sentiments of this conference to that body, and the prospective success attained by his mission.

The report of Bishop-elect Jones was given as follows:

REPORT
of the
DELEGATE TO THE M.E. GENERAL CONFERENCE AT CHICAGO, ILL.

Bishops and Members of the General Conference of the A. M. E. Zion Church in America:

Having attended to the object of my mission to the General Conference of the M. E. Church sitting in Chicago, I beg leave to report that I arrived in that city on the evening of the 21st May, and on the following day repaired to the Conference and learned that a Committee to receive the Colored Delegation from Washington, D. C., had been appointed by the Conference, with Dr. A. M. Osborn at its head. After a short interview with the Committee, I requested to be introduced to the Conference to which my credentials were accredited. The Committee reported to the Conference immediately, and all other orders were suspended for the purpose of receiving the Delegate from the A. M. E. Zion Church. The following from the *Daily Christian Advocate* of the following day will give you a corrected account of the proceeding:

In the General Conference of the M. E. Church held in Chicago, Ill. May 22, 1868, Bishop Scott presiding the following proceedings were had to wit:

"A. M. Osborn desired to request the Committee on reception of delegates from the African M. E. Zion Church, and African M. E. Church to meet immediately.

A. M. Osborn announced that the delegate from the African M. E. Zion Church had arrived with his papers, and, if necessary, desired that the Conference should take action so that the desires of this body and that of the African M. E. Zion Church should be furthered.

W. Heddy moved that the delegate from that body be immediately introduced to the Conference. Carried.

W. H. Ferris moved the time be extended. Carried.

A. M. Osborn, the Chairman of the Committee on Reception, then came upon platform in company with Bishop Singleton T. Jones, of the African M. E. Zion Church, amid the cheers of the Conference and congregation." The Secretary then read the credentials of Bishop Jones, and also a personal communication from himself, as follows:

ADDRESS OF THE AFRICAN METHODIST EPISCOPAL ZION CHURCH

To the Bishops of the Methodist Episcopal Church, Greeting:

I am instructed by the General Conference of the African Methodist Episcopal Zion Church, in America, to say that the M. E. Church is still regarded the mother of our organization, and that, as we were induced to leave her, simply because she made a distinction among her children which seriously affected our interests, we are ready to return, if we can be assured that no individual distinction will be made in regard to us.

We are ready, therefore, to enter into arrangements by which to affiliate on the basis of equality, and to become one and inseparable, now and forever.

Aside from the condition of full equality with the most favored of the Church, we desire the further stipulation that a sufficient number of those we may select to exercise the Episcopal oversight of the colored element of the body may be set apart to that office, on the basis of perfect equality with all other Bishops of the Methodist Episcopal Church.

As we have practically demonstrated that a lay representative, especially in the law-making department of the Church, is at once sound, safe, and productive of harmony among the people, we hope, if at all compatible with your views of religious progress, that you will adopt the same as the rule of the Church.

SINGLETON T. JONES

Delegate, African Methodist Episcopal Zion Conference
Chicago, May 19, 1868

BISHOP JONES' ADDRESS

Venerable Bishops and Brethren of the Methodist Episcopal Church,

I greet you.

I come from a body which represents 164,000 members of the family of Methodism, 694 ministers and sixteen Annual Conferences, marshalled under six executive officers. A century has passed since the immortal Wesleys and their illustrious compeers laid the foundations of Methodism upon the indestructible basis of Bible purity and Bible equality. (Applause). How far the Church in America has degenerated from those principles, the sad story of that Church will tell. But, in the providence of God events have rolled on, and now the State taking the land of the Church, has settled herself down upon the broad principles of the Declaration of Independence, that a man is a man. (Applause). And I am happy to say that it is the understanding of the body from which I come that your Church, in its recent action, has re-echoed the same sentiment, and is ready to announce everywhere that man is a man, and that a Christian is a Christian, whether he be a colored man or a white man.

I am here, therefore, to ascertain whether we can live together again. We have found no difficulty in living together as master and slave; let us hope in God's name we can find no difficulty in living together as freemen and Christians. (Applause.) We ask for equality because, as members of the Christian Church, and as "partakers of the divine nature," we dare not, for the dignity of our Christian principles, we dare not ask for anything less than equality. (Applause.) By that equality, however, we mean not, Mr. Chairman, to thrust ourselves upon you, sir, nor yet to permit you to thrust yourselves upon us. (Long continued and vociferous applause.) We propose, sir, to walk into your parlors and sit down there as men, but not till you invite us to do so, and we do not propose that you shall walk into our parlors and sit down there till we invite you. (Applause.) I think that the Conference will understand that we are sensible on this subject. (Renewed applause.)

We have asked that certain brethren whom we know, but whom you cannot know, might be designated by us to exercise Episcopal authority over us, not because we have any objection to these bishops who sit around me now, but because, sir, we suppose that the Church is not ready to allow *me*, as a bishop to sit in authority over *you;* so we claim that black men shall be authorized to preside over us, and that the Episcopal honors shall be shared in common by black and white, and just as far as there can be an *interchange,* let us have it. (Great applause.)

We do not propose to force this matter, but to let time work it out, and we think that time—and more than all, sir—that *Christianity* will eventually work out this problem satisfactorily to all.

Having said this much, sir, I need add no more. I will only say, however, that if it can be laid down in this Conference that this white organization and this colored organization can become one and inseparable, now and forever, on broad principles of equality, we shall heartily rejoice in it, and the second century of Methodism will commence on a grand basis, that will make it, not only in this land, but in all lands, the great and formidable engine in the hands of God to evangelize and christianize the world. (Applause long continued.)

On motion of J. M. Reed, it was resolved that we have heard with the greatest pleasure the communication and address of our Reverend Brother who has just taken his seat, and that the papers he has presented to this body, be, and they hereby are, referred to the Committee already appointed upon that subject.

A member said he had understood that the brother who has just spoken is a bishop of the African M. E. Zion Church, and asked if this were so.

The brother who had just spoken being appealed to to answer the question whether he was a bishop, said: "I am not right certain about that, sir. They told me just as I was coming to the cars, that the General Conference had done that awkward thing." (Applause.)

A second meeting of the committee was called and held at 2 o'clock P.M. of the same day, and the propositions which were read to the Conference, as well as the sentiments expressed in the address before that body, were freely discussed, and it was agreed that the several members of the committee and also myself should pen down a permanent basis, which might enable the committee to report a final plan of union which should be acceptable to all parties concerned.

A third meeting of the committee was agreed on and held on the morning of the 23rd instant, at which I presented the following propositions as a basis, to wit:

STIPULATIONS OF AFFILIATION AND UNION BETWEEN THE M. E. AND THE A.M.E. ZION CHURCHES

1st. That the M. E. Church receive the A.M.E. Zion brethren on the basis of absolute and unqualified ecclesiastical equality.

2nd. That the superintendents or bishops just chosen by the General Conference of the A.M.E. Zion Church shall continue their episcopal authority as arranged by that body, until the next General

Conference of the M. E. Church, at which time their functions shall cease, and the said General Conference shall designate the persons who shall have the episcopal oversight of such Annual Conferences as are or may be composed, in whole or in part, of colored persons; *Provided,* that at least three of the persons thus designated shall be *colored men,* who shall exercise general episcopal authority in common with all other Bishops of the M. E. Church, and especially in the Council of Bishops and in the General Conferences; leaving the question of their presiding over Annual Conferences composed otherwise than those above named, to the election or choice of the same.

3rd. That a commission be appointed by this body to so merge the several conferences, that whenever it may be practicable, there may be but one colored Conference in each State.

4th. That said commission be empowered to constitute presiding elders and assign them their fields of labor, and also, to appoint such other officers as may be necessary to harmonize the uniting body with the rules and regulations of the M. E. Church.

5th. That upon the adoption of these stipulations by the two General Conferences respectively, the union shall be understood as final.

Upon the presentation and reading of the foregoing stipulations, it was found that the result of the labors of the members of the Committee who had drawn up propositions, were to some extent in harmony with these, and that the vital point of difference was in reference to the three Episcopal officers. After long consultation and discussion, it was agreed that the colored element of the Church should have a pro rata representation in the Episcopal Council according to the proportion which the white members have to the existing Bishops of the M. E. Church.

It was understood that a report would be made in harmony with these stipulations, and so the Committee separated on Saturday morning, May 23rd. On Monday, the 25th inst., at quarter to eleven o'clock A.M., the Chairman of the Committee, Dr. Osbon, having given previous notice of his intention so to do, and having informed me of the motives which induced the committee to change the character of the report from what was originally contemplated, in consequence of the ascertained opposition to that view of it, and the protracted discussion likely to ensue at that advanced stage of the

Conference,—made the following report to the M. E. General Conference, which was adopted:

A. M. Osbon moved to suspend the rule in order to listen to some parting words from the delegate of the African M. E. Zion Church. Carried.

A. M. Osbon presented the Report of the Committee on proposals of the African M. E. Zion Church with the Methodist Episcopal Church, as follows: The Committee appointed to receive and confer with the delegate of the African Methodist Episcopal Zion Church, report that they have had a free conference with the Rev. Singleton T. Jones, who is duly accredited to this body, and beg to present the following resolutions for your adoption, viz:

1. *Resolved,* That we, having received the official communication of the African M. E. Zion Church, proposing union with the Methodist Episcopal Church of the United States, and also the representations of the Rev. S. T. Jones on the same subject, with great satisfaction, hereby express to them our Christian regards and deep interest in their programs and prosperity as a church of the Lord Jesus Christ.

2. *Resolved,* That this Conference entertain favorably the proposal of union between the two bodies aforesaid.

3. *Resolved,* That whereas the time of the sessions of these two General Conferences is so far spent that it will be impracticable to have the necessary negotiations and to discuss and determine the details of the union before adjournment, that eight members of this body be appointed, who, with the Bishops, shall constitute a Commission to meet and confer with a similar Commission of the A.M.E. Zion Church, and report to the next General Conference.

4. *Resolved,* That a copy of the foregoing action of this body be given to the delegate, and by him be forwarded to the General Conference of the A.M.E. Zion Church.

Rev. Dr. Slicer opposed the motion to adopt the report at considerable length, claiming a union impracticable: 1st, because it would change the Ecclesiastical polity of the M. E. Church; 2nd, because it proposed to add six Bishops; 3rd, because it would be to ignore the claims of these colored persons who had always stood by the Church, some of whom would make very good black Bishops; 4th, because it would bring in lay delegations etc.

Not feeling at liberty to correct these mistatements of the facts in the case in open Conference, I availed myself of the privilege of sending to the *Daily Chicago Republican* the following Note on the morning of the next day.

Editor Chicago Republican:

Sir,—Believing that the very remarkable speech of Dr. H. Slicer, delivered in the M. E. General Conference yesterday, in opposition to the report of the Committee on proposals of union between the M. E. and the A.M.E. Zion Churches, has however, unintentionally, conveyed an impression by no means complimentary to my own sense of propriety, nor that of the Body I have the honor to represent, I desire, in all kindness to say, that no such propositions as were discussed by Dr. Slicer were ever entertained,—much less submitted by me, as the Committee can testify.

No proposition of mine, either to Conference or Committee ever contemplated a "change in the ecclesiastical polity of the M. E. Church," or the bringing of "six additional bishops," or the disregarding of the rights of those colored brethren now in the M. E. Church; nor was "Lay Delegation" insisted on.

What I asked in behalf of my constitutents as a condition of union was 1st, equality; 2nd, to be represented in the Episcopal Board by Black Bishops, on an equal footing with the other bishops of the church, in the same proportion to the number of colored members (as well those now in the church, as those who shall unite with it) as the Bishops of that church now sustain to the number of white members in it.

Lay representation, though respectfully recommended, was never insisted on as a fundamental condition of union.

The failure of any member of the committee to explain these simple propositions, and thus to relieve me and my church from the odium of the charge unwarrantable assumption, is my apology for this note.

Yours respectfully,
S. T. Jones, *Delegate*

Chicago, May 26th. 1868

The following note was sent to the *Daily Christian Advocate,* an organ of the M. E. General Conference, published in Chicago, after I had read Dr. Slicer's speech in that paper, on the morning of the 26th of May, and appeared in the issue of the 27th:

AN EXPLANATION

Editor Daily Christian Advocate:

Dear Brother:—I very much regret the necessity which compels me to ask permission to remove, an impression which, in my judgment, the remarkable speech of the Rev. Dr. Slicer, published in your issue of today, is likely to have made on the public mind; but it seems to be due to myself and the Church I represent, that it should be known, that I proposed no change in the "Ecclesiastical polity of the M. E. Church," but on the contrary, asked to be received into that Church, not as inferiors but equals, elders, deacons, preachers, officers and members; and having been received, to have not "six bishops," but a *pro rata* representation, in the person of black men in the Episcopal Board.

"Lay Representation" was only recommended as indicating a preference to that element in the Church, and not as a fundamental condition of union. A paper, embracing these simple, and, as I think, reasonable propositions, was at the instance of Dr. Osbon, presented to his committee on the morning of the 23rd instant.

The failure to "make junction with the African Methodist Episcopal Church," though not pertinent to the subject discussed by the Doctor, and forming no part of the proposition presented by me, was the failure of that Church to submit the "platform" and, thereby, to secure the consent of the people, and is no fault of ours.

Respectfully yours,
SINGLETON T. JONES

Chicago, May 26, 1868

The report of the committee was, however, adopted by a very large majority, and I was informed by Bishop Ames, presiding, that the Conference would be pleased to hear any parting words I might desire to speak. I give you the correct report from the *Daily Christian Advocate* of that city.

BISHOP JONES

Bishop Jones then arose, and when the applause with which he was greeted had subsided, said:

Mr. Chairman: I am thankful, to you and to the Conference for the cordial—I may say enthusiastic—manner in which you have received me; so much as a compliment to myself, as a recognition of the fact that those whom I represent are a part of the great Methodist family. I know for myself, and I hope for my connection—that the kindness will always be reciprocated by us. I do not know that I rightly comprehend the action of your Conference just passed. If I am to regard it as an indication that the grand old ear of Methodism is so obstructed by past alliances that it cannot proceed properly with a black man in it, (Response of "no," "no,") I heartily regret it; not so much for myself, nor for the people whom I represent, as for the light in which it will be regarded by the civilized world. If, however, I am to regard it as a mere necessary arrangement for the purpose of affecting and adjusting the details of this proposed union, so that it shall be all the more strong and permanent when it is made, (in which light I am much more disposed to regard it than the former) (applause) why then, sir, I go back to my Conference and people, telling them that the M. E. Church is moving on. (Applause.)

I need add no more, sir. The Commission has been raised. To this Commission all this question may be safely entrusted. We have borne the Methodist banner for half a century. We have come to you with it untarnished. We have sustained the dignity of Methodism. We shall sustain it, God helping us, whether with the old Church, or alone. (Applause.)

Hoping that wisdom and prudence may guide your counsels, sir, and that nothing may be done here to retard the progress of Methodism, so grand in its first century, I leave you with God's blessing. Adieu. (Applause.)

The Chairman said that it occurred to him that there was a word omitted in the last resolution, which it would be desirable to insert, viz: to meet a *similar* commission from the A.M.E. Zion Church. This was inserted by general consent.

Having obtained an authenticated copy of the original document adopted by the Conference, I made the necessary arrangements and left the City of Chicago, on the morning of the 27th inst., arriving here this morning at 5 a.m.

I will only add that I was treated with distinguished consideration by the Conference, Committee, and all connected with the Body, as well as by the community generally. I, therefore, hope this report may be satisfactory to the Conference and to the entire Church, and that each and all may give their personal influence to the union of these two Christian Bodies so that we may be one at no distant day.

Respectfully submitted,
S. T. JONES, *Delegate*

Washington, D.C., May 29th, 1868

The report was unanimously adopted; the thanks of the Conference was voted to the delegate for his highly successful mission, and a Commission consisting of 8 members of the Conference and the Board of Bishops, was ordered and appointed. The names of the two Commissions will be published in the *Zion Standard and Weekly* Review, with the time and place of meeting, as soon as they are obtained from the Secretary of the Board of Bishops of the M. E. Church.

As an indication of the public interest manifested in this movement, we insert the following from the Chicago *Republican* of Sunday, May 24th, 1868:

BISHOP JONES

"One of the most interesting incidents in connection with the Methodist General Conference, now in session in this city, was the speech of Bishop Jones before the Conference, on Friday last.

Bishop Jones is one of the Bishops of the African M. E. Zion Church, whose General Conference is now in session in Washington City.

A few days since, the General Conference in session in this city received a telegram from the General Conference above named, asking if this General Conference would receive a delegation from that Conference, with propositions for affiliation and union. The Chicago Conference immediately answered, by telegraph, that such a delegation would be received.

Friday, the delegation in the person of Rev. Singleton T. Jones, Bishop-elect of the Church he represents, arrived, and was introduced to the Conference, and delivered his address.

His speech was one of the happiest efforts. He did not occupy the floor more than ten minutes, and his remarks elicited the most enthusiastic applause.

Bishop Jones represents a Church with 164,000 members, 690 ministers, 16 Annual Conferences, and 6 bishops. Mr. Jones' proposition is that this Church is ready to come into the communion of the Methodist Episcopal Church just as soon as they can come in on terms of perfect equality. On the subject of equality, however, he says his people are sensible. They do not propose to force themselves upon their white brethren, nor do they propose to have the whites force themselves upon them. The adjustment of these equitable relations he is satisfied time and Christianity will be able to effect.

It is difficult to see how the General Conference of the Methodist Episcopal Church can refuse to accept these colored brethren on the terms they propose. They cannot, in conscience or reason, ask them to come in on any other terms. In theory, the Methodist Episcopal Church has expelled from her communion all caste. Now the opportunity is given to test her faith by her works on a large scale; and we have too much respect for the common sense, the patriotism, the piety of that Church, to believe that she will retrograde from her present exalted position, but on the contrary, believe that such action will be taken in this matter as will show that she believes in the language of Bishop Jones, that a man is a man, and a Christian is a Christian, irrespective of the color of his skin. Let the different branches of the great Methodist family become one and undivided, now and forever, on the broad principles of Bible purity and equality, and she becomes an engine in the hands of God for the evangelization of the world that would be irresistible.

The matter is in the hands of a competent committee, who will report on Monday morning, and from present indications the consideration of the questions promises to be more interesting than any which has been yet before the Conference."

The above report and account of the conversations with the Methodist Episcopal Church, in a sense, need background which is not easy to supply, but one may safely state that the movement was not one which began with the telegram sent by the Zion Methodist General Conference to the General sessions of the Methodist Episcopal Church in Chicago. The Baltimore Annual Conference Minutes of 1866 may give us the link necessary to fill the gap.

On page 12 of these Minutes appears the following:

Whereas, a convention of delegates from the A. M. E. Zion and the Colored Societies of the M. E. Church met in Zion Church in Philadelphia in November, 1865 for the purpose of deliberating upon the subject of a union between the two bodies there represented and

Whereas, said convention, in its resolves, gave favorable expression of its sentiments in regard to the subject, therefore
Resolved, That we have with great satisfaction (noted) this indication of a disposition to form a union between the two bodies and that the movement has our sympathy and hearty cooperation.

The same Minutes call attention to an earlier meeting between some groups but since they are not named we are at a loss to clearly interpret them. The resolution referred to states:

Resolved, that in keeping with the resolves of the Executive session held in Philadelphia in March, we will use all our efforts to have said platform officially endorsed throughout this Conference District.

The resolution was moved by Singleton T. Jones and seconded by W. F. Butler.

The action then, of the 1868 General Conference as it pertained to the Methodist Episcopal Church, North, was evidently the results of conversations originating certainly as early as 1864 or 1865. One will note the points of opposition as recorded in the account of Singleton Jones' mission to the Methodist Church in Chicago. The opposition from within the Methodist Episcopal Church, itself could have been sincere on all points but the Negro wind, whose loyalty is lauded, had no demonstration to the point of serious consideration of leadership, evidently. One wonders was this a mark of dissatisfaction within the black segments of the Church itself. Jones, while clearly stating Zion's belief in lay representation, appeared not to push the issue and one raises the question of lay reaction had the matter come to a vote.

This then brings a new dimension to the confusion of 1872. Two groups stood to lose as Singleton T. Jones called one faction of the General Conference to meet in New York City where the General Conference of the Methodist Episcopal Church, North, was scheduled to meet. The lay people of Zion Church might well have seen the successful battle of 78 years lost while the Board of Bishops of the Church no doubt would have been drastically reduced.

Whatever the intent of Bishop Jones, he evidently had a change of heart. That which Hood says, in instances, is kind, but a doubt arose as to the strength of each of the two factions. However, regardless of the intent, the Church appears to have arisen to new heights as it debated the matter, made its decision and then proceeded to re-elect Singleton T. Jones a Bishop of the Church.

Returning again to the work of the General Conference of 1868; the next day, Thursday, May 14th, the afternoon session was given over to the reception of a committee from the A.M.E. Church. After the presentation of their message, the Conference was to take action.[16]

A resolution was submitted by David Stevens on the subject of the General Conference communicating with the General Conference of the Methodist Episcopal Church, then meeting in Chicago.[17] The results have been given above.

The following day, in executive session, the General Conference drew up this resolution:[18]

> *Whereas,* This General Conference has been officially informed by a committee from the African Methodist Episcopal Bethel Church that they are not prepared to unite with us on the plan agreed upon by the convention of the two connections held at Philadelphia in 1864, and submitted to the Annual Conferences of each connection for ratification; and
> *Whereas:* They decline uniting on the basis agreed upon, but now ask us to meet with them to unite on some other basis or plan; and
> *Whereas:* Our people in adopting the plan proposed by the said convention did it in good faith and did not authorize us to offer or accept any other plan; therefore
> *Resolved;* That we deem it inexpedient to meet with them according to their proposal.[19]

Final action on the report of the A.M.E. Committee did not come, it appears, until the Tenth Day of the session when the report of the A.M.E. Committee was reviewed. In addition to the resolutions of the Executive Session of the Conference the following official action was taken:

> *Whereas:* The A. M. E. Bethel Conference say in their communication or document that while they are willing for a union, they are not ready to unite upon the platform agreed upon by the convention in Philadelphia in 1864; therefore
> Resolved that the whole matter lay on the table until 1872.[20]

With this action the General Conference appointed a committee consisting of J. P. Hamer, W. F. Butler, J. J. Moore, J. Holliday and M. B. Coss who were instructed to convey the final action of the Con-

---
[16] *Minutes of the General Conference of* 1868.
[17] *Ibid.*
[18] *Ibid.*
[19] *Ibid.*
[20] *Minutes of the General Conference of* 1868.

ORGANIC UNION AND ZION METHODISM

ference to the A.M.E. General Conference and the following communication to accompany it:

> To the General Conference of the A. M. E. Bethel Church:
> We have been appointed a committee to inform your honorable body that according to the action of your body on the subject of consolidation, taken on Saturday last, a copy of which is herewith presented, that our body must respectfully and peremptorily decline to take any further action on the subject at the present session.
> WILLIAM F. BUTLER, *Chairman*[21]
> J. P. HAMER, *Secretary*

Close scrutiny of Zion Methodism would lead one to put stress on the place of lay people in the organization. While Zion oftentimes refers to James Varick as her founder a grave question comes to the student's mind when he notes that Peter Williams and Francis Jacobs were the ones to apply for and obtain the charter. Both of these men were lay people and at the time James Varick had to be in the same category. One then wonders why he was not one of those to so apply. Later, he took up the ministry, however, and became the first Superintendent, not Bishop. Being clear on this point is vital in that it entered the matter of the first effort at union.

This difference of Zion Methodism from all other ventures in Methodism appears to have been a studied intent. Early writers of Zion's history attribute this as the reason for slow expansion. A lay movement church has not the mobility or the zeal of a clergy-inspired people.

Another structural difference was in the leadership of the new venture. These Superintendents were never meant to be the equal of a Bishop. They were elected for four years with the possibility of re-election. The Church, according to the Minutes of 1848 stressed this difference. As late as 1851, for example, the following annual conferences called attention to the Superintendency: the Baltimore, the Philadelphia and the New England. Only the New York Conference ignored the matter. The Baltimore Conference stated:

> 3. *Resolved.* That this Conference consider the use of the word Bishop, and the Third Ordination as set forth in the New Discipline of 1851 as inconsistent with our form of Church government (P. 6).

The Philadelphia Conference in its Minutes of the same year stated:

---
[21] *Ibid.*

> *Resolved.* That this Conference consider the word *Bishop* as set forth in our New Discipline of 1851, and the idea of a Third Ordination, to be inconsistent with our form of Church Government, and was an oversight in publishing the Disciplines.

It should be remembered that the Zion Methodist Church was jealous of lay privileges and rights to the extent that for some reason the thinking is evident in the charter mentioned above and reached deep concern at the time of the Stillwell Secession. The letter sent to Bishop McKendree by Joshua Soule states clearly the impact of this movement.

> You will doubtless see Bishop George in Baltimore or its vicinity and receive from him a narrative of the disastrous events which have transpired in this station. Suffice it to say that several hundred have separated themselves from the fellowship of our church, established an independent congregation embodied under a system of government which secures a perfect equality of right and power to every member, male and female—properly speaking, and ecclesiastical democracy in the most extensive sense of the word. (Life of Joshua Soule by Horace M. DuBose, ed. by Bishop Warren A. Candler (Nashville, 1911) p. 161.)

The Reverend William Stillwell was the minister of Zion and Asbury Churches at the time.

To this point we have endeavored to state two main items; there was a difference in organization and there was a greater emphasis on lay people in the Zion Church. It was this organization and emphasis upon lay participation which brought about the defeat of the 1864 attempt at organic union.

It may never be known when the first effort was broached, but in the Superintendents' Address to the A.M.E. Zion General Conference of 1864 the following appears:

UNION

The union or consolidation of these two great religious bodies, viz., the A.M.E. Church and the A. M. E. Zion Church, permits us to remark that it is our opinion that such union is essentially necessary, and while we would most respectfully recommend and advise cautiousness, discretion and prudence on our part, we would nevertheless urge our delegates at the Convention to spare no pains on their part to bring about the much desired and long prayed for union.

Grace be with you all.
W. H. BISHOP
J. J. CLINTON
Superintendents

(Minutes of the General Conference of 1864, 6)

Noting the wording of the address it is hard to state just when the conversations began. The same Minutes (P. 11) takes note of a special Committee from the A.M.E. Church consisting of a Rev. A. McIntosh, M. Sluby and a Dr. Watts who brought the message on Organic Union. According to the statement of the Committee the A.M.E. Church had appointed a Committee of Nine along with two Bishops to meet with a similar committee from Zion. This joint Committee should work out the plan of further study for union, and, if they saw their way clear to do so, a convention was to be called to determine the conditions *upon which the Union shall be consummated.*

The Zion Committee was subsequently named and met with the Committee of Bethel. One error in the report of the Bethel Committee was reported by Zion's Committee. Instead of the two Bishops from the A.M.E. Church, it was to be the "Bench of Bishops."

On the Seventh Day of the General Conference the following is noted:

> A discussion upon the union was inaugurated from a remark made by some of the lay delegates, who deemed it essential that some instruction should be given the delegates, in order that they might know what course to adopt.
>
> (P. 23)

Reverend Singleton Jones stated that the General Conference had no right to discuss the matter, or to dictate the delegates what to do, "or in any way forestall the matter; but wait the decision of the Convention, which would be submitted to the Annual Conferences of each body, whose action should be final.

"The opponents of the course alluded to by the previous speaker, urged that it was essential to discuss the matter, because in this convention there were no lay delegates admitted, and at the annual Conferences their privileges were limited; hence it was only in the General Conference where the right of expressing themselves was allowed. If then no representation in the Convention is allowed, no privilege granted them to free their minds, and the terms agreed upon in the convention, ratified by the Annual Conferences, did not suit the laity, they could not be compelled to yield to what may prove detrimental to their interests."

(Minutes of 1864, P. 23)

The Zion Church was not opposed to the Union as noted in the

Minutes of the Baltimore Conference (1866—Schomberg Collection)

>   1st, *Resolved*. That it is the sense of this executive session that it will be to the interest of the A.M.E. Zion Church to adopt the third ordination in our Episcopal form and that an extra session of the General Conference by the Superintendents for that purpose as soon as the consent of the majority of the Annual Conferences shall have been secured.
>   2nd. *Resolved*. That in the event such a General Conference being convened, it is the wish of this session that one of the Bishops of the M. E. Church be secured to ordain them for us, but failing in that, it is our purpose to ordain them in the same manner in which the M. E. Church, originally ordained Bishop Asbury.
>   (Baltimore Conference Minutes 1866, 12)

A BRIEF ACCOUNT OF THE PROPOSED UNION BETWEEN THE A.M.E. AND THE A.M.E. ZION CHURCHES
By Reverend Singleton T. Jones

In a Convention held for the purpose in Philadelphia in June, 1864, articles of union and consolidation were agreed on between the two above named churches. These were to be submitted to the people for their approval according to the 10th article of the "platform." The result of such submission having been determined by a committee of the General Conference of the A.M.E. Zion Church:

The Committee on Consolidation, consisting of Revs. S. T. Jones, J. J. Moore and Wm. H. Decker, proceeded to the General Conference of the A.M.E. Church, in session in Israel Church, May 14, 1868, and after being introduced, their Chairman (S. T. Jones) presented the following address:

"Bishops and Brethren of the General Conference of the A.M.E. Zion Church: We are here as a committee authorized by the General Conference of the A.M.E. Zion Church in America, to communicate the very gratifying intelligence that a majority of the Annual Conferences under its jurisdiction have ratified the Article of Consolidation agreed on as a basis of Union and Consolidation in the Convention of 1864, and that said act of ratification has been endorsed by a vote almost unanimously by the same now sitting in this city; and we are instructed to inquire whether the church of which you are the representative body have agreed to said articles, and if so, at what time you will be ready to consummate the union."

Bishop Wayman replied "that there was a committee on the subject, and thought they would report today."

The following was received by the General Conference on the day following:

RESPONSE OF (TO) THE A. M. E. Z. CHURCH

A Committee from the A.M.E. (Bethel) General Conference consisting of Revs. Cain, Johnson, Young, Walker and Warner, were announced; after being introduced, they presented the following communication upon the

Union of the A. M. E. Bethel and A. M. E. Zion Connections:

Whereas, A Convention of the A. M. E. Zion and the A. M. E. Churches, held in Philadelphia, Pa., on the 14th and 16th of June, 1864, for the purpose of forming a plan for the Consolidation of the Connections. And,

Whereas, There were certain propositions laid down by said Convention, which were submitted to the people; giving the interval of four years to canvass and take a vote of the people on the various portions of both Connections. And,

Whereas, There has not been the fullness of expression by the members of our Church, which is their right. And,

Whereas, Those Congregations which have voted on the subject, have expressed a willingness for Union, but averse to the General plan which has been put forth by the Convention. Therefore, be it

Resolved, That this body do not deem it politic or wise in us to form a Consolidation on the basis laid down in '64, lest we thereby interfere with the interest of our Church and create a dissatisfaction among our own membership.

Resolved, That we are willing to form a Union, but with such provisions and arrangements as will meet the wishes of our whole Connection, as well as satisfy the demand of the age.

Resolved, That the information in our possession warrants us in believing, that to Consolidate this Union on the basis laid down, after it has been rejected by a large body of our Churches where it has been submitted, and where it has not been submitted, the people are not prepared to submit to the Union on the basis laid down.

Resolved, Therefore, that we meet the members of the A. M. E. Zion Church and arrange a new plan which we believe will meet the wishes of the people of both Connections.

Resolved, That as ministers we claim not entire jurisdiction over the people of our Churches, but as the spiritual advisors and conservitors of our people's interests are bound to them by every consideration of Christian affection; we, with them, claim to be satisfied with whatever arrangements, we, as their pastors make.

Resolved, That the Committee appointed to wait on the Zion Conference, be hereby instructed to lay before that Body these resolutions and opinions expressed, and invite that Body here, in accordance with the resolutions and directions given to the Conference, according to No. 10 in Articles of Arrangements.

REJOINDER OF THE A.M.E. ZION GENERAL CONFERENCE

Subsequent to which, the report of the committee of the A.M.E. Church was taken up, and Elder J. W. Hood, offered the following resolution:

> *Whereas,* This General Conference has been officially informed by a committee from the A. M. E. (Bethel) General Conference, that they are not prepared to unite with us on the plan proposed by the Convention of the two Connections held in 1864, and submitted for the ratification or rejection of the Churches or Conferences of the two Connections. And,
>
> *Whereas,* They have asked us to meet with them for the purpose of uniting upon some other plan. And,
>
> *Whereas,* Our people in adopting the plan prepared by the aforesaid Convention, did not authorize us to offer or accept any other plan. Therefore,
>
> *Resolved,* That we deem it inexpedient to meet with them according to their request.
>
> On motion of W. F. Butler, the Conference went into Executive session.

The following article from Zion's Standard and Weekly Review, the organ of the A.M.E. Zion Church, will indicate the sentiment of the church on the subject:

CONSOLIDATION OF THE A.M.E. BETHEL AND A.M.E. ZION CHURCHES

This subject, of which so much has been said during the last four years, was finally brought to a sudden termination last Saturday, by the series of Resolutions passed by the Zion General Conference after the reception of the Report from the Bethel General Conference, which we publish in full in another column.

We confess that we are much surprised that after four years incessant toil, attended by vexations and bitter rebukes, that the subject should be so suddenly disposed; we were at a loss to understand how it was, that the matter had not been presented to several of the Bethel Churches; but when we were publicly informed in Conference, by one of the Committee, that he was in the next Town or State, adjoining that of a brother who had for four years been peddling the "Articles of Consolidation" around the country, and never sent him one, then we understood the whole matter. We therefore urge the people to examine the whole subject. The A. M. E. Zion Connection, having carefully kept within the bounds of the Platform as agreed upon by the two Connections, comes forward to make good her agreement and say "We are ready," ready to unite upon one common Platform. We are ready to make common cause with you for the up-building of the Church of Christ. We are ready to meet the demands of the people; for the good

of the People, we are ready to sacrifice all our own interest, views, differences and mode of electing Executives, that the cause of Christ and His people shall be advanced here on earth. We are ready to meet with you and to sacrifice our connectional name, that we may present to the world a United African Methodist Church in America, and the response is for the "ADOPTION OF A NEW PLATFORM;" to this we demur; to this our Connection demurs. We now leave the matter, and let it never be said, that Zion was the cause of the future division between the A. M. E. and A. M. E. Zion Connections, for WE WERE READY.
———Editorial, May 20th, 1868

CHAPTER XVIII

Organic Union After 1868

THE Board of Bishops Episcopal Address to the Eleventh General Conference meeting in Charlotte, North Carolina in 1872, no doubt brings to light at least one of the reasons why unification with the Methodist Episcopal Church was not persued.

In part it stated:

> Dear Brethren, you can more fully appreciate our need of money to extend and support our connection, when we remind you of the two great monied religious bodies we have to grapple with—the M.E. Church north, and the M.E. Church south, who make their money a means of proselyting our preachers, in many cases, especially the former body, and the step taken by our body at our last General Conference toward consolidation with the M.E. Church has been used by unscrupulous agents of that church to proselyte our ministers and members, creating distraction among us and sometimes ruptures in our churches, which course no Christian body could sanction, in the light of the golden rule: "Do unto others as you would have them do unto you." In relation to the question of affiliation and consolidation with the M.E. Church, we could wish, as expressed in our General Conference in 1868, that all branches of Methodists on this continent were united; but from the unfortunate developments connected with this movement, we are compelled to recommend the suspension of future action on the subject until the great obstacle to this happy result is farther removed; that is, the prejudice of caste that still exists in the mother (the M.E.) church; yet we shall still cultivate a friendly and Christian feeling toward our mother until she has reached the proper position on this question of caste.[1]

It may have been an oversight but at least one member of the Board of Bishops who signed this address could have well recalled the fact that several of the A. M. E. Zion Churches were, at one time, members of that vast group of Negro Methodist Episcopal Churches connected with the Southern wing of Methodism. In truth, it would have been well to recall that this was the opening period of deep concern where the Southern wing of Methodism was involved which led to the formation of the Colored Methodist Episcopal Church. While the Address states that the major movement to wean away from Zion Methodism churches and ministers on the guise of eventual unification came from the Methodist Episcopal Church, North, there would

---
[1] Moore, *loc. cit.*, 286.

ORGANIC UNION AFTER 1868

be evidences of strain in certain conferences where the soon to be created Colored Church within the Southern fold exerted pressure.[2] And this, from past history was to be expected.

While there is a record of reports from churches accepting the union with the A. M. E. Church (note) the matter of the merging of the two denominations appears to have been dropped for the next several years. When the General Conference met in New York City, in 1884 (Mother Zion Church), Thomas Fortune, Editor-in-chief of the New York *Globe* again opened the subject of the unification of all Methodists, stating that such a move would not only be for the best Christian interests, but would be an economically sound move.

John Dancy was called upon to answer the address or rather respond to it. In part, Dancy stated: "It was agitated at our General Conferences in 1864, 1868, 1872, 1876 and 1880, and there does not seem to be any great hindrance in the way of its success now, except perhaps in the designation and selection of the General Officers who would have to be chosen as the result of the union. If it were possible I would be willing for a committee to be appointed to go from this conference to the A. M. E. Conference at Baltimore, and meet a similar committee and confer on the subject."[3]

Bishop Jones likewise made a statement in which he declared: "I will take the opportunity notwithstanding our time is precious, just to say the A. M. E. Zion Church has placed itself squarely on the record for the union of Methodists in America. That record stands as it has stood for over twenty years and we are ready now as we were twenty years ago, and on every day and at every hour to form an honorable, fair union with colored Methodists or with white Methodists."[4] Bishop Hood informed the Conference that the matter of union had been approved by the Quarterly Conferences of the denomination as well as the Annual and General Conferences, "with but two dissenting votes."[5]

On May 25 the Reverends Chambers and Scott, and presumably others, offered the following resolution: "Whereas: Much has been

---

[2] *Ibid.*, 174, 175. Note defections in the Kentucky Conference of 1868.
Note: See recorded vote at the end of this chapter.
[3] *Daily Proceedings of the Seventeenth Quadrennial Session* of the A.M.E. Zion Church, May 1884 14, 15.
[4] *Ibid.*, 15, 16.
[5] *Ibid.*, 16.

said upon organic union, therefore be it resolved that we appoint a committee of seven to confer with a like committee from any other body of Methodists wishing organic union." The resolution was adopted.[6] On May 21, 1884 a telegram was read by Bishop Hood from Mr. T. Thomas Fortune of the A. M. E. General Conference, in session in Baltimore, Maryland to the General Conference of the A. M. E. Zion Church stating that the said General Conference had appointed a Committee of Ten on Organic Union with the A. M. E. Zion Church.[7] The Zion General Conference, following the reading of the telegram, appointed a like number to confer with the A. M. E. Committee. The following were named: the Rev. J. C. Price, New England Conf., Rev. R. R. Morris, New England Conf., Rev. John Holliday, Allegheny Conference, Rev. Jacob Thomas, New York Conf., Hon. John C. Dancy, Tarboro, N. C., Rev. C. C. Petty, East Ala. Conf., Rev. J. S. Cowles of the Phila. and Balto Conf., Rev. A. J. Warner, Kentucky Conf.[8] On a suggestion of the Chairman Elder J. C. Price, Bishop Singleton T. Jones and Bishop J. W. Hood were added to the group.[9]

When the General Conference met in Pittsburgh, Pennsylvania in 1892, Bishop Cicero Harris offered the following resolution on Organic Union:

> *Whereas:* A large majority of the African Methodist Episcopal Zion Churches are desirous for the union of these two great bodies of Methodism: therefore, be it
> *Resolved:* 1. That we send a delegate to the General Conference of the African Methodist Episcopal Church now in session in Philadelphia, Pa. to express our readiness to confer with them as to the appointment at once of a Commission on Organic Union, if they favor such a movement; said commission to consist of seven members (or more) together with a similar commission to be appointed by this body, which shall arrange a basis of union between the two churches aforementioned.
> 2. That said commission, if appointed, shall sit in Harrisburg, Pa., or at some other place convenient of access, for a period not exceeding six days from the time of their appointment, at the end of which time the basis of union, if agreed upon, shall be presented to the two General Conferences now in session.
> 3. In case both of the General Conferences shall adopt the basis of union thus presented, or as it may be modified by concurrent action of

---

[6] *Ibid.*, 88.
[7] *Minutes of the Seventeenth Quadrennial Session of the General Conference,* 1884, 103.
[8] *Ibid.*, 4.
[9] *Ibid.*, 103.

ORGANIC UNION AFTER 1868

both bodies, the said basis shall be submitted to all the Annual and Quarterly Conferences of both Churches; and upon being ratified by a majority vote in all the Annual Conferences and by three fourths of all the Quarterly Conferences in each connection, the union shall be declared effected and a united General Conference called by a joint session of the Board of Bishops of the two Churches.

C. R. HARRIS [10]
J. W. HOOD

In the discussion of these resolutions which followed, Joseph Charles Price stated that at the last Ecumenical Methodist Conference held in Washington, D. C., it was agreed that unification was necessary. In that conference, according to Price, there were representatives of all Methodist bodies. He spoke of the Commission appointed in 1884 of which he was chairman. The group had met in Washington and thoroughly discussed the question. Twenty-three out of twenty-four agreed on a basis of union which had been worked out, but the Board did not agree on a name (of the new or proposed denomination) and, "hence the whole matter fell into a prolonged silence until the meeting of the Ecumenical Conference." [11]

The vote to accept the resolution was 92-49.

The fraternal greeting of the A. M. E. Church was brought to the General Conference of 1892 on Tuesday, May 17th and received the following response:

Resolved, That our best thanks be hereby tendered to Rev. A. M. Green, D.D. and Rev. C. Asbury, D.D. fraternal delegates from the African Methodist Episcopal Conference, now in session, for their warm words of praise and congratulation, expressing for them and for their General Conference our heartiest regard, and a pledge that we will again meet them on the safe half-way ground referred to, to plan for complete and permanent union.[12]

The resolution was adopted unanimously.

Bishop Harris suggested that Bishop Hood offer the following:

Resolved: That, in order to carry out the proposition made to the African Methodist Episcopal General Conference, this General Conference remain in session until May 25, or until the report of the Commissioners is made to both General Conferences.

This resolution, too, was adopted.[13]

---

[10] *Minutes of the General Conference* of 1892, *loc. cit.,* 57.
[11] *Minutes of the General Conference* of 1892, *loc. cit.,* 58.
[12] *Ibid.,* 96.
[13] *Minutes of the General Conference* of 1892, *loc. cit.,* 97.

At the close of the afternoon session the Commissioners on Organic Union were named as follows: Bishop C. R. Harris, C. C. Petty, Alexander Walters; from the First District: N. J. Green, Second District, William Howard Day, who because of indisposition declined in favor of G. W. Offley; who was accepted by the Board of Bishops; Third District, W. H. Goler; Fourth District, J. C. Price; Fifth District, F. M. Jacobs; Sixth District, A. J. Warner; Delegates at large: J. C. Dancy, E. H. Curry, F. Killingsworth.[14]

The next day, May 18, a telegram was received from the A. M. E. General Conference. It requested:

> On account of ordinations of Bishops here tomorrow (Thursday), will your Commissioners meet at Harrisburg Friday?
>
> Cornelius Asbury[15]

The General Secretary was ordered to answer this telegram.

On Saturday, May 21, the Commissioners of the Church on Organic Union reported, with the Hon. J. C. Dancy reading the report:

> Harrisburg, Pa.
> May 20, 1892
>
> By authority of the General Conferences of the African Methodist Episcopal and African Methodist Episcopal Zion Churches a joint meeting of the commissions representing these two Methodist bodies, consisting of twelve members each, was held at the African Methodist Episcopal Zion Church at Harrisburg at noon on Friday, May 20, for the purpose of formulating a basis of union to be submitted to the two General Conferences for their consideration. The following were present.
>
> African Methodist Episcopal Zion—Bishops C. R. Harris, C. C. Petty, A. Walters, and Revs. N. J. Green, G. W. Offley, W. H. Goler, J. C. Price, F. M. Jacobs, A. J. Warner, Hon. J. C. Dancy, E. H. Curry and F. Killingsworth.
>
> African Methodist Episcopal—B. W. Roberts, L. H. Smith, J. I. Evans, S. T. Mitchel, Bishops H. W. Turner, B. T. Tanner, B. F. Lee, R. F. Hurley, P. A. Hubbard, J. A. Johnson, D. A. Draper.
>
> Bishops C. R. Harris, D. D., of the African Methodist Episcopal Zion Commission, lined the hymn "Jesus, The Name High Over All," which was sung with much spirit.
>
> Bishop H. M. Turner, D.D., LL.D., of the African Methodist Episcopal Commission, read selections from the Psalms with comments, enforcing impressively the truth, "How good and how pleasant it is for brethren to dwell together in unity."

---

[14] *Ibid.*, 98.
[15] *Ibid.*, 99.

ORGANIC UNION AFTER 1868

Bishop C. C. Petty, D.D., of the African Methodist Zion Commission, led in a fervent prayer.

On motion of Bishop A. Walters, D.D., of the African Methodist Episcopal Zion Commission, Bishop H. M. Turner of the African Methodist Episcopal Commission, was elected chairman for the session, and John C. Dancy of the African Methodist Episcopal Zion Commission, was elected Secretary.

On motion, The Rev. J. A. Johnson of Bermuda, of the African Methodist Episcopal Commission was also elected Secretary at the suggestion of Secretary Dancy.

Bishop Turner made some timely remarks on assuming the chair on the necessity of the union of the two great colored Methodist bodies. "In view of the lynchings and outrages committed against us," said he, "all Negro Methodists and all Negro organizations of a religious name should be one and work for a common end."

Bishop Pettey moved the appointment of a Committee of three from each Commission to consider points of difference and agree upon a basis of union, and submit to the full joint commission for action.

By suggestion of Dr. J. C. Price, of the African Methodist Episcopal Zion Commission, and Bishop B. F. Tanner, DD., of the African Methodist Episcopal Commission, the proposed committee was deferred until the points of differences are adjusted.

Bishop Tanner read at length from the Discipline of the African Methodist Episcopal Church the statutory and fundamental laws of the same, and points of differences were noted and reserved, to be harmonized and settled by the General Conference.

The question of name was then taken up.

Bishop Tanner proposed the name of African Methodist Episcopal Church United.

John C. Dancy proposed the name United Methodist Episcopal Church.

Dr. J. C. Price proposed United African Zion Methodist Episcopal Church, or if not, then delete both Zion and Bethel and leave it the United Methodist Episcopal Church.

Bishop Tanner made a lengthy, strong and forcible speech in favor of the name African Methodist Episcopal Church.

Dr. J. C. Price made an eloquent plea for union without reference to the word African and proposed Methodist Episcopal United Church.

Bishop Lee said he was so anxious for union that he was willing to sink all differences as to name, and made a vigorous speech for the consummation of the union without reference to name. He also alluded to the difficulty likely to arise out of the name agreed upon.

Bishop Harris proposed Episcopal Methodist African Zion Church.

Bishop Tanner proposed African Zion Methodist Episcopal Church.

Reverends A. J. Warner and L. H. Smith proposed African Zion Methodist Episcopal Church.

The name Negro Methodist Episcopal Church was also proposed.

Bishop Pettey said the commission must either retain both names or strike out the disputed points of each.

The main points of harmony and difference were then noted

1. Considerations of Discipline. 2. Catechism of Wesley. 3. Band Societies. 4. General Rules. 5. Class Meetings. 6. Class Leaders (appointed by pastor, a point of difference decided to be statutory). 7. General Conference Annual and District Conferences. 8. Ordinations of Deacons, Elders and Bishops. 9. Dollar Money. 10. Trustees.

On motion of Professor Price and Bishop Tanner it was recommended, since we are one constitutionally, that all statutory differences be relegated to the first United General for settlement.

Bishop Turner opened discussion on the relation of trustees to Quarterly Conferences in the respective African Methodist Episcopal and African Methodist Episcopal Zion Churches.

Bishop C. R. Harris felt that there could be no union if either body insisted upon retaining the distinctive name to the exclusion of the other, and proposed "African Zion Episcopal Methodist." Or, if union could be consummated in two years we could probably be united with the Colored Methodist Episcopal in four years.

Rev. L. H. Smith moved and A. J. Warner seconded, that the name be African Zion Methodist Episcopal Church. Amended by Bishop Walters, that the name be Episcopal Methodist African Zion Church.

Professor Dancy urged that concession was necessary to union. Why not make it and have union? The leaders are in the way. There ought to be compromise. He grew very eloquent.

Rev. Bell suggested United African Methodist Episcopal and African Methodist Episcopal Zion Church. Dr. Hurley favored the long name.

African Methodist Episcopal and Zion Church was proposed by Bishops Tanner and Harris.

Bishop Harris put the several names to vote, with the result as follows:

First Ballot

The name African Zion Episcopal Methodist received no votes; African Zion Methodist Episcopal Church, 6 votes; the Episcopal Methodist African Zion Church, 1 vote; United African Methodist Episcopal and African Methodist Zion Church, no vote: The United Methodist Episcopal Church, 7 votes; The African Methodist Episcopal and Zion Church, 10 votes; total east, 24

Second Ballot

African Methodist Episcopal and Zion Church, 7 votes; African and Zion Methodist Episcopal Church, 0; United Methodist Episcopal Church 10; African-Zion Methodist Episcopal Church, 6; African and Zion Methodist Episcopal Church, 1.

Third Ballot

The African-Zion Methodist Episcopal Church, 13; United Methodist Episcopal Church 8; African Methodist Episcopal and Zion Church, 2; not voting 1.

ORGANIC UNION AFTER 1868

Fourth Ballot

The United Methodist Episcopal Church, 0; The African-Zion Methodist Episcopal Church 22; The African Methodist Episcopal and Zion Church, 1; not voting 1.

African-Zion Methodist Episcopal Church was then agreed upon by the 22 votes above alluded to.

Reverend Hubert was present voting in the negative and Bishop Turner absent.

Adjourned until 8:30 o'clock.

JOHN C. DANCY, Secretary
Respectfully submitted,
C. R. HARRIS, Chairman

The foregoing is correct,

(Signed on part of African Methodist Episcopal Zion Church)

C. C. PETTEY	G. W. OFFLEY
A. WALTERS	N. J. GREEN
J. C. PRICE	W. H. GOLER
F. KILLINGSWORTH	F. M. JACOBS
E. H. CURRY	A. J. WARNER[16]

With the conclusion of the reading of the Report of the Joint-Commission proceedings the enthusiastic General Conference voted to adopt the basis for union as agreed to by the Joint Commission.[17] On motion by Bishop Cicero Harris the General Secretary was ordered to telegraph the A. M. E. General Conference in Philadelphia of this action with the suggestion that as soon as Zion was informed of similar action on the part of that body the proposition would be submitted to the Quarterly and Annual Conferences "in accordance with the" preliminary plans already adopted by each Conference.[18]

The telegram sent was as follows:

General Conference Room
Pittsburgh, Pa., May 21, 1892

To Bishop Tanner, African Methodist Episcopal General Conference, Sixth Street, near Lombard, Philadelphia, Pa.

General Conference has adopted basis of union agreed upon by Joint Commission.

William Howard Day
General Secretary[19]

---

[16] *Journal of the General Conference of 1892, Nineteenth Session,* 172-174.
[17] *Journal of the Nineteenth Quadrennial Session, A.M.E. Zion General Conference,* 1892, 114.
[18] *Ibid.,* 115.
[19] *Ibid.,* 115.

The African Methodist General Conference replied to the above telegram on May 24th:

Philadelphia, Pa.

Bishop C. R. Harris, D.D., African Methodist Episcopal Zion General Conference, Pittsburgh, Pa., African and Zion Methodist Episcopal Church nearly unanimously adopted. We are one.

B. W. ARNETT, H. M. TURNER[20]

At the suggestion of Bishop C. C. Pettey, the doxology was sung by the General Conference upon the receipt of this telegram.

The Hon. J. C. Dancy made an eloquent speech after which Bishop Walters moved that the Board of Bishops join with the Board of Bishops of the A. M. E. Church in preparing the platform to be submitted to the Quarterly and Annual Conferences of the two denominations. In the discussion which followed it was finally agreed that the following be the statement of the Conference: "We have heard with pleasure the acceptance of the name for the proposed church union, and that the proposed platform be submitted to the Quarterly and Annual Conferences and to the churches for their approval. The Board of Bishops of the African Methodist Episcopal Zion Church are hereby authorized to represent this General Conference in such meeting and for said purposes." [21]

Dr. Price's substitute was adopted, and the following telegram was sent:

Pittsburgh, Pa.
May 24, 1892

To Bishops H. M. Turner and B. W. Arnett, African Methodist Episcopal General Conference, Sixth Street near Lombard, Philadelphia, Pa.

Knowledge of acceptance of "African and Zion Methodist Episcopal Church" enthusiastically received. Our Board of Bishops stands ready for perfecting arrangements looking to consummation of union.

(Attest)

C. R. HARRIS, *Presiding Bishop*
WILLIAM HOWARD DAY, *General Secretary*

The resolutions of the session contained as well the following statement from the Commission on Union:

---

[20] *Jounal* of Nineteenth Session, General Conference, 1892, 125 Secretary's note states this was proposal of A.M.E. Zion Board of Bishops as title of proposed denomination.

[21] *Ibid.*

ORGANIC UNION AFTER 1868

In view of the proceedings and actions of the joint commission of the two churches, the African Methodist Episcopal and the African Methodist Episcopal Zion, we, the members representing the latter, do recommend that, as in all constitutional elements the commission decided the two churches are virtually one, all statutory provisions be relegated to the United General Conference for adjustment.

Since it was also agreed, by a vote of twenty-two to two, that the name of the united body be the *African-Zion Methodist Episcopal Church*, we agreed upon the basis of union already adopted by both General Conferences.

(Signed)

C. R. HARRIS, *Chairman*	F. M. JACOBS
J. C. DANCY, *Secretary*	A. WALTERS
F. KILLINGSWORTH	C. C. PETTEY
N. J. GREEN	G. W. OFFLEY
E. H. CURRY	A. J. WARNER
W. H. GOLER	Commissioners[22]

The Reverend Dr. J. Harvey Anderson, Editor and Compiler of the Official Directory of 1895-1896 no doubt wrote the concluding word on this endeavor for Organic Union: He stated: "The A. M. E. Zion Church's attitude in her contact and relations with other churches has been such as to modify friction, preclude controversy and prevent antagonism, and to encourage a spirit of fraternity, reciprocal helpfulness and mutual cooperation in efforts to advance the common cause of Christianity and Methodism. Her history stands for that which is most likely for race elevation and development and that contributes well to the national prosperity.

Her attitude upon questions of Amity and Organic Union with other Episcopal Methodists has ever been affirmative, ready to unite with other like bodies on amicable, fair and equal terms—nothing more, nothing less. In the negotiations which she has carried on with several sister denominations with a view to Organic Union, she manifested a disposition to sacrifice everything but honor and fairness, believing that it was necessary to race progress, religious progress, and the salvation of the people, and she has always been the last to leave the platform of counsel and hope—never leaving until the negative party had gone. Her hopes and efforts to secure a union with other Episcopal Methodists is now being rapidly displaced with a desire for her own advancement, and the utility of her own possibilities. It is not at all likely that she will take the initiative in proposals for Organic Union again unless the profoundest impulses

---

[22] *Journal,* Nineteenth Session, *loc. cit.,* 128.

are aroused by a most favorable prospect for success. As regards the recent efforts to secure the Organic Union of the A. M. E. and the A. M. E. Zion churches, a profound and ominous silence has taken the place of sensational enthusiasm and wild Union desire." [23]

The disposition to lay the blame of failure upon one group, however does not seem logical in the light of the following statement made by the Fraternal Delegate from the New York Conference to the sessions of the Genesee Conference of 1894, Reverend E. G. Clifton:

> "For a number of years organic union has been the theme discussed between the A.M.E. and A.M.E. Zion Churches. The subject drew the attention of wise, learned, and good men in all parts of the country; and it would have been accomplished had not a few on both sides resorted to methods which directly caused its abortion,—" [24]

As noted, very little was said in the General Conference of 1896 where Organic Union was concerned. Bishop Alexander Walters, evidently gave the report from the Annual Conferences and many of the Quarterly conferences. Thirty-one Annual Conferences sent in reports, with the closeset vote being reported from the Philadelphia and Baltimore Area, and even there the proposition carried with an affirmative vote 32 to 25 against the proposition. Twenty of the Annual Conferences reported no adverse vote at all while the highest number standing against the proposition was noted in the large conference of West Alabama where only eight were so noted to 122 for. (The Philadelphia and Baltimore Conference vote, as noted above was the greatest adverse vote with only 57 votes being cast.).

Totals showed a voting strength of 1,722, with 1,569 voting, registering 1,512 for Organic Union and 57 against.[25] The full Conference vote is recorded at the conclusion of this chapter.

While the Quarterly Conference reports are too numerous and detailed to list here, a sampling showed that the New Haven congregation rejected Organic Union while Hartford had a tie vote. In the New Jersey Conference, Trenton and Asbury Park rejected the proposition, tie votes were recorded in Eatontown and Paterson while Somerville and Rossville accepted Organic Union by one vote.

---

[23] J. Harvey Anderson, *Official Directory*, 1895-1896 (New York), 1895, 45.
[24] *Minutes of the Genesee Conference* (Now the Western New York) Ithaca, New York, 1894, 45.
[25] *Minutes of the Twentieth Quadrennial Session of the General Conference, A.M.E. Zion Church* (Charlotte, N.C.), 1896, 229.

ORGANIC UNION AFTER 1868

The Philadelphia and Baltimore Conference recorded negative votes in Harrisburg, Second Church, Carlisle, Chambersburg and South Media. Williamsport reported a one vote acceptance. The North Carolina Conference recorded three rejections—at White Oak, Beaufort, and James City, Swansboro Circuit accepted the proposition by one vote. Jumping Run stood 42 for to 2 against. Only one church in West Alabama voted against Organic Union, Jerusalem. East Alabama had only three churches voting—all for the proposition, while the churches of South Georgia were all for the proposition. The Allegheny Conference showed two churches against, Mt. Pleasant and Altoona.

The Missouri Conference reported a tie in four churches—Jones Tabernacle, Indianapolis, Manson's Tabernacle, Sebree, Ky., and Smith Mills. The South Mississippi had no adverse votes while every church in the California Conference accepted the proposition including Paso Robles who reported a 16 to nothing vote. The Ohio Conference reported one church, Sewickley, favorable. Ponchatoula reported the same as the only one from Louisiana Conference.[26]

Many individual churches also reported the vote of their memberships—we list a few of them here:

Church	Membership	Voting		
John Wesley, Pittsburgh, Pa.	300	211	196	15
Mt. Pisgah, Bedford, Pa.	74	74	74	0
Lewistown, Pa.	24	24	24	0
Sewickley, Pa.	72	52	50	2
Conway Chapel (Arlington, Va.)	48	48	48	0
Union Wesley, Wash.	260	25	14	11
Fresno, Cal.	45	40	40	0
First, San Fran.	190	86	80	6
Ebenezer Ct., Ala.	137	137	137	0
Little Nazarene (Citronelle, Ala.)	130	100	100	0
State Street	707	706	706	0
Long's Chapel (Washington, Ala.)	200	142	128	14
Little Zion, Mobile	850	370	370	0
Clinton Chapel (New Bern)	228	39	20	19
Mt. Zion, Augusta, Ga.	300	300	300	0
Piney Grove	103	75		75

[26] *Minutes of the Twentieth Quadrennial Session of the General Conference, loc. cit.,* 229-234 incl.

Red Springs, N.C. 158	158	158	0
Zion Temple, Craven Co. 90	71		71
Sharon Circuit, Miss. 237	196	196	0
Jones Temple, Aiken, S. C. 25	25	25	0
St. Paul, Canton, Miss. 54	48	48	0
North Corner, S. C. 112	112	112	0[27]
Steven Grove .... 120 (Spartanburg)	80	80	0

---

[27] Minutes, Twentieth Session, *loc. cit.*, 233-234.

CHAPTER XIX

Organic Union After 1868

THE MAZE of situations where Organic Union is concerned may have a tendency to so involve the thinking of the casual reader that he loses sight of the common thread of effort which appears to have been present. To aid one, therefore, in clear thinking, it may be well to refer to a paper or address delivered before the Fourth Annual Pastors' and Christian Workers' Conference, Lincoln University (Pa.) on July 13, 1939 by the then Reverend Dr. Stephen Gill Spottswood, now Bishop of the denomination. In part, Reverend Spottswood stated: "It seems that the spiritual implications of Organic Union—the mere categorical visioning of the spiritual forces which would be released through the merger of Negro Methodists—should give us sufficient impulse to proceed deliberately toward this high goal of unity."

"The Historic Position of the A.M.E. Zion Church on Organic Union"

"The attitude of the African Methodist Episcopal Zion Church on Organic Union is expressed in the following anecdote of more than sixty years ago. Eight hundred members withdrew from the African Methodist Episcopal Church in Columbia, South Carolina and sent for our Bishop Singleton T. Jones, then presiding over the Zion Conferences in the Palmetto state, to receive them. Because Organic Union was under discussion, Bishop Jones refused to receive the withdrawing members."

Bishop Spottswood, then Reverend Spottswood goes on to say: "twenty-eight years later (after the 1864 effort at union) a formidable movement was undertaken, known as the Joint-Council on Organic Union, which met in Washington, D.C. July 27, 1892. The sub-committee appointed on the basis of union by the bishops of the two churches was (for the A.M.E. Church): B. T. Tanner, J. A. Handy and B. F. Lee: (for the A.M.E. Zion Church): J. W. Hood, C. R. Harris and C. C. Petty. Seven articles of agreement were reached and these were remanded to the annual and quarterly Conferences of the two denominations. Subsequently when the bishops of the A.M.E. Zion Church met in Knoxville, Tennessee, October

18, 1892, blanks were distributed to the Bishops for use in compiling the local ballot on the proposed organic union. To illustrate the attitude of the African Methodist Episcopal Zion Church on organic union, let us cite for example the case of churches in Wilkes-Barre, Pennsylvania, and Elmira, New York. In both of these cities Zion and Bethel had churches. The Negro population being small it was felt unwise to have two Negro Methodist Churches operating in the same city, so the bishops of each denomination met and agreed, because of the discussion of organic union was then extant, to the following compromise. The Zion Church was to abandon the field in Wilkes-Barre where the Bethel Church was the stronger and the Bethel Church was to abandon the field in Elmira where the Zion Church was the stronger. Zion promptly withdrew at Wilkes-Barre but Bethel has not withdrawn from Elmira unto this day (July 12, 1939). Zion still retains the ascendency in Elmira but the work of the Kingdom is retarded by the unnecessary competition. We have never attempted any retaliatory tactics in Wilkes-Barre."

Reverend Spottswood continued: "Joint Commissions on Organic Union of the three major Negro Methodist bodies have been formed repeatedly during the Twentieth Century. In each of these the A.M.E. Zion Church has ever been ready to conciliate for union. Commissions met in Washington, D. C. in 1910, Mobile, Alabama in 1912, and Louisville Kentucky, in 1918. The last great surge for Organic Union in the A.M.E. Zion Church occurred about twenty years ago, following spectacular meetings of the bishops of Negro Methodism at Montgomery and Baltimore. Commissions were organized in each denomination and finally a joint commission, representing all three of the denominations involved was created. Articles of Agreement were reached and these articles were remanded to the annual and quarterly conferences for referendum. I know that the A.M.E. Zion Church voted by a substantial majority for this proposed union, which vote was ratified by our General Conference. What became of the vote in the other denominations I do not know." [1]

One gathers the idea from Reverend Spottswood's presentation that the Church, far from being discouraged after the debacle of 1892, returned again to the idea of Union with somewhat of an open

---

[1] *The A.M.E. Zion Quarterly Review*, Vol. XLIX, No. 4, July 1939, 27, 28, 29, 30.

ORGANIC UNION AFTER 1868

mind. However, a distinctly different approach is to be noted in the next few years prior to the undertaking of another major attempt at bringing the churches together. The Board of Bishops of the denomination, in their quadrennial report to the General Conference (1908) stated: "The joint meeting of the Bishops of the A.M.E. Zion, A.M.E. and C.M.E. Churches resulting in a plan of federation among the chief pastors of these energetic branches of the great Methodist family, and the adoption of an agreement which provides for a common hymnal and catechism and a uniform service and other commendable propositions stand out among the notable doings of the quadrennium." [2]

Four years later, when the General Conference met in Charlotte, North Carolina they stated: "The United Council of the Board of Bishops of the A.M.E., A.M.E.Z., and C.M.E. Churches met in Big Zion Church, Mobile, Ala., with the following named Bishops present: H. M. Turner, W. B. Derrick, C. T. Shaffer, B. F. Lee, L. J. Coppin, E. Tyree, C. S. Smith, H. P. Parks, J. W. Wood (evidently Hood), C. R. Harris, A. Walters, G. W. Clinton, J. W. Alstork, J. S. Caldwell, G. L. Blackwell, A. J. Warner, Isaac Lane, L. H. Holsey, R. S. Williams, Elias Cottrell, C. H. Phillips, M. F. Jamison, G. W. Stewart.

Absent Bishops: J. A. Handy, sick; B. T. Tanner, retired; M. B. Salters, sick; J. S. Flipper, called home; J. A. Johnson, Africa; W. H. Heard, Africa.

"Concord and peace dwelt in our midst. Fraternal ties are being drawn closer and closer. These three churches understand each othr as never before. Let us hope that we shall ever go on in this good way. We still intend to bring out the common hymn and tune book.

"That we will not receive preachers from other churches unless they come recommended by the Bishop. That the C Recorder, Star of Zion and Christian Index be exchanged with the Bishops of each church gratis. That we shall get out a common form of service and catechism." [3]

In the fraternal message of the A.M.E. Church delivered to this

---

[2] *The Quadrennial Address of the Bishops of the A.M.E. Zion Church* to The Delegates of the Twenty-Third Session of the General Conference, Philadelphia, Pa. 1908, 9.

[3] *Official Journal of the Twenty-fourth Quadrennial Session* of the General Conference, A.M.E. Zion Church, Charlotte, N.C. 1912, 145, 146.

session of the General Conference a more detailed report of the Washington Conference on Organic Union is noted. The meeting was held, February 12, 1908 and seven different subjects were taken under consideration: 1, Federation; 2, Religious Affairs; 3, Civil and Religious Conditions of the colored people; 4, Liturgy and uniformity of service; 5, Common hymnals; 6, Catechisms and 7, Clerical vestments. This evidently, was the first meeting of the group, for a second is noted convening in Mobile, Alabama, February 8, 1911. This was said of the second session: "Bishop Hood offered a resolution for the three Methodist branches to unite in the work of Africa and be known on that continent. The United Episcopal Methodist Church in Africa might prove to be the forerunner of a more united effort on this side of the ocean.[4]

Little was said in the Quadrennial Message of the 25th Session of the General Conference. In truth, it appears that the leaders of the Church were more interested in the Federal Council of Churches than they were in Organic Union, or at least, more time was spent dealing with this subject. However, it was stated: "When the Bishops of Colored Methodism organized their Federal Council ours were there in active cooperation. . . . A standing Committee or commission should be ordered by our General Conference at this session with authority to treat with any similar body on any question that means getting together in a closer compact for aggressive work on the part of any Christian body." [5]

More concrete action is observed in the Twenty-sixth Session held at Knoxville in 1920 when the following is noted: *SPECIAL ORDER:* Consideration of the plan for Organic Union of the A.M.E., C.M.E. and A.M.E. Zion Churches. Bishop G. W. Clinton presented Dr. S. G. Atkins to read the plan arranged by the joint Commission. The Plan as presented by Dr. Atkins follows, and a motion was offered by Dr. F. M. Jacobs which was seconded by Dr. W. L. Hamblim that the document as read be adopted." The motion to adopt passed after discussion by a vote of 378—5.[6] This was occasioned by greater activity in this field in the years leading up to the

---

[4] *Ibid.,* 545.
[5] *Minutes of The Twenty-fifth Session of the General Conference,* Louisville, Ky. 1916, 35.
[6] *The Minutes of the Twenty-sixth Session of the General Conference,* A.M.E. Zion Church, Knoxville, Tenn., 1920, 94.

ORGANIC UNION AFTER 1868

session. The Board of Bishops intimate this in their Quadrennial Message.

In part, they stated:

"Some progress has been made during the quadrennium toward Organic Union of the three leading independent bodies of Methodism—the A. M. E. Zion, the A. M. E. and the C. M. E. Churches. At a meeting in Louisville, Ky., February 1918, of the Tri-Council of the Board of Bishops of these three communions, all the thirty-two bishops, excepting two, and two absent ones, agreed to a plan of Organic Union. A committee was appointed on ways and means composed of three bishops, three elders, and three laymen from each church, which met in Birmingham, Alabama, April 7, 1918, and unanimously agreed on the basis for union. Their report will be presented at this session of our General Conference for action. The C. M. E. General Conference meeting in Chicago in 1918 adopted the basis and agreed to unite. It remains to be seen what action will be taken at our General Conference and the General Conference of the A. M. E. Church which is meeting at this time at St. Louis, Mo. In February of this year the Bishops of the A. M. E. Church and the A. M. E. Zion Churches met in Baltimore in their semi-annual meeting. Episcopal courtesies were extended on the part of our Board by a formal visit, and these courtesies were reciprocated by the A.M.E. Bishops. There was no attempt at holding a joint meeting, and yet the sentiment created in favor of organic union was more potential than on any previous occasion. The frank and clerical greetings, the recognition of each other as equals, the general repudiation of the ideas of the old school which have prevented union hitherto, the forceful enthusiastic speeches made in favor of the union, the minimizing of the reasons why we should not and the cogency of the reasoning why we should be united, culminated in a veritable love feast and an informal wedding of the two great Methodist bodies together. The sentiment formulated in favor of organic became so irresistible that it obliterated what pessimism there was, and every bishop on both sides was convinced of the feasibility of unification of these three large bodies of Negro Methodists. Your Board of Bishops holds the opinion that organic union of the A. M. E, the A. M. E. Zion and the C. M. E. branches of the Methodist family should be affected:

First, because our doctrines are the same, and the little difference in polity can easily be adjusted.

Second, because in a very large measure we cover the same territory, and thus it will obviate the overlapping of areas.

Third, for economic reasons in running the machinery of the church.

Fourth, because of the increased efficiency it would add in the crystalizing sentiment politically in favor of our race.

Fifth, for the salutory effect it would have upon the economic, religious and business life of the Negro in America, in the Isles of the seas and in Africa.[7]

Writing in the A.M.E. Zion Quarterly Review in 1922, the Editor, Cameron Chesterfield Alleyne said:

"The Commissioners on Organic Union of the A. M. E., A. M. E. Zion and C. M. E. Churches, met at Washington in the John Wesley Church in June. The meeting brought together a number of earnest, hopeful men, their hearts afire with the glow of union; men whose hearts the Lord has touched, who, in their inmost souls desire to see Black Methodism marching as one army of the Living God.

"The results, however, were somewhat disappointing. It seems to us that the Commissioners work too leisurely and yet too hurriedly. They give themselves but little time and then consume that time in useless and wasteful argument.

"An Un-wise choice of a chairman well-nigh ruined this meeting. It was only when Bishop J. S. Caldwell of the Zion Church, took the chair that a little business was transacted. Unfortunately this was late in the day; and although scheduled to meet the next day; the Commissioners had, in many cases, made other engagements, hence a quorum could not be gotten together.

"We were much puzzled by the absence of the A. M. E. Bishops and ministers at the evening service when an elaborate programme was staged, and fine speeches made on the vital subject of union. This was the bright spot in the meeting. Dr. Emmett Scott and Dr. H. Tobias were eloquent in their delivery. Dr. Bray, Educational Secretary of the C. M. E. Church, responded in a neat speech full of epigrams and characterized by logic. Dr. E. D. W. Jones presided in a masterly manner.

"We ought to decide whether we really want union, if we do then we should get down to business and stop wasting time. Remember the Master reminded us that there are but twelve hours in the day.' 'The opportunity of a lifetime lasts only during the lifetime of the opportunity.' Coming together without a definite programme, and not prepared to give sufficient time to the consideration of the important details connected with the venture, making fine speeches and then on leaving forgetting all that was said, will never bring us nearer the desired goal." [8]

If anything, the Board of Bishops revealed a restrained attitude on Organic Union as they addressed the 1924 General Conference. Whether this was born of discouragement or despair is not revealed. The Board reiterated the basic desire of the Church to bring about Organic Union but it called attention to the great enthusiasm on the

---
[7] *Minutes of the Twenty-sixth Session, loc. cit.*, 61, 62.
[8] *The A.M.E. Zion Quarterly Review*, Vol. XXXIII, No 2 (Second Quarter, 1922 62).

ORGANIC UNION AFTER 1868

part of the General Conference of 1920 as the Birmingham Plan was approved and never materialized. Patiently, it was stated: "That Organic Union of Negro Methodists in America has not been effected is no fault of the A.M.E. Zion Church. The blame must be laid at the door of the other denominations who were parties to the triangular proposition." [9]

However, the report on Church Federation and Organic Union was read, considered, and after editing to clearly reveal the mind of the denomination, was approved.[10]

It is not clear as to the implications of this vote of approval for it appears that the General Conference had now in mind a wider movement of unification than that which involved the three original participants. This is revealed in the subsequent action of the Secretary of the Conference as he was instructed to convey the action taken to the Methodist Episcopal General Conference then in session in Springfield, Mass.[11]

In the official documents of the Church it is to be noted that a rebirth of interest in the subject came in the General Conference of 1928 as the delegates met in St. Louis, Missouri. Reference to this and recommended action in 1932 with an explanation as to why so little progress was made appears in the Address of the Board of Bishops in 1932: "Our last General Conference submitted to the annual conferences and to the churches in order, a plan for the unification of the A.M.E. and the A.M.E. Zion denominations. We entered upon the matter of Organic Union in all good faith and are pleased to report, that a large majority of the conferences voted to adopt the plan. Just when we were ready to submit the vote on unification through your commission and the Annual Conferences to our churches and congregations, there came upon us the unheralded and unexpected necessity to give almost all of our attention to conserving and sustaining our institutions and other denominational enterprises. Every other subject was forced to be held in abeyance, while Bishops, pastors and people organized to meet the tremendous task of keeping the doors open throughout our Zion. Today we do not hesitate to again proclaim our time honored approval of Organic

---

[9] *The Minutes of the Twenty-seventh Quadrennial Session,* of the General Conference, Indianapolis, Ind., 1924, 115, 116.
[10] *Ibid.,* 91.
[11] *Ibid.,* 92.

Union, with our Sister Methodism, and refer again, this vital question to you for action, as you deem advisable and expedient.[12]

The Committee on Church Federation and Organic Union submitted its report to the 1932 General Conference in two sections, the first dealing with the Federal Council of Churches and the second with the temporarily abandoned work of Organic Union. The group referred to the statement of the Board of Bishops and went on to suggest that since they had been advised that the A.M.E. Church recommended the completion of the vote in that denomination, they would urge the Board of bishops of Zion Methodism to "authorize the Commission on Organic Union to submit the proposition of Organic Union with the African M.E. Church to the local congregations in accordance with the action taken by the General Conference on this proposition in 1928." [13]

The Committee also suggested that the "Commission on Organic Union be empowered to conduct negotiations toward Organic Union in accordance with our law with any and all Evangelical Protestant denominations demonstrating interest in union with us. Particularly do we recommend that the said Commission consider seriously and promptly the possibility of the union of American Methodism." [14]

It will be recalled that the Board of Bishops at an earlier time had decided upon a plan of action which would allow for cooperation along other vital lines. The General Conference Committee appeared to have turned again to these suggestions as it urged: "For cooperation with other denominations in the establishment of an Inter-denominational Theological Seminary," "Cooperative efforts in the production of a common hymnal and Church School Literature, and other publications"; Cooperation in the Home and Foreign Mission fields and cooperation in the establishment of training schools for ministers and lay people." [15]

The late Bishop Paris Arthur Wallace prepared and read the Quadrennial Address of the Board of Bishops to the Thirtieth Session of the General Conference which met in Greensboro, North Carolina

---

[12] *The Minutes of the Twenty-ninth Quadrennial Session* of the General Conference, Pittsburgh, Pa., 1932, 93.
[13] *Ibid.*, 232.
[14] *Ibid.*
[15] *The Minutes of the Twenty-ninth Quadrennial Session* (Pittsburgh, Pa., 1932 *loc. cit.*, 232.

in May 1936. By this time the denomination appeared well on its way of working out of the economic dilemma but evidently had given up immediate hope of Organic Union. In truth, nothing on this subject appeared in the message, while references were found to interdenominational cooperation across racial lines, and this attitude evidently sought to point the way ahead for the next immediate years, and this has proved correct. A Committee on Church Federation and Organic Union was appointed and was chaired by the Reverend J. W. Brown. However, if a report were drawn it does not appear in the minutes as recorded.

In the message of 1940, when the Quadrennial session met in Washington, D. C., the Bishops said: "The A.M.E. Zion Church, for many years has led the way for organic union of all Negro Methodist Churches in America. She is thoroughly committed to an honorable union with any or all of her Sister denominations.

"We your chief pastors cannot see any good reason for the A.M.E. Zion and the C.M.E. Churches remaining apart as separate and distinct organizations. We believe that a commission should be appointed by this General Conference to study the plan of the United Methodist Church, to see if there is ground for a similar union under the plans of its jurisdiction for the uniting of all the Negro Methodist Churches of America. We believe that the Commission should immediately be appointed and that contacts be made with the two General Conferences now in session, and express to them our desire to see a oneness in Methodism.[16] The Committee on Organic Union and Church Federation agreed to recommend this action.[17]

The Bishops' Quadrennial Address of 1944 was prepared and delivered by Bishop William Jacob Walls when the Thirty-Second Session met in St. Paul Church, Detroit, Michigan.

Again the outlook of the denomination appeared to be involvement in the Interdenominational matters rather than fondly looking forward to Organic Union. A new note, as well, is seen—the determination to strengthen the denomination from within. For example: the report urged "But what we most need in these days of scientific unification and movements of international cooperation, is a new

---

[16] *Official Journal, The Thirty-First Quadrennial Session,* General Conference of the A.M.E. Zion Church, Washington, D.C., 1940, 92, 93.
[17] *Ibid.,* 228.

lesson of unity." [18] And while the Bishops appeared willing to keep an open mind as far as Organic Union was concerned they said: "To this end we admonish that far more important than any movement toward external union, is our duty to make the A.M.E. Zion strong, indeed as strong as true faith, loyal hearts and ready hands can make her. It has been written by some publicists that union in the Negro Methodist groups would have come before now had not the A.M.E. Zion Church always defeated it. The statement is historically false and blandly reflects dumbness on his part." . . . We want a union of souls and wills so that it will stay when it comes."

The address went on to list the areas in which the Church was cooperating with other denominations: "Herein we are active members in the Federal Council of Churches, The Councils of Christian Education, Christian Endeavor, and interdenominational and national youth movements, the world's Sunday School Association, and pay our proportionate means to support them." [19]

Work, however, had been going forward on a proposed Combined Hymnal, A Joint Commission had been appointed and the following Resolution was proposed at this session of the General Conference: Whereas: The A.M.E. Zion Church and the A.M.E. Church Commission on Combined Hymnal has completed the manuscript for said combined hymnal, and has approved of a plan for the publication of said hymnal;

> BE IT RESOLVED: (1) That this General Conference go on record as endorsing the work of the combined Commission; (2) It hereby authorizes the Ways and Means Committee of the Commission on Combined Hymnal to publish 50,000 copies of said combined hymnal on a joint and equitable basis with the A. M. E. Church Commission on Combined Hymnal, with joint ownership of manuscript, plates and sales interest on a 50% basis; (3) That the General Conference hereby authorizes the Board of Finance of the A. M. E. Zion Church to provide one-half of the funds necessary for the publication of said hymnal, according to details worked out by the combined commission.[20]

From 1948 to 1968, as far as the official action of the General Conferences was concerned, only ordinary action was taken in the matter of Organic Union. The 1948 session re-affirmed Zion Methodism's interest and expectation of the movement and further urged that a

---

[18] *Official Journal of the Thirty-Second Quadrennial Session*, Detroit, Mich., 1944, 220.
[19] *Journal, Thirty-Second Session, loc. cit.*, 223.
[20] *Ibid.*, 191.

ORGANIC UNION AFTER 1868

special committee be set up to deal with the matter,[21] while no marked enthusiasm is to be found in the action of the General Conference four years later when the delegates gathered in Brooklyn, New York. However, similar action was taken by the Committee.[22]

The Thirty-fifth session approached Church union on a much broader basis than ever before. It urged maintenance of active ties with every interdenominational venture not only by the denomination itself, but through each of the varied departments. It recognized too, the necessity of active participation in city, state, national and world councils. It insisted that a frank view be taken of the deeper differences which may exist between denominations but urged a careful study leading towards the clarification and interpretation of these matters. Finally, it urged Organic Union among all Negro Methodists and eventually, all Methodism.[23]

In 1960, the Committee sought to call attention of the Church to the happenings around the Nation where Church mergers were to be noted. It called attention, for example, to the final Consummation of the union of the American Lutheran Church and suggested that the dream for Organic Union among the three Negro denominations should not be laid aside. Towards this goal it offered recommendations and further urged that the "unofficial" report from the Methodist Church looking towards unification of all Methodism be actively fostered.[24] Another significant move was *that* to encourage the abandonment of small church units and to emphasize the interracial nature of the church itself.

In the State of the Country Message of the 1964 Minutes, when the General Conference met in Indianapolis, Ind., a request is made again for a Special Commission on Organic Union.[25] However, the issue of Church Union was not one of the *burning* type.

Were it not for the fact that the denomination could not long overlook its traditional stand and efforts toward Organic Union, perhaps this writing on Church Merger would end on a despairing

---

[21] *Official Journal* of the Thirty-Third Quadrennial Session, Louisville, 1948, 297.

[22] *Official Journal Thirty-Fourth General Conference*, Brooklyn, N.Y., 1952, 433.

[23] *Official Journal of the Thirty-Fifth Session*, Pittsburgh, Pa., 1956, 458-460.

[24] *Official Journal, The Thirty-Sixth Quadrennial Session*, Buffalo, N.Y., 1960, 431, 432.

[25] *Official Journal, Thirty-Seventh Quadrennial Session*, Indianapolis, Ind., 1964, 507.

note. However, it is necessary to deal with two major movements and to merely mention the present efforts at union that we in no way, handicap the possibilities of success.

The great dream of a massive Protestant Church involving at least nine, and perhaps more denominations, has now been underway for several years. The joy of the Church in the participation of Zion Methodism in this venture is unbounded, for even if there is no ultimate success, and we firmly believe this ultimate success will be achieved, the exchange of ideas, the re-structuring of denominations, the re-examination of theological concepts along with the interpretation of denominational knowhow, will be a thrilling blessing to every group participating. The Consultation on Church Union, therefore, is not only being actively noted but earnestly prayed for.

The Second Great matter involves the revived hopes for Organic Union among Negro, or Black Methodists, as a step toward the eventual union of all Methodists. Involved is a new group of ministers and laymen—many with ideas which transcends petty differences, to the point of actually aiding in the achievement of God's Kingdom on Earth. Pushed relentlessly by two students of Ecumenics, John H. Satterwhite of the A.M.E. Zion Church and Charles S. Spivey for the A.M.E. Church along with the Rev. W. Clyde Williams of the C.M.E. Church the time and situation is favorable.

However concerned differences do exist. Two of these three denominations have, in their restructuring programs, provided for The Judicial Council, thereby, limiting the power of the Episcopacy. One has rejected the matter in one way or another. Two of these denominations have taken a liberal view of the matter of divorce. The third has endeavored to re-affirm its traditional stand of the past sixty years. The third major difference involves financial system, which we believe, will be the easiest difference to adjust.

It is painful that so many times the three denominations have appeared to have come close to an agreement on union without achieving it for one reason or another. Certainly sentiment has been favorable in many influential circles. For example: the Sunday School Bulletin spoke of one such effort in 1918: "The Board of Bishops of the A.M.E. Zion, the A.M.E. and the C.M.E. Churches met in joint session in Louisville, Ky., February 15 and 16. This is the third meeting of its kind ever held. The effort for the calling of this meeting was started in Chicago last Summer when the resource-

ORGANIC UNION AFTER 1868

ful Bishop J. S. Caldwell offered such a motion to the Connectional Council of the A.M.E. Zion Church, which was unanimously adopted by that body composed of the Bishops and General Officers." [26]

Three years later the same periodical carried the following letter; dated January 3, 1921:

Bishop C. S. Smith, D. D.
Detroit, Michigan
Dear Bishop:
Your letter received. Replying, will say that the vote for Organic Union failed in our church. My conferences went almost unanimously against it. Some of the men in Bishops Cottrell's and Cleaves' conferences voted for it, but the great majority went against it. I understand that Bishop Carter's conferences did not vote on it at all.

There are many reasons for this, chiefly the attitude of Bishop Phillips and some of the unwise or rather indirect things that came out in the papers of the C. M. E. and A. M. E. Churches. As ardent as I was for the Union and am yet, so far as that is concerned, I lost interest for I saw more harm would come than good if we undertook to force the question,

I hope and pray that the day will yet come when these three churches will unite for the good of the race, the salvation of the people and the glory of God. I am

Yours in His Name
(Signed) R. S. WILLIAMS
Bishop[27]

Thus the conversations with the C.M.E. Church which evidently began as far back as the Second Wednesday in May, 1878 (Washington, D. C.) came again to failure. As late as March 1918, great hopes and enthusiasm had been expressed at Louisville, Ky., when only two dissenting votes against the measure had been voiced. The Resolution offered by Bishop George C. Clement was signed by such individuals as Bishops Caldwell, Coppin, Cottrell, Williams and Beckett. The special commission had been appointed consisting of three Bishops, three elders and three laymen from each of the three denominations and on the first of April had been called to meet that eventually their work could be submitted to the General Conferences meeting subsequently.[28]

Many times the lack of communication handicaps the realization of dreams and plans and no doubt this can be said to be the case

---

[26] *The Sunday School Bulletin,* January 1918.
[27] *The Sunday School Bulletin,* February, 1921.
[28] *Ibid.,* March 1918.

where Organic Union is concerned. The Colored Methodist Episcopal Church has, throughout its entire history, spoken of union with the other Negro Methodist bodies. When it is realized that the first and organizing General Conference of that denomination took place in 1870 and men in that church were talking of union in 1876, the subject could not have been a light one. The Christian Index of that year stated:

> Our last General Conference, inspired and prompted by the Spirit of God, expressed its desire for Organic Union with all Colored Methodists, and appointed a committee and invested it with absolute power to effect fraternal or organic union. The African Methodist Episcopal Zion Church will hold its General Conference in Louisville, Ky., and we doubt not that some proposition will be presented or some plan adopted that will tend to bring about organic union. There already exists the most cordial feeling between these two churches. The members are closely connected in the bonds of Christian love, and we can see no reason why a union of Church, as well as a union of hearts, should not be speedily consummated.[29]

The following month (June) the Editor stated:

> This Church and our Church are on the most fraternal terms, and it is thought by many that a union of the two will be effected, if not at this session, at least at an early date.

THE ARTICLES OF AGREEMENT OF THE BIRMINGHAM PLAN OF ORGANIC UNION

Preamble

Historically speaking, it is seen that the African Methodist Episcopal, the African Methodist Episcopal Zion, and the Colored Methodist Episcopal Churches originated in a similarity of causes and therefore resulted in a similarity of effect, as regards their respective organizations.

Then are there any good and sufficient reasons for keeping separate these three Methodist Churches that have never had any ecclesiastical differences among themselves? If it be true that each and all of us are utilizing every means at our command to consummate the same great commission to disciple the world, then it naturally follows that our usefulness in Christian work would be manifold multiplied by working together as a united force.

---

[29] *The Christian Index*, May, 1876.

ORGANIC UNION AFTER 1868

Believing as we do, that organic union is practicable, desirable, and feasible, we recommend:

1. That the African Methodist Episcopal Church, the African Methodist Episcopal Zion Church, and the Colored Methodist Episcopal Church, unite organically into one body, under the denominational title of the United Methodist Episcopal Church.

2. That this recommendation for organic union be presented for ratification to the General Conferences of the three above-named denominations in their order of meeting, namely: To the General Conference of the Colored Methodist Episcopal Church, which meets in Chicago in May, 1918; to the African Methodist Episcopal General Conference meeting in St. Louis, Mo., May, 1920; and to the African Methodist Episcopal Zion General Conference, meeting in Knoxville, Tenn., May, 1920.

3. Should these three named denominations at their quadrennial meetings aforesaid approve and ratify the recommendations herein named, we further recommend that said articles so approved be sent for ratification to the annual conferences of the three named denominations in the order of their annual meetings next following ratification by the two General Conferences meeting in May, 1920.

4. The copies of these recommendations be carried by each presiding elder and pastor from the Annual Conference to the district or charge to which he may be assigned, namely: each district, circuit, station, and mission. That said pastor, upon taking charge of his station, circuit, or mission, as the case may be, inform the people that upon a certain day and date, allowing at least thirty days' notice, and not later than ninety days thereafter, they would be called together to vote upon the resolution touching organic union between the three denominations above named; and at said called meeting, after at least thirty days' notice had been given, the above resolution No 1 be read and after mature deliberations voted upon.

5. Should three-fourths of the members of the annual conferences present and voting, and a majority of the members of each local Church or congregation present and voting, vote for the said resolution No. 1 on organic union, then it shall be declared and adopted by said Annual Conferences and local Churches or congregations.

Correct copies of the minutes bearing on this matter of union by all the Conferences, and congregations, giving date of meeting at which the vote was taken, the number of voting for and the number voting against, shall be presented to the next ensuing General Conferences of the three denominations aforesaid, meeting respectively in May, 1922 and May, 1924.

6. That a true and accurate record of this said meeting of each congregation shall be made and kept, showing the date and place of meeting, the number voting for and the number voting against the said resolution on organic union, and one copy of the same duly signed by the pastor and attested by the Church Clerk or Secretary of said meeting, shall be forwarded by mail to the Secretaries of the commission designated by the General Conferences, above named, and one copy duly signed by the pastor and attested by the Church Clerk or Secretary

of said meeting, shall be deposited with the pastor and by him presented for record at the next ensuing Annual Conference of which he is a member.

7. If it be found that the number of conferences and congregations necessary for ratification have voted for approval and the measure has thus passed, General Conferences of the three bodies shall be called to convene at such time and place as shall be determined by the joint commission to be named by the General Conferences of the three denominations above named.

(8. Appears to be missing. Ed.)

9. The business of the said United General Conference to be the same as any other legislative body, to legislate for the government of the united church, provided, however, that nothing fundamental to Methodism in the way of doctrinal tenets and constitution shall be changed.

10. That we agree to share alike the benefits and liabilities of each connection that is a party to this union; and that the title of all properties now held in the name of each separate organization be transferred to the United Methodist Episcopal Church, and, as far as possible, all deeds and legacies be taken over by the United Methodist Episcopal Church, either by the decision of the courts and special enactments, when necessary, or by such officers and authorities as may have legal right to do so. The details of such transactions to be worked out by the General Conferences of the three denominations above named.

11. That the bishops in office at the time of the approval of these articels in the three-above-named Churches shall continue in the same in accordance with the laws and regulations covering the official tenure of bishops in their respective Churches.

Present Federation

12. Be it recommended to our several denominations that during the period of these organic negotiations, that the spirit and plan of federation as outlined in the Bishops' Louisville Address, or any plan which may suggest itself to the parties concerned in this union, be encouraged; and in all cases that the closest bonds of association and fellowship be maintained between our membership, an exchange of pulpits, where possible among our ministers: and upon request of any of the bishops of the three Churches, there be an exchange of ministers to serve as pastors, and that the said pastors when so exchanged, shall have the same standing in the Church to which he is sent as was held in the Church from which he was sent.

That we encourage the exchange of fraternal messengers to Annual and District Conferences, Sunday School Conventions, and Women's Missionary Meetings, particularly in states where the three or even two denominations operate.

That our bishops invite bishops of either denomination to sit and counsel with them at Annual Conferences, to the end that we may become acquainted with the spirit and policy of our Churches and that a feeling of oneness of purpose and accomplishment might be easier and more rapidly grown.[30]

---

[30] C. H. Phillips, *loc. cit.,* 605-608.

CHAPTER XX

The Church and Ecumenical Ties

SO LITTLE reference has been made through writings concerning the ecumenical ties of the denomination that this is really a study in itself. One gathers, however, that the A. M. E. Zion Church was influenced by the discussions of the time. The early movement at something akin to union began, no doubt, as a result of the Lambeth articles which gathered together the ideas of the Bishops of the Church of England. By 1888 union and cooperation of churches were being discussed freely. We would hasten to state that cooperation of churches on many levels was not new. In the matter of Sunday Schools, for example, lay people were caught up in the matter of working together regardless of denomination.

A Mr. H. K. Carroll, special agent of the eleventh census of churches, made a study regarding unification. During the closing two decades of the Nineteenth Century he published a result of his studies. He stated, for example, that at the time there were 134 different denominations in the United States. He listed seven groups of Adventists, thirteen groups of Baptists, 12 groups of Lutherans, seventeen of Methodists and twelve Presbyterians. He did not state how many other smaller groups there were.

Carroll proposed that there should be three groups of Methodists instead of the seventeen existing organizations. However, we have stated sufficient to reveal the nature of the discussions of the time.

In an old copy of the A.M.E. Zion Quarterly Review (1894) the Editor speaks of the passing of Bishop John Jamison Moore. He states that he first met Bishop Moore in London in 1879. This is surprising for we have been wont to date Zion's cooperation in ecumenical affairs from the date of the participation of Bishop Alexander Walters. The Editor of the Review stated: "We met him in London in 1879, while he was raising money for the book concern. He attended a conference of Wesleyan ministers."

According to the Souvenir Program of the Twenty-first Quadrennial Session of the General Conference, the major advocate of Zion Methodism's participation in ecumenical church life was Alexander Walters, who pastored Mother Zion Church at one time after serving churches in the South and in California. In 1889, he was elected by the Board of Bishops and the Sunday School Association of New York to represent them in the World's Sunday School Convention in London, England in July of that year.[1] Two years later, in 1891, he was a member of the Methodist Ecumenical Conference which met in Washington, D. C. These assignments took place prior to his being elected to the episcopacy in 1892. By 1895 Bishop Walters had been elected a Trustee of the United Society of Christian Endeavor and three years later he was recognized for his interests across denominational lines by being elected President of the National Afro-American Council, which he evidently founded.

The Ecumenical Methodist meeting in Washington in 1891 gave a rich opportunity for several to attend the Conference. We note that no Bishops' meeting could be held for the lack of a quorum because of the sessions. George W. Clinton, for example, was also in attendance at this session.

While little is said of the Ecumenical Conference of 1881, it appears that Bishop Joseph P. Thompson had been invited to England in that year, and, according to Hood "was invited to read a paper before the Ecumenical Conference of Methodist Churches." [2] It appears that some 400 representatives attended this first venture in World Methodism.[3] Joseph Charles Price was also a delegate.[4]

The fact that the church was adequately represented in the first Ecumenical Conference no doubt allowed for the favorable reception of the following when the General Conference met in New York City in 1884:

> To the Bishops and Members of the African Methodist Episcopal Zion Church General Conference, assembled in New York City.
> Dear Fathers and Brethren: The undersigned, the Secretaries of the Ecumenical Methodist Conference, held in City Road Chapel, London, Eng., September 7-20, 1881, transmit to you the resolutions adopted by that body in regard to a second Ecumenical Conference, that you may take such action thereon, as in your godly wisdom may seem most likely

---

[1] Rev. W. H. Snowden, ed., *Souvenir Program of the Twenty-first Quadrennial Session, of the General Conference* (Washington, D.C. 1900) 41.
[2] Bishop J. W. Hood, *One Hundred Years of the A.M.E. Zion Church* (1895) 190.
[3] Emory Stevens Bucke, ed., *The History of American Methodism* (in three vols.) Vol. II, (Abingdon Press, 1964) 698.
[4] *The A.M.E. Zion Quarterly Review*, 1894, 219.

to promote the glory of God, and to secure the unity and prosperity of His Church.

JOHN BOUD,
S. S. WITHINGTON,
A. C. GEORGE,
A. SUTHERLAND,
Secretaries

RESOLUTIONS ADOPTED BY THE ECUMENICAL METHODIST CONFERENCE LONDON, ENGLAND, SEPT., 29, 1881

In accordance with the suggestion of Bishop M. Simpson, and the approval of the Business Committee, the following resolutions were unanimously adopted:

Resolved: That it is expedient that a second Ecumenical Conference be assembled, and, if practicable, in the United States in the year 1887.

Resolved 2d, That in order thereto, and for the promotion of Christian fraternity, the several Methodist bodies are earnestly desired to create an Executive Committee, as now constituted, subject to such changes in its membership as they, in their wisdom, may ordain, beginning with the British Wesleyan Conference in the year 1883.

Resolved 3d, That the Executive Committee constituted in accordance with these resolutions, shall determine the time and place of holding the Second Ecumenical Conference, the number of delegates to be chosen, and the ratio of their distribution amongst the respective bodies, shall prepare a programme of exercises, and rules and regulations for the government of the Conference, and shall make all other necessary arrangements.

The communication was received, and concurred in by vote of the General Conference and a committee of three on correspondence appointed, consisting of Bishop S. T. Jones, J. C. Price and J. C. Dancy.[5]

The Bishops' message of 1892 looked back with a sense of pride on this entrance of the denomination into ecumenics as they declared:

"In place of the self-taught preachers of 1863 we now have a considerable number of cultured theologians. In place of a few old-fashioned houses of worship we have now hundreds of temples. Our Church was then hardly known, except in New England, New York, Pennsylvania, Baltimore and Washington city. Now it is known in all parts of the world. It was the very first to contribute its full quota in support of the Second Ecumenical Conference, for which it was especially commended by the chairman of the Finance Committee. It furnished the only colored layman who read an address before that body, and address acknowledged to be the equal of any one delivered. It furnished the first colored president of that body, (evidently, American section) and there are only three of the sixteen branches of Methodists

---

[5] *Proceedings of the Seventeenth Quadrennial Session of the General Conference,* 1884, 120.

on this side of the ocean which have a larger number of the committee to arrange for the next meeting. The three bodies which have a larger representation are the Methodist Episcopal Church, The Methodist Episcopal Church, South, and the Methodist Church of Canada.[6]

Bishop J. W. Alstork, a beloved prelate in the State of Alabama wrote concerning the Third Ecumenical Methodist Conference of which he was a member. The sessions were held in London, England, September 4-17, 1901. He lists the delegates or attendants from Zion Church as follows: Bishops: C. R. Harris, G. W. Clinton, T. H. Lomax, J. B. Small, J. W. Alstork and Alexander Walters. Others were Reverends J. McH. Farley, J. S. Caldwell, G. L. Blackwell, J. F. Moreland, F. M. Jacobs, J. B. Colbert, M. C. B. Mason, Prof. S. G. Atkins, Hon. Williams, Reverends M. A. Bradley, Florence Randolph, Madames E. V. Walters, M. L. Clinton, M. M. Alstork, and M. C. B. Mason.[7]

The Fourth Ecumenical Conference met just prior to the General Conference of 1912. The dates listed were, Toronto, Canada, October 4-17, 1911. The sessions evidently were held in Queen Street Metropolitan Church at the time. The Bishops message to the General Conference stated: "The entire Methodist family of the world was represented in that great meeting. The red man, the black man, the yellow man, the brown man and the white man, were all there (in the original). The following were the delegates of our Zion: Bishops C. R. Harris, A. Walters, G. W. Clinton, J. W. Alstork, J. S. Caldwell, G. L. Blackwell, A. J. Warner; Prof. S. G. Atkins, Hon. J. C. Dancy, Reverends J. S. Jackson, R. A. Fisher, J. J. Smyer, G. C. Clement, C. S. Whitted, J. E. Mason, W. H. Goler W. H. Coffey, B. G. Shaw, R. R. Ball, B. W. Swain, Dr. W. L. Lee, Mrs. A. W. Blackwell, Mrs. J. W. Alstork. Mrs. P. H. Jackson, Mrs. M. E. Blackwell, and Dr. T. W. Wallace."[8] The Bishops went on to say "In appearance our delegation reflected credit upon itself and the Church it represented. In proportion to subjects and the delivery of them, they were second to none."

"In executive ability and grace, as presiding officers, Bishop A. Walters and Hon. Jno. C. Dancy received the encomiums of the conference.

---

[6] *Minutes of the General Conference of* 1892, Pittsburgh, Pa. 20.
[7] Bishop J. W. Alstork, *Notes Gathered by the Way as We Traveled Through Europe.*
[8] *Official Journal of the Twenty-fourth Quadrennial Session, General Conference,* 1912, 144.

"The address of Bishop Clinton on 'The Missions of Methodism in the Backward Races,' was a masterpiece which reflected great credit upon the Bishop and the church he represented.

"Prof. S. G. Atkins in his wonderful address, 'The Laymen's Movement,' was never more at himself than when delivering this matchless address. It clearly brought out the fact that the A.M.E. Zion Church has in her lay rank men of superior ability who are also great orators."

It is noteworthy too, that the Board of Bishops mentioned other Inter-church gatherings in which the denominations were involved. For example, there was the Inter-Race Conference which met in London. The Board stated: "Wishing to send a strong representative to represent our Zion we delegated that thorough scholar and conservative thinker, Prof. W. B. Crittenden." Then, in June 1911, they mentioned the Sunday School Convention held in San Francisco, California. Bishop G. W. Clinton represented the Church. In another chapter we have noted the participation of other Zion people in Sunday School affairs.

With pride, the Board told the General Conference about its continuing interest in Organic Union, pointing out the fact that a meeting had been held in Mobile, Alabama of the three Boards of Bishops from the Black denominations. Every member of these boards had been present except for those who were ill or out of the country. It appears that one other had been called home. One of the major aims of these denominations was a common hymn and tune book.

Among the agreements reached was one concerning the transfer of ministers across denominational lines. It was agreed that no individual would be accepted without the recommendation of the Bishop. It was likewise agreed that each Bishop would receive copies of the various periodicals of the denominations involved. The third agreement had to do with the issuance of a common worship service and catechism.[9]

First mention of the Church's affiliation with the Federal Council of Churches of Christ in America, one of the constituting bodies of the National Council of Churches was made in the Twenty-fifth Quadrennial session. Again, it was the Board of Bishops Message to to which we turn: "The Federal Council of the Churches of Christ in

---

[9] *Official Journal of the Twenty-fourth Quadrennial Session*, 145, 146.

America is composed of thirty-six (36) denominations having a membership of sixteen million (16,000,000) men and women who are marching in a solid phalanx against the common foe in the world. The Federation was born of the conviction that Churches of Christ were great in more things and in things more important than those in which they differ, and that they could do their best work, not in separation, but in heart-felt cooperation; hence the voice of the Church is heard through sixteen million (16,000,000) Christian men and women who have become members one of another. This united force is not concerning itself very much about uniformity, but is striving to bring forth in each of its constituent bodies the very best that is in them in brotherhood, in peace, in education and in evangelism.[10a]

The following session of the General Conference not only mentioned again the Federal Council of Churches but spoke of the revived hope of organic union, going into detail in reference to the Birmingham Meeting (April 7, 1918) and providing reference to the Louisville Meeting (February, 1918). For the first time, the Inter-Church World Movement came in for a share of interest. The Bishops spoke of the survey of the world's needs, the interest and concern of John D. Rockefeller and the efforts of the Churches to underwrite a suitable budget.[10]

A year following the 1920 General Conference (1921) the Fifth Ecumenical Conference of World Methodism was held in London, England, and again Zion Methodism was well represented. At home, the Church was actively a part of the new International Council of Religious Education (organized in 1910) as noted in the Superintendent's report of the Sunday School Department.[11]

Little was said about world cooperation in Christianity in 1928 but emphasis again was placed on the Federal Council of Churches. Bishop Clement, who was so very vitally concerned about the Council read the message so naturally took time to emphasize the Church's interest in it. In part he stated: "At the initial meeting held in Cooper Union, 1905, which looked toward the organization of the Federal Council of Churches as well as in 1908 at Philadelphia when the organization was perfected, and in all the succeeding years the

---

[10a] *Minutes of the Twenty-fifth Quadrennial Session of the General Conference,* 34.
[10] *Minutes of the Twenty-sixth Quadrennial Session* (1920) 62, 63.
[11] *Minutes of the Twenty-seventh Quadrennial Session,* 213.

THE CHURCH AND ECUMENICAL TIES

A.M.E. Zion Church has actively and heartily participated in the Federal Council of Churches in America. We are one of the Twenty-nine Protestant bodies of which the Council is composed. The scope and influence of this federated body in an advisory and cooperative way have grown and strengthened and we count it a privilege to share in all that has made for fellowship and service in its activities. Missionary enterprises, national and international peace and good will and other major questions have engaged the attention of the Federal Council." [12]

Concern for race relations evidently had developed in the intervening years since the denomination had turned mainly to internal development and missions. By 1932 the Bishops were saying: "The relations of the races in this country must be considered by your chief pastors. Among the questions foremost in public thought today, is that of interracial attitudes. The Christian religion knows no race, color or class. Jesus sent his disciples forth to teach all nations, and he proclaimed that whosoever believeth in him regardless of race or color should be received and baptized in his name. The brotherhood of faith is primary and fundamental wherever the Gospel is believed. We bow our heads in shame and sorrow when we read the records of the gruesome lynchings that occur annually in the United States. We offer our protest against man's inhumanity to man. Justice, equality of appointment, cooperation, racial understanding and the sacredness of personality, are to be stressed now more than ever before in our land. We ask that this General Conference place its record against all lawlessness and crimes, and that we appeal to the Congress of the United States to make lynching a Federal crime." [13]

Perhaps in this respect, the significance of this message fell upon deaf ears so far as America was concerned. One would not argue the point that the Nation was slow to react to this type of racial behaviour while less than forty years later the Nation cannot understand the restlessness of a people who finally have become impatient. A full generation and more has had the opportunity to bring itself more in line with the teachings of Christ where this one item is concerned, but it is still far from the goal. Fearfully, we await a future

---

[12] *Official Journal of the Twenty-eight Quadrennial Session of the General Conference* (1928) 45, 46.
[13] *Journal of the Twenty-ninth General Conference*, 1932, 93.

which, in all too many ways is indicative of violent destruction. For one to conclude that there were not adequate signs in 1932 is to do a disservice to himself. We would cite one instance of this critical situation where ecumenical affairs are concerned.

One of the Departments of the Church, the Christian Education Department, has, for the past fifty years, endeavored in every way to attack this matter of racial segregation. The late James W. Eichelberger had the philosophy that participation of the church in these areas was vital and should be vigorous where inequity was concerned. This writer, for example, has participated in interdenominational conferences which were limited in possible meeting places because of race situations. A favorite point for meeting, for example, was Grand Rapids, Michigan, as Negroes were accepted in the hotels of that city. The line of acceptance finally moved to Columbus, Ohio, even at a time when Chicago hotels had their problems. Eventually, Cincinnati, St. Louis, Louisville, Omaha, and Dallas, Texas were utilized without the fear of racial problems. In this light it should be recognized that the International Council of Religious Education and the National Council of Churches have been great instruments in the breaking down of these walls.

In the midst of this struggle, as stated above was the Christian Education Department under Dr. James W. Eichelberger. Quoting from several sources we would present the crisis which obtained in the International Sunday School Convention in 1926:

MAGILL—A HYPOCRITE

Last April the International Sunday School Convention held its sessions in Birmingham, Alabama, at which time delegates from all over the world and of all denominations in Christendom assembled together to deliberate on burning religious issues and problems affecting the Sunday Schools.

Unfortunately, the three hundred delegates of the black race were compelled to retire from the convention and leave for their respective homes. They could not, as exponents of Christ consent to be segregated and Jim Crowed, and they flatly refused to submit to the establishing of these un-Christian systems in the Sunday School Convention.

According to delegates, Hugh S. Magil, at that time an official of the convention and at this time "Independent" Republican Candidate for United States Senator from Illinois, was one of the parties responsible for the segregation.

Dr. W. H. Alexander, a white southerner and a Christian gentleman, arose to the floor and vigorously protested the Jim Crow rule. He was supported by other white southerners and men from the north who were free from the taint of racial hate. Magill from Illinois made no fight, he showed no resentment and we are not now in the frame of mind to receive his belated apology. Magill would like to "confess and avoid" but the insult still burns and in our minds Magill is stamped and tagged as being too narrow minded to aid our cause in the Senate.

The Northwestern Christian Advocate and the Christian Century have rebuked the officials of the convention editorially, and the papers published by black people have, with the customary, philosophical bitterness, offered their litanies, received no answer. It does appear providential, however, that Hugh Magill should now lay himself liable to public condemnation. It seems that the powers from above have given the black people an opportunity to reject and repudiate this man at the polls who did not have enough Christian courage to drive him out of a Sunday School Convention.

Magill is a reform candidate who feels it necessary to run because Colonel Frank L. Smith, regular Republican nominee, spent a few thousand dollars in the primaries. We feel that Colonel Smith's policies are not honorable, but he is willing to whitewash his own substitution of "policy for principle" in Birmingham. Colonel Smith has never compromised his principles in such a shameful manner. He has never allowed himself to be a party in a programme that would humiliate, embarrass and ridicule a body of Christian workers with black skins. From what we know of Frank L. Smith, he is a man too honorable to indulge in religious hypocrisy.

If Magill is so amenable to southern influence, if he is so willing to compromise his ideals for the well known southern attitude he certainly can be of no service in Washington. We would expect little support from him in wiping out segregation in the Federal Departments, we could expect little from him in passing a Federal law against lynching. In our opinion he would either absent himself from any rollcall in the senate when issues concerning us might arise or allow himself to be filibustered to death by the southern Democrats. In our opinion Mr. Magill has been guilty of gross hypocrisy and his cry for reform politics is a mockery and a travesty. Frank L. Smith, whom he flays, for using a fat campaign fund comes to us with cleaner hands and a freer conscience.[14]

An Editorial in the Boston Post for Friday, February 12, 1926, had heralded the crisis by stating in an article headed: SUNDAY SCHOOL COLOR LINE? "The report that colored church denominations are not to send any delegates to the International Sunday School convention to be held in Birmingham, Alabama, next April, if those delegates are to be segregated in galleries, as planned, makes us wonder if such an intent can possibly be in the minds of those who are to handle the meeting." The article went on to

---

[14] The *Chicago Whip* (Editorial) October 23, 1926.

declare: "One would think that in such a movement as this, if any, the color line would fall. Simply because the great convention, represented by men and women from all parts of the world, happens to be held in a southern city, shall those of a darker skin be insulted by such a herding apart." We would like more definite confirmation of the assertion."

On April 29, 1926, the Northwestern Christian Advocate wrote, under the title: *Difficult, But Not Impossible,* the following:

> Since our comment of last week on the absence of Negro delegates from the Birmingham Convention, a statement on the subject by the executive committee of the International Council of Religious Education has been sent to this office.
>
> This statement shows that there were very great difficulties in the way of providing for the Negro delegates, and that the blame for an essentially un-Christian incident should not be placed upon any one group, white or colored.
>
> The Northwestern knew this to be the fact. Our comment was made with full understanding that the complications which resulted in the refusal of Negro churches to take part were due to Negro obstinacy almost as much as to Caucasian faltering.
>
> But there are more important facts. The Negro insistence on his rights is a sign of that progress for which Caucasian Christians have prayed and labored. The various compromises and accommodations put forward at Birmingham in the attempt to satisfy the Negro delegates without offending local sentiment, were admittedly makeshifts. They will be increasingly difficult and unsatisfactory as the Negro comes to a still larger measure of racial self-estimate. And the Caucasian is showing him the way.
>
> What have the efforts of all denominations which work among the Negroes been aiming at, if not to produce a new racial self-respect? True, this self-respect, now that it is coming into full view, does not always express itself with New Testament gentleness. But the point is one which white Christians consenting to the segregation of their brothers in Christ, will scarcely wish to press home.
>
> The executive committee proves to our complete satisfaction that in the Birmingham incident it was more sinned against than sinning. But it spoils much of the explanation by two sentences, which will be read everywhere with no little amazement and nowhere with more than in the South.
>
> Having accepted the invitation of a Southern city for the convention, we have no escape from the conformity to be the established laws of those providing for our entertainment. *This should be born in mind in choosing the place of meeting for future quadrennial conventions."*
> (Italics ours)
>
> The Northwestern, in its severest moments, has never brought such an indictment as this against any American city. In effect, the committee says convention organizers must bear in mind that there are places

in this country in which, because of local customs and laws, it is impossible to hold a gathering of all races and peoples and tongues which shall be truly Christian in its arrangements and associations.

We know that the thing is difficult: but we do not so completely despair of Christianity in any section of America as to believe it impossible.

The Christian Century published the following on March 25, 1926:

COLORED CHURCHES WILL SHUN BIRMINGHAM

Intense resentment has broken out in various colored denominations against the plans for the quadrennial convention of the International council of religious education, scheduled to open in Birmingham, Alabama, April 12. Sunday School officials of the African Methodist Episcopal Church, the Colored Methodist Episcopal Church, and the African Methodist Episcopal Zion Church have already declared the withdrawal of those churches from all participation in the convention. The trouble arises out of the action of the Committee in charge of the convention in providing a separate block of seats for the colored delegates. This was done, it is said, to conform with a city ordinance requiring segregation between races at meetings held in the city auditorium.

PROGRAM NOT CHRISTIAN

"If white protestantism in America countenances segregation in the convention," said James W. Eichelberger Jr., director of the religious education department of the African Methodist Episcopal Zion Church, "then what message has it for the heathen world?" Segregation is neither Christian nor democratic. The theme of the Birmingham meeting is "Building Together Christian Citizenship." To assume that such a program may be Christian is a travesty on the Christian religion.

The storm over the treatment of the colored delegates to the Birmingham gathering has blown up with a suddenness that shows how tense is the feeling in Negro groups today. The action of the city council of Birmingham is said to have been taken since the first of March and the agreement of the local committee to adjust its plans to the city council's demands for segregation is, therefore, a recent matter. But three Negro churches have already withdrawn, and it looks as though the entire Negro constituency may come to consider itself insulted and follow the example of the three Methodist bodies. The issue thus raised is said to be proving an embarrassing one to President Coolidge, who has agreed to make the opening address of the convention.

As indicative of the state of mind among Negro church members, this editorial from the Star of Zion, weekly published by the African Methodist Episcopal Zion Church is of interest:

"The companions of Christ and leaders of His kingdom should have rejected the segregation of Christians as incompatible with the teachings of him in whose name they meet, for it is not written that Jesus ever sacrificed a principle to accommodate a prejudice. For nearly one hundred and thirty years, the A.M.E. Zion Church has protested against proscription and segregation in any form. Its first organized protest was registered in 1796. However much we may miss by our failure to attend this convention we cannot violate our history and traditions; we cannot sacrifice nor surrender our principles. What we did in 1796 we will do in 1926. We will not consent to segregation, nor have aught to do with the convention."

"We are puzzled to know by what authority any person or persons, committee or comittees of or acting for the international council should presume to proceed with arrangements for the quadrennial convention when such person or persons, committee or committees discovered that by ordinance, or custom or tradition, or agreement the representatives of any cooperating denomination or state council shall be prohibited from exercising the rights and privileges of a member of the convention in violation of the practices and the expressed action of the executive committee?

"Have Massachusetts, Maine, Rhode Island, Connecticut, New York, Pennsylvania, Illinois, Ohio and the other states where for years Negroes have shown an abiding loyalty to the state association (now council) bowed to race discrimination, segregation and tolerance, or will they sidestep it by sending all white delegates?

THE PLACE OF NEGRO BISHOPS

"Should Bishop Robert E. Jones, or Bishop M. W. Clair of the Methodist Episcopal Church be named in the quota to represent their denomination, they would stay in a 'Negro's place,' while their white colleagues sit on the platform. Bishop McDowell, it is reported, is to be one of the speakers. Should Bishop George C. Clement, chairman of the commission on church and race relations of the federal council of churches, attend the international convention, he would be forced to sit in a 'Negro's place.' Should Bishop L. W. Kyles, trustee-at-large of the united society of Christian Endeavor, who is the first colored man to be thus honored since the death of Booker T. Washington—and Washington was the first of the race to get this recognition—attend the Birmingham convention his place would be a 'Negro's place.'

"The Congregational Church refused to hold a banquet in Washington because their Negro members could not be provided for. They adopted a lofty creed expressive of racial brotherhood. What will be the reaction of their Sunday School agency to race discrimination in the international convention at Birmingham?"

Thus it is seen that all did not run smoothly in ecumenical affairs. However, the Church perservered in these struggles until much of this sort of situation has been overcome.

The World Methodist Conference met in London, England again in 1921, as has been noted. Ten years later, the meeting was held in Atlanta, Georgia. In 1947, a large delegation from the denomination

THE CHURCH AND ECUMENICAL TIES

was in attendance at Springfield, Massachusetts, while in 1951 an equally large group attended the session in Oxford, England.

As was the custom the Ecumenical Conference met in America at Lake Junaluska in 1956, again with a large Zion Methodist delegation, both as members and as observers and visitors since the Connectional Council had been called to meet at near-by Asheville, at Hopkins Chapel Church prior to the Conference. Among the official delegates were the following: Bishops W. C. Brown, C. C. Coleman, R. L. Jones, H. T. Medford, Herbert Bell Shaw, Stephen Gill Spottswood, William Andrew Stewart, Charles Eubank Tucker and William Jacob Walls. Others listed as voting members were: Dr. W. O. Carrington, James W. Eichelberger and J. Clinton Hoggard.[15]

It appears that there were others who held membership in this session of the World Methodist gathering, among them being: Walter R. Lovell, David P. Wisdom, David H. Bradley, Bishop Joseph Dixon Cauthen, Charles H. Foggie, Bishop Daniel Carleton Pope, George L. Smith, Bishop W. W. Slade, William Milton Smith, Samuel E. Duncan, J. S. N. Tross, C. L. Wilcox, Daniel W. Andrews, Alexander Barnes, F. R. Blakey, Mrs. C. E. Tucker, J. H. Brockett, Miss Dorothy Jordan, W. S. Dacons, J. R. Funderburke, A. P. Morris, U. S. Johnson, R. W. Sherrill, F. Claude Spurgeon and Mrs. H. T. Medford.[16]

The listed delegates to the Tenth Session of World Methodism were as follows: Dr. C. L. Wilcox (in place of Dr. W. O. Carrington), James W. Eichelberger, J. C. Hoggard, Abbie Clement Jackson, Bishop R. L. Jones, Willa Mae Rice, Bishop D. C. Pope, Bishop H. B. Shaw, Bishop W. M. Smith, Bishop Stephen Gill Spottswood, Bishop William A. Stewart, Bishop W. J. Walls and Mrs. Ann Pate (James Clair) Taylor, and Bishop Felix S. Anderson (in place of Bishop Stewart). Attending also, as youth delegate was Miss Belinda Benson of the Shiloh Church, Englewood, N. J. [17]

According to the roll as noted in the Conference the following also were in attendance: Mrs. Felix S. Anderson. Rev. Louis J. Baptiste, Rev. Elizabeth Green, Mrs. Clinton Hoggard, Mrs. Raymond Jones, Mrs. H. T. Medford, Mrs. C. E. Tucker, and Mr. David P. Wisdom.[18]

---
[15] *Proceedings of the Ninth World Conference* (Methodist) 13.
[16] *Ibid.*, 32, 33.
[17] From Official Listing.
[18] *Proceedings of the Tenth World Methodist Conference, Oslo,* 1961, 21.

More than one hundred members of the Church attended the sessions in London, England, in 1966, so that it is impossible to give a complete listing here.

The Zion Methodist Church has been represented in each and every world gathering of Christians since 1881. Beginning with the Amsterdam Conference, the Church has likewise involved its youth in these world gatherings. Miss Margatet Lewis, Martin L. Harvey and Buford F. Gordon (later Bishop) were among those attending the Amsterdam sessions,[19] Majorie Stiggers, as Youth Council President, was involved in the great Conferences held in India, while at the second such meeting Rena J. Weller as Associate Director of Youth Work and James W. Eichelberger Jr. attended. This session was held in Oslo. Miss Violet Gaskin of Mother Zion Church was also a delegate to this session from the Protestant Youth Council of New York City. Even in the field of scouting, Zion found a place as Ira A. Daves of New Bern and another representative of First Church, Brooklyn attended the World Jamboree held at Moissons, France.

The First Assembly of the World Council of Churches met in Amsterdam, Holland, in 1948. In attendance were: Bishops: B. G. Shaw, W. J. Walls, Dr. D. P. Thomas, Dr. George F. Hall, Mrs. Abbie Clement Jackson, James W. Eichelberger and Reverend J. Clinton Hoggard.[20]

The Second Assembly of the World Council of Churches was held in Evanston, Ill. More than 1,000 Zion Methodist people attended the great gathering in Soldiers Field when upwards of 120,000 people were in attendance. Zion people were also in attendance at the Nineteenth World Conference on Christian Education which met in Tokyo, Japan, August 6-13, 1958. Marian Marsh was the youth delegate.

The delegates to the Third World Conference of Christian Youth gathered in Travancore, India at the close of the year, 1952. Mrs. Majorie Stiggers Lyda (married since her attendance at the conference) was the official representative of Zion Methodism. Because of the lack of records we have not the exact date of meeting held in India at which our official youth delegate was Enoch B. Rochester.

Perhaps the most extensive of the Church in interdenominational

---

[19] *Proceedings of the Thirty-first Quadrennial Session of the General Conference*, 1940, 182. Charles Black was the fourth member of this group.
[20] *Official Journal, Thirty-fourth Quadrennial Session, General Conference*, 1952, 212.

and ecumenical endeavors has been its involvement in the Consultation on Church Union, a venture of at least eight and possibly more denominations leading to eventual union. The Church sent observers to the early sessions in 1962, as the planning groups met in Washington, D. C. Subsequent meetings were held in Obelin (1963), Princeton (1964) and Lexington, Ky. (1965). It was decided that Zion Methodism would become a member of the movement in 1965. Bishop Walls and the Reverend Dr. John H. Satterwhite are the official representatives.

CHAPTER XXI

The Church Through the Years

AT THE suggestion and order of the General Conference the establishment of the Bishops' Meeting was only the forerunner of another major move in 1900 when the recommendation was made that the Connectional Council should be established. The Suggestion appeared as Number 5 on the list and stated:

> We recommend that there be instituted a Connectional Council of the Church to be composed of the Bishops, all of the General Officers and the Presidents, Secretaries and Treasurers of the Boards and Schools whose officers are elected by the General Conference. Said Council shall meet annually. They shall form the Board of Apportionment and make appropriations of the moneys of the following departments: Education, Missionary, Church Extension, Widows and Orphans and Contingencies.

By 1904, the full organization of the Council had been spelled out as the Discipline stated that the President of the Board of Bishops should be the Chairman while the General Secretary of the Church should be the Secretary. The time specified for the meeting should be "once a year at the time and place of the Fall meeting of the Board of Bishops." This, necessarily had to be changed as it interfered with the holding of the Fall Conferences.

This move was merely one of several as the Church endeavored to perfect organization. As early as 1876, for example, the word, "male" was stricken from the Discipline. This occurred in the General Conference meeting in that year in Louisville, Ky. Women preachers who were admitted to "orders" soon followed. In 1884, Bishop James Walker Hood ordained Mrs. Julia A. Foote as a Deacon in the New York Annual Conference.[1] Ten years later the second woman was ordained a deacon by Bishop Alexander Walters at York, Pa., 1894. She was the Mrs. Mary J. Small.

Two ministers were elevated to the Episcopacy in 1888. (It appears that no persons were elected in either 1880 (new) or 1884.) Cicero R. Harris and Charles Calvin Pettey were selected in that year.

---

[1] Cicero R. Harris, *Zion's Historical Catechism for use in Families and Sunday Schools*, (Charlotte, N.C.) 20.

CICERO R. HARRIS

Cicero R. Harris was born in Fayetteville, North Carolina, August 25, 1844. His father died when he was but three years of age. At six, his family moved to Chillicothe, Ohio where he began his education. In 1851 he had a narrow escape from drowning and thereafter considered this a "special manifestation of providential care." In 1854, the family moved to Delaware, Ohio and three years later, removed again to Cleveland, Ohio. He completed the course in Cleveland High School in 1861. Two years later he joined the American Wesleyan Church, the Reverend Adam Crooks, pastor. Returning to Fayetteville, he joined the A.M.E. Zion Church in 1867 and, "under commission of the American Missionary Association" he began to teach. He was licensed to preach in 1872 and joined the North Carolina Conference, thereafter contributing much to the success of the work of Bishop Hood, the establishment of Livingstone College and the Church periodical, *The Star of Zion*. He was ordained a deacon in 1874 and in December of the same year, an elder at Concord, N.C. Reverend Harris served over the years as Business Manager of the *Star of Zion*, General Steward of the Church, General Secretary and Principal of Zion Wesley Institute, being responsible for the removal to Salisbury (of Livingstone College). He was elected and consecrated a Bishop of the Church in 1888 when the General Conference met in New Bern, North Carolina. He served until his retirement, along with Bishop Hood, in 1916. He passed away, in June, 1917.[2] He was the author of the *Centennial Catechism, Historical Catechism* and *Chart Primer*.

CHARLES CALVIN PETTEY

Charles Calvin Pettey was born December 1849 at Wilkesboro, North Carolina. After completing his grade and high school training he entered that which was known as Biddle University (now Johnson C. Smith) at Charlotte, North Carolina. He was not only a preacher but taught school for a great many years as well. He began his ministry around 1871 and was ordained deacon and elder by Bishop James W. Hood. He was elected to the Episcopacy in 1888 and served until December 8, 1900 when he passed away.[3]

---

[2] *James Walker Hood, One Hundred Years of the A.M.E. Zion Church*, 202-207 and other sources.
[3] *Souvenir Program of the Twenty-first Quadrennial Session*, General Conference, 1900, 40.

One would not list the General Conference of 1892 as startling in its work. And yet, it will no doubt go down in history as mainly occupied with the thoughts of Organic Union for it was at this session that the two churches, the A.M.E. and the A.M.E. Zion came closer to union. Elected at this conference were Alexander Walters, and Isom C. Clinton. This was the Conference, which brought into official existence the A.M.E. Zion Quarterly Review, the second oldest periodical of the denomination.

ALEXANDER WALTERS

Alexander Walters was the son of Henry and Harriet Walters, born August 1, 1858 at Bardstown, Kentucky. Here, he attended the public schools for eight years, later attending school in San Francisco, Calif. One writer states that he completed his Theological training in that city but another source states that he completed this work in Indianapolis, Ind., when he joined the A.M.E. Zion Church in that city in 1870. He was licensed to preach in 1877, ordained deacon in 1879 and elder in 1882. He pastored in the South, in California and then the famed Mother Zion Church in New York City. While pastoring here he was selected by the Board of Bishops to represent the denomination at the World's Sunday School Convention in London, England (1889). In 1891, he was likewise a delegate to the Methodist Ecumenical Conference held in Washington, D.C. In 1898, he was elected President of the National Afro-American Council (of which he was founder) an organization dealing with the conditions of Black people. In 1895, he was elected a Trustee of the United Societies of Christian Endeavors. He was elected to the Episcopacy and consecrated a bishop of the Church in 1892. He died February 19, 1917.[4]

ISOM CALEB CLINTON

Reverend Isom Caleb Clinton was one of the outstanding General Stewards of the denomination when this office was of such high importance to the work of the Church. He was born in Lancaster, South Carolina, May 22, 1830, the slave of Irvin Clinton, who was at one time a foremost lawyer at the Lancaster Bar, and one of the leading citizens of upper South Carolina. Unlike many owners of slaves

---

[4] *Quadrennial Souvenir Program, Twenty-first session*, 1900, 41.

of the period, he was never severe in his treatment of slaves and it is said "he never did bar them from gaining knowledge from books." Instead of hindering them he took delight in assisting them. Because of his assistance Isom received a firm foundation in education. During slavery, for example it is stated that "I. C. Clinton was the trusted foreman and confidant of his master and continued to live with him after emancipation, having the chief oversight of his business affairs." Later, Isom acquired property of his own.

Through the aid of his former master he was privileged to open a school on the plantation so that many other Negro boys and girls received a basic education. Through this same former master the A.M.E. Zion Church not only received land and a building for worship but also a school. Many today will recall and know of Mount Carmel Church where, at one time one of the largest camp meetings in the South was held for many years.

Isom Clinton not only aided in the formation of the South Carolina Conference but was one of the first in that area to receive an appointment from Bishop Joseph Jackson Clinton. Through his efforts some 30 churches were established. He was consecrated a bishop in 1892 and died, October 8, 1904. He will be remembered too as the father of Dr. W. D. Clinton who practiced medicine in Wheeling, West Va., and Pittsburgh, Pennsylvania and Presiding Elder F. A. Clinton who served on the Mobile District.[5]

Many persons will look upon the General Conference of 1896 as one of the quiet sessions of the Church. While this was the centennial year of the denomination it was decided to meet in Mobile rather than Mother Zion as several persons had suggested. The total plans for the Anniversary appear not to have been realized as only here and there do we see results of it. No doubt the Publishing House is the one exception to this thinking.

Elected to the Episcopacy were John Holliday, John B. Small, and George Wylie Clinton.

JOHN (JEHU) HOLLIDAY

John or Jehu Holliday was born in Columbia County, Ohio, December 25, 1827. He was converted in November, 1860 and joined the church under the Rev. Joseph Armstrong who did pioneer work

---

[5] *The Church Quarterly*, 1891, later known as the *A.M.E. Zion Quarterly Review*, ed. by George W. Clinton.

for the church in that area. He joined the Allegheny Conference in 1861, was ordained a deacon in the morning and an elder at night, in 1862. The bishop of the area at the time was Joseph Jackson Clinton, then known as a Superintendent. Reverend Holliday pastored several of the older churches of the Conference, our personal recognition being the matter of seeing his picture hanging in the village (Zion) Church of Bedford, Pa. as one of the former pastors. He was consecrated a Bishop in 1896 and served until March 2, 1899 when he passed away.[6]

JOHN BRYAN SMALL

John Bryan Small was born, March 14, 1853 in St. Josephs Parish, Barbadoes, British West Indies. In another section of this book we have mentioned his early life and training, culminating with his work in West Africa. He was taught in early life by his half-sister and later entered St. John Lodge on the recommendation of Bishop Perry of the Church of England. He completed the course, graduating at the head of a class of 56 after four years study. Four years later he completed the work outlined at Codrington College (B.W.I.) as an honor student. In 1871, on his way to England he came by the United States and decided to join the A.M.E. Zion Church (on suggestion). He served as the Secretary of the New England Conference for several years and also served as Presiding Elder. He transferred to the Philadelphia and Baltimore Conference and served as Presiding Elder there as well, being the Presiding Elder of the Author's father. Somewhere in the files of this family is a letter of admonition written by John Bryan Small, which for many years was a cherished possession. So far as is known he was the author of two works: *Psyacticle and Exegetical Pulpiteer* and *Code of the Discipline*. He was consecrated a bishop of the Church in May, 1896 and passed away, January 15, 1915 (see also chapters on Foreign Missions)[7]

GEORGE WYLIE CLINTON

George Wylie Clinton was born in Lancaster County, South Carolina, March 28, 1859, his father dying when he was but two years old. As a result he was reared in the home of his grandparents with whom he and his mother lived until he was sixteen years of age.

His basic education was received in that which was known as a

---

[6] Hood, *loc. cit.*, 542 etc.
[7] *Souvenir of the Twenty-first Quadrennial Session of the General Conference*, 43.

"subscription school" established when the free schools were closed. Here he studied under a West Indies native school teacher who was hired by the Negro people at the time. In 1874 he entered South Carolina University at Columbia which was open to black students at the time. He won here a $200 scholarship for four years. Two years later, in 1876, Wade Hampton became the Democratic party governor of the state and all Negro students were forced to withdraw from the State Institution. George then returned home, taught school for a few years and then registered in Brainard Institute of Chester, South Carolina.

At some time during these years George Wylie Clinton took up the study of law and served as a clerk in the office of C. P. Pelham, Auditor of Lancaster County. In following these studies he became interested as well in the study of the Bible so by 1879 (February 14) was licensed to preach. Leaving the study of law he preached and taught school until 1888 when he was appointed by Bishop Singleton T. Jones to the then most important church west of New York. Here, he entertained the General Conference of 1892.

While in Pittsburgh, George Wylie Clinton became interested in the publishing work and began editing that which was called "The Quarterly." Successfully managing this magazine, he turned it over to the General Conference in 1892 and it became the *A.M.E. Zion Quarterly Review.* Earlier he had edited that which was known as the *Afro-American Spokesman.* The 1892 General Conference placed him in charge of the *Star of Zion.*

A great amount of credit is given George Wylie Clinton for the organization of the Sunday School work in the Church as he is noted as being associated with this work especially around 1905 and 1908. He is listed as Vice President, for example, of Negro Work in this period.

George Wylie Clinton was at one time a lecturer at Tuskegee Institute, President of the Young Peoples Educational and Religious Congress and interested in Christian Endeavor work. One of his major published contributions was "Christianity Under the Searchlight." George Wylie Clinton was consecrated as a bishop in 1896 and died May 12, 1921.[8]

Controversy over the qualifications of the Episcopacy appears to

---

[8] Hood, *loc. cit.,* 268-274; Theodore and Hamilton Flood, ed., *Lives of Methodist Bishops* (New York, 1882) 397.

have entered the thinking of the Church in the last decade of the Nineteenth Century. Several persons wrote on this subject with nothing being done of a concrete nature until after the election of 1900. At that time John Wesley Alstork was elected.

JOHN WESLEY ALSTORK

John Wesley Alstork was born in Talladega, Alabama, September 1, 1852. His education appears to have been secured at Logwood Institute and Talladega College. He joined the A.M.E. Zion Church in 1873, but for some reasons was not converted until 1878 unless the writer of these facts is in error. At any rate it is recorded that he was licensed to preach in that year and joined the Alabama Conference the next, 1879.

In 1882 he was ordained a deacon by Bishop J. P. Thompson and an elder by Bishop J. W. Hodd in 1884. He was elected presiding elder in 1889 and served on the Montgomery District. He was one of the few presiding elders elected to the episcopacy, in recent years.

John Wesley Alstork traveled extensively in Cuba, and at one time suggested that he be assigned to the establishment of the Church there. In 1901, he was a delegate to the Ecumenical Methodist Conference in London England, and spent some time abroad as a result. He was consecrated a bishop in 1900, the only one elected at that time. He died suddenly in July 1920.[9]

In the General Conference of 1904, two individuals were elected to the Episcopacy, John W. Smith and Josiah S. Caldwell.

JOHN W. SMITH

One account of John W. Smith states that he was born, January 27, 1861 in Fayetteville, North Carolina. Another states he was born January 27, 1862.[10] Facts in the accounts appear to agree that he was reared by his grandmother after the early death of his mother. He was converted in a massive event conducted by the Rev. J. W. Davis in 1880, after completing his normal school education in 1878. Three hundred persons were received into full connection June 6, 1880 as a result of this evangelistic campaign.

In 1881 he was admitted into the Central North Carolina Conference on trial. In the same year he was ordained deacon and the

---

[9] *Souvenir Program of the Twenty-first Quadrennial Session*, loc. cit., 58.
[10] Hood, loc. cit., 240; *Souvenir Program of the Twenty-first Quadrennial Session*, 67.

following year, 1882, elder. After serving churches in Louisville, Ky., Baltimore, Md., Washington D. C., Harrisburg and Carlisle, Pennsylvania, he was elected the Editor of the Star of Zion, serving until 1904, when he was elected and consecrated a bishop of the Church. He died October 10, 1910.[11]

JOSIAH S. CALDWELL

There are again two dates given for the birth of another bishop of the Church, Josiah S. Caldwell. Hood declares that he was born in Meckenburg County, North Carolina in August, 1862. Another account states that he was born in Charlotte, North Carolina, August 2, 1861. Bishop Hood states that he was able to attend school but two months a year while another account states that he was able to spend four months a year in school until his sixteenth year. He was converted at the age of nineteen and married at twenty. Meanwhile, by working and saving his money he was able to register at Livingstone College in 1883. He graduated with high honors in 1888. He was ordained a deacon in 1886 and elder in 1888. He was elected and consecrated a bishop of the Church in May, 1904. He served until his death, in 1935.[12]

It will be noted that the elections of 1908 were to see no more additions or replacements on the Board of Bishops until retirement came in 1916. Those placed on the Board in that year were: Martin R. Franklin, George Lincoln Blackwell and Andrew J. Warner.

MARTIN R. FRANKLIN

Martin R. Franklin was born near Macon, Georgia, January 8, 1853. His parents were sold while he was still an infant, separating him from them for the rest of his life. He came North in 1865, after Sherman's army had literally destroyed that part of the South. For a time he resided in Illinois, near Chicago and then, on removing to Washington, D.C. he entered Wayland Seminary there where he studied for two years (1879-1881). While in Washington he joined Asbury Church but on moving to Boston in 1881 he joined Zion Church. He was licensed to preach the same year. Three years later he was a member of the Central North Carolina Conference and began his active ministry as pastor of the church at Laurinburg. By

---

[11] *Ibid.*, and other sources.
[12] Hood, *loc. cit.*, 222, 223. *Souvenir Program of the Twenty-first Quadrennial Conference*, 48, 49.

1896 he was pastor of historic Avery Mission Church, Pittsburgh. He was elected and consecrated a bishop in 1908 and served until May, 1909 when he passed away.[13]

GEORGE LINCOLN BLACKWELL

George Lincoln Blackwell was born in Henderson, North Carolina, July 3, 1861. He was one of eleven children born to Aley and Catherine Blackwell. His father passed away in 1885 and his mother five years later. Subsequently George Lincoln was reared in Granville, County, near Oxford and went to school in that area. He was converted in 1876 and joined the A.M.E. Zion Church. In 1881 he joined the North Carolina Conference and was appointed to Morehead City Circuit. The following year he asked to be relieved of a pastoral charge in order that he might attend Livingstone College. Attending the college, later, Bishop Hood assigned him to the Manchester Circuit in the Central Conference. Again, in 1884, he gave up the active ministry to devote more time to study. George Lincoln Blackwell was the outstanding student of the second class to graduate from this department.

He pastored in New England, studying at Boston University School of Theology, graduating from that institution in 1892. Elsewhere in this work we have listed his work within the denomination prior to his being elected to the Episcopacy in 1908. He passed away in March, 1926.[14]

George Lincoln Blackwell is credited for much progress of the Church in this period, being interested in several areas of the Church's activities.

ANDREW J. WARNER

Andrew J. Warner was born March 4, 1850 in Washington, Ky. He was born in slavery like so many other persons of this period. When he was 13 years of age he ran away from his owners and enlisted in the 27th Ohio Colored Volunteers. At the end of the war he returned to Washington, attending school at night and working during the day. Later, he attended high school in Cincinnati, Ohio. Still later, he attended Wilburforce College.

He was converted in 1870 and licensed to preach in 1875. Two

---

[13] Hood, *loc. cit.*, 597.
[14] *Ibid.*, 245.

years later he joined the Kentucky Conference, pastoring many of the churches in that area. Perhaps one of his most significant achievements was the acquisition of St. John Church in East St. Louis. When Bishop Jones called for men to labor in Arkansas he was one of the volunteers, constructing the building for St. Paul Church, Little Rock. It is said that through his efforts Bishop Jones was able to organize the Arkansas Conference. To his credit is the Logan Temple Church, Knoxville, Tenn., and that which was known as Thompson Temple in Birmingham, Alabama. By 1900 he was pastoring the historic Clinton Chapel Church, Charlotte, North Carolina where he added 500 members. In 1896 he was elected Secretary of the Missionary and Church Extension Departments by the General Conference meeting in that year. He worked hard for organic union in the efforts of 1884 and 1892. The Church long recalled his famous speech in the Auditorium at Asbury Park in 1898. He was elected and consecrated a bishop of the Church in 1908, and passed away May 31, 1920.[15]

MARY JANE SMALL

As one thinks of the outstanding persons of this period of the Church's history the second woman to be ordained a deacon of the denomination should not be overlooked. Mary Jane Small was born in Murfreesboro, Tenn., October 20, 1850. It is said that she was always a lover of the church, even before her conversion as she worked in the Finance Department of the denomination. She later stated that there had been a long ambition in her mind since childhood that of being a missionary to lands and peoples overseas. However, she was not converted until she was 23 years of age.

One of the strange things about her conversion was that she married the then Rev. John B. Small in Bridgeport, Conn., October 23, 1873 while still unsaved. Three days later she was converted.

Mary Jane Small heard the call to preach as early as the opening of the last decade of the 19th century but refused to answer. Finally, January 21, 1892, while signing the Christian Endeavor pledge she surrendered to the summons. She was licensed to preach by Dr. John E. Price, Presiding Elder of the Second District, as it was then called, Philadelphia and Baltimore Conference. The year was 1892. She was

---

[15] *Souvenir Program of the Twenty-first Quadrennial Session*, 1900, 55.

ordained by Bishop Alexander Walters, Sunday, May 19th, 1895. Three years later, in 1898, she was ordained an elder by Bishop Calvin C. Pettey in Baltimore, Maryland, May 23, 1898.[16] For a number of years Reverend Small was confined to a nursing home in Pittsburgh, Pennsylvania. It appears that she died in the vicinity of Pittsburgh.

---
[16] *Souvenir Program of the Twenty-first Quadrennial Session*, 1900, 46.

CHAPTER XXII

The Church Through the Years

NO organization which endeavors to meet constant challenges and seeks to progress ever has smooth sailing. This, naturally, has been so of Zion Methodism. From the outset there were differences of opinion which brought about crises, such as the formation of the second African Chapel, called Asbury, in the City of New York, and the concern over the entrance to the city of Bishop Richard Allen. In a sense, these were minor matters and easily adjusted. The first major controversy came over two items—the matter of the Superintendent, or rather, the Superintendent who was to assist the regularly elected one. The second part of the controversy hinged on the name of the organization—the word *African*. The second situation was not adjusted until the decision of the Lycoming County Court was heard. The first, since so many of the members of the General Conference saw its effect, was finally discarded and all Superintendents were elected with equal rank.

The second half of the Nineteenth Century opened with another controversy concerning the Superintendency. The Reverend Peter Ross had been elected for a four year term but because he could not make a living he sent in his resignation and went back to making shoes.

Superintendent Joseph Jackson Clinton brought the situation before the General Conference of 1864 at its fourth session.[1] A committee to handle the matter was eventually appointed consisting of the Reverends Singleton T. Jones, Abraham Cole, James Walker Hood, Charles Carter and Samson Talbot.[2]

The committee reported on Monday, May 30, 1864. Its report follows:

Report

Your committee appointed to inquire into the nature of the resignation of the Rev. Peter Ross, would submit the following report:

Your Committee do not consider that they have any jurisdiction in the premises, inasmuch as the Constitution of our connection provides:

---
[1] *Minutes of the General Conference of 1864*, 14.
[2] *Ibid.*, 15.

That in the event of a Superintendent ceasing to travel during the interval of the General Conference the Annual Conference shall take action, and finally determine all such cases.

Your Committee are of the opinion that the Rev. Ross is not entitled to a seat in this General Conference, until his case is determined by the Annual Conference according to the rule.

S. T. JONES, *Chairman*
A. COLE
CHAS. J. CARTER
JAS. W. HOOD

When the report was read by the Committee the General Conference raised a question about their interpretation of the law. For some reason the delegation thought that Rev. Ross was before the Committee for examination. He, himself, stated that he was not. In making his statement Rev. Ross aroused the ire of the Committee, especially when he stated that the group had ignored certain facts. He went on to state that while he *forgave* the Committee, he could not *forget* the matter. As a result of this controversy, the Committee requested the opportunity to place in writing their position. The Conference agreed to this.[3] The motion to adopt the report of the Committee was lost.

The Special Committee again reported in the Sixth Session, Tuesday, May 31, 1864. The report follows:

REPORT OF SPECIAL COMMITTEE ON ROSS' CASE
To the Superintendent and General Conference of the A. M. E. Zion Church in General Conference Assembled:

We, your Committee, to whom was referred the investigation of the cause or causes by which the Rev. Peter Ross was induced to publish himself no longer a Superintendent in said Connection, beg leave to report: That we have carefully examined the affairs, and obtained substantially the following:

1. That the said Peter Ross was pecuniarily embarrassed; the field of labor to which he was first assigned after his election to the Episcopal office was well gleaned by his seniors in office, as their due, which is said to have been so decided by the last General Conference. That he has no disposition to beg for his support, and that his salary, while he acted in said capacity, would not amount to more than two hundred dollars, excluding traveling expenses; that on his return home in June of 1863, from the New England Conference, such was his straightened circumstances that he concluded to resign from the superintendency, which he published to the connection through the *Anglo-African*, August 17th, 1863, and purchased a set of shoe-makers' tools to return to his trade, cancel his debts, and thereby prevent

---
[3] *Minutes of the General Conference of* 1864, 19.

scandal and reproach; also, that accidentally, Colonel Nelson Viele, of 14th Rhode Island Heavy Artillery came up with him about Ang., 20th, 1863, and requested him to act as post Chaplain for said 14th regiment while it remained in that region, which he accepted, and was thereby enabled to disembarrass himself.

2. We are of the opinion, that under the circumstances surrounding the case, Rev. Ross is not culpable, and might have continued his position. We therefore consider him a member of this General body.

REV'S. J. D. BROOKS,
J. H. LOGUEN,
G. H. WASHINGTON,
JEPTHA BANCROFT,
JOS. HICKS
Committee

It will be noted, although the Minutes do not mention the change, that this Committee is different from the one first reporting. The report of this Committee was "received and adopted." [4]

Peter Ross thanked the Committee for its work and fairness. Evidently he would have been better off to have said nothing for his statements created a second controversy in which it was even suggested that he be impeached. Superintendent Bishop, who was mentioned in the matter, however, felt that "there was an amicable understanding between him and his associate, and if there had been any difficulty they could settle it themselves." [5] At this juncture the Chairman of the first investigating committee requested the privilege of "making their defense, agreeable to notice already given." This privilege was granted.

The Conference, however, insisted that the Superintendents make a statement which they proceeded to do. Superintendent Bishop "Saying that there was the best of feeling between him and his associate." This statement the Conference accepted. The report of the first Committee appears not to have been drawn up and printed.

The second great confrontation within the Church is dealt with in the Chapter headed: *The General Conferences of 1872 and 1876.*

The Seventeenth Quadrennial Session of the General Conference was called to meet in Mother Zion Church, New York City, May 7, 1884. Incidentally, listed were the delegates to the Centennial of Methodism in Baltimore, Maryland, scheduled for February, 1884. The following were listed: Bishops S. T. Jones, J. W. Hood, and

---

[4] *Minutes of the General Conference of* 1864, 21.
[5] *Ibid.*, 22.

Reverends: G. B. Walker, (Kentucky), George E. Smith, (N.J.), J. C. Price, (N. C. Conf.), J. B. Small (N. C. Conf.), Jehu Holliday (Allegheny), A. Walters, (California), R. S. Rives (Central North Carolina), W. G. Strong (East Ala.), J. H. Anderson (N. E.), J. W. Smith (Phila. and Balto.), Jacob Thomas (N. Y.), J. McH. Farley (Virginia). Along with these delegates were the following lay people: Hon. J. J. Smith (Boston), J. C. Dancy (Tarboro, N. C.), J. T. Williams (Charlotte, N. C.), Charles Jenkins (St. Louis), John H. Butler (Baltimore), and E. V. C. Eato (New York City).[6]

The most significant of trials within the Church occurred at this session. The Board of Bishops intimated that which might transpire as they listed in their message the matters which had handicapped or hindered the progress of the denomination. Among them were suggested the financial system and "the publicly-tarnished and shamefully damaging reputation and character of one of our highest functionaries, one sharing with us the honored and fearful trust, the awful responsibility of a Bishop of the A.M.E. Zion Church."[7]

The Address went on to state that the Bishop in question had been responsible for remarks and rumors in the first two years following the rise of the last General Conference (1880). The Board declared: "His colleagues were met in every section, alike by ministers and laymen, by friends and foes, and confronted by what were no longer regarded as mere rumors, but what were rehearsed in detail as facts." They went on to state that they had tried counseling with the Bishop to no avail. Reluctantly, they had decided to investigate some of the minor charges. They further stated that "No event has ever transpired in the history of our Episcopal existence that has been attended with such demoralizing effects."

The above did not end their statement on the matter for they went on to declare that the situation was a distinct hindrance to the progress of the denomination. "No greater hindrance to our progress, no fouler stain upon our connectional name, no greater reflection upon our ecclesiastical choice, judgment and selection, no more alarming exhibition of either our ignorance or our disregard of the law of our church, no instance of a more general loss of reverence and respect

---

[6] *Daily Proceedings of the Seventeenth Quadrennial Session of the General Conference*, (New York, 1884) 6.
[7] *Daily Proceedings of the Seventeenth Quadrennial Session* (1884) 28.

for the time-honored usages of Methodism has ever resulted from any example as has resulted from this:" [8]

The Message was read the third day of the Conference and immediately after its reading Reverend L. J. Scurlock moved that the matter of Bishop W. H. Hillery be taken up. With the acceptance of the motion by the General Conference, the review of the facts began, a matter which should occupy the attention of the sessions for most of the time of the sitting.

The opening statement appears to have been made by Bishop James Walker Hood, who described in detail some of the allegations against Bishop Hillery, as well as denying that charges filed against him (Hood) had been legally drawn. One of the accusations against Bishop Hillery was the supposed sale of appointments. It appears that a second charge was immorality. Bishop Hood had proceeded to California to look into conditions and received from the hands of one George F. Norton, a member of the San Francisco Church (then styled, Starr King Church) the following:

> First. I charge him with drinking whiskey at a public grocery bar, at the corner of   and Union Streets.
> Second. I charge Bishop Hillery with owing a bill of groceries at the same place.[9]

Bishop Hood went on to state that "Old Mrs. Catherine Hinds has the Bishop's bill posted in sight, with Bishop Hillery's name attached to it. Mrs. Hinds has made a sworn statement of the fact before a notary public and signed it herself." Later he intimated that Bishop Hillery had been accused of *drunkenness.* He stated that he had suggested to Bishop Hillery on his (Hood's) return to Kentucky that if Hillery mended his ways he would "do all I can for you."

Bishop Hood was a candid speaker as he stated: "The minutes of the California Conference were published without alluding to him. I invited him to sit with me at the Allegheny Conference. He was sober all that week; refused to drink wine at an entertainment, and I really thought he was cured. However, he did not come to the Allegheny Conference, and when he came to the Kentucky Conference he came rushing up to me saying, "What is against me here? I told him I could not help trying the charges, but reminded him I

---

[8] *Ibid.,* 29.
[9] *Daily Proceedings of the Seventeenth Quadrennial Session,* 37.

had said I would do all I could for him, if he would quit drinking and added, but you are drunk now. He said, I came down on the train late last night. I would not have drank anything if I had not had to lie out on the river bank." [10]

It appears that the first charge against Bishop Hillery, that regarding the acceptance of money for appointments, was not sustained in the Kentucky Conference.[11] This charge appeared to hinge around the giving of eighty dollars to the Bishop at the hands of Elder Warner. The statement was made that Bishop Hillery "exacted exhorbitant amounts for traveling expenses. Bishop Hillery said it was general fund. Elder Warner said it was not."

The affidavit signed by Mrs. Hinds was then taken up by the Special Judicial Committee. The Proceedings of the General Conference stated: "The affidavit was then read, stating that Bishop W. H. Hillery was in the habit of taking drinks at her bar, of going behind the counter and helping himself to whisky, paying for the same, and that he was then in debt to her for groceries and liquor sold and delivered to him. Signed before Thomas Murphy, Notary Public. Then followed the affidavit, made by John E. Merritt, Samuel Hargo, and Samuel E. Freeman, showing that they had examined the books of Mrs. Hinds, and found entries showing that drinks were very frequent (giving the dates), charged against Bishop Hillery, while in San Francisco." [12]

Both the books of Mrs. Hinds and the affidavits were forwarded to the Kentucky Conference and were available at the trial. The Judicial Committee met and after hearing the evidence as presented voted that the charges against Bishop Hillery had not been sustained. The next day, the Annual Conference heard the report of the Committee but evidently took no action. Bishop Hood stated that as the Committee voted on the question Bishop Hillery was writing down the names of the men. In his judgment, since the Annual Conference did not take action on the Committee's action the law allowed the Chairman to dissent and carry "the matter to the quarterly Conference" where accusations were brought against a member. As Chairman, therefore he felt it his right and duty to carry the matter to a higher court, which in this case, was the General Conference.

---

[10] *Daily Proceedings of the Seventeenth Quadrennial Session*, 1884, 38.
[11] *Ibid.*, 38.
[12] *Ibid.*, 39.

It should be stated that two other charges were mentioned in the session of the General Conference, that of rape and immorality. We utilize the word "mentioned" as this writer is not clear as to the full province of the General Conference. It would seem that the body had the right to consider W. H. Hillery *unfit* to serve in the Episcopal office but there its basic function would cease. It appears that this was recognized in the action of the General sessions. A close look at the entire action is vitally necessary, however, appearing, as it does to many as hesitating.

The statement of two members of the Kentucky Conference is important in the matter even though one is inclined to believe "pressure" may have been used against some or all of the members of the Conference. It follows:

> Inasmuch, as the majority of this Conference have voted that the charges preferred against Bishop Hillery had not been sustained. Inasmuch as we believe that it is contrary to the discipline and usage of the Methodist Church to allow the counsel for the church the right of appeal, as we believe such right to be reserved solely to the accused. Therefore, the attempt of the counsel for the church in the aforesaid case, to make appeal to the General Conference is in our opinion, illegal and without precedent, and therefore cannot effect the standing of the defendant.
>
> J. E. PRICE
> A. J. WARNER[13]

Elder Warner attested to the correct nature of the document and then went on to state that "The Kentucky Conference, all the members thereof, understood that it was an executive session. It was so regarded in the minutes. It was composed of all the members in full connection. Whether you call it a judicial committee, or whatever you may name, it was the Kentucky Conference, composed of the only members who had the right to act in its name, and they did vote *pro* and *con* in this case." [14]

The question of jurisdiction in the Hillery case appears to have bothered many of the outstanding leaders of the period as careful note of the minutes of the period will prove. The Conference, after prolonged discussion, went into Executive Session. Several matters were agreed to—first, for example, that the case reached the General Conference through the presiding officer of the Kentucky Con-

---
[13] *Daily Proceedings of the Seventeenth Quadrennial Session,* 72.
[14] *Proceedings of the Seventeenth Quadrennial Session,* 72.

ference rather than through the Annual Conference itself. A second item which appears to have been acknowledged is that the General Conference had jurisdiction only in the area of Bishop Hillery serving as a Bishop. By the fifth day of the session the Board of Bishops acknowledged that "it is of the opinion of the bishops, however, that this General Conference cannot investigate the conduct, nor *try* the person before us." They went on to state that "you have authority over his Episcopal functions, but not beyond that." [15]

Bishop Hillery, after the statement of the Board offered the following:

> Mr. Chairman, I desire to present the following:
> To the officers and members of the Seventeenth General Conference of the A. M. E. Zion Connection in America. Take notice that I here tender my resignation as bishop, to take effect immediately."

It will be noted that in preceding General Conferences a special Committee had reported on the character of the Bishops prior to their re-election. At the instance of Bishop Singleton T. Jones (see elsewhere in this work we have listed this statement) the practice had been discouraged. In this matter a great amount of hard feeling would have been avoided had the Committee been activated. Incidentally, one must raise the question as to where characters of the Bishops are examined. In the case of ministers and General Officers this is done in the Annual Conference. While Bishops do have a "home" Conference, it is not understood that the character of a bishop is *passed* at the time of that of other persons.

Bishop Harris stated that the resignation of Bishop Hillery had come too late. He declared "Had he offered his resignation before we had gone into this matter, before it had been laid before this Conference, I should have been more in favor of accepting it. But we have heard the statements for and against Bishop Hillery, and I think it is too late to accept the resignation. It is my conviction that we ought to proceed at once—and if I had obtained the floor, I would have made the motion that we immediately proceed to try Bishop Hillery for conduct unworthy of a bishop." [16]

The motion to accept the resignation was laid on the table.

Several of the members of the General Conference appeared against the motion which was finally passed—that the Bishop be

---
[15] *Ibid.*, 75.
[16] *Daily Proceedings of the Seventeenth Quadrennial Session,* 1884, 75.

removed as a member of the Episcopacy and that the entire matter of trial be returned to the Kentucky Conference. It appears that the objection was not to the first idea but rather to trial and referral. J. C. Dancy moved to strike out *Kentucky* and insert New York since Bishop Hillery lived there. Elder Biddle wanted the whole matter turned over to a special Committee in the light that the Kentucky Conference had already voted action. Bishop Hood insisted that the Kentucky Conference had not acted. In the final analysis the "previous question" (that "Bishop Hillery, by this General Conference, be defunct of the office of Bishop, and that he be sent to the Kentucky Conference for the trial of his Christian character.") was called for and sustained with the change that Bishop Hillery would be tried by the Genesee Conference. As many of the men did not vote, several were individually *polled* by Bishop Hood, Elder Biddle, Mark M. Bell were among those who voted against the motion. The final vote stood 120 for and five against. The records were therefore sent down to the Genesee Conference for action.

Several questions naturally were raised by this affair. As one looks back into the account one does wonder about the idea of "Double Jeopardy." Certainly the case had a great deal to do with the issuance of the two interpretations of the discipline, one by Singleton T. Jones and the other by John Bryan Small. The question in the minds of posterity is not the eventual guilt or innocence of Bishop Hillery but rather the modes utilized and, in a sense, the evidences of several insincere statements on the part of the leaders of the Church.

It should be noted that great segments of early disciplines were given over to the protection and rights of the membership of the Church, and this included that of the ministry. The Church must always remember its emphasis on *grace* and it cannot exist without the *grace* of God. At the same time it cannot exist without the exhibition of *grace* on its part. It has the duty and right to promote action which accomplishes its mission, but having so acted, it must assume a position of willingness of *grace*. In all too many controversies this has been lacking. Violations of Christian conduct are not limited to personal ideologies. If one sin hinders, all matters considered sinful or unacceptable to the Church must be approached in the same manner. To do other than this is to move away rather than closer to the spirit of Jesus Christ.

THE PRESIDING ELDER SYSTEM

Just when the Presiding Elder system began and where in Zion Church is not known. As early as 1848 some beginnings along this line are noted in Zion Methodism. The precedent for such an arrangement could have come down through the original system of Methodism in New York City where, because of the lack of elders, John Street Church had that which was called "The Ruling Elder." Under him, *naturally*, would be the preachers of the Chapels who, evidently, carried on the functions of the Church as they had authority. In 1848 (Conference Minutes) the designations appear to follow out this system. For example: Pittsburg Circuit, Jacob Trusty, in his charge Isaac Coleman, William Burley. Bedford Circuit, Shadrach Golden. Lewistown Circuit, Joseph Sinclair, in his charge, Peter Fulman, Charles J. Carter. Chambersburg Circuit, Basil Mackall, in his charge, Jesse Boulden. Harrisburg Circuit, Solomon T. Scott, in his charge, John B. Cox, York Circuit, Moses Gale, in his charge, Jacob P. Hamer. Newtown Circuit, Nelso H. Turpin.[17] The appointment of the stations were as follows: Alleghany, David Stevens, Washington, Joseph Jackson Clinton, Baltimore, John J. Moore, Wilmington, Abram Cole, Philadelphia, George Gelbreth and Burlington and Timbucto, under the supervision of Edward Johnson.

The same pattern is noted in the New York Annual Conference of that period. For example, Flushing Circuit, L. I. J. C. Spence, in his charge Richard Carman. Jerusalem Circuit, E. H. Bishop, in his charge, B. Hambleton. Newburg Circuit, John Dungy, in his charge, R. Eastep. Poughkeepsie Circuit, S. Talbot, in his charge George Washington, H. Hicks, James Davis. Syracuse Circuit, J. W. Loguin, in his charge, William H. Decker, C. Booha, Ed H. Goodman. Bath Circuit, John Tappan, in his charge Francis Thompson. Rochester Circuit, John A. Williams. George Garnett is left without an appointment.

It is interesting to note also that this session of the New York Conference stated that when a minister requested permission to be left without a charge that he likewise must cease to function as a deacon or elder for the time of his inactivity.[18] A second interesting matter were the requirements for the ministry; or Holy Orders: A consistent

---
[17] *Minutes of the Philadelphia Annual Conference*, 1848, 18.
[18] *Minutes of the New York Annual Conference*, 1848, 22.

knowledge of the English language; A consistent knowledge of the "doctrines of our church, as contained in the Discipline and of the Scriptures generally," and that "they point out to the satisfaction of the Conference the difference between Arminianism, Calvinism and Universalism." [19] In the same year the New England Conference, speaking on another subject stated: *"Resolved* that each Circuit and Station furnish a house for the elders and preachers." [20] A close examination of this resolution shows that the Conference meant exactly as was stated for they called attention to the "moving of furniture."

As one follows the extant Minutes we have been able to run across the matter of elder and preachers especially in circuits is to be noted. This is true in Minutes of 1851 and those of 1853.

It appears that the system of Presiding Elders, then, grew out of this arrangement. As the work of the elder increased, especially in the absence of the Bishop (who was expected to travel extensively—some listing as high as 80,000 miles in a four year period) the custom grew to elect from the Annual Conference elders one of the number. The titles were varied. In instances the word "Oversight" is noted. In others the title given was "Presiding Elder." As late as 1880, or even 1884, the system was not denominationally wide for the Discipline of the General Conference of 1884 stated:

> Section I Should the Bishop and Annual Conference decide to adopt the Presiding Elder system, as provided for in Chapter I, Article I, the said Annual Conference shall be divided into a suitable number of districts for that purpose.[20]

The writer is unable to discover the reference of Chapter I, Article I. Revisions made may have changed the intended order. Once the system was established a later General Conference provided that the Presiding Elder should be appointed rather than elected. However this did not come about until after the 1896 General Conference had voted to have the office remain an elective one. Several were interested in the change and many of the Bishops favored appointment rather than election.

The Reverend Owen L. W. Smith attempted the change then he brought the matter to the attention of the Mobile sessions. His

---

[19] *Ibid.,* 22
[20] *The Doctrines and Discipline of the A.M.E. Zion Church in America,* (1886) 67.

efforts were based upon the mode of "other Methodist groups."[21] Despite statements by Prof. J. P. Scott of Harrisburg, Pa.; Reverend S. G. Adams of New York as well as Reverend C. Fairfax of the same Conference and at least one of the Bishops, the General Conference refused to vote for a change. The matter came up at the opening of the Twentieth Century and was accepted.

By 1904 it was no longer a matter of choice as to whether there should be a Presiding Elder as the Discipline stated:

> P. 198. Every Annual Conference shall adopt the residing Elder System, and it shall be divided into a suitable number of districts for that purpose.[22]

It should be noted that by this time also the matter of appointment had been accepted as that accorded to the bishop.

It is unfortunate that the Minutes of the Twenty-fifth and Twenty-sixth Quadrennial sessions were so reduced in content that they are mere outlines of these sessions. A second criticism is the poor quality of paper utilized. This is true also of the 1924 Minutes. Echos are still had by word of mouth concerning the controversy over retirement in 1916. It was merely the beginning of a struggle over retirement which should bring the Church face-to-face with this question in 1944, 1952, 1960, 1964 and in 1968. In this last year a law was passed stating that there would be no recall but that a bishop would serve to the General Conference nearest his seventy-sixth birthday. At that time retirement would not be a matter of decision for the General Conference but would be automatic.

The matter of retirement had been debated throughout the denomination for the years following the General Conference sessions in 1912. The 1916 sessions therefore met in the midst of tension. The report of Bishop James Walker Hood was read by his daughter before the Twenty-fifth session as it met in Louisville, Ky. The Conference took note of the progress made in the Episcopal area while the full report was listened to with "marked attention." [23] A few days later, one of the most powerful of sermons was preached by Bishop Cicero R. Harris and much rejoicing was heard.

Following the Bishops' reports, the Reverend James Edward Mason called the Conference's attention to the fact that an effort was

---

[21] *Minutes of the Twentieth Quadrennial Session*, 1896, Mobile, 96, 97.
[22] *The Doctrines and Discipline of the A.M.E. Zion Church*, 1905, 119.
[23] *Minutes of the Twenty-fifth Quadrennial Conference*, Louisville, 1916, 5.

made in the 1912 General Conference to eliminate the Bishops' reports. On investigation it was noted that a Committee to consider this matter had been appointed.[24]

A new resolution was subsequently offered by Dr. Mason on this subject. It was referred. He likewise offered a second resolution limiting the period over which a bishop could preside over a given area.[25]

As one looks back at the scanty records noted a question arises concerning the decision of Dr. William Harvey Goler who announced that he wished to be relieved of the presidency of Livingstone College. Evidently his decision was made prior to the settlement of the retirement situation.

An interesting angle appears to have developed as the Conference made its decision on the number of bishops to be elected *before* deciding on retirement. The results of the election on the number of bishops appeared to be (for two) 157; (for four) 193.[26]

On May, 11th, one day after this vote, Dr. W. D. Clinton offered a motion providing for the retirement of Bishop James Walker Hood and Bishop Cicero R. Harris. His motion was supported by the Reverend A. P. Petty. In the resultant controversy it was finally agreed that each side would be accorded one hour for debate of the issue. It is not clear as to whether the statements of Bishops Hood and Harris were a part of this time allocation, however. One of the most ardent spokesman for retirement, it is alleged, was the Reverend Dr. J. J. Smyer. The resultant balloting showed 168 against retirement and 187 for. Bishops Hood and Harris were therefore retired.[27]

Elected to replace Bishops Hood and Harris and fill the two additional places were: Lynwood Westinghouse Kyles, Robert Blair Bruce, W. L. Lee and George C. Clement.

LYNWOOD WESTINGHOUSE KYLES

Lynwood Westinghouse Kyles, the son of Burrell and Mary Kyles was born in a small village called Ivey Depot, in Albemarle County, about seven miles from the county seat, Charlottesville, Virginia. He received his early training in a log cabin country school house. He

---

[24] *Ibid.,* 6.
[25] *Minutes of the Twenty-fifth Quadrennial Session,* 6.
[26] *Ibid.,* 14.
[27] *Ibid.,* 17.

worked on the farm seven months during the year for twenty-five cents a day, and thus he was able to buy his shoes and clothes for the winter and the things needed for his schooling.

At the age of fourteen, having listened to an address by a Baptist minister on education, he was moved to better prepare himself for a more useful life. Thus in September of the same year he entered Hampton Normal and Industrial Institute where he worked in the wheelwright and Blacksmith shop until he had finished his trade. Then he went to Paterson, New Jersey and worked at his trade for a while. He removed to Somerville and later Flemington, New Jersey, where he had charge of a large Wheelwright and Blacksmith shop. While here he married Jennie V. Smith, from which union two sons and one daughter were born.

Later, he moved to Ridgewood, New Jersey where he connected himself with the A. M. E. Zion Church and served as Sunday School teacher, class leader, trustee and Superintendent of the Sunday School. It was during his activities in this church that he became conscious of his call to the ministry, and readjusted his life to fully accept his new task.

Shortly after the realization of his call he was licensed as an exhorter in the Ridgewood (Metropolitan) A. M. E. Zion Church on the Third Sunday of September, 1895, and a local preacher on the 17th of September of the same year. He was asked to take charge of the Mission at Bethlehem, Pa., but refused because he felt that he did not have adequate experience for the task.

He was recommended to the New Jersey Annual Conference which was held at Trenton, New Jersey, the latter part of April, 1896, and was appointed to the church at Englewood. In 1897, he managed to enter Lincoln University (Penna.) where he took both College and Seminary work, pastoring Media, Pa. and, at the end of his Junior Seminary year, John Wesley in Washington, D. C. In 1901 he was awarded the A. B. Degree and in 1904, he received his S. T. B. degree from Lincoln. Other churches served were Center Street, Statesville, N. C.; Goler Memorial, Winston-Salem, Big Zion, Mobile, Ala. In 1908, he married Luella M. Bryant, his first wife having died in 1905. To this union two daughters and two sons were born. She passed away in St. Louis, Mo. in 1922. Reverend Kyles pastored Big Zion for six years and in that time added 1600 members to the church. He served at two different times as a General Officer, the first as Secretary-Treasurer of the Ministerial Brotherhood and Relief, appointed to that office by the Board of Bishops and then in 1912, after having served as Associate Editor, he became Editor of the A. M. E. Zion Quarterly Review. From these two joint officers he was elected to the Episcopacy in 1916. He died in Winston-Salem, July 8, 1941. His wife, Mrs. Josephine (Humbles) Kyles and two additional children also survive.

BISHOP ROBERT BLAIR BRUCE

Robert Blair Bruce, long-time Editor of Church School Literature for the A. M. E. Zion Church was born June 26, 1861 in a place called Charlie Hope, Brunswick County, Virginia. He received the major part of his education in Petersburg, Virginia. He was converted in Charlie Hope, Virginia and joined the A. M. E. Zion Church. He was licensed to preach in 1884 by the Virginia Conference and ordained Deacon and elder at Petersburg, Va., and Charlotte, North Carolina. At one time he was Dean of the Theological Seminary at Livingstone College. He died July 9, 1920.

BISHOP W. L. LEE

It does not appear that we have a full account of Bishop Lee's life. He was born, evidently, August 8, 1866, was consecrated bishop in May, 1916 and died July 9, 1927.

BISHOP GEORGE C. CLEMENT

George C. Clement was born, December 23, 1871 in Mocksville, North Carolina. He was educated in the public schools of that area and later attended Livingstone College where he met his future wife, Emma Clarissa, who later became the Mother of the Year in 1946 (Golden Rule Society election). Reverend George entered the ministry September 18, 1888 and was ordained a deacon in 1893. Two years later he was ordained an elder. He purchased the property of Broadway Temple, Louisville and for a time published a Zion Methodist paper. He was a public school teacher for several years and later became Editor of the Star of Zion, the Church weekly. He was elected to this office May 20, 1904. In 1916, he was consecrated a bishop of the Church and served until 1934, when he passed away. To our knowledge, all of his children attended Livingstone College in the footsteps of their father and mother, many of them graduating from the College and at least two from the Seminary.

Three of these children have been outstanding in the Church, Rufus, one-time Dean of the College and later President of Atlanta University, Abbie Clement Jackson, President of the Woman's Home and Foreign Missionary Society, after serving eight years as its executive Secretary and James, who taught in the Seminary and served as a Chaplain in the United States Army. At present he is pastoring, as his brother Rufus has done, in the Church.

In 1920, the General Conference convened in historic Logan Temple Church, Knoxville, Tennessee. Elected to the Episcopate at this session were: John W. Wood and Paris Arthur Wallace, E. D. W. Jones.

JOHN WESLEY WOOD

John Wesley Wood was born in Tolbert County, Georgia, May 10, 1865. He was the son of Isom B. and Amanda (Tignor) Wood. In 1891 (February 10) he married M. Janice Edmond to which union was born five children.

Bishop Wood was educated at La Grange Academy, Georgia, completing the work there in 1882. He then attended Morris Brown College in Atlanta, Georgia (1896). In 1911 and 1912 he was found studying in the Moody Bible Institute in Chicago. In 1920, he was elevated to the Episcopacy and served until his death, April 18, 1940.

He is the author of Lyrics of Sunshine, published in 1922. It should be stated that prior to his election to the Episcopacy he was Secretary of Foreign Missions for the denomination, having served from the time of his election in 1912 until 1920.

PARIS ARTHUR WALLACE

Paris Authur Wallace was born in Maryville, Tenn., April 17, 1870, according to one account.[28] Another states that he was born in 1869, but he, himself, stated the year 1870. The church will long recall his statement in Detroit in 1944: "I was born April 17, 1870. At the General Conference in Louisville, Kentucky, 1916, the law

---

[28] Flood, *Lives of the Methodist Bishops, loc. cit.,* 111.

fixing the age for retiring a bishop was enacted. I have reached that age."

Paris Arthur Wallace was born in Maryville, Tennessee and after his public school career had the opportunity of attending Maryville, Tenn. College in 1895, before so many schools were closed to Negroes. Three years later he was at Lincoln University (Pennsylvania) studying. He had begun his ministry in his home state in 1894. In 1896 he was ordained a Deacon in St. Louis, Mo. and was ordained an elder at Chambersburg, Pa. in 1897. At one time he pastored the Metropolitan Church, Washington, D. C. and of course that which is now First A. M. E. Zion, Brooklyn, New York. He was elected and consecrated a Bishop in 1920 and passed away, February 21, 1952.

Bishop Paris Arthur Wallace was this writer's first Bishop as he entered the ministry, 1929. Bishop Wallace was the type of prelate who could honestly differ with anyone and yet never hold this difference against him. He was an ardent believer in education, being one of the Early pioneers in Minister's Institutes and Leadership Education Schools. His purchase of the Long Branch House where educational endeavors were held was perhaps one of the earliest of these types of ventures. At the same time Paris Arthur Wallace was world minded aligning himself with every forward looking venture where the church was concerned. Mrs. Ida Wallace who passed away after her husband's death ended a long union to which two daughters were born.

CHAPTER XXIII

Laymen and the Church

ONE OF the major controversies of the Zion Methodist Church has been the interpretation of the part played by its lay people over the years as one follows the full span of her history. For a great part of that time, since the passing away of the original leadership, the subject has been debated pro and con with many attempts at total or partial denial of this phase of development. The great sponsor of the lay thesis was the late Cameron Chesterfield Alleyne, Bishop of the Church, who staunchly declared that this was one segment of our development which could not be overlooked. This writer would suggest setting before clergy and laity alike the facts which seem to bear our Bishop Alleyne's thesis.

It is hard, for example, to ignore, as we have said elsewhere, the fact that preachers were not the ones who applied for the Articles of incorporation, a document still extant for all to note.[1] Here, it will be noted, that Peter Williams and Francis Jacobs were the ones to sign. Both were laymen, even though we can find no obstacle which prevented the preachers (there were three in the city at the time) from filing the application. While the Church has historically suggested that James Varick was the founder, two matters are irrefutable—he did not sign these papers and he was not a preacher at the time of formation.[2] Rush and each of the early writers list only Abraham Thompson, June Scott and Thomas Miller. William Miller was an exhorter.

To accept James Varick as a silent founder may be reasonable, but at the same time we must accept him as a layman, not a preacher, at the time of formation. So the conclusions are unavoidable. Bishop John Jamison Moore, who was close to the period lists Francis Jacobs, William Brown, Peter Williams, Abraham Thompson and June Scott as those who had a meeting with Bishop Asbury. James Varick, however, is mentioned by Superintendent Rush in his work

---

[1] Christopher Rush, *Rise and Progress of the African M.E. Church*, (New York, 1866) 14. Original may be found in Records of the Clerk of the City of New York Lib. No. 1 of the Record of Incorporation of Religious Denominations, 28 (Dated March 9, 1801).
[2] Rush, *loc. cit.*, 10.

(he lists Samuel Pontier, Thomas Miller, James Varick and William Hamilton) as being with this group.

We would call attention to the agreement eventually drawn with the Methodist Episcopal Church. Here again, those signing were not preachers. They included Francis Jacobs, Thomas Sipkins, George E. Moore, George White, George Collins, Peter Williams, Thomas Cook, William Brown and David Bias.

The denomination came on the scene at a time when the entire country was caught up in a war of liberation. People were talking about the Bill of Rights, they were talking against taxation without representation, the rights of the individual, so one can only conclude that these references and contentions spilled over into the thinking of free men and freed men alike as they considered their spiritual existence. At the same time, this thinking had to effect the imaginations of slaves as well. The movement indeed, was not confined to this New World, but the germs of unrest were found in Europe as evidenced by the French Revolution. No one can say therefore, that privileges and rights were conversations of one segment of American society alone.

The first Discipline of Zion Methodism appears to have been drawn up by a special Committee. They met at the residence of William Miller (the exhorter) who would logically be a member of the Committee. Rush states that "they did not do much" in this first meeting but resolved to call "to their assistance John Dungy and Abraham Thompson" for their second session. The reason for the selection of Thompson was "They hoped that Father Thompson would be better satisfied by his being on the Committee to form or select the discipline, as he seemed to be somewhat wavering." George Collins, a layman, was to draw up the preamble. It was he also who placed the discipline in final shape for the printer after the session of September 20, 1820.[3]

One must constantly remind himself that the Stillwell Movement climaxed an early struggle between clergy and lay people when the Methodist Episcopal Church appeared to overlook the world around it as well as the current beliefs in building its ecclesiastical forms. Mother Methodism was progressing down the highway of human dignity but appeared to desire a stopping point. Her enthusiastic fostering of the Great Revival in which she was partially born,

---
[3] Rush, *loc. cit.*, 44.

brought about the freeing of many slaves as well as her early stand on the subject of slavery.

Strange, then, is the wording of her agreement with the African Chapel. She stated for example, all property which might accrue to these African Trustees should be held by them and their successors, duly elected. No white person, according to the agreement, could become a trustee of the corporation—"It is provided that none but Africans or their descendants shall be chosen as Trustees of the said African Methodist Episcopal Zion Church."[4] But only male members could be members of the corporation. Here the clergy of the Mother Church appears to have given to the African Trustees more latitude than they were willing to concede to their counterparts, the white trustees of the churches of the city.

When the great controversy within the Zion Church came in 1852 over the Church name, it was the trustee board of the Williamsport (Pennsylvania) Church which instituted the suit against the Wesleyan wing. Laymen, too were present in the highly significant session of the General Conference of 1864. Listed were Philip Buchanan of Wesley Church, Philadelphia, William Wilson, John Wesley Church, Washington, D. C., George Brooks of Zion Wesley, Washington, D. C., Edward Hill, New Berne, N. C., Plato Gale, Oyster Bay, New York, James T. Butler, Baltimore, Md., John J. Smith, Boston Church, Mass., Mr. Pulpress, Alleghany, Pa.[5]

According to Bishop E. D. W. Jones, laymen first began participating in the sessions of the General Conference in 1852. He states: "In 1852, thus obviating the difficulty of delay in making law by sending actions down to the quarterly Conferences requiring four years to shape before any law became final. This also gave lay members their rights in legislating for the whole connection." [6]

Singleton T. Jones turned again to the lay participation angle when, with a tinge of timidity, he suggested that the Mother Methodist Episcopal Church should make provisions for lay people in the law-making body of the Church. This appears to have had a great deal to do with the failure of Church Unification both with this body and the A. M. E. Church. In the latter case the lay people were very outspoken as they declared that the General Conference

---

[4] Rush, *loc. cit.*, 18.
[5] *Minutes of the General Conference of the A.M.E. Zion Church*, 1864, 8.
[6] E. D. W. Jones, *Comprehensive Catechism of the A.M.E. Zion Church*, 38.

floor gave them their only opportunity to express their feelings on organic union since the rights of speech were limited in the Annual Conference.

One must give the Church credit for a certain degree of liberalism as the Nineteenth Century progressed. Time and again the subject of lay participation was discussed even after the Church established the principle of two laymen from each Annual Conference seated in the General Session.

A high point under this system was reached in 1920 when it is noted that W. D. Clinton was selected to head the powerful Episcopal Committee.[7]

By 1880 the early interpretation of lay rights and privileges were somewhat stabilized. The Discipline of that period states: "Section I. How shall the rights and privileges of the Laity be more permanently and effectually secured?" "Ans. By making it a party through representation in legislating for the better government of the church; therefore each station and each circuit shall have the privilege of sending a lay delegate to the Annual Conference. All such delegates shall be elected by the Quarterly Conference or the members of the circuit or station which they represent, and shall be entitled to a seat in the Conference upon the showing of their credentials, properly authenticated by the officers of the meeting in which they were elected: Provided, that their privileges shall be restricted to making known to that body the wants and wishes of their various charges. Nevertheless, the District Conference, which immediately precedes the meeting of the Annual Conference, may elect not more than three lay delegates, to represent the laity of the district in the next Annual Conference, and the delegates so chosen shall be entitled to all the rights and privileges of other members of the Annual Conference."[8]

As was the case in many instances where there were no District Conferences, the delegates were priviledged to meet on the first day of the Annual Conference and select "a number of representatives equal to one-fourth of all the circuits and stations included in the rights and privileges of other members of the Annual Conference."[9]

The work of the Annual Conference at the time was a broadened

---

[7] *Ibid.*, 77.
[8] *The Doctrines and Discipline of the A.M.E. Zion Church*, 1880, 134.
[9] *Ibid.*, 135.

scope of the present Disciplinary Questions, the Conference beginning with the first question and working through the entire list until it reached the question: Where are the preachers stationed? Among the questions asked was "Number of taxable members?" At the time there was a listing of *poor* members who were not expected to pay general fund.

Perhaps of extreme interest was the work of both the Quarterly Conference and the Leaders' Meeting. These, today, have been abreviated far beyond those of yesteryears.

Surprisingly enough, there was a time, too, when a member in good standing could object to the admittance of a person. There have been statements made that this type of admittance was un-Methodistic but those who are critical should recall the period when this was common practice.[10]

In the Twenty-seventh quadrennial session of the General Conference the Board of Bishops stated:

> The demand for increased lay representation in the Annual and General Conferences is a question which should command our serious consideration at this session of our law-making body. That the laity, as well as the ministry have rights that should be respected, is too obvious for discussion here. The idea of the right of self-determination has gripped the world. Taxation without representation is abhorrent. The restlessness of the laity of our Church is a manifestation of that resistance to the restrictions of individual and community rights so hateful to the American people. The Board of Bishops have not seen fit to make any recommendations regarding this subject at this session of our General Conference.[11]

The Church, however, thought seriously of this matter for the Reverend H. W. Swain offered a resolution on the subject. The same day, Mrs. Missouri Moore submitted a second resolution.[12] Several days later, the Reverends A. C. Cook and T. W. Wallace submitted measures for the Conference's consideration.[13]

The Conference rejected "equal lay representation" but the Revision Committee suggested the following change:

> "Amended to read": Lay delegates shall consist of three delegates from Conferences having five or more ministerial delegates.[14]

---

[10] *The Doctrines and Discipline of the African Methodist Episcopal Zion Church,* 1884, 148.
[11] *Minutes of the Twenty-seventh Quadrennial Session of the General Conference,* A.M.E. Zion Church, 105.
[12] *Ibid.,* 30.
[13] *Ibid.,* 37.
[14] *Ibid.,* 85.

There, the matter rested until four years later.
In 1928, the Bishops stated:

> You will be expected to deal with the question of equal representation. As to the merits of this question as it appears for immediate solution your chief pastors are not agreed, although there is a unanimous desire to be impartial and just with both laymen and clergy. Our Church has led all Methodism in the treatment of lay members, especially in granting equal rights to women. Ours is a democratic Church with a traditional reverence for the heritage of the fathers, and we are confident that after close study and unprejudiced action this General Conference will be true to itself and its constituency on this question.[15]

Accordingly, the Rev. S. W. Hamilton offered a resolution on Equal Lay Representation. The Reverends W. C. and William Anderson submitted resolutions on lay membership. We have no way of knowing the contents of these two resolutions. George Gaines submitted another measure on lay representation as did the Reverends A. C. Cook and R. J. Crockett.[16]

The importance of the question was pointed up in the vote, evidently passed, that "any decision would be registered by secret ballot.[17] The Committee on Revision, through R. F. Fisher, reported recommending "Equal Lay Representation. On motion of the Rev. H. L. Holt with a second by Rev. T. J. Houston the matter was recommended for the working out of details involved in the measure." [18]

The Committee then reported as follows; noting the corrections of Bishop Kyles and Bishop Clement:

> The General Conference shall be composed of ministerial and lay delegates meeting in the same session. Revision of Paragraph 65 was approved upon motion of Rev. T. A. Harvey, seconded by Rev. C. P. S. Harrison to read as follows:
> "The ministerial delegates shall consist of one delegate from every ten pastoral charges up to twenty, and one delegate for every fifteen charges above twenty and two-thirds. Such delegates shall have traveled at least four years from the time he was received into an annual conference of the African Methodist Episcopal Zion Church and is in full connection at the time of the holding of the General Conference. It is provided, however, that no conference will be denied the privilege of at

---

[15] *Official Journal of the Twenty-eight Quadrennial Session of the General Conference*, 1928, 47, 48.
[16] *Ibid.*, 54, 62, 65.
[17] *Ibid.*, 77.
[18] *Ibid.*, 78.

least two ministerial and two lay delegates. All ministerial delegates shall be members of the Annual Conference which elects them at the time of election."

Paragraph 71 was revised to read as follows upon motion of Rev. H. P. Lankford, seconded by W. L. Hamblin: "The lay delegates shall consist of one layman for each minister elected by the Annual Conference and must have been a member of the African Methodist Episcopal Zion Church for four years and must be twenty-one years of age, and such lay delegate shall be a member of the A. M. E. Zion Church residing in the territory of the Annual Conference in which he or she is elected.

Upon motion of Rev. T. A. Harvey seconded by Rev. W. M. Anderson, Paragraph 73 was revised to read as follows: "The electoral college shall be composed of one layman from each circuit or station within the bounds of the Annual Conference. Upon assembling the electoral college shall organize by electing a chairman and secretary of their own number. Such laymen composing the lay college to be chosen by the Third Quarterly Conference preceeding the assembling of the Annual Conference. The electoral college shall meet the year preceeding the sitting of the General Conference at the time and place of the Annual Conference. At the Annual Conference at which delegates are elected to the General Conference, the District Conference cannot send up representatives but the delegates must come from each circuit or station."

Paragraph 83 was revised to read as follows: on motion of Rev. H. D. Tillman, seconded by Rev. M. C. Glover: "The following persons are members of the General Conference: The regularly elected ministerial and lay delegates from the Annual Conferences of the African Methodist Episcopal Zion Church. (Bishops and General Officers are to be accorded the privilege of the floor but will not have the power to vote, except that the Bishop may vote on the day he presides) .[19]

So thus, equal lay representation came to the denomination and the people of the Church sat with companionate responsibility in the highest law making body of the organization. New areas had to be achieved, however, as questions were asked and answered in the succeeding years. To what extent does equal representation go? Certainly this is to be applied in the lesser committees of the Conferences, including the all-important ones of budget and finance. In the General session, the precedent has already been set where the Episcopal Committee is concerned as Dr. Clinton rose to the chairmanship of this powerful group as early as 1920.

It will be noted too, that the Woman's Home and Foreign Missionary Society quietly widened its doors in a departure from the

---

[19] *Official Journal of the Twenty-eighth Quadrennial Session of the General Conference,* 88, 89.

original concept of executive officers. This has been true in the General Officer personnel of the denomination itself. A new definition remains, it is believed in the strict interpretation of laymen and women. Is the clergyman's wife to be considered eligible under these present rules as a lay person, or, is she so closely related to the ministerial role that she becomes *clergy* in her thinking?

Twenty years after the acceptance of Equal Lay Representation in the General Conference that body approved the establishment of a Laymen's Council in the denomination. The proposition called for the setting up of Councils on every level, the local church, the district, the annual conference and the denomination. The opening statement is explanatory of the purpose:

> Par. 547 The General Conference of the A. M. E. Zion Church directs that there shall be a Layman's Council for the purpose of deepening the spiritual life of the Laymen of the Church, to assist the ministers in promoting the interest of the Church, to dissiminate information and cultivate denominational loyalty, to expand the denomination through education and evangelism and to promote any other interest of the Kingdom of God. The Laymen's Council shall be under the control of the Board of Lay Activities, which Board shall be appointed by the Board of Bishops.[20]

The General Conference ordered the Laymen's Committee "to bring to the next session of the General Conference its Constitution and By-Laws for adoption by said General Conference." [20] The Committee complied and reported the Constitution to the Brooklyn general Conference (1952).[21]

---

[20] *Official Journal of the 33rd Quadrennial Session,* 1948, 291, 292.
[21] *Official Journal of the 34th Quadrennial Session,* 1952 396-398.

CHAPTER XXIV

These Concluding Years

THE Church will recall with a sense of vividness the era ushered in by the General Conference of 1924 as the General sessions met in Indianapolis, Indiana. There was, as has been noted, the crisis in Foreign Missions and then the election of five bishops, the largest number ever elected to the bench in any one session. In 1856, four Superintendents were selected and in 1916 the same number of bishops were consecrated. Those selected in 1924 were: Benjamin Garland Shaw, Edward D. W. Jones, William Jacob Walls, John W. Martin and Cameron Chesterfield Alleyne.

BENJAMIN GARLAND SHAW

Benjamin Garland Shaw was born in Pope Mississippi, August 26, 1878, the son of Charles and Bridget Shaw. He was educated at Philander Smith College, Little Rock, Arkansas and received degrees from the Louisville Medical College (1907) and Livingstone College (1911). He began his active ministry in 1898, and continued in the traveling ministry as pastor and evangelist until his election to the bishopric in 1924.

Bishop Shaw held charges in Cotton Plant Miss., Payne Chapel, Little Rock, Ark., Hood Temple, Evansville, Ind., and Washington Metropolitan Church, St. Louis, Mo. In his last church significant success of lasting merit was achieved.

In 1920 Bishop Shaw was made the Director of the Bureau of Evangelism. He held this position until his election to the episcopacy in 1924. He died April 14, 1951.[1]

WILLIAM JACOB WALLS

William Jacob Walls was born in Chimney Rock, Rutherford County, North Carolina, on May 8, 1885, the son of Edward and Hattie (Edgerton) Walls and the grandson of John and Patsey Edgerton. He was educated at Allen Industrial School of the Methodist Episcopal Church, Asheville, North Carolina and attended Livingstone College, Salisbury, North Carolina, receiving his A.B.

---
[1] *The A.M.E. Zion Quarterly Review* LIX No. 3, 1949, 101.

degree in 1908 and his D.D. in 1913. He studied at Columbia University where he majored in journalism and philosophy. In 1939 he received his A.M. degree from the University of Chicago, having studied under Dr. W. C. Bower and many others.

Bishop Walls began his public ministry as a boy evangelist on September 10, 1889, and preached in practically every section of the country. He pastored at Cleveland, N.C. from 1905 to 1907; Lincolnton, N.C., 1908-1913 and Broadway Temple Church, Louisville, Ky., where he built the present church structure, from 1913 to 1920. In 1916, he entertained the General Conference of the denomination in this Church.

On leaving Broadway Temple, he was elected Editor of the *Star of Zion,* the weekly denominational newspaper. He placed this paper on exchange with leading religious journals and tripled its circulation. He was elected to the bishopric in 1924.

The activities of Bishop Walls have been many and varied. He has always taken an interest in the affairs of the Church from an interdenominational standpoint. In 1928, he was the fraternal messenger to the General Conference of the Methodist Episcopal Church in session at Kansas City, Mo. As early as 1918, however, he had been our Fraternal Messenger to the Methodist Episcopal General Conference, South as it met in Atlanta, Georgia. He has been a member of the Ecumenical Methodist Conference several times. He has also been interested in the work of the World Council of Churches as well as the National Council. He likewise has been vitally concerned with the work of the International Council of Christian Endeavor. He was retired by the General Conference of 1968 after having been recalled in 1960, and 1964.[2] Bishop Walls is married to the former Miss Dorothy Jordan.

JOHN WILLIAM MARTIN

In that class of 1924 five men of different temperament were elected. John W. Martin was known as the philosopher of the group. Few people in the A.M.E. Zion Church will ever forget his unique way of telling fundamental truths and great principles. Born, June 30, 1879, in Russell County, Virginia, near Lebanon, much of his keen philosophy for which he was known, was inherited from his mother Nancy. His father, Cornelius, was an industrious man who

---

[2] *The A.M.E. Zion Quarterly Review,* LIX, No. 3, 102.

worked hard to take care of twelve full brothers and sisters of John William, as well as three half-sisters and one half-brother. A coincidence is that his mother's maiden name was Martin also. Nancy Martin proved to be an excellent director of destiny for her children and soon after her marriage and the birth of their children insisted upon the family moving from Virginia to Johnson City, Tenn., "Where," she said, "my children can get schooling."

John William Martin attended Langston High School, Johnson City, Tenn., and after graduation matriculated at Lincoln University, Pennsylvania, taking both the college and seminary work there. Later, after being made a bishop of the Church, he spent two years in Post-Graduate study at the University of Southern California at Los Angeles, Cal.

John Martin pastored churches St. Mark Church (Now Walters Chapel) Indianapolis, Ind., and other places. While in Indianapolis, Bishop George W. Clinton insisted that he become head of Atkinson College in Madisonville, Ky. In 1916, he became Secretary of Education. He was elected a bishop eight years later. Bishop Martin passed away October 16, 1955.[3]

EDWARD D. W. JONES

Elected the second Bishop in that class of five in 1924 was the son of Bishop Singleton T. Jones, E. D. W. Jones. He was born September 11, 1871 and received his early education in the schools of Washington, D. C. Later, he attended Livingstone College. He was converted at the college as a student in 1887. As a member of John Wesley Church, Washington he was licensed to preach in 1891 and joined the Western North Carolina Conference in 1892. The following year, 1893, he was ordained a deacon and an elder in 1894. By this time he was located in Tennessee and therefore was ordained at Athens.

Bishop Jones will be remembered as the editor of the Comprehensive Catechism which has proved a very valuable work in these latter years. He evidently had planned to publish a full history of the denomination but did not live to accomplish this. He died in 1935.

---

[3] *The A.M.E. Zion Quarterly Review, loc. cit.,* 104-105.

CAMERON CHESTERFIELD ALLEYNE

Cameron Chesterfield Alleyne was born September 3, 1880 in Bridgetown, Barbadoes, British West Indies. He was the son of Robert Henry and Amelia (Clarke) Alleyne. He was educated at Naprima College, Port Au Spain, Trinidad, B. W. I., having matriculated there between 1889 and 1903. He attended Tuskegee Institute in Alabama in 1903-1904 and received his A.M. degree from Livingstone College in 1915. Howard University honored him with a degree in 1924 (D.D.) and Wilburforce did the same in 1942.

Cameron Chesterfield Alleyne was ordained deacon in 1904 and an elder the following year. He pastored some of our most important churches among them being: Anniston, Alabama, St. Elmo, Tenn., John Wesley, Washington, D.C., Providence, Rhode Island, Grace Church, Charlotte, N.C. and New Rochelle, New York. He was elected Editor of the A.M.E. Zion Quarterly Review in 1916 and served until his election to the bishopric in 1924 when he was assigned to Africa as our first resident bishop. In June, 1905, he married Annie Lucille Washington of Charlotte, North Carolina who passed away soon after the General Conference of 1944. Later, he married Bettylee Roberts. Bishop Alleyne died March 24, 1955.[4]

Of this group of five, the late Bishop Taylor wrote: "For the first time in one hundred and twenty-eight years, five bishops were elected. Another significant aspect of that election was that the three main emphases of Methodism were represented by these men: Preaching—two pastors and an evangelist at large; Education—a college president; Literature—two editors. All of these men had felt the attraction of the office of a bishop." [5]

It should be said that the influence of these five would be felt throughout the church, in many respects, over the next half-century. Four of them observed twenty-five years and more as Bishops of the Church. One, Bishop William Jacob Walls, served actively until 1968, or forty-four years, thus serving as long as that great expansionist, James Walker Hood who was elected in 1872 and retired in 1916.

The General Conference of 1928 is recalled by many as the significant session according equal lay representation to the members of the Church. While lay people were found in the General Sessions as ear-

---
[4] *A.M.E. Zion Quarterly Review*, loc. cit., 106, 107.
[5] *Ibid.* 111.

ly as 1852 they were first accorded representation evidently based upon attendance. By the end of the Nineteenth Century one notes that there were two lay people in attendance from each of the Annual Conferences. This prevailed until 1928. At this session too, William W. Matthews and Frederick M. Jacobs were elected bishops.

WILLIAM W. MATTHEWS

William W. Matthews was a lay preacher in 1893, evidently having been converted in 1893.

A chronological roll of the bishops of the Church lists him as having been born in 1871. On the Seventh day of the Thirty-second quadrennial session (1944) the following is noted:

> At this point, Dr. Rufus E. Clement raised the question of Bishops' ages—suggesting that because there had been considerable confusion over the age of Bishop Matthews, that he be requested to give some convincing statement concerning the age given in the Book of Minutes of the General Conference of 1908. Bishop Matthews stated that this was not printed upon any information given by himself. Dr. Clement then read a telegram from Mrs. Caroline Matthews, mother of Bishop Matthews, which telegram was sent to the General Secretary, stating that the Bishop was born in Batesville, Mississippi in 1876.[6]

The account noted from which this biography is taken, suggests his birthdate as October 28, 1871. He attended Branch Normal School in Pine Bluff, Arkansas from 1890 to 1900, and studied at New Orleans University from 1900-1902.

William W. Matthewes joined the Arkansas Conference in 1904 and was ordained a deacon at Solgohatchie, Arkansas. He was ordained an elder in Little Rock in December of the same year. In 1906, we note him on the West Coast serving his Church. He was elected Secretary of Foreign Missions in 1920 and served in this capacity until 1928 when he was elevated to the episcopacy.

The question of his age was raised at the General Conference of 1944 when Bishop Paris Arthur Wallace was retired. At that time he produced a telegram from his mother covering this aspect.

On May 7, 1948, the following charges against Bishop Matthews were filed:

---

[6] *Official Journal of the Thirty-second Quadrennial Session* (1944) 54.

To the Rt. Rev. W. J. Walls
President 33rd Session General Conference,
A.M.E. Zion Church in Session.

Greetings:

The undersigned a member of the African Methodist Episcopal Zion Church, complains to you that William Walter Matthews, a member of the same church, has been guilty of forgery and also of uttering a forged instrument of writing knowing the same to be forged.

COUNT NO. 1

Specification No. 1—That on divers times in May 1944 the said William Walter Matthews, a Bishop of the African Methodist Episcopal Zion Church, in the City of Detroit, at a session of the 32nd General Conference, exhibited a government visa or passport number 68030, which in words and figures showed that he was born on October 28, 1876—the said figures 1876 being changed from 1871—as appears in the application upon which the said passport was issued on July 22nd, 1921, and at that time the said William Walter Matthews swore to an affidavit that he was born at Batesville, Mississippi on the 28th day of October 1871—which affidavit was corroborated by his mother, Mrs. Caroline Matthews, who also swore that the said William Walter Matthews, the applicant for said passport was born in Panola County, Mississippi, on October 28th, 1871, her mark being witnessed by J. E. Hill a notary public.

The said forged and altered passport was presented to divers members of the Episcopal Committee for the purpose of deceiving the Episcopal Committee and the General Conference for the purpose of continuing him in office as an active Bishop of the African Methodist Episcopal Zion Church and for the purpose of making the Episcopal Committee believe that he, the said William Walter Matthews was 67 years, 6 months and not subjected to retirement at that time, when as a matter of truth and fact the said William Walter Matthews was at that time over 72 years and 6 months and eligible for retirement according to the law of the African Methodist Episcopal Zion Church and that by reason of said forgery and the publishing of a forged document of writing, the said William Walter Matthews was continued as an active Bishop although eligible for retirement under the law, and that if the General Conference and Episcopal Committee had had before it the real facts concerning the said age of William Walter Matthews he would have been retired from active service. And further that at the time that the said William Walter Matthews presented the forged and altered visa and passport to the Episcopal Committee that he then and there knew that the same was forged and altered, and that he continued to deceive and to perpetrate a fraud upon the said Episcopal Committee and General Conference, against the Discipline of our denomination and against the peace and dignity of the African Methodist Episcopal Zion Church.

COUNT NO. 2
Immoral conduct

Specification No. 1—The undersigned a member of the African Methodist Episcopal Zion Church complains that the said William Walter Matthews, a member of the same church has been guilty of immoral conduct and he is hereby charged therewith as follows:

That the said William Walter Matthews did openly associate with one Etoria Dryver during the life-time of his late wife, Mrs. Alice J. Matthews—which association occasioned divers and sundry rumors and it is believed contributed to the death of the said Mrs. Alice J. Matthews, who was alleged grieved because of the alleged association of her husband William Walter Matthews with the Etoria Dryver, who he later appointed as Episcopal Supervisor of the 5th Episcopal District, and further that in pursuance of the alleged relationship between himself and Mrs. Etoria Dryver that on January 28, 1947—he entered into a marriage contract at Malvern, Arkansas, with the said Etoria Dryver, said marriage being performed by Rev. K. S. L. Cook. It is further alleged that the said Etoria Dryver has two divorced living husbands, against the Discipline and precedents of our Denomination and against the peace and dignity of the African Methodist Episcopal Zion Church.

(Signed) J. R. FUNDERBURK

SUMMARY STATEMENT
By Dr. Rufus E. Clement

1. W. W. Matthews was found guilty by the Trial Committee on both counts of the charges brought against him.
2. Subsequently by action of the General Conference W. W. Matthews was "retired as a Bishop of the A.M.E. Zion Church" by unanimous vote.
3. This action is to be interpreted as follows:

   a. W. W. Matthews has no status as a Bishop of the A.M.E. Zion Church.
   b. W. W. Matthews is not a "Retired Bishop" in the usual, official use of this title or term.
   c. W. W. Matthews is prohibited from functioning as a Bishop in the A.M.E. Zion Church in any sense at any time in the future, beginning now.

4. As an act of mercy and out of consideration for his many years of service in the Church, it is recommended that W. W. Matthews be given an annual stipend of $2100 (one-half of his former annual salary as a Bishop) for the remainder of his life and so long as his character is passed by the Annual Conference of the A.M.E. Zion Church in which he may be holding membership as an Elder.
5. In view of the fact that W. W. Matthews does not have regular status as a Retired Bishop of the A.M.E. Zion Church there is no con-

sideration to be given his widow, other than that given to the widow of any Elder in good standing in the church.[7]

Bishop Matthews made a statement before the General Conference on May 13, 1948. He declared that the charges were based upon "suspicion and rumor." He denied having altered the visa or passport or presenting same to the Episcopal Committee in Detroit. He stated that this document was passed around from hand-to-hand on the grounds. Some of the persons seeing the document were not members of the Episcopal Committee. He went on to state that the passport was not presented to the General Conference and he was not called upon to appear before the Committee. He declared that the passport carried "an erroneous date of my birth, but I accepted it when I went to Europe in 1921. I used it because no crime or intent of such was involved or meant to be involved." [8]

Bishop Matthews admitted that he had been called before the Episcopal Committee at Detroit and requested to give evidence of his age. He went on to state: "I dispatched a message to my mother at Tucker, Arkansas, and she made a new and corrected affidavit of my birth date and sent the information by telegraph to the secretary of the General Conference at Detroit. The General Conference received that information from the Secretary (Ed. note: The statement was read not by the Secretary but by Dr. Rufus Clement), and then ordered that I register with the Episcopal Committee and along with the other bishops, so ordered to register, my name and place and date of my birth." [9]

Bishop Matthews then asked for a review of this material by the General Conference. Evidently, it was at this point that the General Conference was dealing with the matter and Bishop Matthews was speaking under a point of personal privilege, the decision of the Committee not having been read at the time.[10] The point of personal privilege appears to have been denied, however and then the Bishop was privileged to make his statement *after* the report of the Committee was heard. The report of the Committee stated:

We, the Committee, beg to make our report as may be found enclosed in these two envelopes.

---

[7] *Official Journal of the Thirty-third Quadrennial Session* 301, 302.
[8] *Ibid.*, 303.
[9] *Official Journal, 33rd Quadrennial Session, General Conference*, 303.
[10] *Ibid.*, 53.

We have done all possible, in the name of God, and trust that the report may be considered in that light.

We find the defendant Bishop W. W. Matthews, according to the evidence given, guilty on both counts and we recommmend the defendant to the mercy of the General Conference now in session.

Your Committee
F. R. Blakey, *Chairman*
A. P. Morris, *Secretary*

On motion of Reverend F. Thomas Roberts with a second by the Rev. D. F. Martinez, the report was received.[11]

As this writer would suppose, the statement of Bishop Matthews had a place *before* the report of the Committee. It appears that the Reverend Dr. C. E. Tucker expressed this thinking following the statement. However, regardless to position we now allude to the second charge and Bishop Matthews statement.

The Bishop stated that the charge on "Count 2" was "false and malicious and was designed to besmirch the good name and the character of myself and of another person who is entirely innocent of any such ugly, and malicious attack to have been made upon one who deserves better treatment. I say this because not one scintilla of truth has been stated." He further declared that the basic cause of the divorce of Mrs. Dryver was "Scriptural" and according to Discipline although this was not stated in the divorce complaint in order to save the reputations and feelings of involved persons.

The Bishop asked that he be given the status of a Retired Bishop and that the last statement of Dr. Rufus Clement be deleted. This, the Conference refused to do.

The General Conference of 1948 did not close the Matthews affair for it appeared again on the floor of the Thirty-fourth Quadrennial session which met in Brooklyn.

As the writer is not a student of ecclesiastical law he hesitates to suggest the possibility of error on the part of the General Conference as it turned again to the Matthews matter in Brooklyn. However, it appears to him that the intent and purpose of the General Conference of 1948 was clear and evidently mis-interpreted in 1952.

Bishop Matthews appealed to the Thirty-fourth Quadrennial session thereby making it necessary for the matter to be reviewed. The recorded documents of 1948 were studied again (many of the

---

[11] *Official Journal, 33rd Quadrennial Session,* 53.

participants of 1948 were on hand at the time) and these along with any new evidence were placed before the Judiciary Committee. The Committee called in the plaintiff's attorney, Dr. C. Eubank Tucker, as well as the attorney for the defendant, Bishop Matthews' Attorney S. A. Burnley. Three other attorneys were consulted: James A. Crumlin, Dr. W. A. Cooper and Mrs. Ruth Whitehead Whaley. They came to the conclusion that the Thirty-fourth Quadrennial Session had no jurisdiction in the case. They therefore recommended that the petition of Bishop Matthews be dismissed.[12] The point to which the writer alludes has to do with the statement of Dr. Rufus Clement before the Thirty-third session, a statement accepted by that body.

The review of the trial of Bishop Matthews brought into focus an item which should be recalled by the Membership of the Church,—the decisions of the General Conference. We note the necessity of deep recognition of the work each General Conference as it influences the work of a succeeding one. However, to us, there must be a maneuvering ground where new evidence is concerned or error involved.

Bishop Matthews died in Washington D.C. in 1962, March 15.

FREDERICK M. JACOBS

Dr. Frederick M. Jacobs (He was a medical doctor) was born July 15, 1865 in Camden, South Carolina. He attended Jackson College and, evidently Charleston Military College. It is not clear as to whether he took private lessons at this institution. He was converted in Charleston, S.C. and later joined the A.M.E. Zion Church in 1882 in Charlotte, North Carolina. He began preaching the same year and joined the Central North Carolina Conference. In 1884 he left North Carolina proceeding to Washington and entered Howard University, graduating from that institution in 1888. He was made a Deacon in the Philadelphia and Baltimore Conference in 1886 and an elder two years later. He later completed work at the New York Medical College.

Dr. Jacob pastored churches in Baltimore, later re-organizing Clinton Church in that city also, Wesley Union, Harrisburgh, Hopkins Chapel, Asheville, North Carolina, Logan Temple, Knox-

---

[12] *Official Journal of the Thirty-fourth Quadrennial Session* of the General Conference, 1952, 410-418.

ville etc. He was a member of many of the General Conferences from 1892. He was elected and consecrated a bishop in 1928 and died in 1931.[13]

No elections were held in 1932 as the General Conference met in Wesley Center Church, Pittsburgh, Pennsylvania.

The denomination was recovering somewhat from the Depression as the delegates of the Church gathered in Trinity Church, Greensboro, North Carolina in 1936. Problems which the Conference faced were therefore multiplied. Barely had the sessions opened when a protest was filed regarding the delegates from the North Alabama Conference. The protest was signed by Reverend W. E. Jenkins, Miss Elizabeth Tucker and others. The move to appoint a Credentials Committee (Dr. E. J. Magruder, the mover of the motion and Dr. D. G. Garland, supporting) was challenged by Dr. W. A. Cooper and Dr. Walter R. Lovell, who offered a motion that the matter be referred to the Executive and Judiciary Committee was lost by a tabling motion made by J. R. Wingfield with a second by E. A. Abbott, so the original motion prevailed. The following were appointed as a Credentials Committee: A. L. Martin, A. Jackson, M. P. Sawyer, William Murphy, D. F. Martinez, J. V. Catledge, W. W. Long, W. A. Steward, J. C. Lewis, A. C. Little John, W. S. Dacons, S. D. Leverette.[14]

The Committee on Credentials reported the next day, after the reading of the Minutes. It stated: "We your committee on credentials beg to make the following report: According to the evidence submitted to us we recommend that the protest set up in the petition with reference to the illegal or irregular election of delegates in the North Alabama Conference be denied and the delegates be seated." [15] The report was approved.

A protest was made by the Rev. C. E. Tucker against the placing of General Secretary H. C. Weeden on the Districting Committee. This matter was first referred to Bishop Walls and then he, in turn, referred the matter to the General Conference. In the end the matter was referred to the Committee on Judiciary and Executive.

The third day of the Conference charges were filed against Bishop Benjamin Garland Shaw by the Reverend J. R. Wingfield. The

---
[13] *Hood, loc. cit.,* 346-353, and other sources.
[14] *Journal of the Thirtieth General Conference,* Greensboro, N.C. 1936, 27, 28.
[15] *Ibid.,* 28.

charges were as follows: 1. Placing a Presbyterian Minister, Rev. William Sample, to the pastorate of Metropolitan Church, Birmingham; 2, Misappropriating the sum of $1,100; 3, Misappropriating $1,200. Again, an effort was made to assign this matter to the Committee on Judiciary and Executive Matters. On referral to the law of the Church a Trial Committee was appointed consisting of Rev. C. P. S. Harrison, D. G. Garland, E. S. Hardge, F. W. Riley, James Clair Taylor, H. Leo Johnston, D. C. Pope, W. Roy Smith, A. C. Cook. The Committee was instructed to begin its work at 8:00 A.M. the following day.

The Committee reported Monday, May 11, 1936 as follows:

REPORT OF THE TRIAL COMMITTEE OF BISHOP BENJAMIN GARLAND SHAW

We, your Trial Committee, elected by the Thirtieth Quadrennial Session of the General Conference of the A.M.E. Zion Church, do hereby submit the following report:

We met, heard the evidence as presented by the prosecution and defense in reference to the following charges against Bishop Benjamin Garland Shaw, to:

1. Maladministration in office.
Specification: The said Bishop Benjamin Garland Shaw did appoint one Rev. William Samples of the Presbyterian Church, pastor of our Metropolitan Church (A.M.E. Zion) of Birmingham, Ala., on Sunday night September 29, 1935 in violation of the law of our church.
2. Misappropriation of funds.
a. That on December 5, 1930, during the sitting of the North Alabama Conference, J. R. Wingfield and H. T. Medford were appointed as a committee, at said Annual Conferences by Bishop Benjamin Garland Shaw, to draw up a resolution authorizing the Conference to borrow $1200 to be paid on the mortgage of Thomas Chapel A.M.E. Zion Church, which had been foreclosed. That instead of taking up the mortgage, he used the money for purposes otherwise than that for which it was obtained.
b. The said Benjamin Garland Shaw took $1100 out of the General Claims raised during the said North Alabama Conference, and sent to Dr. W. H. Goler, then the Financial Secretary of the A.M.E. Zion Church, a note for that amount payable in ninety days with the statement that he was forced to take one thousand and one hundred dollars out of the General Claims to save the situation.

Charge No. 1: We find this charge and specification sustained.
Charge No. 2 a. We find this charge and specification are not sustained.

b. We find, according to strict interpretation of the law as provided by our Discipline, page 67, Article 4, that this specification is sustained.

Your Committee recommend mercy.

Respectfully submitted,

Signed: H. LEO JOHNSON, D. C. POPE, F. W. RILEY, W. ROY SMITH, E. S. HARDGE, A. C. COOKE, C. P. S. HARRISON, JAMES CLAIR TAYLOR, Secretary, D. G. GARLAND, Chairman.[16]

On a motion by James W. Eichelberger with a second by Dr. W. A. Blackwell, the report was referred to an Executive Session. This action was taken immediately. While a move to suspend Bishop Benjamin Garland Shaw was supported a substitute motion prevailed, submitted by W. A. Blackwell and M. C. Glover, in which Bishop Shaw was required to make restitution within twelve months,[17] and that he resign the appointment.

The Bishops elected at Greensboro were: E. L. Madison, W. C. Brown and James W. Brown.

ELIJAH L. MADISON

Elijah Lovette Madison was born near Montogomery, Alabama, May 28, 1876. He entered Livingstone College while the late Dr. W. H. Goler was president of that institution. In 1898, he joined the Western North Carolina Conference as he followed his calling as a minister. He pastored such churches as Hopkins Chapel, Asheville, N. C., Clinton Chapel, Charlotte, Metropolitan Church, Greensboro, First Church, High Point, and St. Luke, Wilmington, N.C. In 1920 he assumed charge of John Wesley Church, Pittsburgh, Pa. and under his leadership the present Wesley Center Church was constructed. In 1932 he was elected Financial Secretary of the denomination and served until he was elected to the Episcopacy in 1936.

Bishop Madison was stricken while holding the Allegheny Conference and lingered for some time. He died June 26, 1946.[18]

WILLIAM CORNELIUS BROWN

William C. Brown was born June 24, 1877, according to one account. Another states that he was born in 1879. His birthplace was Chowan County, North Carolina. He was converted in Canaan's Temple in that community and afterwards removed to New England

---
[16] *Journal of the Thirtieth General Conference,* 283.
[17] *Ibid.,* 36, 37.
[18] *Official Journal, Thirty-third Quadrennial Session,* 309.

where the major part of his schooling was secured. He joined the Church in September 18, 1900 and was licensed to preach. He was ordained a deacon in Providence, R.I. in May 1901 and an elder at Cambridgeport, Mass., in June, 1904. He pastored several of the outstanding churches of the denomination, including Washington, D.C. and Brooklyn, New York. He was intensely interested in the Ministerial Pension Service, a great amount of credit going to him for the formation of the present system.

Bishop Brown was retired at the General Conference of 1960. He passed away, in January of 1964.

JAMES W. BROWN

Of James Walter Brown the Editor of the A.M.E. Zion Quarterly Review wrote: "The accidental death of Bishop James Walter Brown took from our midst a choice spirit. He acquired, early in his ministry, the reputation of being 'a builder.' It was the writer's good fortune to pastor for seven years in a community which still bears the impress of Bishop Brown's personality. For twenty-three years he labored in a city in which, as Channing once said of London,

> ". . . the distance of a few streets only will carry you from one stage of civilization to another, from the excess of refinement to barbarism, from the abodes of cultivated intellect to brutal ignorance, from what is called fashion to the grossest manners."

And left as a monument to his labors the imposing structure which houses the congregation of the Mother A.M.E. Zion Church." [19]

James Walter Brown was born July 10, 1872 in Elizabeth City, North Carolina. He was elevated to the Episcopacy in May 1936 at Greensboro, North Carolina, and was tragically killed as he crossed a busy New York city street in 1941, February 27th.

Bishop Brown was educated at Shaw University, Lincoln University in Pennsylvania and held an honorary degree from Livingstone College. The tragic death of this Bishop to Africa (two terms of assignment) left a distinct gap in leadership.

Some note of the General Conference of 1940, held in the National Church of Zion Methodism has already been taken. There were no elections, as has been stated, a matter which may have changed the entire course of events of the denomination. Outstand-

---

[19] *The A.M.E. Zion Quarterly Review*, Vol. LI, No. 2, 83, 84.

ing details have been given of the 1944 General Conference and the question of retirement and its attendant controversy likewise has been mentioned. However, with the death of Bishops James Walter Brown and Lynwood Westinghouse Kyles and the retirement of Bishop Paris Arthur Wallace, three places on the Board of Bishops were open and it was determined that they should be filled. Accordingly, Walter William Slade, Frank W. Alstork and Buford F. Gordon were selected for this honor.

BISHOP WALTER WILLIAM SLADE

Walter William Slade was no doubt one of the firmest friends this new Editor had as he began the strange and responsible position as Editor-Manager of the A.M.E. Zion Quarterly Review. Bishop Slade's counsel, and we were wont to consult him time and again, brought us through many *trying* situations as we struggled to fulfill the mandate of the General Conference of 1948. Bishop Slade came from a long line of churchmen and was thoroughly engrained in the work of the Master. One of our greatest regrets is that his knowledge and understanding he had of men and community was never passed along to posterity. The Church, in this respect, is all poorer.

Walter William Slade's father was one of those old Zion pioneers of which little is spoken, the Reverend Walter Slade. The combined experiences of father and son made of Walter William one of the great preachers and leaders of the denomination. The warmth of fellowship really glows as one recalls his relating of experiences, and oftentimes, his involvement of the individual in them. This Editor recalls with a bit of mirth, which was not funny at the time, of his saying to us. "Take over and hold this Conference until I return." One hour passed and then two and into the third hour, and by this time we had done everything we knew to do, and then he came in and concluded the session of the year. That which we received from Walter William Slade, just from observation, is one of the richest contributions to our living.

Walter William Slade was elevated to the episcopacy after serving many of the most outstanding churches of the denomination, among them being, Fayetteville, North Carolina (Evans Metropolitan) and Wesley Center, Pittsburgh, Pa. He was one of the ablest of Presiding Elders, who, when he made his quarterly visit, really inspired the hearts of people. He was an able General Officer, first as Connectional Evangelist and later as Financial Secretary. He died in 1963. His wife Mrs. S. Mae Slade Survives.

FRANK W. ALSTORK

It is hard for a writer to avoid over-doing the situation as he thinks of those with whom there has been a personal association. Frank W. Alstork was the type of person who deeply impressed one as to his religious convictions. Perhaps his standing in this area appears high simply because one has always held the idea that Bishops were of a special calibre. When one's personal faith either in situations or men wavered, then one should look to higher leadership. The serious approach Frank W. Alstork took to leadership for the type of assurance needed.

Frank Wesley Alstork was born in 1885 and died July 9, 1948.

BUFORD F. GORDON

According to the order of election, Buford F. Gordon was the second bishop elected in 1944. He was one of the most progressive ministers in the denomination, and perhaps, did his greatest task in the ministry at Akron, Ohio. We recall his appointment as Editor of the Church School Literature by the Board of Bishops, so, as he completed the Conference year at Wesley Temple, he brought his reports by the Annual Conference, then meeting in Avery Memorial Church, Pittsburgh, to carry the same type of enthusiasm into the work of editing literature. The fresh approach of illustrations and identification gave a new impetus to this area of Church work. His election at Detroit in 1944 was a blessing to the Church.

Perhaps one of the added attributes of Buford F. Gordon, beyond his enthusiasm for hard work, was his evaluation placed upon work assignment. We recall his refusal to attend a meeting in Europe in 1951 simply because he saw work at home to accomplish. Many, however might wish to state that his refusing this assignment was based upon his already having been abroad, but this would not be the full picture. In his stead he insisted that James Clair Taylor, another Bishop, should take his place.

Just days prior to his death, we worked with him in a Christian Education Board meeting in St. Louis, and here too, saw the diligence with which he approached a task.

Buford F. Gordon was born in Pulaski, Virginia, August 24, 1893.

He passed away January 19, 1952. His wife, Thelma and seven children survive.

E. B. WATSON

E. B. Watson was born in 1874. The General Officer in charge of the Secretarial work of the Church stated at his death: "Shortly after the close of the Bishops' Meeting in Philadelphia, Pa. where Bishop Edgar Bennett Watson had presided with such grace and dignity, and the business had been dispatched in such orderly manner, when a phone call to our office gave the shocking news that this servant of God had passed. His life had been one of piety and devotion to duty. His labors in the episcopacy had been successful and outstanding. He rounded out his educational budget and reported the entire Golden-Diamond Jubilee apportionment from all conferences over which he presided before his home going."

Edgar Bennett Watson served many of the outstanding churches of the denomination, his last pastorate being Norfolk Virginia (Metropolitan Church). He was elected to the epsicopacy in 1944 and passed away in 1951, just as the year got underway.

Bishop Watson was assigned Texas, Oklahoma, Liberia, West Gold Coast, East Gold Coast and Nigeria in the beginning quadrennium after his election. In 1948 he was assigned Central North Carolina, Pee Dee, and East Tennessee and Virginia. This was his area at the time of his passing.

The General Conference of 1948 met in Louisville, Kentucky. The restlessness of the Church appeared to be more in evidence at this time as can be noted by its actions. Some of the matters coming before the session have been noted in another chapter. The Conference appeared to be in no mood for dictation and set about its work in that spirit. James Clair Taylor, Raymond L. Jones and Hampton Thomas Medford were elevated to the bishopric.

JAMES CLAIR TAYLOR

James Clair Taylor was born in Cambridge, Mass., May 3, 1893. His parents were James Madison and Harriette Ann Taylor. He was the oldest of four children. When his father died James Clair was but six years old.

He graduated from the elementary and high school in Cambridge and at the age of 15 years was converted and baptized at St. Paul Baptist Church (now Peoples Baptist Church) in Boston, Mass., which was the home church of his parents. His father, for example, served as a licensed minister and ordained deacon until his passing. His mother was a former school teacher in Virginia.

As an active minister in his church, James Clair devoted much time to singing and serving as a leader of the youth group.

In 1912 he was married to Alma Jackson of Boston. To this union one son, Durward St. Clair Taylor, was born.

During the depression he and his family moved to Maine and settled in Portland. Since the only church of their race was the A.M.E. Zion, he and his family affiliated with this congregation. It was while in Portland that James Clair felt the call to preach and began preparing for the same. He began his studies at Bates College at Lewiston and later went on to study at Chicago Theological Seminary and later at Union Theological Seminary, New York City.

James Clair Taylor was ordained both deacon and elder in the New England Conference, the first ordination taking place when the Conference met in Cambridge, June, 1918. His first charge was Meriden, Conn. He later served churches in Goldsboro, North Carolina, Moores Chapel, Salisbury, N.C., Rutherfordton, N.C. Memorial Church, Rochester, N.Y., Wesley Union, Harrisburg, Pa. and First Church, Paterson, N.J.

After the death of his first wife, Rev. Taylor was married to Anne Pate of Goldsboro, N.C. during his pastorate at Rochester, N.Y.

In 1936, James Clair Taylor was elected the Editor-manager of the A.M.E. Zion Quarterly Review, a post he held with the highest distinction, bringing the periodical to an extraordinary level of attainment. He held this post until he was elevated to the bishopric in Louisville, Ky. in 1948. He died July 1954.

RAYMOND LUTHER JONES

Raymond Luther Jones, a son of the Rev. James and Callie Victoria (Bradford) Jones, was born April 7, 1900 in Chattanooga, Tenn. He was converted in Logan Temple Church, Knoxville in 1906. He preached his trial sermon in September 1917 in Logan Temple and was ordained deacon in Little Rock Church, Charlotte, N.C. in November 1922. Two years later, in Winston-Salem, N.C. he was ordained an elder. He was elected and consecrated a bishop of the Church in Louisville, Ky. in 1948.

Raymond Luther Jones pastored the following churches prior to his elevation to the bishopric: Second Greek Circuit, Salisbury, N.C., Marable Memorial, Kannapolis, Grace Church, Charlotte and Hopkins Chapel, Asheville, all in North Carolina. In Tennessee he served the following churches: St. Paul, Johnson City, and finally, Broadway Temple, Louisville, Ky.

Bishop Jones received his education in the elementary schools of Knoxville, and his College and seminary training at Livingstone College and Hood Theological School, completing his work in the last named institution in 1924. Bishop Jones married Carrie L. Smith in 1924 and upon her death, married Mabel L. Miller in 1956. His children are: Sujette Victoria, Raymona and Millicent Luthia. Bishop Jones has been a delegate to three world Methodist Meetings, Oxford, England, Lake Junaluska, N.C. and Oslo, Norway. He declined to attend the London, England meeting because of the expense it would have caused the denomination.

HAMPTON THOMAS MEDFORD

Hampton Thomas Medford, the 56th Bishop of the denomination was born in McDonald County, North Carolina, Jan., 29, 1886. Born in extreme poverty, he was not privileged to attend school until he was fourteen years of age. He was able, because of his quick and ready mind, to secure a good education despite this late start and for a time served as a teacher in the North Carolina School system. For a time, too, he was an insurance agent and a store keeper.

His first marriage was to Mary Elizabeth Camp who passed away in 1951. Five children were born of this marriage, two of whom survive.

Hampton Thomas Medford was converted and joined Doggettee Grove Zion Methodist Church. Later he felt the call to preach and entered upon a very successful ministry. To prepare himself for this vocation he registered at Livingstone College.

Bishop Medford's last pastorate was John Wesley Church, Washington, D.C., now the National Church of Zion Methodism. From this post he was elected Secretary of Foreign Missions, serving as a General Officer until his election to the episcopacy in 1948.

On May 6, 1952 he was married to Mrs. Savannah Jones. Bishop

Medford died in September, 1964, after having been retired at the General Conference of 1960.

One could feel the mounting interest and concern as the Zion Methodist Church prepared to open its Thirty-fourth quadrennial session in Brooklyn, New York (1952). There was a grim attitude toward changes in the budget while an equally firm attitude was developing in the matter of retirement. If a poll of delegates had been possible on these two items it might have been astonishing to note the undercurrents of feelings. The writer, for example, experienced illness to the extent that he could not be on hand at the opening sessions and, finally, on attending, was forced to rest rather than take any major or active part in proceedings. A phone call to the seat of the Conference evinced this statement from the late Dr. James W. Eichelberger: "We have everything under control, so do not worry about anything." This was indeed so to the point that the great part of the Conference, evidently without adequate leadership, was really dominated by the segment which knew where it was going and how it would attain it.

The Episcopal Committee, through a member of the group, Reverend M. S. Rudd, came to the session on Monday, May 12th seeking some instructions and some enabling legislation. They requested the endorsement of twelve episcopal districts, the power to assign the best and most suitable person to the African work with the understanding that the person so designated would be required to reside in Africa with no assignments of American Conferences to him. It was also asked that the power to state the person so designated for the African work should return to America no more than once during the quadrennium except for the General Conference or some emergency.[20]

Approval was given to these suggestions on motions made by W. M. Smith with a second by J. W. Shaw and others, which attended to the general endorsement of these matters.

A statement was made by Rev. J. R. Funderburk re: the W. W. Matthews case as follows:

> Please permit me to say first of all that I am not a candidate for any office but that I stand before you as one who means to do what is right towards all men.

[20] *Official Journal, 34th Quadrennial Session*, General Conference, 51, 52.

In regard to the petition presented by Bishop W. W. Matthews I want you to know that I have nothing in my heart against him. And, if he can give the proper satisfaction that may be required by this General Conference, I will not oppose any favorable consideration that may be given him.[21]

Elsewhere, we have indicated the situation hinging on the Matthews case.

The matter of retirement, as stated, was one of vast interest to the General Sessions. On the second day, following the reading of the Quadrennial Address, Dr. James W. Eichelberger made the following motion: "Mr. Chairman, I move that there shall not be any retirement of Bishops at this time, the 34th quadrennial session of the General Conference of the African Methodist Episcopal Zion Church at Brooklyn, New York, May 7-22, 1952 and that the General Secretary shall be instructed and directed not to announce to the General Conference the age of Bishops when they have finished their reports as required under Par. 192, Section I of our Discipline and that the Presiding Officer(s) be instructed and directed not to declare any Bishop retired because of age." [22]

The motion was seconded by Mrs. Abbie Clement Jackson. Intense debate followed during which an amendment to the motion was offered by the Rev. Dr. C. Eubank Tucker providing for the tabling of the motion.[23] The amendment was lost with the motion being carried by a vote of 312 to 32.

The result of the voting does not clearly indicate the temper of the Conference. The controversy regarding this move was debated for many years. Perhaps it should be stated that this was the high point of the influence of James W. Eichelberger, as he, himself, would have noted. The three Bishops who would have fallen under the law of the denomination, W. C. Brown, W. W. Slade and J. W. Martin, expressed their thanks to the Conference.

Elected to fill vacant places on the Board created by the deaths of Benjamin Garland Shaw, Frank Wesley Alstork and Buford F. Gordon, were: Herbert Bell Shaw, Stephen G. Spottswood, William Andrew Steward and Daniel Carleton Pope.

---

[21] *Official Journal, 34th Quadrennial Session,* 52.
[22] *Official Journal of the 34th Quadrennial Session,* 43.
[23] *Official Journal of the 36th Quadrennial Session* (1960) 78.

HERBERT BELL SHAW

Herbert Bell Shaw was born in Wilmington, North Carolina, in 1908 the son of John Henry and Lummie Virginia (Hodges) Shaw. He was converted in St. Luke Church, Wilmington, June 13, 1920. He preached his trial sermon on July 12, 1927 and was ordained deacon in Washington, N.C., May 10, 1928. Two years later he was ordained elder, November 15, 1930. He has served the following churches: Bowen's Chapel, St. Andrews, Price Memorial, all in North Carolina. He served as a General Officer, in charge of Ministerial Brotherhood, Thomas Walker Wallace having passed in September, 1942. Through his work and that of Bishop William Cornelius Brown the new structure for the Brotherhood Pension Service was designed.

Herbert Bell Shaw was educated in several institutions, receiving the degrees of Ba.A., B.D. and D.D. over the years. He married Mrs. M. Ardelle Shaw in September 1931. He has two children, John Herbert and Maria A. He is Vice President of the World Methodist Conference to which he has been a delegate three times, Oslo, Lake Junaluska and London.

Herbert Bell Shaw has done great work in the reopening of our work in areas of West Indies, establishing new conferences as well as re-constituting others which had been abandoned for almost three quarters of a century.

STEPHEN GILL SPOTTSWOOD

Stephen Gill Spottswood was born July 18, 1897, the son of Abraham and Mary Elizabeth (Gray) Spottswood. He is a graduate of Albright College and Gordon Divinity School. He did graduate work also at Yale University. He married Viola Estelle Booker (deceased). He is the father of five children. He spent thirty-four years in the pastorate, serving the following points: Portland, Maine, West Newton and Lowell, Mass., New Haven, Conn. Jones Tabernacle, Indianapolis, Ind., Golder Memorial, Winston-Salem, N.C., St. Luke, Buffalo, N.Y. and John Wesley, Washington, D.C., the Church he was serving when elected to the Episcopacy.

Stepehn Gill Spottswood has been closely identified with the National Association for the Advancement of Colored People, serving for several years as the chairman of the Board. He has likewise served as the head of the denominational Board of Finance (Chairman) and as a Trustee of Livingstone College. He has four children.

WILLIAM ANDREW STEWART

William Andrew Stewart was born in 1894, the son of Eli and Allie Stewart in Evergreen, Alabama. He is a graduate of Phelps Hall Training School and Tuskegee. He also attended Livingstone College. Later he undertook study at Howard University in Washington, D.C. Upon graduation from Tuskegee, he taught school in Macon County and Tuskegee, Alabama for several years.

He transferred to the Western North Carolina Conference and pastored under Bishop Lynwood Westinghouse Kyles. During his pastorate he completed study at Livingstone College and Hood Theological Seminary. He married Miss Sula Cunningham and to this union seven children were born.

His pastorates were always successful as he built churches and parsonages where needed, paying off debts in other cases. His great work was achieved in Washington, D.C. where he constructed a building for Union Wesley Church.

William Andrew Stewart was elected to the episcopacy in 1952. His new duty gave him a chance to discover and give men large opportunities in the ministry.

Over the years, Bishop Stewart has been vitally interested in community service. While at Old Ship Church, Mongomery, Ala., he brought about changes in the attitude of the Louisville and Nashville Railroad and the Western Railway of Alabama. In still another instance, through his efforts, two young men, imprisoned for rape in that State were released.

Bishop Stewart has several children. His wife, Sula, passed away several years ago.

DANIEL CARLETON POPE

Daniel Carleton Pope was born in 1887. He and his wife spent the period between 1923 and 1930 serving in Liberia and lost a child while laboring in this part of the world. Upon his election to the episcopacy he evinced a desire to return to this work and was accordingly placed by the Episcopal Committee.

Daniel Carleton Pope had been one of the most successful of

ministers. He had labored in several sections of the Church after his return to America. Meanwhile, he suffered his second loss, that of his wife. One of the officials of the church had declared that no doubt the loss of his son was due to the rigors of the Missions field and the lack of adequate facilities where health was concerned.

In 1948, upon the election of Thomas Hampton Medford, Daniel Carleton Pope was elected Secretary of Foreign Missions. It was from this office that he was elected to the bishopric in 1952. He was re-assigned this work in 1956.

Bishop Pope came up for retirement in 1960 and was re-called by the Buffalo General Conference. In the assignment of Conferences the work which he had accomplished for the two quadrenniums appeared not to have influenced the Episcopal Committee. His district was therefore that which was not contended for by others. Bishop Pope made the statement that if this was the best which could be done he would just as well accept retirement.[23] Thereupon Bishop Tucker suggested the transfer of the East Tennessee and Virginia Conference from his listing to Bishop Pope. The suggestion was accepted.

Bishop Pope passed away, March 4, 1964, just a few months prior to the convening of the General Conference. His final acts were to endeavor to straighten out some grievous conditions, utilizing his own salary to do so.

CHAPTER XXV

The Storm Breaks

THE interesting thing about organizations and movements is that so frequently the swift currents of life are those least visible to the hurrying observant. Perhaps in this, the grave danger lies. There is small doubt that the turning aside from major purposes of such groups as the Church not only weakens their intended end views but lends an opportunity to an ever-present hostile force to thrive and grow. In all too many instances the group at hand returns to its given task bewildered because of the strength of opposing forces. Internecine controversies therefore, ought to be discouraged as leadership, fulfilling its basic function, interprets clearly the development of complaint prior to its show of strength. We endeavor to say that signs of discontent and restlessness must always be noted early by those in authority, and those in authority must understand the possibility and imperative of compromise.

One of the great weaknesses of the Protestant Church over the years had been its slowness of change. Too frequently the morals of the State run by the morals of Church, while the Church is busily debating course and action. In these situations the Church is no longer the catalytic agent which society so vitally needs. The Black Church does not and did not appear to clearly understand the rapidly marching demands for change and the pressure this would bring upon its own organization. Coupled with this world of change are conditions working for and against it. The new *integrated* thrust may or may not be beyond the Church's thinking. It is a question as to whether the Black Church has looked forward to the day when it itself will be out of existence as it faces that integrated society. Certainly, the Church has educated and urged education upon its membership only to note that those she trains linger a short time within her vaulted roof. This then is a handicap, for this merely states that those who could lend the best aid merely *escape*.

The one *enceinte* is the reliance on that which may well be the temporary emphasis on *Black is beautiful,* or the longer and wiser course change.

Pittsburgh, Pennsylvania had clear lessons for Zion Methodism.

At least two of the Bishops, and probably more, sensed this. The struggle was between one demanding change and another, adherence to an older system. It should be said that the denomination, in all of its unpleasant confrontations, is guilty not of haste but of the willingness to avoid unpleasantness. At times this has vigorously worked against her. Her Methodist sisters, for example, have dealt time and again with situations with the attitude of the surgeon.

Any student of Zion Methodism could have anticipated Pittsburgh, that is, if he looked closely at Louisville. He would have more clearly understood Buffalo and Indianapolis. It is hoped that Detroit began a new understanding.

In a former chapter we have stated that one can see in the finances of the Church and the attitude of the Church to those finances, something understandable. The Thirty-fifth Quadrennial session was able to move the budget upward only with the great aid of careful pre-study, the wisdom of the committee and good floor leadership. These would have come to a collective failure, no doubt, had not the Budget Committee restricted the amount of assessments a local annual conference could levy. They stated: "the asking assessment, or requirements on a church, charge, pastor or persons within a church, for use within an annual conference to an amount which does not exceed the equal of 40% of the General Claims. . . ." [1]

The second matter which came to the front at Pittsburgh was the Judicial Council proposal. The Church reasoned that all other Methodist bodies had finally come to the point of adopting such a plan and Zion should do so as well. Again, this writer would point out that the move was suggested out of a very current belief that two matters had to be faced by the denomination: the supremacy of the General Conference and the curtailment of the power of the episcopacy. One would state that the confrontation could well have been avoided by reason.

The Reverend Dr. Felix S. Anderson was the Chairman of the Revisions Committee. On May 16, he reported out of his committee Resolution Number 211, providing for the establishment of a Judicial Council. The Committee concurred with the resolution. The proposed Resolution follows:

---

[1] *Official Journal, 35th Quadrennial Session,* 1956, 440.

I move the adoption of the following:

There shall be established a JUDICIAL COUNCIL of the A. M. E. Zion Church, as follows:

Article I—Members

The Judicial Council shall be composed of nine members, five of whom shall be ministers and four shall be laymen. They shall be (1) at least forty years of age, (2) members in good standing in the A. M. E. Zion Church for at least twenty years, (3) an officer in the local church for at least ten years, or a member of the Annual Conference for at least six years, or a delegate to the General Conference for at least two times. The term of office shall be eight years; provided, however, 1/2 that a member of the Council shall cease to function at the General Conference nearest his seventy-fourth birthday, and be released from membership responsibility in the Council regardless of the date of expiration of his term of office. Members of the Council shall be nominated and elected in the following manner. The Bishops shall nominate twice the number of elders and laymen to be elected by the Conference and shall submit their report on the third day of the General Conference, and the General Conference shall proceed immediately to elect by secret ballot, and without debate, the members of the Judicial Council. The three elders and two laymen receiving the highest number of votes above a majority shall be elected for the full term of eight years. The two elders and two laymen receiving the next highest number of votes above a majority shall be elected for a term of four years. Thereafter, alternately, each General Conference shall elect two elders and two laymen (four members) and three elders and two laymen (five members) respectively.

Election of members shall be held at each session of the General Conference for only the number of members whose terms expire at such session.

Article II—Alternates

There shall be six alternates, three elders and three laymen and their qualifications shall be the same as that for membership in the Judicial Council. The term of office for alternates shall be eight years with the same provision as that for members of the Judicial Council.

The alternate members shall be elected in the following manner: the nominees having the next highest number of votes in each classification shall be elected alternates.

Article III—Vacancies

1. For malfeasance in office or for conduct adjudged to be of such nature and kind as to reflect dishonor upon the Judicial Council and/or the A.M.E. Zion Church, the Judicial Council by a two-third vote may terminate the services of a member of the Council at any time between sessions of the General Conference. The General Conference may take such action by a two-third vote at any quadrennial session.

2. If a vacancy in the Judicial Council occurs during the interim

between sessions of the General Conference, it shall be filled by the alternate of the same class in the order of election. The alternate holding such vacancy shall hold office for the unexpired term of the member he succeeds. In event of any vacancy, it shall be the duty of the President and Secretary of the Judicial Council to notify the alternate entitled to fill it.

Article IV—General

The term of office of members of the Council and of Alternates expire upon the adjournment of the General Conference at which their successors are elected.

1. Members of the Council shall be ineligible for membership in the General Conference or on administrative boards or in any connectional office.

2. The Judicial Council shall provide its own methods of organization and procedure. It shall meet at the time and place of the General Conference and shall remain in session until the adjournment of that body. It shall meet at such other times and places as it may seem necessary. Seven members shall constitute a quorum. An affirmative vote of at least six members of the Council shall be necessary to declare an act of the General Conference unconstitutional. On other matters a majority vote shall be sufficient.

Article V—Powers

1. The Judicial Council shall determine the constitutionality of any act of the General Conference upon an appeal of the majority of the Board of Bishops, or one-third of the members of the General Conference.

2. The Judicial Council shall have jurisdiction to pass upon the constitutionality of any proposed legislation when such declaratory decision is requestioned (ed. note: requested?) by the General Conference or the Board of Bishops.

3. The Judicial Council shall hear and determine the legality of any action taken therein by a General Conference Committee, or Administrative Board, upon appeal by one-third of the members thereof, or upon request of the Board of Bishops.

4. The Judicial Council shall hear and determine any appeal from a Bishop's decision on a question of law made in the Annual Conference when said appeal has been made by one-fifth of that conference present and voting.

5. The Judicial Council shall meet at least once a year and pass upon decisions of law made by the Bishops in Annual Conferences upon questions submitted to them in writing, and reported in writing to the Council with a syllabus of each case, and affirm, modify, or reverse them. Before affirmation, no episcopal decision shall be authoritative in the case pending. When the decisions are affirmed, they shall become the law of the Church.

6. The Judicial Council shall hear and determine an appeal of the Bishop when taken from the decision of the trial court in his case.

7. The Judicial Council shall have such other duties and powers as may be conferred upon it by the General Conference.

8. All the decisions of the Judicial Council shall be final. However, when the Judicial Council shall declare any act of the General Conference unconstitutional, that decision shall be reported back to the General Conference immediately.

9. When the General Conference shall have passed any act or legislation that appears to be subject to more than one interpretation, or when any paragraph or paragraphs of the Discipline seem to be of doubtful meaning or application, the Judicial Council, on petition as hereinafter provided, shall have jurisdiction to make a ruling in the nature of a declaratory decision as to the meaning, application and effect of such act, legislation or paragraph or paragraphs of the Discipline; and the decision of the Judicial Council thereon shall be as binding and effectual as a decision made by the Judicial Council on appeal under the law relating to appeals to the Judicial Council.

The following bodies of the A. M. E. Zion Church are hereby authorized to make such petitions to the Judicial Council for declaratory decisions:

1. The Board of Bishops; 2 Any General Conference Committee on matters relating to or affecting the work of such committee; 3 Any Annual Conference, or matters relating to the Annual Conference of the work therein; 4. Any Administrative Board; 5 The various departments of the A.M.E. Zion Church; 6. The General Conference; 7. The Connectional Council.

10. Any minister, layman or member, or deaconess shall have a right of appeal to the Judicial Council after first exhausting the present existing legal machinery of the A. M. E. Zion Church.

11. In any case the Judicial Council shall determine from the facts in the case whether or not it has jurisdiction to hear and determine the same.

12. When a declaratory decision is sought, all persons or bodies who have or claim any interest which would be affected by the declaration shall be parties to the proceeding, and the petition shall name such parties. If the Council determines that other $\frac{1}{2}$ parties not named by the petition would be affected by such a decision, such additional parties shall also be added; and the petitioners or petitioners shall then be required to serve all parties so joined with a copy of the petition within fifteen days after the filing of the same with the Judicial Council. In like manner any interested party may on his or its own motion intervene and answer, plead, or interplead.

13. All parties shall have the privilege of filing briefs and arguments, and presenting evidence, under such rules as the Council deems necessary to a complete understanding of the facts, in any proceeding in the nature of a petition for declaratory action and decision, it may hear evidence (either orally or by affidavits filed) or statements of facts agreed upon by the adverse parties, or it may designate one or more of its members to hear evidence and report the same to the Judicial Council.

14. Up to the level of the Annual Conference, the present judicial laws of the church remain operative.

15. The decisions of the Judicial Council on questions of law, with a summary of the facts and of the opinion, shall be filed with the Secretary of the Board of Bishops, General Secretary of the A.M.E. Zion Church and published in the *Star of Zion* and entered in the General Secretary's minutes.

ARTICLE VI—EXPENSE

1. Members of the Judicial Council shall serve without pay, but will be entitled to reasonable transportation expense to and from session, and reasonable board and lodging expense while actually in session. The Financial Secretary of the A. M. E. Zion Church is hereby authorized and ordered to pay such expense, including reasonable secretarial expense.

ARTICLE VII

All paragraphs and sections of present law of the A. M. E. Zion Church in conflict with the above amendments are hereby repealed.

On motion by Dr. Victor J. Tulane, supported by the Rev. H. H. Sink, to sustain the Committee, the matter was before the house. Dr. Rufus Clement offered an amendment to the measure. This was seconded by the Rev. Emory Proctor. Unreadinesses were heard from the following: Mr. S. A. Burnley, Bishop C. C. Coleman, Bishop W. C. Brown, Dr. S. E. Duncan, Mr. W. M. Steele and Bishop W. J. Walls. Another motion made by Mr. John P. Sawyer and seconded by Mr. W. M. Steele calling for the end of debate and the presentation of the previous question was carried. Rev. J. E. McCall moved that the matter be deferred. This motion did not receive a second.

As the time for the noonday message had arrived a short devotional period was observed and the Conference returned to the question at hand.[2]

Bishop Walls then "spoke to a privileged question." "The motion to adopt the report with stated recommendations was carried by a vote of 365 for and 57 against.

The above resolution bore the signatures of the following: J. R. Funderburk, William Steele, S. L. Hopkins, G. L. Smith, J. C. Canty, G. L. Fauntleroy, G. F. McMurray, Harold A. L. Clement, B. M. Montgomery, Arthaniel E. Harris, Elias S. Hardge.[3]

The motion of Dr. Samuel E. Duncan which pertained to the Judicial Council Resolution was as follows:

---

[2] *Official Journal of the 35th Quadrennial Session,* 125, 126.
[3] *Official Journal of the 35th Quadrennial Session,* 450.

Motion by Dr. S. E. Duncan, that the Bishops be authorized and are hereby instructed to constitute the Judicial Council by appointing the members of the same for the quadrennium 1956-60 under the eligibility regulations for membership, thereon as approved in legislation passed by in the 35th General Conference on May 16, 1956.

The motion of Dr. Duncan was seconded by Mrs. Bettye Lee Alleyne and Reverend John Miller.[4]

When the Connectional Council met in Asheville, North Carolina (Hopkins Chapel) on August 24, 1956 the decision of the Board of Bishops stated that the legislation concerning the "Judicial Countil was incomplete and ineffective until repassed by the 1960 General Conference and submitted to the Annual Conferences for approval, as set forth in the decision." [5]

The full statement of the Board of Bishops is not included here, since the above will clearly state the case at hand.

The tenor of the Church's attitude as its official family (The Connectional Council collected its material and moved on to Lake Junaluska (to attend the Ecumenical World Methodist Conference) was not one to bring about forceful advancement. From areas normally at one with the program and policy of the Church statements were noted which indicated the real depth of the cleavage. Recalling the attitude of the late William Bascom (Presiding Elder of long standing in Alabama) and the late Dr. Rufus Early Clement (President of Atlanta University) it may be understood that few groups within the church were satisfied with the decision of the Board of Bishops.

The second day of the Thirty-sixth session saw the intent of the General Conference in the matter. "Mr. Oscar W. Adams, North Alabama Conference, brought a point of unfinished business from the 1956 General Conference. The Chair ruled that Mr. Adams was out of order and that his question would come later in the legislative session; that preliminaries would come before such questions.

"Mr. Adams appealed from the decision of the Chair. The Chair asked the house whether it would sustain its decision and the question was put to vote whether or not the decision of the Chair would be the rule of the house. The stated count of the delegates was:

---

[4] *Ibid.*, 450, 451.
[5] *Ibid.*, 451.

77—For

225—Against

"Bishop Walls stated that the vote had disrupted the program.

"A motion was made by Mr. Adams that action be taken to implement the action of the 1956 General Conference regarding the appointing of members of the Judicial Council by the Board of Bishops. The Council is to consist of five elders and four laymen, and that we do now to proceed to elect same."

The Chair refused to entertain the motion and explained his position by stating that the Board of Bishops is responsible for the interpretation and no organic legislation is final until it has gone through the constitutional process.

"Mr. Adams then read Sections 73 and 77 of the A.M.E. Zion Discipline: Section 77 of the Discipline regarding the General Conference—'*it also finally determines the correct interpretation of any question or opinion of law or any ruling on the part of the Bishop in any lower court.*'

"Section 73. '*The General Conference shall have power to revise and amend rules whenever it may deem it necessary for the General interest of the Connection: and all such rules shall become valid immediately after the sanction of that body.*"

"Mr. Oscar Adams asked the Chair to put to the body an appeal from the Chair's ruling that the motion was unconstitutional.

"The Chair refused to put the appeal and read from the 1956 Discipline, Page 33, paragraph 84, of the Discipline, also Paragraph 88 and Paragraph 90, section 3, to sustain his ruling." †

In the session of the afternoon the same day, Mr. Adams again made a motion that the General Conference proceed to the election of the members of the Judicial Council. It will be noted that at the morning session it was stated that the Quadrennial Episcopal Address was scheduled. Bishop Walls now stated that the resolution could not be followed because: "It would mean no law passed by the General Conference could be interpreted by the Bishops. . . . The Discipline authorizes the Bishops to make interpretation of all laws before they can be put into the Discipline. . . . The Discipline delegates to the Board of Bishops the interpretation of all laws. . . . Technicalities in laws are not finally decided by legislative bodies." ††

---

† *Official Journal of the Thirty-sixth Quadrennial Session*, 1960, 41.
†† *Official Journal of the Thirty-sixth Quadrennial Session*, 43.

"Mr. Adams read from Section 77 of the Discipline regarding the General Conference 'it also finally determines the correct interpretation of any question or opinion of law or any ruling on the part of a Bishop in any lower Court.'

" 'Section 73. The General Conference shall have power to revise and amend rules whenever it may deem it necessary for the general interest of the Connection; and all such rules shall become valid immediately after the sanction of that body.' "

In the discussion which followed Bishop Walls stated that the matter of the Judicial Council had been brought back to the General Conference for reconsideration and revision. The Reverend Dr. W. A. Cooper requested that the statement of the Board of Bishops re: the Judicial Council be read. Bishop Tucker stated that the measure was not unconstitutional but incomplete. Dr. Cooper then moved that a committee be appointed to "put the resolution in proper form." The General Conference insisted that a set time be noted for the Committee to report. This time was set for 2:30 P.M. Monday, May 9th.§

As the committee was constituted the following were named: Bishops W. J. Walls, S. G. Spottswood, H. B. Shaw, R. L. Jones, H. T. Medford; Reverends E. Franklin Jackson, W. A. Cooper, R. W. Bullette, G. W. McMurray, W. T. Kennedy, R. A. G. Foster, I. B. Pierce, R. E. Stevens, H. H. Little, J. H. Satterwhite, J. H. Miller; Mr. Oscar W. Adams, D. D. Garrett, Melvin Johnson, S. A. Burnley, Oliver Francis, Mrs. Abbie Clement Jackson, Mrs. Lucy T. David, G. W. Lawrence and P. C. Moore.⁶ At least four of these individuals were lawyers. At the suggestion of Bishop Walls, who stated that he did not think it proper for bishops to serve, these names were removed from the committee. On motion of Rev. E. Franklin Jackson, seconded by J. W. Watson, the committee was approved.

"The Judicial Council Committee reported. The report was read by Mr. Oscar W. Adams, who moved the adoption of the report. The Chair would not entertain a motion to adopt the report, stating that the report would have to be reviewed by the Executive and Judiciary Committee. Mr. Adams appealed to the Chair's ruling. The Chair stated that until identical facts were presented to the Board of Bishops and the General Conference, he could not accept a motion. The Presiding Officer (then) referred the report of the Special Committee on the

§ *Ibid.*, 43.
⁶ *Official Journal, 36th Quadrennial Session*, 43, 44.

THE STORM BREAKS

Judicial Council to the Committee on Executive and Judicial Business. A proposal was made to defer this matter until the General Conference delegates had an opportunity to read the report, after mimeographed copies had been distributed. No action was taken." [7]

On Tuesday, May 10, 1960, a motion was made by Dr. Rufus Clement ordering the Judicial Committee to "report Wednesday, May 11, at 3:00 P.M. This motion was seconded by Mr. Oscar Adams.[8] It appears that Dr. Jackson distributed copies of the Resolution on Judicial Council before the end of the session. It also appears that the report was not ready or, at least, was not called for at the time. However, Mr. Oscar Adams moved that the first order of the day, May 12, at 10:00 A.M. should be the report of the Executive and Judiciary Committee. The motion, supported by E. Franklin Jackson, was carried.[9] This was to come immediately after the reading of the Minutes.

With Bishop Stephen Gill Spottswood presiding, the matter of the Judicial Council came before the Conference again, Thursday, May 12th. The Chair, this time, called for the order of the day. The Board of Bishops' statement was read by Bishop C. E. Tucker:

BOARD OF BISHOPS' STATEMENT
Regarding the Judicial Council

According to our organic law, this legislation, undoubtedly must be ratified by the Annual Conferences to become an established amendment according to the Constitution.

That it is the unanimous decision of the Board of Bishops that a Bishop give only objective official attention to the legislation on the Judicial Council as should be done on matters of referral of organic law to the Annual Conferences.

Provided, however, that it is the duty of the Chairman of any meeting or the Bishop of any Conference to give objective explanation without comment or effort to influence votes.

Furthermore, it is the opinion of your Board of Bishops that this referral can be processed in the interim probably within one and one-half years from the rise of this General Conference.

We would then follow our established custom of nominating Boards and presenting them to the Connectional Council for election when the General Conference so orders and further, in submitting their names for election to the succeeding General Conference.[10]

---

[7] *Ibid.*, 55.
[8] *Ibid.*, 56.
[9] *Ibid.*, 60.
[10] *Official Journal of the 36th Quadrennial Session*, 62.

Attorney George W. Lawrence requested the opportunity to discuss the statement of the Bishops. The Chair ruled that the report of the Executive-Judicial Committee should be read first. A motion of E. Franklin Jackson with a second by Attorney Lawrence stated that the opinion of the Board of Bishops be discussed. Mr. Adams stated that the statement was merely an opinion. "That report to be read is a report and does not reflect opinion of Special Committee appointed by the General Conference."

Dr. Clement called for a point of procedure. The Executive and Judiciary Committee evidently had decided that a statement from the Board should be heard first along the same line. Dr. Clement read this statement agreeing that the members of the Board of Bishops should not oppose the passage or procedure of the resolution in the Annual Conferences; that the vote would be by secret ballot and the results reported in the Connectional Council of 1961. Mr. Adams did not agree with the statement made, declaring that there was no law whereby matters had to be handed down to the Annual Conferences. He then stated that he would offer the following amendment to the report: "1. Proposals made by the Special Committee regarding impeachment of members of Judicial Council be included: 2. Judicial Council have no operation on Annual Conference level be included. Amendment seconded by Dr. E. Franklin Jackson." [11]

"Dr. S. E. Duncan said he is willing to go along with the compromise if Bishops are unanimous in their desire to see that the Judicial Council go through the Annual Conferences. The Chair requested Bishop Walls to answer. Bishop Walls said the Bishops are friendly to the movement and we will preside objectively as Chairmen and not fight it. I state this as my opinion." [12]

Mrs. Abbie Clement Jackson endeavored to expedite matters by suggesting, through motion that the following prevail: 1. Time limit on each speaker. 2. No person to speak more than once, on the subject before all who wished to do so had spoken. 3. Have hour for closing. 4. Next order of business vote on recall of Bishops.[13] This motion passed.

Dr. Rufus Clement moved that a time limit be placed on each

---

[11] *Official Journal, 36th Quadrennial Session,* 62.
[12] *Ibid.,* 62, 63.
[13] *Official Journal, 36th Quadrennial Session,* 63.

speaker and that at 4:00 P.M. the vote be taken on the Judicial Council. "Mr. Oscar Adams asked for clarification regarding the amendment made to adopt report of Executive-Judicial Committee since the Chair had ruled no appeal from a judicial decision of the Bishops. To deny appeal was to deny democratic rights. Rev. E. F. Jackson withdrew his second of the amendment in light of the Board of Bishops' ruling, taking exception, and Mr. Adams withdrew the motion for amendment with the same exceptions." [14]

A substitute motion made by K. Melvin Taylor that the General Conference accept the report of the Committee as read was seconded by R. W. Gullette. Under an unreadiness, M. F. Ward asked the question: "Why refer the question of the Judicial Council to the local conferences and not refer the General budget to the local conferences?" The Chair stated that the budget was not a constitutional matter. Dr. Taylor then asked the needed percentage of the Annual Conferences for ratification. The answer was two-thirds.

The Rev. E. F. Jackson moved that this General Conference upon nomination of the Board of Bishops elect two (2) elders from each Episcopal District to draw up a constitution for the A.M.E. Zion Church, said constitution to be presented at the 1964 General Conference. Mr. Adams amended the motion so as to include equal lay representation. The motion and the amendment were carried.[15]

The Conference then proceeded to the matter of the recall of Bishops.

The 1960 Minutes of the General Conference lists the following on the Judicial Council (P. 65):

MOTION: Re Judicial Council

It was moved:

1. That the General Secretary of the A. M. E. Zion Church at the rising of the 1960 General Conference send down to each Annual Conference the statutes forming the Judicial Council as passed by the 1960 General Conference, for action upon the same by each Annual Conference. The vote on the same is to be by secret ballot by the members of the Annual Conferences. A simple majority vote will determine the action of each conference. A two-thirds majority vote of the total number of Annual Conferences the (the statement is evidently unfinished, Ed.)

2. The Secretary of each Annual Conference will immediately notify the action of the General Church (should be, Annual Con-

---

[14] *Ibid.*, 63.
[15] *Official Journal of the 36th Quadrennial Session,* 64.

ference) General Secretary of the action of the Annual Conference. When ratified the Bishops shall nominate the interim Judicial Council to the Connectional Council of August 1961. When elected this group shall serve until May 1, 1964 at which time the statutes as passed will become operative thereafter.
Attested To:
Bishop Stephen G. Spottswood
Presiding Officer

Mrs. Willie G. Alstork
General Secretary
Buffalo, New York
May 12, 1960[16]

The writer assumes the privilege to make a statement of fact in one instance as this order was sent down to the Annual Conferences. While no person in the Allegheny Conference, meeting in Uniontown, Pa., was unaware of the stand of Bishop Stephen Gill Spottswood where the Resolution was concerned, it should be said, without fear of contradiction, that nothing was placed in the way of a fair and free vote of those with that privilege. As a result, every Annual Conference under Bishop Spottswood voted *for* the Judicial Council. The official vote as issued by the General Secretary of the Church is listed:

RESULTS OF THE VOTE ON THE
JUDICIAL COUNCIL

Conference	Yes	No
Bishop W. J. Walls, 1st Dist.		
New York	14	82
Western New York	11	27
New England	2	45
Western North Carolina	56	50
Bishop R. L. Jones, 2nd Dist.		
Phila. and Balto.	46	16
West Cent. N. C.	80	9
Central N. C.	56	50
Bishop H. B. Shaw, 3rd Dist.		
Cape Fear	16	46
New Jersey	24	44
Palmetto	14	18
South Florida	0	15
Bahama	0	2
Bishop Stephen G. Spottswood, 4th Dist.		
Ohio	88	5
Allegheny	21	9

[16] *Official Journal, 36th Quadrennial Session,* 65.

THE STORM BREAKS

Michigan	91	5
Indiana	29	3

Bishop W. A. Stewart, 5th Dist.

Virginia	38	19
Blue Ridge		No
Albemarle		No
North Carolina		No
Tennessee	47	7

Bishop D. C. Pope, 6th Dist.

Pee Dee	Yes
South Carolina	Yes
Georgia	Yes
South Georgia	Yes
East Tenn. and Va.	Yes

Bishop C. E. Tucker, 7th Dist.

Kentucky	9	32
West Tenn. and Mississippi	2	25
South Miss.	2	24
West Alabama	4	32

Bishop Joseph D. Cauthen, 8th Dist.

California	8	32
South-West Rocky Mountain	5	18
Oregon-Washington	3	2
Missouri	2	32

Bishop Felix S. Anderson, 9th Dist.

Alabama	28	11
North Alabama	59	2
Cahaba	27	1
Central Alabama	29	4
South Alabama	27	3

Bishop W. M. Smith, 10th Dist.

Texas	0	13
Louisiana	1	32
Florida	3	16
Arkansas	0	31
North Arkansas	1	24
Oklahoma	0	13
Colorado	1	6
South America		No
Virgins Islands	(Forgot to take vote)	

Bishop S. Dorme Lartly, 11th Dist.

Liberia		No
West Ghana	4	35

Bishop W. A. Hilliard, 12th Dist.
East Ghana .... Yes
Nigeria .... Yes

    Number of conferences voting yes 23
    Number of conferences voting no 28
    Total number of conferences 52
    Necessary for approval .... 35 [17]

Thus the Judicial Council resolution was defeated.

What will be the end product of this venture? Naturally no one person can say. There is the possibility that many persons of the denomination now look upon reform as a hopeless task. If this is true then the Church can expect a weakening of its appeal. This writer has repeatedly stated that the Church must follow its own precepts into every single action. The Zion Methodist Church has often been spoken of as the *Freedom Church,* and in truth, it was, for history will note that at one time every outstanding advocate of freedom was numbered in her membership. One endeavors to assess the absence of many leaders of 1960 in the 1964 sessions. It is to be hoped that this is not the type of indication it appears to be.

One wonders if the Church, somewhere, lost the zeal of its major calling, over and above power and prestige, and in this struggle over the Judicial Council it allows too much thinking in that direction. The Church has one major purpose for existence. It dare not turn aside from that purpose and endure.

One final note where the matter of the Judicial Council is concerned. This writer asked a Bishop of a sister denomination about the Judicial Council. Then, as now, we were all, supposedly, working for one Black Methodist Church. His words will remain with us a long time as he stated his denomination would never give up the Judicial Council. Our efforts then at Organic Union must await a change of heart on the part of the Annual Conferences of Zion Methodism.

Thus, with the defeat of the measure of the Judicial Council, the second great thrust of the Church at limitation failed. The first, it will be recalled, was the attempt to limit the *askings* in Annual Conferences from local congregations. There would come an even greater thrust in the Connectional Budget only that this too, would be severely weakened.

---

[17] *Report of the General Secretary,* Mr. E. M. Graham to the Connectional Council.

CHAPTER XXVI

The Authority of the General Conference

THE elections of 1956 will be long remembered by all Zionites. Anyone desirous of examining the real causes would not have far to look. It is this writer's opinion that many of the delegates to the Thirty-fifth Quadrennial session of the General Conference were basically interested in the welfare of the denomination. Every confrontation pointed to this thesis. A firm indication of this was the matter involving Editor Walter R. Lovell of the Star of Zion. The General Conference heard the statement of the Board of Bishops in the Episcopal address and promptly voted Walter R Lovell back into office by a resounding 272 votes out of a possible 388. Six other candidates could muster no more than 26 votes each. This did not say that every one of them was not a worthy successor to Dr. Lovell but the delegates were no longer concerned in approving the action of his removal. They listened to the reasons and did not listen.

The balloting for the episcopacy began on the Tenth Day with Bishop William Andrew Stewart in the Chair. Earlier, it was understood that several candidates were not approved for running since the law of 1900 would not permit this from one who had "two living wives," i.e. a divorced person. This rule applied too, to the wife of the individual, if she were divorced, unless in either case, the candidate or his wife, obtained such a divorce on Scriptural grounds. It appears that an understanding of prohibition had been issued and that this understanding was to have been handed to the delegates of each Episcopal District. At least two or three of the Bishops made no effort to push this prohibition in their delegations.

It is not the purpose of this work to go into the background of these matters. In truth, any documents available are not easily accessible. So we return to that which appears in the public records.

It should be stated that in at least one case the matter of divorce and re-marriage did not enter, or this appears to be so from the records.

Let us then look at the record:

Tellers were named by the bishops and district leaders, and at this time, Bishop Stewart ordered the election without further delay. He stated there were persons disqualified, and read the declaration of the Board of Bishops' ineligible ministers: Reverends Charles Foggie, Alfred G. Dunston, and Fred D. Porter.

Reverend Foggie asked for the floor on the point of personal privilege. After some debating, Reverends Foggie, Dunston and Porter were granted permission to speak. Both Reverend Foggie and Reverend Dunston spoke eloquently and intelligently on the status of their marital situations, which disqualified the three men. Bishop Herbert Bell Shaw read a document (see notarized document [Ed. note: the document appears not to have been included in the published Minutes]) that the Rev. A. G. Dunston Jr. submitted to the Board of Bishops, and reading was requested by the Board.

"Rev Porter of Detroit was granted the floor on his point of personal privilege, He stated that his marital position since being in Zion, had been in accordance with the laws of the church. He had appeared before the Board of Bishops as the Revs. Dunston and Foggie and waited for the decision of the Board."[1]

It was necessary to restore order as several individuals were endeavoring to speak to this point. Rev. James Clement suggested prayer and forgiveness at the hands of God and of the men. A question was asked by E. S. Hardge regarding the possibility of appeal. The ruling was that there was no appeal. "Mr. Levi Saunders was given the floor to state a point of accuracy on the matter of divorce being both moral and legal. Mr. Melvin Johnson obtained the floor but was ruled out of order."[2] The Conference began balloting. It is intimated that any ballots for any of the three men named by the Board of Bishops were to be thrown out.

"A motion to appeal from the decision of the Board of Bishops by Reverend A. G. Dunston with a second by Reverend Foggie, was ruled out of order on the grounds it was a ruling of the Board of Bishops and not the Chairman's individual opinion."[3]

It is intersting to note the reaction of the General Conference, when, on the Fourth Ballot, the Reverend Dr. Charles Eubank Tucker was elected. The Secretary wrote: "Shouts of joy and many cheers went out in honor of his promotion."[4] The General Conference left little to guess work where his election was concerned.

---

[1] *Official Journal of the 35th Quadrennial Session of the General Conference*, 101.
[2] *Official Journal 35th Quadrennial Session*, 101.
[3] *Ibid.*, 102.
[4] *Ibid.*, 106.

On the sixth ballot, the Reverends Joseph Dixon Cauthen and Charles Cecil Coleman were elected.

CHARLES EUBANK TUCKER

Charles Eubank Tucker was born in Baltimore, Maryland, January 12, 1896, the son of William A. and Elivia (Clark) Tucker. In 1922 he married Amelia Moore. One daughter was born to this union, Bernice. He was educated at Beckford and Smith College, Jamaica, West Indies, completing his work in 1913. He attended Lincoln University (Pennsylvania) completing work at this institution in 1917, after which he attended Temple University for the next two years. He studied law under the Hon. Charles Gogg at Point Pleasant, Virginia. He began the practice of Criminal Law in Louisville, Ky., in 1929, and was a candidate for the Assembly of that State in 1933. He began his pastoral work early in life, serving the following churches: Middletown, Delta and Williamsport, Pa., Hilliard Chapel, Montgomery, Alabama, Sharon, Mississippi, Augusta, Georgia, Key West, Florida, Stoner Memorial, Louisville, Ky., Jones Temple, New Albany, Ind., and as Presiding Elder in the Philadelphia and Baltimore, the Kentucky and Indiana Conferences. From this last post he was elected to the episcopacy.

JOSEPH DIXON CAUTHEN

It appears that we do not have as much as we would like on Bishop Cauthen for his attitude in the work of Christ has been one of the high points of the denomination. His ministry has been colored with the problems of few men. He was born, February 21, 1887 in Kershaw, South Carolina. He attended Lancaster Normal and Industrial School, Clinton Junior College in Rock Hill, South Carolina and received his A. B. degree from Livingstone College, Salisbury, N. C. He also received his B. D. degree from Hood Theological Seminary, Salisbury, N. C. In 1921 he married Miss Ruth Smith of Concord, N.C. To this union a son was born, the mother passing away when the child was 16 months of age in 1929.

In 1940, Joseph Dixon Cauthen married Miss Georgia Little of Mobile, Alabama. To this union a daughter was born. Mrs. Cauthen passed away in Jan. 1964.

Bishop Cauthen pastored the following churches: Gethsemane, Charlotte, N. C., State Street in Mobile, Ala., Varick in Philadelphia,

Pa. and Metropolitan in Norfolk, Va. He was elevated to the episcopacy in 1956.

CHARLES CECIL COLEMAN

Charles Cecil Coleman was born in Key West, Florida in 1906. He received his early education at that city and then determined to secure advance work away from home. He came to Livingstone College, Salisbury, N. C. and in 1929 received his A. B. degree with highest honors.

Charles Cecil Coleman married Miss Alcestis McCullough. Meanwhile, he had been pastoring churches in North and South Carolina. He was elected to the episcopacy in Pittsburgh in 1956. He passed away July 17, 1958.

When the General Conference met in Buffalo, four men were elevated to the episcopacy among them being the first native African ever to be so honored by the church. Bishop Lartey, whose biography appears in the appendix of this work, died in Monrovia in August 1969.

FELIX S. ANDERSON

Felix S. Anderson was born in Wilmington, North Carolina, October 3, 1893, the son of Charles and Betty (Foye) Anderson. He was educated in the elementary schools of Boston, Mass. completing his high school work in the same city. He did his college work at Livingstone College, Salisbury, North Carolina and his seminary training at Western Theological Seminary, Pittsburgh, Pennsylvania.

On April 28, 1920 he married Bessie B. Bizzell. To this union six children were born.

Felix S. Anderson was converted February 10, 1910 in Boston, Mass. and decided to enter the ministry, preaching his trial sermon in August 1913, at Clinton Chapel Church, Charlotte, N. C. He was ordained a deacon November 15, 1915 and an elder Nov. 17, 1917. He has served the following churches: Rocky Creek Circuit, Mainville Circuit in the Western North Carolina Conference, Cedar Grove, Gilmore Chapel, Big Zion, Albemarle, N. C., Mt. Washington, Pittsburgh, Pa., Trimble Chapel, Oakdale, Pa., First, Providence, R. I., Mt. Lebanon, Elizabeth City, N. C., Kedesh Church, Edentown, N. C., Hunter Chapel, Tuscaloosa, Ala., Shaw Metropolitan, Atlanta, Ga., Union Chapel, Athens, Ga., St. Peter Church, Trinity, Southern Pines, N. C., Big Zion, Mobile, Ala. and Broadway Temple, Louisville, Ky. He served three terms in the Kentucky Legislature. He was elevated to the episcopacy in 1960.

WILLIAM M. SMITH

William Milton Smith was born in Baldwin County, Alabama, December 18, 1915, a son of George and Elizabeth Smith. He attended Lomax-Hannon High School and received his B. S. degree from Alabama State College at Montgomery. He received his A. M. degree from Tuskegee and the B. D. degree from Hood Theological Seminary, Salisbury, North Carolina. He later studied at the Perkins School of Theology, Southern Methodist University, Dallas, Texas.

He is married to Ida M. Anderson and has one daughter.

Bishop Smith is a member of the Board of Directors of the following, Chamber of Commerce, Red Cross of Mobile County, Mobile County Mental Health Association, Mobile General Hospital, Multiple Sclerosis Committee. He is also on the Board of Directors of the Gulf Federal Savings and Loan Bank of Mobile. He was a delegate to the Ecumenical World Methodist Conferences of 1956 and 1966.

He has pastored the following churches: St. Thomas and Zion, Perdita and Atmore, Alabama, Zion Star and Zion Fountain, the latter in Brewton, Ala., Ebenezer, Montgomery and Big Zion in Mobile. He was elevated to the episcopacy in 1960.

EXTRAORDINARY

The Government of Liberia announces with profound regrets the death in his seventy-fourth year of:[*]

THE RT. REV. DR. SOLOMON DORME LARTEY
D.D., LITT.D., PH.D., G.B.S.A., K.G.B.

Bishop of the African Methodist Episcopal Zion Church,
Ninth Episcopal District, West Africa and
Former Postmaster, Monrovia Post Office

This sad event occurred at the ELWA (Eternal Love Winning Africa) Hospital, Paynesville, Sunday, August 3, 1969, at the hour of three o'clock post meridian.

The late Dr. Lartey was born at Christiansborg, Accra, Ghana, on

---
[*] 71st year (according to family records)

September 12, 1895,** unto the union of the late Mr. Dorme Lartey and Mrs. Amelia Arhuma Lartey.

Bishop Lartey obtained his education from the Presbyterian Mission School in Accra, Ghana, where he majored in Mathematics. Thereafter, he worked for various mercantile enterprises and became an outstanding accountant in that community.

In August 1928, Reverend Lartey travelled to Liberia where he decided to settle. A few years thereafter, he became a naturalized citizen.

Dr. Lartey's public career commenced in Liberia when he was appointed Inspector of Internal Revenues, Treasury Department, in which position he served efficiently until he was appointed Accountant of the Bureau of Internal Revenues. He served efficiently in this capacity for fourteen years. In 1946, President Tubman was pleased to commission him Postmaster of the Monrovia Post Office. In this post he rendered outstanding services until his retirement from Government in 1960.

In his religious affiliation, Dr. Lartey was a Presbyterian and served for many years as a Stated Supply of a few churches, prior to his coming to Liberia. Following his arrival in Liberia, he continued his services as a Presbyterian until 1939, when, during the administration of Bishop James Walter Brown, he severed his membership with that denomination and became a member of the African Methodist Episcopal Zion Church.

Reverend Lartey launched a vigorous program and spearheaded the building of the first A.M.E. Zion Church in Monrovia (Brown Memorial A.M.E. Zion Church, Benson Street), and served as its pastor for many years. Reward for his devoted services came when Dr. Lartey was elevated to the position of Presiding Elder and later as Bishop's Deputy. In 1960, he had the distinguished privilege of being elected and consecrated the first African Bishop in the history of the African Methodist Episcopal Zion Church. He was designated and assigned as Bishop of Liberia, West and East Ghana, and the Federal Republic of Nigeria. He served in this exalted position with distinction and reverence until his demise.

During his encumbency, Bishop Lartey built the Zion Academy, Benson Street, Monrovia, which today molds the lives of many young men and women and opened Po-River Station where an

---
** 1898 (according to family records)

institution is under construction. He also built the Cartwright Memorial A.M.E. Zion Church in Brewerville and a number of other churches, and educational institutions in Liberia and Ghana. He served as a Trustee of Livingstone College, U.S.A.; Chairman of the International Justice and Goodwill; Worship and Ritual; Vice Chairman of Christian Education, Home and Church; Executive Officer of World Methodist Council; Executive Officer of the World Council of Churches; Chairman of the Board of Bishops; as well as a founding member of the Christian Ministers' Association of Liberia. In the latter organization he served as its first secretary.

In his fraternal association, Dr. Lartey was Past Master of St. John's Lodge, Past Grand Secretary and Grand Chaplain of the Most Worshipful Grand Lodge of Masons of Liberia; Past Master of the Order of United Brothers of Friendship, and Council Member of the Grand United Order of Odd Fellows.

In recognition of his meritorious services to the Church and the State, President Tubman decorated him with the distinctions of Grand Band, Star of Africa and Knight Great Band of the Humane Order of African Redemption. He received the following honorary degrees from Livingstone College, U.S.A., and the University of Liberia; Doctor of Literature, and Doctor of Philosophy and Doctor of Divinity, respectively. He also received a Spanish Decoration of Knight of the DOMAIN OF NEPTUNUS REX—Ruler of the Raging Main.

Dr. Lartey was married twice: first to Mrs. Caroline Lewis, which marriage was later dissolved; on September 12, 1945, he was married the second time to Miss Alicia Ethel Smith, daughter of the late Vice President of Liberia, James S. Smith.

The deceased is survived by his wife, his mother, eight children: Janet, Nadu, David Dorme, Helena Nadu, Victoria Nadu, Nora, Benjamin Dorme, Annie Nadu, and Louise Marie; many grandchildren, one sister, one brother, ten foster children, and other relatives.

The funeral sentences over his remains will be said at the Centennial Memorial Pavilion, Monrovia, on Sunday, August 10, 1969, at the hour of 10 o'clock ante meridian. Thereafter, his body will be borne to the Po-River Station for interment.

As a mark of last respect to the late Rt. Reverend Dr. Solomon Dorme Lartey, D.D., LITT.D., Ph.D., G.BSA., Bishop of the African Methodist Episcopal Zion Church, Ninth Episcopal District, West Africa and former Postmaster, Monrovia Post Office, it is hereby ordered and directed that on the day of interment the flag of the Republic be flown at half-staff from all public buildings in the City of Monrovia from eight o'clock ante meridian to six o'clock post meridian.

BY ORDER OF THE PRESIDENT
J. RUDOLPH GRIMES
Secretary of State

Department of State
Monrovia, Liberia
August 6, 1969

WILLIAM ALEXANDER HILLIARD

William Alexander Hilliard, elected to the Episcopacy in Buffalo, New York, May, 1960 is a product of Texas having been born in that State, September 14, 1904, the son of John H. and Carrie (Hicks) Hilliard. At an early age his parents took him to Kansas City, Kansas, where he spent several years. Later, the family removed to Des Moines, Iowa where William Alexander completed his elementary school education. His high school training was taken in Kansas City, Kansas. His college work was done at Western University in Quinders, Kansas and his Seminary work at the same institution. Later he did additional work at Wayne University, Detroit, Michigan. In 1948 he was honored with a D. D. degree from Livingstone College, Salisbury, North Carolina, for outstanding services to the denomination.

In 1927, the then Reverend Hilliard married Miss Edra Mae Mael of Kansas City, Mo.

Bishop Hilliard pastored the following churches: St. Matthew Church, Kansas City, Mt. Zion Church, Argentine, Kansas, Metropolitan Church, Kansas City, Metropolitan Church, Chester, S. C., St. John, Wilson, N. C., and St. Paul, Detroit, Mich. The first quadrennium as a bishop of the Church was spent as one of the resident bishops of Africa. His work was in Ghana and Nigeria.

As the General Conference of Buffalo opened two matters were of extreme importance. We have traced in detail the matter of the Judicial Council and will now turn to the second matter—that of the election of bishops. We have, above, given the biographical sketch of three of them, the fourth, Bishop Lartey, will be found in the appendix.

It is ironic that again Bishop William Andrew Stewart was in the chair as the balloting for bishops got underway. Again it was his task to announce: "the Board of Bishops had declared the following ministers ineligible to contest for the bishopric: Reverends, A. G. Dunston Jr., R. A. G. Foster, J. A. Babington-Johnson and A. G. Anonye.

"Bishop C. E. Tucker stated that he wished to state disagree in the Dunston matter as follows:

"Bishop Tucker stated that he did not see anything in the discipline that would disqualify Rev. Dunston from being a candidate, but did not contest the decision of the Board of Bishops.

"Bishop stated copies of the decision made four years ago by the bishops would be on the ground tomorrow if anyone wanted them.

"Bishop W. C. Brown stated 'There is no law that makes Rev. A. G. Dunston ineligible. The opinion of the Board of Bishops should state it was a majority decision. Rev. A. G. Dunston was asked for a transcript of his divorce, but he hasn't brought it. I am not going to say he is ineligible, but he hasn't done what the Board of Bishops asked him to do.'

"Dr R. E. Clement, 'We have reached an impasse in an interpretation of the law, only one thing we can do. I call for the order of the day.'

"Point of personal privilege by Dr. Dunston. Chair, 'you may not.' Dr. Dunston: 'Why?' Chair: 'the order of the day is to vote.' The Chair states: 'We insisted upon Dr. Dunston giving us new evidence in this matter. The evidence given was not sufficient to clear the matter. We asked him to bring new evidence. He came to the Bishops' meeting in January and wanted to appear before us.'

"Dr. Dunston asked for a point of personal privilege, he wished to read a statement regarding his case. The presiding officer refused to grant permission, stating the order of the day is to proceed to vote. 'Additional evidence from Rev. A. G. Dunston has been requested by the Board of Bishops. This has not been complied with by Rev. Dunston.' Rev. Dunston stated the matter was left with one of the bishops to instruct him about the letter he should have sent the Board; this was not done. Rev. A. G. Dunston asked: 'Is it not up to the General Conference to hear this appeal?' Will you not let the house speak?' The Chair again refused. Rev. Dunston asked, 'Will you allow the ballots be impounded until this question of law is settled?' The Chair answered, 'No.' Rev. Dunston insisted he had the right of appeal to the General Conference to be heard, and stated the Chair was taking away his right, the right of any member of the Church, more so of an elder in good standing. The Chair asked for the calling of the roll while Rev. Dunston continued to call for recognition by the Chair, finally stating 'I wish to be relieved of my seat in the General Conference.' The Chair answered, 'Thank you.' " [5]

---

[5] *Official Journal, 36th Quadrennial Session,* 68.

While the balloting began and was concluded in the election of four persons in Buffalo, the matter did not end here. That which was said and done was merely an interlude. A statement of one of the bishops in Pittsburgh, Pa., four years before, is recalled. "You may as well settle the matter now for it will come up again." While this writer is not sure as to the author of that statement he believes it was Bishop Andrew Stewart.

As one looks through the Zion Methodist Church, he notes she faces another situation where Organic Union and union of all Methodists is concerned, her stand on divorce and re-marriage. Bishop Spottswood has stated that in order to live up to the Discipline, the applicant's status must begin in the local church with the church member and follow through to the ministry. The Church, too, must bring her written words on the subject in line with that of the state or agree to the possibility of disobedience. One will note that the Discipline states: "As far as it respects civil affairs, we believe it the duty of Christians, and especially all Christian ministers, to be subject to the supreme authority of the country where they may reside." While this is not speaking directly on the subject of marriage and divorce, the Church must know that marriage is both a civil and a religious matter. One does not exist without the other.

The Church, under present conditions, states that a divorced and re-married person is living in sin. On the other hand, the State brings no punishment on the party or parties whom it legally separates. The State, on the one hand declares that a person "taken in adultery" is guilty of crime and must be punished. The Church on the other may be aware of such conditions and remain silent. It then suggests a rating of moral standards and we believe the standards of the Church should be the higher which, at the present, they are not.

Bishop William Milton Smith was presiding on Saturday, May 16, 1964 at Indianapolis, Indiana, as the subject of the episcopacy came up again. The record states:

> The ballot for the election of the bishop was prepared for distribution by districts. Rev. Harlee Little asked of the General Secretary if certified copies of the birth certificates of the candidates had been submitted. The General Secretary answered in the affirmative. Rev. George Leake inquiring of the candidates asked if the name of the Rev. Alfred G. Dunston appeared on the ballot. The question was answered in the negative by the Chairman, that being so for the same reason that it did not appear on the ballot in the previous General Conference eight

years ago. The Chairman ruled everything on the matter out of order. On point of personal privilege, Bishop C. Eubank Tucker appealed the denial of the Chair and appealed to the house for a decision. A discussion relative to the eligibility of candidates for the Bishop was entered upon.[6]

It should be stated that in the General Conference of 1960 the rule of balloting had been changed. Two general ballots were to be prepared by the General Secretary, one containing the listings of the candidates for Bishop and the other, a listing of candidates for General offices. Fees were to be charged each person listed to defray the cost of preparing the ballots. The General Conference of 1964 saw the first use of this procedure.[7]

In the discussion which followed Bishop C. E. Tucker called the General Conference's attention to its past acts stating that it had elected J. W. Brown (note change of initials) who had been divorced (ed. note:) and James Clair Taylor whose wife was divorced.[8]

The discussion, with all of its ramifications, brought the Church to one of its greatest crises since 1852, a matter of 112 years. At one point, as the Presiding Officer vacated the Chair, the General Conference threatened to elect its own Chairman and proceed. The Bishops returned and resumed the session. At another, there were open threats to bring in civil law to settle matters within the Church. One can use his own interpretation as to the mood of the Conference. The Conference called for the reading of the records where the Rev. A. G. Dunston and Rev. Charles Foggie were concerned. The crux of the matter was clearly stated by the Reverend R. L. Speaks as he said: "that something greater than individual position was involved. We are trying to decide whether the Bishops or the General Conference is supreme." The writer is not sure as to the origin of these words found in the Minutes:

> It was observed that we have two issues that might have been settled separately. (1) Where lies the ultimate authority of the Church and (2) the question of a marital status of a person. It was observed that the Conference was prepared to vote on this issue at this moment and that the hour has come when we must decide whether or not the General Con-

---
[6] *Official Journal, 37th Quadrennial Session*, 6, 59, 60.
[7] *Discipline of the A.M.E. Zion Church*, 1960, 126; 1964, 133.
[8] *Official Journal, 37th Quadrennial Session*, 60.

ference has the final say on any question. This General Conference must settle this issue.⁹

It was observed that Rev. Dunston was pastoring the "highest Church in the denomination" and "the Bishop who assigned him should be tried at this conference." Reverend Long declared "It seems that one side is not going to yield to either side." He suggested that an appeal be made to the courts of the land bringing about an injunction. The Chairman said that he would have no objection to such action." ¹⁰

Perhaps for Zion Methodism, God intervened as the Church went to worship and prayer after a Saturday of confusion and hostility. The very crucial session of Monday, May 18 saw in the Chair the African Bishop, S. Dorme Lartey and on the following day, his companion in African work, Bishop William Alexander Hilliard. Bishop Lartey was priviledged to serve but two full quadrenniums but it may be that he was *called* especially for his task of May 18.

The report of the Budget Committee was heard as well as that of the Episcopal Committee, who provided for the election of one bishop. The calmness and fairness of Bishop Lartey brought the church through an awesome crisis.

On Tuesday, May 19, Bishop William Alexander Hilliard took the Chair. After the election of the Connectional Budget Board, there was but one task open—the return to the disturbing problem of the previous Saturday.

The Conference refused to go into Executive session and began debate on the matter. At long last, Bishop William Jacob Walls offered a motion that the Rev. A. G. Dunston's character be passed by this General Conference. The motion was not seconded.¹¹

One would note a point of law here. The Church, in the 19th Century, declared that only an appeal could be brought before the General Conference. Trial, and therefore guilt or absolution is a matter for the Annual Conference and not an item for the General Conference. The General Conference, therefore, can merely accept or reject a candidate but has not the power to place the individual on trial without the action of a lower court. The simple matter to be

---
⁹ *Ibid.*, 63.
¹⁰ *Ibid.*, 63.
¹¹ *Official Journal,* 37th Session, 83, 84.

decided by the General Conference was whether the names of Reverends Dunston and Foggie should be placed on the ballot. On this motion the vote was as follows: Number of votes cast: 471. Void, 7, Necessary for the passing of the motion, 263. Affirmative votes (for the motion) 377. Against the motion, 87.[12]

The names of the Rev. Dunston and Rev. Foggie were therefore placed on the ballot.

The balloting began at the night session. Reverend Dunston received 153 votes on this ballot. Reverend Foggie received 8. It should be stated that only one bishop was to be elected. On the second ballot Reverend Dunston received 237 votes. Again there was no election. "Rev. William Coleman of Los Angeles suggested that Bishop William Alexander Hilliard be given a rising vote of thanks for the remarkable way in which he had presided today. It was done." [13]

Bishop William Jacobs Walls presided on Wednesday, May 20. The Minutes show that "A statement of opinion was read by the presiding officer. Rev. M. P. Linder observed that the opinion should be taken up as a separate item. Rev. W. A. Cooper, rising to a point of procedure, stated that "the opinion of the presiding officer has no place in Tuesday's minutes but could be inserted in Wednesday's morning minutes." Rev. J. Dallas Jenkins was interrupted by Rev. F. R. Blakey on a point of procedure in that the opinion was not a part of the minute. The Rev. E. Franklin Jackson stated that the minutes should show that the conference indulged the reading of the opinion and that the conference did not approve or disapprove the statement, there being no action taken.[14]

The Chair announced the conference would proceed with the election of a bishop.

The report of the third ballot showed no election.

"Moved by Rev. A. Marshall and seconded by Rev. James Clement that the Rev. Alfred G. Dunston be elected by acclamation. Dr. J. Clinton Hoggard and Rev. J. W. Wactor withdrew with thanks. Rev. Richard Council withdrew with thanks.[15] The motion to elect by acclamation was carried.

---

[12] *Official Journal, loc. cit.,* 84.
[13] *Ibid.,* 86.
[14] *Ibid.,* 87.
[15] *Official Journal of the 37th Quadrennial Session,* 88.

STATEMENT OF OPINION—PRESIDING OFFICER
Bishop W. J. Walls, May 20, 1964

Once in the seventh decade in the history of our church there was a split that threatened our existence. The price was that we fell behind other churches of the race founded in the same period as our Zion. A motion passed yesterday on an illegal, basis that is:

"Paragraph 77, A.M.E. ZION DISCIPLINE—'The General Conference shall have power to ratify or reverse the decision of the lower court, to try charges against a Bishop during its sitting, to acquit, expel, or disrobe him of his Episcopal authority, or remand his case to lower court for decision; it also constituted a court of appeals for Traveling Ministers in full connection who have been convicted by a lower court; it also finally determines the correct interpretation of any question or opinion of law or any ruling on the part of a Bishop in any lower court.

That was passed presumptive that it applied to decisions of the Board of Bishops who are governed by the Law.

"Para. 90 Section (3)—The Board of Bishops shall have authority to hand down interpretations of existing church law; and explanations of methods for administering the law, when so interpreted."

The matter is unsettled. It matters less who is elected or not elected in that motion. It still remains that the judicial authorities of the bishops and the General Conference have struck a grit of confusion, and this matter must be settled.

It will come a day, sooner than we expect, that the bishops may render a decision which will be acceptable to two contending factions (ed. note, omission of the prefix *un* or *not,* appears possible). It will have the seeds of splitting the Church, and we must prevent this by settling the matter before we leave this crisis, which is still in our hands any supreme council of the church which the bishops constitute now, since there is no other, must be protected against a body merely legislative.

The suggestion is that a representative group meet with the Board of Bishops to iron out this matter with legal assistance, and if possible, short of any court decision except that of the church.

Signature
W. J. WALLS
Chairman Gen. Conference
May 20, 1964 [16]

One should note that the above statement does go beyond that of legislation. The General Conference likewise can constitute itself a court, so in this, it takes upon itself a second function—judicial.

The Indianapolis General Conference recalled Bishop Walls by a vote of 250 for to 233 against. Two Hundred forty-two votes were needed for recall.[17]

---

[16] *Official Journal, 37th Quadrennial Session,* 88.
[17] *Ibid.* 50.

THE AUTHORITY OF THE GENERAL CONFERENCE

The General Conference of 1968, meeting in Detroit accomplished little. In the recall vote, the following were retained for another four year term:

BISHOP WILLIAM ANDREW STEWART
BISHOP S. E. TUCKER
BISHOP FELIX S. ANDERSON
BISHOP JOSEPH DIXON CAUTHEN

As has been stated elsewhere, Bishop Walls failed of recall.

In the subsequent election for the one place on the Board of Bishops the Rev. Charles Foggie was elected by the General Conference.

ALFRED GILBERT DUNSTON

Alfred Gilbert Dunston was born June 25, 1915 in Coinjock, N. C., the son of Reverend Alfred G. and Cora Lee (Charity) Dunston. He was converted in Elizabeth City, N. C., preached trial sermon, September 4, 1935, at Mt. Lebanon Church, Elizabeth City, N. C. He was ordained a Deacon in July 1937, Salisbury, N. C. and Elder at Cornelius, N. C., June 1938. He was consecrated a Bishop at Indianapolis, Indiana May 21, 1964. He was educated in the Elementary and High Schools of Elizabeth City, N. C., Livingstone College, A. B., 1935, and pursued graduate studies at Drew University, Madison, N. J. 1938-39 and 1941-1942. He was awarded the D. D. degree by Allen University in 1960 and the D. C. L. from Monrovia College, Monrovia, Liberia. He married Permilla R. Flack, June 18, 1940. His children are: Carol Jean, Aingred Chislaine, Armayne Garrinetta. He served as United States Army Chaplain in World War II and is a Reserve Major. He is a member of Alpha Phi Alpha Fraternity. He pastored the following churches: Mt. Sinai Circuit, Advance, N. C., St. John, Thomasville, N. C., Wallace Temple, Bayonne, N. J., Price Memorial, Atlantic City, Wallace Chapel, Summit, N. J., Logan Temple, Knoxville, N. C., Wesley, Philadelphia, Pa., Mother Zion, New York City.

CHARLES HERBERT FOGGIE

Charles Herbert Foggie was born in Sumter South Carolina, August 12, 1912. He was reared in Boston, Massachusetts and received his education at Livingstone College (A.B., 1936), Boston University (A.M. 1938), Boston School of Theology (S.T.B. 1939 and S.T.M. 1942) and D. D. Livingstone College, 1949.

Charles Foggie pastored the following churches prior his election: Wadsworth Street Church, Providence, R. I., Rush Church, Cambridge, Mass. and Wesley Center Church, Pittsburgh, Pa. He serves many boards and commissions in his resident city, Pittsburgh. He was elected to the Episcopacy, May 13, 1968. His wife Madeline and daughter comprise the family.

CHAPTER XXVII

The Church's Program and Beliefs
1796-1968

AS THE concluding chapter of this work is reached the author finds it necessary to depart from the relatively safe paths of historical fact to one of interpretation. In an effort to draw together that which appears to have been and is the intent of Zion Methodism in the evolvement of the Kingdom of God this is necessary. The accepted task is not easy and may well assure harsh criticism from many sources. We are confident, however, that here and there during these more than one hundred and seventy-five years of history (assuming that the faint indications that the first church came into being through frequent prayer services as early as 1780s) we can point to evidences supporting that which may be stated.

Every Zion Methodist has an obligation to keep clearly in his or her mind the reasons for the establishment of the Mother Church, and, subsequently, the denomination. To lose sight of these basic facts is to miss a great reason for the existence of the Negro Church. The effort to achieve a significant dignity of personality, both from the spiritual, social and economic standpoints, had to be high in the minds of the Church founders. These items presented the incentive needed and set the goal for each generation as it came upon the scene.

A discerning student will see with clarity these basic principles. They were exhibited in the Stillwell movement and Zion's reaction to it, for the intent of this movement merely enunciated the thinking of the Negro group. Too little attention, too, has been given the agreement of the Church with the Mother Church along these lines, for close scrutiny will reveal a great deal beyond common belief.

To state that the Zion Church was swept along with the controversy over slavery which broke American Methodism into two factions is, in a sense untrue, for its membership was so vitally involved in the conflict that the organization was a rallying point for every outstanding Negro abolitionist of the Century. Dedicated to the belief of a common Fatherhood of God and the brotherhood of man these men and women were privileged to develop under the autogenic direction of the Church,

Zion Youth will do well to recall the work of Sojourner Truth, who began a long line of Negro abolitionists which included Frederick Douglass, who began in the Zion Church as a local preacher in New Bedford, Mass.; then moved on to publishing his *North Star* in the Memorial Church of Rochester, New York. The Reverend Thomas James, his mentor, labored in that city, as well. To the East, at Auburn there was the famed Harriet Tubman, who later willed her property to the Zion Church, and to the West, there was Catherine Harris at Jamestown, likewise a member of the Church.

Many of these early abolitionists rose to significant position in the Church. Jermain Loguen, an escaped slave, became a Bishop, as well as John Jamison Moore, well schooled and trained by his benefactors who aided his escape from slavery, the Fishertown (Pennsylvania) Quakers. Christopher Rush had important connections in North Carolina where the opening wedge of Zion Missions of the South began. James Varick, the first Superintendent and a founder, definitely had slave connections as did Peter Williams, who signed the incorporation papers.

Scarcely had the first wave of Zion Methodism's humanitarians slowed pace when a new generation of workers arose to carry on this mission of human dignity. William Howard Day (born Oct. 16, 1825) was a different type of abolitionist. He demonstrated the possibility before any Negro youth, as he matriculated at Oberlin University in 1843, graduating in 1847 and received his Master of Arts degree from that institution in 1859. It was he who stubbornly fought the separate but equal thesis in Pennsylvania where public schools were concerned. Baptized by James Varick, he lived most of the century in close relationship with the Church.

James Walker Hood appears to have confined his major work to the post-Civil War period, being first, a missionary to Nova Scotia and then to the South, chiefly North Carolina, where he fathered the Public School laws of that State and began the successful venture of Zion Methodism in Education.

Under the direction of Bishop Hood the Zion Church finally established the beginnings of her school and college program as well as the successful Star of Zion, a weekly publication.

THE CHURCH'S PROGRAM AND BELIEFS 1796-1968

And there were others—the account of whom would provide a significant work in itself. Among these were John C. Dancy, Collector of Customs at the Port of Wilmington, North Carolina, one-time Editor of the Star of Zion and for many years, Editor of the second periodical, The A.M.E. Zion Quarterly Review. Bishop John Bryan Small added a new dimension to the missionary effort of the denomination by his interest in the development of the African work and his unique method of developing indigenous leadership in that continent. Through him and others, such leaders as J. E. K. Aggrey and F. A. Osam-Pinanko were brought over and educated, returning later to aid their people. Others educated were the Reverend Dr. Fiawoo, J. A. Babington-Johnson, A. A. Adjahoe, Walter K. Dolly, Charles Acolate, Beresford Cole, Charity Zomolo, Isaac D. Osabutey, Princess Ayina Adamah, Skyne Uku and others who since have been sponsored by Bishop Dunstan, and who are completing their work here in America.

Perhaps the second great point in Zion Methodism's progress was that of education. Trained minds, both in pulpit and pew were a necessity so the preachers were urged to study, books were to be provided in each local church and education in general was to be fostered.

One must look with a clear interpretation on other facts which one would not attempt to deny. It is conceded, for example, that there was an undeniable master-slave relationship which eventually entered into all the endeavors of the Church. While John Street Church was distinctly a bi-racial experiment, it did not allow for the basic increments needed for full Christian development. So these early Church leaders of Zion sought a fellowship worthy of the Church of God.

They recognized the impossibility of this necessity within the Methodist Episcopal Church and sought to gain it for themselves. One would not state that from within the Church this may have been possible for a few, but the masses of slaves and freedmen would naturally have been excluded. Along with this fellowship would go greater efforts in evangelism, interpreting to the full the Christ mandate to his disciples. They recognized too, that no Christian or religious experience was possible without the unrestricted exercise of their faith—the development of expression and belief. John Street

Church could, at best, provide only limited movement in these directions, so the decision to form the new organization.

To say that the leaders of the new church were not well acquainted with all the problems faced within and without the church would bring to them a disservice. They knew, for example, that any organization with a sizable number of Negroes, would in time, be working at a disadvantage among all groups, and, as time wore on they knew that the zeal of evangelism within the Mother Church on the existing terms became a question mark as she struggled to gain status among other denominational enterprises.

It appears to this writer that Zion should understand as the History of the denomination is studied that the final separation from the Mother John Street Church did not come about because of the race question, but was caught up in the Stillwell movement,—a struggle within the Church over property rights and the eventual rights of lay people—their power over against the authority of the clergy and the control of real estate.

So frequently, we ignore the significant words one sees in the permitted paper of Incorporation for Zion Church and that which evidently was denied the Church in general. In the agreement with the Mother Church there are likewise significant statements which bring amazement to the discerning reader in the light of the existing relationship between clergy and lay people. And, finally, we dare not overlook the statement of the congregation as it severed its ties with the Mother Church.

> "Whereas, a very grievous schism has taken place in the Methodist Episcopal Church in this City, in consequence of a resolution of the last General Conference, and that resolution acted upon by the annual conference of the New York District—the substance of which is (as we are informed) that a memorial shall be drawn up . . . ." (the full text of which has been recorded in the first volume of this History, Page 77, 78.)

The position of the New York Conference, or subsequent stands of that body did not allow for the eventual development of a Negro clergy. The formation of the African Chapel provided for the attainment of this end, first, through actual experience and membership action and, second through the very definite efforts at establishing a school. Training and apprenticeship were imperative, but as in so many Labor Unions of our time, doors were effectively closed to the securing of these opportunities.

Evidently in the back of the minds of our founding fathers was likewise the thought of economic development. Certainly, the promoting of the institution of the church served here as well.

Too infrequently Zion people turn to the Doctrines and Discipline of the Church with merely a passing nod. The late W. H. Davenport in his work: Membership in Zion Church states: "An eminent American scholar and minister has written a book, "Beliefs That Matter," in which he shows that beliefs affect conduct, character and destiny. One must believe something. It is important therefore, what he believes, and in whom he believes." For that reason both priest and people should be well conversant with the Articles of Religion. These, in essence, have not changed over the centuries while we do concede that the General Rules of the Denomination need to be reviewed.

At this point in the world's history the common interpretation and mission of the Church is vital to every decision and act of the present and we would urge not only the study of our beliefs and organization but a sincere effort to see to it that our purposes and intent are kept relevant to our understanding of the past and the challenges of the future as well as the present.

The development of materials and literature to promote the purpose and program of the Church is rather hard to trace. It is known that the first discipline was produced in 1820 and in the development of this work a layman, George Collins, served along with Christopher Rush. Twelve hundred copies of this work were distributed. A Discipline appears to have been published following the General Conference of 1848 as reference to an 1851 Discipline are noted. As was customary, the General Rules and Articles of Religion appeared in both of these publications. The writer has noted a Discipline of 1852 and its successor the revisions of 1856. That which happened in 1860 and 1864 is not known as is true of 1868. It appears, however, that no discipline was issued in 1872—the revisions being carried in a leaf which was to be pasted in older disciplines. The sheet sold for five cents. Disciplines for 1880 to the present have been noted, each carrying the Articles of Religion and the General Rules.

Hymnbooks for the use of the Church likewise came into being. This Bishops' Address appeared in the 1872 issue:

> Members and Friends of the African Methodist Episcopal Zion Church in America
>
> Beloved Brethren: In consequence of the great difficulties our societies have labored under for the want of a suitable Collection of Hymns, the General Conference at its session of 1872, adopted the following book as used by the Methodist Episcopal Church. That the Triune God may make it a blessing to all into whose hands it may come is the sincere and earnest prayer of your humble pastors and companions in tribulation, and in the kingdom and patience of Jesus Christ.
>
>
> JOSEPH JACKSON CLINTON
> SAMPSON D. TALBOT
> J. W. LOGUEN
> S. T. JONES
> JOHN J. MOORE
> J. W. HOOD
> *Bishops*
>

A new hymnal for the use of the worship services of the Church was issued around 1892. The interesting portion of the Committee's address, a part of the preface is here recorded.

> What is the first requisite to congregational singing? Let the people provide themselves with hymn and tune books, at least one for every two worshipers.
>
> What kind of books should be procured? Such books as contain the hymns of our own denominations. All the different evangelical Churches now have their own hymns set to tunes, and published by their respective societies.
>
> How can the people sing who do not read music? Every Church should hold stated singing meetings, for the purpose of rehearsing the tunes for the coming Sabbath, for the general improvement in music; and the whole congregation, with the choir, should attend these meetings.
>
> How should such meetings be conducted? Let them be opened with prayer by the Pastor, closed with the doxology, and the music under the direction of the chorister, who should be well paid for his work unless he is able and willing to give the Church his services free.
>
> What is the duty of the chorister, quartette, or choir? To lead the congregation in the singing of all the hymns which are read or announced from the pulpit.
>
> Should choirs ever monopolize the service of song in our Churches? Never, no more than a few should monopolize the prayers of our Churches.
>
> Should organ voluntaries be used in our church services? While the people are taking and vacating their seats a good organ voluntary is always acceptable.

Should interludes be played between the verses while singing the hymns? In some few cases a very short one may serve as a rest; but in most cases a silent pause is better, and more impressive.

Should anthems and set pieces ever be sung by the choir or quartette alone? Just before the minister begins his first service, and immediately at the close, a good, appropriate—but spiritual—set piece or anthem will produce a good effect when well rendered by the choir.

How can general interest be awakened in our service of praise? By obtaining the best chorister you can, if possible a devoted Christian, whose duty it should be not only to have charge of the music in Church and Sabbath-School, but also to teach and drill the people at the stated singing meetings. The Pastor can do much to urge the attendance, and make interesting the praise meeting and in carrying out the above suggestions.

Let the people praise thee, O God, let all the people praise thee.

COMMITTEE

Accompanying this preface was a Formula of Worship for the African M.E. Zion Church. This was arranged by the Rev. J. Wesley Brown for the Book Concern. We give it as outlined:

1. Organ Prelude
2. Hymn
3. Reading Psalms, by Congregation
4. Scripture Lesson
5. Invocation
6. Organ Interlude, Anthem
7. Beatitudes or Ten Commandments (Congregation standing)
8. Chant (Lord's Prayer)
9. Hymn
10. Sermon
11. Invocation
12. Singing
13. Collection During Singing
14. Notices
15. Apostles' Creed (Congregation standing)

Most of these early efforts at producing a hymnal were merely the utilizing of the hymnals of the Methodist Episcopal Church, with the preface and endorsements furnished by the Church.

The first effort at the production of a distinctly African Methodist hymnal began in the middle decades of the Twentieth Century—1930-1960. Progress was at first made with the idea of the three Black Methodist denominations working to produce a common book. Later, the A.M.E. and the A.M.E. Zion Church appeared very close to the obtaining of such a work, much of the material having been collected and put together. Keen disappointment was expressed when it became known that the A.M.E. Church was already proceeding towards the production of such a work without following through on the basic cooperation with Zion. Reasons for this decision are not known at this time.

When the General Conference met in Pittsburgh in 1956, after some ten years of cooperative effort and eventual frustration, the Reverend J. W. Watson made a statement concerning the publishing of a Church Hymnal and stated that Zion Church should proceed to develop such a work. Bishop Stephen Gill Spottswood, who had been one of the most active in the venture, stated that because of the difficulty with the A.M.E. Church, we had been delayed in producing our hymnal, "but since the order of the 1952 General Conference, we have not lost any time in planning to have a hymnal for our church, and if we are able to get the money, we will have the hymnal in the near future." [1]

The order of the General Conference of 1952 referred to by Bishop Spottswood was based on a resolution offered by the Reverend J. E. McCall which read:

> *Whereas,* the A.M.E. Zion Church, like other churches has use of Hymnals in its service for the choir and congregation;
> *Whereas,* it has been quite some time since we have had any hymnals printed;
> *Whereas,* the services of our churches will be greatly enhanced by the use of our own hymnals, Be it
> *Resolved:* that a committee be appointed to work with the manager of the Publication House in printing new hymnals for the A.M.E. Zion Church; be it further
> *Resolved:* that a campaign be launched to sell, at least two thousand copies before they are printed.
> The resolution was referred to the Commission on Hymnals:
> The following names were given the secretary by Bishop W. J. Walls as members of the Commission on Hymnals:

Bishop W. J. Walls	Rev. L. L. Boyd
Bishop C. C. Alleyne	Dr. James W. Eichelberger
Bishop S. G. Spottswood	Rev. G. L. Fauntleroy
Dr. W. A. Cooper	Dr. T. W. Tobin[2]
Dr. J. Van Catledge	

By 1960 the hymnal was off the press and was considered to be superior to many in use. The statement follows:

---
[1] Official Journal of the Thirty-fifth Quadrennial Session, (1956) 127.
[2] Official Journal of the 34th Quadrennial Session, 1952, 76, 77.

THE CHURCH'S PROGRAM AND BELIEFS 1796-1968

The New A.M.E. Zion Hymnal has been published in two editions. It contains a large selective number of hymns including many by Charles Wesley, John Wesley, Isaac Watts, Ancient Hymns and Canticles, Modern Authors, Spirituals, Zion Methodist Authors; Hymns for children, and for youth. In addition, there is part of the ritual, responses and sentences, Responsive Readings and eight Indices.

It was published by the A.M.E. Zion Hymnal Commission in two bindings, regular and deluxe. Each is on sale by the Financial Department, Publishing House, Departments, and other depositories.

Our new hymnal is a credit to the Hymnal Commission that prepared and published it, and to the entire denomination.[3]

RE: COMMISSION ON COMBINED HYMNAL

Whereas: The A.M.E. Zion Church and the A.M.E. Church Commission on Combined Hymnal has completed the manuscript for said combined hymnal, and has approved of a plan for the publication of said hymnal;

Be it Resolved:

1. That this General Conference go on record as endorsing the work of the combined commission;

2. It hereby authorizes the Ways and Means Committee of the Commission on combined hymnal to publish 50,000 copies of said combined hymnal on a joint and equitable basis with the A.M.E. Church Commission on Combined Hymnal, with joint ownership of manuscript, plates and sales interest on a 50% basis;

3. That the General Conference hereby authorizes the Board of Finance of the A.M.E. Zion Church to provide one-half of the funds necessary for the publication of said combined hymnal, according to details worked out by the combined commission.[4]

[3] *Official Journal of the 36th Quadrennial Session,* (1960) 322.
[4] *Official Journal, 32nd Quadrennial Session of the General Conference,* 1944, 191.

Bibliography

PRIMARY SOURCES

Anderson, J. Harvey, *Official Directory of the A. M. E. Zion Church, 1895-96*
Alstork, Bishop J. W. *Notes Gathered by the Way as We Traveled Through Europe*
Bradley, David H. Sr., *A History of the A. M. E. Zion Church, 1796-1872* (Nashville, 1956)
Bruce, Richard Blair, *Quadrennial Report of the Sunday School Department, A. M. E. Zion Church, May 6, 1908*
The Church Extension Society of the A. M. E. Zion Church, a pamphlet
Colbert, Rev. Jesse, *History of the Varick Christian Endeavor Society*
Daily Journal of the Sixteenth Quadrennial Session of the General Conference of the A. M. E. Zion Church, Montgomery, Ala. 1880
Daily Proceedings of the Seventeenth Quadrennial Session of the General Conference of the A. M. E. Zion Church, New York, 1884
Dancy, John C. *The Quarterly Almanac, 1894*
Doctrines and Discipline of the African Methodist Episcopal Zion Church, 1852, 1880, 1884, 1889, 1905, 1924, 1928, 1932, 1936, 1940, 1944, 1948, 1952, 1960, 1964.
Eichelberger, James W. *Quadrennial Reports of the Christian Education Department, 1940, 1944, 1948, 1952, 1956, 1960, 1964.*
Eichelberger, James W. *Interviews with*
The General Conference of the African Methodist Episcopal Zion Church (Minutes) *of 1864 with appendix* (Hartford, Conn., 1864)
Graham, Mr. E. M. *Report of the General Secretary to the Connectional Council.*
Harris, Bishop Cicero R. *Zion's Historical Catechism—For use in Families and Sunday Schools* (Charlotte, N. C.)
Hood, Bishop J. W.—*One Hundred Years of the African Methodist Episcopal Zion Church* (New York, 1895)
Hood, Bishop J. W. *Sketch of the Early History of the African Methodist Episcopal Zion Church with Jubilee Souvenir and Appendix* (1914)
Informer, The, Of the Church Extension Society and Corresponding Secretary's Report
Jones, Bishop E. D. W. *Comprehensive Catechism of the A. M. E. Zion Church* (Washington, D. C. 1934)
Jones, Reverend Singleton T. *Stipulations of Affiliation and Union Between the A. M. E. and the A. M. E. Zion Churches*
Jones, Rev. Singleton T. *A Brief Account of the Proposed Union Between the A. M. E. Zion and the Methodist Episcopal Churches.*
Jones, Singleton, T. (Rev.) *Report of the Delegate to the M.E. General Conference at Chicago*
Journal of the Twenty-ninth Quadrennial Session of the General Conference, Pittsburgh, Pa., 1932
Journal of the Thirtieth Quadrenial Session of the General Conference of the A. M. E. Zion Church, Greensboro, N. C. 1936
Journal of the Thirty-third Annual Session of the Allegheny-Ohio Conference
Minutes of the General Conference of 1848 (of the A.M.E. Zion General Conference)
Minutes of the General Conference of 1868
Minutes of the General Conference of 1888 (New Bern, N. C.)
Minutes of the General Conference, Nineteenth Quadrennial Session, Pittsburgh, Pa. 1892
Minutes of the Twentieth Quadrennial Session of the General Conference, Mobile, Alabama, 1896
Minutes of the Twenty-third Quadrennial Session of the General Conference of the A. M. E. Zion Church, Philadelphia, May 6-22, 1908

BIBLIOGRAPHY

Minutes of the Twenty-fifth Quadrennial Session of the General Conference of the A. M. E. Zion Church, Louisville, Ky. 1916

Minutes of the Twenty-sixth Quadrennial Session of the General Conference of the A. M. E. Zion Church, Knoxville, Tenn. 1920

Minutes of the Twenty-seventh Quadrennial Session of the General Conference, of the A. M. E. Zion Church, Indianapolis, Ind., 1924

Minutes of the Twenty-eighth Quadrennial Session of the General Conference of the A. M. E. Zion Church, St. Louis, Mo. 1928

Minutes of the Twenty-ninth Quadrennial Session of the General Conference, A. M. E. Zion Church, Pittsburgh, Pa. 1932

Minutes of the Baltimore Conference, 1848, 1850, 1851, 1852, 1853, 1866

Minutes of the Genesee Annual Conference, 1851, 1853, 1894

Minutes of the New England Annual Conference, 1848, 1850, 1853

Minutes of the New York Annual Conference, 1848, 1850, 1851, 1853

Minutes of the New Jersey Annual Conference, 1874, 1875

Minutes of the North Carolina Annual Conference, (Tenth Session) 1873, 1874, 1876, 1877

Minutes of the North Carolina Annual Conference 1871

Minutes of the Sixteenth Annual Session of the North Carolina Annual Conference, 1879 (Lincolnton, North Carolina)

Minutes of the Philadelphia Annual Conference 1848, 1850, 1851, 1853

Minutes of the Philadelphia and Baltimore Annual Conference, 1888,

Moore, Bishop John Jamison, History of the A.M.E. Zion Church (York, Pa. 1884)

Moore, William J., Autobiography of

Official Journal of the Daily Proceedings of the Twenty-first Quadrennial Session of the General Conference of the A. M. E. Zion Church, Washington, D. C. 1900

Official Journal of the Twenty-fourth Quadrennial Session of the A. M .E. Zion Church (Charlotte, N. C. 1912)

Official Journal of the Thirty-first Quadrennial Session of the General Conference of the A. M. E. Zion Church, Washington, D. C. 1940

Official Journal of the Thirty-second Quadrennial Session of the General Conference of the A. M. E. Zion Church, Detroit, Michigan, 1944

Official Journal of the Thirty-third Quadrennial Session of the General Conference A. M. E. Zion Church, Louisville, Ky., 1948

Official Journal of the Thirty-fourth Quadrennial Session of the General Conference, A. M. E. Zion Church, Brooklyn, N. Y. 1952

Official Journal of the Thirty-fifth Quadrennial Session of the General Conference, A. M. E. Zion Church, Pittsburgh, Pa. 1956

Official Journal of the Thirty-sixth Quadrennial Session of the General Conference, A. M. E. Zion Church, Buffalo, N. Y., 1960

Official Journal of the Thirty-seventh Quadrennial Session of the General Conference, A.M.E. Zion Church, Indianapolis, Ind., 1964

Powell, Reverend Jacob. Bird's Eye View of the 1916 General Conference

Program of the General Religious Education Convention, 1915

Quadrennial Address of the Bishops of the A. M. E. Zion Church to the Delegates of the Twenty-third Session of the General Conference, 1908

Quadrennial Missionary Convention Program, 1911

Report of the A. M. E. Zion Brotherhood, June 1, 1908-December 31, 1909

Rogerson, Idonia, Ed. Historical Synopsis of the Woman's Home and Foreign Missionary Society, 1967

Rush, Supt., Christopher, A Short Account of the Rise and Progress of the African Methodist Episcopal Church in America (New York 1943)

Sixth Quadrennial Report of the Woman's Home and Foreign Missionary Society, 1924-1928

Small, Bishop John Bryan, Code of the Discipline of the African Methodist Episcopal Zion Church (York Dispatch Press, 1898)

Smith, Reverend J. W. *The First Biography of Bishop Singleton T. Jones*
Souvenir Program of the A. M. E. Zion Church, San Francisco, Calif., Rev. L. Roy Bennett, Pastor
Souvenir Program of the Twenty-first Quadrennial Session of the General Conference, Washington, D. C. 1900
Spurgeon, F. Claude, ed. *A. M. E. Zion Handbook, 1952-1956*
Supplement to the Discipline of 1884
Walters, Bishop Alexander, *My Life and Work* (1917)
Wheeler, Rev. Benjamin F. *The Varick Family* (Mobile, Ala., 1906)

PERIODICALS

A. M. E. Zion Quarterly Review, 1894, 1896, No. 1, 1904, No. 3, 1906, XXXIII, 2, 1922, X, 2, XLIX, 4, 1939, LI, 2, LIII, 1, 2, 1942, 1943, LIX 3, 1949
The Chicago Whip, Oct. 23, 1926
The Christian Index, May, 1876
The Church Quarterly (Later the A. M. E. Zion Quarterly Review) 1891
Ladies Home Journal, Sept. 1968
The Sunday School Bulletin, Jan. 1918, March 1918, Feb., 1921
The Star of Zion
A Harrisburg Newspaper (Zerox material)

GENERAL WORKS

Alleyne, Bishop Cameron Chesterfield, *Gold Coast at A Glance* (Norfolk, Va.)
Bucke, Emory Stevens, ed. *The History of American Methodism*, in three vols. (Abingdon, 1964)
Encyclopaedia of Sunday Schools and Religious Education, in three vols. (Thomas Nelson, 1915)
Flood, Theodore and Hamilton, ed. *Lives of Methodist Bishops* (New York, 1882)
Wesley, John, *Live and Times of*, 1872 (reprint)
Minutes of the Common Council of the City of New York (1784-1831)
Moede, Gerald F., *The Office of Bishop in Methodism* (Publishing House of the Methodist Church, Zurich, Switzerland, 1964)
Penn, I. Garland, *The Afro-American Press and Its Editors* (Springfield, Mass, 1891)
Phillips, Bishop C., H., *The History of the Colored Methodist Episcopal Church in America* (Jackson, Tenn., 1925)
Proceedings of the Ninth World Methodist Conference
Proceedings of the Tenth World Methodist Conference, 1961
Walls, Bishop William Jacob., *Joseph Charles Price* (Christopher Press, 1943)
Wesley, John, *The Works of* (Zondervan Press, 1872, reprint)

APPENDIX

Added Notes on the Church Extension Department

The Church Extension Society of the A. M. E. Zion Church was first incorporated in the State of Pennsylvania in July (10) 1905. The Charter of the same follows:

Whereas, we, the undersigned, all of whom are citizens of the commonwealth of Pennsylvania whose names are subscribed to this charter or certificate of incorporation, having associated ourselves together for the purpose and upon the terms and by the name herein stated, under the provisions of an Act of the General Assembly of the Commonwealth of Pennsylvania, entitled, "An Act to provide for the incorporation and regulation of certain corporations," approved the twenty-ninth day of April, in the year of our Lord, one thousand eight hundred and seventy-four and several supplements thereto, we therefore set forth and declare that:—

1. The name of the Corporation is "General Committee of the Church Extension Society of the African Methodist Episcopal Zion Church."

2. The purposes for which this Corporation is formed are to promote the general welfare of the members of the African Methodist Episcopal Zion Church; to extend the teaching, tenets and faith as promulgated by the Discipline of said Church among the people of the community at large; to remodel, build, erect, purchase, hold and own real estate for the purpose of Divine Worship, and for parsonages; to receive, take, hold, own and dispose of by deed, gift, conveyance, bequest, lease or otherwise, in trust, for the African Methodist Episcopal Zion Church any real, personal or mixed property of any kind or description whatsoever and wheresoever situated without limit as to amount, except as fixed by law, and to have and to hold, and to exercise as such owner, all of the rights, titles, duties and authority as any natural person could or might do for the purpose and to the use hereinbefore stated, and to sue and be sued, to plead and be impleaded in any court of law or equity, here or elsewhere, and generally to do all and singular the matters and things which shall be lawful for the said corporation to do, touching and concerning the well-being and management of its property and affairs as any natural person could or might do, subject however, to the laws and discipline of the African Methodist Episcopal Zion Church.

3. That it shall be lawful for the said Corporation to accept contributions to the funds of said Corporation from any person or persons making such donations; *Provided, however,* That all amounts so received shall be

loaned by said corporation on adequate securities; and *Provided,* further, That the aggregate amount of annuities that the said Corporation shall assume to pay, shall never be allowed to exceed the annual interest receivable on the loans made by the said Corporation, and the amount in the Loan Fund.

4. The principal office for the transaction of the business of this Corporation shall be in the City of Philadelphia, and the Corresponding Secretary of the Church Extension Society of the African Methodist Episcopal Zion Church shall be the executive Representative of this Corporation.

5. This Corporation shall have and use a comomn seal in the transaction of its business and the same at will to change, alter or renew.

6. This Corporation shall have perpetual succession by its corporate name, and the successors in the office shall be appointed by the Board of Bishops of the African Methodist Episcopal Zion Church as provided by the Discipline of said Church and By-Laws of this Corporation, and the said Corporation shall be under the direction and control of the General Conference of the said Church.

7. This Corporation has no capital stock nor are there any shares of stock. The names and residences of the subscribers appear by their signatures hereunto.

8. The number of Committee of Managers of this Corporation is fixed at nine, and the names and residences of those who are chosen managers for the first year are as follows:

George W. Clinton, 415 North Myers St., Charlotte, N. C.
James W. Hood, Fayetteville, N. C.
Alexander Walters, 28 Oak Street, Jersey City, N. J.
Josiah S. Caldwell, 763 S. 15th St., Phila., Pa.
William H. Coffey, 420 S. 11th St., Phila., Pa.
George L. Blackwell, 624 S. 16th St., Phila., Pa.
Martin R. Franklin, 420 S. 11th St., Phila., Pa.
Richard A. Morrisey, 1216 Catherine St., Phila., Pa.
John P. Scott, 413 Filbert St., Harrisburg, Pa.

9. There are no pecuniary benefits to its members to be derived from the business of this Corporation.

From the pamphlet: *Church Extension Food,* published by the Rev. William H. Coffey. Date of Incorporation: July 10, 1905.

INDEX

A

Adams, Oscar, 165
Adams, Oscar W., 450, 451, 452, 453, 455
Adamson, Dr. C., 98
Adjahoe, A. A., 243
Advocate Endeavor, 209
African Bishop, 240
African Chapel, 414
African Methodist Episcopal Zion Church, 346, 347
African Mission, 60
African Missions Schools, 117
African Zion Episcopal Methodist, 346
African Zion Methodist Episcopal, 346, 347
Afro American Spokesman, 204
Agard, James A., 248
Aggrey, James Emman Kwegyir, 243, 244
Alabama Conference, 57, 61
Alexander, Dr. W. H., 376
Allegheney Conference, 21, 54, 60, 111, 149, 316, 388
Allegheney Ohio Conference, 77, 248
Allegheney Station, 21
Allen, Richard Bishop, 97, 314
Allen, Mrs. J. B., 118
Allended American, 100
Alleyne, Bishop Cameron Chesterfield, 241, 244, 251, 285, 287, 290, 358, 412, 420, 422
Alleyne, Mrs. Betty Lee, 450
Alstork, Bishop Frank W., 286, 434, 435, 440
Alstork, Bishop J. W., 62, 145, 238, 247, 248, 355, 372, 390
Alstork, Mrs. Willie G., 152, 181
Altoona, 351
A. M. E. Church, 314, 317, 332, 350
A. M. E. Z. Historical Society, 182, 184
A. M. E. Z. Quarterly Review, 136, 173, 204, 206, 207
Anderson, A., 155, 156
Anderson, Mrs. Annie, 225, 237
Anderson, Charles, 149
Anderson, Felix S., 82, 186, 297, 445, 462, 473
Anderson, J. Harvey, 59, 112, 139, 156, 166, 208, 349
Anderson, Jacob, 316
Anderson, William, 418
Andrews, D. W., 165, 381

Andrews, Emma, 71
Anglo African, 190, 214, 396
Annual Conference Fund, 169
Anonye, A. C., 467
Apostolic, 147
Argyle, E. M., 279
Arkansas Conference, 59
Arlington Heights, 55
Arnette, B. W., 348
Arthur, Rev. Frank, 249
Articles of Agreement, 354
Articles of Agreement—Birmingham Plan, 366, 367
Articles of Consolidation, 338
Asbury, Cornelius, 343, 344
Asbury, Bishop Francis, 146, 412
Asbury Park, N. J., 238, 350
Atkins, Dr. S. G., 115, 117, 164, 356, 372
Atkinson College, 112, 176
Auburn, 24
Auditing Committee, 155
Auditor, 166, 167
Avery Memorial Church, 237

B

Babcock Hall, 114
Babington-Johnson, J. A., 467
Bahama Conference, 32, 58
Bahia Brazil, 249
Baker, Josephus, Samuel, 231
Ball, R. R., 372
Baltimore, 357
Baltimore Annual Mission Board Report, 211, 212
Baltimore Conference, 11, 23, 55, 65, 149, 211, 216, 333
Baltimore District, 15
Bancroft Jepthahog, 397
Bank, Rev. O. H., 79
Baptiste, Louis J., 381
Baptized Children, 92
Barbar-Scotia Seminary, 110
Barber Camp, 179
Barnes, Alexander, 186, 380
Bath Circuit, 22
Beamen, Jehial C., 187
Beckett, Bishop, 475
Bedford Circuit, 21, 404
Bell, Mark A., 93, 154, 232, 346
Bellize, 242
Benson, Belinda, 381

Berean Series, 69
Bermuda Conference, 32, 232
Bethel Church, 335, 337
Biddle, Eli George, 208
Biddle, William J., 37, 196
Big Zion, 354
Birchmore, Samuel C., 32, 60
Bird, F. K., 158
Birmingham, Alabama, 241, 257, Plan, 359, 366
Bishop, Edward, 12
Bishop, William H., 11, 12, 20, 27, 29, 37, 47
Bishop, Senior, 47
Bishop's Salary, 256
Black, Charles, 81
Black, Harry, 97
Black, J. L., 177
Blackmen, J. H., 108
Blackwell, Annie, 235
Blackwell, Bishop George Lincoln, 63, 71, 157, 251, 355, 371, 392
Blackwell, George, 117
Blackwell, W. A., 88, 202
Blair, Montgomery, 31
Blairsville, 22
Blake, A. J., 309
Blakey, D. L., 159, 428
Blakey, F. R., 428
Bleeker Street, 157
Blockson, L. D., 167
Blue Ridge, 61
Blunt, Rev. Nathan, 153
Board of Bishops, 47, 70, 136, 151, 152, 159, 167, 173, 177, 179, 203, 204, 276, 277
Board of Christian Education, 115
Board of Home and Foreign Missions, 232
Board of Managers, 170
Board of Publication, 158, 159
Bolding, B. J., 90, 209
Booha, Cyrus, 27, 30
Book Agents, 132, 153, 154, 156
Book Concern, 152
Book Room, 157
Book Steward, 153, 154
Boulware, R. J., 118
Bowens, William B., 222
Boyd, S. B., 118
Bradley, Daniel Francis, 74
Bradley, David H., Sr., 27, 83, 177, 183, 184, 207, 380
Bradley, Mark Anthony, 206
Brannon, Leroy, 37
Bray, Dr., 358
Brewerville, 227
Bridgewater, 21

Bridwell, Richard, 37
Brightwood Mission, 55
British Honduras, 242, 249
Brockett, John Henry, 113, 203, 381
Brook, Noah, 27
Brooklyn, 241
Brooks, Bishop J. D., 54, 57, 149, 315, 397
Brotherhood—Brotherhood Pension Service, 172, 175, 203
Brown, A. L., 186
Brown, Aaron, 81, 90
Brown, J. M., 315
Brown, Bishop James W., 136, 160, 251, 261, 381, 432, 433
Brown, Bishop W. C., 178, 179, 381, 432, 433
Brownsville, 21
Bruce, R. B., 71, 74, 79, 407, 409
Buchanon, Philip, 414
Budget Board, 309
Budget Committee Report, 278, 288
Burksville, 37
Burnley, S. A. Attorney, 449, 452
Bureau of Public Statistics, 184
Burnett, William, 27
Busle, Matilda, 224
Butler, W. F., 31, 36, 38, 99, 149, 191, 217, 256, 316, 331, 338

C

Cahaba Conference, 62
Calibar, 243
California, 37, 54
California Conference, 351
Caldwell, Bishop J. S., 89, 166, 209, 355, 358, 365, 372, 390, 391
Canada and Michigan Conference, 36
Candler, Bishop Warren F., 334
Cape Conference, 62, 242, 249
Cape Coast Conference, 62
Cape Fear Conference, 62
Cape Palamas, 226, 227
Carlisle, 21, 351
Carrington, W. O., 381
Carroll, H. K., 369
Carter, Bishop R. A., 247
Carter, Charles, 316, 395
Cartwright, Andrew, 60, 225, 226, 231, 250
Cauthen, Bishop J. D., 380, 460, 461, 472
Centennial Celebration, 53
Center Street Church, Louisville, Ky., 37, 39, 40
Central Alabama Conference, 61
Central Committee, 75
Central North Carolina, 59

INDEX

Chambers, R. W., 341
Chambersburg, 21
Champlain Lake, 14
Chansford, 21
Chester, F. M., 166
Chester, South Carolina, 73
Chicago Urban League, 85
Children's Day Fund, 115
Christian Endeavor, 105
Christian Endeavor Advocate, 88
Christian Education Department, 376
Christian Index, 366
Christian Recorder, 355
Church Extension Dept., 159, 164, 280
Church Organ, report of committee, 194
Church Quarterly, 205, 206
Church School Herald Journal, 209
Circular on Revision, 13
Claiborne, Smith, 116
Clair, Bishop Matthew W., 380
Clark, Francis E., 88
Clay, Asland, 227
Clement, Bishop George C., 78, 158, 201, 249, 407, 408, 417
Clement, H. A. L., 449
Clement, James, 460, 471
Clement, R. E., 182, 285, 287, 424, 426, 449, 453, 454, 467
Clifton, E. G., 350
Clifton Conference, 77
Clifton, Mass., 75
Clinton Chaple Church, 42, 163, 269
Clinton College, 84, 112
Clinton, Bishop G. W., 157, 201, 372, 373, 387, 388
Clinton, H., 160
Clinton, I. C., 342, 386, 387
Clinton, Joseph Jackson, 11, 12, 24, 36, 41, 44, 50, 57, 58, 99, 138, 215, 217, 223, 334, 395, 404
Clinton, Dr. W. D., 407
Coffey, W. H., 163, 372
Colbert, Jesse, 88, 99, 157, 209, 241
Cole, Abram, 12, 55, 395
Cole, Baresford, 243
C. M. E. Church, 39, 247, 248, 356, 358, 364
Coleman, Bishop Charles Cecil, 293, 381, 449, 461, 462
Coleman, Isaac, 21, 154, 316
Coleman, Dr. S. C., 294
Collins, George, 149, 479
Collins, Leonard, 188
Collins, S., 24
Colorado, Conference, 63, 64
Columbia, 21

Columbia Circuit, 55
Combined Hymnal, 362
Committee on Church Federation, 360
Committee on Church Extension, 160, 161
Committee on Complaints, 102
Committee on Episcopacy, 140
Committee on Miscellaneous Matters, 170
Committee on Revision, 13
Comprehensive Catechism, 99
Connectional Council, 171, 185, 384, 454
Connectional Journal, 187, 197, 198, 452
Conrad, Bell Riley, 79
Consolidation of the A. M. E. Bethel and A. M. E. Zion Churches, 338
Constitution of Baltimore Annual Conf. Mission Fund, 219
Consultation on Church Union, 364, 382
Cook, A. C., 417, 431
Cooper, W. A., 452
Cooperative Curriculum, 83
Coppin, Bishop L. J., 355
Cornwallace, 211
Corrothers, J. C., 290, 294
Cottrell, Bishop Elias, 355, 365
Coss, M. B., 193
Council, R. A., 471
Courts of Appeal, 139
Cowan, Creola B., 236
Cowles, J. S., 342
Cox, John, 55, 316
Crenshaw, Thomas, 67
Crittenden, W. B., 373
Crockett, R. J., 417
Crockett, J. W., 158
Crook, A. A., 249
Culver, Dwight, 33
Curry, C. H., 163, 347, 349

D

Dacons, W. S., 168, 381
Daily Christian Advocate, 326
Dancy, John C., 74, 106, 108, 141, 143, 164, 173, 200, 201, 206, 341, 342, 344, 345, 348, 349, 477
Davenport, W. H., 209, 479
David, Mrs. Lucy F., 452
Davis, Elizabeth, 309
Davis, Henrietta, 236
Davis, James, 27
Davis, J. W., 160, 195
Davis, Tomas E., 250
Daughters of Conference, 224
Daughters of Varick, 225
Day, Alfred, 128, 155
Day School, 215

Day, William Howard, 48, 67, 77, 99, 100, 151, 191, 193, 196, 198, 265, 344, 347, 348, 372, 476
Deane, C. C., 247
Deane, Glascoe, 247
Deane, W. A., 247
Decker, William H., 27, 29, 154, 156, 193
Delaney, Martin R., 188
Demerara, 20
Department of Education, 115
Detroit, Michigan, 59
Derrick, Bishop W. B., 255
Dinwiddie Institute, 112, 117
Discipline of 1851, 56
District Conference, 70
District Sunday School Convention, 70
Dodge Hall, 114
Dolly, Walter, 243, 477
Double Jeopardy, 403
Douglas, F. D., 167, 190, 195
Duck, Joseph, 55
Dudley, Samuel Madison, 209, 286
Duncan, Samuel E., 82, 112, 308, 449, 450, 454
Dungy, John, 11, 27, 29, 404, 413
Dunsten, Bishop Alfred G., 241, 243, 251, 293, 460, 467, 468, 471
Dyson, R. H., 138, 256, 316
Dyson, William, 218

E

East Alabama Conference, 60, 351
Eastern North Carolina Institute (Industrial Academy), 112, 117
East Tenn. and Virginia Conference, 60
Eato, Sarah J., 224
Eato, Timothy, 12, 14, 20, 27, 153
Eatontown, N. J., 350
Edenton High School, 112, 117
Educational Department, 115, 116
Educational Evangelism, 82
Egan, Mattie D., 309
Eichelberger, James W., 8, 72, 77, 84, 117, 119, 209, 289, 376, 379, 382, 432, 440
Ellis, C. C., 177
Elliott, Samuel, 37
English, A., 230
Ennals, Sarah, 224
Episcopal Supervisor, 234, 235
Erie, Lake, 14
Essequebo, 54
Essex County, 15, 98
Essex School, 15
Evans, Aurora, 223, 224, 225
Evans, J. I., 344
Evans, R. S., 160

Evangelism, Bureau and
Evangelism, Department, 167
Executive Judiciary Committee, 244

F

Farley, J. Mc H., 150, 195, 200
Federal Council of Churches of Christ, 487, 488
Federal Council of Negro Churches, 464
Female and Male, 384
Fergerson, Katy, 67
Fergeson, W. H., 150, 160
Ferris, W. H., 321
Fiawoo, F. K., 243, 477
Fifth Ecumenical Conference of World Methodism, 374
Fifteenth Street Church, 48
Financial Plan, 271
Finch, Jane, 224
First Discipline, 149
Fisher, 204
Fisher, R. A., 372
Fisher, R. Farley, 152
Fisher, Richard L., 8
Fishertown, 476
Flack, P. R.,
Fleet Street Church, 88
Flemingsburg, 37
Flemington Swamp, 51
Flipper, Bishop J. S., 355
Florida, 36, 57
Flushing, L. I., 223
Foggie, Bishop Charles H., 7, 291, 381, 460, 469, 477
Fontleroy, G. L., 449
Fonville, P. K., 207
Foote, Julia, 384
Foreman, W. A., 127, 160
Fortune, Thomas, 341
Foster, R. A. G., 452, 467
Francis, Oliver, 452
Francis, W. D., 250
Frankfort, Kentucky, 37
Franklin, Bishop Martin R., 391
Frazier, J. W., 286
Freeman, Samuel E., 400
French, Edgar N., 8
Friendship Village, 54
Fulman, Peter, 12, 21
Funderburke, J. R., 296, 381, 426, 449

G

Gaines, S. M., 118
Gales, Moses, 12, 404
Gardner, Eliza Ann, Sr., 224

INDEX

Garland, D. G., 250, 282, 431
Garnett, Henry, 42, 191
Garrett, D. D., 452
Garrett, G. E., 285
Gaskin, Violet, 382
Gelbreth, George (Galbraith), 11, 12, 13, 25, 56, 66, 188, 404
General Conference Delegate, 48, 49, 150
General Financial Steward, 151
General Funds, 268, 276
General Mission Board, 160
General Secretary, 47, 149
General Sunday School Convention, 78
General Superintendent African Work, 239
Genesee Conference, 14, 22, 29, 36, 51, 54, 149, 350
Gennett, George, 12
George, A. C., 371
George, Bishop, 334
Georgia, 63
Ghesson, Rev. Henry, 250
Gibson, R. A., 316
Giles, S. M., 149, 154, 218, 315, 316
Glasgow, Kentucky, 37
Globe, New York, 341
Gloucester, J. N., 320
Glover, M. C., 418, 432
Gold Coast, 239
Golden, Shadrach, 12, 404
Goler Metropolitan, Winston Salem, 241
Goler, William H., 32, 118, 272, 344, 347
Goosely, Rev. Stephan, 32
Gordon, Bishop Buford, 72, 81, 209, 307, 434, 435, 440
Grand Rapids, Michigan, 59
Graham, E. M., 152
Gray, Richard, 309
Gray, S. T., 11, 12
Green, A. M., 343
Green, Elizabeth, 381
Green, N. J., 166, 344, 347
Greensboro, North Carolina, 76
Greensburg, Kentucky, 37
Greenville College High School, 112, 117
Gullett, R. W., 452, 455

H

Haiti, 32
Halifax, Nova Scotia, 22, 32, 54
Hall, G. F., 287, 382
Hamer, J. P., 44, 160, 316, 333
Hamilton, Bermuda, 222
Hamilton, Robert, 191
Hamilton, Thomas, 190
Hamilton, S. W., 417
Hamilton, William G., 191

Hamlin, W. L., 167, 356, 418
Handy, J. A., 353
Harmony Cemetery, 31
Hardge, Elias S., 168, 288, 431, 449, 460
Harper, James, 24
Harris, A. E., 8, 449
Harris, Catherine, 476
Harris, Bishop Cicero R., 62, 105, 108, 109, 110, 150, 167, 198, 199, 229, 230, 343, 344, 347, 353, 354, 372, 385, 407
Harris, Robert, 150
Harrisburg, Pa., 351
Harrisburg Circuit, 404
Harrison, C. P. S., 417, 431
Hartford, Conn., 350
Harvey, Martin, 81
Harvey, T. A., 417
Harvard College (University), 184
Hauser, M. A., 236
Hartshorn, W. N., 75
Hazel, C. D., 119
Heard, Bishop W. H., 355
Heckerman, Henry, 75
Heinz, H. J., 75
Henderson, Robert Charles, 20, 54
Hensen, Thomas, 12, 13
Hill, E. H., 35, 262
Hill, F. H., 167
Hill, J. M., 158, 159
Hilliard, Bishop William A., 8, 241, 243, 251, 294, 466
Hilliard, Mrs. William A., 243
Hillery, Bishop William, 52, 138, 139, 150, 399, 400, 401
Hines, Maggie, 298
Historical Catechism, 60
Historical Synopsis, 225
Hockman, William, 248
Hoggard, J. Clinton, 208, 241, 293, 294, 381, 382
Holiday, Bishop Jehu (John), 61, 157, 387, 388
Hollidaysburg, Pa., 14, 21
Holland, W. J., 144
Holsey, Bishop L. H., 354, 355
Hood, Bishop J. W., 31, 35, 41, 43, 50, 53, 109, 133, 138, 191, 198, 223, 224, 316, 342, 353, 355, 395, 406, 407
Hood, Mrs. K. P., 236
Hood, Temple Church, Richmond, Va., 82
Hooper, John, 106
Hopkins, Chapel Asheville, N. C., 450
Hopkins, T. A., 160

Home Missions Dept., 159, 164, 178, 179, 181
Home Missions Pension and Relief, 169, 177
Home and Foreign Missions, 211, 232
Houston, I. J., 417
Howard, Samuel, 192
Hubbard, P., 344
Hunter, Chaplain, 317
Hymnal, Combined, 362
Hymnal Commission, 483
Hymn Book, 46, 153, 155

I

Iboland, 244
Ikot Ekan, 243
Indiana Conference, 69
Indianapolis, 307
Inter-denominational Theological Seminary, 360
International Christian Endeavor Society, 88
International Council of Religious Education, 83, 374, 378, 379
International Lessons, 69
International Sunday School Association, 74, 376
Irwin, T. C., 119

J

Jackson, Anthony, 155, 156
Jackson, Abbie Clement, 236, 294, 296, 309, 382
Jackson, E. Franklin, 292, 296, 299, 452, 453, 455, 471
Jackson, George, 156
Jackson, H. R., 165
Jackson, J. S., 72, 271, 372
Jacobs, B. F., 75
Jacobs, F. M., 68, 74, 152, 166, 344, 347, 349, 372, 424, 429
Jacobs, Francis, 413
Jamaica Conference, 64
James, Thomas, 217, 476
James City, 351
Jamison, M. F., 355
Janifer, Sarah, 98
Jenkins, J. Dallas, 8, 82, 168, 471
Jersey City, N. J., 90
John Wesley Church, Pittsburgh, Pa., 115, 140, 204
Johnson, A. F., 309
Johnson, Daisy, 236
Johnson, Edward, 11, 15
Johnson, Henry, 12
Johnson, Bishop J. A., 345

Johnson, Melvin, 452, 460
Johnson, Rural (Memorial) School, 112
Johnson, U. S., 381
Johnson, William, 55
Johnston, H. Leo, 431
Johnstown, Pa., 21, 205
Joint Commission on Organic Union, 318, 347
Jones Chapel, 84
Jones, Edgar F., 8
Jones, Bishop E. D. W., 60, 129, 153, 157, 209, 225, 414, 420, 422
Jones, James A., 48, 150
Jones, Mary J., 236
Jones, Bishop Raymond L., 210, 437, 452
Jones, Mrs. Raymond L., 381
Jones, Bishop Singleton T., 37, 41, 42, 44, 57, 99, 132, 138, 143, 150, 191, 193, 223, 315, 316, 317, 321, 327, 331, 335, 341, 342, 395, 402, 403
Jones Tabernacle, 299
Jones, William, 12
Jones University, 112
Jordan, Miss Dorothy, 381
Journal, Committee on, 196
Journal Secretary, 151
Judicial Council, 364, 445, 455, 466, 472
Jumping Run, 351

K

Kell, M. S., 144
Kennedy, Dempsey, 26, 27, 28
Kennedy, W. T., 452
Kennett Township, 53
Kentucky, 214
Kentucky Conference A. M. E. Zion Church, 51, 401
Kentucky Conference C. M. E. Church, 40
Kesley, A. G., 106
Keta, 243
Key West, 31
Keys, Elsie G., 236, 293
Killingsworth, F., 344, 347
King, John A., 11, 12, 13, 14, 149, 153
King, Lord, 120
Kyles, Lynwood Westinghouse, 63, 175, 206, 247, 279, 286, 380, 407, 417, 434

L

Lacey, Rev. J. W., 32
Ladies Home and Foreign Missionary Society (See Woman's Home and Foreign Missionary Society)
Lancaster Normal and Industrial School, 118
Lane, Bishop Isaac, 355

INDEX

Lankford, H. P., 418
Lartey, Bishop S. Dorme, 463, 470
Lawrence, Att. G. W., 452
Laws, P. G., 316
Lay Rights and Privileges, 415
Lay Representation, 326, 327, 416, 418
Leake, George J., 468
Lee, 204
Lee, B. F., 353, 355
Lee, Dr. J. Francis, 71, 81, 209
Lee, M. D., 118, 152
Lee, R. H. C., 152
Lee, W. L. Bishop, 407, 409
Levingston, James, 27, 29
Lewis, G. W., 144
Lewis, Margaret L., 81
Lewistown, 21
Lewistown Circuit, 21, 404
Liberia, 62
Lincoln University, 33, 112, 353
Literary Connectional Convention, 98
Little, H. H., 452
Little Falls, 22
Little Rock, 59
Little Rock Church, 51
Liturgy in Organic Union, 356
Liverpool, Nova Scotia, 23, 211
Livingstone College, 33, 53, 112, 113, 117, 187
Lockport, 22
Loguen, Jermain W., 12, 14, 24, 37, 39, 41, 50, 57, 215, 316, 317, 397, 404
Lomax, Hannon, 112, 118
Lomax, R. S., 204
Lomax, Bishop Thomas H., 51, 107, 109, 138, 223, 372
Louisiana Conference, 36, 54, 215, 351
Louisville, Kentucky, 37, 218
Lovell, Walter R., 202, 204, 381, 459
Lycoming County, 30, 395
Lyman, Dr. H. C., 77
Lyons, Rev. William, 167

M

Macon High School, 117
Madison, Bishop E. L., 432
Manly, J. H., 241
Manning, Rev. G., 150
Manual Labor School, 15
Marcus, G. H., 75
Marsh, Marian, 81
Marshall, Arthur J., 292, 471
Marshall, Wesley C., 55
Martin, Bishop J. W., 117, 249, 286, 293, 420, 421
Martinez, Daniel, 186

Maryland and District of Columbia, 213
Mason, James Edward, 485
Mattocks, J. H., 106
Matthews, Bishop W. W., 208, 239, 241, 251, 285, 424, 439
Maxwell, L. B., 15
Meeks, N. L., 8
Medford, B. T., 204
Medford, Bishop H. T., 208, 241, 251, 381, 438, 452
Medford, Mrs. H. T., 381
Memorial A. M. E. Zion Church, 194
Merritt, John E., 400
Methodist Ecumenical Conference, 370
Methodist Episcopal Church, 320
Methodist Episcopal Church North, 34, 39, 43, 45, 47
Methodist Episcopal Church South, 34, 39
Metropolitan Wesley, Washington, D. C., 143, 144
Meyersdale, Pa., 74
Michigan and Canada Conference, 52, 59, 63
Michigan Avenue Church, 80
Michigan Conference, 8, 63
Miles, Bishop William H., 37, 38, 39, 40
Miller, J. H., 450, 452
Miller, William, 149, 254, 413
Millersburg, Ky., 37
Ministers' and Laymen's Association, 183, 296
Ministers' Mutual Benefit Society, 19
Ministers' Salaries, 257
Minutes of the General Conference of 1852, 153
Missionaries, 216, 217
Missionary Seer, 207, 208, 236
Missouri Annual Conference, 37, 61, 351, 461
Mitchel, S. T., 344
Mitchell, Silas, 27
Mobley, Marvin, 309
Moede, Gerald F., 150
Monrovia, 226
Montgomery, Alabama, 44
Montrose, 22
Moore, Bishop J. J., 11, 12, 13, 31, 38, 41, 51, 57, 58, 60, 129, 149, 153, 189, 205, 223, 320, 369, 404
Moore, P. C., 452
Moore, W. J., 106
Moreland, John F., 158, 163, 172, 173, 282, 372
Morgan, E. E., 8
Morris, A. P., 181, 381, 428
Morris, Robert R., 32, 69, 70, 154, 223, 342

495

Morrisey, R. A., 241
Mother Zion, 44, 82, 97, 138, 157, 341
Mount Olivet Church, 73
Mount Pleasant, Pa., 351
Mount Zion Church, 89
Murphy, Thomas, 400
Mutual Benefit Society, 170
Mystery, 22, 188, 189

Mc

MacKall, Basal, 12
McCall, J. E., 293, 444, 482
McClain, T. B., 145
McCreary, Henry III, 8
McIntosh, A., 335
McLeese, A., 167
McMillan, J. T., 90, 209
McMullen, J. H., 144
McMurray, G. F., 449, 452

N

National Afro American Council, 370
National Baptist Publishing Board, 80
National Standard, 196
Negro Methodist Church, 345
Neuby, A., 160
New Bern, 34, 36
New England Conference, 11, 23, 28, 31, 34, 36, 55, 66, 149, 333
New England District, 15
New England Mission Board, 218
New Haven, Connecticut, 350
New Jersey Conference, 36, 57, 66
New York Conference, 11, 23, 25, 26, 68, 149, 155, 258, 333, 350
North Carolina Annual Conference Minutes, 187, 351
North Carolina Conference, 36, 45, 48, 51, 149, 214
North Carolina Mission, 55
North Louisiana Conference, 61
North Star, 194
Norton, George F., 399
Nova Scotia, 36, 52, 54, 223
Nyenfuah, Chief Brown, 309

O

Offly, G. W., 344, 347
Ofosuhene, Rev. P. D., 243
Ogwas Owerri Province, Nigeria, 243
Ohio African University, 98
Ohio Conference, 36, 351
Oklahoma Conference, 61
Ontario, Lake, 14
Organic Union, 342, 343, 344, 349, 357, 362

Organic Union Commissioners, 358, 360, Vote 350, 351
Oregon Conference, 61
Oregon-Washington Conference, 62
Osabutey, Isaac D., 243, 477
Osam-Pinauko, Frank A., 239, 243, 477
Osbon, A. M., 321, 325
Oslo, Norway, 81
Ottley, Rev. O. E., 248
Owensville, Kentucky, 37

P

Palmetto Conference, 61
Parks, Bishop H. P., 355
Paso Robles, 351
Paterson, N. J., 350
Patton, E. B., 309
Peach Bottom, 21
Peacock, Rev. S. W., 250
Pee Dee Conference, 63
Petty, A. P., 407
Petty, Calvin C., 61, 138, 140, 143, 144, 151, 198, 344, 345, 347, 353, 384, 385
Petty High School, 111, 112
Penn, I. Garland, 204
Pension Plan, 178
Pension Service, 177
Periodicals Committee (Publishing Committee), 203
Perryville, 21
Peter, R. E. (Rev. and Mrs.), 239, 245, 250
Petersburg, Va., 199, 226
Petition from West African Missions, 245
Phoebus, Dr. William, 122
Philadelphia and Baltimore Conference, 8, 21, 67, 74, 127, 149, 150
Philadelphia Conferences, 22, 28, 55, 58, 65, 258, 316, 333
Phillips, Bishop C. H., 355
Phillips, H. C., 195
Pierce, I. B., 452
Pierce, J. J., 250
Pile, Rev. and Mrs. R. F., 250
Pine and Palm, 191
Pitts, William H., 49, 154, 316
Pittsburgh, 21
Pope, Bishop Daniel C., 208, 250, 381, 43. 440, 442
Porter, Fred D., 460
Preachers Institutes, 71
Presiding Elder System, 404
Price, J. C., 33, 113, 128, 155, 342, 344, 345, 347, 370
Price, Mrs. J. C., 274
Price, J. E., 193, 401

INDEX

Pringle, Mrs. Louisa, 79
Proctor, Emory, 449
Progressive Literary Society, 88
Protestant Film Commission, 82
Providence, Rhode Island, 217
Public Relations and Social Service, 184
Publishing House, 153, 157, 158, 291
Pulpress, B., 414
Purnell, Elizabeth, 224

Q

Quadrennial Address, 172, 202, 205, 206, 271, 274, 340
Quittah Station, 329

R

Raleigh, North Carolina, 76
Raleigh Plan, 70
Randolph, Florence, 234, 236, 240, 243, 372
Reddy, W., 321
Redford, Rev. A. H., 39
Redpath, James, 191
Reed, J. M., 323
Reid, Mrs. Dancy, 187
Rejoinder of the A.M.E. Zion General Conference, 338
Report of Andrew Cartwright, 227
Report of Committee on Home and Foreign Missions, and Church Extension, 231
Report of the Delegate to the M. E. General Conference, 320
Republican, Chicago, 329
Respass, J. R., 292
Revision Comm., 185
Reynolds, R. J. Foundation, 114
Rice, Willa Mae, 381
Richardson, A. S., 109, 110
Richardson, Jacob, 187
Richardson, Rev. John D., 153
Richardson, Victoria, 237
Richmond, Virginia, 82, 217
Ricks, A. W., 250
Rieves, R. S., 106, 195, 201
Riley, F. W., 431
Rio de Janeiro, 249
Roberts, Mary, 224
Robeson, B. C., 287
Robinson, Dr. Ernest, 296
Robinson, M. B., 204
Robinson, Miss A. G., 250
Rochester Circuit, 22
Rochester, Enoch, 82
Rockton, 24

Rogers, L. R., 309
Ross, Peter, 11, 12, 14, 18, 27, 29, 98, 135, 153, 395
Royal, Mrs. Alice F., 8
Rudd, M. S., 285, 439
Rush Academy, 15, 49, 117, 154
Rush, Christopher, 11, 12, 13, 20, 27, 29, 34, 47, 55, 66, 98, 122, 129, 149, 476
Rush University Fund, 105

S

Sackets Harbor, 25
Salters, Bishop M. B., 355
Sanford, William, 99, 149, 316
San Jose, 38
Satterwhite, John, 8, 364, 383, 452
Sawyer, John F., 186
Sawyer, John P., 449
Sawyer, M. P., 177
Scott, A. L., 200
Scott, Rev., 341
Scott, Bishop Solomon T., 11, 54, 55, 98, 132, 404
Scott, Emmett, 358
Scurlock, L. J., 399
Seay, Solomon S., 183
Secretary General, 150, 183, 207, 209
Selectman, I. W., 144
Severies, J. L. H., 128
Sewickley, 351
Sexton, G., 160
Shaffer, C. T., 355
Sharpsburg, Ky., 37
Shaw, Ardelle M., 309
Shaw, Bishop Benjamin Garland, 167, 381, 382, 420, 431
Shaw, Bishop Herbert Bell, 64, 82, 177, 178, 179, 381, 440, 441, 452
Shaw, J. W., 294, 439
Shepherd, J. E., 73, 75
Sherman, Samuel, 138
Sherrill, R. W., 158, 381
Sherwood Orphan School, 112
Shipman, Dr. F. George, 113
Shippensburg, 21
Shurman, Samuel, 37, 138
Sierre Leone, 242
Simmons, H. L., 172
Simmons, James, 11, 12, 15, 20, 48, 153
Simmons, R. H., 49, 109
Sims, Oliver, 250
Simpson, Bishop M., 371
Sinclair, Joseph, 12, 13, 21, 404
Sink, Henry, 449
Slade, Bishop W. W., 203, 381, 434
Slicer, Dr. H., 325

Small, Bishop John Bryon, 142, 151, 155, 207, 248, 372, 387, 388, 398
Small, Mary Jane, 78, 233, 236, 384, 393
Smith, Almena J., 250
Smith, Frank L., 377
Smith, Garret, 98
Smith, J. H., 191, 316
Smith, J. J., 191
Smith, Joseph G., 154
Smith, J. W., 201, 390
Smith, Leven, 27, 29
Smith, L. H., 344, 345, 346
Smith Mills, 351
Smith, W. C., 200
Smith, Bishop W. M., 241, 299, 381, 439, 463, 468
Smith, W. Roy, 431
Smyer, A. P., 106
Smyer, J. J., 372
Snowden, W. H., 141, 144
Social Education and Action, 83
Social Service, Public Relations, 184
Soldier Relief Association, 218
Sons and Daughters of Zion, 88
Soule, Joshua, 334
South Alabama Conference, 62
Southeast Alabama Conference, 63
South Carolina Conference, 36
South Florida Conference, 61
South Georgia Conference, 63, 351
South Mississippi Conference, 61, 351
Southwest Virginia Conference, 62
Southwest Rocky Mt. Conference, 63
Southern Conference, 55
Southern Department, 191
Spaulding, Carrie, 309
Speaks, R. L., 469
Special Committee Investigation, 202
Spence, J. C., 12, 27, 29
Spencer, John C., 25
Spivey, Charles, 364
Spottswood, Bishop Stephen Gill, 8, 63, 241, 353, 354, 381, 441, 452, 468
Springfield, Kentucky, 38
Spring Street Chapel, 55
Spruill, J. E., 309
Spurgeon, E. Claude, 152, 381
Spywood, George A. (Supt.), 12, 13, 154, 316
Squirrel, Robert, 55
Stanford, A. L., 317
Stanback, J. S., 72
Stansbury, J. B., 37
Stanton, Edward M., 31, 35
Star, King, Rev., 38

Star King Church, 38, 399
Star of Zion, 53, 78, 109, 151, 157, 187, 194, 195, 198, 199, 201, 203, 204, 355
Statistical Secretary, 60, 63, 151, 166, 201
Steele, W. M., 449
Stevens, David, 13, 188
Stevens, Ellen, 224
Stevens, R. E., 452
Stevenson, Abel, 131, 146
Steward, General, 116, 151, 205, 261
Stewart, C. C., 167
Stewart, G. W., 355
Stewart, Bishop W. A., 381, 440, 467, 468
Stiggers, Marjorie (Lyda), 81, 382
Stillwell Secession Movement, 135, 413
Stillwell, William, 253
Stipulations of Affiliations between CME and AME Churches, 323
Stitt, R. H., 88, 209
Story, M. W., 205
Strength of My Life, 210
Strong, W. G., 31, 32, 36, 262
Student Union Bldg., 114
St. John's Church, Cincinnati, 82
St. Louis, 357
St. Marc, 32
St. Paul Church, Cleveland, 80
St. Paul Church, Detroit, 152, 361
St. Paul Parish, 20
Sunday School, 215, Association, 370
Sunday School Bulletin, 209
Sunday School Constitution, 93, 94
Sunday School Convention, 67
Sunday School Choirs, 68
Sunday School Council of Evangelical Denominations, 80
Sunday School Headlight, 73
Sunday School Literature, 71, 79, 91
Sunday School Union, 85, 86
Superannuated Ministers, 151
Superannuated Preachers' Fund, 169, 258
Superintendent, 135, Senior, 187
Superintendent of African Missions, 151
Superintendent of Sunday Schools, General, 85
Suggs, D. C., 113, 201
Sutherland, A., 371
Sutton, William, 118
Swannsboro Circuit, 351
Swain, B. W., 372
Syracuse, 23
Syracuse Circuit, 22

T

Talbot, Bishop Sampson, 12, 21, 36, 57, 149, 316

INDEX

Tampa, Florida, 32
Tanner, Bishop B. T., 344, 345, 347, 355
Tappan, John, 12, 14
Tasker, A., 160
Taylor, Bishop James Clair, 146, 183, 207, 431, 436, 469
Taylor, James Clair, Mrs., 381
Taylor, H. V., 118
Taylor, Joseph Drybauld, 243, 250
Teachers Journal, 209
Tennessee Conference, 60, 215
Texas Conference, 8
Theological Circle, 119
Theological Seminary, 111
Tillman, H. D., 418
Tillman, Harold, 8
Thomas, D. P., 382
Thomas, Jacob, 128, 154, 155, 193, 316
Thomas, John, 316
Thompson, Abraham, 122, 254, 412
Thompson, C. R., 309
Thompson, John, 14, 20
Thompson, Francis, 404
Thompson, Bishop J. P., 11, 12, 14, 26, 28, 31, 50, 52, 58, 74, 127, 192, 193, 223, 370
Thurber, W. H., 106, 110, 138, 160
Tobias, Dr. H., 358
Tompkins, Rev. R., 217
Tredwell, George, 12
Trent Gymnasium, 114
Trent, W. J., 82, 113, 114, 183
Tross, J. S. N., 381
Trusty, Jacob, 12, 21, 24, 44, 193, 214, 256, 316, 404
Truth, Sojourner, 224
Tubman, Harriet (Home), 179, 476
Tucker, Bishop C. E., 286, 430, 440, 461, 467, 469
Tucker, C. E., Mrs., 381
Tulane, Victor, 113, 449
Tunstal, J. W. I., 182
Turner, Bishop H. M., 344, 345, 348, 355
Turpin, N. H., 121, 160, 404
Tuskegee Industrial College, 99, 100
Tyler, J. A., 195, 198, 200
Tyler, J. C., 108
Tyree, E., 355

U

UKU, Skyne, 243, 477
Union, South Carolina, 73
United African Methodist Episcopal Church, 346
United Council of the Board of Bishops, 355
United Methodist Episcopal Church, 346
United General Conference, 349

V

Van Catledge, Dr. J., 72
Vandevere, Daniel, 2, 20
Vanhass, Peter, 12
Varick, Alliance, 88
Varick Auditorium, 114
Varick Christian Endeavor, 78
Varick, James, 149, 254, 412
Varick Memorial Bldg., 266
Varick Memorial Fund, 266
Varick Monument, 276
Viele, Col. Nelson, 397
Vincent, Bishop, 69
Virgin Islands, 241
Virginia, 213, 214
Virginia Conference, 60
Vogalson, Marie, 224

W

Wactor, J. W., 309
Wales, S. S., 342
Wallace, Bishop Paris Arthur, 281, 360, 410, 524
Wallace, Thomas, 175, 177, 372
Walls, Bishop William J., 65, 73, 78, 89, 113, 176, 183, 201, 286, 287, 361, 381, 382, 420, 449, 470
Walters, Bishop Alexander, 60, 62, 68, 89, 90, 92, 142, 157, 229, 237, 247, 251, 344, 350, 369, 372, 386
Walters Institute on Walter's Southland, 79, 112
Wannamaker, John, 75
Ward, M. F., 455
Warner, Bishop A. J., 38, 163, 342, 344, 345, 347, 349, 355, 392, 400, 401
Warren, Edward K., 75
Washington, Booker T., 99
Washington, G. G., 154
Washington, George H., 99, 155, 156, 193, 261, 316
Washington Metropolitan Church, 78
Washington Penn, 21
Watkins, S. D., 158
Watson, Bishop E. B., 251, 436
Watson, Emma B., 236, 237
Watson, J. W., 292
Watts, Dr., 335
Weathington, P. A., 69, 70
Weaver, E., 316
Weeden, H. C., 152, 207
Weekly Witness, 198
Weller, Rena J., 81
Wells, John, 29
Wesley Center, 21
Wesley Church, Philadelphia, 154, 315, 414

Wesley, John, 120, 135
Wesley Zion, 149
Wesley Zion Washington, 318, 414
Wesleyan, 30, 414
West Alabama, 351
West, C. E., 77
West Central North Carolina Conference 62
West Coast, 38
West Gold Coast Conference, 62
West India Mission, 54, 159, 232
West Indies, 222, 223, 247
West Kentucky Conference, 36
West Tennessee-Mississippi, 58, 59
Western North Carolina, 61
Western Star of Zion, 276
Wheeler, Rev. B. F., 117, 118, 144
White, J. H., 166
Whitesville, N. C., 51
Whitted, Rev. C. S., 175, 372
Widows and Orphans Board (Fund), 171
Wilcox, C. L., 296, 381
Wilkes-Barre, Pa., 354
William J. Walls Center, 114
Williams, Rev. C. H., 249
Williams, Eugene, 309
Williams, Rev. J. A., 12, 14, 24, 25, 316
Williams, J. H., 315
Williams, Rev. John, 31, 34
Williams, Rev. M. C., 296
Williams, Rev. N. H., 138
Williams, Rev. Peter, 413
Williams, Rev. P. H., 166
Williams, Rev. R. S., 355, 365
Williams, Rev. W. Clyde, 473
Williamsburg, L. I., 25, 27
Williamsport, Pa., 21, 351, 414
Wilson, A. M., 155
Wilson, William, 256
Windsor, Ontario, 59

Wingfield, Jr., 118, 430
Wisdom, David P., 82, 381
Women's Home & Foreign Missionary Society, 78, 247, 418
Women's Home & Foreign Missionary Treasury, 203
Wood, Bishop J. W., 208, 234, 239, 241
Woodyard, Prof. W. E., 119
World Council of Churches, 382
World Council of Christian Education, 82
World Methodist Conference, 82
World Sunday School Association (Convention), 69, 73

Y

Yates, Walter L., 226, 249
Yearbook, 152
York, 21
York, A., 106, 138
Younge, J. W., 117
Young, Archibong, 243
Youth Council President, 81
Youth Movement, 91

Z

Zion-Asbury Group, 122
Zion Church Advocate, 193
Zion Church, New York, 26
Zion's Church, 27
Zion Collegiate Institute, 99
Zion High School, 112
Zion Hill Collegiate Institute, 103, 111
Zion Institute, 117
Zionite Institute, 112
Zion Standard and Weekly Review, 191, 194, 228
Zion Temple, 243
Zion Wesley Institute, 107, 108, 109, 111, 112, 113, 115, 187
Zomolo, Charity, 243, 477

www.ingramcontent.com/pod-product-compliance
Lightning Source LLC
Chambersburg PA
CBHW052111010526
44111CB00036B/1635